# TRADE SECRET LAW IN THE UNITED STATES: CASES AND COMMENTS

# TRADE SECRET LAW IN THE UNITED STATES: CASES AND COMMENTS

**Paul E. Krieger**
*Partner, Morgan, Lewis & Bockius LLP*
*Adjunct Professor, University of Houston School of Law*

LexisNexis®

ISBN: 978-0-7698-4724-5
Looseleaf ISBN: 978-0-7698-5994-1
eBook ISBN: 978-0-3271-7762-3

**Library of Congress Cataloging-in-Publication Data**

**Krieger, Paul**
**Trade Secret Law in the United States: Cases and Comments / Paul Krieger.**
**p. cm.**
**Includes index.**
**ISBN: 978-0-7698-4724-5**
**1. Trade secrets--Law and legislation--United States. I. Title.**
**KF3197.K75 2012**
**346.7304'8--dc23**

2012035847



NOTE TO USERS
To ensure that you are using the latest materials available in this area, please be sure to periodically check the LexisNexis Law School web site for downloadable updates and supplements at www.lexisnexis.com/lawschool.

Editorial Offices
121 Chanlon Rd., New Providence, NJ 07974 (908) 464-6800
201 Mission St., San Francisco, CA 94105-1831 (415) 908-3200
www.lexisnexis.com

MATTHEW BENDER

(2012–Pub.3359)

# *ACKNOWLEDGMENTS*

This book would not have been completed without the generous offer by two of my former students, Audrey Guaqueta and Hillary Lewis, to help me organize and edit the jumble of cases I had been collecting and using in my Trade Secret class at the University of Houston Law Center for many years. I think they wanted to save future students from having to read all the extraneous material in the unedited cases I assigned for each class. They helped me with research and preliminary editing for several years until they had their own professional lives to lead. After I completed the bridge sections and finalized selecting and editing the cases, Deborah Selden took time from her busy schedule as the attorney for the state court judges in Harris County, Texas, to review and edit my writings to make them much more readable. Also, many thanks to Deborah Rypacek for taking the numerous drafts I generated and finalizing them, and to Elizabeth Ducote for cite and quote checking the final draft. Of course, I am fully responsible for all the materials and written content.

# TABLE OF CONTENTS

# Chapter 1

# INTRODUCTION TO TRADE SECRETS AND HISTORICAL BACKGROUND

## A. INTRODUCTION TO TRADE SECRET LAW

Trade secrets are unique. They are the only traditional form of intellectual property right that cannot be enforced universally. The holder of a patent, trademark or copyright may enforce these intellectual property rights against the world. Before a trade secret may be enforced, however, there must be some form of underlying contractual obligation, trust relationship or legal duty between the property owner and the alleged infringer.[1] [2]

This actual or imputed connection between the trade secret owner and recipient is what makes trade secrets an interesting and challenging form of intellectual property. For more than a century, American jurisprudence has debated and struggled with the question of what makes a trade secret an enforceable right.[3] Regardless of whether a court places its emphasis on the nature of the property right in question or the relationship of the parties, enforcement of trade secret rights requires proving that the alleged infringer (or alleged misappropriator) violated a legal right of the owner beyond using information available through legal and appropriate means, such as by reverse engineering or independent development.

---

[1] *See* Morison v. Moat (1851) 68 Eng. Rep. 498, 500, 9 Hare 241, 258-59 ("[I]t may well be, that the Plaintiffs have no right against the world in general, and may yet have a good title against this Defendant"); *see also* Kewanee Oil Co. v. Bicron Corp., 416 U.S. 470, 475 (1974), ("The protection accorded the trade secret holder is against the disclosure or unauthorized use of the trade secret by those to whom the secret has been confided under the express or implied restriction of nondisclosure or nonuse.").

[2] The doctrine of misappropriation, which is dealt with in a separate chapter below, is not considered to be a traditional form of intellectual property right because it applies to information in the public domain and depends on unfair competition principles, or as a type of "quasi property right," not as a type of "intellectual property." *See* Int'l News Serv. v. Associated Press, 248 U.S. 215, 236 (1918). Although the right of publicity has been characterized as an intellectual property right (*see* Henley v. Dillard Department Stores, 46 F. Supp. 2d 587, 590 (N.D. Tex. 1999)), it is not a traditional form of intellectual property. The right of publicity's roots lay in the tort of invasion of privacy and do not necessarily involve the creative intellectual aspect that forms the basis for the traditional intellectual property rights. Many famous people who have expended considerable money and effort in creating the persona they use to distinguish themselves from others, however, may disagree.

[3] *Compare* E.I. DuPont de Nemours Powder Co. v. Masland, 244 U.S. 100, 102 (1917) ("The property may be denied, but the confidence cannot be."), *with* Nat'l Starch Prods. Inc. v. Polymer Indus., Inc., 79 N.Y.S.2d 357, 361 (N.Y. App. Div. 1948) ("There is no betrayal of confidence unless there is a [trade] secret to be imparted.").

It is reported that some form of trade secret protection has been available since ancient times, when a slave owner had legal recourse against another who derived confidential business information from the slave without the slave owner's permission.[4] In the early 1800s, as limits on restraints of trade were developing[5] and the Industrial Revolution was taking root,[6] protection of confidential business information was recognized in England,[7] followed several years later by the United States.[8]

From the beginning, trade secret rights have consisted of three basic elements: (1) the trade secret is information that provides a business advantage over competitors who do not know it; (2) the information has at least some degree of secrecy; and (3) a competitor or unrelated third party who knows about the information must have a contractual obligation, trust relationship, or legal duty vis-à-vis the owner against unauthorized disclosure or use of the information. In short, trade secret protection is based on a legally enforceable right that is personal against the accused party or parties, and not on universal enforcement; thus the basis for the early debate as to whether trade secret protection should be based on the breach of legal duty, or on the infringement or theft of a property right.

The earliest English cases involved improper use of a trade secret by an employee or someone in privity with the owner. Courts considered such a use to be unlawful as a violation of a property or contract right or a breach of trust.[9] Since that time, the law of trade secrets has evolved to protections based on much broader principles. In the seminal case, *Kewanee Oil Co. v. Bicron Corp.*, the U.S. Supreme Court expressed the rationale for trade secret protection as: "[T]he maintenance of standards of commercial ethics and the encouragement of invention are the broadly stated policies behind trade secret law."[10] The *Kewanee* Court explained that trade secret law encourages the dissemination of ideas through confidential disclosures, and industrial espionage cannot be condoned because it violates "[a] most fundamental human right" of privacy.[11]

---

[4] *See* A. Arthur Schiller, *Trade Secrets and the Roman Law; The Actio Servi Corrupti*, 30 COLUM. L. REV. 837 (1930); *but see* Alan Watson, *Trade Secrets and Roman Law: The Myth Exploded*, 11 TUL. EUR. & CIV. L.F. 19 (1996).

[5] *See* Mitchell v. Reynolds (1711) 24 Eng.Rep. 347, 350, 1 P.Wms 181, 191 ("[W]hat does it signify to a tradesman in London, what another does in Newcastle?"); *Rousillon v. Rousillon*, (1880) 14 Ch.D. 351 (the issue of whether an unlimited restraint is void is whether it went further than necessary).

[6] LUCAS, ROBERT E., JR., LECTURES ON ECONOMIC GROWTH 109-10 (Harvard Univ. Press 2002).

[7] *See* Yovatt v. Winyard, (1820) 37 Eng.Rep. 425, 426, 1 Jac. & W. 395 (Ch.) (An injunction was granted based on Plaintiff's argument that the case involved "an instance of breach of confidence towards an employer, in the manner of acquiring the knowledge, contending that though the Court might not protect a secret from disclosure by one to whom the proprietor had himself communicated it, yet it would, when the person sought to be restrained had clandestinely possessed himself of it.")

[8] *See* Vickery v. Welch, 36 Mass. 523, 526 (1837) (holding, "[t]he plaintiff was to become the proprietor of the mills, and also of the secret mode of manufacture which the bond supposes was used and possessed by the defendant.").

[9] *See* Morison v. Moat, (1851) 68 Eng.Rep. 492, 498, 9 Hare 241; ("In some cases [the exercise of jurisdiction was based on] property, in others to contract, and in others, again, it has been treated as founded upon trust or confidence.").

[10] 416 U.S. 470, 481 (1974).

[11] *Id.* at 487.

Unlike trade secrets, the other traditional types of intellectual property rights (i.e., patents, trademarks, and copyrights) are different because they are rights that can be enforced universally within the applicable jurisdiction against anyone who violates or trespasses on them, regardless of whether the violator knows about their existence or has any type of relationship or legal duty to the owner. Patents and copyrights are sanctioned by Article 1, § 8, of the U.S. Constitution, which provides that Congress has the power "to promote the progress of science and the useful arts, by securing for limited times to authors and inventors the exclusive right to their respective writings and discoveries." Trademarks, like trade secrets, do not fall under the federal Constitutional umbrella, but are subject to various state and federal laws.[12]

**Patents:** The Patent Laws enacted by Congress in Title 35 United States Code[13] grant inventors an exclusive right in the form of a patent. This allows the inventor to exclude all others, for a specified period of time, from making, using, selling, and offering for sale any invention that is covered by the claims of the patent. The federal government grants this protection in exchange for full disclosure of the invention and satisfaction of novelty and other requirements established by the Patent Laws. In 1974, after years of controversy, the Supreme Court found that the Patent Laws do not preempt state enforcement of trade secret rights.[14]

**Copyrights**: Copyright Laws found in Title 17 United States Code,[15] provide for copyright protection on any "original works of authorship fixed in any tangible medium"[16] for the life of the author plus 70 additional years,[17] against any unauthorized reproduction, distribution, public performance, public display, or creation of derivative works. Copyrights and trade secrets may offer overlapping protection in some instances, particularly for technology such as computer software. Similar to the Supreme Court's decision regarding patents, the Copyright Laws have been held not to preempt state enforcement of trade secret rights.[18]

**Trademarks**: A combination of federal laws (i.e., the Lanham Act[19]), state statutes (so-called little Lanham Acts), and state judicial precedent (reflected in the RESTATEMENT (THIRD) OF UNFAIR COMPETITION)[20] provide civil protection of trademarks. There are also criminal penalties for counterfeiting.[21]

---

[12] 15 U.S.C. § 1051-1141.

[13] 35 U.S.C. §§ 1-376 (2006).

[14] *See* Kewanee Oil, 416 U.S. at 492 (holding "[n]either complete nor partial pre-emption of state trade secret law is justified.").

[15] 17 U.S.C. §§ 101-1332 (2006).

[16] *Id.* § 102.

[17] *Id.* § 302.

[18] *See* Warrington Assocs., Inc. v. Real-Time Eng'g Sys., Inc., 522 F. Supp. 367, 369 (N.D. Ill. 1981). (holding, "the likelihood of preemption, between patent and trade secret law is stronger than between trade secret and copyright law," and "state law provides an area of protection extending beyond copyright" because "trade secrets tort is premised on concepts of breach of trust and confidentiality, and not copying.").

[19] 15 U.S.C. §§ 1051-1141.

[20] RESTATMENT (THIRD) OF UNFAIR COMPETITION §§ 9-37 (1995).

[21] 18 U.S.C. § 2318 *et seq.*

Trademarks are any type of identifier or indicia ("any word, name, symbol, or device, or any combination thereof . . ."[22]) that can be used to identify the source of products or services. The term "trademark" has been used to encompass trademarks that are used on "goods" (including trade dress for product shapes and containers), and service marks used on commercially available services,[23] as well as certification marks for certifying characteristics of goods or services performed by members of a group and collective marks indicating membership in an organization.[24] In addition to traditional forms of trademarks such as words, letters, drawings, objects, and product shapes and packaging, trademark protection on color,[25] sound,[26] and scent[27] have been upheld.

Trademark rights may be acquired through use alone. Federal and state laws provide additional rights through respective registration processes. Trademarks can be enforced against anyone who uses the same or similar mark in a way that causes likelihood of confusion,[28] or deception,[29] or is likely to dilute the strength of the mark,[30] or registers a domain name that infringes a registered mark.[31] Federal counterfeiting laws also protect owners of federally registered marks from knock-offs that use identical or "substantially indistinguishable" marks.[32]

**Trade Secrets**: Trade secrets are protected primarily by state statutory law. For years, state common law followed the RESTATEMENT OF TORTS § 757,[33] which was superseded by the RESTATEMENT (THIRD) OF UNFAIR COMPETITION §§ 39-45.[34] As of 2012, 46 states have some version of the Uniform Trade Secrets Act.[35]

Courts have also allowed trade secret enforcement actions under the Lanham Act's section on unfair competition by applying the doctrine of "passing off," in which a party is allegedly guilty of deception by representing that someone else's trade secret is its own. Actions filed in the International Trade Commission under

---

[22] 15 U.S.C. § 1127.

[23] *Id.*

[24] *Id.*

[25] *See* Qualitex Co. v. Jacobson Prods. Co., 514 U.S. 159 (1995) (i.e., green-gold color for industrial machine mats).

[26] *See* U.S. Patent & Trademark Office, Reg. No. 76307773, American Life Assurance, duck quacking the word "AFLAC."

[27] *See* In re Clarke, 17 U.S.P.Q.2d 1238 (T.T.A.B. 1990) (i.e., thread having the smell of plumeria blossoms).

[28] 15 U.S.C. § 1114(1)(b).

[29] 15 U.S.C. § 1125(a).

[30] 15 U.S.C. § 1125(c).

[31] 15 U.S.C. § 1125(d).

[32] *See* ANTI-COUNTERFEITING CONSUMER PROTECTION ACT OF 1996, Public Law 104-153, 104th Congress, July 2, 1996.

[33] RESTATEMENT OF TORTS § 757 (1939).

[34] RESTATEMENT (THIRD) OF UNFAIR COMPETITION §§ 39-45 (1995).

[35] UNIFORM TRADE SECRET ACT §§ 1-12 (1985) ("UTSA"). The UTSA was initially approved in 1979. Four Official Amendments were approved in 1985. As of 2012, versions of the UTSA were enacted in 46 states, the District of Columbia, and the Virgin Islands.

§ 1337 of the Tariff Act[36] to bar foreign imports can be based on alleged trade secret misappropriation. Federal civil provisions under the Racketeer Influenced & Corrupt Organizations Act (RICO)[37] and the Computer Fraud and Abuse Act[38] have also afforded protection for trade secrets. Additionally, federal criminal laws such as mail and wire fraud laws,[39] the Economic Espionage Act,[40] and the Computer Fraud and Abuse Act,[41] as well as state criminal laws, afford trade secret protection and enforcement.

As a testament to the durability of the common law, the basic theories of trade secret laws and the arguments in modern case law remain much the same as those found in the earliest English cases.[42] While trade secret law has, in one sense, remained relatively static, it has also remained a topic of considerable debate and evolving nuance. Accordingly, the study of some of the important cases from Georgian and Victorian England will provide a sound introduction to the basic principles underlying trade secret protection and enforcement.

## B. HISTORICAL ROOTS OF TRADE SECRET PROTECTION

### YOVATT v. WINYARD

(1820) 37 Eng. Rep. 425 (Ch.)

Injunction to restrain a Defendant from communicating certain recipes for medicines and vending them granted, on the ground that he had obtained a knowledge of the mode of preparing them by a breach of trust.

Mr. Wetherell moved, upon certificate of the bill filed and affidavit, to restrain the Defendant from making use of or communicating certain recipes for veterinary medicines, and from printing and publishing certain papers of directions for the mode of administering them, and of managing the animals while taking them.

The Plaintiff, who was the proprietor of the medicines, had employed the Defendant for some time as an assistant or journeyman, under an agreement, by which he was to have a salary, and to be instructed in the general knowledge of the business, but was not to be taught the mode of composing the medicines; he, some time since, left the Plaintiff, and entered into business for himself, and the Plaintiff had lately discovered that he had, while in his service, surreptitiously got access to his books of recipes, and copied them, and was now selling the medicines, with printed papers for administering them, which were almost literal copies of those

---

36 19 U.S.C. § 1337.

37 18 U.S.C. § 1962 (2006).

38 18 U.S.C. § 1030 (2012).

39 18 U.S.C. §§ 1961-68 (2006).

40 18 U.S.C. § 1831.

41 18 U.S.C. § 1030.

42 *Compare* Morison v. Moat (1851), 68 Eng.Rep. 492 *with* Kewanee Oil, 416 U.S. 470 (1974).

composed by the Plaintiff. The Defendant had afterwards offered, for a small salary, to agree not to divulge the recipes.

Mr. Wetherell, in support of the motion, distinguished the case from *Newberry v James* (2 Mer. 447), *Williams v. Williams* (3 Mer. 157), as being an instance of breach of confidence towards an employer, in the manner of acquiring the knowledge, contending that though the Court might not protect a secret from disclosure by one to whom the proprietor had himself communicated it, yet it would, when the person sought to be restrained had clandestinely possessed himself of it. In those cases the knowledge was communicated for a particular purpose, and it was attempted to prevent the party from using it for any other; but here the first discovery was obtained by a breach of duty, and in violation of a positive agreement.

The Lord Chancellor granted the injunction, upon the ground of there having been a breach of trust and confidence; but confined it so as not to prevent the Defendant from administering the medicine to any animals then under a course, it being stated in the papers of directions that a sudden discontinuance would be prejudicial.

* * *

## MORISON v. MOAT

(1851) 68 Eng. Rep. 498, 9 Hare 241

* * *

The Vice-Chancellor [Sir G. J. Turner]. The Plaintiff's case was rested in argument upon the ground that the Defendant had obtained this secret by breach of faith or of contract on the part of Thomas Moat. The subsidiary ground brought forward by the bill, of the Defendant's selling his medicines under the original name and description, was relied upon rather in support of the case of breach of faith and of contract than as a separate and distinct ground for the interference of the Court. Upon that part of the case it is sufficient, therefore, to observe that there might be difficulty in maintaining it, at all events, until the Plaintiffs should have established their right at law. The true question is whether, under the circumstances of this case, the Court ought to interpose by injunction, upon the ground of breach of faith or of contract.

That the Court has exercised jurisdiction in cases of this nature does not, I think, admit of any question. Different grounds have indeed been assigned for the exercise of that jurisdiction. In some cases it has been referred to property, in others to contract, and in others, again, it has been treated as founded upon trust or confidence, meaning, as I conceive, that the Court fastens the obligation on the conscience of the party, and enforces it against him in the same manner as it enforces against a party to whom a benefit is given the obligation of performing a promise on the faith of which the benefit has been conferred; but, upon whatever grounds the jurisdiction is founded, the authorities leave no doubt as to the exercise of it.

* * *

It was much pressed in argument, on the part of the Defendant, that the effect of granting an injunction in such a case as the present would be to give the Plaintiffs a better right than that of a patentee; and the case of *Canham v. Jones* (2 V. & B. 218) was cited on the Defendant's behalf; but what we have to deal with here is, not the right of the Plaintiffs against the world, but their right against the Defendant. It may well be that the Plaintiffs have no title against the world in general, and may yet have a good title against this Defendant; and the case of *Canham v. Jones* does not appear to me to touch the question. In that case the allegation was, not that the Defendant was compounding the syrup according to the recipe, but that he did not know the recipe, and was compounding and selling a spurious preparation, falsely describing it under the title by which the true preparation was known, and thereby damaging the character of that preparation. The case, therefore, did not depend upon any breach of confidence, for there was no confidence reposed, but depended wholly on a supposed right of property in the medicine; and it is clear, from the judgment, that the distinction between that case and a case like the present had not escaped Sir Thomas Plumer's attention; for he observes that the case then before him was not one "in which the Court has restrained a fraudulent attempt in one man to invade another's property" (2 V. & B. 221).

Such being the state of the authorities upon this subject, I have now to consider whether the circumstances of this case bring it within the range of those authorities, and whether the Court ought to interfere by injunction; for which purpose it is necessary to examine the case as it has stood at several different periods.

It does not appear to be disputed that James Morison was the inventor, and, down to the 23d of June 1830, the sole depository of the secret in question. Upon the 23d of June 1830 the partnership deed between him and Moat, and the two bonds, were executed; and the first question to be considered is, what was the effect of those instruments? It was contended, on the part of the Defendants, that the effect of them was to constitute the secret an asset of the partnership; but, looking at the deed alone, apart from the bonds, I am much disposed to think it could not have that effect; and taking the deed, as I think it must be taken, in connexion with the bonds, I think it clear that it could not so operate. The question, I apprehend, is one of intention, like the question whether there is a partnership in mines, or only in the minerals which are raised and manufactured by parties working the mines; and this deed, I think, contains indications that the secret was not intended to belong to the partnership; for although it contemplated the introduction of new partners, and expressly provides for the communication of the secret by James Morison to Thomas Moat, it leaves it to the option of James Morison whether he will communicate the secret to persons introduced either by himself or by Moat, according as the word "he" in the clause referred to may apply to one or the other (a point which is not material); and it is difficult to conceive that a secret which one partner had a discretion to withhold from others could be intended to be a partnership asset. Again, the clause as to accounts seems to look to matters which would properly and without difficulty be the subject of account, and not to such an asset as this secret would be. An account was to be taken upon a new partner coming in. Is it conceivable that, if this secret had been contemplated as an asset of the partnership, there would have been no provision as to what should then be done respecting it, no provision for valuing it, either then or at the termination of the partnership? But, however this question might have stood upon the deed alone, the bonds seem to me to conclude it; for, by Moat's bond, he is not to communicate the secret to any person whomsoever; and by Morison's bond he is not to communicate it except to persons whom he or Moat may introduce into the partnership, or for the purposes of the foreign trade; and how then could it be in the contemplation of the parties that it should be an asset of the partnership in which case it would be liable to be sold when the partnership determined. The true effect of these instruments appears to me to be that Morison reserved to himself the secret against all the world except Thomas Moat. Morison had power to introduce partners into the concern; Moat had the like power with the concurrence of Morison, but not otherwise. It was entirely at the option of Morison whether he would communicate the secret to any partner introduced either by himself or by Moat. Moat was also bound not to reveal the secret to any person whatsoever.

At this stage of the case, therefore, there was, according to the authorities to which I have referred, a perfect right, on the part of Morison against Moat, to restrain him from divulging the secret. It is to be seen whether what has since passed has destroyed that right; and, if not, whether the Plaintiffs are entitled to enforce it against the Defendant?

The next stage in the case which we have to consider is the transaction of July and August 1835. At that time both the Plaintiffs had become partners in the concern, and the secret was communicated to them. Moat, who had been the acting partner, had fallen into bad health; and an agreement was entered into by all parties that the Defendant, the son of Moat, should come into the office as his father's servant; and by deed, dated the 8th of August 1835, and attested by Morison, the Defendant was appointed to be a partner in the business after the death of his father, which occurred a few days afterwards. It is not pretended that Morison ever communicated the secret to the Defendant; and the case does not appear to me to be at all altered by anything which appears on these instruments of 1835; for, if I am right in the conclusion at which I have before arrived, the fact of the Defendant's becoming a partner in the concern gave him no right to the knowledge of the secret, and certainly he could derive no such right from the agreement that he should come into the office as the servant of his father. The very language of the agreement, so far as it has any bearing upon the question, leads, I think, to the opposite conclusion; for it is that he is to transact the business so far as he is able so to do, not being a partner.

These instruments, however, although nothing material appears upon the face of them, have an important bearing upon the case; for the Defendant says that, under the provisions of the agreement, he attended the office and gained a knowledge of the ingredients used in the medicines; and that afterwards, having become a partner on the death of his father, he for two months superintended the business in common with his co-partners, and during that time saw the mode and manner of compounding the medicines and the ingredients thereof, and the proportions in which such ingredients were used, and acquired a complete practical knowledge of the mode of compounding and mixing them; and it is insisted on his part that he has the right to use that knowledge.

Undoubtedly, if the facts thus stated by the Defendant be proved — if the Defendant, after he became a partner in the concern, openly took part in compounding the medicines, and used the secret for the purpose — if, with the knowledge and concurrence of the partners, he was permitted to acquire, and did acquire, a full knowledge of the mode of compounding these medicines and of the secret process in the manufacture of them, it would be difficult for any of those partners afterwards to restrain him from using any knowledge so acquired or any secret so disclosed; they would, I think, in such a state of circumstances, be considered to have waived any right to preserve the secret for their separate benefit. But how does the evidence stand upon these facts?

[Editor's note: The following narrative was included in the reported decision.] [His Honor then stated the substance of the affidavits on this point, *see* pages 251, 253, *supra*; and concluded that, if the Defendant did in fact, after he became a partner in the concern, acquire by practice the knowledge of the mode of mixing the medicines (but which His Honor said he did not believe he did), he acquired that knowledge surreptitiously and without the sanction of his partners.]

The case then in this stage stands thus: — The Defendant admits that the secret was communicated to him by Thomas Moat. His allegation that he acquired a knowledge of it by acting as partner in the concern is disproved; and it is shewn that, if he did acquire such knowledge, he did so surreptitiously. The question then is whether there was an equity against him; and I am of opinion that there was. It was clearly a breach of faith and of contract on the part of Thomas Moat to communicate the secret. The Defendant derives under that breach of faith and of contract, and I think he can gain no title by it. In *Green v. Folgham*, upon a trust admitted, an account was decreed against the party to whom the secret had been divulged; and it cannot, I think, make any difference whether the trust is admitted or proved; and the cases of *Tipping v. Clarke* and *Prince Albert v. Strangeshew* that the equity prevails against parties deriving under the breach of contract or duty.

It might indeed be different if the Defendant was a purchaser for value of the secret, without notice of any obligation affecting it; and the Defendant's case was attempted to be put upon this ground. It was said that, as appointee, he came in as purchaser under the deed of the 23d of June 1830, and that he had no notice of the bond; but I do not think that this view of the case can avail him, for, in whatever character he may stand as appointee, he has no consequential right in the secret. So far as the secret is concerned he is a mere volunteer deriving under a breach of trust or of contract.

There having been then this equity against the Defendant, has it been displaced by what has since occurred? The Defendant contends that it has; for he says that the deed of 1837 was entered into with full knowledge, on the part of the Plaintiffs and of James Morison, that he had possession of the secret. He has proved, I think, sufficient to shew that the fact of his having become a sleeping partner under that deed furnishes no inference against such knowledge, there having been other disputes between the parties. For proof of his knowledge the Defendant relies on the covenant in the deed against divulging the secret having been made applicable to him. The alleged conversations, and the covenant in the deed, which is of more importance, are, I apprehend, to be regarded as evidence of the knowledge imputed by the Defendant to the Plaintiffs and their father, and to be weighed against the other evidence in the cause; and, in determining the weight due to the evidence on the part of the Defendant, it is material to be observed that he nowhere states that he told the Plaintiffs and their father that he had possession of the secret, and that he gives no detail of the conversations to which he refers. On the other hand, there is a denial by the Plaintiffs of any such conversations with them, and, to their belief, with James Morison; and the grounds of the denial are stated, and are not controverted by the Defendant. There is also the fact that, if the Plaintiffs and their father had known that the Defendant was in possession of the secret, there appears to be no reason why he should not have participated in the business of mixing the medicines, which I consider it to be proved that he did not; and there is, besides, the conduct of the Defendant at a subsequent period, to which I shall next refer. These facts, in my opinion, far outweigh the Defendant's statement as to the conversation and the covenant in the deed, which might well be inserted by way of precaution; and I think, therefore, that the Defendant's case upon the deed of 1837 cannot be supported. If the covenant in the deed was inserted as a protection against the Defendant's divulging a knowledge which he was known to have already acquired, surely the fact of his having acquired that knowledge would have been recited in the deed.

We come now to the death of James Morison who died in May 1840. Soon after his death disputes arose between his executors, the widow and administratrix of Moat, and the surviving partners; and these disputes were compromised upon the terms, amongst others, of an annuity of £100 being paid to the widow of Moat out of the profits of the business, so long as the business continued, and out of the proceeds of the sale of the secret, if it should be sold under the trusts of Morison's will. Three deeds were executed for carrying into effect this compromise; and each of those deeds recited the will of Morison, with the recital contained in it that he was the inventor and sole proprietor of the medicine, and with the trusts for sale of the secret declared by it; and by one of those deeds the annuity was secured in manner above mentioned. The Defendant was a party to each of these deeds; and it is clear, therefore, that he did not then claim any right or interest in the secret adverse to the title under the will of Morison.

Nothing further appears to have occurred until the determination of the partnership except that, in 1846, the Defendant, through his solicitor, complained of a paper which had been published by the Plaintiffs in America containing a statement to the effect that Thomas Moat had not revealed the secret, and distinctly stated that he was in possession of it; but nothing ensued upon the complaint, and, the partnership being then still subsisting, it is difficult to see what could, on either side, have been done upon it. Upon the determination of the partnership on the 25th of March 1851 the stock was divided; but this was according to the provisions of the partnership articles, and therefore could not affect the rights of either party.

The Defendant, by his affidavit, attempts to set up a further case upon the ground that great expenses have been incurred in advertisements, and that this will be for the benefit of the Plaintiffs alone, if he be not permitted to carry on the business; but I do not think he can maintain his case upon this ground. It has been the practice of the partnership, and he and his father have had the benefit of it during its subsistence.

The last point urged in the Defendant's behalf was the delay on the part of the

Plaintiffs: but I think there has been no such delay as disentitles the Plaintiffs to the interposition of the Court; for, at the dissolution of the partnership, the Defendant had distinct notice that his claim would be resisted; and there has since been the question with the Stamp Office — the suit in this Court, and, as it would appear, some negotiation for a compromise; and, besides, he had clearly the right to sell the medicine and use the labels allotted to him at the termination of the partnership.

Upon the whole, therefore, I am of opinion that the Plaintiffs have made out their case for an injunction. I think, however, the injunction cannot go to the extent which is asked for by the notice of motion. It should, I think, go to the extent of restraining the Defendant from selling, under the title or designation of "Morison's Universal Medicine," or "Morison's Vegetable Universal Medicine," any medicine made or manufactured by him, proceeding to this extent, not upon the mere use of the name, but because this is clearly the mode in which the Defendant is availing himself of the breach of faith and contract; and upon the authorities, and particularly *Yovatt v. Winyard*, I think it should also go to the extent of restraining the Defendant from making or compounding any medicines according to the secret, and from in any manner using the secret of compounding the medicine. But I cannot grant it to restrain the Defendant "from in any manner using the name of Morison in the manufacture or sale of any medicine;" as, in my view of the case, it would very much depend upon the purpose for which and the mode in which the name may be used whether the injunction would be due or not; nor can I grant it to restrain the communication of the secret, there being no evidence or even allegation of an intention to communicate it.

Restrain the Defendant, his agents, &c., from selling, or causing or procuring to be sold, under the title or designation of "Morison's Universal Medicine," or "Morison's Vegetable Universal Medicine," any medicine made or manufactured by the Defendant, or by or under his order or direction; and restrain the Defendant, his agents, &c., from making or compounding any medicines according to the secret in, &c., and from in any manner using the secret of compounding the said medicines or any part thereof.

* * *

## PEABODY v. NORFOLK

98 Mass. 452 (1868)

* * *

The bill set forth that, for many years prior to the filing of the same, Peabody was secretly engaged in making experiments, inventing and adapting machinery, and originating and perfecting a process, to manufacture gunny cloth from jute butts, and at last succeeded in perfecting machinery and a process to do so profitably, such a manufacture having never before been attempted, so far as he knew; that thereupon he built a large factory on Bridge Street in Salem to carry on such manufacture with such machinery and process, and filled it with such machinery, and invested a large sum in the building, and the machines, material and business; that, both in all his experiments, and in the construction of the machines for the factory and the setting up and running of the same, he employed Norfolk, who was a machinist, to give his whole time and skill for a salary; that, in the course of this employment, Norfolk became confidentially possessed of knowledge of the machinery and process, well understanding that such knowledge was to be kept wholly secret; and that, at the solicitation of Norfolk while so employed, Peabody made a written agreement with him, dated June 24, 1865, which was annexed in full to the bill, and the material parts whereof were as follows:

"Said Norfolk agrees to serve the said Peabody as the engineer of his jute factory in Bridge Street so far as he is required to do so by said Peabody, and particularly for that part which relates to the running and construction of the engines and boilers, and of the machinery used in the manufacture of the goods, also in the construction and repairs of the buildings that are required;" and "agrees that he will not give any parties information, directly or indirectly, in regard to the machinery, or any portions of it," which had been used in the experiments, or should be used in the factory, but "will consider all of said machinery as sacred to be used only for the benefit of said Peabody or his assigns, and that by all the means in his power he will prevent other persons from obtaining any information in regard to it such as would enable them to use it."

"Said Peabody on his part agrees to pay the said Norfolk the sum of one thousand dollars annually in monthly instalments of eighty-three dollars and thirty-three cents each, to be received in full compensation for above described services, provided the said Norfolk shall render his services acceptable to said Peabody as he has heretofore done, and that said Peabody or his assigns or agents shall continue the business of manufacturing jute goods in said mill in Bridge Street or elsewhere."

The bill further alleged that, on January 1, 1867, Norfolk left his said employment, and had made arrangements with persons unknown to Peabody to build another factory for the manufacture of gunny cloth from jute butts, and to furnish these persons with machinery to be built on the models of the machinery of Peabody, and impart to them Peabody's secret process of manufacturing, and aid and assist them in manufacturing by that process; and that he had taken from the possession of Peabody the original drawings, or copies thereof, of said machinery, and intended to use them in carrying out his said arrangements.

The prayer of the bill was for an injunction to restrain Norfolk from carrying out any such arrangements, or communicating to any person any knowledge of said machinery and process derived by him in the course of his said confidential employment; and to oblige him to return to Peabody said drawings or copies. Upon this bill an injunction was issued in conformity with its prayer.

On June 8, 1867, Peabody filed a supplemental bill, reciting said prayer and the issue of the injunction, and alleging that he had learned for the first time, since the service of the injunction on Norfolk, that James P. Cook was one of the persons with whom Norfolk had made his said arrangements; and further, that Cook and his associates, knowing the relations between Peabody and Norfolk, and knowing the fact of the injunction, were nevertheless proceeding to build machinery to manufacture gunny cloth from jute butts by Peabody's secret process; that Cook was pretending to build the machinery in his own name, upon information, models and drawings obtained from Norfolk before or about the time of the service of the injunction, but that, in fact, long before he ever made any arrangements with Norfolk on the subject, he had notice of all Peabody's relations with and claims on Norfolk; and that, although Norfolk was falsely pretending to obey the injunction, yet in fact he was one of Cook's present associates in the building of such machinery.

* * *

It is the policy of the law, for the advantage of the public, to encourage and protect invention and commercial enterprise. If a man establishes a business and makes it valuable by his skill and attention, the good will of that business is recognized by the law as property. If he adopts and publicly uses a trade mark, he has a remedy, either at law or in equity, against those who undertake to use it without his permission. If he makes a new and useful invention of any machine or composition of matter, he may, upon filing in a public office a description which will enable an expert to understand and manufacture it, and thus affording to all persons the means of ultimately availing themselves of it, obtain letters patent from the government securing to him its exclusive use and profit for a term of years. If he invents or discovers, and keeps secret, a process of manufacture, whether a proper subject for a patent or not, he has not indeed an exclusive right to it as against the public, or against those who in good faith acquire knowledge of it; but he has a property in it, which a court of chancery will protect against one who in violation of contract and breach of confidence undertakes to apply it to his own use, or to disclose it to third persons. The jurisdiction in equity to interfere by injunction to prevent such a breach of trust, when the injury would be irreparable and the remedy at law inadequate, is well established by authority.

In the earliest reported case of this class, Lord Eldon indeed refused to grant an injunction against imparting, in violation of an agreement, the secret, not only of a patent which had been obtained and had expired, and which the whole public was therefore entitled to use; but also that of making a certain kind of pills, for which no patent had been procured; and stated, as a reason for the latter, that, if the art and method of preparing them was a secret, the court could not, without having it disclosed, ascertain whether it had been infringed. *Newbery v. James*, 2 Meriv. 446. But the same learned chancellor afterwards considered the general question as still an open one, whether a court of equity would restrain a party from divulging a secret in medicine, which was not protected by patent, but which he had promised to keep; and in such a case dissolved an injunction of the vice-chancellor, upon the sole ground that the defendant made affidavit that the secret was not derived from the plaintiff. *Williams v. Williams*, 3 Meriv. 157. And in a later case he unhesitatingly granted an injunction against one who by the terms of his agreement with the plaintiff was not to be instructed in the secret, and who had obtained a knowledge of it by a breach of trust. *Yovatt v. Winyard*, 1 Jac. & Walk. 394.

Sir John Leach decreed, in one case, specific performance of an agreement by a trader to sell the good will of a business and the exclusive use of a secret in dyeing; and, in another, an account of the profits of a secret for making a medicine against a son of the inventor, holding it in trust for his brothers and sisters. *Bryson v. Whitehead*, 1 Sim. & Stu. 74. *Green v. Folgham*, *Ib.* 398.

In a more recent case, Morison, the inventor and sole proprietor of a medicine, for which no patent had been obtained, entered into partnership with Moat, to whom he communicated the secret of making the medicine, but did not make the secret a part of the assets of the partnership, and reserved it to himself as against all other persons, and Moat covenanted not to reveal it to any person whomsoever; by subsequent agreement Morison's sons and a son of Moat were admitted as partners in the business; and the secret was surreptitiously obtained from Moat by his son. After the death of both the original parties, on a bill brought by Morison's sons, who were also legatees of the secret, against Moat's son, Vice-Chancellor Turner, in an elaborate judgment reviewing all the English authorities, granted an injunction restraining the defendant from using the secret in any manner in compounding the medicine; and refused to restrain him from communicating the secret, simply for want of any allegation or evidence of an intention to communicate it. *Morison v. Moat*, 9 Hare, 241. The defendant appealed; but the order was affirmed; and Lord Cranworth, delivering the opinion of the court of appeal, said: "The principles that were argued in this case are principles really not to be called in controversy. There is no doubt whatever, that when a party who has a secret in trade employs persons under a contract express or implied, or under duty express or implied, those persons cannot gain the knowledge of the secret and then set it up against their employer." 21 L. J. (N. S.) Ch. 248.

Mr. Justice Story states the doctrine in the broadest terms, that "courts of equity will restrain a party from making a disclosure of secrets communicated to him in the course of a confidential employment; and it matters not, in such cases, whether the secrets be secrets of trade or secrets of title, or any other secrets of the party important to his interests." 2 Story Eq. § 952. In this court, it is settled that a secret art is a legal subject of property; and that a bond for a conveyance of the exclusive right to it is not open to the objection of being in restraint of trade, but may be enforced by action at law, and requires the obligor not to divulge the secret to any other person. *Vickery v. Welch*, 19 Pick. 523. *Taylor v. Blanchard*, 13 Allen, 373, 374. In *Jarvis v. Peck*, 10 Paige, 118, such a bond was held valid in equity. And by the Gen. Sts. c. 113, § 2, this court has not only jurisdiction in equity of suits for enforcing and regulating the execution of trusts, or for the specific performance of written contracts by and against either party and his representatives and assigns, but also full equity jurisdiction, according to the usage and practice of courts of equity, in all other cases where there is not a plain, adequate and complete remedy at law.

The contract between Peabody and Norfolk was, on the part of Norfolk, to serve Peabody as engineer in his jute factory so far as required, and particularly in the construction and running of the machinery, and not to give any third person information directly or indirectly in regard to any portion of the machinery, but to "consider all of said machinery as sacred to be used only for the benefit of said Peabody or his assigns, and by all means in his power prevent other persons from obtaining any information in regard to it such as would enable them to use it;" and, on the part of Peabody, to pay Norfolk an annual salary "in full compensation for the above described services," provided he should render his services acceptable to Peabody as he had theretofore, and Peabody or his assigns should continue the business of manufacturing jute goods. The "above described services" clearly include, not only the affirmative promise to serve as an engineer, but the negative promise not to disclose the secret, and to do his best to conceal it; and the salary is a legal and sufficient consideration for all the agreements of Norfolk.

The plaintiffs do not ask for specific performance of Norfolk's promise to serve as engineer. It is therefore unnecessary to consider whether that promise is limited in point of time or determinable at pleasure, or is capable of being specifically enforced. Whatever may be the limit or effect of his obligation to serve, he is bound by his contract never to disclose the secret confidentially imparted to him during the term of his actual service. And this part of his agreement may be specifically enforced in equity, even if the other part could not. *Lumley v. Wagner*, 1 De Gex, Macn. & Gord. 604.

The bill alleges that the invention and the process of manufacture have been kept secret, and that the secret is the property of the original plaintiff and of great value to him, and was confidentially imparted to Norfolk; and on demurrer these allegations must be taken to be true. Although the process is carried on in a large factory, the workmen may not understand or be intrusted with the secret, or may have acquired a knowledge of it upon the like confidence. A secret of trade or manufacture does not lose its character by being confidentially disclosed to agents or servants, without whose assistance it could not be made of any value. Even if, as is argued in support of the demurrer, the process is liable to be inspected by the assessor of internal revenue or other public officer, the owner is not the less entitled to protection against those who in, or with knowledge of, violation of contract and breach of confidence, undertake to disclose it or to reap the benefit of it. The danger of divulging the secret in the course of a judicial investigation affords in our opinion no satisfactory reason why a court of equity should refuse all remedy against the wrongdoers.

The supplemental bill alleges, and the demurrer admits, that Cook, with notice of the relations between Peabody and Norfolk, has made arrangements to have the secret communicated to him by Norfolk, and together with him to use it for their own benefit. Upon such a state of facts, Cook has no better equity than Norfolk.

The executors of the will of the original plaintiff succeed to his rights, and appear on the allegations of the bills to be entitled to the relief prayed for. *Morison v. Moat*, above cited.

*Demurrer overruled.*

* * *

## NOTES AND QUESTIONS:

1. The early English cases illustrate how the focus for trade secret protection began in England as a vehicle for protecting confidential business information from a recipient's bad faith in the form of a breach of a promise to reveal or use confidential information, which was described in *Yovatt* as a "breach of duty, and in violation of a positive agreement." 37 Eng.Rep. at 426. The court in *Morison* expanded this focus by observing that "[d]ifferent grounds have indeed been assigned for the exercise of that jurisdiction [such as property, contract and breach of confidence]." 68 Eng.Rep. at 498. Such an expansion was necessary as the court found the evidence showed that Moat had received the secret formula "surrepti-

tiously," not from the breach of an agreement. *Id.* at 501. As a practical matter, does the ultimate outcome depend on which rationale a court applies? Why was it so difficult for courts in the early cases in England to agree on how trade secret rights should be protected?

2. *Newberry v. James*, (1817) 35 Eng.Rep. 1011 (Ch.), a case decided before *Yovatt*, was mentioned in *Peabody* as the first reported trade secret case in England. The court in *Newberry*, however, denied the plaintiff's request for an injunction. The court could not make a determination as to whether the alleged trade secrets had been misappropriated because the plaintiff would not disclose them to the court. Why would a party refuse to disclose a trade secret to a court when claiming a violation of its property rights? It is difficult to see how this problem could arise in today's courts. Now, courts routinely grant protective orders in cases where confidential business information might have to be produced during discovery, in court filings, to experts, or at trial. A typical protective order defines the terms under which confidential information is to be handled during and after resolution of the case before the court. Some federal courts, such as the U.S. District Court for the Eastern District of Texas, use a form protective order. *See* copy of form *infra*, Chapt. 2(C)(2), n.5. Usually, disputes regarding protective orders involve issues such as the creation of different classes of trade secrets (typically labeled as "Highly Confidential — Attorneys Eyes Only" or "Confidential"), and whether individuals employed by the parties may access the information.

3. The *Peabody* case reflects American jurisprudence's adoption of the English approach to the protection of trade secret rights. Does enforcement of employment agreements, like the one in *Peabody*, affect the ability of employees to find a new job? How strong was the defendant's argument that his employment agreement was a restraint of trade?

4. In an earlier U.S. case, *Vickery v. Welch*, 36 Mass. 523, 19 Pick. 523 (1837), the defendant argued that when an agreement to transfer an exclusive interest in his trade secrets to the plaintiff prevented him from communicating them to a third party when no such promise was made, the obligation was void as being a restraint of trade. The court rejected this argument by reasoning that if the "public are not prejudiced by the transfer of the [trade secret] . . . it is of no consequence to the public whether the secret art be used by the plaintiff or the defendant." *Vickery*, 19 Pick. at 527.

## C. NATURE OF TRADE SECRET PROTECTION (FIDUCIARY RELATIONSHIP v. PROPERTY RIGHT)

### PRESSED STEEL CAR CO. v. STANDARD STEEL CAR CO.

60 A. 4 (Pa. 1904)

* * *

[Editor's note: After reproducing the trial court's extensive findings of fact, the court of appeals affirmed the judgment for the plaintiff with a substantially truncated description of the facts.]

The very elaborate opinion of the learned trial judge renders unnecessary an extended review of the questions involved in this case. We are satisfied that the evidence fully justifies his findings of fact, and we are equally well convinced that his conclusions of law on the facts are correct. The drawings or tracings of the parts of the cars and the blue prints, except the "secondary prints," were made by the appellee company to be used in connection with, and were necessary for, carrying on the business in which the company was engaged. The court finds as follows: "In connection with the designing and construction of these cars, the company prepares drawings or tracings showing the various parts of the cars to be built, and how the different railway specialties and appliances can be successfully applied to cars which it manufactures. Blue prints of these drawings are sent to the railroad companies proposing to purchase cars, so as to enable them to ascertain whether or not the cars which it is proposed to build will meet their requirements, each order of cars being especially designed to meet the particular requirements of the railroad for which they are built. During the manufacture of the cars, copies of these blue prints are frequently furnished to the railroad companies for the purpose of inspecting the cars, to see that they are built in accordance with the drawings. And after the cars are built and delivered, or contemporaneously therewith, blue prints of the cars are furnished to the railroads, so as to enable them either to order parts necessary for repairing the cars, or to make the repairs on the cars themselves. It is common practice with the railroads to order from the plaintiff company and keep in stock with their storekeepers, a large number of such parts of the cars as will most likely be needed for repairs, and for this purpose it has been customary to, and it is necessary that they should, have these blue prints. All of the blue prints so sent out by the plaintiff company were sent out only in connection with the carrying on of its business in the manner and for the purpose stated, and receipts for them were generally required to be given by the persons by whom they were obtained."

The drawings and blue prints in controversy were therefore not sold or given to the railroad companies, but were the property of the plaintiff and made by it for the purpose of carrying on its business, and were sent out in connection with the business of the company. Part of these blue prints were sent to the three railroad companies in connection with orders for cars made by the plaintiff company for the railroads, but, as found by the court, only "for their information and use, as a necessary part of the transaction, and also for their use in ordering repair parts." The remainder of the prints were sent by the plaintiff to one W. H. Miner, draft rigging manufacturer, for his use in adapting and applying the rigging to cars made by the plaintiff company. Notwithstanding the fact that these prints were delivered by the plaintiff to the parties for the purpose stated in the finding of the court, they delivered them to the defendant, a rival company, which is now making use of them in carrying on a competing business. While there was no expressed restriction placed on the ownership of the prints, or any expressed limitation as to the use to which they were to be put, it is clear, as observed by the trial court, that the purpose for which they were delivered by the plaintiff was understood by all parties. The facts of the case warrant no other conclusion. There is no evidence to sustain the contention that the delivery of the prints by the plaintiff to the railroad companies was absolute and unconditional. As suggested above, there was no expressed agreement on the subject, but the facts clearly support the finding of the trial court that the prints were sent in connection with the orders for cars for the information and use of the purchasers, as a necessary part of the transaction, and also for their use in ordering repair parts. The blue prints, therefore, remained the property of the plaintiff after delivery to the railroad companies, whose use of them was restricted to the purpose for which they were delivered, and a chancellor will sustain a bill to enjoin the use of them for another purpose by the railroad company or the defendant company to which, without the plaintiff's consent, they were delivered.

We see no grounds whatever upon which the appellant can claim ownership in the prints, or the right to use them in its business of manufacturing and selling steel cars and car parts in competition with the plaintiff. It is not pretended that the defendant company paid any consideration for them to the plaintiff or to the parties from which it received them. The right to hold them as against the plaintiff is based simply on the fact that the prints were delivered to the defendant company by the railroad companies so that they might obtain their cars and car parts from the defendant instead of the plaintiff, and thus, by the use of the plaintiff company's own designs, enable them to give their trade to its rival competitor. In other words, the prints which had been delivered to the railroad companies to enable them to purchase and use the cars and car parts manufactured by the plaintiff were delivered by the railroad companies to the defendant company so that the latter might manufacture and sell cars and car parts from designs and drawings which had been prepared by the plaintiff for exclusive use in its own business. This was clearly a violation, not only of the property rights of the plaintiff in the prints, but also of the trust and confidence with which they were received by the railroad companies. This unauthorized act and breach of confidence resulted in great advantage to the appellant and loss to the appellee. The court finds that "these prints, both originals and copies, are of great value and use to the defendant company, and their possession by it is a damage to the interests of the plaintiff company." These facts will, on reason and authority, as shown by the learned trial judge, confer jurisdiction on a court of equity, which will restrain the defendant company from making use of the prints in its business, and give such other and adequate relief as the rights of the injured party may require.

* * *

## E.I. DUPONT DE NEMOURS POWDER CO. v. MASLAND

244 U.S. 100 (1917)

* * *

MR. JUSTICE HOLMES delivered the opinion of the court:

This is a bill to prevent the defendant Walter E. Masland from using or disclosing secret processes the knowledge of which was acquired by the defendant while in the plaintiffs' employ. The defendant admits that he intends to manufacture artificial leather, to which some of the plaintiffs' alleged secret processes relate, but denies that he intends to use any inventions, trade secrets, or secret processes of the plaintiffs that he may have learned in any confidential relation, prefacing his denial, however, with the averment that many of the things claimed by the plaintiffs are well known to the trade. A preliminary injunction was refused at first. But before the final hearing the defendant proposed to employ one or more experts and to make such disclosures to them as the preparation of the defense might require. Thereupon the district court issued a preliminary injunction against disclosing any of the plaintiffs' alleged processes to experts or witnesses during the taking of proofs, but excepting counsel, with leave to move to dissolve the injunction if occasion to consult experts arose. Later a motion to dissolve was denied and the hearing was continued for a decision by the appellate court. The circuit court of appeals reversed the decree. Before any further order was entered the writ of certiorari was granted by this court.

The case has been considered as presenting a conflict between a right of property and a right to make a full defense; and it is said that if the disclosure is forbidden to one who denies that there is a trade secret, the merits of his defense are adjudged against him before he has a chance to be heard or to prove his case. We approach the question somewhat differently. The word "property" as applied to trademarks and trade secrets is an unanalyzed expression of certain secondary consequences of the primary fact that the law makes some rudimentary requirements of good faith. Whether the plaintiffs have any valuable secret or not the defendant knows the facts, whatever they are, through a special confidence that he accepted. The property may be denied, but the confidence cannot be. Therefore the starting point for the present matter is not property or due process of law, but that the defendant stood in confidential relations with the plaintiffs, or one of them. These have given place to hostility, and the first thing to be made sure of is that the defendant shall not fraudulently abuse the trust reposed in him. It is the usual incident of confidential relations. If there is any disadvantage in the fact that he knew the plaintiffs' secrets, he must take the burden with the good.

The injunction asked by the plaintiffs forbade only the disclosure of processes claimed by them, including the disclosure to experts or witnesses produced during the taking of proofs, but excepting the defendant's counsel. Some broader and ambiguous words that crept into the decree, seemingly by mistake, may be taken as stricken out and left on one side. This injunction would not prevent the defendant from directing questions that should bring out whatever public facts were nearest to the alleged secrets. Indeed, it is hard to see why it does not leave the plaintiffs' rights somewhat illusory. No very clear ground as yet has been shown for going further. But the judge who tries the case will know the secrets, and if, in his opinion and discretion, it should be advisable and necessary to take in others, nothing will prevent his doing so. It will be understood that if, in the opinion of the trial judge, it is or should become necessary to reveal the secrets to others, it will rest in the judge's discretion to determine whether, to whom, and under what precautions, the revelation should be made.

Decree reversed and case remanded for further proceedings in conformity with this opinion.

* * *

## NATIONAL STARCH PRODUCTS, INC. v. POLYMER INDUSTRIES, INC.

273 A.D. 732, 77 U.S.P.Q. 644 (N.Y. App. Div. 1948)

VAN VOORHIS, JUSTICE.

The defendants appeal from an order striking out two affirmative defenses. The action is by respondent National Starch Products, Inc., for an injunction to restrain the individual defendants, who were former employees of said corporation engaged in research, production and sales, from disclosing secret processes, formulae, and other trade secrets including lists of customers and methods of manufacture, use, application and sale of its products, and to restrain the use of these in the business of defendant Polymer Industries, Inc., in competition with plaintiff.

* * *

The defendants ought to be allowed to plead these affirmative allegations as defenses, leaving it to the trial to determine whether they can be sustained. With respect to the first defense, it is of course true, as plaintiff's counsel contends, that there are other trade secrets than secret processes and formulae, such as customers' lists. A motion to strike out portions of an answer does not furnish a suitable occasion to draw nice distinctions between the exact coverage of these terms, especially when they have been employed more or less indiscriminately in the complaint.

To the extent that the trade secrets sought to be protected relate to secret formulae, or industrial know-how in the processes of manufacture, or lists of customers, it is plain that the defendants should be enjoined from using them or communicating them to others to be used in competition with plaintiff — provided that they are truly secret. It is well established in the law of this subject that in order that a property right may inhere in a secret process or formula, it must be kept secret; that does not mean that a considerable number of persons may not know about it, provided that such information was imparted to them in confidence; on the other hand, if there has been a voluntary disclosure by plaintiff, or if the facts pertaining to the matter are a subject of general knowledge in the trade, then any property right has evaporated.

In the language of Judge Taft, later Chief Justice of the Supreme Court of the United States: "The property in a secret process is the power to make use of it to the exclusion of the world. If the world knows the process, then the property disappears. There can be no property in a process, and no right of protection if knowledge of it is common to the world." (Quoted with other pertinent citations in *Sachs v. Cluett, Peabody & Co., Inc.*, 265 App.Div. 497, 501, *aff'd.* 291 N.Y. 772.)

The complaint herein is comprehensive in scope and embraces a large number of specific activities that are sought to be enjoined on the part of the defendants, not all of which are comprised by any single category above mentioned. The first affirmative defense, in alleging that plaintiff's processes and formulae are generally available to the trade without charge from the manufacturers and suppliers of the various raw materials used, states facts from which, if true, unless counteracted by other facts not mentioned the conclusion of law flows that there is no property right in such processes and formulae belonging to plaintiff. The complaint does seek to enjoin more activities than the disclosure and utilization of such alleged secret formulae and processes; but the circumstances that plaintiff has prepared an omnibus complaint ought not to prevent the defendants from setting forth such defenses as they have against being enjoined from engaging in any of the particular activities alleged in the complaint. That does not mean that these are partial defenses; it means that, if established, they are complete defenses against being restrained from doing that particular thing. Thus, while the formulae and processes of the plaintiff do not comprise all of its alleged trade secrets, a defense which alleges that neither said formulae nor processes are secret is a complete defense against being enjoined from disclosing or utilizing those particular alleged trade secrets.

An earnest argument has been made in plaintiff's behalf to the effect that it is not essential to the protection of these processes and formulae that they be secret, provided that they have been learned by the defendants while in the plaintiff's employ. In support of that argument portions of the opinion in *Kaumagraph Co. v. Stampagraph Co.*, 235 N.Y. 1, have been quoted to the effect that "the question before us is not whether defendants make use of some process not generally known to the public but peculiarly within the knowledge of plaintiff and themselves, but whether defendant's knowledge of the process was obtained by them through and by means of the fact that Chadwick and Turner had been in plaintiff's employ. Employees may not gain knowledge of a secret and avail themselves of it for their private advantage against their employer. But there is no betrayal of confidence when no secret is imparted." [235 N.Y. at 7-8.]

The last sentence furnishes the key to what was decided, and the effect of the decision is to support the first defense herein. There is no betrayal of confidence unless there is a secret to be imparted. Chadwick and Turner were defendants; the proof showed that they had been in the employ of an English company which had patented the process prior to their coming to the United States and entering the employ of Kaumagraph Company. It was held that they could not be restrained by plaintiff therein from disclosing or utilizing for themselves formulae and process which they had not learned from that plaintiff, whether secret or not; in the instant case the plaintiff, in attacking the first affirmative defense, is asking the court to hold the converse of that proposition, that former employees are to be restrained if they learned the information from the plaintiff, regardless of whether such information was secret or not. No such conclusion is to be drawn from *Kaumagraph* case. The earlier part of the opinion therein points out that negative covenants unlimited as to time or place are valid as a basis for equitable relief only as they protect trade secrets acquired during a confidential employment; that means only where, in the language of the opinion, "plaintiff was employing in its business a secret process either developed by itself or the sole right to use which had been acquired by it from the discoverer of the process. . . . A 'secret' is nothing more than a private matter; something known only to one or a few and kept from others."

Likewise, *DuPont Powder Co. v. Masland*, 244 U.S. 100, points in an opposite direction from plaintiff's contention. It is true that in the opinion by Justice Holmes the court said that "Whether the plaintiffs have any valuable secret or not the defendant knows the facts, whatever they are, through a special confidence that he accepted. The property may be denied but the confidence cannot be. Therefore the starting point for the present matter is not property or due process of law, but that the defendant stood in confidential relations with the plaintiffs, or one of them. These have given place to hostility, and the first thing to be made sure of is that the defendant shall not fraudulently abuse the trust reposed in him." The context in which this language was employed is not what one might assume from reading respondent's brief. The court was not reviewing a final judgment; it was reviewing an order pendente lite which sought to manage the difficult problem of how to enable the defendant to present his defense without publishing what would be a trade secret if plaintiff were to prevail in the action. The suit was brought to enjoin defendant from using or disclosing secret processes of plaintiff's business, and the defense was what the first defense is in this action, namely, a denial that the said processes were secret and an allegation that they were well known to the trade. The United States Supreme Court apparently considered that to be a valid defense, if established, and the order appealed from was merely to regulate the procedure in trying out that question, which appears to have been regarded as the controlling issue in the action; the decision of the court permitted the defendant to make disclosure to his attorney and to the court, leaving it to the discretion of the court to permit revelation of the secrets later to expert witnesses, if it should appear to the court necessary for the defendant to call them. Thus the case cited is really an authority for the appellants.

It is to be borne in mind that the injunction sought herein is unlimited by time or place insofar as disclosure of what are alleged to have been trade secrets is concerned. Whether or not such an injunction is proper depends upon whether they are truly secrets. If they, or some of them, are already in the public domain, then no relationship of trust and confidence pertaining to such disclosed features is threatened. [Citations omitted.] If, as defendants allege, respondent's processes and formulae are well known in the trade, no injunction in reference thereto can be obtained.

While it is possible that disclosure of the customers' list and some other details of the business might, after a trial, be held to be prohibited, even if the formulae and processes of manufacture be public property, that would not void the first affirmative defense insofar as the formulae and processes are involved. It simply alleges that the formulae and processes are public, nor is this converted into a partial defense respecting them simply because plaintiff did not separately state and number its causes of action.

The circumstance that it might be possible to raise this point by denials is not controlling, as is stated in the opinion at Special Term. Respondent's argument has been that the content of the defense is insufficient in law. Section 242 of the Civil Practice Act authorizes the pleading of all grounds of defense which, if not raised, would be likely to take the opposing party by surprise. The defendants were not obliged to run the risk that their proofs would not be accepted at the trial for the reason that they had not apprised their adversary of the nature of their attack upon the validity of the causes of action alleged in complaint, on which issue in some respects they have the burden of proof. *Brearton v. DeWitt*, 252 N.Y. 594; *see esp. Murray v. Cooper*, 268 App.Div. 411, *aff'd without opinion*, 294 N.Y. 658.

This does not depend upon the rule of clean hands; the point is that defendants have a right to allege affirmatively that plaintiff has no property right in the main items which it seeks to prevent defendants from utilizing or disclosing.

* * *

## RUCKELSHAUS v. MONSANTO CO.

467 U.S. 986 (1984)

Over the past century, the use of pesticides to control weeds and minimize crop damage caused by insects, disease, and animals has become increasingly more important for American agriculture. [Citations omitted.] While pesticide use has led to improvements in productivity, it has also led to increased risk of harm to humans and the environment. [Citations omitted.] Although the Federal Government has regulated pesticide use for nearly 75 years, FIFRA was first adopted in 1947. [Citation omitted.]

Justice Blackmun delivered the opinion of the Court.

In this case, we are asked to review a United States District Court's determination that several provisions of the Federal Insecticide, Fungicide, and Rodenticide Act (FIFRA), 61 Stat. 163, as amended, 7 U.S.C. § 136 et seq., are unconstitutional. The provisions at issue authorize the Environmental Protection Agency (EPA) to use data submitted by an applicant for registration of a pesticide in evaluating the application of a subsequent applicant, and to disclose publicly some of the submitted data.

As first enacted, FIFRA was primarily a licensing and labeling statute. It required that all pesticides be registered with the Secretary of Agriculture prior to their sale in interstate or foreign commerce. [Citations omitted.] The 1947 legislation also contained general standards setting forth the types of information necessary for proper labeling of a registered pesticide, including directions for use; warnings to prevent harm to people, animals, and plants; and claims made about the efficacy of the product. [Citations omitted.]

Upon request of the Secretary, an applicant was required to submit test data supporting the claims on the label, including the formula for the pesticide. §§ 4(a) and (b). The 1947 version of FIFRA specifically prohibited disclosure of "any information relative to formulas of products," §§ 3(c)(4) and 8(c), but was silent with respect to the disclosure of any of the health and safety data submitted with an application.

In 1970, the Department of Agriculture's FIFRA responsibilities were transferred to the then newly created Environmental Protection Agency, whose Administrator is the appellant in this case. [Citation omitted.]

Because of mounting public concern about the safety of pesticides and their effect on the environment and because of a growing perception that the existing legislation was not equal to the task of safeguarding the public interest [Citations omitted.] Congress undertook a comprehensive revision of FIFRA through the adoption of the Federal Environmental Pesticide Control Act of 1972, 86 Stat. 973.

The amendments transformed FIFRA from a labeling law into a comprehensive regulatory statute. H.R.Rep. No. 92-511, at 1. As amended, FIFRA regulated the use, as well as the sale and labeling, of pesticides; regulated pesticides produced and sold in both intrastate and interstate commerce; provided for review, cancellation, and suspension of registration; and gave EPA greater enforcement authority. Congress also added a new criterion for registration: that EPA determine that the pesticide will not cause "unreasonable adverse effects on the environment." §§ 3(c)(5)(C) and (D), 86 Stat. 980-981.

For purposes of this litigation, the most significant of the 1972 amendments pertained to the pesticide-registration procedure and the public disclosure of information learned through that procedure. Congress added to FIFRA a new section governing public disclosure of data submitted in support of an application for registration. Under that section, the submitter of data could designate any portions of the submitted material it believed to be "trade secrets or commercial or financial information." § 10(a), 86 Stat. 989. Another section prohibited EPA from publicly disclosing information which, in its judgment, contained or related to "trade secrets or commercial or financial information." § 10(b). In the event that EPA disagreed with a submitter's designation of certain information as "trade secrets or commercial or financial information" and proposed to disclose that information, the original submitter could institute a declaratory judgment action in federal district court. § 10(c).

The 1972 amendments also included a provision that allowed EPA to consider data submitted by one applicant for registration in support of another application pertaining to a similar chemical, provided the subsequent applicant offered to compensate the applicant who originally submitted the data. § 3(c)(1)(D). In effect, the provision instituted a mandatory data-licensing scheme. The amount of compensation was to be negotiated by the parties, or, in the event negotiations failed, was to be determined by EPA, subject to judicial review upon the instigation of the original data submitter. The scope of the 1972 data-consideration provision, however, was limited, for any data designated as "trade secrets or commercial or financial information" exempt from disclosure under § 10 could not be considered at all by EPA to support another registration application unless the original submitter consented. *Ibid.*

The 1972 amendments did not specify standards for the designation of submitted data as "trade secrets or commercial or financial information." In addition, Congress failed to designate an effective date for the data-consideration and disclosure schemes. In 1975, Congress amended § 3(c)(1)(D) to provide that the data-consideration and data-disclosure provisions applied only to data submitted on or after January 1, 1970, 89 Stat. 755, but left the definitional question unanswered.

Much litigation centered around the definition of "trade secrets or commercial or financial information" for the purposes of the data-consideration and data-disclosure provisions of FIFRA. EPA maintained that the exemption from consideration or disclosure applied only to a narrow range of information, principally statements of formulae and manufacturing processes. In a series of lawsuits, however, data-submitting firms challenged EPA's interpretation and obtained several decisions to the effect that the term "trade secrets" applied to any data, including health, safety, and environmental data, that met the definition of trade secrets set forth in Restatement of Torts § 757 (1939). [Citations omitted.] These decisions prevented EPA from disclosing much of the data on which it based its decision to register pesticides and from considering the data submitted by one applicant in reviewing the application of a later applicant. [Citations omitted.]

Because of these and other problems with the regulatory scheme embodied in FIFRA as amended in 1972, [citations omitted], Congress enacted other amendments to FIFRA in 1978. These were effected by the Federal Pesticide Act of 1978, 92 Stat. 819. The new amendments included a series of revisions in the data-consideration and data-disclosure provisions of FIFRA's §§ 3 and 10, 7 U.S.C. §§ 136a and 136h.

* * *

Appellee Monsanto Company (Monsanto) is an inventor, developer, and producer of various kinds of chemical products, including pesticides. Monsanto, headquartered in St. Louis County, Mo., sells in both domestic and foreign markets. It is one of a relatively small group of companies that invent and develop new active ingredients for pesticides and conduct most of the research and testing with respect to those ingredients.

These active ingredients are sometimes referred to as "manufacturing-use products" because they are not generally sold directly to users of pesticides. Rather, they must first be combined with "inert ingredients" — chemicals that dissolve, dilute, or stabilize the active components. The results of this process are sometimes called "end-use products," and the firms that produce end-use products are called "formulators." See the opinion of the District Court in this case, *Monsanto Co. v. Acting Administrator, United States Environmental Protection Agency*, 564 F.Supp. 552, 554 (E.D.Mo.1983). A firm that produces an active ingredient may use it for incorporation into its own end-use products, may sell it to formulators, or may do both. Monsanto produces both active ingredients and end-use products. *Ibid.*

The District Court found that development of a potential commercial pesticide candidate typically requires the expenditure of $5 million to $15 million annually for several years. The development process may take between 14 and 22 years, and it is usually that long before a company can expect any return on its investment. *Id.*, at 555. For every manufacturing-use pesticide the average company finally markets, it will have screened and tested 20,000 others. Monsanto has a significantly better-than-average success rate; it successfully markets 1 out of every 10,000 chemicals tested. *Ibid.*

Monsanto, like any other applicant for registration of a pesticide, must present research and test data supporting its application. The District Court found that Monsanto had incurred costs in excess of $23.6 million in developing the health, safety, and environmental data submitted by it under FIFRA. *Id.*, at 560. The information submitted with an application usually has value to Monsanto beyond its instrumentality in gaining that particular application. Monsanto uses this information to develop additional end-use products and to expand the uses of its registered products. The information would also be valuable to Monsanto's competitors. For that reason, Monsanto has instituted stringent security measures to ensure the secrecy of the data. *Ibid.*

It is this health, safety, and environmental data that Monsanto sought to protect by bringing this suit. The District Court found that much of these data "contai[n] or relate to trade secrets as defined by the Restatement of Torts and Confidential, commercial information." *Id.*, at 562.

Monsanto brought suit in District Court, seeking injunctive and declaratory relief from the operation of the data-consideration provisions of FIFRA's § 3(c)(1)(D), and the data-disclosure provisions of FIFRA's § 10 and the related § 3(c)(2)(A). Monsanto alleged that all of the challenged provisions effected a "taking" of property without just compensation, in violation of the Fifth Amendment. In addition, Monsanto alleged that the data-consideration provisions violated the Amendment because they effected a taking of property for a private, rather than a public, purpose. Finally, Monsanto alleged that the arbitration scheme provided by § 3(c)(1)(D)(ii) violates the original submitter's due process rights and constitutes an unconstitutional delegation of judicial power.

After a bench trial, the District Court concluded that Monsanto possessed property rights in its submitted data, specifically including the right to exclude others from the enjoyment of such data by preventing their unauthorized use and by prohibiting their disclosure. 564 F.Supp., at 566. The court found that the challenged data-consideration provisions "give Monsanto's competitors a free ride at Monsanto's expense." *Ibid.* The District Court reasoned that § 3(c)(1)(D) appropriated Monsanto's fundamental right to exclude, and that the effect of that appropriation is substantial. The court further found that Monsanto's property was being appropriated for a private purpose and that this interference was much more significant than the public good that the appropriation might serve. 564 F.Supp., at 566–567.

The District Court also found that operation of the disclosure provisions of FIFRA constituted a taking of Monsanto's property. The cost incurred by Monsanto when its property is "permanently committed to the public domain and thus effectively destroyed" was viewed by the District Court as significantly outweighing any benefit to the general public from having the ability to scrutinize the data, for the court seemed to believe that the general public could derive all the assurance it needed about the safety and effectiveness of a pesticide from EPA's decision to register the product and to approve the label. *Id.*, at 567, and n.4.

After finding that the data-consideration provisions operated to effect a taking of property, the District Court found that the compulsory binding-arbitration scheme set forth in § 3(c)(1)(D)(ii) did not adequately provide compensation for the property taken. The court found the arbitration provision to be arbitrary and vague, reasoning that the statute does not give arbitrators guidance as to the factors that enter into the concept of just compensation, and that judicial review is foreclosed except in cases of fraud. 564 F.Supp., at 567. The District Court also found that the arbitration scheme was infirm because it did not meet the requirements of Art. III of the Constitution. *Ibid.* Finally, the court found that a remedy under the Tucker Act was not available for the deprivations of property effected by §§ 3 and 10. 564 F.Supp., at 567-568.

The District Court therefore declared §§ 3(c)(1)(D), 3(c)(2)(A), 10(b), and 10(d) of FIFRA, as amended by the Federal Pesticide Act of 1978, to be unconstitutional, and permanently enjoined EPA from implementing or enforcing those sections. *See* Amended Judgment, App. to Juris. Statement 41a.

We noted probable jurisdiction. 464 U.S. 890 (1983).

In deciding this case, we are faced with four questions: (1) Does Monsanto have a property interest protected by the Fifth Amendment's Taking Clause in the health, safety, and environmental data it has submitted to EPA? (2) If so, does EPA's use of the data to evaluate the applications of others or EPA's disclosure of the data to qualified members of the public effect a taking of that property interest? (3) If there is a taking, is it a taking for a public use? (4) If there is a taking for a public use, does the statute adequately provide for just compensation?

For purposes of this case, EPA has stipulated that "Monsanto has certain property rights in its information, research and test data that it has submitted under FIFRA to EPA and its predecessor agencies which may be protected by the Fifth Amendment to the Constitution of the United States." App. 36. Since the exact import of that stipulation is not clear, we address the question whether the data at issue here can be considered property for the purposes of the Taking Clause of the Fifth Amendment.

This Court never has squarely addressed the applicability of the protections of the Taking Clause of the Fifth Amendment to commercial data of the kind involved in this case. In answering the question now, we are mindful of the basic axiom that " '[p]roperty interests . . . are not created by the Constitution. Rather, they are created and their dimensions are defined by existing rules or understandings that stem from an independent source such as state law.' " *Webb's Fabulous Pharmacies, Inc. v. Beckwith*, 449 U.S. 155, 161, 101 S.Ct. 446, 451, 66 L.Ed.2d 358 (1980), *quoting Board of Regents v. Roth, 408 U.S. 564, 577, 92 S.Ct. 2701, 2709, 33 L.Ed.2d 548 (1972).* Monsanto asserts that the health, safety, and environmental data it has submitted to EPA are property under Missouri law, which recognizes trade secrets, as defined in § 757, Comment *b*, of the Restatement of Torts, as property. [Citations omitted.] The Restatement defines a trade secret as "any formula, pattern, device or compilation of information which is used in one's business, and which gives him an opportunity to obtain an advantage over competitors who do not know or use it." § 757, Comment *b*. And the parties have stipulated that much of the information, research, and test data that Monsanto has submitted under FIFRA to EPA "contains or relates to trade secrets as defined by the Restatement of Torts."

Because of the intangible nature of a trade secret, the extent of the property right therein is defined by the extent to which the owner of the secret protects his interest from disclosure to others. [Citations omitted.] Information that is public knowledge or that is generally known in an industry cannot be a trade secret. Restatement of Torts, *supra*. If an individual discloses his trade secret to others who are under no obligation to protect the confidentiality of the information, or otherwise publicly discloses the secret, his property right is extinguished. [Citations omitted.]

Trade secrets have many of the characteristics of more tangible forms of property. A trade secret is assignable. [Citations omitted.] A trade secret can form the res of a trust, [citations omitted], and it passes to a trustee in bankruptcy. [Citation omitted.]

Even the manner in which Congress referred to trade secrets in the legislative history of FIFRA supports the general perception of their property-like nature. In discussing the 1978 amendments to FIFRA, Congress recognized that data developers like Monsanto have a "proprietary interest" in their data. S.Rep. No. 95-334, at 31. Further, Congress reasoned that submitters of data are "entitled" to "compensation" because they "have legal ownership of the data." H.R.Conf.Rep. No. 95-1560, p. 29 (1978), U.S.Code Cong. & Admin. News 1978, pp. 1966, 2045. This general perception of trade secrets as property is consonant with a notion of "property" that extends beyond land and tangible goods and includes the products of an individual's "labour and invention." 2 W. Blackstone, COMMENTARIES; *see generally* J. Locke, THE SECOND TREATISE OF CIVIL GOVERNMENT, ch. 5 (J. Gough ed. 1947).

Although this Court never has squarely addressed the question whether a person can have a property interest in a trade secret, which is admittedly intangible, the Court has found other kinds of intangible interests to be property for purposes of the Fifth Amendment's Taking Clause. [Citations omitted.] That intangible property rights protected by state law are deserving of the protection of the Taking Clause has long been implicit in the thinking of this Court:

> "It is conceivable that [the term "property" in the Taking Clause] was used in its vulgar and untechnical sense of the physical thing with respect to which the citizen exercises rights recognized by law. On the other hand, it may have been employed in a more accurate sense to denote the group of rights inhering in the citizen's relation to the physical thing, as the right to possess, use and dispose of it. In point of fact, the construction given the phrase has been the latter." *United States v. General Motors Corp.*, 323 U.S. 373, 377–378, 65 S.Ct. 357, 359, 89 L.Ed. 311 (1945).

We therefore hold that to the extent that Monsanto has an interest in its health, safety, and environmental data cognizable as a trade-secret property right under Missouri law, that property right is protected by the Taking Clause of the Fifth Amendment.[43]

---

[43] [9] Contrary to EPA's contention, Brief for Appellant 29, Justice Holmes' dictum in *E.I. du Pont de Nemours Powder Co. v. Masland*, 244 U.S. 100, 37 S.Ct. 575, 61 L.Ed. 1016 (1917), does not undermine our holding that a trade secret is property protected by the Fifth Amendment Taking Clause. Masland arose from a dispute about the disclosure of trade secrets during preparation for a trial. In his opinion for the Court, the Justice stated:

> The case has been considered as presenting a conflict between a right of property and a right to make a full defence, and it is said that if the disclosure is forbidden to one who denies that there is a trade secret, the merits of his defence are adjudged against him before he has a chance to be heard or to prove his case. We approach the question somewhat differently. The word property as applied to trade-marks and trade secrets is an unanalyzed expression of certain secondary consequences of the primary fact that the law makes some rudimentary requirements of good faith. Whether the plaintiffs have any valuable secret or not the defendant knows the facts, whatever they are, through a special confidence that he accepted. The property may be denied but the confidence cannot be. Therefore the starting point for the present matter is not property or due process of law, but that the defendant stood in

## NOTES AND QUESTIONS:

1. Was the outcome in *Pressed Car* based on the plaintiff's property rights in the freight car design, or was it based on the defendant's breach of confidence? Does it matter which basis was used?

2. Did Mr. Justice Holmes' decision in *Masland* intend for trade secrets not to have any property attributes whatsoever? Can you make an argument that *Masland* and *National Starch* are not inconsistent with each other (double negative intended)? Why do you think the court in *National Starch* cited a New York appellate court opinion that quoted future Chief Justice of the Supreme Court, William Howard Taft, and even mentioned his future position on the Court, as saying that "[t]he property in a secret process is the power to make use of it to the exclusion of the world." *Id.* at 735. Note the Court's explanation in *Ruckelshaus*, at n.9, that in *Masland*, "Justice Holmes did not deny the existence of a property interest; he simply deemed determination of the existence of that interest irrelevant to resolution of the case."

3. Why was the issue about whether trade secrets are property still being debated in 1984, when *Ruckelshaus* was decided?

4. The "*prima facie* tort theory" is a legal principle that was developed in the early 1900s to obviate the need to bend nontraditional causes of action into defined categories (called "code pleading"), which was carried over from the early common law pleading in England. This principle was articulated by Justice Holmes in *Aikens v. Wisconsin*, 195 U.S. 194, 204 (1904), where he stated:

> It has been considered that prima facie the intentional infliction of temporal damages is a cause of action, which, as a matter of substantive law, whatever may be the form of pleading, requires a justification if the defendant is to escape.

The "prima facie tort theory" developed as a way to allow the law to evolve and encompass new situations that did not quite fit in the traditional notions of actionable torts and the common law cause-of-action pigeonholes. What influence do you think the prima facie tort theory had on the development of trade secret law in the United States? Note that Mr. Justice Holmes wrote his decision in *Masland* in 1917.

---

confidential relations with the plaintiffs." *Id.*, at 102, 37 S.Ct., at 575. Justice Holmes did not deny the existence of a property interest; he simply deemed determination of the existence of that interest irrelevant to resolution of the case. In a case decided prior to *Masland*, the Court had spoken of trade secrets in property terms. *Board of Trade v. Christie Grain & Stock Co.*, 198 U.S. 236, 250–253, 25 S.Ct. 637, 639–640, 49 L.Ed. 1031 (1905) (Holmes, J., for the Court). *See generally* 1 R. Milgrim, TRADE SECRETS § 1.01[1] (1983).

* * *

## D. CONSTITUTIONAL PREEMPTION ISSUES

### KEWANEE OIL CO. v. BICRON CORP.

416 U.S. 470 (1974)

We granted certiorari to resolve a question on which there is a conflict in the courts of appeals: whether state trade secret protection is pre-empted by operation of the federal patent law. In the instant case the Court of Appeals for the Sixth Circuit held that there was pre-emption. The Courts of Appeals for the Second, Fourth, Fifth and Ninth Circuits have reached the opposite conclusion.

Harshaw Chemical Co., an unincorporated division of petitioner, is a leading manufacturer of a type of synthetic crystal which is useful in the detection of ionizing radiation. In 1949 Harshaw commenced research into the growth of this type crystal and was able to produce one less than two inches in diameter. By 1966, as the result of expenditures in excess of $1 million, Harshaw was able to grow a 17-inch crystal, something no one else had done previously. Harshaw had developed many processes, procedures, and manufacturing techniques in the purification of raw materials and the growth and encapsulation of the crystals which enabled it to accomplish this feat. Some of these processes Harshaw considers to be trade secrets.

The individual respondents former employees of Harshaw who formed or later joined respondent Bicron. While at Harshaw the individual respondents executed, as a condition of employment, at least one agreement each, requiring them not to disclose confidential information or trade secrets obtained as employees of Harshaw. Bicron was formed in August 1969 to compete with Harshaw in the production of the crystals, and by April 1970, had grown a 17-inch crystal.

Petitioner brought this diversity action in United States District Court for the Northern District of Ohio seeking injunctive relief and damages for the misappropriation of trade secrets. The District Court, applying Ohio trade secret law, granted a permanent injunction against the disclosure or use by respondents of 20 of the 40 claimed trade secrets until such time as the trade secrets had been released to the public, had otherwise generally become available to the public, or had been obtained by respondents from sources having the legal right to convey the information.

The Court of Appeals for the Sixth Circuit held that the findings of fact by the District Court were not clearly erroneous, and that it was evident from the record that the individual Respondents appropriated to the benefit of Bicron secret information on processes obtained while they were employees at Harshaw. Further, the Court of Appeals held that the District Court properly applied Ohio law relating to trade secrets. Nevertheless, the Court of Appeals reversed the District Court, finding Ohio's trade secret law to be in conflict with the patent laws of the United States. The Court of Appeals reasoned that Ohio could not grant monopoly protection to processes and manufacturing techniques that were appropriate subjects for consideration under 35 U.S.C. § 101 for a federal patent but which had been in commercial use for over one year and so were no longer eligible for patent protection under 35 U.S.C. § 102(b).

We hold that Ohio's law of trade secrets is not preempted by the patent laws of the United States, and, accordingly, we reverse.

* * *

The first issue we deal with is whether the States are forbidden to act at all in the area of protection of the kinds of intellectual property which may make up the subject matter of trade secrets.

Article I, § 8, cl. 8, of the Constitution grants to the Congress the power,

> "(t)o promote the Progress of Science and useful Arts, by securing for limited Times to Authors and Inventors the exclusive Right to their respective Writings and Discoveries . . ."

In the 1972 Term, in *Goldstein v. California*, 412 U.S. 546, 93 S.Ct. 2303, 37 L.Ed.2d 163 (1973), we held that the cl. 8 grant of power to Congress was not exclusive and that, at least in the case of writings, the States were not prohibited from encouraging and protecting the efforts of those within their borders by appropriate legislation. The States could, therefore, protect against the unauthorized rerecording for sale of performances fixed on records or tapes, even though those performances qualified as "writings" in the constitutional sense and Congress was empowered to legislate regarding such performances and could pre-empt the area if it chose to do so. This determination was premised on the great diversity of interests in our Nation-the essentially non-uniform character of the appreciation of intellectual achievements in the various States. Evidence for this came from patents granted by the States in the 18th century. 412 U.S., at 557, 93 S.Ct., at 2310.

Just as the States may exercise regulatory power over writings so may the States regulate with respect to discoveries. States may hold diverse viewpoints in protecting intellectual property to invention as they do in protecting the intellectual property relating to the subject matter of copyright. The only limitation on the States is that in regulating the area of patents and copyrights they do not conflict with the operation of the laws in this area passed by Congress, and it is to that more difficult question we now turn.

The question of whether the trade secret law of Ohio is void under the Supremacy Clause involves a consideration of whether that law "stands as an obstacle to the accomplishment and execution of the full purposes and objectives of Congress." [Citations omitted.] We stated in *Sears, Roebuck & Co. v. Stiffel Co.*, 376 U.S. 225, 229, 84 S.Ct. 784, 11 L.Ed.2d 661 (1964), that when state law touches upon the area of federal statutes enacted pursuant to constitutional authority, "it is 'familiar doctrine' that the federal policy 'may not be set at naught, or its benefits denied' by the state law. [Citation omitted.] This is true, of course, even if the state law is enacted in the exercise of otherwise undoubted state power."

The laws which the Court of Appeals in this case held to be in conflict with the Ohio law of trade secrets were the patent laws passed by the Congress in the unchallenged exercise of its clear power under Art. I, § 8, cl. 8, of the Constitution. The patent law does not explicitly endorse or forbid the operation of trade secret law. However, as we have noted, if the scheme of protection developed by Ohio respecting trade secrets "clashes with the objectives of the federal patent laws,"

*Sears, Roebuck & Co. v. Stiffel Co., supra*, 376 U.S., at 231, 84 S.Ct. at 789, then the state law must fall. To determine whether the Ohio law "clashes" with the federal law it is helpful to examine the objectives of both the patent and trade secret laws.

The stated objective of the Constitution in granting the power to Congress to legislate in the area of intellectual property is to "promote the Progress of Science and useful Arts." The patent laws promote this progress by offering a right of exclusion for a limited period as an incentive to inventors to risk the often enormous costs in terms of time, research, and development. The productive effort thereby fostered will have a positive effect on society through the introduction of new products and processes of manufacture into the economy, and the emanations by way of increased employment and better lives for our citizens. In return for the right of exclusion-this "reward for inventions," *Universal Oil Co. v. Globe Co.*, 322 U.S. 471, 484, 64 S.Ct. 1110, 1116, 88 L.Ed. 1399 (1944) — the patent laws impose upon the inventor a requirement of disclosure. To insure adequate and full disclosure so that upon the expiration of the 17-year period "the knowledge of the invention enures to the people, who are thus enabled without restriction to practice it and profit by its use," *United States v. Dubilier Condenser Corp.*, 289 U.S. 178, 187, 53 S.Ct. 554, 77 L.Ed. 1114 (1933), the patent laws require that the patent application shall include a full and clear description of the invention and "of the manner and process of making and using it" so that any person skilled in the art may make and use the invention. 35 U.S.C. § 112. When a patent is granted and the information contained in it is circulated to the general public and those especially skilled in the trade, such additions to the general store of knowledge are of such importance to the public weal that the Federal Government is willing to pay the high price of 17 years of exclusive use for its disclosure, which disclosure, it is assumed, will stimulate ideas and the eventual development of further significant advances in the art. The Court has also articulated another policy of the patent law: that which is in the public domain cannot be removed therefrom by action of the States.

"(F)ederal laws require[ ] that all ideas in general circulation be dedicated to the common good unless they are protected by a valid patent." [Citations omitted.]

The maintenance of standards of commercial ethics and the encouragement of invention are the broadly stated policies behind trade secret law. 'The necessity of good faith and honest, fair dealing, is the very life and spirit of the commercial world.' *National Tube Co. v. Eastern Tube Co.*, 3 Ohio Cir.Cr.R., N.S. at 462. In *A. O. Smith Corp. v. Petroleum Iron Works Co.*, 73 F.2d, at 539, the Court emphasized that even though a discovery may not be patentable, that does not

> "destroy the value of the discovery to one who makes it, or advantage the competitor who by unfair means, or as the beneficiary of a broken faith, obtains the desired knowledge without himself paying the price in labor, money, or machines expended by the discover."

In *Wexler v. Greenberg*, 399 Pa. 569, 578-579, 160 A.2d 430, 434-435 (1960), the Pennsylvania Supreme Court noted the importance of trade secret protection to the subsidization of research and development and to increased economic efficiency within large companies through the dispersion of responsibilities for creative developments.

Having now in mind the objectives of both the patent and trade secret law, we turn to an examination of the interaction of these systems of protection of intellectual property — one established by the Congress and the other by a State — to determine whether and under what circumstances the latter might constitute "too great an encroachment on the federal patent system to be tolerated." *Sears, Roebuck & Co. v. Stiffel Co.*, 376 U.S., at 232, 84 S.Ct., at 789.

As we noted earlier, trade secret law protects items which would not be proper subjects for consideration for patent protection under 35 U.S.C. § 101. As in the case of the recordings in *Goldstein v. California*, Congress, with respect to nonpatentable subject matter, "has drawn no balance; rather, it has left the area unattended, and no reason exists why the State should not be free to act." *Goldstein v. California, supra*, 412 U.S., at 570, 93 S.Ct. at 2316 (footnote omitted).

Since no patent is available for a discovery, however useful, novel, and nonobvious, unless it falls within one of the express categories of patentable subject matter of 35 U.S.C. § 101, the holder of such a discovery would have no reason to apply for a patent whether trade secret protection existed or not. Abolition of trade secret protection would, therefore, not result in increased disclosure to the public of discoveries in the area of nonpatentable subject matter. Also, it is hard to see how the public would be benefited by disclosure of customer lists or advertising campaigns; in fact, keeping such items secret encourages businesses to initiate new and individualized plans of operation, and constructive competition results. This, in turn, leads to a greater variety of business methods than would otherwise be the case if privately developed marketing and other data were passed illicitly among firms involved in the same enterprise.

Congress has spoken in the area of those discoveries which fall within one of the categories of patentable subject matter of 35 U.S.C. § 101 and which are, therefore, of a nature that would be subject to consideration for a patent. Processes, machines, manufactures, compositions of matter and improvements thereof, which meet the tests of utility, novelty, and nonobviousness are entitled to be patented, but those which do not, are not. The question remains whether those items which are proper subjects for consideration for a patent may also have available the alternative protection accorded by trade secret law.

Certainly the patent policy of encouraging invention is not disturbed by the existence of another form of incentive to invention. In this respect the two systems are not and never would be in conflict. Similarly, the policy that matter once in the public domain must remain in the public domain is not incompatible with the existence of trade secret protection. By definition a trade secret has not been placed in the public domain.

The more difficult objective of the patent law to reconcile with trade secret law is that of disclosure, the quid pro quo of the right to exclude. [Citation omitted.] We are helped in this stage of the analysis by Judge Henry Friendly's opinion in *Painton & Co. v. Bourns, Inc.*, 442 F.2d 216 (CA2 1971). There the Court of Appeals thought it useful, in determining whether inventors will refrain because of the existence of trade secret law from applying for patents, thereby depriving the public from learning of the invention, to distinguish between three categories of trade secrets:

> "(1) the trade secret believed by its owner to constitute a validly patentable invention; (2) the trade secret known to its owner not to be so patentable; and (3) the trade secret whose valid patentability is considered dubious." *Id.*, at 224.

Trade secret protection in each of these categories would run against breaches of confidence — the employee and licensee situations — and theft and other forms of industrial espionage.

As to the trade secret known not to meet the standards of patentability, very little in the way of disclosure would be accomplished by abolishing trade secret protection. With trade secrets of nonpatentable subject matter, the patent alternative would not reasonably be available to the inventor. "There can be no public interest in stimulating developers of such (unpatentable) know how to flood an overburdened Patent Office with applications (for) what they do not consider patentable." *Ibid.* The mere filing of applications doomed to be turned down by the Patent Office will bring forth no new public knowledge or enlightenment, since under federal statute and regulation patent applications and abandoned patent applications are held by the Patent Office in confidence and are not open to public inspection. 35 U.S.C. § 122; 37 C.F.R. § 1.14(b).

Even as the extension of trade secret protection to patentable subject matter that the owner knows will not meet the standards of patentability will not conflict with the patent policy of disclosure, it will have a decidedly beneficial effect on society. Trade secret law will encourage invention in areas where patent law does not reach, and will prompt the independent innovator to proceed with the discovery and exploitation of his invention. Competition is fostered and the public is not deprived of the use of valuable, if not quite patentable, invention.

Even if trade secret protection against the faithless employee were abolished, inventive and exploitive effort in the area of patentable subject matter that did not meet the standards of patentability would continue, although at a reduced level. Alternatively with the effort that remained, however, would come an increase in the amount of self-help that innovative companies would employ. Knowledge would be widely dispersed among the employees of those still active in research. Security precautions necessarily would be increased, and salaries and fringe benefits of those few officers or employees who had to know the whole of the secret invention would be fixed in an amount thought sufficient to assure their loyalty. Smaller companies would be placed at a distinct economic disadvantage, since the costs of this kind of self-help could be great, and the cost to the public of the use of this invention would be increased. The innovative entrepreneur with limited resources would tend to confine his research efforts to himself and those few he felt he could trust without the ultimate assurance of legal protection against breaches of confidence. As a result, organized scientific and technological research could become fragmented, and society, as a whole, would suffer.

Another problem that would arise if state trade secret protection were precluded is in the area of licensing others to exploit secret processes. The holder of a trade secret would not likely share his secret with a manufacturer who cannot be placed under binding legal obligation to pay a license fee or to protect the secret. The result would be to hoard rather than disseminate knowledge. *Painton & Co. v.*

*Bourns, Inc.*, 442 F.2d, at 223. Instead, then, of licensing others to use his invention and making the most efficient use of existing manufacturing and marketing structures within the industry, the trade secret holder would tend either to limit his utilization of the invention, thereby depriving the public of the maximum benefit of its use, or engage in the time-consuming and economically wasteful enterprise of constructing duplicative manufacturing and marketing mechanisms for the exploitation of the invention. The detrimental misallocation of resources and economic waste that would thus take place if trade secret protection were abolished with respect to employees or licensees cannot be justified by reference to any policy that the federal patent law seeks to advance.

Nothing in the patent law requires that States refrain from action to prevent industrial espionage. In addition to the increased costs for protection from burglary, wire-tapping, bribery, and the other means used to misappropriate trade secrets, there is the inevitable cost to the basic decency of society when one firm steals from another. A most fundamental human right, that of privacy, is threatened when industrial espionage is condoned or is made profitable; the state interest in denying profit to such illegal ventures is unchallengeable.

The next category of patentable subject matter to deal with is the invention whose holder has a legitimate doubt as to its patentability. The risk of eventual patent invalidity by the courts and the costs associated with that risk may well impel some with a good-faith doubt as to patentability not to take the trouble to seek to obtain and defend patent protection for their discoveries, regardless of the existence of trade secret protection. Trade secret protection would assist those inventors in the more efficient exploitation of their discoveries and not conflict with the patent law. In most cases of genuine doubt as to patent validity the potential rewards of patent protection are so far superior to those accruing to holders of trade secrets, that the holders of such inventions will seek patent protection, ignoring the trade secret route. For those inventors 'on the line' as to whether to seek patent protection, the abolition of trade secret protection might encourage some to apply for a patent who otherwise would not have done so. For some of those so encouraged, no patent will be granted and the result

> "will have been an unnecessary postponement in the divulging of the trade secret to persons willing to pay for it. If (the patent does issue), it may well be invalid, yet many will prefer to pay a modest royalty than to contest it, even though Lear allows them to accept a license and pursue the contest without paying royalties while the fight goes on. The result in such a case would be unjustified royalty payments from many who would prefer not to pay them rather than agreed fees from one or a few who are entirely willing to do so." *Painton & Co. v. Bourns, Inc.*, 442 F.2d, at 225.

The point is that those who might be encouraged to file for patents by the absence of trade secret law will include inventors possessing the chaff as well as the wheat. Some of the chaff — the nonpatentable discoveries — will be thrown out by the Patent Office, but in the meantime society will have been deprived of use of those discoveries through trade secret-protected licensing. Some of the chaff may not be thrown out. This Court has noted the difference between the standards used by the Patent Office and the courts to determine patentability. *Graham v. John*

*Deere Co.*, 383 U.S. 1, 18, 86 S.Ct. 684, 694, 15 L.Ed.2d 545 (1966). In *Lear, Inc. v. Adkins*, 395 U.S. 653, 89 S.Ct. 1902, 23 L.Ed.2d 610 (1969), the Court thought that an invalid patent was so serious a threat to the free use of ideas already in the public domain that the Court permitted licensees of the patent holder to challenge the validity of the patent. Better had the invalid patent never issued. More of those patents would likely issue if trade secret law were abolished. Eliminating trade secret law for the doubtfully patentable invention is thus likely to have deleterious effects on society and patent policy which we cannot say are balanced out by the speculative gain which might result from the encouragement of some inventors with doubtfully patentable inventions which deserve patent protection to come forward and apply for patents. There is no conflict, then, between trade secret law and the patent law policy of disclosure, at least insofar as the first two categories of patentable subject matter are concerned.

The final category of patentable subject matter to deal with is the clearly patentable invention, i.e., that invention which the owner believes to meet the standards of patentability. It is here that the federal interest in disclosure is at its peak; these inventions, novel, useful and nonobvious, are "the things which are worth to the public the embarrassment of an exclusive patent." *Graham v. John Deere Co., supra*, at 9, 86 S.Ct., at 689 (quoting Thomas Jefferson). The interest of the public is that the bargain of 17 years of exclusive use in return for disclosure be accepted. If a State, through a system of protection, were to cause a substantial risk that holders of patentable inventions would not seek patents, but rather would rely on the state protection, we would be compelled to hold that such a system could not constitutionally continue to exist. In the case of trade secret law no reasonable risk of deterrence from patent application by those who can reasonably expect to be granted patents exists.

Trade secret law provides far weaker protection in many respects than the patent law. While trade secret law does not forbid the discovery of the trade secret by fair and honest means, e.g., independent creation or reverse engineering, patent law operates "against the world," forbidding any use of the invention for whatever purpose for a significant length of time. The holder of a trade secret also takes a substantial risk that the secret will be passed on to his competitors, by theft or by breach of a confidential relationship, in a manner not easily susceptible of discovery or proof. *Painton & Co. v. Bourns, Inc.*, 442 F.2d, at 224. Where patent law acts as a barrier, trade secret law functions relatively as a sieve. The possibility that an inventor who believes his invention meets the standards of patentability will sit back, rely on trade secret law, and after one year of use forfeit any right to patent protection, 35 U.S.C. § 102(b), is remote indeed.

Nor does society face much risk that scientific or technological progress will be impeded by the rare inventor with a patentable invention who chooses trade secret protection over patent protection. The ripeness-of-time concept of invention, developed from the study of the many independent multiple discoveries in history, predicts that if a particular individual had not made a particular discovery others would have, and in probably a relatively short period of time. If something is to be discovered at all very likely it will be discovered by more than one person. [Citations omitted.] Even were an inventor to keep his discovery completely to himself, something that neither the patent nor trade secret laws forbid, there is a high probability that it will be soon independently developed. If the invention, though still a trade secret, is put into public use, the competition is alerted to the existence of the inventor's solution to the problem and may be encouraged to make an extra effort to independently find the solution thus known to be possible. The inventor faces pressures not only from private industry, but from the skilled scientists who work in our universities and our other great publicly supported centers of learning and research.

We conclude that the extension of trade secret protection to clearly patentable inventions does not conflict with the patent policy of disclosure. Perhaps because trade secret law does not produce any positive effects in the area of clearly patentable inventions, as opposed to the beneficial effects resulting from trade secret protection in the areas of the doubtfully patentable and the clearly unpatentable inventions, it has been suggested that partial pre-emption may be appropriate, and that courts should refuse to apply trade secret protection to inventions which the holder should have patented, and which would have been, thereby, disclosed. However, since there is no real possibility that trade secret law will conflict with the federal policy favoring disclosure of clearly patentable inventions partial pre-emption is inappropriate. Partial pre-emption, furthermore, could well create serious problems for state courts in the administration of trade secret law. As a preliminary matter in trade secret actions, state courts would be obliged to distinguish between what a reasonable inventor would and would not correctly consider to be clearly patentable, with the holder of the trade secret arguing that the invention was not patentable and the misappropriator of the trade secret arguing its undoubted novelty, utility, and nonobviousness. Federal courts have a difficult enough time trying to determine whether an invention, narrowed by the patent application procedure and fixed in the specifications which describe the invention for which the patent has been granted, is patentable. Although state courts in some circumstances must join federal courts in judging whether an issued patent is valid, *Lear, Inc. v. Adkins, supra*, it would be undesirable to impose the almost impossible burden on state courts to determine the patentability — in fact and in the mind of a reasonable inventor — of a discovery which has not been patented and remains entirely uncircumscribed by expert analysis in the administrative process. Neither complete nor partial pre-emption of state trade secret law is justified.

Our conclusion that patent law does not pre-empt trade secret law is in accord with prior cases of this Court. [Citations omitted.] Trade secret law and patent law have co-existed in this country for over one hundred years. Each has its particular role to play, and the operation of one does not take away from the need for the other. Trade secret law encourages the development and exploitation of those items of lesser or different invention than might be accorded protection under the patent laws, but which items still have an important part to play in the technological and scientific advancement of the Nation. Trade secret law promotes the sharing of knowledge, and the efficient operation of industry; it permits the individual inventor to reap the rewards of his labor by contracting with a company large enough to develop and exploit it. Congress, by its silence over these many years, has seen the wisdom of allowing the States to enforce trade secret protection. Until Congress takes affirmative action to the contrary, States should be free to grant protection to trade secrets.

Since we hold that Ohio trade secret law is not preempted by the federal patent law, the judgment of the Court of Appeals for the Sixth Circuit is reversed, and the case is remanded to the Court of Appeals with directions to reinstate the judgment of the District Court.

* * *

MR. JUSTICE DOUGLAS, with whom MR. JUSTICE BRENNAN concurs, dissenting.

Today's decision is at war with the philosophy of *Sears, Roebuck & Co. v. Stiffel Co., 376 U.S. 225, 84 S.Ct. 784, 11 L.Ed.2d 661* and *Compco Corp. v. Day-Brite Lighting, Inc.*, 376 U.S. 234, 84 S.Ct. 779, 11 L.Ed.2d 669. Those cases involved patents-one of a pole lamp and one of fluorescent lighting fixtures each of which was declared invalid. The lower courts held, however, that though the patents were invalid the sale of identical or confusingly similar products to the products of the patentees violated state unfair competition laws. We held that when an article is unprotected by a patent, state law may not forbid others to copy it, because every article not covered by a valid patent is in the public domain. Congress in the patent laws decided that where no patent existed, free competition should prevail; that where a patent is rightfully issued, the right to exclude others should obtain for no longer than 17 years, and that the States may not "under some other law, such as that forbidding unfair competition, give protection of a kind that clashes with the objectives of the federal patent laws," 376 U.S., at 231, 84 S.Ct. at 789.

The product involved in this suit, sodium iodide synthetic crystals, was a product that could be patented but was not. Harshaw the inventor apparently contributed greatly to the technology in that field by developing processes, procedures, and techniques that produced much larger crystals than any competitor. These processes, procedures, and techniques were also patentable; but no patent was sought. Rather Harshaw sought to protect its trade secrets by contracts with its employees. And the District Court found that, as a result of those secrecy precautions, "not sufficient disclosure occurred so as to place the claimed trade secrets in the public domain"; and those findings were sustained by the Court of Appeals.

The District Court issued a permanent injunction against respondents, ex-employees, restraining them from using the processes used by Harshaw. By a patent which would require full disclosure Harshaw could have obtained a 17-year monopoly against the world. By the District Court's injunction, which the Court approves and reinstates, Harshaw gets a permanent injunction running into perpetuity against respondents. In *Sears*, as in the present case, an injunction against the unfair competitor issued. We said: "To allow a State by use of its law of unfair competition to prevent the copying of an article which represents too slight an advance to be patented would be to permit the State to block off from the public something which federal law has said belongs to the public. The result would be that while federal law grants only 14 or 17 years' protection to genuine inventions, *see* 35 U.S.C. §§ 154, 173, States could allow perpetual protection to articles too lacking in novelty to merit any patent at all under federal constitutional standards. This would be too great an encroachment on the federal patent system to be tolerated." 376 U.S., at 231-232, 84 S.Ct. at 789.

The conflict with the patent laws is obvious. The decision of Congress to adopt a patent system was based on the idea that there will be much more innovation if discoveries are disclosed and patented than there will be when everyone works in secret. Society thus fosters a free exchange of technological information at the cost of a limited 17-year monopoly.

A trade secret, unlike a patent, has no property dimension. That was the view of the Court of Appeals, 478 F.2d 1074, 1081; and its decision is supported by what Mr. Justice Holmes said in *DuPont de Nemours Powder Co. v. Masland*, 244 U.S. 100, 102, 37 S.Ct. 575, 576, 61 L.Ed. 1016:

> "The word property as applied to trade-marks and trade secrets is an unanalyzed expression of certain secondary consequences of the primary fact that the law makes some rudimentary requirements of good faith. Whether the plaintiffs have any valuable secret or not the defendant knows the facts, whatever they are, through a special confidence that he accepted. The property may be denied but the confidence cannot be. Therefore the starting point for the present matter is not property or due process of law, but that the defendant stood in confidential relations with the plaintiffs, or one of them. These have given place to hostility, and the first thing to be made sure of is that the defendant shall not fraudulently abuse the trust reposed in him. It is the usual incident of confidential relations. If there is any disadvantage in the fact that he knew the plaintiffs' secrets he must take the burden with the good."

A suit to redress theft of a trade secret is grounded in tort damages for breach of a contract-a historic remedy[.] [Citation omitted.] Damages for breach of a confidential relation are not pre-empted by this patent law, but an injunction against use is pre-empted because the patent law states the only monopoly over trade secrets that is enforceable by specific performance; and that monopoly exacts as a price full disclosure. A trade secret can be protected only by being kept secret. Damages for breach of a contract are one thing; an injunction barring disclosure does service for the protection accorded valid patents and is therefore pre-empted.

From the findings of fact of the lower courts, the process involved in this litigation was unique, such a great discovery as to make its patentability a virtual certainty. Yet the Court's opinion reflects a vigorous activist antipatent philosophy. My objection is not because it is activist. This is a problem that involves no neutral principle. The Constitution in Art. I, § 8, cl. 8, expresses the activist policy which Congress has enforced by statutes. It is that constitutional policy which we should enforce, not our individual notions of the public good.

I would affirm the judgment below.

* * *

## WARRINGTON ASSOCIATES, INC. v. REAL-TIME ENGINEERING SYSTEMS, INC.

522 F. Supp. 367 (N.D. Ill. 1981)

Plaintiff, Warrington Associates, Inc. ("Warrington"), a designer and marketer of computer software programs for banks and other financial institutions, has filed this action alleging the wrongful appropriation and use of its trade secrets and proprietary materials by defendant, Real-Time Engineering Systems, Inc. ("Real-Time"). More specifically, in its five-count amended complaint, Warrington alleges that Real-Time, individually and in conspiracy with others, misappropriated Warrington's secret computer software programs (Count I), unlawfully interfered with and conspired to breach contractual assurances of confidentiality owed to Warrington (Counts II and III), infringed Warrington's copyrights (Count IV), and engaged in unfair competition (Count V).

* * *

A. Legal Issues: Preemption.

The scope of federal preemption of state law by the Copyright Act is prescribed by that statute itself. In Section 301(b), the Act provides:

> Nothing in this title annuls or limits any rights or remedies under the common law or statutes of any State with respect to
>
> (3) activities violating legal or equitable rights that are not equivalent to any of the exclusive rights within the general scope of copyright as specified by section 106.

An analysis of the interests secured by Copyright and trade secret law makes plain that the claims are not "equivalent" as intended by the Congress. It is well-settled that copyright protection extends not to an idea itself, but rather to the particular expression used by its author. [Citations omitted.] In contrast, the protection provided by the common law of trade secret misappropriation extends to the very ideas of the author, subject, of course, to the requirement that the idea has some originality and is as yet undisclosed or disclosed only on the basis of confidentiality. [Citations omitted.] The practical distinction between the two interests is manifest. While disclosure of the expression does not vitiate rights secured by copyright law, that same disclosure may well strip the underlying idea of its confidentiality, and thus its status as a trade secret. To a certain degree the two respective rights in intellectual property interact. To the extent a work has been copyrighted and published, the chances of unprivileged disclosure may increase. But the mere fact that an expression is copyrighted does not, in and of itself, disclose the trade secret or eliminate its mantle of confidentiality.

In light of the analysis expressed above, it is hardly surprising that neither Congress nor the courts have viewed the federal Copyright Act as preempting the common law of trade secret misappropriation. For example, in the legislative history of the Copyright Act, the House Committee Report states:

> The evolving common law rights of "privacy," "publicity," and trade secrets, . . . would remain unaffected so long as the causes of action contain elements such as an invasion of personal rights or a breach of trust or confidentiality . . . .

H.Rep.No. 94-1476, 94th Cong., 2d Sess. 132 (1976) reprinted in 5 U.S.Code Cong. & Admin.News at 5746-5747 (1976).

Both federal and state courts have concurred. In an analogous context, the Supreme Court found nothing incompatible between the law of trade secrets and federal patent statutes. *Kewanee Oil Co. v. Bicron Corp.*, 416 U.S. 470, 94 S.Ct. 1879, 40 L.Ed.2d 315 (1974). If anything the congruence and, concomitantly, the likelihood of preemption, between patent and trade secret law is stronger than between trade secret and copyright law. [Citations omitted.] Finally, whether Wisconsin or Minnesota law is applied, state law provides an area of protection extending beyond copyright. The highest courts of both states have continued to recognize causes of action for trade secret misappropriation subsequent to the amendment of the federal Copyright Act in 1976. The common law of each of these forums stresses that the trade secrets tort is premised on concepts of breach of trust and confidentiality, and not copying. [Citations omitted.]

Accordingly, the court holds that the Copyright Act does not preempt Warrington's common law tort claims in this action.

* * *

## AARONSON v. QUICK POINT PENCIL CO.

440 U.S. 257 (1979)

We granted certiorari, 436 U.S. 943, 98 S.Ct. 2843, 56 L.Ed.2d 784, to consider whether federal patent law pre-empts state contract law so as to preclude enforcement of a contract to pay royalties to a patent applicant, on sales of articles embodying the putative invention, for so long as the contracting party sells them, if a patent is not granted.

In October 1955 the petitioner, Mrs. Jane Aronson, filed an application, Serial No. 542677, for a patent on a new form of keyholder. Although ingenious, the design was so simple that it readily could be copied unless it was protected by patent. In June 1956, while the patent application was pending, Mrs. Aronson negotiated a contract with the respondent, Quick Point Pencil Co., for the manufacture and sale of the keyholder.

The contract was embodied in two documents. In the first, a letter from Quick Point to Mrs. Aronson, Quick Point agreed to pay Mrs. Aronson a royalty of 5% of the selling price in return for "the exclusive right to make and sell keyholders of the type shown in your application, Serial No. 542677." The letter further provided that the parties would consult one another concerning the steps to be taken "[i]n the event of any infringement."

* * *

In June 1961, when Mrs. Aronson had failed to obtain a patent on the keyholder within the five years specified in the agreement, Quick Point asserted its contractual right to reduce royalty payments to 2 1/2% of sales. In September of that year the Board of Patent Appeals issued a final rejection of the application on the ground that the keyholder was not patentable, and Mrs. Aronson did not appeal. Quick Point continued to pay reduced royalties to her for 14 years thereafter.

The market was more receptive to the keyholder's novelty and utility than the Patent Office. By September 1975 Quick Point had made sales in excess of $7 million and paid Mrs. Aronson royalties totaling $203,963.84; sales were continuing to rise. However, while Quick Point was able to pre-empt the market in the earlier years and was long the only manufacturer of the Aronson keyholder, copies began to appear in the late 1960s. Quick Point's competitors, of course, were not required to pay royalties for their use of the design. Quick Point's share of the Aronson keyholder market has declined during the past decade.

In November 1975 Quick Point commenced an action in the United States District Court for a declaratory judgment, pursuant to 28 U.S.C. § 2201, that the royalty agreement was unenforceable. Quick Point asserted that state law which might otherwise make the contract enforceable was preempted by federal patent law. This is the only issue presented to us for decision.

Both parties moved for summary judgment on affidavits, exhibits, and stipulations of fact. The District Court concluded that the "language of the agreement is plain, clear and unequivocal and has no relation as to whether or not a patent is ever granted." Accordingly, it held that the agreement was valid, and that Quick Point was obliged to pay the agreed royalties pursuant to the contract for so long as it manufactured the keyholder.

The Court of Appeals reversed, one judge dissenting. 567 F.2d 757. It held that since the parties contracted with reference to a pending patent application, Mrs. Aronson was estopped from denying that patent law principles governed her contract with Quick Point. Although acknowledging that this Court had never decided the precise issue, the Court of Appeals held that our prior decisions regarding patent licenses compelled the conclusion that Quick Point's contract with Mrs. Aronson became unenforceable once she failed to obtain a patent. The court held that a continuing obligation to pay royalties would be contrary to "the strong federal policy favoring the full and free use of ideas in the public domain," *Lear, Inc. v. Adkins*, 395 U.S. 653, 674, 89 S.Ct. 1902, 1913, 23 L.Ed.2d 610 (1969). The court also observed that if Mrs. Aronson actually had obtained a patent, Quick Point would have escaped its royalty obligations either if the patent were held to be invalid, *see ibid.*, or upon its expiration after 17 years, *see Brulotte v. Thys Co.*, 379 U.S. 29, 85 S.Ct. 176, 13 L.Ed.2d 99 (1964). Accordingly, it concluded that a licensee should be relieved of royalty obligations when the licensor's efforts to obtain a contemplated patent prove unsuccessful.

On this record it is clear that the parties contracted with full awareness of both the pendency of a patent application and the possibility that a patent might not issue. The clause de-escalating the royalty by half in the event no patent issued within five years makes that crystal clear. Quick Point apparently placed a significant value on exploiting the basic novelty of the device, even if no patent issued; its success demonstrates that this judgment was well founded. Assuming, *arguendo*, that the initial letter and the commitment to pay a 5% royalty was subject to federal patent law, the provision relating to the 2 1/2% royalty was explicitly independent of federal law. The cases and principles relied on by the Court of Appeals and Quick Point do not bear on a contract that does not rely on a patent, particularly where, as here, the contracting parties agreed expressly as to alternative obligations if no patent should issue.

Commercial agreements traditionally are the domain of state law. State law is not displaced merely because the contract relates to intellectual property which may or may not be patentable; the states are free to regulate the use of such intellectual property in any manner not inconsistent with federal law. [Citations omitted.] In this as in other fields, the question of whether federal law pre-empts state law "involves a consideration of whether that law "stands as an obstacle to the accomplishment and execution of the full purposes and objectives of Congress." *Hines v. Davidowitz*, 312 U.S. 52, 67 [61 S.Ct. 399, 404, 85 L.Ed. 581] (1941)." *Kewanee Oil Co.*, *supra.*, 416 U.S., at 479, 94 S.Ct., at 1885. If it does not, state law governs.

In *Kewanee Oil Co., supra*, at 480-481, 94 S.Ct., at 1885-1886, we reviewed the purposes of the federal patent system. First, patent law seeks to foster and reward invention; second, it promotes disclosure of inventions, to stimulate further innovation and to permit the public to practice the invention once the patent expires; third, the stringent requirements for patent protection seek to assure that ideas in the public domain remain there for the free use of the public.

Enforcement of Quick Point's agreement with Mrs. Aronson is not inconsistent with any of these aims. Permitting inventors to make enforceable agreements licensing the use of their inventions in return for royalties provides an additional incentive to invention. Similarly, encouraging Mrs. Aronson to make arrangements for the manufacture of her keyholder furthers the federal policy of disclosure of inventions; these simple devices display the novel idea which they embody wherever they are seen.

Quick Point argues that enforcement of such contracts conflicts with the federal policy against withdrawing ideas from the public domain and discourages recourse to the federal patent system by allowing states to extend "perpetual protection to articles too lacking in novelty to merit any patent at all under federal constitutional standards," *Sears, Roebuck & Co. v. Stiffel Co.*, 376 U.S. 225, 232, 84 S.Ct. 784, 789, 11 L.Ed.2d 661 (1964).

We find no merit in this contention. Enforcement of the agreement does not withdraw any idea from the public domain. The design for the keyholder was not in the public domain before Quick Point obtained its license to manufacture it. *See Kewanee Oil Co., supra*, 416 U.S. at 484, 94 S.Ct. at 1887. In negotiating the agreement, Mrs. Aronson disclosed the design in confidence. Had Quick Point tried to exploit the design in breach of that confidence, it would have risked legal liability. It is equally clear that the design entered the public domain as a result of the manufacture and sale of the keyholders under the contract.

Requiring Quick Point to bear the burden of royalties for the use of the design is no more inconsistent with federal patent law than any of the other costs involved in being the first to introduce a new product to the market, such as outlays for research and development, and marketing and promotional expenses. For reasons which Quick Point's experience with the Aronson keyholder demonstrate, innovative entrepreneurs have usually found such costs to be well worth paying.

Finally, enforcement of this agreement does not discourage anyone from seeking a patent. Mrs. Aronson attempted to obtain a patent for over five years. It is quite true that had she succeeded, she would have received a 5% royalty only on keyholders sold during the 17-year life of the patent. Offsetting the limited terms of royalty payments, she would have received twice as much per dollar of Quick Point's sales, and both she and Quick Point could have licensed any others who produced the same keyholder. Which course would have produced the greater yield to the contracting parties is a matter of speculation; the parties resolved the uncertainties by their bargain.

No decision of this Court relating to patents justifies relieving Quick Point of its contract obligations. We have held that a state may not forbid the copying of an idea in the public domain which does not meet the requirements for federal patent protection. [Citations omitted.] Enforcement of Quick Point's agreement, however, does not prevent anyone from copying the keyholder. It merely requires Quick Point to pay the consideration which it promised in return for the use of a novel device which enabled it to pre-empt the market.

In *Lear, Inc. v. Adkins*, 395 U.S. 653, 89 S.Ct. 1902, 23 L.Ed.2d 610 (1969), we held that a person licensed to use a patent may challenge the validity of the patent, and that a licensee who establishes that the patent is invalid need not pay the royalties accrued under the licensing agreement subsequent to the issuance of the patent. Both holdings relied on the desirability of encouraging licensees to challenge the validity of patents, to further the strong federal policy that only inventions which meet the rigorous requirements of patentability shall be withdrawn from the public domain. *Id.*, at 670-671, 673-674, 89 S.Ct. at 1911, 1912-1913. Accordingly, neither the holding nor the rationale of *Lear* controls when no patent has issued, and no ideas have been withdrawn from public use.

Enforcement of the royalty agreement here is also consistent with the principles treated in *Brulotte v. Thys Co.*, 379 U.S. 29, 85 S.Ct. 176, 13 L.Ed.2d 99 (1964). There, we held that the obligation to pay royalties in return for the use of a patented device may not extend beyond the life of the patent. The principle underlying that holding was simply that the monopoly granted *under a patent* cannot lawfully be used to "negotiate with the leverage of that monopoly." The Court emphasized that to "use that leverage to project those royalty payments beyond the life of the patent is analogous to an effort to enlarge the monopoly of the patent . . ." *Id.*, at 33, 85 S.Ct., at 179. Here the reduced royalty which is challenged, far from being negotiated "with the leverage" of a patent, rested on the contingency that no patent would issue within five years.

No doubt a pending patent application gives the applicant some additional bargaining power for purposes of negotiating a royalty agreement. The pending application allows the inventor to hold out the hope of an exclusive right to exploit the idea, as well as the threat that the other party will be prevented from using the idea for 17 years. However, the amount of leverage arising from a patent application depends on how likely the parties consider it to be that a valid patent will issue. Here, where no patent ever issued, the record is entirely clear that the parties assigned a substantial likelihood to that contingency, since they specifically provided for a reduced royalty in the event no patent issued within five years.

This case does not require us to draw the line between what constitutes abuse of a pending application and what does not. It is clear that whatever role the pending application played in the negotiation of the 5% royalty, it played no part in the contract to pay the 2 1/2% royalty indefinitely.

Our holding in *Kewanee Oil Co.* puts to rest the contention that federal law pre-empts and renders unenforceable the contract made by these parties. There we held that state law forbidding the misappropriation of trade secrets was not pre-empted by federal patent law. We observed:

> "Certainly the patent policy of encouraging invention is not disturbed by the existence of another form of incentive to invention. In this respect the two systems [patent and trade secret law] are not and never would be in conflict." 416 U.S., at 484, 94 S.Ct., at 1887.

Enforcement of this royalty agreement is even less offensive to federal patent policies than state law protecting trade secrets. The most commonly accepted definition of trade secrets is restricted to confidential information which is not disclosed in the normal process of exploitation. *See* Restatement of Torts § 757, Comment *b*, p. 5 (1939). Accordingly, the exploitation of trade secrets under state law may not satisfy the federal policy in favor of disclosure, whereas disclosure is inescapable in exploiting a device like the Aronson keyholder.

Enforcement of these contractual obligations, freely undertaken in arm's-length negotiation and with no fixed reliance on a patent or a probable patent grant, will

> "encourage invention in areas where patent law does not reach, and will prompt the independent innovator to proceed with the discovery and exploitation of his invention. Competition is fostered and the public is not deprived of the use of valuable, if not quite patentable, invention." (Footnote omitted.) 416 U.S., at 485, 94 S.Ct., at 1888.

The device which is the subject of this contract ceased to have any secrecy as soon as it was first marketed, yet when the contract was negotiated the inventiveness and novelty were sufficiently apparent to induce an experienced novelty manufacturer to agree to pay for the opportunity to be first in the market. Federal patent law is not a barrier to such a contract.

Reversed.

**Mrs. Aronson's key holder**

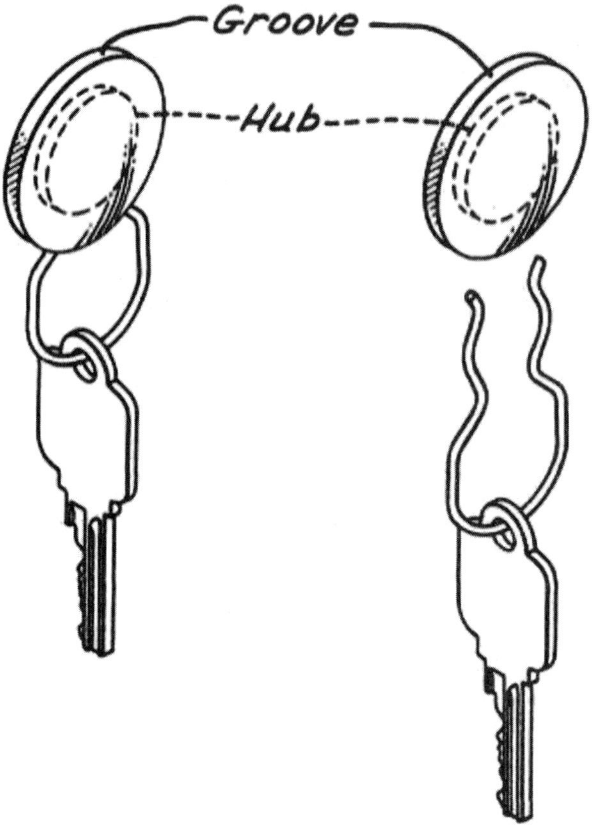


## NOTES AND QUESTIONS:

1. Why do you think there was still a question about whether trade secrets were preempted by the patent laws in 1974 when *Kewanee Oil* was decided? You might consider Judge Motley's district court decision in *Painton & Co. v. Bournes, Inc.*, 309 F.Supp. 271 (S.D.N.Y.1970), *rev'd*, 442 F.2d 216 (2dCir.1971), and the Sixth Circuit's decision in *Kewanee*, at 478 F.2d 1074. Was Mr. Justice Douglas' dissent in *Kewanee Oil* convincing? Was his approach realistic in view of the importance of trade secrets in protecting technology in our modern industrial age?

2. Preemption by the federal copyright laws, which are also sanctioned in art. 1, § 8, cl. 8. of the U.S. Constitution, was raised as a defense against using state trade secret laws for protecting confidential computer software in *Warrington.* In deciding that state trade secret protection is not preempted by the copyright laws, the court in *Warrington* noted that "the likelihood of preemption, between patent and trade secret law is stronger than between trade secret and copyright law," and "state law provides an area of protection extending beyond copyright" because "trade secrets tort is premised on concepts of breach of trust and confidentiality, and not copying." Couldn't this latter rationale have been used in *Kewanee Oil* to

find that state trade secret protection was not preempted by the patent laws?

3. Were there any trade secrets involved in *Aronson*? Why were trade secret rights important in *Aronson*? Would the outcome have changed if Mrs. Aronson's key holder was known to the public when she signed her agreement with Quick Point Pencil Co.? If so, what would have been the legal rationale for that outcome?

4. The large footprint of the Patent Laws was illustrated in *Bonito Boats, Inc. v. Thunder Craft Boats, Inc.*, 489 U.S. 141 (1989), in which the Supreme Court held that the patent laws preempted a Florida law prohibiting the direct copying of boat hulls, which seems to be nothing more than an elaborate form of reverse engineering. *Kewanee Oil* was distinguished as a case that involved a "breach of trust or secrecy." *Bonito Boats, Inc.*, 489 U.S. at 166. The strength of the boat lobby was reflected in the Vessel Hull Design Protection Act, 17 U.S.C. §§ 1301-1332 (1998), which was passed after *Bonito Boats* was decided. This statute provided protection for 10 years, similar to that in the Florida law the Supreme Court struck down.

# Chapter 2

# SUBSTANTIVE ASPECTS OF TRADE SECRET LAW

To explore the substantive aspects of trade secret law, one must develop an understanding of the three basic components of trade secret protection: (1) the property component, (2) secrecy, and (3) the relationship between the parties. Separate sections of this Chapter will deal with the legal issues involved in these components.

Section A will discuss how the legal definition of a trade secret in American jurisprudence evolved. Over the years, the rudimentary principles developed to protect confidential business information during the English Industrial Revolution have become broader and more inclusive in response to evolving technologies and e-commerce. The cases and materials trace the struggle to develop a uniform definition of a "trade secret" from the initial attempt in § 757 of the Restatement of Torts to the currently accepted definitions found in the Uniform Trade Secrets Act (UTSA) and the Restatement (Third) of Unfair Competition.

The cases in Section B were selected to: (1) illustrate the wide range and types of information courts have found to be trade secrets; (2) reflect the multitude of scenarios where trade secret issues may arise; and (3) examine the issues of novelty, concreteness, improvements, and actual use in a business.

Section C explores an essential component of trade secret law — secrecy. The issues discussed involve (1) what degree of secrecy is required, (2) the principles to be used when determining whether the requisite level of secrecy exists, and (3) what measures can be taken to maintain the secrecy of a trade secret.

Materials in Section D deal with one of the most complicated aspects of trade secret law — the circumstances under which a relationship or obligation can be created in which an individual may not disclose or use a trade secret without the owner's permission. This section will also (1) discuss the tort of misappropriation, (2) explore the limited protection of business information in the public domain, and (3) examine the circumstances under which trade secret protection may be available against a party who does not have a confidential relationship with the originator of the information.

## A. LEGAL DEFINITION — TRADE SECRET

### (1) Restatement (Second) of Torts § 757 (1939), cmt. b (1965-79)

b. *Definition of trade secret.* A trade secret may consist of any formula, pattern, device or compilation of information which is used in one's business, and which gives him an opportunity to obtain an advantage over competitors who do not know or use it. It may be a formula for a chemical compound, a process of manufacturing, treating or preserving materials, a pattern for a machine or other device, or a list of customers. It differs from other secret information in a business (see § 759) in that it is not simply information as to single or ephemeral events in the conduct of the business, as, for example, the amount or other terms of a secret bid for a contract or the salary of certain employees, or the security investments made or contemplated, or the date fixed for the announcement of a new policy or for bringing out a new model or the like. A trade secret is a process or device for continuous use in the operation of the business. Generally it relates to the production of goods, as, for example, a machine or formula for the production of an article. It may, however, relate to the sale of goods or to other operations in the business, such as a code for determining discounts, rebates or other concessions in a price list or catalogue, or a list of specialized customers, or a method of bookkeeping or other office management.

### (2) Uniform Trade Secrets Act ("UTSA")

(4) "Trade secret" means information, including a formula, pattern, compilation, program, device, method, technique, or process that:

(i) derives independent economic value, actual or potential, from not being generally known to, and not being readily ascertainable by proper means by, other persons who can obtain economic value from its disclosure or use, and

(ii) is the subject of efforts that are reasonable under the circumstances to maintain its secrecy.

### (3) Restatement (Third) of Unfair Competition (1995)

§ 39. Definition of Trade Secret

A trade secret is any information that can be used in the operation of a business or other enterprise and that is sufficiently valuable and secret to afford an actual or potential economic advantage over others.

## NOTES AND QUESTIONS:

1. When § 757 of the Restatement of Torts was written, the comments stated that "[a]nalogy [to trade secret protection] is sometimes found in the law of 'literary property,' copyright, patents, trade-marks and unfair competition. The suggestion that one has a right to exclude others from the use of his trade secret because he has a right of property in the idea has been frequently advanced and rejected. The theory that has prevailed is that the protection is afforded only by a general duty of good faith, and that the liability rests upon the breach of the duty; that is, breach of contract, abuse of confidence or impropriety in the method of ascertaining the secret." Restatement (Second) of Torts, § 757 cmt. a. However, the property component cannot be ignored as we saw in *National Starch* and *Ruckelshaus.* Why is the property component important?

2. Comment a also states that trade secret protection "is in some respects greater and in some respects less than that afforded by the patent laws." Is this statement at odds with the Supreme Court's observation in *Kewanee Oil* that "[t]rade secret law provides far weaker protection in many respects than the patent law?" 416 U.S. at 489-90. How are trade secrets weaker than patents? How are they stronger? What did the Court in *Kewanee Oil* mean when it said "[w]here patent law acts as a barrier, trade secret law functions relatively as a sieve"? *Id.* at 490.

3. Section 757 of the Restatement of Torts distinguished trade secrets from "other secret information in a business (see § 759) in that it is not simply information as to single or ephemeral events in the conduct of a business." Section 759 of the Restatement of Torts deals with procuring information by improper means and "applies to information about one's business whether or not it constitutes a trade secret." Restatement (Second) of Torts, § 759 cmt. b. In view of the broader scope of what constitutes a "trade secret" in the UTSA and the Restatement (Third) of Unfair Competition, does the distinction between trade secrets and other information used in one's business have any practical effect? Is there any real difference in these modern definitions of what constitutes a trade secret between what have been called trade secrets, proprietary information, confidential business information, know-how, etc.?

4. The Uniform Trade Secret Act (USTA) was initially promulgated in 1979 (and amended in 1985). As of 2012 it has been adopted in some form in 46 states, the District of Columbia, and the Virgin Islands. What law is applied in the other states? Note that in *Kewanee Oil* the Supreme Court observed that, "Ohio has adopted the widely relied-upon definition of a trade secret found at Restatement of Torts, § 757, Comment b (1939)." *Kewanee Oil*, 416 U.S. at 474.

5. When the American Law Institute was redrafting the new Restatement of Torts, it decided to remove many aspects of unfair competition law and place them into the Restatement (Third) of Unfair Competition. The name Restatement (Third) of Unfair Competition was selected to reflect that it was drafted in parallel with the Restatement (Third) of Torts, even though there had never been a First or Second Restatement of Unfair Competition.

# B. PROPERTY COMPONENT OF TRADE SECRETS

## (1) Categories of Trade Secret Information

### (a) Technical Information and Customer Lists

#### STANDARD BRANDS, INC. v. ZUMPE
264 F. Supp. 254 (E.D. La. 1967)

RUBIN, DISTRICT JUDGE.

A nationally known manufacturer of food and related products here seeks to enjoin a former employee from working for a competitor engaged in the coffee and tea business principally in Louisiana and Tennessee and in the areas surrounding each of these states, and from disclosing confidential information and trade secrets learned during his employment.

Through what is known as its Chase and Sanborn Division, the plaintiff develops, processes, and manufactures coffee and tea products. It distributes these under advertised and well known brand names, such as Chase & Sanborn, Tender Leaf, Instant Chase & Sanborn, Instant Siesta Decaffeinated, Instant Tender Leaf Tea, and Instant Tender Leaf Iced Tea. The plaintiff conducts research in coffee and tea processes and products at research laboratories in New Orleans, Louisiana and Stamford, Connecticut. It operates a pilot plant in New Orleans, where it seeks to improve its coffee and tea products. It also operates a manufacturing plant in New Orleans where it makes all of the instant coffee sold by it throughout the nation.

Walter T. Zumpe, who is one of the defendants, began to work for Standard in 1946 as a shipping clerk. Although he has had no technical education, he has a talent for dealing with people. He was promoted successively until in 1954 he was transferred to New Orleans where he became Plant Manager of Standard's Chase & Sanborn Production Division in New Orleans.

Because Zumpe's work afforded him access to information that Standard considered confidential, Zumpe signed two agreements, one in 1959 and the other in 1964. These agreements, similar in terms, provided that, in consideration of his employment by Standard, Zumpe agreed:

> 2. That except as required in the performance of his duties to the Company, he will not disclose or use at any time during his employment any of the Company's manufacturing processes, techniques, types of machinery and equipment used together with improvements and modifications thereof, product formulae and ingredients, including raw materials used, discoveries, inventions, ideas, . . . projects or programs, customer lists or any information disclosed to him in confidence or any information held in secret by the Company, of which he became informed during the term of his employment with the Company; and
>
> 3. That he will not disclose or use at any time after the termination of his employment any of the foregoing information which may be trade secrets

or confidential information of the Company unless he shall first request and obtain the written consent of the Company.

As Plant Manager, Zumpe received reports from Standard's Research and Development laboratories covering the work being done by them. He also conferred from time to time with research and technical personnel regarding methods of production and areas of research in which they were engaged. The information that he received included trade secrets and confidential information as well as much that was routine.

The defendant, William B. Reily & Company, Inc., is a family firm engaged in the coffee and tea business and in the distribution of other food products. It operates a plant in New Orleans located only a few hundred yards from the plaintiff's plant. Its New Orleans plant specializes in coffee with chicory, which is marketed under the trade name "Luzianne." It also sells both roasted and instant pure coffee and tea under the trade names Arobrand and Crescent Club. It has a subsidiary in Knoxville, Tennessee, which sells only roasted and instant pure coffee and tea products. Reily manufactures its own instant coffee. It purchases decaffeinated coffee and instant tea from other manufacturers.

Reily needed a Production Manager. It was particularly interested in finding someone who could work well with people. One of its executive officers heard favorable reports about Zumpe, looked him up, and, after a series of conferences, engaged him as Reily's Vice-President and General Manager in charge of production. His duties include coordination of production at both the Knoxville and New Orleans plants. He was hired principally as an executive and to take charge of production processes, not to engage in improvement of coffee or tea products, research, or new product development. But Standard contends that in seeking properly to discharge his duties for Reily Zumpe will inevitably disclose the secret and confidential information that he learned while working for Standard, and that he cannot so "compartmentalize his mind" as to avoid disclosure however good his intentions.

The legal problems created when an employer seeks to protect his trade secrets from disclosure by a former employee were familiar to judges long before they learned the delight of a fragrant cup of coffee. The Romans recognized an action for enticement to communicate business secrets. But it was not until the end of the Third Century, one legend tells, that monks, fleeing persecution, escaped to the highlands of Abyssinia, across the Red Sea from Arabia, and by accident discovered the virtues of the coffee bean.[1]

---

[1] [3] One story says that one night one of the shepherd fathers came pale and trembling to the monastery from his night vigil with the flock. He was convinced the sheep were bewitched because they were jumping and playing as if it were a spring morning. When the friar went to investigate, he found the animals romping in the moonlight instead of sleeping. Watching night after night, the friar at last learned that the sleeplessness resulted when the sheep ate the leaves and fruit of an unfamiliar shrub. When he picked the ripe, cherry like fruit and chewed the seeds, he felt an unusual exhilaration and was wakeful. That at least is the way the tale is told in Compton's Encyclopedia, verbo Coffee, page 426.

However fanciful the legend, Abyssinia and Arabia were the original home of the coffee shrub. By the 15th century, pilgrims to Mecca used to drink a brew made from roasted coffee beans to prevent drowsiness during religious services. From Arabia the practice passed to Constantinople, then to Venice,

The coffee purchased by the consumer is a blend, compounded usually by a secret formula to achieve that flavor and aroma the coffee maker considers his own. Courts have recognized the need for blending conflicting interests in trade secret cases, too, although they are still struggling with the proper adjustment of the balance between employer and employee.

An employer who discloses valuable information to his employee in confidence is entitled to protection against the use of these secrets in competition with him. But the employee who possesses the employer's most valuable confidences is apt to be highly skilled. The public is interested in the reasonable mobility of such skilled persons from job to job in our fluid society, which is characterized by and requires the mobility of technically expert persons from place to place, from job to job and upward within the industrial structure. And the employee himself must be afforded a reasonable opportunity to change jobs without abandoning the ability to practice his skills. The resolution of the issues in this case first requires determining how much Zumpe knows that can be properly considered Standard's "trade secrets or confidential information" as distinguished from those things that he has absorbed as part of his general managerial and professional background.

NATURE OF THE INFORMATION IMPARTED TO ZUMPE

A part of the trial was held in camera because the plaintiff contended that the testimony would necessarily disclose its trade secrets. By agreement of the parties, when the testimony dealt directly with information that the plaintiff considered secret, all persons were excluded from the courtroom except a representative of the plaintiff, the plaintiff's counsel, Zumpe, defendants' counsel, and the reporter. In order to preserve the confidentiality of the record, the documents alleged to be secret were presented in envelopes which were separately sealed. When the testimony required an answer the plaintiff considered secret, the witness wrote it instead of answering orally so that the reply itself would not appear in the transcript. Finally, because the plaintiff contended that even after these efforts a clever competitor might piece together confidential information from other testimony, the transcript itself was ordered not to be disclosed to the public.

The defendant acquiesced in these efforts to maintain secrecy but it contended that relatively little of the information identified by the plaintiff as secret or confidential was truly either one or the other.

Standard offered evidence that Zumpe had received confidential information or trade secrets regarding each of the following:

1. Development of a new dry coffee concentrate.

2. Processes for aroma and flavor recovery.

3. Instant coffee extraction equipment, developmental in nature, to produce best balance between quality and yield.

4. Standard's processes specifically for instant coffee production, including aroma oil, extraction and foam control, and maintenance of flavorability.

---

and then through Europe, spread with the aid of Turkish ambassadors. *Ibid.*

5. Decaffeinization.

6. Instant tea processes.

7. New instant dry tea concentrate.

8. Process and equipment development for freeze drying.

9. Research and other reports.

Zumpe testified that he had received information in each of these areas, that he considered relatively little of it to be secret since he thought a good deal of it was known to technical experts in the trade, but that Standard did consider this information confidential. It is clear that Standard had spent a good deal of money to develop this information and made a major effort to prevent its disclosure. Copies of reports relating to these subjects were kept in locked cabinets. The documents were not available to employees generally. Standard thought the information was of value to its competitors — not only because of the information concerning successful experiments or other work underway, but also because even the information about unsuccessful experiments had 'negative value': a competitor who knew that a certain experiment had been fruitless could save the time and expense of repeating it. In addition, the evidence is clear that in regard to development of new products, merely being able to offer the product first — a few weeks or months ahead of competitors — may give a food manufacturer a substantial advantage.

Defendants sought to minimize the value of this information in three ways:

First, they denied that much of it was of any interest to Reily. Thus, for example, they contended that Reily had no interest in developing a new dry coffee concentrate; therefore even if this information were secret, Reily had no interest in it.

Second, they sought to show that new product processes could be duplicated rapidly once a new product was marketed because competitors could buy the new product, analyze it, and repeat the process.

Finally, they sought to show that some of the information could be readily obtained elsewhere — through trade publications, equipment manufacturers, and other trade sources.

Nonetheless, the evidence is convincing that the information available to Zumpe in these nine areas is valuable, it is not readily available elsewhere, and, even if none of it is of present interest to Reily, the disclosure of the information would violate Zumpe's contract with Standard.

INEVITABILITY OF DISCLOSURE

In his new position, Zumpe will be responsible for managing production. He will participate in deciding whether Reily should manufacture products or buy them elsewhere. It cannot be doubted that he will try to do the best job possible. Standard contends that, under these circumstances, Zumpe will inevitably disclose some of the confidential information learned while he worked for Standard.

However, this conclusion is not warranted by the evidence. It is doubtless true that Zumpe may be tempted to use his confidential information to Reily's benefit, but, because of the nature of Reily's business, it does not follow that disclosure is inevitable. This conclusion is reached by considering each of the 'confidential areas' separately and specifically. The evidence presented to the court indicates that the nature of Reily's business both with respect to pure coffee and coffee with chicory, instant and roasted, as well as with respect to tea, make it entirely possible for Zumpe to work for Reily for the two years estimated by Standard as the useful life of its confidential information without disclosing any of it.

By comparison with Standard, Reily is a small firm. It is not now engaged in new product research and does not intend to market a new dry coffee concentrate in the foreseeable future. (Confidential Group No. 1.) It is conducting no experiments to improve aroma and flavor recovery. (Confidential Group No. 2.) It is not engaged in experiments to improve its instant coffee extraction equipment. (Confidential Group No. 3.) It has a working process of instant coffee production and it has no experiment underway to alter this nor any intention of doing so in the future. (Confidential Group No. 4.) It purchases decaffeinated coffee from another manufacturer who uses its own process (Confidential Group No. 5), and it likewise purchases its instant tea. (Confidential Group No. 6.) It is not interested in a new dry tea concentrate. (Confidential Group No. 7.) It has no intention of engaging in freeze drying. (Confidential Group No. 8.)

Reily therefore is not now engaged in work that would permit the ready application of the confidential information known to Zumpe. While Standard's witnesses testified that he would inevitably do his best whenever a problem came up because he is an able, ambitious man, the testimony that his disclosure of confidential information would be inevitable rests upon the conclusion that doing his best would entail disclosure of such information. This conclusion does not follow from the evidence presented.

Standard's brief sums up this testimony by saying that "Zumpe could not stand by and watch Reily's personnel use poor techniques, knowing the secret, more efficient, and newer techniques and know-how of Standard for processing instant coffee and tea." But this assumes first that Reily has poor techniques, a fact not proved, and secondly that the "newer techniques and know-how" can be applied to Reily's processes. The nature of the confidential information and the methods used by Reily in its operations do not justify these conclusions.

It is true that it is possible for Zumpe to use Standard's confidential information. For example, he might pass on knowledge of an improvement in decaffeinization learned from Standard to Reily's manufacturer. This however would be a conscious and deliberate act, not merely the inevitable result of normal efforts to do an efficient production job. And it would inevitably be detected. For Standard is now running periodic chemical analyses of Reily's products and will learn promptly of any change in their composition or method of manufacture.

* * *

In this case Standard suggests that Zumpe has general managerial skills and that an injunction against his employment in the areas of instant coffee and instant tea research, processing and manufacturing would not unduly restrict his employment opportunities "in the instant coffee and tea business in any nonsensitive area like sales, personnel or even in coffee plants devoted solely to roasting and grinding coffee; nor from working in Reily's (or other competitors) chemical, salad oil, or general food divisions as plant manager, production executive or in any other position."

But there can be no doubt that Zumpe is peculiarly well qualified to handle production work in the coffee and tea business. Even an injunction limited in the manner thus sought by Standard would enforce at least in part a contract not to compete and would prevent Zumpe from working in the "field for which he is particularly fitted."

* * *

## WEIL-MCLAIN CO. v. ANDRO CORP.

200 U.S.P.Q. 538 (N.D.N.Y. 1977)

* * *

Weil-McLain contends that any nonpatented device in the public domain can be copied. Since all of Andro's alleged trade secrets were obvious from an inspection of its products, and since these products were sold on the open market, Andro possessed no trade secrets. Andro argues that its trade secrets were not merely the particular features which its products incorporated but, rather, the efficiencies of these features which had been discovered through research and economic analysis.

* * *

B. Pendent Jurisdiction.

Along with its claims of patent infringement, Andro's complaint alleges three state claims entitled unfair competition, contract, and pricing. Weil-McLain has moved to dismiss these claims for want of pendent jurisdiction. 28 U.S.C. § 1338(b) provides that, "[t]he district courts shall have original jurisdiction of any civil action asserting a claim of unfair competition when joined with a substantial and related claim under the . . . patent . . . laws." Further, the power to exercise pendent jurisdiction exists wherever a substantial federal claim and a pendent state claim "derive from a common nucleus of operative fact." *United Mine Workers v. Gibbs*, 383 U.S. 715, 725 (1966).

Weil-McLain concedes that the "common nucleus of operative fact" test governs both the unfair competition claim, under 28 U.S.C. § 1338(b), and the other state claims as well. However, Weil-McLain contends that the only possible common nucleus is the gas burner to which both patents relate. Contending the state claims refer entirely to matters other than the gas burner, Weil-McLain argues that they lack a common nucleus and, thus, that no pendent jurisdiction exists.

This interpretation of the common nucleus requirement misses the mark. Andro's claim under the patent laws is one of *infringement* of the patent arising out of the alleged unfair conduct of its former employee, Grether. Grether was Andro's Manager of Engineering and later allegedly defected to Weil-McLain, where he became its Manager of Engineering. Andro claims that Grether then constructed furnaces and air conditioners which were copies of Andro's, which infringed two of Andro's patents, and which utilized Andro's trade secret information. Grether's alleged conduct supplies the "common nucleus of operative fact."

This Circuit has declined to take a restrictive view of pendent jurisdiction in the patent context, *see A. H. Emery Co. v. Marcan Products Corp.*, 268 F.Supp. 289, 153 U.S.P.Q. 337 (S.D.N.Y. 1967), *aff'd*, 389 F.2d 11, 156 U.S.P.Q. 529 (2d Cir.), *cert. denied*, 393 U.S. 835, 159 U.S.P.Q. 799 (1968), and has opted instead for the broader reading advocated by Professor Moore. *See* 1 J. Moore, FEDERAL PRACTICE ¶ 60.60 [8.-7] at 658-59 (2d Ed. 1976). The identity of proof test has been rejected for a more liberal test requiring overlap in the factual bases of the two claims. *Channel Master Corp. v. JFD Electronics Corp.*, 260 F.Supp. 568, 151 USPQ 498 (E.D.N.Y.1966). In a case involving very similar facts, the Fifth Circuit held that pendent jurisdiction was appropriately exercised. *River Brand Rice Mills, Inc. v. General Foods Corp.*, 334 F.2d 770, 142 U.S.P.Q. 185 (5th Cir. 1964), *cert. denied*, 379 U.S. 998, 144 U.S.P.Q. 781 (1965). An employee was alleged to have left the plaintiff to work for defendant. He then developed processes for defendant which allegedly infringed patents and utilized trade secrets of his former employer. The court refused to apply section 1338(b) restrictively.

The power to exercise pendent jurisdiction exists, and its exercise seems proper here. The patent claims have not been dismissed.[4] Judicial economy will best be served by trying Andro's patent claims and related state claims in one proceeding. Therefore, Weil-McLain's motion to dismiss these state claims for want of jurisdiction is denied.

C. Trade Secrets.

Andro's "unfair competition" claim alleges misappropriation of its trade secrets. Insofar as these secrets were incorporated in Andro's Janitrol furnace, Weil-McLain argues that they were not secrets at all and were not entitled to any protection. Weil-McLain contends that the alleged secrets were obvious to anyone who inspected a Janitrol furnace. Since the furnace was marketed, the information was placed in the public domain and cannot be characterized as secret. *See Scharmer v. Carrollton Manufacturing Co.*, 525 F.2d 95, 99, 187 U.S.P.Q. 736, 738-739 (6th Cir.1975); Restatement of Torts § 757, comment *b* at 5-6 (1939). Weil-McLain further argues, relying on *Sears, Roebuck & Co. v. Stiffel Co.*, 376 U.S. 225, 140 U.S.P.Q. 524 (1964), that once Andro placed its furnace on the market, all unpatented features could be copied by anyone.

There are two problems with Weil-McLain's argument. First, its characterization of Andro's trade secrets is too narrow. Weil-McLain contends that the secrets are, in fact, obvious features in the construction of the furnace, e.g. the use of screwing parts together rather than welding. However, Andro asserts that the secrets are not the particular features used but, rather, the economic efficiencies and engineering benefits derived from such features. Cost analysis had shown screwing to be much cheaper than welding; engineering studies indicated that the obvious pie-pan dimple on the heat exchanger reduced stress and cracking. The Second Circuit has held that similar nonobvious benefits and properties of marketed products may constitute trade secrets. *See A.H. Emery Co. v. Marcan Products Corp.*, 389 F.2d 11, 156 U.S.P.Q. 529 (2d Cir.), *cert. denied*, 393 U.S. 835, 159 U.S.P.Q. 799 (1968). Secondly, a confidential relationship existed between Andro and its Manager of Engineering, Mr. Grether. Weil-McLain's argument presupposes that an unrelated third-party has copied a marketed product. That is not the case here. The undisputed facts show that a high level employee was hired by a competing firm. The inference of trade secret theft, rather than permissible copying, has been raised.

Weil-McLain has *argued* that unpatented products may be copied by anyone, citing *Sears, Roebuck & Co.*, 376 U.S. 225, 140 U.S.P.Q. 524 (1964). However, *Sears* did not entirely incapacitate state unfair competition laws. Sears had committed no commercial espionage, nor had it procured information from one of Stiffel's employees. It merely copied a product on the open market. However, where a breach of commercial ethics has occurred, unfair competition laws still have an important function, independent of federal patent policy. Ten years after *Sears* was decided, the Supreme Court upheld trade secret protection of unpatented processes. *Kewanee Oil Co. v. Bicron Corp.*, 416 U.S. 470, 181 U.S.P.Q. 673 (1974). Unlike what occurred in *Sears*, in *Kewanee Oil* the copying was done by former employees who had learned secret processes and then had defected to form their own company, where these processes were utilized. The confidential relationship between Andro and Grether distinguishes this case from Weil-McLain's simple scenario of permissible copying. Where a confidential relationship has been breached, trade secret law still protects the injured party. *See Rite off, Inc. v. Contact Industries, Inc.*, 350 N.Y.S.2d 690, 181 U.S.P.Q. 330 (2d Dep't 1973); *Spiselman v. Rabinowitz*, 61 N.Y.S.2d 138, 69 U.S.P.Q. 192 (1st Dep't 1946). Copying, otherwise permissible, becomes forbidden when accomplished by unfair means.

Because the trade secrets may not have been obvious to anyone examining Andro's Janitrol furnace, and because of the inference that Mr. Grether relied on these trade secrets in developing competing products for Weil-McLain, summary judgment in Weil-McLain's favor would be inappropriate.

Insofar as Weil-McLain's motion relates to trade secrets allegedly incorporated into Andro's air conditioner, summary judgment is equally inappropriate. Clear questions of fact exist as to when Andro's new air conditioning units were developed. Also, Weil-McLain's contention that Andro's method of construction was common knowledge in the industry should be supported not merely by affidavit, but by a fuller exploration of the facts, including expert testimony.

* * *

## LEO SILFEN, INC. v. CREAM

278 N.E.2d 636 (N.Y. 1972)

The judgment should be reversed and the complaint dismissed. Plaintiffs have failed to prove a physical appropriation or copying of confidential information, or wrongful disclosure or use of a trade secret. In particular, no trade secret protection is warranted since plaintiffs' customers are likely, if not known, users of the employers' merchandise and engaged in business at advertised locations.

Plaintiff corporations are engaged in selling building maintenance supplies to industrial and commercial users. Plaintiffs purchase their inventory from independent supply houses and then, at a substantial markup, resell to customers under their own label. Plaintiff Silfen sells soaps, polishes, waxes, finishers, and disinfectants, while plaintiff Formula 33 Corporation specializes in ice and snow melting compounds.

In 1949 defendant Cream joined Silfen, then engaged only in the paper and twine business. Cream was assigned and became solely responsible for the development of a cleaning and maintenance chemical supply division. During its formative years Cream interviewed and hired salesmen, developed products, and found suppliers. Initial customer solicitation consisted of direct contact and media advertising. Meeting little success he employed the services of mailing houses which provided lists of prospects to whom brochures and business reply cards were forwarded. Eventually, an average of one million mailings were made annually with a reply rate of 0.6%. Of those replying 25% Became customers at an average cost per new customer in 1967 of $45. Over the years, some 15,000 customers were obtained.

For each customer a separate file was kept containing: name of purchasing agent and other personnel at customer's office; temperament of purchasing agent; gratuities given; particular requirements; and past purchases. In 1961 these customer profiles were consolidated into a central filing system and measures were taken to insure that each salesman had access only to that portion of the files containing his customers. So concerned were plaintiffs in the protection of this information that in the employment agreement with each salesman hired after 1961 it was provided: "(The salesman) acknowledges that the list of the Corporations' customers is a unique asset of their respective businesses, and . . . will not, during or after the term of his employment, appropriate to his own use or disclose to others for any purpose, any names on such list or any confidential information obtained by him during his employment." Vigilance is also demonstrated by a form required to be signed by each salesman after contact with a customer: "The names of all the company customers ever called by me, and those appearing on the face of this telephone report sheet, were obtained from leads furnished by the company and remain the property of the company and will not be disclosed to any unauthorized persons in violation of the trust placed in me by the company."

In 1965, on the death of the principal of Silfen and the taking of control by his widow, Cream was named executive vice-president and general manager of plaintiff corporations for a term of 12 years. The written agreement between the parties provided for a base salary of $26,000 plus 25% of the aggregate net profits. The corporations reserved the right to discharge Cream if the aggregate net profits in any one year failed to exceed $35,000. It was also provided that if Cream terminated the agreement he would "not, for one year thereafter . . . engage in the sale to the corporations' customers of any products competing with the corporations' products." Since Cream was discharged this restriction is not controlling. The agreement contained no comparable provision to cover Cream's discharge.

On November 17, 1967, Cream was discharged purportedly because of a decline in net profits. Cream, however, urges that he was discharged in order to make room for the new husband of the widow, the former Mrs. Silfen. Thirteen days after his discharge he set up Real Estate Maintenance Chemical Specialty Corporation and engaged in the same business as plaintiffs except limited to building owners and building managers. About three months later, in March, 1968, plaintiffs brought this action to enjoin defendants' solicitation of plaintiffs' customers. The complaint alleged that defendants had been soliciting plaintiffs' customers, that Cream had made copies of plaintiffs' secret and confidential customer files, and was using such information in his solicitation. Cream admits that of a list of 1,100 customers submitted by plaintiffs defendants had solicited 47. Defendants, however, contend that the names of these customers were procured from available commercial lists compiled by commercial list houses. Defendants allege in their answer and assert in their testimony that the customers are openly engaged in business at advertised locations and their names are well known to plaintiffs' competitors.

Notably, plaintiffs did not attempt to sustain their allegation that Cream had made copies of plaintiffs' secret and confidential files, or used the recorded detail in those files with respect to each customer's "profile". The solicitation of plaintiffs' customers was at most the product of casual memory, or, as defendants would have the court believe, coincidence. If there has been a physical taking or studied copying, the court may in a proper case enjoin solicitation, not necessarily as a violation of a trade secret, but as an egregious breach of trust and confidence while in plaintiffs' service [citations omitted]; former Penal Law, § 553, subd. 6). Nor is there any allegation or evidence of other wrongful or fraudulent tactics employed by Cream in connection with the solicitation of plaintiffs' customers. If there had been, a court might award damages and enjoin further similar conduct as constituting unfair competition. [Citation omitted.] All that remains, therefore, on the theory alleged in the complaint or developed on the trial is whether plaintiffs' customer list, exclusive of the recorded detail about each customer, classifies as a trade secret rendering defendants' solicitation of customers on that list improper, sufficient to warrant injunction and damages.

Generally, where the customers are readily ascertainable outside the employer's business as prospective users or consumers of the employer's services or products, trade secret protection will not attach and courts will not enjoin the employee from soliciting his employer's customers. [Citations omitted.] Conversely, where the customers are not known in the trade or are discoverable only by extraordinary efforts courts have not hesitated to protect customer lists and files as trade secrets. This is especially so where the customers' patronage had been secured by years of effort and advertising effected by the expenditure of substantial time and money. [Citations omitted.]

The customers solicited by defendants, as apparently found by the trial court, are openly engaged in business in advertised locations and their names and addresses may readily be found by those engaged in the trade. Indeed, plaintiffs' counsel apparently conceded as much at the conclusion of the trial, but thought that circumstance irrelevant unless defendants had actually obtained the prospects from commercially available lists and not from Cream's prior service with plaintiffs. Relying upon this court's opinion in *Town & Country House & Home Serv. v. Newbery*, 3 N.Y.2d 554, 170 N.Y.S.2d 328, 147 N.E.2d 724, *Supra*, the trial court apparently believed that commercial notoriety of defendant's prospects as users of this type of service is not controlling, misapplying, it is suggested, the *Town & Country* case to make an exception where there has been substantial effort by plaintiffs in acquiring their patronage.

Indeed, the *Town & Country* case presents an interesting contrast. Plaintiff in that case was engaged in the business of house and home cleaning by contract with individual householders. After three years of operation it had acquired 240 customers. Defendants left its employment, established a competing corporation, and solicited 38 of plaintiff's customers. Only plaintiff's customers were solicited. The court marked the type of customer that the parties serviced.

"(T)he customers of plaintiff were not and could not be obtained merely by looking up their names in the telephone or city directory or by going to any advertised locations, but had to be screened from among many other housewives who did not wish services such as respondent and appellants were equipped to render, but preferred to do their own housework. In most instances housewives do their own house cleaning. The only appeal which plaintiff could have was to those whose cleaning had been done by servants regularly or occasionally employed, except in the still rarer instances where the housewife was on the verge of abandoning doing her own work by hiring some outside agency." (3 N.Y.2d at p. 559, 170 N.Y.S.2d, at p. 332, 147 N.E.2d, at p. 726).

"It would be different if these customers had been equally available to appellants and respondent, but, as has been related, these customers had been screened by respondent at considerable effort and expense, without which their receptivity and willingness to do business with this kind of a service organization could not be known." (*Id.*, at p. 560, 170 N.Y.S.2d, at p. 333, 147 N.E.2d, at p. 727).

Unlike the customers in the *Town & Country* case (*supra*), plaintiffs' customers were readily ascertainable as likely prospects. Although plaintiffs have demonstrated an investment of time and money in developing a patronage of approximately 15,000 enterprises, the investment was not an attempt to create a market for a new type of service as was the case in the *Town & Country* case. Rather, that investment reflected simply widespread canvassing of an obvious and highly competitive market. Indeed, consider the comparable investment in the distribution of soap and soap products to the individual consumer.

A better parallel than the *Town & Country* case is *Abdallah v. Crandall*, 273 App.Div. 131, 76 N.Y.S.2d 403, *Supra*. In *Abdallah* the plaintiff employer was engaged in the dairy business and the defendant employee made deliveries on some of plaintiff's retail milk routes. When the defendant left plaintiff's employment, he joined a competing business and solicited his former customers. In dismissing the former employer's action to enjoin such solicitation, the court noted; "In some instances a list of customers may be a trade secret but it would be straining the meaning of the word beyond any reasonable limit to hold that the list transferred in this case came within that category. The plaintiff himself conceded on the trial of the action that every householder in both of the communities involved either bought milk or was a potential customer for it. It was also conceded, and it is a matter of common knowledge, that the delivery of milk from the very nature of the business is open and notorious. A trade secret, like any other secret, is nothing more than private matter; something known to only one or a few and kept from the general public; and not susceptible to general knowledge. *Kaumagraph Co. v. Stampagraph Co.*, 235 N.Y. 1, 138 N.E. 485. A list of milk customers in a small city like Cortland, and a village like Homer, hardly meets such a definition. We are therefore constrained to hold with the referee that the list of Brown's milk customers was not a trade secret according to the accepted meaning of that term." (pp. 133-134, 76 N.Y.S.2d, at p. 406).

In the absence of express agreement to that effect between the parties, or a demonstration that a customer list has the several attributes of a trade secret, courts, without more, should not enjoin an ex-employee from engaging in fair and open competition with his former employer. The limiting effects upon the former employee with respect to his ability to earn a living are marked and obvious. [Citations omitted.] Moreover, the issuance of the permanent injunction in the present case has an untoward consequence. By discharging Cream plaintiffs obtained greater protection than they would have had under their agreement with him, if he had terminated the employment. It was observed earlier that the 1965 employment agreement provided that Cream would not solicit plaintiffs' customers for one year following his termination of the employment. This provision suggests that the parties considered Cream's role as a future competitor, and, more important, were satisfied to provide protection for only one year.

In concluding, it may be stated expressly what was earlier implied, namely, that if defendants had been shown to have appropriated by copying, studied memory, or by some other manner which does not now come to mind, the detailed information in the customer files there would be a case quite different from this. The record shows no such appropriation with respect to a single customer, let alone many customers to an extent barring reliance on casual memory. Instead, it shows that defendants solicited 47 of the 1,100 customers submitted on a list prepared by plaintiffs from its confidential files. The point is that in the circumstances described names of customers alone involved no trade secret and there was no wrongful conduct by defendants. If trade secrets there were, they consisted of the data in the carefully secured and segregated files.

Accordingly, the judgment appealed from should be reversed and the complaint dismissed, with costs in all courts.

* * *

## PHONEDOG v. KRAVITZ
No. C-11-03474 MEJ, 2011 U.S. Dist. LEXIS 129229
(N.D. Cal. Nov. 8, 2011)

* * *

The relevant allegations, taken from PhoneDog's Complaint, are as follows.

PhoneDog is an "interactive mobile news and reviews web resource," that reviews mobile products and services and provides users with resources needed to research, compare prices, and shop from mobile carriers. Compl. ¶ 8. PhoneDog uses a variety of social media, including Twitter, Facebook, and YouTube, to market and promote its services to users. *Id.* ¶ 9.

Beginning in April 2006, Mr. Kravitz began working for PhoneDog as a product reviewer and video blogger. *Id.* ¶ 14. PhoneDog alleges that "[a]s an employee of PhoneDog, [Mr. Kravitz] was given use of and maintained the Twitter account "@PhoneDog_Noah" (the "Account")." *Id.* ¶ 15. As part of Mr. Kravitz's employment, he submitted written and video content to PhoneDog, which was then transmitted to its users via a variety of mediums, including PhoneDog's website and the Twitter Account. *Id.* ¶ 14. Mr. Kravitz accessed the Twitter Account using a password and used the Account to disseminate information and promote PhoneDog's services on behalf of PhoneDog. *Id.* According to PhoneDog, all @PhoneDog_Name Twitter accounts used by its employees, as well as the passwords to such accounts, constitute proprietary, confidential information. *Id.* ¶ 12. PhoneDog avers that, during the course of Mr. Kravitz's employment at PhoneDog, the @PhoneDog_Noah Account generated approximately 17,000 Twitter followers. *Id.* ¶ 16.

In October 2010, Mr. Kravitz ended his employment with PhoneDog. *Id.* ¶ 17. At that time, PhoneDog requested that he relinquish use of the Twitter Account. *Id.* In response, Mr. Kravitz changed the Account handle to "@noahkravitz," and continues to use the Account. *Id.* As a result, PhoneDog alleges that it has suffered at least $340,000 in damages. *Id.* at 9.

Based on these allegations, on July 15, 2011, PhoneDog filed this lawsuit against Mr. Kravitz, asserting claims under California law for: (1) misappropriation of trade secrets; (2) intentional interference with prospective economic advantage; (3) negligent interference with prospective economic advantage, and (4) conversion. *Id.* at 3-7.

Mr. Kravitz now moves to dismiss PhoneDog's Complaint pursuant to Rule 12(b)(1) for lack of subject matter jurisdiction and pursuant to Rule 12(b)(6) for failure to state a claim.

* * *

a. Misappropriation of Trade Secrets Claim

Mr. Kravitz challenges PhoneDog's misappropriation of trade secrets claim.

Mr. Kravitz first argues that the claim is subject to dismissal because "the identity of the Account followers and the 'password' to the Account which PhoneDog alleges were misappropriated by Kravitz are not a 'trade secret' within the meaning of the California Uniform Trade Secrets Act ("UTSA")." 1 Mot. at 14. Specifically, he argues that "[t]he followers of the Account are not secret because they are and have been publicly available for all to see at all times." *Id.* With respect to the password to the Account, Mr. Kravitz contends that passwords to Twitter accounts do not derive any actual or potential independent economic value under the UTSA because they do not provide any substantial business advantage. Mot. at 15. Rather, he argues that the passwords merely allow the individual logging on to view information already widely known. *Id.* Mr. Kravitz also argues that he — not PhoneDog — initially created the password and that PhoneDog did not make any reasonable efforts to maintain the secrecy of the password. *Id.*

Additionally, Mr. Kravitz contends that PhoneDog has failed to allege any act by him that falls within the definition of misappropriation. 2 Mot. at 16. Rather, he argues that "PhoneDog only makes the conclusory allegation that Kravitz used 'improper means, as such are defined in Civil Code § 3426.1(a), to obtain and misappropriate the Confidential Information' without providing any factual support of the actual alleged improper act committed by Kravitz." *Id.* (quoting Compl. ¶ 23).

Finally, Mr. Kravitz argues that PhoneDog has failed to plead misappropriation with particularity, as required by Rule 9(b) for any claim sounding in fraud. Mot. at 16. Again, Mr. Kravitz asserts that PhoneDog has not alleged any facts regarding his conduct, but has merely alleged that he used "improper means" to obtain and misappropriate the Twitter password. Mot. at 16-17.

In its Opposition, PhoneDog contends that it has sufficiently stated its misappropriation of trade secrets claim, arguing that it has alleged the existence of a trade secret in paragraphs 12 and 22 of the Complaint. Opp'n at 10. It also contends that it has alleged that when it requested that Mr. Kravitz relinquish use of the Account, he "merely changed the Twitter handle on the Account," continued to use the Account, and "used improper means, as such are defined in Civil Code section 3426.1(a), to obtain and misappropriate the Confidential Information." Opp'n at 11 (citing Compl. ¶¶ 17, 23).

PhoneDog also disputes that Rule 9(b)'s heightened pleading standard applies to the misappropriation of trade secrets claim because the claim does not sound in fraud or mistake. *Id.*

Finally, PhoneDog argues that Mr. Kravitz's challenges to whether PhoneDog has a protectable trade secret are beyond the scope of a 12(b)(6) motion and should be addressed on summary judgment. Opp'n at 12.

The Court has carefully considered the parties' arguments and finds that Mr. Kravitz has not shown any basis for dismissal of the misappropriation of trade secrets claim under Rule 12(b)(6). With respect to the applicable pleading standard, although courts have applied conflicting standards, the Court finds that PhoneDog's misappropriation claim does not sound in fraud or mistake and thus Rule 9(b) does not control. *See TMX Funding, Inc. v. Impero Tech., Inc.*, 2010 U.S. Dist. LEXIS 60260 (N.D. Cal. June 17, 2010). PhoneDog has sufficiently described the subject matter of the trade secret with sufficient particularity and has alleged that, despite its demand that Mr. Kravitz relinquish use of the password and Account, he has refused to do so. At this stage, these allegations are sufficient to state a claim. Further, to the extent that Mr. Kravitz has challenged whether the password and account followers are trade secrets and whether Mr. Kravitz's conduct constitutes misappropriation requires consideration of evidence beyond the scope of the pleading. Thus, such challenges should be raised at summary judgment on a fully-developed evidentiary record. The Court therefore DENIES Mr. Kravitz's request to dismiss PhoneDog's misappropriation of trade secrets claim.

[Editor's note: The court also granted Kravitz's motion to dismiss PhoneDog's claims for intentional interference with prospective business advantage and negligent interference with prospective business advantage, but denied Kravitz's motion to dismiss its claim for conversion.]

## EARLY, LUDWICK & SWEENEY, LLC v. STEELE

No.CV 98040963S, 1998 Conn. Super. LEXIS 2256 (Conn. Super. Ct. Aug. 7, 1998)

Plaintiff, Early, Ludwick & Sweeney, LLC ("ELS"), a law firm specializing, inter alia, in pediatric lead paint poisoning cases, brings suit against John-Henry Steele ("Steele"), an attorney formerly employed by ELS, and the law firm of Brown, Welsh, & Votre, P.C. ("BWV"), Steele's current employer. Plaintiff's complaint is in four counts. The First Count alleges misappropriation of trade secrets in violation of Connecticut's Uniform Trade Secrets Act, ("UTSA") General Statutes, Sections 35-50ff; the Second Count, wilful violation of said trade secrets act; the Third Count alleges that said misappropriation is a violation of the Connecticut Unfair Trade Practices Act (CUTPA), General Statutes, Sections 42-110a ff. The Fourth Count alleges tortious interference with business expectancies, in that defendants solicited clients of the plaintiff following defendant Steele's departure from ELS.

* * *

From December 1991 defendant Steele worked as an attorney for ELS and its predecessor firm. ELS, its predecessor and its principal, James F. Early, have concentrated on representing clients in toxic tort cases, including asbestos disease and lead paint poisoning cases. The firm's specialty in pediatric lead poisoning cases had its genesis in the beginning of this decade and the firm has acquired experience, expertise and a client base in this area of the law. ELS has over 100 such cases pending. Defendant Steele began working for the firm circa 1991 and his practice was predominantly in the area of pediatric lead poisoning cases. In December 1997, Steele left the employ of ELS and joined BMV. At the time of his departure, Steele was in charge of the firm's lead poisoning cases under the supervision of Early.

By letters dated January 2, 1998, Steele notified sixteen clients of ELS that he had moved from ELS to BMV and in most of said letters indicated his willingness to continue handling that client's lead poisoning case. (The letters were, for the most part, directed at the parents or guardians of child victims of lead paint poisoning). The plaintiff asserts that the names, addresses and telephone numbers, guardians, blood lead levels, and insurance coverage of said clients constitute a trade secret, namely a client list, misappropriated by defendants. This court is not persuaded.

III

"Trade secret" is defined by statute (General Statutes, Section 35-51(d)) as "information, including a formula, pattern, compilation, program, device, method, technique, process, drawing, cost data or customer list that: (1) Derives independent economic value, actual or potential, from not being generally known to, and not being readily ascertainable by proper means by other persons who can obtain economic value from its disclosure and use, and (2) is the subject of efforts that are reasonable under the circumstances to maintain its secrecy."

"Misappropriation" means: "(1) Acquisition of a trade secret of another by a person who knows or has reason to know that the trade secret was acquired by improper means; or (2) disclosure or use of a trade secret of another without express or implied consent by a person who (A) used improper means to acquire knowledge of the trade secret; or (B) at the time of disclosure or use, knew or had reason to know that his knowledge of the trade secret was (i) derived from or through a person who had utilized improper means to acquire it; (ii) acquired under circumstances giving rise to a duty to maintain its secrecy or limit its use . . . ; or (iii) derived from or through a person who owed a duty to the person seeking relief to maintain its secrecy or limit its use; or (C) before a material change of his position, knew, or had reason to know that it was a trade secret and that knowledge of it has been acquired by accident or mistake." General Statutes, Section 35-51(b).

"Improper" means "includes theft, bribery, misrepresentation, breach or inducement of a breach of duty to maintain secrecy, or espionage through electronic or other means." (S.35-51(a).)

Thus, in the context of the facts of this case, plaintiff claims that defendant Steele used a trade secret of the plaintiff without plaintiff's express or implied consent when at the time of use Steele knew that this knowledge of the trade secret was acquired under circumstances giving rise to a duty to maintain its secrecy or limit its use; while defendant BMV knew that its knowledge of the trade secret was derived from or through a person who owed a duty to the person seeking relief to maintain its secrecy or limit its use.

IV

A list of customers may be a trade secret, *Town & Country House & Homes Service, Inc. v. Evans*, 150 Conn. 314, 318, 189 A.2d 390. Nevertheless, a substantial element of secrecy must exist, to the extent that there would be difficulty in acquiring the information except by the use of improper means, *Id.* at 319, 189 A.2d 390. Factors to be considered in determining if information is a trade secret include (1) the extent the information is known outside the business; (2) the extent to which it is known by employees or others involved in the business; (3) the extent of measures taken by the employer to guard the secrecy of the information; (4) the value of the information to the employer and to his competitors; (5) the amount of effort or money expended by the employer in developing the information; (6) the ease or difficulty with which the information could be properly acquired or duplicated by others, *Id.* [citation omitted], *Robert S. Weiss & Associates, Inc. v. Wiederlight*, 208 Conn. 525, 538, 546 A.2d 216. Applying these factors to the facts of this case, that element of secrecy simply has not been shown here. Twelve of the sixteen clients' matters had been put into suit; their names and their claims are public knowledge. They were certainly known to the defendants in their respective lawsuits. Plaintiff obtained many of its clients by referral from the Connecticut Citizen's Action Group (CCAG), a nonprofit advocacy organization concerned, inter alia, with aiding victims of lead paint poisoning. There was no showing that CCAG considered the names and addresses of, or information relating to, people it referred to plaintiff as trade secrets, nor that such information would not be available to others on inquiry to CCAG. Of the four clients whose cases were not in suit, two elected to stay with ELS. ELS turned the files of a third over to Steele and Steele took the remaining file from ELS openly and with the knowledge of ELS attorneys.

Defendant Steele acquired the client list by proper means, in the course of his work for plaintiff. Having worked on the cases in question and established relationships with these clients, Steele was entitled to notify them of his change of employer and to signify his willingness to represent them if they so desired. ELS, if asked, was obligated to inform these clients as to where they could contact Steele. See Rules of Professional Conduct, Rule 5.6 There was no evidence that Steele contacted any of ELS's clients before his departure to solicit their business. Defendant Steele acquired expertise and experience during his stay with ELS. He was entitled to use those skills and knowledge after his departure from ELS.

The efforts made by ELS to maintain secrecy of the alleged trade secrets appear to be no more than the usual precautions taken by a law firm to ensure clients' files remain confidential. Not all confidential information meets the definition of trade secret. The existence in the firm's computer system of separate icons for asbestos and lead paint poisoning files is not persuasive evidence of security measures undertaken to protect trade secrets. The court finds no misappropriation of a trade secret by defendants.

V

The plaintiff insists that the Rules of Professional Conflict are irrelevant to this matter and that defendants are barred from relying on said rules and certain informal opinions of the Committee on Professional Ethics of the Connecticut Bar Association (Informal Opinions Nos. 88-23; 97-14; and 97-15) as bases for their defense. Plaintiff relies on disclaimer language in the Rules' Preamble and in the last paragraph of Informal Opinion 88-23 (January 9, 1989) and cites *Noble v. Marshall*, 23 Conn.App. 227, 231, 579 A.2d 594 and *Mazzochi v. Beck*, 204 Conn. 490, 500-01, 529 A.2d 171, in further support of its position.

Plaintiff overstates his case. *Noble v. Marshall, supra*, holds that the Rules of Professional Conduct do not of themselves give rise to a cause of action. *Mazzochi v. Beck, supra*, noting that "every court that has examined this question has concluded that the Code of Professional Conduct does not, per se, give rise to a third party cause of action for damages," held that on that basis the plaintiff's complaint did not state a cause of action for legal malpractice. To posit that the holdings in these cases require the conclusion that the Rules of Professional Responsibility are irrelevant in the instant case is untenable.

The Rules of Professional Conduct, as adopted by the judges of the Superior Court, have the force of law, *Mazzochi v. Beck, supra*, at 501, fn. 7, 529 A.2d 171 [citation omitted]. The Rules provide moral and ethical guidelines for lawyers engaged in the practice of law. Compliance with the Rules may not constitute a complete defense in a given case, but when, as here, a claim is made that an attorney improperly solicited clients of another, thus engaging in tortious interference with business expectancies, it is valid for a defendant to assert his actions complied with the Rules of Professional Conduct and for the court to consider evidence regarding such assertion. Courts may use the Rules in assessing an attorney's conduct in a given case. *See, eg, Sorrentino v. All Seasons Services, Inc.*, 245 Conn. 756, 775, where the court applied the factors listed in Rule 1.5(a) of the Rules of Professional Conduct in determining that a fee agreement was reasonable.

VI

Apart from the factors enumerated in *Town & Country House & Homes Service, Inc. v. Evans, supra*, other considerations militate against plaintiff's claims. The plaintiff asks this court to recognize that the issues facing it in this case concern only the purely entrepreneurial or commercial side of the practice of law.

In discussing the application of CUTPA to the practice of law our Supreme Court has made it clear that an attorney is not exempt from CUTPA, *Haynes v. Yale New Haven Hospital*, 243 Conn. 17, 34, 699 A.2d 964; but the court held that CUTPA covers only the entrepreneurial or commercial aspects of the profession of law, *Id* at 35, 699 A.2d 964. Accordingly, "the noncommercial aspects of lawyering-that is, the representation of the client in a legal capacity-should be excluded for public policy reasons," *Id.* As with CUTPA, so with UTSA.

Applying the standards of *Haynes* the court finds that the dispute presented here is not purely entrepreneurial or commercial. The dispute between the parties here is as to who is entitled to represent the clients concerned. It necessarily implicates the clients' rights, including their right to choose their lawyers. The general rule is that a client may terminate the relationship between himself and his attorney with or without cause. [Citations omitted.]

Other aspects of the instant dispute demonstrate that the claim that the dispute is purely commercial or entrepreneurial cannot withstand scrutiny. Testimony established that in one or more cases plaintiff and defendants are engaged in a battle for representation in court, with competing appearances being filed. Such a conflict must necessarily involve "the representation of the client in a legal capacity" and could affect the progress of said clients' cases. It is more urgent to protect clients from attorneys than to protect attorneys from successor attorneys, *Perkins & Mario, P.C. v. Annunziata*, 45 Conn.App. 237, 241, 694 A.2d 1388. The central issue in the case-the use by Steele of the client list-and the relief sought by the plaintiff-an order enjoining Steele from using the list-directly implicate the said clients' right to choose their representation. "While a law firm has a legitimate interest in its own survival and economic well-being and in maintaining its clients, it cannot protect those interests . . . by, in effect, restricting the choices of the clients to retain and continue the withdrawing member as counsel. [Citation omitted.]. *Cohen v. Lord, Day & Lord, supra*, at 413.

Were the court to grant the relief requested, the clients' right to change counsel would be restricted. This would clearly be contrary to public policy.

Were plaintiff to prevail, a subclass of clients would be created, who, because of the complexity or esoteric nature of their problems, were limited in their right to change counsel. This, too, would be contrary to public policy.

The court notes in passing it is highly unlikely that the clients in question, in choosing ELS to represent them, contemplated that ELS thus acquired a proprietary interest in their names, addresses, telephone numbers, medical conditions and blood lead levels such as to restrict said clients' freedom to change lawyers as the clients see fit.

For the foregoing reasons, plaintiff's claim must fail. There being no violation of the Uniform Trade Secrets Act, there can be no wilful violation of the same. Since the plaintiff's CUTPA claim is predicated solely on the claimed violation of the Uniform Trade Secrets Act, this claim fails also.

VII

In its Fourth Count, plaintiff alleges tortious interference with business expectancies, in that defendants solicited clients of the plaintiff following Steele's departure from ELS. Plaintiff failed to brief this claim, and the court may deem the claim abandoned, *Sachem's Head Ass'n v. Lufkin*, 168 Conn. 365, 366, 362 A.2d 519. Because the claim is predicated on the same set of facts as are the other three counts, the court will address the merits.

A cause of action for tortious interference with contract rights or other business relations has long been recognized. However, not every act that disturbs a business expectancy is actionable. For a plaintiff successfully to prosecute such an action it must prove that the defendant's conduct was in fact tortious. This element may be satisfied by proof that the defendant was guilty of fraud, misrepresentation, intimidation or molestation or that the defendant acted maliciously. An action for intentional interference with business relations requires the plaintiff to plead and prove at least some improper motive or improper means (citations omitted.) The court finds that defendants' contact with the clients in question did not constitute solicitation, nor was improper motive or means shown.

Based on the evidence and testimony presented, plaintiff failed to establish, by a fair preponderance of the evidence, that defendants, by their conduct, tortiously interfered with plaintiff's reasonable business expectancies.

VIII

The court finds that the plaintiff has failed to establish, by a fair preponderance of the evidence, its allegations that the defendant's conduct violated General Statutes, Section 35-50 et seq., the Uniform Trade Secrets Act. That being the case, plaintiff has failed to establish, by a fair preponderance of the evidence, a wilful violation of the Uniform Trade Secrets Act.

Because plaintiff's CUTPA claim is predicated solely on defendants' violation of the Uniform Trade Secrets Act, plaintiff's CUTPA claim must also fail. Plaintiff has failed to establish, by a fair preponderance of the evidence, that defendants, by the conduct complained of, violated General Statutes, Section 42-110a et seq. Finally, plaintiff has failed to establish, by a fair preponderance of the evidence, that the defendants tortiously interfered with the reasonable business expectancies of the plaintiff.

Accordingly, the relief requested is denied and judgment on all four counts may enter for the defendants, John-Henry Steele and Brown, Welsh & Votre, P.C.

* * *

## NOTES AND QUESTIONS:

1. Judge Rubin's careful analysis of whether it was "inevitable" that Mr. Zumpe would use Standard Brands' trade secrets illustrates how fact-sensitive trade secret disputes can be. It is a credit to Mr. Zumpe's lawyers that they were able to present a winning defense in the face of persuasive evidence that Mr. Zumpe possessed valuable secret information, which had the potential of being useful to a competitor. The court's consideration and rejection of the "inevitability" of Mr. Zumpe's use of Standard Brands' trade secrets is a precursor to the "inevitable disclosure doctrine" covered separately in Chapter 4, B, *infra.* Judge Rubin's playful discussion in footnote 3 regarding the discovery of the stimulating effects of coffee by early shepherds should be a delight to coffee lovers and non-drinkers alike.

2. In *Standard Brands*, the court observed that, "information about unsuccessful experiments had 'negative value.' " 264 F.Supp. at 260. What is this so-called negative information and why might it have value? THE RESTATEMENT (THIRD) OF UNFAIR COMPETITION, § 39, cmt. *e* (Reporter's Notes), like n.6 in *Standard Brands*, indicates that the "use" requirement under the RESTATEMENT (SECOND) OF TORTS § 757, would "place[] into doubt protection for so-called 'negative' information that teaches conduct to be avoided," which is developed before a product was actually marketed. However, this problem was eliminated by the UTSA, which dropped the "use" requirement and noted, "the results of lengthy and expensive research which proves that a certain process will *not* work would be of great value to a competitor." Uniform Trade Secrets Act § 1, cmt. The value of such "negative information" was recognized in *Ashland Oil, Inc. v. Fed. Trade Comm'n*, 409 F.Supp. 297 (D.D.C. 1976), discussed below in Chapt. 2, B, 1, c, where the court held that a competitor would find geophysical data to have "a 'negative' value." *Id.* at 304.

3. Customer lists were considered important enough to be listed specifically in RESTATEMENT (SECOND) OF TORTS § 757. Why was there a distinction made between customer lists and other information that was characterized in § 757 as "simply information as to single or ephemeral events in the conduct of the business"? This other information would include, but not be limited to, secret bid information, employee salaries, security investments, or the date fixed for announcing a new policy or product.

4. The Uniform Trade Secret Act and the RESTATEMENT (THIRD) OF UNFAIR COMPETITION broadened the definition of a trade secret to eliminate the distinction between the traditional forms of secret information defined in § 757 and "the single and ephemeral events." Why do you think that distinction was discarded? In the next section, note the court's discussion in *Cybertek Computer Products, Inc. v. Whitfield* regarding the defendant's attempt to "delineate the difference between confidential matter on the one hand and trade secrets on the other hand." 203 U.S.P.Q. 1020, 1023 (Cal.App.Dep't Super.Ct. 1977). Of special interest is the *Cybertek* court's conclusion that in "the factual context of this case [involving computer software], this may amount to a distinction without a difference."

5. An important subject of trade secret protection has been technical information that is not apparent from an examination of a product in the public domain. The *Weil-McLain* court described such information as "economic efficiencies and engineering benefits derived from such features . . . [as] screwing to be much

cheaper than welding . . . [and] the obvious pie-pan dimple on the heat exchanger reduced stress and cracking." 200 U.S.P.Q. at 543. Why should this type of information about a product in the public domain be protected? Why should other information that is available from a close scrutiny and/or testing of the product not be protected? The *Weil-McLain* court's decision was whether summary judgment should be granted. Accordingly, would *Weil-McLain* have any precedential value in persuading a court to find that this type of information was a protectable trade secret?

6. Unless the party asserting its rights has expended "extraordinary efforts" to develop customer information beyond names on a list that are "readily ascertainable," protection of customer lists can be difficult. *Compare Webcraft Techs., Inc. v. McCaw*, 674 F.Supp. 1039, 1045 (S.D.N.Y.1987) (printer's customer information held to be trade secret where "it is a long, difficult process to educate and convert a prospective customer to the benefits" of the in-line services at issue), *with Nalco Chem. Co. v. Hydro Techs., Inc.*, 984 F.2d 801 (7th Cir.1993) ("The group of purchasers for Hydro and Nalco Watergy products is neither fixed nor small. The products are used in such common items as industrial boiler, heating, and cooling systems, and processed waste treatment systems. The target market for the products is broad, encompassing commercial buildings, universities and schools, hospitals and clinics, and industry.").

7. In *Silfen*, the court observed that if the defendant had "appropriated [detailed information in customer files] by copying [or by] studied memory . . . there would be a case quite different from this." The distinction between "studied memory" and information "retained" in a former employee's memory is dealt with in the RESTATEMENT (THIRD) OF AGENCY, § 396, cmt. b, which provides that an employee is normally allowed to compete with a former employer and use customer names retained in his memory. Otherwise, a departing employee would be forced to "perform a frontal lobotomy on himself or herself." *Fleming Sales Co., Inc. v. Bailey*, 611 F.Supp. 507, 514 (N.D.Ill.1985). How do the "readily ascertainable" and "casual memory" tests mentioned in *Silfen* square with each other with regard to customer lists? Note that the court in *Cybertek*, which is excerpted in the next section, commented that "the weight of authority indicates that appropriation by memory will be proscribed under the same circumstances as an appropriation via more tangible means." *Cybertek*, 203 U.S.P.Q. at 1025.

8. In *Silfen*, the defendant had a non-competition clause in his employment agreement. Why wasn't that clause dispositive of the case? What did the court mean when it said that "[b]y discharging Cream plaintiffs obtained greater protection than they would have had under their agreement with him, if he had terminated the employment." 278 N.E.2d at 641. Non-competition clauses or covenants not to compete are discussed below in Chapt. 2, D, 1, nn.3-5.

10. Did the decision in *PhoneDog* hold that Twitter data and information were trade secrets, or merely put that decision off to another day? Can a Twitter password be a trade secret, or is it the key to the real trade secrets? *PhoneDog* seems to be on the front edge of a wave of future enforcement actions involving the new forms of social media.

11. As shown in *Early, Ludwick & Sweeney*, customer (or client) lists are tough to enforce against departing lawyers. Law firms have also been unsuccessful in causes of action for an inducing breach of contract theory against departing associates, based on engagement letters of firm clients. *See Koeppel v. Schroder*, 122 A.D.2d 780, 783 (N.Y.App.1986) ("a client has an absolute right on public policy grounds to terminate the attorney-client relationship at any time without cause,").

### (b) Computer Software

## CYBERTEK COMPUTER PRODUCTS, INC. v. WHITFIELD

203 U.S.P.Q. 1020 (Cal. App. Dep't Supr. Ct. 1977)

Very briefly, and by way of an overview without attempting to set forth the facts in any considerable detail, the dispute essentially arises out of the prior employment of defendant Whitfield by plaintiff, and his subsequent employment by defendant Tracor in the same field of endeavor. Plaintiff was formed in 1969 for the purpose of engaging in the business of furnishing computer related services to the life insurance industry. Defendant Whitfield was one of the founding officers of plaintiff, and had a substantial background and expertise in computer software, as specifically related to its use in the life insurance business. He purchased shares in plaintiff, and in his capacity as an employee of plaintiff, directly participated in the design and development of plaintiff's on-line new business computer system known as the Auto/Issue System, his responsibilities including the specific design of some major portions of the system. For a time he had management responsibility for this system, and subsequently was a senior analyst involved in its design, programming and testing.

In connection with his employment, defendant Whitfield executed an Employee Nondisclosure Agreement, dated December 2, 1970, which provided among other things that the techniques and methods relating to plaintiff's products were trade secrets and confidential, and that he would not at any time disclose to anyone outside of plaintiff any information about plaintiff's products which related to the design, use or development of such products. The agreement specifically made reference to the Auto/Issue System. He voluntarily terminated his employment and relationship with plaintiff on March 31, 1971, at which time he acknowledged in writing that he understood his agreement with plaintiff not to disclose confidential information, and that he had returned all confidential material to plaintiff. He thereafter did some consulting work for defendant Tracor between July and October, 1971, commenced full-time employment with said defendant on November 15, 1971, and ever since that time has remained in said defendant's employ. His duties with defendant Tracor have included responsibility for the development of an insurance on-line new business system, which would provide substantially the same capabilities as plaintiff's Auto/Issue System, and which was to be marketed in direct competition to plaintiff's Auto/Issue System.

Plaintiff developed its Auto/Issue System over a period of approximately two years, from November, 1969 through approximately November, 1971. Since that time it has been marketing the system. Defendant's similar system, which it has named Trac/70, has been substantially though not completely developed, but is nevertheless being marketed at the present time in competition with plaintiff's Auto/Issue System. It was stipulated by the parties that plaintiff and defendant Tracor have each expended in excess of $500,000 in the development of their respective systems.

II.

Plaintiff has at all times maintained and *enforced* a corporate policy which requires its employees to execute Employee Nondisclosure Agreements such as that executed by defendant Whitfield, and which further requires its potential and actual licensees to execute nondisclosure agreements prior to receiving Auto/Issue documentation other than marketing material. Plaintiff also at all times material herein maintained additional reasonable measures of security which clearly demonstrate plaintiff's intention to keep information concerning its products, including the Auto/Issue System, confidential, such as the marking of documentation relating to its products as confidential, the use of registration numbers in connection with copies of its documentation, and permitting only authorized personnel to have access to its Auto/Issue documentation other than marketing materials. Defendant Tracor has likewise taken similar steps relating to security in order to protect the confidentiality of its on-line new business system known as Trac/70.

III.

It is plaintiff's contention that during defendant Whitfield's consultations and employment with defendant Tracor, he has been substantially and directly involved in the design of said defendant's Trac/70 System, in connection with which he has utilized and disclosed plaintiff's trade secrets and confidential information in violation of his duty to plaintiff, and in breach of his specific Nondisclosure Agreement with plaintiff. Both defendants deny any responsibility to plaintiff, and contend that the alleged trade secrets and confidential matter claimed by plaintiff are in fact not trade secrets or confidential, but rather are well known concepts in the computer industry, that they are, therefore, not confidential, and that defendant Whitfield has merely utilized his substantial degree of skill and experience in his employment by defendant Tracor which he had developed prior to his employment with plaintiff and which he has the right to so utilize.

IV.

There are a number of basic thresh hold issues to be determined by the Court, which appear to involve mixed questions of law and fact. Among these are the following: Do any or all of the 12 items set forth in plaintiff's Exh. 1A (said exhibit purports to enumerate the areas of design and development of the Auto/Issue System which constitute the confidential information and trade secrets concerning which plaintiff is entitled to protection), or any combination thereof, constitute confidential information or trade secrets? If they fail to reach the dignity of trade secrets, do they nevertheless constitute confidential matter entitled to protection under the law? Is the nondisclosure contract executed by defendant Whitfield with plaintiff a valid and binding agreement? What was the intention of the parties under said nondisclosure agreement? Was any of said alleged confidential matter or trade secrets disclosed by defendant Whitfield to defendant Tracor in connection with the development of the Trac/70 System?

V.

While there may have been a question in the past as to whether or not computer software is susceptible of protection under the trade secret doctrine, it is clear that such protection is available today in practically all jurisdictions. See 38 George Washington Law Review 909, and cases cited by both plaintiff and defendants in their respective trial briefs, all of which make it amply clear that computer software is protectible under the trade secret doctrine, given appropriate facts and circumstances.

VI.

It should be noted at the outset that plaintiff and defendant Whitfield executed a document entitled "Cybertek Employee Non-Disclosure Agreement" on December 2, 1970, which as already indicated purports to restrict the disclosure by defendant Whitfield of certain information concerning plaintiff's products, including the Auto/Issue System. Plaintiff places considerable importance on this agreement in this litigation, and defendant Whitfield contends that the agreement is not binding upon him for a number of reasons, including the contention that the agreement was executed without consideration. While it is true that the nondisclosure agreement was executed a number of months after the commencement of defendant Whitfield's employment with plaintiff, plaintiff contends that this is of no moment because when plaintiff was first formed by its founding officers consisting of Vaughn Morgan, Nancy Wilten and defendant Whitfield, it was clearly understood and agreed that the on-line new business system which would be developed by plaintiff would be confidential and not disclosed to any outsiders without the necessary controls to insure the confidentiality of such system, and that the subsequent execution of the written nondisclosure agreement was only to memorialize their prior oral agreement. A consideration of all of the evidence leads the Court to conclude and find these to be the true facts, and that, therefore, the contention of a lack of consideration must fail. The evidence demonstrates without question that from the very inception, it was always the intention of said principals that their development of the Auto/Issue System would be considered to be highly confidential matter, and this is supported not only by the said nondisclosure agreement of December 12, 1970, but also by the agreement executed with Pacific Mutual Life Insurance Company as well as the agreement with I.S.A., both of which contained language clearly indicating such confidentiality.

The contention has also been advanced by defendants that said nondisclosure agreement is violative of the Public Policy of California, as articulated in Section 16600 of the Business and Professions Code. Defendants cite no authorities to support this position. A distinction must be drawn between contracts which prohibit an employee from competing with his former employer, which subject to certain exceptions do violate said Business and Professions Code section, and agreements which seek to prohibit an employee from disclosing confidential information and trade secrets, which do not come within the ambit of said section. [Citations omitted.] Thus, the Court concludes that the nondisclosure agreement is valid and binding upon defendant Whitfield.

VII.

Said nondisclosure agreement is not ideally drafted, and leaves some room for interpretation. Plaintiff concedes that it was not its intention to prohibit the disclosure of any and all information relating to its products, but only such information which would reasonably be deemed to be confidential or in the nature of a trade secret. The Court agrees with this interpretation, and finds that the parties intended by said agreement to prohibit defendant Whitfield from disclosing any information concerning its products which would reasonably be deemed confidential to the point where it should not be revealed to outsiders without some contractual control and limitations. The Court does not believe or find that the parties intended any distinction between the use of the words "trade secrets" on the one hand and "confidential" on the other hand, but rather used these terms interchangeably to indicate information which should reasonably be withheld from outsiders. Thus the task of the Court will be to determine whether the nondisclosure agreement, so interpreted, has been violated by the defendant Whitfield during his employment by Tracor.

VIII.

The Court having concluded that the nondisclosure agreement is indeed a valid and subsisting agreement, it is necessary to determine the effect of said agreement in the factual context of defendant Whitfield's activities on behalf of defendant Tracor. A fair reading of the cases would seem to indicate that considerable importance is placed upon the existence of such contracts, as compared to situations where no agreement exists between the employer and his former employee. *See Futurecraft Corp. v. Clary Corp.*, 205 C.A.2d 279, where in denying relief to the plaintiff on the trade secrets theory, the court pointed out that the trial court had found that there was no agreement of nondisclosure between the employer and the employee, and further cited in support of its position the case of *Wexler v. Greenberg*, 160 A.2d 430, 125 USPQ 471 where relief was also denied, one of the grounds again apparently being that there was no express covenant between the parties relating to nondisclosure of the confidential information. There is a clear inference from both of these cases that relief may well be denied in the absence of a covenant of nondisclosure between the parties. While the existence or nonexistence of such a contract is not determinative, and relief may under some circumstances be granted even in the absence of a contract, the existence of a contract makes it more probable that the employer will be granted relief for breach of contract, and this may be so even if the confidential information, knowledge or technology, does not rise to the dignity of a trade secret. *Structural Dynamics Research Corporation v. Engineering Mechanics Research Corporation*, 401 Fed.Supp.1102 so held, and specifically pointed out that a former employee may be liable for breach of contract if he uses confidential information gained while employed with a former employer, even though such information was not itself a trade secret. In view of these cases, the Court has concluded that considerable weight must be given to the fact that plaintiff and defendant Whitfield executed the nondisclosure agreement in question.

## IX.

The above observations of the Court must lead to the conclusion that if confidential matter relating to the Auto/Issue System was disclosed by defendant Whitfield to defendant Tracor, particularly if that confidential matter was in the nature of trade secrets, liability would have to be imposed. Considerable time was expended during the course of trial by counsel in an effort to delineate the difference between confidential matter on the one hand and trade secrets on the other hand, but at least in the factual context of this case, this may amount to a distinction without a difference, and in the Court's view a proper disposition of this case does not necessitate the drawing of such a fine line.

## X.

Simply stated, plaintiff's position is that some 12 areas of development and design in its Auto/Issue System set forth in extremely technical language in Exh. 1A constitute trade secrets, or at least highly confidential matter which should be protected either on the theory that defendant Whitfield breached his confidential duty to plaintiff or breached his express covenant of nondisclosure. To determine this issue, it is necessary to attempt to glean a definition of a trade secret from the authorities and case law, and that examination of the authorities and cases makes it immediately obvious that while the simplistic definitions found therein are easily understood, the application thereof to a highly technical area such as computer software programs is extremely difficult. Section 757 of the Restatement of Torts, Comment b, generally defines a trade secret as any formula, pattern, device or compilation of information which is used in one's business, and which gives him an opportunity to obtain an advantage over competitors who do not know or use it. In spite of this simple definition, it further states that an exact definition of a trade secret is not possible, and lists some factors to be considered in determining the existence or nonexistence of a trade secret. Briefly stated, these include the extent to which the information is known by others outside of the business or employees of the business, the extent of measures taken to guard the secrecy of the information, the value of the information, the effort and expense involved in developing it, and lastly the ease or difficulty with which the information could be properly acquired or duplicated by others. As to some of the latter factors, plaintiff clearly comes within their ambit, as the evidence is virtually uncontradicted that reasonably strict security measures were taken to guard the secrecy of the Auto/Issue System, in excess of $500,000 was expended by plaintiff to develop it, license fees of somewhere between $100,000 and $200,000 are charged plaintiff's customers for the right to use the system, and a formidable and expensive task is faced by any competitor who might desire to properly acquire or duplicate it. The serious conflict in the evidence arises, however, in connection with the factor dealing with the issue as to the extent to which the information is known to others outside of plaintiff's business. Defendants essentially contend that we are not dealing with trade secrets, nor for that matter even confidential matter to any degree, because all the alleged items set forth in Exh. 1A are not secret or confidential information but rather consist of well known concepts in the computer and data processing industry, and consequently cannot by any stretch of the imagination be considered confidential or secret. This issue was joined in the traditional battle of the experts, with Dr. Gilbert and others testifying on behalf of plaintiff to the effect that Exh. 1A indeed did include unique and confidential approaches not known to the computer industry in general, and Mr. Shafto and others testifying on behalf of defendants to the contrary. The technical nature of their testimony would be mind boggling to the average lay person, as it was to the court, and this is amply demonstrated by the fact that Mr. Shafto, an obviously well qualified expert in the computer field, testified that he had great difficulty in even understanding the meaning of the descriptive language of the alleged trade secrets found in Exh. 1A. The Court has carefully considered all of the testimony, and has concluded that at least to some degree, defendants' position is correct in that some of the approaches utilized in the Auto/Issue System, standing separately, are general concepts known to experts in the computer industry. The cases indicate, and plaintiff concedes that general concepts are not protectible, per se, as trade secrets. However, the cases further indicate that while general concepts are not protectible, the specific implementation involving a particular combination of general concepts may well amount to a trade secret. *See Winston Res. Co. v. Minnesota Mining & Mfg. Co., supra*, involving the manufacture of a tape recording device, supporting this theory. That court pointed out that the same general concepts had been used in developing defendants' machine as had been used in plaintiff's machine, that such development involved the use of general concepts and approaches which were known in the industry, and were, therefore, not in and of themselves susceptible of trade secret protection. However, the court further pointed out that while the general approach and the basic mechanical elements thereof were not trade secrets, that the specifications of these basic mechanical elements and their relationship to each other embodied in plaintiff's machine were not publicly known, were arrived at only after painstaking research and extensive trial and error, and therefore, constituted a trade secret entitled to protection. In other words, the court found that the specific embodiment of the general concepts and approach into a combination of parts was protectible, even though all or some of them might well be known to the industry. *Also see By-Buk Co. v. Printed Cellophane Tape Co.*, 163 C.A.2d 157, 118 USPQ 550. The Court believes that the principle annunciated in these cases applies to our case, and that while some of the concepts set forth in Exh. 1A are general concepts not susceptible of protection, that the entire bundle or combination of these concepts as developed and utilized by plaintiff in its Auto/Issue System do constitute trade secrets which are protectible under the circumstances. As pointed out in the above mentioned Restatement of Torts, as well as in 80 Harvard Law Review 1432, at page 1452, any information which provides a competitive advantage over competitors may well constitute a trade secret, and in the Court's view it is obvious that the combination of factors involved in the Auto/Issue System must give the plaintiff its protection under this doctrine.

XI.

Having concluded that the confidential matter in question should not have been disclosed by defendant Whitfield, the next issue which must be determined is whether in fact there was such a disclosure by him in connection with his work on the development of Tracor's Trac/70 System. Defendant Whitfield contends that since he took away no actual documentation or physical material relating to the Auto/Issue System, it must follow that he did not disclose or use any confidential information relating thereto, but rather merely made use of his expertise and general know-how in the development of Trac/70. Putting it in another way, defendants contend that Trac/70 was independently developed, and was not copied from plaintiff's Auto/Issue System. This presents an extremely close question of fact for the Court to determine, and the Court is not unmindful of the classic confrontation in the law of the policy which strives to extend some protection to an employer from the breach of confidence of a former employee in taking away and utilizing trade secrets with the policy of the law which protects an employee in his right to carry on his trade or profession after he leaves his employer. The Court also has considered the well recognized principle that where a defendant in a trade secret case claims independent development, that the burden then shifts to the defendant and places upon the defendant a heavy burden of persuasion to show that the production was a result of independent development and not from the use of information confidentially secured during the prior employment. This principle has been articulated in many cases, including *Bolt Associates, Inc. v. Alpine Geophysical Associates, Inc.*, 365 Fed.2d 742, 151 USPQ 520.

Looking to the evidence, it is not seriously controverted, and the Court finds that there are in fact substantial similarities in the Auto/Issue System and the Trac/70 System. Such similarity, while not determinative of the issue, is of obvious importance, and must be given weight. Granted that the systems are not identical, many cases indicate that such identity is not required, and that trade secrets need not be exactly copied in order to impose liability. Likewise, the conceded difference in terminology utilized in the systems is not significant.

Defendants have also *argued* that many of the similarities are purely coincidental, since there were relatively few options which every expert in the field would consider in arriving at methods of approach for a new business on-line system. However, plaintiff presented evidence to the effect that there were in fact significant design choices, and that similar choices utilized by defendants would, therefore, indicate copying rather than independent development. This again is a question of fact, and the Court accepts Dr. Gilbert's testimony to the effect that there were significant design choices, and not as indicated by defendants, choices only as to insignificant details. Furthermore, even if the Court resolves the conflict in the evidence regarding whether or not defendant Whitfield took away with him documentation concerning the Auto/Issue System in favor of defendant Whitfield, the cases are clear that documentation need not be taken in order to establish liability, since appropriation by memory alone is proscribed. As pointed out in 38 George Washington Law Review, page 909 at pages 938 and 939, the weight of authority indicates that appropriation by memory will be proscribed under the same circumstances as an appropriation via more tangible means.

When the Court considers all of the above factors, and adds thereto the ingredient sustained by the evidence that defendant Whitfield had complete knowledge and understanding of plaintiff's system, and in addition supervised and oversaw the development of defendants' system, the Court concludes and finds that defendant

Whitfield did disclose and utilize substantial aspects of plaintiff's Auto/Issue System in the development of the Trac/70 System.

XII.

Defendant Whitfield's liability having been established, the Court must finally determine whether defendant Tracor also has liability under the circumstances. The cases indicate, as does Section 757 of the Restatement of Torts, that a new employer may also be liable for misappropriation of trade secrets, provided that he utilizes the information with notice of the secret nature thereof and with notice that the employee has disclosed it in breach of his duty to the former employer. *See By-Buk Co. v. Printed Cellophane Tape Co., supra.* The evidence indicates that before any substantial development of the Trac/70 System was begun, defendant Whitfield had been placed on notice by plaintiff by letter concerning a possible trade secret violation, and defendant Tracor was apprised of said demand by defendant Whitfield. In addition, it is conceded by defendants that the instant lawsuit was actually filed before any substantial development of the Trac/70 system. Under these circumstances, the Court finds that defendant Tracor was on notice of the potential liability in this matter, and consequently the Court finds that defendant Tracor has liability herein along with defendant Whitfield.

## COM-SHARE, INC. v. COMPUTER COMPLEX, INC.

338 F. Supp. 1229 (E.D. Mich. 1971)

The case before us arises out of a dispute between the parties to a contract related to the operation of computers.

* * *

Certain background materials are necessary not only to an understanding of the issues (which, legally, are not complicated) but as well to the explanation of certain of the unique meanings given words commonly employed in every day speech. Thus the word "languages", as used in this operation is a collection of programs that individually allow a user to develop programs of his own in a language something like English, but which is susceptible to translation into such computer languages as NEWBASIC, XTRAN, and QED.

* * *

The contract between the parties concerned the business each was engaged in, namely, offering the use of computer systems on a "time sharing" basis. This business and its mechanisms are so set up that different customers can use the computer system simultaneously from their places of business through the use of telephone facilities. Both parties are also engaged in developing and marketing what is known as "software". This word, as here employed, refers to the programs and controls which are used in the computer. It is clear that this business of computer time sharing is a fast moving operation. Developments in the technology and improvements thereof are frequently made and are important not only for the service of existing customers but in attracting potential customers for the systems.

The agreement before us, concerning which the dispute arises, was entered into on February 10, 1967 and denominated "Technical Exchange Agreement". The negotiations preceding the Technical Exchange Agreement began in or around January, 1967 and were conducted in part by Mr. William D. Mercer, then President of the defendant, who came to Ann Arbor and Detroit for the purpose of these negotiations, which ultimately resulted in the Technical Exchange Agreement. Defendant's stated objective was to obtain workable systems of time sharing software, plaintiff's subsequent new software developments, and all enhancements, and the maintenance of such software. Summarizing briefly, under the Technical Exchange Agreement, so negotiated, plaintiff and defendant agreed to provide to each other during the term of their agreement, all information concerning "hardware" (e.g., specifications, designs, production drawings, changes, improvements, and new designs relating to computer components) and "software" (i. e., programs and controls that are read into a computer) that came into the legal possession of either party and which related to any phase of operating an SDS 940 Time Sharing Computer System, except that the exchange of applications software in any way proprietary to a user was subject to the express permission of the user. The technology was supplied by magnetic tapes, listings, printouts, and other appropriate transfer media.

From, then, approximately February of 1967 through November 1, 1970, in reliance upon and pursuant to the terms of the Technical Exchange Agreement, plaintiff supplied to defendant, in confidence, from and within the State of Michigan, information, systems software developments and technology called for by the Technical Exchange Agreement, including developments, information, training, know how, documents, tapes, tangible things and other technology developed by plaintiff. Such developments and technology as were supplied by defendant to plaintiff under the Technical Exchange Agreement were delivered by defendant to plaintiff in Ann Arbor, Michigan. In addition, certain of the defendant's employees received extensive technical training under the Technical Exchange Agreement at plaintiff's offices in Ann Arbor.

Consistent with the confidential nature of such developments and technology, the Technical Exchange Agreement specifically provided as follows:

"Com-Share and Southern [now Computer Complex, Inc.] each agreed not to lease, sell or otherwise divulge to any third party interest, without the prior written consent of the other, any and all systems software developments supplied to it by the other."

Further to safeguard the information and data thus supplied, the Technical Exchange Agreement also provided that

"Notwithstanding the expiration or termination of this Agreement, the limitations set forth in Section XI (last paragraph) shall continue for a period of 24 months after such expiration or termination."

Differences having arisen between the parties, they agreed by letter dated November 30, 1970 that the Technical Exchange Agreement was terminated effective as of November 1, 1970. This letter, which was drafted by the defendant, provided in part as follows:

"This letter signifies mutual termination of the Technical Exchange Agreement dated February 10, 1967 between our two companies. This termination shall be effective as of November 1, 1970, as of which date neither company requires further performance by the other under the said agreement."

The prayer for a preliminary injunction before us was triggered in large part by the circumstance that on August 5, 1971, defendant publicly announced that it had entered into an agreement with Tymshare, Inc., a California corporation, to sell substantially all of defendant's assets and goodwill related to its computer time sharing operations to Tymshare, Inc. The obligations of Tymshare, Inc. under this agreement, which is dated August 4, 1971, are subject to certain conditions precedent, including the approval of defendant's shareholders. Defendant's shareholders have not yet approved the sale of the assets to Tymshare, Inc., which corporation, we find, is not an indispensable party which must be joined or in the absence of which this action must be dismissed under Fed.R.Civ.P. 19(a) and 12(b)(7). [Citations omitted.]

The plaintiff, obviously disturbed by the implications of the above with respect to its confidential data, wrote to both defendant and Tymshare, Inc., a letter (August 10, 1971) citing to them the provisions of the paragraphs above quoted of the Technical Exchange Agreement, and stating, in addition, that plaintiff presumed that defendant would not divulge to Tymshare, Inc. any information about or pertaining to the systems software developments which had been supplied to the defendant by the plaintiff. Subsequent thereto, the plaintiff took the action before us. On August 27, 1971 it filed for preliminary and permanent equitable relief. On September 13, 1971 defendant filed motions to dismiss the complaint for failure to state a claim upon which relief could be granted, for lack of jurisdiction, and for failure to join an indispensable party. On October 1, 1971, plaintiff filed its motion for a preliminary injunction restraining and enjoining defendant Computer Complex, Inc., its directors, officers, agents and employees, and all other persons acting in concert with them who receive notice of its order, pending the final determination of this action and thereafter until November 1, 1972, from leasing, selling, transferring, disclosing or otherwise divulging to Tymshare, Inc., its directors, officers, agents, and employees, or to any other third party, any of the systems software developments and technology supplied by plaintiff to defendant pursuant to the Technical Exchange Agreement.

With reference to the "systems software developments and technology supplied by plaintiff", the record shows that during the period from 1967 to November 1, 1970, plaintiff delivered to defendant, pursuant to the Technical Exchange Agreement, certain magnetic tapes, symbolics, listings, printouts, documents and other items containing or embodying plaintiff's systems software developments and technology as the use of such was made commercially available by plaintiff. Pursuant to the amendment to the Technical Exchange Agreement dated August 3, 1970, plaintiff also delivered to defendant software developments and technology pertaining to the SDS (XDS) 940 computer while such developments and technology were still in the developmental stages prior to their release to plaintiff's customers in a normal time sharing environment. The systems software supplied by plaintiff to defendant under the Technical Exchange Agreement included the following:

(a) The "Monitor" (a collection of programs that combine to control the various operations of the physical hardware devices that comprise the computer) and the "Executive" (a collection of programs that combine to perform administrative functions and interfacing the user to the machine). The "Monitor" and "Executive" programs supplied by plaintiff to defendant were in three separate series: the "C-00" Series, the "T-00" Series and the "W" Series. The "Monitor" and "Executive" programs in the "W" Series were unique and new programs.

(b) The "Languages", which, as we have noted heretofore, is a collection of programs allowing a user to develop programs of his own, in a language which resembles English but which can be translated into language peculiar to the computer, including XTRAN, QED and NEWBASIC.

These systems software developments and technology so supplied by the plaintiff to the defendant were developed by the plaintiff's Research and Development Division at a cost of some two million dollars to the plaintiff.

Some of the history behind the systems software technology for computer time sharing must be noted at this point since it bears upon defendant's claim that there really isn't anything unique about plaintiff's software. Certain of the original concepts had been developed in 1966 at the University of California in Berkeley in a project called "Project Genie" which had been financed by the Federal Government. The systems software developed in this project was identified as System 1.50 and 1.53 and its principal use was in scientific research rather than for commercial time sharing programs.

Also, representatives of plaintiff, Scientific Data Systems, Inc. (commonly referred to as "SDS" and now wholly owned by Xerox Corporation and referred to as "XDS"), and Tymshare, Inc., assisted by faculty and students from the University of California participated in a joint project in 1966 at the facilities of Tymshare, Inc., in Palo Alto, California, for the purpose of developing a commercial version of the software developed earlier at Berkeley for use on a modified SDS 930 computer (later called a 940 computer after certain hardware modifications were made by Scientific Data Systems). This joint project, which was sponsored by Scientific Data Systems (the manufacturer of the SDS 930 computer) resulted in the development of a more commercially oriented system identified as System 1.82. System 1.82 was available to those firms that participated in the joint project, including plaintiff. Mr. Richard Crandall, now plaintiff's president, participated as an employee of plaintiff in this joint project.

Following Mr. Crandall's return to plaintiff Com-Share, Incorporated, in late 1966, he recruited and assembled a staff of research and development technicians, including Mr. Steven Weiss (later, the principal inventor of the W system technology) and Mr. Ronald Jeffries (later, the inventor of XTRAN), and plaintiff commenced developing and did develop, a number of software systems for use with the SDS 940 computer.

Using separate research and development groups, plaintiff developed software systems along two distinct lines: (1) enhanced versions of System 1.82 (Systems C-00 and T-00) which contained a number of improvements, among the most important of which was the increase in the maximum number of simultaneous users which had theretofore been relatively restricted; and (2) certain totally new software systems, including the W system "Monitor", the W system "Executive", "XTRAN" and Com-Share's version of the "QED" text editor. A great many smaller routines were also developed. The W system Monitor and Executive permit 34 to 40 simultaneous users as compared to the 8 to 10 simultaneous users possible under System 1.82, the 13 to 15 simultaneous users possible under the C-00 system, and the 20 to 25 simultaneous users possible under the T-00 system.

It is our judgment, upon the record before us, that the W system software, XTRAN and plaintiff's version of the QED were invented by plaintiff's employees based upon new principles and concepts with unique engineering, logic and coherence, and did not embody the technology developed by the University of California staff in Project Genie or that developed in the joint project sponsored by Scientific Data Systems. Moreover, with reference to defendant's argument that the software supplied to it by plaintiff was not secret but "instead, in the public domain", it is necessary to note that the existing software systems which are unique in the computer time sharing industry all contain certain elements which perform similar functions and many utilize certain similar fundamental concepts, of a general nature. This is no more than saying that all have a common concept, and, in the most general sense, a common base. Such is common in all engineering. Thus, the concept of vehicular locomotion, involving in one aspect, the basic principles of the internal combustion engine, is common to snowmobiles, ships, airplanes, and automobiles, but there the similarity stops. The varying systems, as patent lawyers so eloquently demonstrate, differ greatly in the steps taken to accomplish the objective. Similarly here. the specific engineering of these software systems, and their particular underlying technologies and design, together with what has been referred to as their "logic and coherence", as well as their speed, accuracy, cost, and commercial feasibility may differ greatly from system to system. They will and do inevitably reflect the peculiar and unique accomplishments and technical skills of the developers thereof. This, in a nutshell, is what the software systems developed by the plaintiff supplied to the defendant under the Technical Exchange Agreement. And while it is true that defendant may have made certain technical changes in software supplied to it by plaintiff under the Technical Exchange Agreement, the defendant did not alter the unique principles, engineering, logic, and coherence developed by plaintiff into such software systems. This software was supplied to the defendant on magnetic tapes in machine readable form known as "selfills" and "symbolics", referred to as "human readable in printed form."

It is clear that the utmost caution was used by plaintiff in protecting the secrecy of this software. Each page of the listings embodying plaintiff's systems contains the words "Com-Share, Inc. Company Confidential." "Passwords", it was testified, are built into the systems to prevent unauthorized access. Magnetic tapes and symbolics are kept locked when not in use. These protections have been built into the systems themselves, not only in order that no customer can have unauthorized access to any other customer's data base or specialized technology, but also in order that no employee of the company itself can have unauthorized access to any system, and possibly betray his employer and client.

The plaintiff's systems, software development, technology, and their underlying engineering, we find, have been, in fact, kept secret and confidential. Disclosures have been made by the plaintiff only to the defendant, and to plaintiff's foreign licensees. With respect to the "C-00" Series and "T-00" Series software there have been disclosures in isolated instances to certain other firms not in the time sharing business, but such exceptions do not impeach plaintiff's allegations of secrecy. It is clear that plaintiff's software has not been made available to competitor companies in the computer time sharing business.

In the conduct of this business, which it is clear is not static, either as to technologies and operations, certain disputes occurred between the parties as to the performance of their respective obligations to exchange technology thereunder. Defendant complains of plaintiff's failure to furnish symbolics, whereas plaintiff established that up to the date of the termination of the Technical Exchange Agreement the defendant had declined to furnish plaintiff with at least one of its hardware design elements, specifically, the "CCI" communications interface device, which would have been of material value to the plaintiff. Defendant argues thus that plaintiff has come into Court with "unclean hands." We do not so find. There is nothing here of morally reprehensible conduct, of acts of such nature that good conscience should not permit the plaintiff to be heard. At the most, there were no more than minor breaches of the contract, neither major nor substantial. It is significant that the parties themselves did not regard such failures as existed as having gone to the root of the contract. At no time prior to November 30, 1970 (the date of the termination letter) nor since that date, has either party threatened to rescind or to commence an action for damages under the Technical Exchange Agreement as a result of any such claims of non-performance. In fact, as of August 3, 1970, the plaintiff and defendant entered into a letter agreement clarifying what were considered by the parties to be ambiguities in the Technical Exchange Agreement. Plaintiff delivered to defendant during the term of the Technical Exchange Agreement substantially all of the technology within its possession or control that was within the scope of the Agreement, and there is no evidence of an anticipatory breach thereof by the plaintiff.

We now come to the termination agreement and its bearing upon the contractual obligations of the parties. This termination, by mutual agreement, was evidenced by a letter dated November 30, 1970, prepared by defendant and executed by both parties. The first paragraph of this letter stated as follows:

> "This letter signifies mutual termination of the Technical Exchange Agreement dated February 10, 1967 between our two companies. This termination shall be effective as of November 1, 1970, as of which date neither company requires further performance by the other under said agreement."

The defendant argues that the parties intended by this agreement to discharge not only their mutual obligations "to perform under the Technical Exchange Agreement" but also the obligations not to disclose to any third party the software developments supplied to each other by the parties. Thus, it is argued, the very clause designed to prevent disclosure upon termination becomes nugatory upon termination. A more complete exercise in contractual futility would be difficult to find. The purpose behind the non-disclosure provisions is self evident. It is to confine the use of the systems software development, researched and formulated at substantial expense, strictly to the other party, to whom it had been furnished.

The difficulty with defendant's suggested interpretation of the letter, to the effect that it terminates as well the non-disclosure provisions, is simply that it does not say so. An agreement to safeguard sale or disclosure for two years following termination will not be read out of a contract by implication. Nor will it be rendered nugatory by an agreement that there will be no "further" performance under the agreement. Restraint on disclosure is not "further" performance of anything. There can be no "further" performance of a clause that does not come into operation until termination. We find no inconsistency here with the terms of the contract and no ambiguities. But should ambiguity there be, it will be recalled that it was drafted by the same party who now insists that contained within it is a mutually-agreed abrogation of the protective provisions of the contract.

But we are not left solely to the four corners of the instrument. Mr. Crandall, of the plaintiff, took the stand. (It was he who signed the letter on behalf of the plaintiff.) He testified that before he signed the letter he obtained verbal confirmation from Mr. C. H. McCall, then defendant's vice president, that the termination letter did not extinguish the provision of the Technical Exchange Agreement prohibiting the sale, lease or disclosure of the software systems developments or technology supplied by plaintiff to defendant for the 24 month period following the date of termination of the Technical Exchange Agreement.

An affidavit from Mr. McCall was filed in support of defendant's motion to dismiss for failure to state a cause of action, which we denied. In it he does not assert that Mr. Crandall's version of the conversation is in error. Mr. McCall simply doesn't recall any conversation that could be so interpreted. Mr. McCall was not produced at the hearing.

It is our conclusion, having seen and heard the witnesses, received the instruments, and having heard arguments of counsel, that the disclosures we are about to describe, made by defendant, were in wilful and deliberate violation of the terms of the Technical Exchange Agreement and for the purpose of relieving the dire financial distress in which defendant found itself, all at the expense of the plaintiff. The plaintiff has thus stated a claim upon which relief can be granted under Fed.R.Civ.P. 12(b)(6).

Disclosure by defendant, to its vendee, Tymshare, has already commenced. Early in August, 1971, shortly after the agreement between the defendant and Tymshare, Inc. had been executed, defendant commenced disclosure of soft fare technology to Tymshare and, in fact, some of defendant's employees have been working in the facilities of Tymshare, Inc. to implement the disclosure and transfer of the software to Tymshare, Inc.

The software so disclosed was invented and developed by plaintiff, and is its principal business asset and its principal means of retaining and servicing its existing customers and obtaining new customers. The plaintiff regards, and the Court finds that, its software systems developments as secret, confidential and proprietary in nature. (Other companies in the computer time sharing industry, including Tymshare, Inc., also regard their own software as secret, confidential and proprietary in nature.)

The competitive situation in the time shared computer business has a direct bearing on the remedy sought. The standard contracts which plaintiff has with the users of its time shared computer services are cancellable by the users on 30 days' notice to the plaintiff. Approximately 40% of the plaintiff's gross revenues are derived from ten customers, some of whom are also customers of Tymshare, Inc. Approximately 50% to 55% of plaintiff's revenues are attributable to time sharing services sold to customers in the areas of Chicago, Illinois; Los Angeles, California; San Francisco, California; Washington, D. C.; New York, New York; and Boston, Massachusetts. Tymshare, Inc., is a principal competitor of plaintiff in each of these areas. Defendant is not a competitor of plaintiff in the Chicago, Washington, D. C., and Boston areas, and is not a major competitor of plaintiff in the New York City, Los Angeles and San Francisco areas.

Tymshare, Inc., has revenues of approximately $1,200,000 a month, compared to plaintiff's revenues of approximately $450,000 a month. Tymshare, Inc., has a sales force approximately three times as large as the sales force of plaintiff and a geographic communications coverage that is approximately twice as large as plaintiff's. Tymshare, Inc., presently has 19 XDS 940 computers, as compared to plaintiff's 8 XDS 940 computers. Defendant has 4 XDS 940 computers.

In the event that defendant is permitted to make further disclosure of plaintiff's software to Tymshare, Inc. and in the event that defendant is permitted to transfer title to plaintiff's software to Tymshare, Inc., Tymshare, Inc., in the absence of legal restraint, would have no obstacles to thereafter offering such software to plaintiff's customers.

Both parties assert financial distress. Defendant pleads that should the Court grant the relief requested, it will have to go into bankruptcy. It therefore argues for a money-damage remedy, should plaintiff prevail, though the utility of such a remedy against a financially precariously situated corporation may well be doubtful. Plaintiff, as well, pleads a desperate financial situation, though it does not go to the lengths of asserting impending bankruptcy should relief not be granted. The plaintiff has sustained operating losses every year since its founding in 1966. At the end of its fiscal year ending June 30, 1970, the plaintiff had working capital (i. e., net current assets) of $147,071. At the end of its fiscal year ending June 30, 1971, plaintiff's working capital position was even less favorable. Since June 30, 1970 plaintiff has been unable to obtain bank or venture capital financing, and plaintiff is dependent upon its operating revenues for the survival of its business. The loss of operating revenues would reduce the plaintiff's cash flow and income to the point where plaintiff would not be able to meet its obligations as they become due and would place plaintiff's business in a position of severe financial jeopardy.

It is clear that in the event that plaintiff would lose customers to Tymshare, Inc., as a result of Tymshare, Inc., offering plaintiff's technology to such customers, the loss of revenues and income therefrom in the future could not be accurately ascertained, nor would it be possible to ascertain the loss of revenues and income that might be attributable to plaintiff's inability to obtain new customers in the future.

* * *

As to the relationship between the parties and the materials furnished, under the laws of the State of Texas (governing this contract) the Technical Exchange Agreement established a confidential relationship between plaintiff and defendant. *Hyde Corp. v. Huffines*, 158 Tex. 566, 314 S.W.2d 763 (1958). The systems software developments supplied by plaintiff to defendant were unique property that constituted trade secrets of plaintiff and were supplied to defendant in confidence under the restraints against sale, lease or disclosure set forth in the Technical Exchange Agreement.

The plaintiff has rendered substantial and satisfactory performance of its obligations under the Technical Exchange Agreement.

There has been no anticipatory breach of the Technical Exchange Agreement by plaintiff. Changes may, indeed, have been necessitated by the nature of the operation but did not alter the unique principles, engineering, logic, and coherence developed by plaintiff into its systems software developments.

With respect to the rights upon termination, the letter dated November 30, 1970, providing for the termination of the Technical Exchange Agreement did not, as we have noted, contain terms inconsistent with the provisions of Section XII, paragraph (e), of the Technical Exchange Agreement and did not supersede or negate the provisions of Section XII, paragraph (e).

The letter dated November 30, 1970 between the plaintiff and the defendant which provided that "termination shall be effective as of November 1, 1970, as of which date neither company requires further performance by the other under the said agreement," is interpreted to mean that as of November 1, 1970 neither plaintiff nor defendant required the other to supply technology to the other under the Technical Exchange Agreement.

The provision in Section XII, paragraph (e), of the Technical Exchange Agreement continuing the restraint against lease, sale or disclosure of systems software developments supplied by plaintiff to defendant for a period of 24 months after termination of the Technical Exchange Agreement, was not extinguished or waived by the termination letter dated November 30, 1970; this provision survives the termination of the Technical Exchange Agreement and is interpreted to mean that defendant is restrained from selling, leasing or disclosing plaintiff's systems software developments to any third party prior to November 1, 1972.

Moreover, as we have previously commented, if there is any ambiguity as to whether the termination letter dated November 30, 1970 extinguished the provisions of Section XII, paragraph (e), the termination letter must be construed against the defendant, the party that drafted the letter, and in favor of the plaintiff. In addition, we state once more that the Court will not imply the waiver of the explicit contractual obligation of defendant to refrain from selling, leasing or disclosing the systems software developments supplied to it by plaintiff for a period of 24 months after termination of the Technical Exchange Agreement.

We are advised that, technically, the sale to Tymshare has not yet been fully consummated. With respect to this sale, it is our legal conclusion that defendant's sale, lease or disclosure prior to November 1, 1972, of the systems software developments and technology supplied by plaintiff to defendant under the Technical Exchange Agreement would constitute a breach of Sections XI and XII(e) of the Technical Exchange Agreement. Such sections of the Technical Exchange Agreement do not permit the sale in their entirety, nor the piecemeal sale, of the systems software developments and technology supplied by plaintiff to defendant under the Technical Exchange Agreement.

The sale prior to November 1, 1972 by defendant to Tymshare, Inc., or to any other third party, of the systems software developments and technology supplied by plaintiff to defendant in confidence and subject to the terms of the Technical Exchange Agreement, would constitute a wrongful disposition of such developments and technology and would unjustly enrich defendant at the expense of plaintiff.

The sale and further disclosure by defendant to Tymshare, Inc. of the systems software developments and technology supplied by plaintiff to defendant under the Technical Exchange Agreement, will if not restrained, cause plaintiff to suffer substantial and irreparable injury, loss and damage to plaintiff's business for which plaintiff will have no adequate remedy at law.

If the sale and further disclosure by defendant to Tymshare, Inc. of plaintiff's systems software developments and technology is not restrained, plaintiff would suffer damages which would be impossible to calculate and which could not be adequately compensated by money damages, and plaintiff's entire business would be placed in a position of severe financial jeopardy.

The sale and further disclosure prior to November 1, 1972 by defendant to Tymshare, Inc., of the systems software developments and technology supplied by plaintiff to defendant should be restrained for the reason that plaintiff's systems software developments and technology are unique property and constitute trade secrets of plaintiff and were supplied by plaintiff to defendant in confidence.

That defendant may be in financial difficulty and may not receive the consideration provided under its August 4, 1971 agreement with Tymshare, Inc., if preliminary relief is granted to plaintiff, does not confer upon it a right to breach its contractual obligation under the Technical Exchange Agreement with plaintiff and cannot prevent the issuance of a preliminary injunction in view of the confidential and secret nature of the plaintiff's systems software developments and technology and the threatened irreparable injury and loss to plaintiff.

In balancing the equities, the threatened irreparable injury and loss to plaintiff that would follow upon the sale and further disclosure of plaintiff's systems software developments and technology by defendant to Tymshare, Inc. outweighs any adverse consequences that might result to defendant by reason of the issuance of the preliminary injunction. We are of the opinion, as well, that there is a reasonable and substantial probability that plaintiff will prevail on the merits.

Defendant has argued that the Court is presented with a *fait accompli*, that the transfer of software to Tymshare and incorporations in its system have already started, that the omelet cannot be unscrambled, that equity never decrees a "vain act" and that it would be a "rather apparent [illusory?] victory for them to get an injunction in this case." Plaintiff, on the other hand, argues that the difficulties in enforcement are not insurmountable, that they are, in effect, those encountered in the usual trade secret, proprietary information, case.

We are not persuaded that modern technology has withered the strong right arm of equity. Moreover, difficulties of enforcement often reflect in direct ratio the recalcitrance or lack thereof in the parties affected by the Court's order. We will not anticipate untoward difficulty. At this moment, the first duty of this Court is to issue a preliminary injunction as the only adequate means of preserving the status quo. This injunction shall provide that, to the extent, if any, that defendant is unwilling or unable to extricate changes made by defendant to any software supplied to it by plaintiff, defendant cannot sell, transfer or disclose the whole or any part of that portion of the technology which defendant cannot or will not separate; that the injunction shall restrain and enjoin defendant, its directors, officers, employees, agents, and all other persons acting in concert with them who receive notice thereof, pending the final determination of this action and thereafter until November 1, 1972, from leasing, selling, transferring or further disclosing to Tymshare, Inc., or to any other third party, any of the systems software developments and technology supplied by plaintiff to defendant pursuant to the Technical Exchange Agreement.

## NOTES AND QUESTIONS:

1. In the face of evolving areas of technology, a skillful combination of trade secret, contract, patent, and copyright law has been essential in the development of intellectual property law protections for computer software. The illustrative cases above clearly demonstrate that trade secret protection has been and is a critical aspect in this developing area of the law.

2. The issues before the courts in *Cybertek* and *Com-Share* involved disputes over two very different agreements that included non-disclosure provisions. The *Cybertek* case dealt with an employment agreement, while *Com-Share* was concerned with a technology exchange agreement. Such contracts are often instrumental in protecting computer software as an important trade secret of the owner.

3. The court in *Cybertek* observed, "[w]hile there may have been a question in the past as to whether or not computer software is susceptible of protection under trade secret doctrine, it is clear that such protection is available today in practically all jurisdictions." 203 U.S.P.Q. at 1022. Why was computer software not immediately accepted as being protectable as a trade secret? How does computer software fit within the definitions of a trade secret in RESTATEMENT (SECOND) OF TORTS § 757 and the UTSA? Is the definition in the RESTATEMENT (THIRD) OF UNFAIR COMPETITION more friendly to computer software than the earlier definition in RESTATEMENT (SECOND) OF TORTS § 757?

4. Attempts to attack contracts with non-disclosure provisions as being anti-competitive have rarely been successful. In *Com-Share*, for example, the court rejected an argument that the non-disclosure obligation in a consulting agreement did not survive termination of the agreement. In an employment agreement, the

*Cybertek* court found that a non-disclosure provision did not violate a California law prohibiting covenants not to compete.

5. Patent protection for software has not been available until relatively recently. Initially, courts and the United States Patent and Trademark Office (PTO) insisted that computer software was non-patentable subject matter. *See Parker v. Flook*, 437 U.S. 584, 592-96 (1978). Justice Stevens wrote that once an algorithm "is assumed to be within the prior art, the application, considered as a whole, contains no patentable invention." *Id.* at 594. A few years later, the United States Supreme Court took a remarkably different view when it decided *Diamond v. Dier*, 450 U.S. 175 (1981). In a majority opinion by Chief Justice Rehnquist, the court granted limited protection for a computer program that used a computer-operated algorithm for determining when the rubber in a tire mold was cured by taking a number of temperature readings inside the tire mold. After many years of not having any clear guidance on the outer boundaries for the computer software patents, the Supreme Court recently decided that the test for determining whether a business method that involved the use of an algorithm is patentable when the claimed subject matter "is tied to a particular machine," or by showing that his claim "transforms an article." *Bilski v. Kappos*, 130 S.Ct. 3218, 3232 (2010). What is wrong with broad patent protection for computer software? The corollary question is: How far should the protection of computer software that is essentially a mathematical algorithm extend? Why would software owners not want to file for a patent instead of trying to protect software as a trade secret?

6. Copyright protection is also available for computer software codes. How does this type of protection differ from that provided by a patent? How is it complementary? Although a copy of the work must be deposited with the Copyright Office when a copyright is registered, these specimens are available for public inspection. 17 U.S.C. § 705(b). When the copyrighted work is a computer program, parts of the specimen that contain trade secrets can be deleted. 37 C.F.R. § 202.20(c)(2)(vii)(A)(2). This can be implemented by depositing the first and last 25 pages of the source code, which must be "reproduced in a form visually perceptible without the aid of a machine or device." Circular 61, U.S. Copyright Office. One way of satisfying this requirement is to mask the portion of the code on the pages that are submitted, as shown below.

```
Pr  am W  _Track
  st
 MaxW  s = 20

{$I  PE.INC
{   VARIPL  NC}
    HELP  C}
$I  IN    NC}
{$I N     NC}
{$I       INC}
{$    I.INC
    PROD_I   C}
    FORM    C}
$I DEF   S.INC
{$I    .INC}
{$I    LCOMP
{$    OMPANY
    PRINT   }
 I PLOT
{$I TI   NC}
{$I    ENU.

BEGIN
  A   (CLF_F    CLF_Fil   ');
        Res   F_File    $I+}
   IORESU     0 then   rite(C     le);
  lose(Cl    e);
  Clrscr   tle;
  Dela    0);
  Te    e(C80);    tCol     low);    ackgr    Blue)
  S  inter;
     at
    Reset(C   le);
    FS :=   Size(C   le);
    Clo   LF_Fi
    do   = fals
      MainM   lect c
       '1'  :    FS >0    unDat     Else     ords;
       '2'     FS >0     RunP    tMenu     NoRe
       '3'    If FS     en Ru    enu E   Reco
       '     RunC     Lease     enanc
             :  Ru    enu;
             :  D    = TRU
     ; {Cas
   RSCR;
   til do
  Writel     ,#27#
END.
```

### (c) Other Business Information

## ASHLAND OIL, INC. v. F.T.C.
409 F. Supp. 297 (D.D.C. 1976)

On or about April 15, 1975, the FTC served upon the plaintiff a 'Natural Gas Survey Special Report' order ('Special Report') issued pursuant to Section 6(b) of the FTC Act (15 U.S.C. § 46(b)). By this order, Ashland was required to file a 'Special Report' and was advised that non-compliance would result in the imposition of penalties under applicable provisions of federal law. On August 27, 1975, Ashland responded by filing with the Commission a completed Special Report containing the information sought by the FTC. Included in the information submitted was highly sensitive competitive data detailing the company's reserve estimates for all of its natural gas leases and contracts nationwide.[2] Ashland's submission was accompanied by a letter from J. Creig Coogan, Vice President of Ashland Exploration Company (a division of Ashland Oil, Inc.) stating that the company's information on gas reserves was confidential and of a proprietary nature, such that disclosure would result in competitive injury and that such information was submitted to the Commission with the specific reservation that plaintiff could claim its right to have the materials therein provided 'accorded confidential treatment and be protected from disclosure.' (Plaintiff's Complaint, Exhibit AA).

On October 6, 1975, Congressman John E. Moss, in his capacity as a member of Congress, requested the FTC to make available to him data gathered by the Commission pertaining to lease extensions on federal lands. (Id., Exhibit A). By letter dated October 24, 1975, Charles A. Tobin, Secretary of the Commission, denied the Congressman's request for the reason that the data sought constituted 'trade secrets and commercial or financial information (and) geological and geophysical information and data, including maps, concerning wells' which were exempt from mandatory disclosure under the Freedom of Information Act (5 U.S.C. § 552(b)(4) and (b)(9)). Consequently, Secretary Tobin concluded that the Commission was without discretion to release such exempt records. (Id., Exhibit B).

On October 29, 1975, Congressman Moss sent a second request to the FTC, but this time in his official capacity as Chairman of the Subcommittee on Oversight and Investigations of the House Committee on Interstate and Foreign Commerce. (Id., Exhibit C). Congressman Moss's letter noted that the Freedom of Information Act was not authority to withhold information from Congress, and that this second request was made not in the Congressman's individual capacity, but 'as Chairman of the Subcommittee on Oversight and Investigations' for the purpose of fulfilling the Subcommittee's general oversight responsibilities.

---

[2] [2] The information contained in Ashland's Special Report included the locations and identities of plaintiff's natural gas leases, together with information revealing the percent ownership of various individuals in such leases and Ashland's internal estimates as to gas reserves in those leases. (See Affidavit of George C. Hardin, Jr., Plaintiff's Memorandum in Support of Motion for Preliminary Injunction).

The FTC treated Congressman Moss's second letter as a formal Congressional request and, by letter of November 18, 1975, advised the Congressman that the natural gas reserve data which he requested would be furnished on November 28, 1975. In this reply, Chairman Engman cautioned that several of the companies involved considered the data 'competitively very sensitive and might constitute trade secrets which the Commission is prohibited from making public under Section 6(f) of the Federal Trade Commission Act,' and that the U.S. Geological Survey also was 'of the opinion that this is confidential, proprietary information.' He went on to mention that the Commission continued to be involved in litigation with companies refusing to provide such data under the Special Report order. Therefore, Chairman Engman emphasized that:

> As a result, your Subcommittee will receive data only from those companies which have voluntarily complied with the Commission's orders. This fact is not lost upon companies faced with information requests from the Commission and will do little to encourage voluntary compliance, especially if any sensitive information is made public.
>
> Therefore, the Commission respectfully but strongly urges your Subcommittee to maintain the confidentiality of the information submitted in response to your request and in particular, the reserve estimates furnished in response to Question 5 of the Natural Gas Energy Study Order. (Id., Exhibit D).

Ashland was advised of the Commission's decision on November 18, 1975. On November 21, 1975, plaintiff received written notice of the Commission's intention to disclose its reserve data to Congressman Moss's Subcommittee. (Id., Exhibit E). On the same day, Ashland was informed by telephone that the Commission intended to turn over the data to Congressman Moss on demand and would not be bound to the November 28th date mentioned in Chairman Engman's letter.

This action was filed on November 24, 1975, and on that date, plaintiff moved for and was granted a temporary restraining order enjoining the Federal Trade Commission from releasing the information in issue, thereby preserving the status quo until the Court considered the merits of Ashland's claims.

On December 2, 1975, the Subcommittee authorized and the Chairman of the Interstate and Foreign Commerce Committee signed a subpoena duces tecum requiring FTC Chairman Engman to appear before the Subcommittee on December 3, 1975, and to bring with him any and all records within the Federal Trade Commission's control or custody or within the Federal Trade Commission's means to produce appertaining to or involving oil and/or gas lease extensions on Federal lands, including Ashland Oil, Inc. and including all correspondence (See H.R.Rep.No.94-756, 94th Cong., Trade Commission and Ashland Oil, Inc. relating in any manner to agreements or proposed agreements to hold such records confidential or to give advance notice of the release thereof. (See H.R.Rep.No.940-756, 94th Cong., 1st Sess., at 3–4 (1975)).

By letter of December 3, 1975, Chairman Moss informed Mr. Engman that the Subcommittee planned 'no enforcement action of this subpoena until after the Court has considered' the questions arising in this case. (Id., at 5).

On December 18, 1975, the House of Representatives assented to House

Resolution No. 899. (121 Cong.Rec. 12, 918–919 (daily ed. December 18, 1975)). Section 1 of the Resolution provides:

Resolved, That the chairman of the Subcommittee on Oversight and Investigations of the Committee on Interstate and Foreign Commerce is authorized to intervene and appear in the pending action entitled 'Ashland Oil Incorporated, plaintiff against Federal Trade Commission, et al., defendant,' Civil Action 75-1956, United States District Court for the District of Columbia on behalf of the Committee on Interstate and Foreign Commerce in order to secure information relating to natural gas reserves now in the possession of the Federal Trade Commission for the use of the committee and the House. (Emphasis supplied.)

On January 16, 1976, after a hearing held in open court, we granted Congressman Moss's motion to intervene pursuant to Fed.R.Civ.P. 24(a).

Plaintiff has moved for preliminary and permanent injunction. Defendants Moss and FTC have filed motions for summary judgment or, alternatively, to dismiss. The Court, sua sponte, advanced and consolidated the hearing on the merits of Ashland's complaint with that on its motion for preliminary injunction. See Fed.R.Civ.P. 65(a)(2).

C. Section 6(f) of the Federal Trade Commission Act

The principal arguments on the merits of this case focus on Section 6(f) of the FTC Act, 15 U.S.C. § 46(f), which empowers the Commission:

To make public from time to time such portions of the information obtained by it hereunder, except trade secrets and names of customers, as it shall deem expedient in the public interest; and to make annual and special reports to the Congress and to submit therewith the recommendations for additional legislation; and to provide for the publication of its reports and decisions in such form and manner as may be best adapted for public information and use.

Ashland maintains that the language employed is unequivocal in prohibiting disclosure of trade secrets by the FTC to any third party, including the Congress; that this construction is buttressed by the legislative history of the Act, by the wording and judicial interpretation of similar statutory provisions, and finally by the 'historical position' of the Attorney's General's Office from 1909 to the present that such language ordinarily indicates an absolute prohibition against executive disclosures of proprietary data to the legislative branch, absent adequate assurances that confidentiality will be maintained.

In addition to specifically invoking confidentiality protection in submission of its reserve estimates to the FTC, Ashland states that it relied upon the belief that the Commission would abide by the mandate of Section 6(f), as well as the FTC's own rules, and refrain from divulging the materials in issue to Congress. Even if the FTC's disclosure to Congress is held pursuant to a lawful subpoena, plaintiff believes that the ultimate result will be a serious infringement of its common law and statutory rights, and a violation of its constitutional guarantees of equal protection, due process and freedom to petition the government.

Congressman Moss and the FTC respond that Section 6(f) clearly does not restrict Congressional access to trade secrets or other types of information collected by the FTC, since such a limitation upon the inherent investigatory power of Congress may not be imposed by implication. The pertinent language of the Section — 'to make public' — does not explicitly refer to Congress, and, thus, according to defendants' argument, cannot be read as an inhibition of Congress' statutory right to 'annual and special reports' or its Article I subpoena power. Also relying on legislative history, defendants Moss and FTC conclude that the Commission was intended to be no more than an extension of the Congressional 'visitorial power,' at least in its information gathering function, and, therefore, a convenient storehouse of information readily accessible to the Congress.

In addition, defendants contend that the Subcommittee's subpoena and the underlying investigation of the natural gas industry are legitimate exercises of the powers conferred upon the Congress under Article I; and that once such constitutional powers have been legitimately invoked by a coordinate branch, the courts are bound to accord great deference and refrain from unwarranted interferences with on-going Congressional investigations. Defendants attempt to dispose of Ashland's remaining arguments in short order, contending that once a legitimate legislative purpose has been established, 'Ashland's constitutional, statutory, and equitable arguments must fall before the legitimate assertion of the constitutional power of the Congress.' (Intervenor's Memorandum in Support of Motion to Dismiss, p. 14).

## II. ASHLAND'S NATURAL GAS RESERVE ESTIMATES

Since plaintiff endeavors to invoke common law and statutory protection for its reserve estimates, the Court must make a threshold determination whether such materials fall within the 'widely relied-upon definition of a trade secret found at 4 Restatement of Torts § 757, comment b (1939), viz.:

A trade secret may consist of any formula, pattern, device or compilation of information which is used in one's business, and which give him an opportunity to obtain an advantage over competitors, who do not know or use it . . . . 4 Restatement of Torts § 757, p. 5 (1939).

According to the Restatement, a more precise definition of what constitutes a trade secret is not possible. However, Comment b does enumerate a number of factors which may assist a court in determining whether particular data rises to the level of a trade secret:

(1) the extent to which the information is known outside of his business; (2) the extent to which it is known by employees and others involved in his business; (3) the extent of measures taken by him to guard the secrecy of the information; (4) the value of the information to him and to his competitors; (5) the amount of effort or money expended by him in developing the information; (6) the ease or difficulty with which the information could be properly acquired or duplicated by others. 4 Restatement of Torts § 757, Comment b, p. 6 (1939).

On the record before the Court, it is evident that Ashland's natural gas reserve estimates satisfy each of these criteria. The data in issue has been compiled at the considerable expense of 'hundreds of thousands of man-hours and millions of dollars' and enables plaintiff to successfully bid on federal natural gas leases, in competition with 'dozens of other companies.' Consequently, such information is 'highly valued and closely guarded,' not only by Ashland, but throughout the natural gas industry. (See Affidavit of George C. Hardin, Jr., Plaintiff's Memorandum in Support of Motion for Preliminary Injunction).

Moreover, the agency with particular expertise in the regulation of natural gas, the Federal Power Commission ('FPC'), has explicitly recognized natural gas reserve estimates to be valuable, proprietary assets. For example, in Amerada Hess Corporation, 50 F.P.C. 1049, 1050 (1973), the agency observed:

To begin with, it must be recognized that a natural gas company's reserve data, much like a patent or trade secret, constitutes a valuable and closely guarded asset. Making this asset available to competitors, without due compensation, would most certainly be inimical to competition, especially in highly competitive areas, as the comments of Ashland Oil, Inc. illustrate:

. . . Ashland Oil, Inc. has obtained leases in Federal off-shore areas by payments to the United States Government of large bonuses. Unleased acreage adjoins and offsets certain of these leases. If significant reserves are discovered and if the reserves extend into unleased areas, Ashland would not disclose the results of such exploration until an opportunity is available to bid in a drainage sale of the offsetting acreage. The information developed on such leases is highly confidential and proprietary in nature and disclosure of such information prior to the drainage sale would destroy Ashland's competitive advantage in bidding at such sale by making available to other companies the results of Ashland's exploration efforts made at great expense of it.

Similarly determining such reserve data to constitute 'valuable property' in *Reliability of Electric and Gas Service*, 49 F.P.C. 1428, 1429 (1973), the FPC discussed the underpinnings of its holding as follows:

The policy reasons underlying our assurance of confidentiality are obvious. In a period when the gas supply shortage is most acute, disclosure of detailed reserve data would undoubtedly inhibit future exploration for new gas reserves since speculators and competitors could equally benefit from the geological and geophysical expenditures of other companies. A competitor would particularly benefit from knowledge of another producer's uncommitted reserves for particular locations, especially in highly competitive areas. In addition, it would be extremely unfair to sellers of gas to disclose such data to potential buyers with whom they negotiate for the sale of gas. Furthermore, we believe that certain reserve data constitutes a valuable property right which should not be taken without due process and just compensation. (Emphasis added).

The federal courts have also acknowledged that detailed competitive information of the type here in issue constitutes trade secrets entitled to protection from public disclosure.

In *Abbott v. United States*, 239 F.2d 310, 314 (5th Cir. 1956), the Court found the geophysical surveys underlying a company's reserve estimates to be of 'almost inestimable practical value in the essential program of continuous exploration and development of mineral resources which is the life blood of an oil producing company.' Moreover, once disclosed, such data possesses 'a 'negative' value' in the hands of a competitor who can use it to 'undertake development, procure leases, and impede or thwart the company's plans.' [Citations omitted.] And in *Continental Oil Co. v. FPC*, 519 F.2d 31, 32, 35 (5th Cir. 1975), the Fifth Circuit voided an FPC order permitting public access to materials submitted by interstate natural gas companies which contained 'detailed intrastate sales information, including the names of purchasers, date and location of the sale, pressure base, annual sales volume and price terms,' and data with reference to 'extent of supply.' The Court held that such information fell squarely within the Freedom of Information Act's 'trade secret' exemption from public disclosure, reasoning that disclosure 'would alter industry custom and existing relationships to the disadvantage of petitioner's competitive positions.'519 F.2d at 35.

After careful evaluation of the Hardin Affidavit, supra, with due deference to the findings of the National Geological Survey, and in consideration of the cases discussed supra, the Court is of the opinion that at least that portion of the data in issue detailing Ashland's natural gas reserve estimates constitutes 'trade secret' information within the purview of Section 6(f) of the FTC Act.

## III. THE SUBCOMMITTEE SUBPOENA

[Editor's note: The court found that the subcommittee subpoena was properly issued as being directly related to and in furtherance of "a legitimate task of Congress."]

Injunctive relief is appropriate only 'to prevent existing or presently threatened injuries' and 'will not be granted against something merely feared as liable to occur at some indefinite time in the future.' *Connecticut v. Massachusetts*, 282 U.S. 660, 674, 51 S.Ct. 286, 291, 75 L.Ed. 602 (1930). *See also, General Fireproofing Company v. Wyman, 444 F.2d 391, 393 (2d Cir. 1971)*. Injunctions will not be granted where the injuries complained of are prospective and 'which may, indeed, never occur.' *Crimmins v. American Stock Exchange, Inc.*, 346 F.Supp. 1256, 1262 (S.D.N.Y.1972). The injury complained of must be of such imminence that there is a 'clear and present' need for equitable relief to prevent irreparable harm. *Hershey Creamery Co. v. Hershey Chocolate Corp.*, 269 F.Supp. 45 (S.D.N.Y.1967); *see also Assn. of Professional Engineering Personnel v. Radio Corp. of America, 183 F.Supp. 834 (D.C.N.J.1960)*. And the required showing of irreparable injury is not eliminated simply by virtue of a claim alleging violation of statutory or constitutional rights (unless the requirement has been specifically eliminated by statute). Thus, in *United Fuel Gas Co. v. Railroad Commission*, 278 U.S. 300, 49 S.Ct. 150, 73 L.Ed. 390 (1928), the Supreme Court noted:

> Suitors may not resort to a court of equity to restrain a threatened act merely because it is illegal or transcends constitutional powers. They must show that the act complained of will inflict upon them some irreparable injury. 278 U.S., at 310, 49 S.Ct., at 152 (Stone, J.). [Citations omitted.]

While Ashland couches its concerns in terms of 'public disclosure,' any irreparable injury to it would result, more precisely, in disclosure to its competitors. Certainly, such injury might logically result as well from general dissemination. But the transfer of such data from the FTC to the Subcommittee and the Subcommittee's review of that information, does not lead inexorably to either public dissemination or disclosure to Ashland's competitors. Moreover, the courts must presume that the committees of Congress will exercise their powers responsibly and with due regard for the rights of affected parties. [Citations omitted.]

Ashland argues that this presumption is rebutted by 'Congressman Moss's own past practices' and the Subcommittee's handling of trade secrets in the past which, according to plaintiff, 'has shown either a total incapacity to protect such trade secrets or a callous indifference to the proprietary nature of those secrets.' (Plaintiff's Reply Memorandum, p. 59). In addition, Ashland suggests that the Court take judicial notice of the fact that throughout the pendency of this action, 'there has been no promise or commitment that Ashland's trade secret data would be given confidential treatment.' Id., at 58. While the Court can appreciate Ashland's concern under these circumstances, it does not appear to the Court that isolated instances of breached confidentiality in the past are sufficient to overcome the continuing presumption of Congressional propriety.

Through its staff counsel, the Subcommittee has indicated that there is 'no indication' that the Subcommittee 'would release information originating from Ashland.' (Affidavit of Michael R. Lemov, Intervenor's Motion to Dismiss). And Chairman Moss, through counsel, has represented:

Of course, the Subcommittee does not seek publication of Ashland's trade secrets; it seeks merely production of documents in compliance with a Congressional subpoena. (Response of Chairman Moss to Ashland's Opposition to Motion to Dismiss, p. 6).

Weighing all of these considerations, it appears to the Court, on balance, that the irreparable injury which Ashland seeks this Court to prevent by the issuance of permanent injunctive relief is neither 'presently threatened' nor 'imminent.' The injuries complained of are, rather, 'prospective' in nature and 'may, indeed, never occur.' *See Crimmins v. American Stock Exchange, supra.*

V. CONCLUSION

If irreparable injury cannot be established, and we hold that it has not been established in this case, injunctive relief is not warranted. It follows that the Court need not consider the other factors outlined in Virginia Petroleum Jobbers Association, supra, nor need we reach the merits of Ashland's complaint, nor dispose of the arguments and counter arguments propounded by the parties in support of their respective positions.

## CONTINENTAL DATA SYSTEMS, INC. v. EXXON CORP.

638 F. Supp. 432 (E.D. Pa. 1986)

* * *

In the instant case, defendant argues that the sales materials acquired from Continental are forms and data which are "standard, common place and well-known to personal injury attorneys." Memorandum for Summary Judgment at 21. Plaintiff's own employees admit that to be true. The information used to select or create the programs' output was obtained from interviews with lawyers who allowed plaintiff to copy their files, and from copying forms from books. (Deposition of Rosenfeld at 43–45). "Plaintiff cannot usurp standard data or forms from another industry and claim it as plaintiff's secret." Memorandum for Summary Judgment at 21. In general, Exxon relies on that portion of the Restatement which states that "[m]atters of public knowledge or of general knowledge in an industry cannot be appropriated by one as his secret. Matters which are completely disclosed by the goods which one markets cannot be his secret."

The fact that individual forms and samples found in the sales materials were compilations of public information does not preclude a finding that the combination of the included elements affords a plaintiff competitive advantage and is not itself in the public domain. *See, Rohm and Haas Co. v. Adco Chemical Co.*, 689 F.2d 424, 433 (3d Cir.1982); *Anaconda, supra*, 485 F.Supp. at 422. The combination of information contained in the sales materials reflected market research performed by plaintiff and decisions to include and exclude elements from a larger pool of data. It is this, rather than the data contained in the individual forms known generally among personal injury lawyers, which may contain a sufficient degree of novelty, however slight, to be excluded from general knowledge, and may qualify the sales manual as a trade secret. *See, Croydon Plastics, supra*, 348 F.Supp. at 812 (slight advance over general knowledge may qualify for trade secret protection).

In addition, Continental took significant precautions to limit the distribution and use of information contained in its sales manuals and the information disclosed to purchasers of its software. Company rules required sales people to obtain approval from Continental's Vice President and assurances of confidential treatment from prospective purchasers before portions of the sale manual were lent to the prospective purchaser. As part of the transaction, the buyer agreed to prevent unauthorized use or dissemination of the software and its manuals. Based on the evidence before me, I am unable to say that the market research information reflected in the selection of output for Continental's software was so freely disseminated that it may not be accorded trade secret status.

The only remaining issue is whether Exxon used the information contained in the sales manual to the detriment of Continental. During the twelve month period following Exxon's introduction of its personal injury application to its records processing software, Continental experienced a significant decline in sales. Exxon used the information acquired from Continental to prepare its personal injury application, but only one customer agreed to purchase from Exxon its personal injury application; it was never delivered.

Continental argues that sales by Exxon of its personal injury application were not necessary to harm Continental. Rather, merely marketing Exxon's personal injury software application, which included information misappropriated from Continental, "increased [Exxon's] credibility with customers in the legal marketplace and decreased Continental's credibility as the sole supplier of the product." Plaintiff's Second Supplemental Memorandum at 14–15. While I foresee substantial difficulties in proving the contention, I believe that plaintiff is entitled to present its evidence on causation.

For the foregoing reasons, I will deny Exxon's motion for summary judgment as to the state law claims presented in this case.

## NOTES AND QUESTIONS:

1. The *Ashland* court had little trouble finding that the compilation of natural gas reserve estimates qualified as a trade secret under RESTATEMENT (SECOND) OF TORTS § 757, particularly since it was "compiled at the considerable expense of 'hundreds of thousands of man-hours and millions of dollars' and enables plaintiff to successfully bid on federal natural gas leases, in competition with 'dozens of other companies.' " *Ashland Oil*, 409 F. Supp at 303.

2. In *Continental Data Systems* there was a different twist, in that all of the forms of the data were in the public domain. The court nevertheless held that the compilation qualified as a trade secret because it "contain[ed] a sufficient degree of novelty, however slight" and "afford[ed] a plaintiff [a] competitive advantage," and *Continental* "took significant precautions to limit the distribution and use of [the] information." *Continental Data Systems*, 638 F. Supp. at 443. How important are factors discussed in *Continental*, in the final analysis, when information involving only "slight" novelty is involved?

### (2) Novelty

## KEWANEE OIL CO. v. BICRON CORP.

416 U.S. 470 (1974)

* * *

Novelty, in the patent law sense, is not required for a trade secret, *W. R. Grace & Co. v. Hargadine*, 392 F.2d, at 14. 'Quite clearly discovery is something less than invention.' *A. O. Smith Corp. v. Petroleum Iron Works Co.*, 73 F.2d 531, 538 (CA6 1934), modified to increase scope of injunction, 74 F.2d 934 (1935). However, some novelty will be required if merely because that which does not possess novelty is usually known; secrecy, in the context of trade secrets, thus implies at least minimal novelty.

* * *

## MOTOROLA, INC. v. FAIRCHILD CAMERA & INSTRUMENT CORP.

177 U.S.P.Q. 614 (D. Ariz. 1973)

This case proceeded to trial on plaintiff's fifty-five page (plus attachments) Amended Complaint filed May 29, 1969. The original complaint was filed August 27, 1968. In the caption the Amended Complaint was entitled: "Complaint for: Unfair Competition; Interference with Advantageous Personnel Relationships; Antitrust Violation; Unjust Enrichment; Constructive Trust upon Benefits Wrongfully Obtained; Damages — Punitive and Compensatory; Breach of Fiduciary Duty by Officer and Director."

During the eight weeks consumed by plaintiff in presenting its case-in-chief some

75 witnesses were called either in person or by deposition, and approximately 560 exhibits were introduced into evidence by plaintiff. Prior to commencement of trial, by stipulation, defendants marked directly into evidence over 850 exhibits, many of which were used in cross-examination of plaintiff's witnesses and in the examination of defendants themselves when called by plaintiff for cross-examination. At the conclusion of plaintiff's case all defendants moved to dismiss pursuant to Rule 41(b), Federal Rules of Civil Procedure, on the grounds that "upon the facts and the law plaintiff has shown no right to relief." The test, simply stated, is that if, from the record as it stands at the end of plaintiff's case, the Court is convinced that the evidence preponderates against plaintiff, the Court is empowered to grant the motion. *Ellis v. Carter*, 328 F.2d 573 (9th Cir. 1964). This Court is so convinced.

The basic dispute arises from the fact that in early August of 1968 eight executives of Motorola's Semiconductor Division at Phoenix, Arizona, resigned to accept employment with one of Motorola's important competitors, Fairchild Camera and Instrument Corporation, at Mountain View, California. While some of these individuals were employed in a similar capacity at Fairchild Camera's Semiconductor Division, others were employed in different and more responsible positions and some with corporation-wide responsibilities. Not all of them have remained with Fairchild Camera.

* * *

Plaintiff alleges a general conspiracy among the defendants to injure plaintiff and profit defendants through misappropriation of plaintiff's trade secrets.

* * *

It was clearly established that Fairchild Camera regularly (both before and after August 1968) purchased and studied all domestic and foreign patents as well as relevant trade literature and competitors' sales and promotional literature and products. The same purchase, study and analysis of competitors' newly marketed products is also a regular and customary practice by all engaged in this highly competitive industry. Because of the rapidly changing technology in this explosive industry it is apparent that such a practice is necessary for survival. Also, with regard to patent disclosure, neither the law nor the above-mentioned nondisclosure agreement limits the "patents" to domestic ones only.

Defendants contend that all of plaintiff's claimed trade secrets in issue at trial were either fully disclosed by patents, domestic or foreign, issued prior to August 1968; or were generally known in the trade and not secrets in fact; or were disclosed in publications prior to August 1968; or are not in fact used by Fairchild Camera; and further that there is no evidence in any event that any particular Motorola employee-defendant disclosed any or all of them.

* * *

Originally there were 140 different alleged trade secret items (covering virtually every step in the semiconductor manufacturing process) in issue in the litigation, as set forth in plaintiff's answer to defendants' interrogatories filed September 6, 1968. Of these original 140 alleged trade secret items, *134* were voluntarily dropped from the case prior to trial, leaving only six: Nos. 6, 23, 24, 71, 95 and 97. On June 26,

1970, Motorola added three new items, Nos. S-1, S-2 and S-3. On February 8, 1971, Motorola added the final and tenth alleged trade secret item introduced at trial, No. § 4.

As categorized by plaintiff, the remaining ten alleged trade secrets relate to the manufacture of two discrete devices — the plastic encapsulated TO-92 (Items 6, 23, 24, 71 and S-4) and the aluminum packaged TO-3 (Items S-1, S-2, S-3, 95 and 97).

While the Motorola employee-defendants had executed the above-mentioned nondisclosure agreement, they were not advised upon execution, either generally or specifically, what, if any, production processes, know-how, or other things plaintiff considered proprietary. At no time during their employment were they so advised. Upon their termination attention of each was called to the existence of the trade-secret agreement. Even in view of the knowledge by plaintiff that they were accepting employment with a competitor, however, they were not advised either generally or specifically what plaintiff considered to be covered by the restrictive nondisclosure agreement. Indeed, the conclusion is inevitable that Motorola did not know what it so considered. The evidence established that there was no list or index of any kind in existence in Motorola's records, or in the records, of their learned patent counsel who was privy to all their patent and alleged trade-secret information, as to what plaintiff considered to be a proprietary trade secret. The evidence also established that in other similar companies in the same industry such restrictive agreements were implemented by furnishing the employee a list of employer-claimed secrets at the time of employment; during employment as additions or deletions were made; and at termination by requiring a signed document acknowledging specifically identified and claimed trade secrets.

In *E. W. Bliss Co. v. Struthers-Dunn, Inc.*, 408 F.2d 1108, 161 USPQ 263 (8th Cir. 1969), a case on facts similar to those here, the Court of Appeals, in setting aside an injunction issued by the lower court which specified general areas or fields of production and product lines in which the employee-defendants could not be employed by the defendant employer, stated, id. at 1114, 161 USPQ at 267:

"The lower court appears inclined to let the defendants reach the legal conclusion that a particular design concept is a 'trade secret' of Eagle. These defendants would then be able to test their legal opinion on the law of trade secrets and their technical opinion on the state of the prior art in a proceeding to show cause why they should not be held in contempt. We feel that the vagueness of this section, even when read in the context of the entire injunction [specifying various 'fields of solid state engineering'], places an unduly harsh burden on the defendants, especially on Struthers [the new employer] which is presumed to know all the confidential technical information of Eagle, . . . ."

The same principle of undue burden and overbreadth would seem to apply to the contract here so as to make it unenforceable without specific advice at some time to employees as to specific trade secrets claimed or some evidence (of which there was none here) from which the Court could find that the employee should know a secret of which his employer did not specifically advise him.

No contract existed between plaintiff and its former employee-defendants restricting or limiting their employment in the same industry following termination.

Particularly appropriate in this case is the principle that the protection allowed trade secrets "is not a sword to be used by employers to retain employees by the threat of rendering them substantially unemployable in the field of their experience should they desire to resign. This shield is not a substitute for an agreement by the employee not to compete with his employer after the termination of employment." *E. W. Bliss Co. v. Struthers-Dunn, Inc., supra*, at 1112-1113, 161 USPQ at 265-267.

It is further the conclusion of the Court that plaintiff's trade secret claims must fail because as to those in issue at trial no real effort was made by plaintiff prior to trial to keep them secret. They were also either revealed in the marketed product; fully disclosed by issued patents; generally known to those skilled in the industry or trade; or consisted of information easily acquired by persons in the industry from patents, literature or known processes freely available as of August, 1968, and in any event prior to any shown use by Fairchild Camera.

From 1965 on and even after 1968 plaintiff's employees regularly conducted tours of the entire TO-92 production line involving that group of claimed trade secrets. Among persons toured were customers (some of whom were also competitors in this same product), employees of competitors in this same product), employees of competitors being considered for employment or attempting to be recruited by plaintiff, and on at least one tour Mr. Fred Kuliche of Kuliche & Soffa (builders of commercial manufacturing equipment of the TO-92 line type claimed as a trade secret) which ultimately built the Fairchild Camera production equipment complained of.

There were no signs in the area warning of trade secrets, no warnings given to those taking the tours, and no statements regarding nondisclosure required to be signed or acknowledged. Persons taking the tour could observe, time, and inquire of operators as to the speed of machine operations and receive honest answers; could operate one of the "secret" machines and observe its "secret process in a separate microscope placed there for this purpose. The line tour disclosed the sequence of manufacturing steps and for a careful observer, knowledgeable in the industry, little would be left unknown following such a tour of the TO-92 group of claimed trade secrets. As testified on cross examination by Dr. Petritz, plaintiff's trade secret expert:

"Q. Isn't it true that if a line is important enough that you want to keep it secret you don't even tour people through the area?

"A. Yes."

Plaintiff also entertained a reporting team from Electronic Procurement Magazine, permitted them to tour and photograph the TO-92 line, resulting in a picture article entitled "Photo Tour of Motorola Plastic Transistor Plant" in its August, 1965, issue, describing the general nature of its TO-92 line with photos of some of the items claimed to be secret.

Plaintiff also produced two movies: one prior to filing the lawsuit, and one after, which were generally shown in the trade and revealed to the skilled observer substantially all of alleged trade secret 71 of the TO-92 group.

Aside from the fact that plaintiff did not know at the time of filing this action what trade secrets it possessed and failed to take any reasonable steps to protect their secrecy, the TO-92 group of claimed secrets were disclosed as to the various individual steps in Motorola's own patents issued prior to August, 1968. The fact that Motorola had established a high-speed, straight-line production program for the TO 92 — and therefore it could be done — was well known in the industry long before August, 1968. The succession and order of manufacturing and testing steps from crystal pulling to packaging was dictated by the nature of the product and necessarily followed by everyone in the industry.

The Ferranti Company in Europe had in operation a high-speed, almost completely automated straight-line production program in 1967 almost identical in every respect to plaintiff's and which was described in detail in their sales literature distributed to the trade in 1967. Most devastating to plaintiff's case, however, was the testimony of their own trade secrets expert, Dr. Petritz, on cross examination (there was no re-direct examination of this witness) that every step of claimed trade secret 71 (of the TO-92 group) was fully disclosed or necessarily implied in the Helda-Lincoln and Lehner patents; that as to claimed trade secret No. 6 of that group the procedure was described in the Da Costa patent, the significance of the process for high-speed production was disclosed in the Lehner patent, and Fairchild Camera uses a different technique than Motorola anyway; that claimed trade secret 23 of that group is disclosed in the Lehner patent (the Ferranti literature and Motorola tours as well as the above-mentioned movies disclose the same matters and procedure).

As to claimed trade secret S-4 of the TO-92 group, it was generally known in the industry prior to August, 1968, and Fairchild does not follow the Motorola steps anyway. There may be some significance here to the fact that this was not even claimed by Motorola to be a trade secret until more than two years after the suit was filed in spite of its blanket claim of 140 items made shortly after this action was filed.

With regard to the TO-3 group of claimed trade secrets: Item 96 was fully disclosed in the Robinson and Boczar-Davis patents. Item 97 is one of the "cook-book" of cleansers, is no longer used by plaintiff and simply does not rise to the level of a "trade secret." Item S-1 when marketed disclosed the materials used (everyone in the industry regularly examines competitors' marketed products for just such purposes) and together with the disclosures of the Robinson and Boczar-Davis patents eliminates any secrecy. Items S-2 and S-3 were generally known in the industry prior to August 1968, were in pilot production at Fairchild Camera prior to August 1968 (using identical epitaxial processes) and are also fully disclosed in the Robinson and Boczar-Davis patents.

There was also testimony at trial (although not mentioned in post-trial memoranda) of the marketing by Fairchild Camera of a device labeled MPS-6500, being a duplicate of plaintiff's device labeled MPS-6500. Plaintiff claimed MPS means Motorola Plastic Semiconductor — defendants claimed it means Moulded Plastic Semiconductor. Both devices were interchangeable in use. There was no evidence of actual confusion by customers, presumably because each Motorola device carried its batwing M logo in addition to the MPS-6500 designation, and each Fairchild device carried its block F stamped logo. All third-party catalogues introduced clearly indicated to any prospective buyer the manufacturing source.

While each Motorola employee-defendant came from a different area of expertise and knowledge at Motorola, there was no evidence from which the Court could find that any particular defendant disclosed any particular information. The closest was the claim that Lehner, who had supervised design and in-house construction of production equipment at Motorola, ordered TO-92 line production equipment from Kuliche & Soffa for Fairchild Camera. There is no evidence that he did more than list ultimate performance criteria for production equipment using a different and Fairchild-patented vertically processed (as opposed to plaintiff's similar horizontally processed) lead frame strip for the Fairchild TO-92 line. The equipment was then designed and built by Kuliche & Soffa and sold to Fairchild for a substantial price. As noted above, the *methods* for performance from which the machines could be independently designed was available from patent and other literature and information readily available in the trade. No one from Kuliche & Soffa was called to testify at the trial regarding the source of their information used in the design and construction of the production line equipment.

As discussed above, plaintiff's trade secrets claims must fail because of lack of implementation of the general trade secrets agreement; because plaintiff did not take reasonable steps to protect its trade secrets and, in fact, did not even know what it was intending to claim; because some were clearly revealed in the marketed product; and because substantially all of the claims were revealed in patents and trade literature or generally known in the trade prior to August 1968, and therefore excepted from restriction under the specific terms of the agreement, and under trade secret law.

## RICHTER v. WESTAB, INC.

529 F.2d 896 (6th Cir. 1976)

Plaintiffs were partners in the firm of Richter & Mracky Design Associates, which created and developed designs for products and marketing concepts. In 1964 Mark Seitman, an employee of Richter & Mracky, observed that the school supplies industry was characterized by drabness and a lack of attractiveness in the various product lines. He believed that a school supply firm could improve its sales by using on notebook covers and binders fashion designs and fabrics which matched clothing being advertised in young women's fashion magazines; that such fashion-oriented supplies could be matched as a package so that the fashion-conscious buyer could purchase all items from one company; and that these lines of school supplies could be advertised in fashion magazines rather than in trade journals as had been the practice with school supplies in the past.

Seitman solicited Westab and arranged a meeting for February 10, 1965, with its officers. Westab was the largest manufacturer of school supplies in the country. At this meeting Seitman presented his concept, which resulted in authorization for Richter & Mracky to produce tentative designs and samples for presentation to Westab sales officials. During the meeting a Westab officer suggested that the notebook binders in the fashion line have interchangeable covers, and Richter & Mracky was also authorized to develop this idea.

After the meeting Seitman discussed with Edgar Stovall, Vice-President of Westab, the matter of compensation which included a royalty of five percent of

Westab's sale price, to be paid on specific designs submitted by Richter & Mracky and used by Westab. It did not include royalties on the mere concept of fashion design.

During the summer of 1965 Richter & Mracky worked to perfect interchangeable binder covers and to produce fashion designs which it named 'Fashion Goes To School.' Samples were submitted to Westab. The interchangeable covers became loose when the notebook was opened, and were not practical. The 'Fashion Goes To School' concept was submitted at a meeting of Westab's salesmen; it called for a retail price of $4.95 for the package.

None of the designs was acceptable to Westab, and the project was rejected in October 1965 when Westab marketing officials balked at the projected retail price of $4.95 for the package. Westab then paid Richter & Mracky for shop expenses and asked that the work product not be given to competitors.

The concept was then presented to Sears, Roebuck and Company by Richter & Mracky, proposing that the binders would be purchased from Westab. Westab agreed to furnish the binders, but Sears declined to purchase the concept.

In 1965 Westab's research and marketing personnel independently developed a package of school supplies with matching plaid covers, packed together in a transparent shrink wrapper, and called 'Campus Mates.' This package was a success. In 1967 Westab introduced paisley-patterned binder covers. In 1968 more paisley patterns and stripe patterns were introduced in the 'Girl Talk' line, promoted by advertisements in the magazine Seventeen. In 1969 Westab coordinated binder fabrics with fashion trends in 'The Wet Look' and 'The Leather Look' lines. In 1970 the fashion binder lines were promoted in fashion magazines as clothing accessories: 'Think of a notebook as something you wear'; 'Westab's got notebook ensembles to go along with all those sharp new clothes you've just bought this fall.' These fashion lines generated sales revenues in excess of $4.6 million in the years 1966-1969.

In 1969 Seitman first noticed that Westab's marketing strategy resembled the concept which he had presented to Westab in 1965. In 1971 the present suit was brought to recover five percent royalties on all sales by Westab of fashion coordinated school supplies.

Two theories of recovery were presented: breach of express contract and breach of implied contract arising from the use of a trade secret. The District Court found that an express contract, partly oral and partly in writing, existed but had not been breached; that the contract did not contain the provisions claimed by Richter & Mracky; and that the concept could not be protected as a trade secret because it did not fit within the definition of a trade secret under Ohio law.

## THE EXPRESS CONTRACT

Richter & Mracky challenges the finding of the District Court that an express contract existed, the terms of which were not breached. This finding must be affirmed if supported by substantial evidence in the record, *Metropolitan Paving Co. v. City of Aurora*, 449 F.2d 177, 181 (10th Cir. 1971), and can be reversed only if clearly erroneous, Fed.R.Civ.P. 52(a), *Northeast Theatre Corp. v. Wetsman*, 493 F.2d 314, 317 (6th Cir. 1974).

If the contract called for Westab to pay a five percent royalty only on binders carrying specific designs furnished by Richter & Mracky no breach of contract occurred. There was substantial evidence to support the finding that the contract required Richter & Mracky to submit specific designs and to be paid only for use of the designs so submitted.

On cross-examination of Seitman the following exchange occurred:

Q: Tell us what you said?

A: How is this to be compensated for us, there is outside work, and you ask how it should be billed for it, and as far as the items that come from the concept Mr. Stovall had clearly said, and I had clearly said, that we would receive a royalty on them.

Q: Let me ask you to do this. If you would, consider yourself a tape recorder, could you play back what you said to Mr. Stovall at that meeting of February 10, 1965 concerning the contract, and what you were to do?

A: Let's take the next step as per the excitement, let's develop these products.

Q: Is that what you said?

A: Yes. You are asking what I said to the man.

Q: Go ahead, tell all that you said to him.

A: He said that we would receive a five percent royalty. I said we would develop the products that showed interest, that there was interest in, we would develop different approaches to the vision as you have expressed in it, as everybody was excited about, and on anything that is used we are to get five percent royalty, and on any work you ask us to do we should bill you outside costs.

That's what I said to him, and that's what he agreed upon. (A. 108-09)

This testimony supports the terms of the contract found by the District Court. In addition, the letters exchanged between the parties in April and May of 1965 can be fairly construed to indicate that a five percent royalty was to be paid for a particular line of binders called 'Fashion Back To School,' which was to be designed by Richter & Mracky, but which was rejected by Westab's sales managers in October. Finally, Stovall testified that the agreement made between himself and Seitman called for Richter & Mracky to be paid a royalty on sales of items designed by Richter & Mracky.

We conclude that the District Court's finding that an express contract existed calling for Richter & Mracky to be paid a royalty for specific designs submitted by them was supported by substantial evidence, including the finding that such contract was not breached. We further conclude that such findings were not clearly erroneous.

## THE TRADE SECRET THEORY

An alternate theory of recovery claimed was that an implied contract arises to pay for use of a trade secret when the secret is divulged as part of a confidential relationship. Even if this principle is a correct statement of Ohio law it cannot create an implied contract in Ohio because the fashion coordinating concept is not a trade secret as defined in [4 Restatement of Torts § 257 Comment b (1939)].

A trade secret may consist of any formula, pattern, device or compilation of information which is used in one's business, and which gives him an opportunity to obtain an advantage over competitors who do not know or use it. It may be a formula for a chemical compound, a process of manufacturing, treating or preserving materials, a pattern for a machine or other device, or a list of customers. . . . A trade secret is a process or device for continuous use in the operation of the business. Generally it relates to the production of goods, as, for example, a machine or formula for the production of an article. . . .

This definition does not include a marketing concept or a new product idea. Trade secret law is designed to protect a continuing competitive advantage, which a company enjoys due to confidential information it possesses, from destruction due to disclosure by a departed former employee. A marketing concept does not by confidentiality create a continuing competitive advantage because once it is implemented it is exposed for the world to see and for competitors to legally imitate.

This conclusion is even more compelling because Richter & Mracky is asking for compensation to cover periods when fashion binders were widely sold on the market by Westab's competitors as well as by Westab. Even if Westab had been paying Richter & Mracky to use the concept, it would have ceased being a trade secret upon introduction of the products, and Richter & Mracky thereafter would have no legal right to the concept.

Any competitive advantage to be gained from use of this concept would last only until a competitor could place similar items on the market. Richter & Mracky would have no remedy against Westab's competitors for their use of the concept.

Prior to sending samples to Westab plaintiffs had disclosed its concept to editorial personnel of fashion magazines, to potential suppliers of fabrics, and to an assistant professor of art at the University of California. When defendant declined to accept plaintiffs' 'Fashion Goes To School' concept plaintiffs disclosed the alleged secret to Sears, Roebuck and Company.

## THE LEGAL PROTECTION OF IDEAS

We must recognize that firms which sell ideas as their product should be able to protect their right to ask for and to receive compensation for their products just as any other business can. These firms have traditionally been protected by patent and copyright laws. However, intangible concepts which are being sold by many consultants today cannot be protected by patent or copyright statutes.

Richter & Mracky suggests that legal protection is sometimes given to advertising slogans, marketing concepts, and television program concepts. This is true, but such relief is not found under the law of trade secrets. The logical means to protect a marketing concept is a tort action for conversion of intellectual property, or a quasi-contract action for wrongful appropriation of intellectual property. Such a cause of action is quite rare in Ohio.

The general rule of law is that ideas are not the property of anyone under federal law unless patented or copyrighted. *Lear, Inc. v. Atkins*, 395 U.S. 653, 668, 89 S.Ct. 1810, 23 L.Ed.2d 610 (1969).

If an idea cannot meet the requirements of patent or copyright laws which entitled it to protection, the states can not render such requirements nugatory by affording such ideas protection under state law. *Sears, Roebuck & Co. v. Stiffel Co.*, 376 U.S. 225, 231, 84 S.Ct. 784, 11 L.Ed.2d 661 (1964). There are exceptions to this rule: state protection of trade secrets is considered to be not inconsistent with patent laws. *Kewanee Oil Co. v. Bicron Corp.*, 416 U.S. 470, 94 S.Ct. 1879, 40 L.Ed.2d 315 (1974), (upholding Ohio law of trade secrets).

With respect to ideas which are colorably patentable the law seems clear that states are limited in their ability to protect items not meeting patent criteria. However, with respect to literary property the failure to meet the criteria for copyright protection does not necessarily preclude protection under state common law. This is particularly true of unfinished program concepts presented to the broadcast media. The reason for this toleration of state law copyrighting is that the federal copyright statutes antedate the development of modern marketing concepts and the broadcast media. The need for legal protection of unfinished marketing and broadcast program concepts has not been met by amendment of the copyright laws, so the common law has once again served to meet new legal problems by finding protection for such concepts. *See* Note, *Beyond the Realm of Copyright: Is There Legal Sanctuary for the Merchant of Ideas?* 41 BROOKLYN L.REV. 284, 297-302 (1974).

Ohio law recognizes the existence of a common law copyright which protects unpublished works from appropriation when exposed in confidence to another. [Citation omitted.]

Common law copyright protection has been held in other jurisdictions to protect not only polished manuscripts but also advertising [citation omitted] and program concepts [Citations omitted.]. However, when protection is to be afforded to a concept rather than to a specific expression, the concept must be both novel and concrete. [Citation omitted.]

The idea of fashion-coordinated designs on binder covers does not appear to meet the test of novelty required in *Stevens v. Continental Can Co.*, 308 F.2d 100 (6th Cir. 1962). There the plaintiff's concept was to place a wood grain design on paper plates and cups. We held that even if wood grain patterns had never been used before on paper plates and cups the idea was not novel because the wood grain design was not novel. The idea of using a design on a particular item is abstract. The design to be used is concrete; but if the design to be used is not novel then no legal protection is available.

In the case at bar Richter & Mracky suggested that Westab apply to their school supplies designs already seen on clothing fashions. Since the designs to be used were not originated by Richter & Mracky, the suggestion lacks novelty according to

Stevens, supra, and the idea that the designs be placed on binders, standing alone, also lacks concreteness.

While there is authority in other jurisdictions for permitting recovery on an implied contract theory for use of an idea which is neither novel nor concrete in the legal sense, [citation omitted] an implied contract theory is inappropriate here because an express contract has been found to exist.

The law does not favor the protection of abstract ideas as the property of the originator. An idea should be free for all to use at least until someone is able to translate such idea into a sufficiently useful form that it may be patented or copyrighted. Thus competition in the use of ideas is a social good, hastening the process of invention.

When a design firm suggests that a particular product be decorated with thematic designs, this act of suggesting should not establish an exclusive right to exploit the idea. Perhaps the design firm will not be sufficiently competent to produce good designs based upon the concept. A concept is of little use until solidified into a concrete application. The idea of fashion designs is useless unless good designs are obtained. If the design firm is incapable of producing good designs the public should not be denied the benefit of the idea if another designer could produce good designs. Thus the principle denying legal protection to abstract ideas has important social interests behind it.

In spite of this policy, firms which specialize in selling abstract concepts may protect their work product by contract. If Richter & Mracky had made a contract with Westab which required Westab to pay a royalty on all fashion binders sold by Westab, the contract would have been enforceable in the courts. Likewise, if the parties had made an agreement in advance of the meeting that any sale arising from the use of concepts presented at the meeting would require royalty payments to Richter & Mracky, the facts here would probably require a judgment for plaintiffs.

We doubt that Westab would ever enter into such a contract, preferring to hear the presentation, or to see the proposed designs, before agreeing to a contract for their use. Such action would merely reflect the fact that an abstract idea has little commercial value until translated into a specific utilization.

Here the contract between the parties called for Richter & Mracky to submit the specific designs called for in the concept, and to be compensated for their acceptance and use. Similarly, when those designs proved to be unsatisfactory, it was the design department of Westab which gave the idea commercial value by developing its own designs which would utilize the concept.

The abstract concept of fashion designs on binders was a sales tool for Richter & Mracky, not a product. Richter & Mracky wished to sell designs, not the concept. The concept was necessary to the firm because it enabled the firm to solicit contracts for the purchase of its designs from a new market, the manufacturers of school supplies. Richter & Mracky obtained value for the idea, and opened up a new market for its design services. However, its design services were not sufficiently superior to the skills of Westab's own designers to cause Westab to purchase Richter & Mracky's product. Westab's own designers produced designs which attracted a significant volume of business, and the company was rewarded by the market for its efforts. The public benefited from this system which permitted competition to develop the best utilization for an abstract idea.

Denying the existence of a legal interest in abstract ideas disclosed in confidence will not as a practical matter impede the flow of ideas between companies. In this case Richter & Mracky never intended to sell its concept of fashion binders; it intended to sell designs to the school supplies industry. The disclosure of the concept was made in soliciting a contract to design binder covers. This disclosure would have occurred regardless of the legal status of the idea disclosed.

We do not find in the circumstances of this case any basis under which Richter & Mracky, or its members, would be entitled to compensation for use by Westab of the fashion design concept.

Affirmed.

## MURRAY v. NATIONAL BROADCASTING CO.

844 F.2d 988 (2d Cir. 1988)

It was almost a generation ago that a young comedian named Bill Cosby became the first black entertainer to star in a dramatic network television series. That program, *I Spy*, earned Cosby national recognition as an actor, including three Emmy Awards (1966, 1967 and 1968) for best performance in a dramatic series, and critical acclaim for the portrayal of a character without regard to the actor's race. Although keenly aware of the significance of his achievement in breaking the color line on network television, Cosby set his sights then on "accomplish[ing] something more significant for the Negro on TV." In an interview in 1965, he envisioned a different approach to the situation comedy genre made popular by *The Dick Van Dyke Show.* The *Daily News* described Cosby's "dream" series as not unlike other situation comedies.

There'll be the usual humorous exchanges between husband and wife . . . . Warmth and domestic cheerfulness will pervade the entire program.

Everything on the screen will be familiar to TV viewers. But this series will be radically different. Everyone in it will be a Negro.

> . . . "I'm interested in proving there's no difference between people," [explained Cosby]. "My series would take place in a middle-income Negro neighborhood. People who really don't know Negroes would find on this show that they're just like everyone else."

Nearly twenty years later, on September 20, 1984, Cosby's dream for a "color-blind" family series materialized with the premier of *The Cosby Show*-a situation comedy about a family known as the Huxtables. Bill Cosby stars in the leading role as Heathcliff ("Cliff") Huxtable together with his TV wife Clair and their five children.

Plaintiff-appellant Hwesu Murray, an employee of defendant-appellee ("NBC"), claims in the instant case that in 1980, four years prior to the premier of *The Cosby Show* on NBC's television network, he proposed to NBC a "new" idea for a half-hour situation comedy starring Bill Cosby. In a written proposal submitted to NBC, Murray described his series called

"Father's Day" as "wholesome . . . entertainment"

> which will focus upon the family life of a Black American family . . . . The leading character will be the father, . . . a devoted family man and a compassionate, proud, authority figure . . . .
>
> . . . The program may well resemble "Father Knows Best" and "The Dick Van Dyke Show." It will be radically different from "The Jeffersons," "Good Times," "Different Strokes," and "That's My Mama." The father will not be a buffoon, a supermasculine menial, or a phantom . . . . The program will show how a Black father can respond with love . . . , and will present . . . a closely-knit family . . . .

On this appeal from an order of the United States District Court for the Southern District of New York (Cedarbaum, J.) granting defendants-appellees' motion for summary judgment, we are asked to determine whether, under New York law, plaintiff has a legally protectible interest in his idea which he maintains was used by NBC in developing *The Cosby Show.* Because we agree with the district court's conclusion that, under New York law, lack of novelty in an idea precludes plaintiff from maintaining a cause of action to prevent its unauthorized use, we affirm the district court's order granting summary judgment and dismissing the complaint.

BACKGROUND

Plaintiff Hwesu S. Murray has been employed in the television industry for the past ten years. Murray holds a Bachelor of Arts degree in English and graduate degrees in broadcast journalism and law. In 1979, defendant-appellee NBC hired Murray as a Unit Manager and financial analyst in its sports division. A year later, plaintiff contacted an NBC official outside of NBC Sports about some "extracurricular" ideas he had for future television programs, and the official apparently instructed him to submit his proposals in writing. Soon thereafter, in June 1980, plaintiff submitted five written proposals, one of which was entitled "Father's Day." Murray allegedly informed NBC that if it were interested in any of the proposals, he expected to be named executive producer and to receive appropriate credit and compensation as the creator of the eventual program. Plaintiff also allegedly told NBC that his ideas were being submitted in confidence.

Murray's proposal for "Father's Day" is the subject matter of this action. The NBC official who originally had requested it encouraged Murray to "flesh out" his proposal and submit it to Josh Kane, then an NBC vice-president and a top official with NBC Entertainment, the division of NBC responsible for network television programming. Plaintiff thereupon submitted to Kane an expanded proposal for "Father's Day." In a two-page memorandum dated November 1, 1980, Murray first suggested that Bill Cosby play the part of the father. At that time, plaintiff also made several other casting suggestions, including roles for a working spouse and five children, and again indicated that the proposed series would "combine humor with serious situations in a manner similar to that of the old *Dick Van Dyke Show*" but "with a Black perspective." Murray's expanded proposal concluded with the observation that, "[l]ike *Roots*, the show will attempt to depict life in a [closely-knit]

Black family, with the addition of a contemporary, urban setting."

NBC apparently decided not to pursue Murray's proposal. On November 21, 1980, Kane returned the "Father's Day" submission to plaintiff and informed him that "we are not interested in pursuing [its] development at this time."

Four years later, in the fall of 1984, *The Cosby Show* premiered on NBC. *The Cosby Show* is a half-hour weekly situation comedy series about everyday life in an upper middle-class black family in New York City. The father, played by Bill Cosby, is a physician, and the mother is a lawyer. In its first season, *The Cosby Show* soared to the top of the Nielsen ratings and has become one of the most popular programs in television history. The show is highly regarded by critics and is also a huge commercial success.

Less than a month after viewing the premier, plaintiff wrote to NBC to advise it that *The Cosby Show* had been derived from his idea for "Father's Day." In January 1985, NBC responded through its Law Department, stating its position that " 'Father's Day' played absolutely no role in the development of 'The Cosby Show' . . . [since m]uch of the substance and style of 'The Cosby Show' is an outgrowth of the humor and style developed by Bill Cosby throughout his career." NBC further maintained that *The Cosby Show* was developed and produced by The Carsey-Werner Company ("Carsey-Werner"), an independent production company and the executive producers of the series.

In his complaint, plaintiff claimed that *The Cosby Show's* portrayal of a strong black family in a nonstereo typical manner is the essence of "Father's Day," and "[i]t is that portrayal of Black middle-class life that originated with plaintiff." Murray also alleged that Josh Kane showed plaintiff's "Father's Day" proposal to his superiors at NBC, including defendant-appellee Brandon Tartikoff, President of NBC Entertainment. Tartikoff, together with Cosby and Carsey-Werner, have been credited with the creation and development of *The Cosby Show.* Plaintiff maintains that NBC and Tartikoff deliberately deceived plaintiff into believing that NBC had no interest in "Father's Day" and then proceeded to develop and eventually produce plaintiff's idea as *The Cosby Show.*

Plaintiff's complaint stated a number of causes of action arising out of defendants' alleged appropriation of his idea. Among those relevant to this appeal are plaintiff's claims of race discrimination under 42 U.S.C. §§ 1981 and 1982, false designation of origin under the Lanham Act, 15 U.S.C. § 1125, and various state law claims, including misappropriation, conversion, breach of implied contract, unjust enrichment and fraud. Plaintiff sought, *inter alia,* damages and declaratory and injunctive relief as the "sole owner of all rights in and to the idea, proposal and property [known as] 'Father's Day.' "

* * *

Our review of the instant appeal is limited to deciding whether the district court properly concluded that there was "no genuine issue as to any material fact" entitling defendants to "judgment as a matter of law." Fed.R.Civ.P. 56(c). Summary judgment is appropriate when, after drawing all reasonable inferences in favor of the party against whom summary judgment is sought, no reasonable trier of fact could find in favor of the non-moving party. [Citations omitted.]

As the district court recognized, the dispositive issue in this case is whether plaintiff's idea is entitled to legal protection. Plaintiff points to "unique"-"even revolutionary"-aspects of his "Father's Day" proposal that he claims demonstrate "genuine novelty and invention," *see Educational Sales Programs, Inc. v. Dreyfus Corp.*, 65 Misc.2d 412, 317 N.Y.S.2d 840, 844 (Sup.Ct.N.Y.Cty.1970), which preclude the entry of summary judgment against him. Specifically, plaintiff contends that his idea suggesting the nonstereotypical portrayal of black Americans on television is legally protectible because it represents a real breakthrough. As he stated in his affidavit in opposition to defendants' motion,

> [w]hen I created "Father's Day", I had in mind . . . a show that . . . would portray a Black family as it had never been shown before on television . . . . I also . . . desire[d] to produce a show with strong and positive role models for the Black community, and to make a statement regarding the love and integrity of the Black family to the world. I think every Black person in this country knows there has been a need for this, and that never before on television had there been a portrayal of a Black family as I created it for "Father's Day."

Murray claims that the novelty of his idea subsequently was confirmed by the media and the viewing public which instantly recognized the "unique" and "revolutionary" portrayal of a black family on *The Cosby Show.*

We certainly do not dispute the fact that the portrayal of a nonstereotypical black family on television was indeed a breakthrough. Nevertheless, that breakthrough represents the achievement of what many black Americans, including Bill Cosby and plaintiff himself, have recognized for many years-namely, the need for a more positive, fair and realistic portrayal of blacks on television. While NBC's decision to broadcast *The Cosby Show* unquestionably was innovative in the sense that an intact, nonstereotypical black family had never been portrayed on television before, the mere fact that such a decision had not been made before does not necessarily mean that the idea for the program is itself novel. *See Educational Sales Programs*, 317 N.Y.S.2d at 843 ("[n]ot every 'good idea' is a legally protectible idea").

Consequently, we do not agree with appellant's contention that the nonstereotypical portrayal of a black middle-class family in a situation comedy is novel because

> [t]o argue otherwise would be the equivalent of arguing that since there had always been baseball, and blacks in baseball, there was nothing new about Jackie Robinson playing in the major leagues-or that since there had always been schools in Little Rock, Arkansas, and blacks in schools, there was nothing new about integrating schools in Little Rock.

As appellees persuasively point out in response to this analogy, Murray has "confuse[d] the 'idea' with its execution . . . . Indeed, the idea of integration . . . had been discussed for decades prior to the actual events taking place." Similarly, we believe, as a matter of law, that plaintiff's idea embodied in his "Father's Day" proposal was not novel because it merely represented an "adaptation of existing knowledge" and of "known ingredients" and therefore lacked "genuine novelty and invention." *Educational Sales Programs*, 317 N.Y.S.2d at 844.

We recognize of course that even novel and original ideas to a greater or lesser extent combine elements that are themselves not novel. Originality does not exist in a vacuum. Nevertheless, where, as here, an idea consists in essence of nothing more than a variation on a basic theme-in this case, the family situation comedy-novelty cannot be found to exist. *Id.; see Surplus Equipment, Inc. v. Xerox Corp.*, 120 A.D.2d 582, 502 N.Y.S.2d 491, 492 (2d Dep't 1986). The addition to this basic theme of the portrayal of blacks in nonstereotypical roles does not alter our conclusion, especially in view of the fact that Bill Cosby previously had expressed a desire to do a situation comedy about a black family and that, as the district court found, Cosby's entire career has been a reflection of the positive portrayal of blacks and the black family on television.

Appellant would have us believe that by interpreting New York law as we do, we are in effect condoning the theft of ideas. On the contrary, ideas that reflect "genuine novelty and invention" are fully protected against unauthorized use. *Educational Sales Programs*, 317 N.Y.S.2d at 844. But those ideas that are not novel "are in the public domain and may freely be used by anyone with impunity." *Ed Graham Productions*, 347 N.Y.S.2d at 769. Since such non-novel ideas are not protectible as property, they cannot be stolen.

In assessing whether an idea is in the public domain, the central issue is the uniqueness of the creation. Murray insists that there is at least a question of fact as to the novelty of "Father's Day" because *The Cosby Show* is indisputably unique. In support of this contention, plaintiff points to the fact that NBC contracted with Carsey-Werner for the right of NBC to broadcast *The Cosby Show.* The contract apparently was executed by the parties before there had been any written development of the proposed series. The "program idea" for *The Cosby Show*, however, was described in the contract as "unique, intellectual property." According to plaintiff, the inescapable conclusion is that the idea-whether it be "Father's Day" or *The Cosby Show*-could not possibly have been in the public domain if NBC expressly contracted to purchase it from Carsey-Werner.

We disagree. The Carsey-Werner contract contemplates a fully-produced television series. The contract refers to, *inter alia*, the program format, titles, set designs, theme music, stories, scripts, and art work as well as to the "program idea." Taken together, these elements no doubt would be considered original and therefore protectible as property. On the other hand, we think it equally apparent that the mere idea for a situation comedy about a nonstereotypical black family-whether that idea is in the hands of Murray, Carsey-Werner, NBC, or anyone else-is not novel and thus may be used with impunity.

Finally, as an alternative attack on the propriety of the district court's order granting summary judgment, plaintiff posits that even if his idea was not novel as a matter of law, summary judgment still was inappropriate because his proposal was solicited by defendants and submitted to them in confidence. In this regard, Murray relies on *Cole v. Phillips H. Lord, Inc.*, 262 A.D. 116, 28 N.Y.S.2d 404 (1st Dep't 1941). Murray contends that *Cole* stands for the proposition that when an idea is protected by an agreement or a confidential relationship, a cause of action arises for unauthorized use of that idea irrespective of the novelty of the subject matter of the contract. Plaintiff's reliance on *Cole* is misplaced in light of subsequent cases, particularly the New York Court of Appeals decision in *Downey v. General Foods Corp.*, 31 N.Y.2d 56, 334 N.Y.S.2d 874, 286 N.E.2d 257 (1972). *See also Ferber v. Sterndent Corp.*, 51 N.Y.2d 782, 433 N.Y.S.2d 85, 86, 412 N.E.2d 1311 (1980) ("[a]bsent a showing of novelty, plaintiff's action to recover damages for illegal use of 'confidentially disclosed ideas' must fail as a matter of law"); *Educational Sales Programs*, 317 N.Y.S.2d at 844 ("[o]ne cannot be forever barred from using a worthwhile but unoriginal idea merely because it was once asked to be treated in confidence").

Consequently, we find that New York law requires that an idea be original or novel in order for it to be protected as property. *See Downey*, 334 N.Y.S.2d at 877, 286 N.E.2d at 259. Since, as has already been shown, plaintiff's proposal for "Father's Day" was lacking in novelty and originality, we conclude that the district court correctly granted defendants' motion for summary judgment.

* * *

GEORGEC. PRATT, CIRCUIT JUDGE, DISSENTING:

Today this court holds that the idea underlying what may well be the most successful situation comedy in television history was, in 1980, so unoriginal and so entrenched in the public domain that, as a matter of law, it did not constitute intellectual property protected under New York law. Because I am convinced that the novelty issue in this case presents a factual question subject to further discovery and ultimate scrutiny by a trier of fact, I respectfully dissent.

At least for purposes of this appeal, it is given that Murray presented NBC with an idea for a television series; that, after showing interest in Murray's initial idea, NBC then asked him to submit a more detailed proposal; and that NBC then actually used his proposal in developing *The Cosby Show*, but at the same time refused to provide any compensation to Murray. The only question on appeal is whether there is evidence to indicate that Murray's idea possessed the novelty and originality required under New York law. [Citation omitted.] Specifically, in order to affirm the district court judgment, this court must conclude that there is insufficient evidence to present a triable issue on novelty. [Citations omitted.]

I agree with the majority that there is some evidence that Murray's idea was not novel. But clearly, there is also evidence indicating novelty. Initially, there is the admission by NBC, in its agreement with Carsey-Werner, that the television series is "unique, intellectual property." Although NBC argues, and the majority agrees, that this clause refers to a "fully-produced television series", and not Murray's program idea, such analysis ignores two important facts.

First, the "unique, intellectual property" language is found in the remedies section of the development agreement. This section gives NBC the right to prevent the loss of its "unique, intellectual property" should Carsey-Werner fail to perform. However, if Carsey-Werner does not perform-that is, if it subsequently refuses to develop the television series-the only "unique, intellectual property" to be protected is the program's underlying idea. In other words, from the outset NBC wanted to make certain that if its relationship with Carsey-Werner faltered, the novel idea it had given Carsey-Werner would be protected from disclosure. And because, for purposes of this appeal, we must assume that NBC got its idea from Murray, the Carsey-Werner development agreement, at a minimum, constitutes admissible evidence that Murray's idea was unique, thus making the novelty determination a question of fact. [Citation omitted.]

That the "unique, intellectual property" mentioned in the agreement refers to Murray's basic idea underlying the series rather than a fully-produced series, also finds support in the second fact the majority ignores. The definition section of the development agreement specifically defines this "property", not, as the majority contends, as "titles, set designs, theme music, stories, scripts, and art work"-indeed, these are separately defined in the agreement as the "elements" to be developed by Carsey-Werner-but rather, the development agreement defines the actual "property" exclusively to be the "story, literary property, program idea, and/or program format *which form(s) the basis*" for the television series. This provision provides additional evidence that it was Murray's underlying idea, not the developed elements of the series as a whole, which NBC desired to protect as unique and novel property.

Nor is the agreement the only piece of evidence indicating an issue of fact as to novelty. In 1985, NBC admitted that Murray had "rights" in his idea, but determined it had no interest in acquiring those rights. At trial, both Cosby and Tartikoff stated that they believed *The Cosby Show* to be novel and unique. NBC admitted that the reason it normally returned rejected submissions, as it did in Murray's case, was that the "material belong [ed] to the submitter." In short, there is substantial evidence, both within and independent of the Carsey-Werner development agreement, which directly conflicts with the majority's holding that, as a matter of law, Murray's idea was not novel.

The fact that the basic idea had been expressed by Cosby some fifteen years before Murray submitted his proposal to NBC does not erase these factual issues. To say, as a matter of law, that an idea is not novel because it already exists in general form, would be to deny governmental protection to any idea previously mentioned anywhere, at anytime, by anyone. I do not believe New York law defines "novelty" so strictly, especially in the area of mass communications, an area long recognized by state courts as "a specialized field having customs and usages of its own" where "a property right exists" in "a combination of ideas evolved into a program." *Cole v. Phillip H. Lord, Inc.*, 262 A.D. 116, 121, 28 N.Y.S.2d 404, 409 (1st Dep't 1941). Indeed, in a market the very existence of which depends on the generation and development of ideas, it may be impossible to formulate a concept that has not previously been expressed by someone, somewhere.

Novelty, by its very definition, is highly subjective. As fashion, advertising, and television and radio production can attest, what is novel today may not have been novel 15 years ago, and what is commonplace today may well be novel 15 years hence. In this instance, where Cosby expressed the concept almost a decade and a half before Murray submitted his proposal, where it was Murray's idea that NBC actually used, where there is no evidence indicating NBC knew anything of the program idea until Murray submitted it, *compare Downey v. General Foods Corp.*, 31 N.Y.2d 56, 60, 334 N.Y.S.2d 874, 877-78, 286 N.E.2d 257 (1972) (no novelty because defendant had "envisaged" *and* "utilized" plaintiff's idea for "years before the plaintiff submitted it") *with Werlin v. Readers Digest Ass'n Inc.*, 528 F.Supp. 451, 466 (S.D.N.Y.1981) (even though plaintiff's idea was in public domain, no evidence that defendant knew about or would have discovered the idea except through plaintiff's proposal; hence, the "idea was novel" as far as defendant was concerned), and where substantial conflicting evidence exists as to the "novelty" of the idea under New York law, there seems to be at least a triable issue.

The majority's decision prematurely denies Murray a fair opportunity to establish his right to participate in the enormous wealth generated by *The Cosby Show.* Accordingly, I would reverse the district court judgment and remand the case for further consideration.

## NOTES AND QUESTIONS:

1. In *Kewanee Oil*, the Supreme Court stated that: "[n]ovelty, in the patent law sense, is not required for a trade secret. . . . However, some novelty will be required if merely because that which does not possess novelty is usually known; secrecy, in the context of trade secrets, thus implies at least a minimal novelty." *Kewanee Oil*, 416 U.S. at 476. Does having a minimal novelty requirement make sense? If so, why? If not, why not? Should there be a sliding scale for novelty? That is — should a sophisticated technology require only a slight advance, whereas a less sophisticated technology must provide a much greater advance before legal protection would be available? Should the court relax the novelty requirement if the facts of the misappropriation involve particularly egregious acts?

2. The *Motorola* opinion blurred the distinction between secrecy and novelty by relying on Judge Yankwich's 1958 opinion in *Sarkes Tarzian, Inc. v. Audio Devices, Inc*, 166 F.Supp. 250, 265 (D.C.Cal.1958). Motorola quotes the opinion's statement that there must be some "discovery" or else "matters which are generally known in the trade or readily discernable by those in the trade cannot be made secret by being so labeled in an agreement." *Motorola, Inc v. Fairchild Camera & Instrument Corp.*, 366 F. Supp. 1173, 1184 (D.C. Ariz. 1973). Could this be the court's rationale for the decision in *Richter*? Or was *Richter* simply a question of contract interpretation?

3. What was the alleged trade secret at issue in *Murray v. N.B.C*, 844 F.2d 988 (2d Cir. 1988)? How many of the *details* of Mr. Murray's proposal were actually in the public domain? Consider whether the holding in *Murray* is consistent with the decision in *Hamilton National Bank v. Belt*, 210 F.2d 706 (D.C.Cir.1953), discussed below in the section dealing with concreteness. Were you convinced by Judge Pratt's dissent in *Murray*? Was the issue of novelty really one for the jury, and not suitable for summary dismissal?

4. As observed in *Ecclesiates* 1:9, "What has been is what will be, And what has been done is what will be done, And there is nothing new under the sun;" accordingly, many trade secrets are made up of a combination of known elements. As succinctly noted by the U.S. District Court for the Eastern District of Pennsylvania, "a trade secret can exist in a combination of characteristics and components, each of which, by itself, is in the public domain, but the unified process, design and operation of which, in unique combination, affords a competitive

advantage and is a protectable secret." *Anaconda Co. v. Metric Tool & Die Co.*, 485 F.Supp. 410, 422 (E.D.Pa. 1980) (quoting from *Imperial Chem. Indus., Ltd. v. Nat'l Distillers & Chem. Corp.*, 342 F.2d 737, 742 (2d Cir. 1965)). The court then found that "[h]ere it was the precise configuration, juxtaposition, and assemblage of components and features set forth in Appendix A, rather than the breaking of heretofore unknown ground, which made plaintiff's [ ] machine unique" and therefore a trade secret. *Anaconda Co.*, 485 F.Supp. at 422. The *Anaconda* court essentially echoed the opinion in *Continental Data Systems*, which held "[t]he fact that individual forms and samples found in the sales materials were compilations of public information does not preclude a finding that the combination of the included elements affords a plaintiff competitive advantage and is not itself in the public domain." 638 F.Supp. at 443.

## (3) Concreteness.

## HAMILTON NATIONAL BANK v. BELT

210 F.2d 706 (D.C. Cir. 1953)

The appellee, Lloyd K. Belt, sued the appellant, Hamilton National Bank, for damages incurred by reason of the Bank's appropriation of a type of radio program which he claimed to have originated and made known to the Bank. The jury returned a money verdict for Mr. Belt and the Bank appeals from the ensuing judgment.

Expressly reserving the right to negotiate with any school, radio station, or sponsor, as well as all other rights, Mr. Belt by letter of October 21, 1949, to the Assistant Superintendent of Public Schools set forth a plan to select student talent by holding auditions in the high schools and with talent thus selected to put on half-hour weekly broadcasts. Each show would be presented first to the student body as an assembly, recorded, and the recording broadcast in the evening. A school atmosphere would be retained by referring to the show as a class, to the acts as class assignments, and to the action as class recitations. A different school would be featured each week. The program would include several pieces by the glee club in addition to the talent. The actual content of each show, with the exception of the glee club and an orchestra, could not be predicted until selection of the talent. Such selection, together with production and presentation of the show, would be subject at all times to supervision and approval by the school authorities. If desired, Mr. Belt would conduct the auditions, production and presentation with such assistance as would be available. There would be a minimum of conversation and introductions, the time being devoted principally to a 'fast moving, first rate, entertaining show', and there would be no commercial 'spots', though the sponsoring firm would be accorded a brief acknowledgment of its sponsorship at the beginning and end of the broadcast.

This plan was proposed by Mr. Belt to several Washington business establishments. They were not interested in sponsoring it. He then presented it to the Bank, which was interested. A contract between the Bank and Mr. Belt was entered into November 1, 1948. Mr. Belt was to be paid $25 a week and was to make the necessary arrangements with the schools for auditions and transcriptions. Should the Board of Directors of the Bank approve transcribed programs and put them on the air a revised agreement covering the duties and compensation of Mr. Belt would be made.

The school authorities did not at first give the necessary approval. Pursuant to the terms of their agreement the Bank thereupon canceled its contract with Mr. Belt, later paying him $50 in full settlement of a controversy over two weeks compensation In March, 1949, the Board of education advised the Bank of its willingness to approve such a program. The Bank then, with the assistance of someone other than Mr. Belt, carried the plan forward with periodical broadcasts for over a year.

Appellant contends (1) the idea was so general and abstract as to be devoid of a property right in the absence of a definite contract, entered into prior to its voluntary disclosure, for compensation for its use; (2) the question whether the idea was sufficiently concrete to warrant legal protection was one of law which the court erroneously submitted to the jury and which this court can decide; (3) to justify legal protection an idea must also be new and novel, a question of fact which the court submitted to the jury without adequate evidence; (4) the court caused improper hypothetical questions to be asked experts who testified as to the market value of the idea.

The problems presented are new in this jurisdiction; but consideration of cases decided by other courts and of the principles involved leads us to conclude that a person has such a property right in his own idea as enables him to recover damages for its appropriation or use by another when the idea is original, concrete, useful, and is disclosed in circumstances which, reasonably construed, clearly indicate that compensation is contemplated if it is accepted and used.

That the idea must be new and novel, or, as sometimes termed, original, is clear. In *Lueddecke v. Chevrolet Motor Co.*, 8 Cir., 70 F.2d 345, 347, recovery was denied in part because the court was not persuaded that the idea was a 'novel and useful' one. *See, also, Soule v. Bon Ami Co., 201 App.Div. 794, 195 N.Y.S. 574, affirmed,* 235 N.Y. 609, 139 N.E. 754. It is not disputed that the issue of novelty is for the jury if the evidence raises a question of fact in that regard. Appellant does contend there was not sufficient evidence of originality to go to the jury. We find, however, that there was conflicting testimony on the subject. Indeed, the trial court thought there was no substantial evidence contrary Mr. Belt's claim of originality.

In addition to being new, novel or original, an idea to be legally protected must also be concrete. The law shies away from according protection to vagueness, and must do so especially in the realm of ideas with the obvious dangers of a contrary rule. An abstract idea, in any event when not the subject of a contract, is so unattached as to be deemed legally without the quality of individual identity or property. Protection of ideas at all, in contrast with inventions, literary productions and trade secrets, the law with respect to which we do not now consider, must be careful to avoid attributing to individual ownership that which is in reality common property; and it would be unwise to place a burden upon communication of ideas by requiring compensation for their adoption and use. But the dangers suggested are sufficiently avoided to warrant the law in placing an idea among protected property rights when it is definite and concrete, new and novel, has usefulness and is disclosed for commercial purposes in circumstances which the parties ought reasonably to construe as contemplating compensation for its use.

Was this plan concrete? The Bank says this is a question of law which was erroneously left to the jury. An ancillary position is that in any event the instructions to the jury on this issue were inadequate. We need not decide whether in every case it is for court rather than jury to answer the question of concreteness, for we think this plan was concrete and that to have defined the term more fully for the jury in the context of this case would have been to describe a pattern into which Mr. Belt's plan necessarily fitted. This being so the submission of the question to the jury, though with inadequate instructions, did not harm the Bank.

If the idea had been merely to broadcast programs of selected student talent it would have been too general and abstract, and perhaps would also have lacked newness and novelty. On the other hand, had the plan been accompanied with a script for each broadcast it would have been sufficiently concrete. Some opinions indicate that such detailing is essential. *See O'Brien v. RKO Radio Pictures, D.C.S.D.N.Y., 68 F.Supp. 13, 14*, where it is said: 'It is the means of expressing these ideas rather than the ideas themselves which warrant protection.' *See, also, Bowen v. Yankee Network, D.C.Mass., 46 F.Supp. 62, 63*, where it is stated: 'Such a right can only exist in the arrangement and combination of the ideas, i.e., in the form, sequence, and manner in which the composition expresses the ideas, not the ideas themselves.' We think, however, that in the field of radio broadcasting concreteness may lie between the boundaries of mere generality on the one hand and, on the other, a full script containing the words to be uttered and delineating the action to be portrayed. Where the plan is for a series of broadcasts the contents of which depend upon selection of talent at different times, a detailed program cannot be presented at the preliminary stages of negotiation. This should not in and of itself deprive the originator of a property right in his plan. [Citations omitted.]

As we have seen, in addition to the utilization of student talent selected for each broadcast from a different high school, the show was to be presented and recorded as a student assembly, retaining the atmosphere of a school by referring to the show as a class, to the acts as assignments and to the action as recitations. There was to be a rendition of several pieces by the school glee club, a minimum of conversation and introductions, a brief acknowledgment of sponsorship at the beginning and end of the broadcasts, and no provision for commercial 'spots'. And a very important element in the plan was the cooperation and participation of the school authorities through the use of school buildings and facilities and the assistance of faculty members. These details, when added to the basic general idea which, alone, would be too abstract, give sufficient concreteness. The cases advanced to support a contrary ruling are of little assistance because of factual differences.

In view of our conclusion that the plan was concrete it is unnecessary to express an opinion as to what protection, if any, should be afforded an abstract idea. Some jurisdictions deny protection in the absence of a contract entered into prior to disclosure and expressly reserving rights in the originator. [Citations omitted.] We leave this question undecided.

A remaining problem is whether the plan, assuming originality, concreteness, and usefulness, the latter of course uncontested because of the use actually made of it, was disclosed to the Bank in circumstances which contemplated compensation for its use. Factually this question is answered by pointing out that when the plan was first disclosed to the Bank it was made the subject of a contract between the parties. This contract, it is true, was largely for Mr. Belt's own personal services, but it nevertheless also placed the disclosure in circumstances indicating that compensation was expected for its use. While the contract itself, as we have said, was terminated, this did not erase the fact of disclosure in those circumstances. Nor did the idea become public property on disclosure to the Bank. [Citations omitted.]

Lastly, we do not think it was reversible error for the court to insist, though it need not have done so, that the hypothetical questions put to expert witnesses as to the value of the idea must include the assumption that it was new, novel and original. To require these witnesses to make this assumption did not prejudge the issue of newness, novelty, and originality; for the court made it clear that the assumption was for the purpose of the hypothetical question, and that before considering value the jury itself must determine the issue of novelty.

Affirmed.

## TATE v. SCANLAN INTERNATIONAL, INC.

403 N.W.2d 666 (Minn. Ct. App. 1987)

Generally, abstract ideas are not protectable property interests. In order for an abstract idea to be the subject of an express or implied contract or to be otherwise protected by the law, it must be novel and concrete. [Citations omitted.] Appellant argues that respondent's idea was neither novel nor concrete, and that the evidence was insufficient to support these findings by the jury.

A. Novelty.

A novel idea is an original idea, something that is not already known or in use. [Citation omitted.] The novelty essential to a protected property right cannot arise solely from the fact that something already known and in use is put to a new use. *Id.* In order for the aggregation of known elements to satisfy the novelty requirement, their conjunction must contribute something, that is, the whole must exceed the sum of its parts. [Citation omitted.]

Appellant asserts that respondent's idea is an obvious combination of previously developed products (Tip Guards, and the Kittner Sponge foam block), and is therefore not novel and not subject to legal protection. This argument requires an analogy to patent cases, in which the question of novelty often hinges on whether the subject of the patent is obvious.

The test for determining obviousness, or anticipation precluding patentability of an idea is whether the prior art discloses all elements of the claimed combinations, or their mechanical equivalents, functioning in substantially the same way, to produce the same result. [Citation omitted.] The linchpin in this analysis is not whether the individual components of the patent were obvious at the time of the invention, but whether the aggregation produced a new or different result or achieved a synergistic effect. [Citations omitted.] In answering this question, secondary considerations tending toward a showing of nonobviousness include commercial success of the product, copying, long felt but unsolved need, and failure of others. [Citations omitted.]

Here, there was no dispute that respondent did not design any of the individual elements of Suture Boots. However, respondent's idea was for a *system* to assist operating room nurses in firmly handling delicate suture. The need for such a product was evidenced by the prior dissatisfaction with the method of cutting catheter tubing to shod clamps. Evidence showed that prior experimentation into a method for achieving such a system had been unsuccessful, and that Suture Boots was a commercially successful product, despite copies which had emerged on the market.

The question of novelty is a question of fact for the jury and it is not a question upon which there is likely to be uniformity of thought in every given factual context. *Belt v. Hamilton Nat'l Bank*, 108 F.Supp. 689, 692 (D.C. Cir.1952). Here, the jury found that respondent's idea was novel. This conclusion finds much support in the evidence and will not be disturbed.

B. Concreteness.

Concreteness of an idea pertains to the requisite developmental stage of the idea when it is presented. [Citation omitted.] An idea is a protectable property interest, if it is sufficiently developed to be ready for immediate use without additional embellishment. *Id.* If an idea requires extensive investigation, research, and planning before it is ripe for implementation, it is not concrete. *Id.*

Appellant argues that since the key to Suture Boots as a new product was the foam block, and respondent admitted she provided only an example, expecting appellant to develop a suitable holder, the idea was not sufficiently developed so as to be usable, and was therefore not concrete.

The evidence here showed that respondent developed an idea for a system of elements, using something like the Kittner foam block to hold plastic, radiopaque, sterile tips to fit on the ends of clamps and provide strength and sensitivity in a convenient, efficient way. Respondent orally presented her specific idea to Scanlan, demonstrating the elements of the product and its goal. Respondent expected Scanlan to develop the idea further-by producing the parts of the product as she had specified. With respondent's help, Scanlan researched the idea and produced just what respondent had ordered in Suture Boots.

Oral presentations and demonstrations of ideas and written proposals of ideas have been held to be sufficiently developed to be "usable," and thus satisfy the concreteness requirement. [Citations omitted.].

The undisputed testimony of Mr. McGoldrick was that "concrete" in the field of medical marketing meant that the concept was very well defined, with reasonable access to all parts necessary to develop it. He also testified that in this field a working model of an idea was rarely presented. A review of the evidence adduced at trial shows that there was more than adequate support for the jury's determination that respondent's idea was usable and was concrete.

## NOTES AND QUESTIONS:

1. How is the level of technical detail in the radio program in *Hamilton Bank* different from the program summary in *Murray* discussed in the preceding section? Are the holdings in these two cases consistent with each other? Where do you think the line should be drawn between "novelty" and "concreteness"?

2. The *Tate* court emphasized that there was undisputed testimony in the record that "concrete in the field of medical marketing meant that the concept was very well defined" and "a working model of an idea was rarely presented" in supporting a decision that the idea in question was concrete enough to protect as a trade secret. See *Tate v. Scanlan Int'l, Inc.*, 403 N.W.2d 666, 672 (Minn.Ct.App.1987). Does this mean that a smart trial lawyer should introduce testimony as to the standard in the particular industry involved as to how far an idea must be developed before it is accepted for a license or acquisition? Could the existence of this type of standard in certain industries help to understand the seemingly inconsistent results in *Hamilton Bank* and *Murray*, even though there was no direct evidence on this point in either one of those cases?

### (4) Improvements

## SIKES v. MCGRAW-EDISON CO.

665 F.2d 731 (5th Cir.), *cert. denied*, 458 U.S. 1108 (1982)

* * *

In late 1974, Charles L. Sikes, an electrical engineer and a "tinkerer," was inspired by observation of the powerful "Weed Eater" mowing tool then being successfully marketed to experiment with developing a light-weight trimmer, usable in tight places where bulkier equipment would not fit. Working with a small trimmer already on the market, he modified it by replacing its metal blade with a nylon monofilament line, inserted in a hole drilled at the end of the power transmission wand and held in place by an enlarged end and the operation of centrifugal force.

In early 1976, Mr. Sikes demonstrated his device successfully to McGraw-Edison and provided it with written material and engineering drawings. Before he did so, the parties entered into a letter agreement providing, in pertinent part:

> This confidential disclosure agreement shall remain in full force and effect between myself and McGraw-Edison Company for a period of two (2) years from date of disclosure, unless such submitted information can be shown by McGraw-Edison Company to have been in its possession, or of public knowledge, or to have been in the public domain prior to such submission . . . .

At this demonstration, which commenced indoors and later proceeded to the plant yard, the McGraw-Edison employees seemed highly enthusiastic about Mr. Sikes' device. As the demonstration progressed, more and more highly placed executives were summoned to watch. Their comments suggested to Mr. Sikes that they had never seen quite such a device before; none gave any indication that any similar one was known to them. Sikes was twice asked how much he wanted for the invention. His response of $50,000.00 cash and a 50 cents per unit royalty produced the rejoinder that the cash asked was a little too high but the royalty seemed about right. Matters concluded with Mr. Sikes' leaving his model and papers with McGraw-Edison for their further study.

About two weeks later, McGraw-Edison invited Mr. Sikes to return to Missouri, where the first demonstration had been held, for further negotiations. He went, accompanied by his brother. At this session, the McGraw-Edison personnel took a somewhat different line.

Though at the earlier conference they had indicated keen interest and had confided both that a somewhat comparable device which they had under development would not be ready for two years and that it was vital that they bring a trimmer out in time for the August 1976 home product show, at this time they advised the Sikes that their own product was already developed. He was told that even so they maintained an interest in his device because their's would cost a few cents more to manufacture. Sikes rejected the offer of this amount-" about 8 cents"-per unit as a royalty. Negotiations faltered and, later, came to a close.

McGraw-Edison met the August deadline with its "Graswhip," a device remarkably similar to that of Mr. Sikes and one which has proved a considerable success. This suit followed in due course, asserting that McGraw-Edison had improperly availed itself of Mr. Sikes' device in bringing out the Graswhip. The jury awarded $900,000 damages. In several points of error, McGraw-Edison urges that it did not use Mr. Sikes' ideas, that they were already known to it, that they were already public knowledge at the time of their disclosure to McGraw-Edison by Sikes, and that the court's instructions to the jury on damages and on the Texas law relating to trade secrets were wrong. It is convenient to take up the last of these points first.

* * *

Little need be said in response to this contention, essentially one that record evidence does not support the jury verdict. Pointing to a different mode of attaching the nylon flail to the end of the Graswhip's power wand, McGraw-Edison argues that this is dispositive of the matter. The Sikes device employed a short length of monofilament having a bulb at one end, threaded through a transverse hole across the wand's full diameter and held in place by centrifugal force. The Graswhip's nylon flail replaced the bulb with an eyelet threaded over an axial peg at the end of the wand, with the length of line passing out through a hole in one side of the wand. We are not convinced.

We have briefly summarized above the evidence that, viewed most favorably to the verdict, amply supports it. Much of it came from employees or former employees of McGraw-Edison. To quote the testimony of one witness only, a former McGraw-Edison Vice-President in charge of tool-division marketing:

Q But, Mr. Sullivan, couldn't you have just taken a Weed Eater and take off the guard or take off its spool for putting a cord in and out and just any man in your shop have come up with this thing in two days?

A I suppose the answer to that is yes, they could have, but the other answer is no, they didn't. They weren't able to. There was no, we had never thought of doing that kind of thing.

Q Had you then been working on that trying to get a lawn trimmer?

A Well, some time in 1975 Mr. Spencer directed that the products policy committee and the engineering department and the manufacturing to cease talking about a nylon line grass trimmer. He didn't want to hear about it any more, for whatever reasons he had. We were unsuccessful, he didn't think we were going to be able to get around the patents that Weed Eater had and he didn't want to hear about it any more . . . . And I think we all got the message, and we were not, we had no time or talents being spent on a nylon line grass trimmer at the time that Mr. Sikes visited our office.

Q . . . I want to ask you, did McGraw-Edison use this (Sikes') tool for some purpose in its development of its own tool?

A I would say that this tool was the start of McGraw-Edison's development of their Graswhip, that this was the tool that we used out in the field for testing, and we took our motors and our envelopes and tried to develop the tool from this product, from this one here.

Any contention that on such evidence the jury could not properly find that McGraw-Edison used the Sikes device in developing its Graswhip is meritless.

* * *

## PRINCE MFG., INC. v. AUTOMATIC PARTNER, INC.

191 U.S.P.Q. 450 (N.J. Sup. Ct. 1976)

Thus, we come now to the third claim of misappropriation, that relating to a venturi-shaped air entraining rubber detent. The concept of a detent in a tennis machine is not new. It was contained in the "Big Prince" machine. It is the fact that it is venturi-shaped and made of rubber which is the basis of plaintiff's claim. The foundation of the claim is the same as the claim relating to the air induction system claim, that is the Church memorandum, Exhibit P-5 in evidence. Therein at page 5 are two drawings of rubber detents. Figure 10 is of a form previously utilized by plaintiff which may be described as a "half venturi" or conical shaped detent. It is this type of detent which is contained in the patent, Exhibit P-6 and the concept of which was admittedly in the public domain at that time. Figure 11 is a venturi-shaped rubber detent and is the basis of plaintiff's claim of misappropriation. At page 5 of the May 10, 1972 Church memorandum, Exhibit P-5, Church discussed these two forms of detent in the context of problems created by the Figure 10 type of detent, which problems resulted from an increase in back pressure within the machine. He discussed Figure 10 as a "bad" design creating an "area of extreme turbulence" and Figure 11 as a "good" design as reducing "back pressure", but recognized that the Figure 10 design might be required for other reasons.

In response to plaintiff's claim of misappropriation defendant argues that the present venturi-shaped rubber detent did not come into existence until the autumn of 1973, more than a year after the submission to the Board of Directors of Exhibit P-5. And they contend that the origin of the venturi shape and the purpose of the Figure 11 design in Exhibit P-5 was the reduction of back pressure and in no sense was it for the purpose or function for which the present detent is utilized. In this connection, Nielsen testified as follows: "The detent in Figure 11 of the Church memorandum shows a venturi-shaped detent the function of which is to provide a minimum of back pressure and to allow for as close as possible laminar flow of air through the detent. While the detent of DN-1 which is in my engineering notebook and is used in the Lob-ster and Automatic Partner machines in evidence was for the function of holding the ball for a predetermined length of time which could be adjustable in order to allow, first, a greater velocity capability so that you could get a stronger shot with everything else being the same, and second, more reliability so that even at very low pressures the ball ultimately would come out, which was a very important feature as far as a machine operation is concerned, because frequently using the detent of Figure 10 the ball could stay forever in the detent never coming out until it was pulled out by hand. If a slight problem occurred with the machine by the development of leakage or something like that."

The present detent as to which plaintiff seeks an assignment of patent applications or injunctive relief contains even further modifications. The venturi-shaped detent apparently in theory could have behind it either a solid mass of malleable rubber which would compress under pressure permitting the ball to pass through the orifice or a body of trapped air which would perform the same purpose. Either would reduce air turbulence as in Figure 11 of Exhibit P-5, but only the one containing trapped air could be the subject to variable pressure or a "bleed hole" as in the modification conceived by Nielsen in 1973. As contained in the Lob-ster machine, Exhibit P-8, the conception of Nielsen is called an adjustable detent or an air entraining detent because it works on the principle of bleeding out of the trapped air while the ball is lodged in and creating a pressure upon the detent and blocking the opening so that pressurized air is building up behind the ball. Through the medium of the adjustable detent, the air trapped behind the detent escapes in a regulated manner through the "bleed hole" and then when the ball is released air comes back in the "bleed hole". By regulating the speed at which the air leaves the "bleed hole" the timing of the machine is also regulated.

This was conceived by Nielsen in the summer of 1973, many months after the termination of his employment with plaintiff. He and Church filed a joint application on another patent containing this conception and that patent is pending in the Patent Office. Plaintiff claims that the detent contained in the pending patent application is the intellectual property of plaintiff. I disagree. The concept of the venturi-shaped detent for the purpose of reducing air turbulence and back pressure to the extent that it is useful, became plaintiff's property through the disclosure to the corporation of Exhibit P-5. And I find, as Mr. Sweeton testified, that Church and Nielsen did discuss at a technical committee meeting of plaintiff problems which they were having with the "Big Prince" detent and the benefits which could be obtained by converting to a venturi-shaped detent. Further the possibility of pressurizing the space between the walls and the side of the detent was also discussed. But I find that this concept is entirely different than and unrelated to the concept later conceived by Nielsen. Plaintiff argues that it is a mere modification and that such modification cannot eliminate the pre-existing property right misappropriated. I agree with the legal principle but not with the factual foundation of plaintiff's argument. The new detent is different in both design and purpose from that shown in Figure 11 of Exhibit P-5 and described in the written words on pages 1 and 4 of that Exhibit. Nielsen testified and I find that the Figure 11 detent was never used in any machine and it could not be for without a "bleed hole" it would not work properly and the ball would be trapped in the machine and would not be discharged. Contrary to the situation in the air induction system previously discussed, the modification constituted the invention. The venturi-shaped detent in Figure 11 was designed for assistance for solving a problem existing in "Big Prince" machine which did not have an air induction system. That problem of back pressure and air turbulence was eliminated by the use of the air induction system as in the Tech-Con prototype which utilized an "air box". The utilization of a venturi-shaped detent in the "Big Prince" machine is a totally different concept than the utilization of the adjustable detent as found in Lob-ster machine. It was actually the creation of a new detent rather than a mere improvement of the old one.

. . . .

## NOTES AND QUESTIONS:

1. The most commonly used approach to determine liability for an improvement of a trade secret is whether the improvement was derived from the trade secret, as discussed in *Sikes.* Liability has been found even where the final product is significantly different, when there was substantial use of the product. *See Superior Flux & Mfg. Co. v. H & S Indus., Inc.*, 210 U.S.P.Q. 669 (N.D.Ohio 1980).

2. The Restatement (Third) of Unfair Competition adopts the "derivation" test, but provides some latitude for the defendant by commenting that "an actor is liable for using the trade secret with independently created improvements or modifications if the result is substantially derived from the trade secret. . . . However, if the contribution made by the trade secret is so slight that the actor's product or process can be said to derive from other sources of information or from independent creation, the trade secret has not been 'used' for purposes of imposing liability. . . ." Restatement (Third) of Unfair Competition § 40 cmt. *c.*

3. While the court almost always finds liability when a party's trade secrets have been improved upon by a competitor, this was not the case in *Prince Manufacturing.* Although the product at issue, a detent (a device for positioning and holding one mechanical part in relation to another so that the device can be released by force applied to one of the parts), in *Prince Manufacturing* was considered to be an improvement, the court did not find liability because the concept of the improvement was "entirely different than and unrelated to the concept later conceived by Nielsen" and that "[t]he new detent is different in both design and purpose" from Prince's trade secrets. 191 U.S.P.Q. at 463. Was the test applied in *Prince Manufacturing* any different from the "derivation" test in *Sikes*?

4. Some cases have applied a test for whether an improvement violated the trade secret owner's rights, which is similar to the doctrine of equivalents test in

patent law, i.e., whether the improvement "functioned substantially the same way and accomplished substantially the same result." *See Sinclair v. Aquarius Elecs., Inc.*, 184 U.S.P.Q. 682, 684 (Cal.Ct.App.1974).

### (5) Use In a Business

## HARRIS MANUFACTURING CO. v. WILLIAMS

157 F. Supp. 779 (W.D. Ark. 1957)

* * *

The mastic or adhesive called 'Harris Mark 10 Adhesive' produced and sold by plaintiff is of a type never before used in the United States for the purpose of cementing parquet flooring, and is claimed to be superior to any other mastic presently available for the purpse of cementing parquet flooring to the subfloor.

* * *

Having concluded that plaintiff's domestic mastic and the V-3 assembly machine are trade secrets and have been unlawfully appropriated by defendants, the Court reaches the remaining question of the relief to which plaintiff is entitled.

The usual relief in a case of this type is an injunction against the defendants, and an order by the Court of an accounting by defendants of the profits received by them as a result of the appropriation and use of plaintiff's trade secrets. *Franke v. Wiltschek, supra*; Annotation, 170 A.L.R. 449, 488.

In the instant case plaintiff contends that it is entitled to an injunction forbidding the use by defendants of the trade secrets in question and from disclosing said secrets to others. Plaintiff futher contends that defendants should be enjoined from using any type of mastic having PVA as its principal ingredient, and that the defendant corporation should be ordered to destroy at least part of the two assembly machines now in its possession.

Defendants argue that plaintiff has discontinued use of the domestic mastic and is entitled to no relief insofar as the mastic is concerned. The defendants also contend that plaintiff is not entitled to an injunction with regard to the assembly machine since it was not a trade secret and was not copied by defendants.

The Court is not impressed with defendants' contention that plaintiff has abandoned use of the domestic mastic and, therefore, is entitled to no relief as to said item. The mere fact that plaintiff is not using the domestic mastic at the present time does not prevent said mastic from being a trade secret and does not give defendants the liberty of appropriating and using said mastic. The domestic mastic is available for plaintiff's use any time it desires to do so, and its failure to use said mastic at the present time does not militate against its right to have the defendants enjoined from copying said mastic and violating plaintiff's trade secret.

On the other hand, the Court is also of the opinion that plaintiff is not entitled to an injunction against the use by defendants of any mastic having PVA as its principal ingredient. Certainly if defendants in good faith could purchase a finished mastic on the open market, they would be free to use such mastic even though it might contain a PVA base.

Therefore, with regard to the mastic, plaintiff is entitled to an injunction enjoining defendants, their agents or assigns from further use of the A.P. No. 7 mastic now being used by defendant corporation, and from the use of any mastic which is based in substantial part on plaintiff's domestic mastic. Plaintiff is also entitled to an injunction enjoining defendants, their agents or assigns from disclosing the ingredients or method of preparation of the domestic mastic to any other person.

## NOTES AND QUESTIONS:

1. Restatement (Second) of Torts § 757 requires that the trade secret be "used in one's business." In *Harris*, the court found that a potential business use, no matter how slight, satisfied the business use requirement.

2. The UTSA discarded the business use requisite by requiring that the trade secret must "derive[] independent economic value actual or potential," while the Restatement (Third) of Unfair Competition indicates that the trade secret must be "sufficiently valuable . . . to afford an actual or potential economic advantage over others."

3. The notes to the Restatement (Third) of Unfair Competition state that the economic advantage does not have to be great, only that it must be "more than trivial." This relaxed standard avoids problems during the R&D stage of product development when a company is not actually "using" the trade secrets in a commercial sense. Restatement (Third) of Unfair Competition § 39 cmt. *e*. Elimination of the "use" requirement also effectively eliminates any potential argument that so-called "negative information" cannot be protected as a trade secret.

4. There are two related and offbeat California opinions deciding whether the Church of Scientology could protect its trade secrets. In 1986, the Ninth Circuit rejected the notion that a spiritual use of the church's secrets qualified them as protectable trade secrets where the church failed to allege a "competitive market advantage" in *Religious Technology Center v. Wollersheim*, 796 F.2d 1076, 1091 (9th Cir. 1986). Three years later, however, the same court reached an opposite result after the church was allowed to amend its complaint to allege use of the secrets in the church's business. *See Religious Tech.Ctr. v. Scott*, 869 F.2d 1306, 1308 (9th Cir.1989).

## C. SECRECY

### (1) Relative Secrecy

### KEWANEE OIL CO. v. BICRON CORP.

416 U.S. 470 (1974)

* * *

The subject of a trade secret must be secret, and must not be of public knowledge or of a general knowledge in the trade or business. *B. F. Goodrich Co. v. Wohlgemuth, supra*, 117 Ohio App., at 499, 192 N.E.2d, at 104; *National Tube Co. v. Eastern Tube Co.*, 3 Ohio Cir.Ct.R., N.S., 459, 462 (1902), *aff'd*, 69 Ohio St. 560, 70 N.E. 1127 (1903). This necessary element of secrecy is not lost, however, if the holder of the trade secret reveals the trade secret to another 'in confidence, and under an implied obligation not to use or disclose it.' *Cincinnati Bell Foundry Co. v. Dodds*, 10 Ohio Dec. Reprint 154, 156, 19 Weekly Law Bull. 84 (Super.Ct.1887). These others may include those of the holder's 'employes to whom it is necessary to confide it, in order to apply it to the uses for which it is intended.' *National Tube Co. v. Eastern Tube Co, supra*, 3 Ohio Cir.Ct.R., N.S., at 462. Often the recipient of confidential knowledge of the subject of a trade secret is a licensee of its holder. *See Lear, Inc. v. Adkins, 395 U.S. 653, 89 S.Ct. 1902, 23 L.Ed.2d 610 (1969).*

* * *

### SMITH v. DRAVO CORP.

203 F.2d 369 (7th Cir. 1953)

In the early 1940s Leathem D. Smith, now deceased, began toying with an idea which, he believed, would greatly facilitate the ship and shore handling and transportation of cargoes. As he was primarily engaged in the shipbuilding business, it was quite natural that his thinking was chiefly concerned with water transportation and dock handling. Nevertheless his overall plan encompassed rail shipping as well. He envisioned construction of ships especially designed to carry their cargo in uniformly sized steel freight containers. These devices (which, it appears, were the crux of his idea) were: equipped with high doors at one end; large enough for a man to enter easily; weather and pilfer proof; and bore collapsible legs, which (1) served to lock them (a) to the deck of the ship by fitting into recesses in the deck, or (b) to each other, when stacked, by reason of receiving sockets located in the upper four corners of each container, and (2) allowed sufficient clearance between deck and container or container and container for the facile insertion of a fork of a lift tractor, and (3) were equipped with lifting eyelets, which, together with a specially designed hoist, made possible placement of the containers upon or removal from a ship, railroad car or truck, while filled with cargo. The outer dimensions of the devices were such that they would fit compactly in standard gauge North American railroad cars, or narrow gauge South American trains, and in the holds of most water vessels.

World War II effectually prevented Smith from developing his conception much beyond the idea stage. Nevertheless blue prints were drawn in 1943, and in 1944, as a result of considerable publicity in trade journals and addresses delivered by Smith before trade associations, Agwilines, one of the principal New York ship operators, displayed great interest in the proposals. Certain refined features, particularly in dimensions and folding legs, were the result of discussions between Smith and Agwilines' officials.

In 1945 production started, and in the fall of that year twelve containers were used by Agwilines in an experimental run. Relative success was experienced, with the result that, by the spring of 1946, Brodin Lines, Grace Lines, Delta Lines and Stockard, in addition to Agwilines, were leasing Safeway containers. (Leathem D. Smith Shipbuilding Company was the owner of the design and manufactured the containers. Safeway Container Corporation purchased the finished containers from the shipbuilding company and leased them to shippers.)

During this period the containers were occasionally seen on the docks. However, in view of their limited number (100) this was far from an every day occurrence. Further more, the details of their construction could not be ascertained by casual, distant appraisal. But, in the quest for acceptance, some minor construction details were revealed in the publicity material distributed throughout the shipping trade, including: the outer dimensions, cubic and weight capacities, placement of the lifting lugs, stacking sockets, double doors and the fact that the legs were folding. Three dimensional perspective illustrations demonstrated the use of the containers.

Up until this time the devices were of a 'knock-down' variety, i.e., they could be taken apart when not in use, thus enabling the user to conserve storage space when hauling a cargo for which they were not adapted. However, in the spring of 1946, having determined that return cargoes for which the containers could be employed were generally available, and that the cost of erecting and dismantling and empty 'knock-down' was greater than the cost of the hold space occupied by an empty container, the design was altered slightly so that future containers would be rigidly constructed. The first of the rigid type was placed in use in early 1947.

On June 23, 1946, Smith died in a sailing accident. The need for cash for inheritance tax purposes prompted his estate to survey his holdings for disposable assets. It was decided that the container business should be sold. Devices in process were completed but no work on new ones was started.

Defendant was interested in the Safeway container, primarily, it appears, for use by its subsidiary, the Union Barge Lines. In October 1946 it contacted Agwilines seeking information. It watched a loading operation in which Agwilines used the box. At approximately the same time, defendant approached the shipbuilding company and inquired as to the possibility of purchase of a number of the containers. It was told to communicate with Cowan, plaintiffs' eastern representative. This it did, and, on October 29, 1946, in Pittsburgh, Cowan met with defendant's officials to discuss the proposed sale of Safeways. But, as negotiations progressed, defendant demonstrated an interest in the entire container development. Thus, what started as a meeting to discuss the purchase of individual containers ended in the possible foundation for a sale of the entire business.

Based upon this display of interest, Cowan sent detailed information to defendant concerning the business. This included: (1) patent applications for both the 'knock-down' and 'rigid' crates; (2) blue prints of both designs; (3) a miniature Safeway container; (4) letters of inquiry from possible users; (5) further correspondence with prospective users. In addition, defendant's representatives journeyed to Sturgeon Bay, Wisconsin, the home of the shipbuilding company, and viewed the physical plant, inventory and manufacturing operation.

Plaintiffs quoted a price of $150,000 plus a royalty of $10 per unit. This was rejected. Subsequent offers of $100,000 and $75,000 with royalties of $10 per container were also rejected. Negotiations continued until January 30, 1947, at which time defendant finally rejected plaintiffs' offer.

On January 31, 1947 defendant announced to Agwilines that it 'intended to design and produce a shipping container of the widest possible utility' for 'coastal steamship application . . . (and) use . . . on the inland rivers and . . . connecting highway and rail carriers.' Development of the project moved rapidly, so that by February 5, 1947 defendant had set up a stock order for a freight container which was designed, by use of plaintiffs' patent applications, so as to avoid any claim of infringement. One differing feature was the use of skids and recesses running the length of the container, rather than legs and sockets as employed in plaintiffs' design. However, Agwilines rejected this design, insisting on an adaptation of plaintiffs' idea. In short defendant's final product incorporated many, if not all, of the features of plaintiffs' design. So conceived, it was accepted by the trade to the extent that, by March 1948, defendant had sole some 500 containers. Many of these sales were made to firms who had shown considerable prior interest in plaintiffs' design and had been included in the prospective users disclosed to defendant.

One particular feature of defendant's container differed from plaintiffs: its width was four inches less. As a result plaintiffs' product became obsolete. Their container could not be used interchangeably with defendant's; they ceased production. Consequently the prospects of disposing of the entire operation vanished.

The foregoing is the essence of plaintiffs' cause of action. Stripped of surplusage, the averment is that defendant obtained, through a confidential relationship, knowledge of plaintiffs' secret designs, plans and prospective customers, and then wrongfully breached that confidence by using the information to its own advantage and plaintiffs' detriment.

* * *

The continued secrecy of the construction plans presents a different question. The District Court entered the following finding of fact: '. . . the record shows that Plaintiffs had published to the world, through public uses of the containers and unrestricted publications by circulars and in trade magazines, complete information concerning the subject-matter with which the material (the patent applications and plans) . . . was concerned.' From this the court concluded that no secrets were confidentially disclosed to defendant.

The publicity material did not, in any way, disclose plaintiffs' design. The outward dimensions were revealed, and the fact that the container employed large double doors, lifting eyelets, stacking sockets and folding legs was publicized. But this was not equivalent to a disclosure of the structural design, the engineering details, of either the container as a whole or its various working parts. These could be obtained only by careful inspection of the article and the drawings. Therefore, in this respect the finding of fact that plaintiffs had, through unrestricted publications in trade magazines and circulars, 'Published . . . complete information concerning the subject', was clearly erroneous and must be set aside.

There is no dispute that 100 of plaintiffs' products had been in public use at the time of the communication. There is, however, serious debate over the legal consequences of this fact. The lower court, in refusing plaintiffs recovery, applied the following conclusion of law: 'There can be no confidential disclosure where, as here, the alleged novel container was being manufactured and sold. . . . and all information concerning its construction was available from an inspection of the container.' Certain cases appear to give support to this broad statement. *See, e.g., Sandlin v. Johnson, 8 Cir., 141 F.2d 660; Northup v. Reish*, 7 Cir., 200 F.2d 924; *Carver v. Harr, 132 N.J.Eq. 207, 27 A.2d 895.* But, close examination reveals that the inquiry is much deeper than whether 'all information . . . was available from an inspection of the containers.'

As a starting point we must look again to Pennsylvania for our guide. In *Pressed Steel Car Co. v. Standard Steel Car Co.*, 210 Pa. 464, 60 A. 4, 7, plaintiff sought to protect its secret construction design for railroad cars. These plans had been obtained by defendant through a known breach of confidence. It was urged by defendant that because it could have obtained the design from an inspection of the car (which was in public use) its use of knowledge gained through improper means would be condoned. In short, defendant suggested, as does defendant here, that the existence of a lawful means of acquiring the information precluded recovery for the employment of unlawful means. The court said:

'. . . these engineers and draftsmen . . . should have been able to measure the cars made by the company, and to produce in a short time detailed and practical drawings from which the cars could be constructed. They did not do this, for the obvious reason that blue prints of drawings were available and were accurate. . . .'

The court then affirmed recovery for the plaintiff.

Thus, Pennsylvania will not deny recovery merely because the design could have been obtained through inspection. Rather, the inquiry in that jurisdiction appears to be: How did defendant learn of plaintiffs' design? And this, we regard as the proper test. It recognizes the very nature of the type of wrong with which we are here concerned. Confidential business information is not given protection merely as a reward to its accumulator. If the creator is entitled to reward it is available to him in the patent and copyright statutes. Nims, Unfair Competition and Trade Marks, Sec. 142. Instead our function is that of condemning 'the employment of improper means to procure the trade secret.' Restatement, Torts, Sec. 757, comment. Those who gain their information improperly are brought to book in recognition of 'the general principle that intentionally inflicted harm is actionable unless privileged.' Protection and Use of Trade Secrets, 64 Harv.L.Rev. 976.

It is unquestionably lawful for a person to gain possession, through proper means, of his competitor's product and, through inspection and analysis, create a duplicate, unless, of course, the item is patented. But the mere fact that such lawful acquisition is available does not mean that he may, through a breach of confidence, gain the information in usable form and escape the efforts of inspection and analysis. 'The fact that a trade secret is of such a nature that it can be discovered by experimentation or other fair and lawful means does not deprive its owner of the right to protection from those who would secure possession of it by unfair means.' Nims, Unfair Competition and Trade Marks, Sec. 148.

This text citation is the distillate of many judicial decisions. Thus, in *A. O. Smith Corp. v. Petroleum Iron Works Co.*, 6 Cir., 73 F.2d 531, 538, the court said: 'The mere fact that the means by which a discovery is made are obvious . . . cannot . . . advantage the competitor who by unfair means, or as the beneficiary of a broken faith, obtains the desired knowledge without himself paying the price in labor, money, or machines expended by the discoverer.' And in *Shellmar Products Co. v. Allen-Qualley Co.*, 7 Cir., 36 F.2d 623, 625, this court announced: 'Whether it would have been possible to have discovered and purchased the Olsen patent, without the information disclosed to appellant in confidence, it is not necessary to determine, because it is clear from the record that by a breach of confidence the information was disclosed and used as a basis for the search that was made.' And in *Tabor v. Hoffman*, 118 N.Y. 30, 23 N.E. 12, 13, this is the language: 'But, because this discovery may be possible by fair means, it would not justify a discovery by unfair means . . . .'

It is, therefore, our conclusion, that the District Court applied an erroneous conclusion of law to the facts at hand. Here was no simple device, widely circulated, the construction of which was ascertainable at a glance. [Citations omitted.] If such were the case our problem would be simple. Instead we are concerned with a relatively complex apparatus; designed to carry large and heavy amounts of cargo; proper inspection of which was, perhaps, accessible to defendant but, in no way shown to have been made. Under such circumstances the District Court's conclusion that plaintiffs no longer possessed a trade secret at the time of their negotiations with defendant was erroneous.

## STEWART & STEVENSON SERVICES, INC. v. SERV-TECH, INC.

879 S.W.2d 89 (Tex. App. 1994)

* * *

The subject matter of a trade secret must be secret. Matters of public knowledge or of general knowledge in an industry cannot be appropriated by one as his secret.

Substantially, a trade secret is known only in the particular business in which it is used. It is not requisite that only the proprietor of the business know it. He may, without losing his protection, communicate it to employees involved in its use. He may likewise communicate it to others pledged to secrecy. Others may also know of it independently, as, for example, when they have discovered the process or formula by independent invention and are keeping it secret. Nevertheless, a substantial element of secrecy must exist so that, except by the use of improper means, there would be difficulty in acquiring the information.

In connection with the issue of "improper use or disclosure of confidential information," the trial judge instructed the jury:

"Confidential information" — Although given information is not a trade secret, one who receives the information in a confidential relation or discovers it by improper means may be under some duty not to disclose or use that information. Because of the confidential relation or the impropriety of the means of discovery, he may be compelled to go to other sources for the information. The duty not to use or disclose "confidential information" may be imposed by employment or contract where one person trusts and relies upon the other. Such information may be a trade secret or similar specific information received under moral or business circumstances that would reasonably require confidentiality. This is determined by the actual facts of the relationship.[3]

All three appellants assign points of error to the trial court's submission of question 7 and the accompanying definition of confidential information, quoted above, because there is no cause of action for misappropriation of confidential information. Question 7 inquired:

Did any defendant engage in an improper use or disclosure of confidential information of Serv-Tech that was a proximate cause of damage to Serv-Tech?

"Improper use or disclosure" means one who discloses or uses another's "confidential information" and:

(a) he discovered the confidential information by improper means; or

(b) his disclosure or use constitutes a breach of confidence reposed in him by the other in disclosing the confidential information to him; or

(c) he learned the confidential information from a third person with notice of facts that it was confidential information and that the third person discovered it by improper means or that the third person's disclosure of it was otherwise a breach of his duty to the other; or

(d) he learned the confidential information with notice of the facts that it was confidential information and that its disclosure was made to him by mistake.

The jury answered "yes" for all three appellants. Thus, the trial court, in submitting the question and the accompanying instructions, created a cause of action for misappropriation of confidential information by changing the requirement in § 757, subsections (a) through (d) that the "trade secret" be *secret* to a requirement that the matter be only "confidential information."

Appellee argues that there is a cause of action for disclosing confidential information even though the information "is not legally a trade secret," citing RESTATEMENT (First) OF TORTS § 757 (1939). Appellee quotes from comment *b* to the section, as follows:

*Information not a trade secret.* Although given information is not a trade secret, one who receives the information in a confidential relation or discovers it by improper means may be under some duty not to disclose or use that information.

---

[3] [3] The first two sentences of this instruction were taken from the last paragraph of comment b to § 757. The source of the final three sentences is unknown.

Because of the confidential relation or the impropriety of the means of discovery, he may be compelled to go to other sources for the information. As stated in Comment *a*, even the rule stated in this Section rests upon abuse of confidence or impropriety in learning the secret. Such abuse or impropriety may exist also where the information is not a trade secret and may be equally a basis for liability.

We do not regard this comment as authority for appellees contention for several reasons. First § 757 provides for liability *only if* the trade secret is *secret.* Second, appellee's quote from comment *b* conspicuously omits the next sentence: "The rules relating to the liability for duties arising from *confidential relationships generally are not within the scope* of the Restatement of this Subject." (emphasis supplied) Thus, what appellee quotes as a Restatement Rule is not a rule at all — it is merely a statement that a duty under the stated facts *may* arise, but that the subject is not covered by the section. Third, earlier on in comment *b*, from which appellee's quote is taken, the comment plainly requires that "The subject matter of a trade secret must be secret." Fourth, in comment *m* to § 757, it is stated that "The actor is subject to liability under this clause only if the information is secret." Finally, we are not directed to any case, and our own research has not revealed any, where the quoted portion of comment *b* has been adopted or even quoted. Thus we reject appellee's argument that the Restatement of Torts provides a basis for a cause of action for misappropriation of confidential information that is not secret.

Next, appellee argues that "Texas courts have recognized liability for misuse of confidential information in addition to liability for misuse of trade secrets,"

* * *

The three appellants, on the other hand, contend there is no cause of action for misappropriation of non-secret confidential information, and they cite a number of cases which they assert support such position.

From all the cases we have been able to find, it appears to be well settled that in order to be entitled to common-law protection, a trade secret must be *secret.*

* * *

Appellee apparently has no dispute with this established principle and, as to the trade secrets issue quoted above, the trial court correctly instructed the jury that the matter must be secret.

The definition of "trade secrets" is very broad and loose language used by some courts have appeared to lessen the requirement of secrecy in some instances. On March 12, 1958, the supreme court decided two trade secret cases: *K & G Oil Tool & Service Co., Inc. v. G & G Fishing Tool Service*, 314 S.W.2d 782 (Tex.1958) and *Hyde Corporation v. Huffines*, 314 S.W.2d 763 (Tex.1958). These cases are the bedrock for trade secret causes of action in Texas. As above pointed out, each of the cases involved an actual *trade secret* that was eventually patented. However, prior to the issuance of letters patent the defendant in each of the cases, as a result of a confidential relationship, learned the details of the trade secret and appropriated the secret to its own use. In *Hyde*, the court stated:

If these details as to construction were received by Hyde Corporation in confidence and that company later attempted to exploit them to Huffines' injury through a breach of confidence, an action lies and *it matters not whether the suit be designated as a "trade secret" case or as a suit for breach of confidence*, which is a term commonly used by Huffines in describing his claim for relief. (emphasis added)

314 S.W.2d at 777. And, in *K & G Oil Tool*, the court stated:

According to the jury's findings, which are not attached, G & G did not learn how to make the Kirby tool or a device similar thereto by observing it in an assembled or unbroken condition but learned of its internal proportions, qualities and mechanisms by taking it apart despite an agreement that it would not do so. *We have here the violation of a confidence and the breach of a contract.* (emphasis added)

314 S.W.2d at 787. The supreme court's "breach" or "violation" of *confidence* terminology has been changed by some of the courts of appeal to "confidential information."

[A number of Texas intermediate appellate court cases were discussed by the court]

While each of these cases, *Welex, Jeter, Richardson, American Precision* and *Dannenbaum*, refer to the basic cause of action as involving "confidential information," all the cases relied upon *Hyde* and/or *K & G Oil Tool.* And each of the cases required that the information be secret or at least substantially secret. Here, however, the trial court neither instructed the jury that the "confidential information" must be secret or substantially secret nor did he submit an inquiry for the jury to make such a finding. From all these cases we conclude that there is no cause of action for misappropriation of confidential information that is not either secret or, at least *substantially* secret.

Since all three appellants objected to the failure of the court to instruct the jury that the confidential information must be secret, a deemed finding to supply this essential element cannot be made to support the judgment. [Citation omitted.] § & S's second and fifth points of error are sustained; OMSI's second point of error is sustained and Ohmstede's second point of error is sustained.

* * *

## NOTES AND QUESTIONS:

1. The *Kewanee Oil* opinion indicates that a trade secret does not have to be absolutely secret, but can be disclosed to others when there is "an implied obligation not to use or disclose it." 416 U.S. at 475 (citation and internal quotation marks omitted). Obviously, the court did not intend to exclude agreements with express non-disclosure provisions or employment agreements containing express secrecy obligations like those signed by Harshaw's former employees.

2. Restatement (Second) of Torts § 757 cmt. b (1965-79) listed the following factors to be considered in determining whether a trade secret exists:

> (1) the extent to which the information is known outside of his business; (2) the extent to which it is known by employees and others involved in his business; (3) the extent of measures taken by him to guard the secrecy of the information; (4) the value of the information to him and his competitors; (5) the amount of effort or money expended by him in developing the information; (6) the ease or difficulty with which the information could be properly acquired or duplicated by others.

These factors were carried over to the RESTATEMENT (THIRD) OF UNFAIR COMPETITION § 39 Rep. Note, p. 444.

3. The RESTATEMENT (THIRD) OF UNFAIR COMPETITION also focuses on whether the "information is not readily ascertainable through proper means and hence is eligible for protection as a trade secret." § 39 cmt. f, p. 432. Various types of circumstantial evidence can be used to establish the requisite level of secrecy:

> [p]recautions taken by the claimant to preserve the secrecy of the information . . . the willingness of licensees to pay for disclosure of the secret, unsuccessful attempts by the defendant or others to duplicate the information by proper means, and resort by a defendant to improper means of acquisition." RESTATEMENT (THIRD) OF UNFAIR COMPETITION, pp. 432-3.

The RESTATEMENT (THIRD) OF UNFAIR COMPETITION also observes that "[w]hen a defendant has engaged in egregious misconduct in order to acquire the information, the inference that the information is sufficiently inaccessible to qualify for protection as a trade secret is particularly strong." *Id.* at 433. This latter comment leads to the mildly cynical observation that motive is an extremely important factor in trade secret cases. Seemingly, the more egregious the alleged misappropriator's conduct, the less secret the information has to be in order for a court to protect it.

4. Absolute secrecy is not necessary in order to protect a trade secret. As illustrated in *Smith v. Dravo Corp.*, 203 F.3d 369 (7th Cir.1953), limited, nonconfidential disclosures can be made to others as long as the information does not become generally known or readily ascertainable to competitors. *See Metallurgical Indus., Inc. v. Fourtek, Inc.*, 790 F.2d 1195, 1200 (5th Cir. 1986) (disclosures that "were not public announcements" and made to two potential customers with whom plaintiff did not have a confidential relationship to "further [plaintiff's] economic interests" did not destroy secrecy). Does this relatively loose standard make sense? To what extent do you believe defendant's blatant disregard for the trade secret owner's rights in *Dravo Corp.* might have contributed to the decision?

5. How does the decision in *Stewart & Stevenson Services, Inc. v. Serv-Tech, Inc.*, 879 S.W.2d 89 (Tex.App.1994), fit into this discussion? Is the court's decision based on a simple technical error in formulating the jury instructions, or is there a broader principle at play? Could RESTATEMENT (SECOND) OF TORTS § 757 be read to support liability for misappropriation of "confidential information" that is not "a trade secret"? Would the same result occur under the rule stated in the RESTATEMENT (THIRD) OF UNFAIR COMPETITION?

## (2) Efforts to Protect Trade Secrets

### USM CORP. v. MARSON FASTENER CORP.

204 U.S.P.Q. 233 (Mass. 1979)

The USM Corporation (USM) seeks an accounting for the alleged misappropriation of a trade secret contained in a machine used in the manufacture of blind rivets. In addition, USM sought relief from each of the defendants by reason of their "wrongful acts" in misappropriating confidential information.

To defeat the claim of misappropriation of a trade secret, the defendants alleged that USM had not kept its information secret. Hearings were held before a master; one of the master's conclusions was that although information embodied in the machine was "of a nature which would constitute it a trade secret if protected, [it] was not sufficiently guarded by USM to entitle USM to recover anything from the defendants." A judge confirmed the master's report, ruling that "the Master's ultimate finding with respect to the adequacy of the measures taken by USM to guard the secrecy of the USM machine is supported by the evidence before the Master, consistent with his subsidiary and other general findings and correct as a matter of law." The judge then ordered the entry of judgment dismissing the complaint with prejudice. USM appeals. We allowed USM's application for direct appellate review.

The main thrust of USM's appeal is that it did pursue a course of conduct reasonably designed to preserve the secrecy of its trade secret. USM contends that it was error to conclude from the master's subsidiary findings that its complaint should be dismissed. USM avers that in any event it was improper to dismiss the complaint since the master's report indicates that the defendants acquired the information improperly. See Restatement of Torts § 759 (1939). We have reviewed the master's report and conclude that it was error for the judge to dismiss the complaint.

We summarize the subsidiary findings of fact on which the master and the judge based their conclusions. Since 1950, USM has engaged in the manufacture and sale of blind rivets. In 1954, employees of USM began development of a new type of blind rivet assembly machine. Development of the machine was completed in 1959.

The USM blind rivet assembly machine ("USM machine" or "machine") is able "to provide a means of reliable and rapid assembly of mandrels and rivet bodies into rivets." USM claims that the combination and relationship of various parts of the machine, along with certain features incorporated into the machine, are the trade secrets and confidential information which the defendants have misappropriated.

The master ultimately found that the development of the USM machine involved considerable time, effort and expense, that the development of the machine was relatively difficult, and that its "combination [of features] was unique and effective when devised and . . . did not constitute a matter of public knowledge or of general knowledge in the industry." Therefore, the master properly concluded that the USM machine was of an appropriate nature to qualify it as a trade secret.

The master also found that Joe Cooper, Irving Cooper, and Louis Lewis were the officers and directors of corporations which distributed USM blind rivets for a period of approximately one year. In 1961, after being denied an exclusive distributionship, the defendants decided to manufacture blind rivets in competition with USM, but they were dissatisfied with the performance of their own blind rivet assembly machines. Eventually, the defendants were able to construct a blind rivet assembly machine like the USM machine because the defendants hired Frank Lahnston, a former junior engineer at the USM Shelton plant and provided him with "a group of about 100 [blue] prints without identifying title blocks but which Lahnston recognized as prints of USM [parts] drawings of the USM Machine." By 1964, Lahnston had succeeded in constructing for the defendants a blind rivet assembly machine which was "substantially the same as the USM Machines."

However, the master concluded that USM was not entitled to claim trade secret protection for its machine because USM had taken inadequate precautions to preserve the secrecy of the USM machine. To reach this result, the master focused on the security measures taken at the USM plant in Beverly, where the USM machine was developed, and at the USM plant in Shelton, where the USM machines were in operation. We therefore summarize the master's findings relating to USM's security measures in some detail.

Between 1954 and 1959 USM carried out the development of its machine at the Beverly plant. The Beverly plant was fenced, and employees and visitors entered the plant through guarded gates. Once inside the plant, employees were expected to remain in their immediate work areas. Supervisors questioned any employee who was discovered outside the employee's work area. While employees were not to remove objects from the plant without permission, guards did not generally inspect employees' brief-cases or lunch boxes as they left the plant.

Visitors to the plant were logged in and out. They were also required to state their business and to wait in a designated reception area. At no time were visitors permitted to walk unescorted through the plant.

During the period of their development, the USM machines were located in a relatively isolated area of the Beverly plant, but USM employed no special security precautions to prevent access to the machines. At all times both during and after their development, USM treated the machines as items of factory equipment. "The term 'factory equipment' defines machines and other equipment developed or adapted by USM to be used internally in production of items to be sold to others and not themselves to be sold or otherwise made available to third persons."

All drawings and blueprints of parts for the USM machines were kept in the engineering department of the Beverly plant, along with 250,000 other drawings of factory equipment. No assembly drawings were ever made for the USM machine. Whenever a print of a particular drawing was required for work being done outside the engineering department, the employee needing the print was to complete a written production order. After receiving the work order, engineering employees stamped the print with the work order number and the phrase "for the above only" before delivering the print to the employee. However, while some USM blueprints were stamped "confidential," no drawings, blueprints, or prints of the USM machine were stamped "confidential" prior to the filing of the complaint in this action.

After USM completed the development of the USM machine, some of these machines were installed at the USM plant in Shelton, Connecticut. With a few variations, USM security precautions at the Shelton plant were similar to those in force at the Beverly plant.

Employee entrances at the Shelton plant were unguarded, and employees did not wear badges. All doors were locked during hours when the plant was not operating, and any employee entering the plant outside of regular working hours was required to have a pass and to be logged in by the watchman.

Visitors to the Shelton plant were always logged in and waited in a reception room which was separated from the production area by an opaque partition. Visitors entering the production area were expected to be escorted at all times.

The USM machines at the Shelton plant were located in the production area of the plant. They were not separated from other plant operations and were visible from the shipping room doors. A set of reproducible drawings for the USM machine was kept at the Shelton plant. The drawings were located in the office of the engineering department, which was separated from the production area by a lockable door.

USM conducted occasional plant tours at Shelton. The tours, however, did not open the plant to the general public and were conducted for the families of employees and for distributors of USM products.

All supervisory, technical, and engineering employees at the Shelton plant signed nondisclosure agreements in early 1963. Similar agreements were signed by research personnel at the Beverly plant.

USM generally did not seek patent protection for any items of factory equipment and sought no such protection for the USM machine or for any of its components. There was also no written policy specifically prohibiting disclosure of information concerning factory equipment, and prior to November, 1963, no USM officer published a formal statement identifying the USM machine or its components as confidential information.

The master concluded that these security precautions did not entitle USM to claim trade secret protection for the USM machine, measured against a standard of conduct which required USM to "exercise a degree of eternal vigilance or pursue an active course of conduct sufficient to maintain the secrecy of the information embodied in the USM Machine."

USM argues that the master's subsidiary findings of fact establish that USM took reasonable precautions to maintain the secrecy of its information, and that such reasonable precautions are all that are required to entitle a plaintiff to claim trade secret protection for its information. Thus USM asserts that the defendants' use of this information constituted a misappropriation of USM's trade secrets and confidential information for which the defendants should be held liable. We agree.

One who possesses a trade secret and wishes to protect it must act to preserve its secrecy.

* * *

However, where a plaintiff has actively sought to protect its trade secret, the question then becomes whether the protective measures are reasonable. "Reasonable precautions against predatory eyes we may require, but an impenetrable fortress is an unreasonable requirement, and we are not disposed to burden industrial inventors with such a duty in order to protect the fruits of their efforts." *E.I. duPont deNemours & Co. v. Christopher*, 431 F.2d 1012, 1017.

* * *

No general rule may be established to determine whether the security precautions taken by the possessor of a trade secret are reasonable. "Relevant factors to be considered include (1) the existence or absence of an express agreement restricting disclosure, (2) the nature and extent of security precautions taken by the possessor to prevent acquisition of the information by unauthorized third parties, (3) the circumstances under which the information was disclosed . . . to [any] employee to the extent that they give rise to a reasonable inference that further disclosure, without the consent of the possessor, is prohibited, and (4) the degree to which the information has been placed in the public domain or rendered 'readily ascertainable' by the third parties through patent applications or unrestricted product marketing." *Kubik, Inc. v. Hull*, 56 Mich. App. 335, 356, 185 USPQ 391 (1974). Additionally, a court should consider the relationship and the conduct of the parties. We think it appropriate to balance a plaintiff's conduct in maintaining its security measures against the conduct of a defendant in acquiring the information. See Restatement of Torts § 757, Comment b (1939) ("a substantial element of secrecy must exist, so that, except by the use of improper means, there would be difficulty in acquiring the information").

The master's subsidiary findings reveal that the information which USM seeks to protect is embodied in certain features of the USM machine, including the internal configuration and arrangement of various component parts. Because this information relates to the machine itself, the marketing of the blind rivets produced by the machine would not disclose the information which USM seeks to protect. Disclosure of this information requires either extended access to the machine itself or access to the detailed parts drawings.

USM required supervisory, technical, and research personnel, including the defendant Lahnston, to sign nondisclosure agreements. See note 8 supra. While the nondisclosure agreements did not list the particular information which USM considered secret, such specificity is not required to put employees on notice that their work involves access to trade secrets and confidential information.

* * *

In the work environment at USM, where employees are on notice that their work may involve access to trade secrets and confidential information, there can be little question that the USM employees knew or should have known that detailed parts drawings and blueprints for factory equipment were considered confidential by their employer. "[I]t is well settled that detailed manufacturing drawings . . . are prima facie trade secrets." *A.H. Emery Co. v. Marcan Prods. Corp.*, 389 F.2d 11, 16, 156 USPQ 529, 531-532 (2d Cir.), *cert. denied*, 393 U.S. 835, 159 USPQ 799 (1968). *See Schulenburg v. Signatrol, Inc.*, 33 Ill. 2d 379, 386-388, 147 USPQ 167 (1965), *cert.*

*denied*, 383 U.S. 959, 148 USPQ 772 (1966). It is not fatal that the blueprints and parts drawings were not labeled "confidential" or "secret" or that USM had not expressly informed its employees that these parts drawings were considered secret by USM. [Citations omitted.]

Similarly, the plant security precautions taken by USM were sufficient to exclude the general public from the production areas of USM's plants, thereby denying access to USM factory equipment, including the USM machine. The fact that USM conducted escorted tours for employees' families and USM product distributors, including certain defendants, does not militate against a finding that USM denied public access to the USM machine. *Compare Plant Indus., Inc. v. Coleman*, 287 F.Supp. 636, 643, 159 USPQ 651, 656-657 (C.D. Cal. 1968) (tours by women's clubs and customers' representatives do not constitute failure to maintain secrecy) and *Franke v. Wiltschek*, 209 F.2d 493, 99 USPQ 431 (2d Cir. 1953) (defendants' tour of plant while negotiating to sell plaintiffs' products does not destroy secrecy), with *Motorola, Inc. v. Fairchild Camera & Instrument Corp.*, 366 F.Supp. 1173, 1186, 177 USPQ 614, 622 (D. Ariz. 1973) (security inadequate where competitors toured plant, operated "secret" machine and "observed its 'secret' process in a separate microscope placed there for this purpose") and *Hamilton Mfg. Co. v. Tubbs Mfg. Co.*, 216 Fed. 401, 404 (W.D. Mich. 1908) (public generally not excluded from production area). [Citations omitted.]

We do not require the possessor of a trade secret to take heroic measures to preserve its secrecy. Rather, "if the person entitled to a trade secret wishes to have its exclusive use in his own business, he must not fail to take all proper and reasonable steps to keep it secret. He cannot lie back and do nothing to preserve its essential secret quality." *J.T.Healy & Son v. James A. Murphy & Son*, 357 Mass. 728, 738, 166 USPQ 443 (1970). [Citation omitted.] The question whether a plaintiff has taken "all proper and reasonable steps" depends on the circumstances of each case, considering the nature of the information sought to be protected *as well as the conduct of the parties.* [Citations omitted.]

Applying this standard, we denied trade secret protection in Healy because the plaintiff had made a conscious policy decision to do nothing to safeguard the confidentiality of its manufacturing processes. *J.T.Healy & Son v. James A. Murphy & Son, supra* at 736-738, 166 USPQ 443. In Healy, the employees were never informed that any of the manufacturing processes were considered secret; employees were not required to sign nondisclosure agreements; the plant was not partitioned into sections; and employees engaged in other work could plainly see the two "secret processes" in operation. *Id.* at 736-737, 166 USPQ 443. The plaintiff in Healy, other than excluding the general public from the manufacturing plant, took no security precautions whatever. *See id.* at 738-739, 166 USPQ 443.

By contrast, in *Eastern Marble Prods. Corp. v. Roman Marble, Inc.*, 372 Mass. 835, 204 USPQ 229 (1977), trade secret protection was afforded a plaintiff who not only *enforced* a separation of the manufacturing area of the plant from the public area but also required all manufacturing employees "to sign an agreement not to disclose the methods and procedures involved in the [plaintiff's] manufacturing processes." Id. While the nondisclosure agreements did not specifically refer to the particular manufacturing processes claimed as trade secrets, we observed that "this agreement by its terms included all the proprietary and secret information involved in the manufacturing process. Such an agreement cannot be disregarded as an empty formality. At the very least it put the employees on notice that secrets were involved." *Id.*

We think that, considering the character of the information which USM sought to protect, the steps taken by USM to preserve the secrecy of its trade secret were reasonable. [Citation omitted.] Until the defendants acquired a set of USM machine parts drawings and a former USM employee, the defendants' efforts to construct a satisfactory blind rivet assembly machine had been unsuccessful. In short, USM's "efforts at secrecy, like the process itself, met the basic criterion of success." *Space Aero Prods. Co. v.R.E. Darling Co.*, 238 Md. 93, 112, 145 USPQ 356, *cert. denied*, 382 U.S. 843, 147 USPQ 541 (1965). *See* Restatement of Torts § 757, Comment b (1939).

Since we have concluded that USM took sufficient reasonable steps to preserve the secrecy of the information embodied in the USM machine, and that USM is entitled to claim this information as a trade secret, the judge's dismissal of the complaint in this action must be *reversed.*

We think it necessary to comment on the judge's action in dismissing the complaint without ruling on the master's finding that Cooper had utilized improper means to procure information about the USM machine. Although we need not base our conclusion on the master's finding of impropriety on the part of Joe Cooper, we will not condone such conduct by our silence.

A plaintiff who may not claim trade secret protection either because it failed to take reasonable steps to preserve its secrecy or because the information, while confidential, is only "business information," may still be entitled to some relief against one who improperly procures such information. The law puts its imprimatur on fair dealing, good faith, and fundamental honesty. Courts condemn conduct which fails to reflect these minimum accepted moral values by penalizing such conduct whenever it occurs. [Citations omitted.]

## ROCKWELL GRAPHIC SYSTEMS, INC. v. DEV INDUSTRIES, INC.

925 F.2d 174 (7th Cir. 1991)

POSNER, CIRCUIT JUDGE.

This is a suit for misappropriation of trade secrets. Rockwell Graphic Systems, a manufacturer of printing presses used by newspapers, and of parts for those presses, brought the suit against DEV Industries, a competing manufacturer, and against the president of DEV, who used to be employed by Rockwell. The case is in federal court by virtue of the RICO ("Racketeer Influenced and Corrupt Organizations") statute. 18 U.S.C. §§ 1961 *et seq.* The predicate acts required for liability under RICO are acts of misappropriation (and related misconduct, such as alleged breaches of fiduciary duty) committed by the individual defendant, Fleck, and by another former employee of Rockwell and present employee of DEV, Peloso. These acts are alleged to violate Illinois law, and in pendent counts Rockwell seeks to impose liability for them directly under that law as well as indirectly under

RICO. The district judge granted summary judgment for the defendants upon the recommendation of a magistrate who concluded that Rockwell had no trade secrets because it had failed to take reasonable precautions to maintain secrecy. Therefore there had been no misappropriation, which in turn was the foundation for the predicate acts; so the RICO count had to be dismissed. With the federal claim out of the case, the district judge relinquished jurisdiction over the pendent counts, resulting in a dismissal of the entire case. 730 F.Supp. 171 (N.D.Ill.1990).

When we said that Rockwell manufactures both printing presses and replacement parts for its presses — "wear parts" or "piece parts," they are called — we were speaking approximately. Rockwell does not always manufacture the parts itself. Sometimes when an owner of one of Rockwell's presses needs a particular part, or when Rockwell anticipates demand for the part, it will subcontract the manufacture of it to an independent machine shop, called a "vendor" by the parties. When it does this it must give the vendor a "piece part drawing" indicating materials, dimensions, tolerances, and methods of manufacture. Without that information the vendor could not manufacture the part. Rockwell has not tried to patent the piece parts. It believes that the purchaser cannot, either by inspection or by "reverse engineering" (taking something apart in an effort to figure out how it was made), discover how to manufacture the part; to do that you need the piece part drawing, which contains much information concerning methods of manufacture, alloys, tolerances, etc. that cannot be gleaned from the part itself. So Rockwell tries — whether hard enough is the central issue in the case — to keep the piece part drawings secret, though not of course from the vendors; they could not manufacture the parts for Rockwell without the drawings. DEV points out that some of the parts are for presses that Rockwell no longer manufactures. But as long as the presses are in service — which can be a very long time — there is a demand for replacement parts.

Rockwell employed Fleck and Peloso in responsible positions that gave them access to piece part drawings. Fleck left Rockwell in 1975 and three years later joined DEV as its president. Peloso joined DEV the following year after being fired by Rockwell when a security guard caught him removing piece part drawings from Rockwell's plant. This suit was brought in 1984, and pretrial discovery by Rockwell turned up 600 piece part drawings in DEV's possession, of which 100 were Rockwell's. DEV claimed to have obtained them lawfully, either from customers of Rockwell or from Rockwell vendors, contrary to Rockwell's claim that either Fleck and Peloso stole them when they were employed by it or DEV obtained them in some other unlawful manner, perhaps from a vendor who violated his confidentiality agreement with Rockwell. Thus far in the litigation DEV has not been able to show which customers or vendors lawfully supplied it with Rockwell's piece part drawings.

The defendants persuaded the magistrate and the district judge that the piece part drawings weren't really trade secrets at all, because Rockwell made only perfunctory efforts to keep them secret. Not only were there thousands of drawings in the hands of the vendors; there were thousands more in the hands of owners of Rockwell presses, the customers for piece parts. The drawings held by customers, however, are not relevant. They are not piece part drawings, but assembly drawings. (One piece part drawing in the record is labeled "assembly," but as it contains dimensions, tolerances, and other specifications it is really a piece part drawing, despite the label.) An assembly drawing shows how the parts of a printing press fit together for installation and also how to integrate the press with the printer's other equipment. Whenever Rockwell sells a printing press it gives the buyer assembly drawings as well. These are the equivalent of instructions for assembling a piece of furniture. Rockwell does not claim that they contain trade secrets. It admits having supplied a few piece part drawings to customers, but they were piece part drawings of obsolete parts that Rockwell has no interest in manufacturing and of a safety device that was not part of the press as originally delivered but that its customers were clamoring for; more to the point, none of these drawings is among those that Rockwell claims DEV misappropriated.

The distinction between assembly and piece part drawings is not esoteric. *A.H. Emery Co. v. Marcan Products Corp.*, 268 F.Supp. 289, 300 (S.D.N.Y.1967), aff'd, 389 F.2d 11, 16 (2d Cir.1968), marks it, and along with other cases declares — what is anyway obvious — that a firm's act in making public some of its documents (or part of a document) does not destroy the status as trade secrets of information contained in other documents (or another part of the same document). *Alexander & Alexander, Inc. v. Drayton*, 378 F.Supp. 824, 833 (E.D.Pa.1974), aff'd without opinion, 505 F.2d 729 (3d Cir.1974); *Ecolaire Inc. v. Crissman*, 542 F.Supp. 196, 206 (E.D.Pa.1982); *Laser Industries, Ltd. v. Eder Instrument Co.*, 573 F.Supp. 987, 991 (N.D.Ill.1983). It is immaterial that Rockwell affixed the same legend enjoining the user to confidentiality to its assembly drawings as it did to its piece part drawings. Perhaps thinking of the doctrine of patent misuse (on which see *USM Corp. v. SPS Technologies, Inc.*, 694 F.2d 505, 510–12 (7th Cir.1982), and cases cited there), DEV suggests that if a firm claims trade secret protection for information that is not really secret, the firm forfeits trade secret protection of information that is secret. There is no such doctrine — even the patent misuse doctrine does not decree forfeiture of the patent as the sanction for misuse — and it would make no sense. This is not only because there are any number of innocent explanations for Rockwell's action in "overclaiming" trade secret protection (if that is what it was doing) — such as an excess of caution, uncertainty as to the scope of trade secret protection, concern that clerical personnel will not always be able to distinguish between assembly and piece part drawings at a glance, and the sheer economy of a uniform policy — but also because it would place the owner of trade secrets on the razor's edge. If he stamped "confidential" on every document in sight, he would run afoul of what we are calling (without endorsing) the misuse doctrine. But if he did not stamp confidential on every document he would lay himself open to an accusation that he was sloppy about maintaining secrecy — and in fact DEV's main argument is that Rockwell *was* impermissibly sloppy in its efforts to keep the piece part drawings secret.

On this, the critical, issue, the record shows the following. (Because summary judgment was granted to DEV, we must construe the facts as favorably to Rockwell as is reasonable to do.) Rockwell keeps all its engineering drawings, including both piece part and assembly drawings, in a vault. Access not only to the vault, but also to the building in which it is located, is limited to authorized employees who display identification. These are mainly engineers, of whom Rockwell employs 200. They are required to sign agreements not to disseminate the drawings, or disclose their contents, other than as authorized by the company. An authorized employee who needs a drawing must sign it out from the vault and return it when he has finished with it. But he is permitted to make copies, which he is to destroy when he no longer needs them in his work. The only outsiders allowed to see piece part drawings are the vendors (who are given copies, not originals). They too are required to sign confidentiality agreements, and in addition each drawing is stamped with a legend stating that it contains proprietary material. Vendors, like Rockwell's own engineers, are allowed to make copies for internal working purposes, and although the confidentiality agreement that they sign requires the vendor to return the drawing when the order has been filled, Rockwell does not enforce this requirement. The rationale for not enforcing it is that the vendor will need the drawing if Rockwell reorders the part. Rockwell even permits unsuccessful bidders for a piece part contract to keep the drawings, on the theory that the high bidder this round may be the low bidder the next. But it does consider the ethical standards of a machine shop before making it a vendor, and so far as appears no shop has ever abused the confidence reposed in it.

The mere fact that Rockwell gave piece part drawings to vendors — that is, disclosed its trade secrets to "a limited number of outsiders for a particular purpose" — did not forfeit trade secret protection. *A.H. Emery Co. v. Marcan Products Corp.*, 389 F.2d 11, 16 (2d Cir.1968). On the contrary, such disclosure, which is often necessary to the efficient exploitation of a trade secret, imposes a duty of confidentiality on the part of the person to whom the disclosure is made. *Jones v. Ulrich*, 342 Ill.App. 16, 25–26, 95 N.E.2d 113, 117 (1950); *Crocan Corp. v. Sheller — Globe Corp.*, 385 F.Supp. 251, 253 (N.D.Ill.1974). But with 200 engineers checking out piece part drawings and making copies of them to work from, and numerous vendors receiving copies of piece part drawings and copying them, tens of thousands of copies of these drawings are floating around outside Rockwell's vault, and many of these outside the company altogether. Although the magistrate and the district judge based their conclusion that Rockwell had not made adequate efforts to maintain secrecy in part at least on the irrelevant fact that it took no measures at all to keep its assembly drawings secret, DEV in defending the judgment that it obtained in the district court argues that Rockwell failed to take adequate measures to keep even the piece part drawings secret. Not only did Rockwell not limit copying of those drawings or insist that copies be returned; it did not segregate the piece part drawings from the assembly drawings and institute more secure procedures for the former. So Rockwell could have done more to maintain the confidentiality of its piece part drawings than it did, and we must decide whether its failure to do more was so plain a breach of the obligation of a trade secret owner to make reasonable efforts to maintain secrecy as to justify the entry of summary judgment for the defendants.

The requirement of reasonable efforts has both evidentiary and remedial significance, and this regardless of which of the two different conceptions of trade secret protection prevails. (Both conceptions have footholds in Illinois law, as we shall see.) The first and more common merely gives a remedy to a firm deprived of a competitively valuable secret as the result of an independent legal wrong, which might be conversion or other trespass or the breach of an employment contract or of a confidentiality agreement. Under this approach, because the secret must be taken by improper means for the taking to give rise to liability, Ill.Rev.Stat. ch. 140, ¶¶ 352(a), (b)(1), (2)(A), (B); Restatement of Torts § 757 (1939); *ILG Industries, Inc. v. Scott*, 49 Ill.2d 88, 93, 273 N.E.2d 393, 396 (1971); *Brunswick Corp. v. Outboard Marine Corp.*, 79 Ill.2d 475, 479, 38 Ill.Dec. 781, 783, 404 N.E.2d 205, 207 (1980), the only significance of trade secrecy is that it allows the victim of wrongful appropriation to obtain damages based on the competitive value of the information taken. The second conception of trade secrecy, illustrated by *E.I. duPont de Nemours & Co. v. Christopher*, 431 F.2d 1012 (5th Cir.1970), and in Illinois by Ill.Rev.Stat. ch. 140, ¶ 352(b)(2)(C), and *Schulenburg v. Signatrol, Inc.*, 33 Ill.2d 379, 387–88, 212 N.E.2d 865, 869 (1965), is that "trade secret" picks out a class of socially valuable information that the law should protect even against nontrespassory or other lawful conduct — in *Christopher*, photographing a competitor's roofless plant from the air while not flying directly overhead and hence not trespassing or committing any other wrong independent of the appropriation of the trade secret itself. [citation omotted]

Since, however, the opinion in *Christopher* describes the means used by the defendant as "improper," 431 F.2d at 1015–17, which is also the key to liability under the first, more conventional conception of trade secret protection, it is unclear how distinct the two conceptions really are. It is not as if *Christopher* proscribes *all* efforts to unmask a trade secret. It specifically mentions reverse engineering as a proper means of doing so. *Id.* at 1015. This difference in treatment is not explained, but it may rest on the twofold idea that reverse engineering involves the use of technical skills that we want to encourage, and that anyone should have the right to take apart and to study a product that he has bought.

It should be apparent that the two different conceptions of trade secret protection are better described as different emphases. The first emphasizes the desirability of deterring efforts that have as their sole purpose and effect the redistribution of wealth from one firm to another. The second emphasizes the desirability of encouraging inventive activity by protecting its fruits from efforts at appropriation that are, indeed, sterile wealth-redistributive — not productive — activities. The approaches differ, if at all, only in that the second does not limit the class of improper means to those that fit a preexisting pigeonhole in the law of tort or contract or fiduciary duty — and it is by no means clear that the first approach assumes a closed class of wrongful acts, either.

Under the first approach, at least if narrowly interpreted so that it does not merge with the second, the plaintiff must prove that the defendant obtained the plaintiff's trade secret by a wrongful act, illustrated here by the alleged acts of Fleck and Peloso in removing piece part drawings from Rockwell's premises without authorization, in violation of their employment contracts and confidentiality agreements, and using them in competition with Rockwell. Rockwell is unable to prove directly that the 100 piece part drawings it got from DEV in discovery were stolen by Fleck and Peloso or obtained by other improper means. But if it can show that the probability that DEV could have obtained them otherwise — that is, without engaging in wrongdoing — is slight, then it will have taken a giant step toward proving what it must prove in order to recover under the first theory of trade secret protection. The greater the precautions that Rockwell took to maintain the secrecy of the piece part drawings, the lower the probability that DEV obtained them properly and the higher the probability that it obtained them through a wrongful act; the owner had taken pains to prevent them from being obtained otherwise.

Under the second theory of trade secret protection, the owner's precautions still have evidentiary significance, but now primarily as evidence that the secret has real value. For the precise means by which the defendant acquired it is less important under the second theory, though not completely unimportant; remember that even the second theory allows the unmasking of a trade secret by *some* means, such as reverse engineering. If Rockwell expended only paltry resources on preventing its piece part drawings from falling into the hands of competitors such as DEV, why should the law, whose machinery is far from costless, bother to provide Rockwell with a remedy? The information contained in the drawings cannot have been worth much if Rockwell did not think it worthwhile to make serious efforts to keep the information secret.

The remedial significance of such efforts lies in the fact that if the plaintiff has allowed his trade secret to fall into the public domain, he would enjoy a windfall if permitted to recover damages merely because the defendant took the secret from him, rather than from the public domain as it could have done with impunity. [Citations omitted.] It would be like punishing a person for stealing property that he believes is owned by another but that actually is abandoned property. If it were true, as apparently it is not, that Rockwell had given the piece part drawings at issue to customers, and it had done so without requiring the customers to hold them in confidence, DEV could have obtained the drawings from the customers without committing any wrong. The harm to Rockwell would have been the same as if DEV had stolen the drawings from it, but it would have had no remedy, having parted with its rights to the trade secret. This is true whether the trade secret is regarded as property protected only against wrongdoers or (the logical extreme of the second conception, although no case — not even *Christopher* — has yet embraced it and the patent statute might preempt it) as property protected against the world. In the first case, a defendant is perfectly entitled to obtain the property by lawful conduct if he can, and he can if the property is in the hands of persons who themselves committed no wrong to get it. In the second case the defendant is perfectly entitled to obtain the property if the plaintiff has abandoned it by giving it away without restrictions.

It is easy to understand therefore why the law of trade secrets requires a plaintiff to show that he took reasonable precautions to keep the secret a secret. If analogies are needed, one that springs to mind is the duty of the holder of a trademark to take reasonable efforts to police infringements of his mark, failing which the mark is likely to be deemed abandoned, or to become generic or descriptive (and in either event be unprotectable). 1 McCarthy, Trademarks and Unfair Competition § 17:50, at pp. 778–80 (2d ed. 1984). The trademark owner who fails to police his mark both shows that he doesn't really value it very much and creates a situation in which an infringer may have been unaware that he was using a proprietary mark because the mark had drifted into the public domain, much as DEV contends Rockwell's piece part drawings have done.

But only in an extreme case can what is a "reasonable" precaution be determined on a motion for summary judgment, because the answer depends on a balancing of costs and benefits that will vary from case to case and so require estimation and measurement by persons knowledgeable in the particular field of endeavor involved. On the one hand, the more the owner of the trade secret spends on preventing the secret from leaking out, the more he demonstrates that the secret has real value deserving of legal protection, that he really was hurt as a result of the misappropriation of it, and that there really *was* misappropriation. On the other hand, the more he spends, the higher his costs. The costs can be indirect as well as direct. The more Rockwell restricts access to its drawings, either by its engineers or by the vendors, the harder it will be for either group to do the work expected of it. Suppose Rockwell forbids *any* copying of its drawings. Then a team of engineers would have to share a single drawing, perhaps by passing it around or by working in the same room, huddled over the drawing. And how would a vendor be able to make a piece part — would Rockwell have to bring all that work in house? Such reconfigurations of patterns of work and production are far from costless; and therefore perfect security is not optimum security.

There are contested factual issues here, bearing in mind that what is reasonable is itself a fact for purposes of Rule 56 of the civil rules. [Citations omitted.] Obviously Rockwell took some precautions, both physical (the vault security, the security guards — one of whom apprehended Peloso *in flagrante delicto*) and contractual, to maintain the confidentiality of its piece part drawings. Obviously it could have taken more precautions. But at a cost, and the question is whether the additional benefit in security would have exceeded that cost. We do not suggest that the question can be answered with the same precision with which it can be posed, but neither can we say that no reasonable jury could find that Rockwell had done enough and could then go on to infer misappropriation from a combination of the precautions Rockwell took and DEV's inability to establish the existence of a lawful source of the Rockwell piece part drawings in its possession.

This is an important case because trade secret protection is an important part of intellectual property, a form of property that is of growing importance to the competitiveness of American industry. Patent protection is at once costly and temporary, and therefore cannot be regarded as a perfect substitute. If trade secrets are protected only if their owners take extravagant, productivity-impairing measures to maintain their secrecy, the incentive to invest resources in discovering more efficient methods of production will be reduced, and with it the amount of invention. And given the importance of the case we must record our concern at the brevity of the district court's opinion granting summary judgment (one and a half printed pages). Brevity is the soul of wit, and all that, and the district judge did have the benefit of a magistrate's opinion; but it is vital that commercial litigation not appear to be treated as a stepchild in the federal courts. The future of the nation depends in no small part on the efficiency of industry, and the efficiency of industry depends in no small part on the protection of intellectual property.

The judgment is reversed and the case remanded to the district court for further proceedings consistent with this opinion (including reinstatement of the pendent counts).

REVERSED AND REMANDED.

## NOTES AND QUESTIONS:

1. *USM Corp. v. Marsten Fastener Corp.*, 204 U.S.P.Q. 233 (Mass.1979), discusses many of the measures that courts have found to be "reasonable" in protecting valuable trade secrets. Obviously the measures do not have to be absolute, only that "reasonable precautions" must be taken. The court in *USM Corp.* made several important points to illustrate this standard, i.e., "an impenetrable fortress is an unreasonable requirement," and "heroic measures" are not necessary. *Id.* at 238-39. The court in *USM Corp.* also made the point that even though a plaintiff might have failed to take reasonable steps to preserve its confidential information, it still may be entitled to some relief against someone who improperly procures the information. Does this provide a sliding scale for finding liability by weighing the steps taken to preserve secrecy against the defendant's conduct?

2. Employment procedures may also be instituted to protect trade secrets. Part of routine pre-employment and exit interviews conducted by human resource or non-technical staff members may incorporate non-disclosure warnings to employees or prospective employees about her or his secrecy obligations. Non-accusatory letters advising new employers of their new hire's confidentiality obligations to their former employer are also a useful precaution to reinforce trade secrecy rights.

3. When information is widely distributed, no precautionary measure will undo the harm and save the trade secret status of the information. How did the court in *Rockwell Graphic Systems, Inc. v. DEV Industries, Inc.*, 925 F.2d 174 (7th Cir.1991), avoid having to reach this conclusion? In his thoughtful opinion, Judge Posner explores the philosophy of trade secret protection while finding a fact question to justify reversing the lower court's summary judgment. He discusses two different "conceptions" of trade secret protection: (i) the deterrent approach, where the goal is to deter the redistribution of wealth from one firm to another, and (ii) the protective approach, where inventive activity is encouraged. *Id.* at 178. What was Judge Posner's difficulty with the lower court's conclusion that Rockwell did not deserve to protect its trade secrets because it had made only "perfunctory efforts" to maintain them? Can this decision be relied on as precedent that trade secrets are not lost even though thousands of documents are in the hands of vendors and customers?

4. To be effective, efforts to maintain secrecy need not be perfect. An occasional lapse does not jeopardize trade secret protection as long as the information does not become generally known as a result. *See ISC-Bunker Ramo Corp. v. Altech, Inc.*, 765 F.Supp. 1310, 1322-24 (N.D.Ill.1990) (where, when computer programs and service manuals were not normally distributed to customers except on request and confidential disclosure agreements were executed, one instance out of several thousand where information leaked was not sufficient to find that the secrets were not protectable).

5. There is always a risk during trade secret litigation that secret information might inadvertently be disclosed. Protective orders are routinely issued by courts spelling out restrictions and procedures for handling secret information. Documents and information in court documents are typically filed "under seal" to maintain the secrecy of information belonging to both parties, which means the

documents containing confidential information are placed in a sealed envelope that is deposited with the clerk and not available in the public court documents. A typical protective order is reproduced below, which is one used by The U.S. District Court for the Eastern District of Texas.

**IN THE UNITED STATES DISTRICT COURT**
**FOR THE EASTERN DISTRICT OF TEXAS**
**TYLER [MARSHALL] DIVISION**

| | |
|---|---|
| Plaintiffs<br>vs.<br>Defendants | CASE NO. |

*(Sample Form)*

**PROTECTIVE ORDER**

This Protective Order is issued to facilitate document disclosure and production under the Local Rules of this Court and the Federal Rules of Civil Procedure. Unless modified pursuant to the terms contained in this Order, this Order shall remain in effect through the conclusion of this litigation.

In support of this order, the Court finds that:

1. Documents or information containing confidential proprietary and business information and/or trade secrets ("Confidential Information") that bear significantly on the parties' claims or defenses is likely to be disclosed or produced during the course of discovery in this litigation;
2. The parties to this litigation may assert that public dissemination and disclosure of Confidential Information could severely injure or damage the party disclosing or producing the Confidential Information and could place that party at a competitive disadvantage;
3. Counsel for the party or parties receiving Confidential Information are presently without sufficient information to accept the representation(s) made by the party or parties producing Confidential Information as to the confidential, proprietary, and/or trade secret nature of such Confidential Information; and
4. To protect the respective interests of the parties and to facilitate the progress of disclosure and discovery in this case, the following Order should issue:

**IT IS THEREFORE ORDERED THAT:**

1. Documents or discovery responses containing Confidential Information disclosed or produced by any party in this litigation are referred to as "Protected Documents." Except as otherwise indicated below, all documents or discovery responses designated by the producing party as "Confidential" and which are disclosed or produced to the attorneys for the other parties to this litigation are Protected Documents and are entitled to confidential treatment as described below.
2. Protected Documents shall not include (a) advertising materials, (b) materials that on their face show that they have been published to the general public, or (c) documents that have submitted to any governmental entity without request for confidential treatment.
3. At any time after the delivery of Protected Documents, counsel for the party or parties receiving the Protected Documents may challenge the

Confidential designation of all or any portion thereof by providing written notice thereof to counsel for the party disclosing or producing the Protected Documents. If the parties are unable to agree as to whether the confidential designation of discovery material is appropriate, the party or parties receiving the Protected Documents shall certify to the Court that the parties cannot reach an agreement as to the confidential nature of all or a portion of the Protected Documents. Thereafter, the party or parties disclosing or producing the Protected Documents shall have ten (10) days from the date of certification to file a motion for protective order with regard to any Protected Documents in dispute. The party or parties producing the Protected Documents shall have the burden of establishing that the disputed Protected Documents are entitled to confidential treatment. If the party or parties producing the Protected Documents do not timely file a motion for protective order, then the Protected Documents in dispute shall no longer be subject to confidential treatment as provided in this Order. All Protected Documents are entitled to confidential treatment pursuant to the terms of this Order until and unless the parties formally agree in writing to the contrary, a party fails to timely move for a protective order, or a contrary determination is made by the Court as to whether all or a portion of a Protected Document is entitled to confidential treatment.

4. Confidential Treatment. Protected Documents and any information contained therein shall not be used or shown, disseminated, copied, or in any way communicated to anyone for any purpose whatsoever, except as provided for below.

5. Protected Documents and any information contained therein shall be disclosed only to the following persons ("Qualified Persons"):

   A. Counsel of record in this action for the party or party receiving Protected Documents or any information contained therein;

   B. Employees of such counsel (excluding experts and investigators) assigned to and necessary to assist such counsel in the preparation and trial of this action; and

   C. The Court.

   Protected Documents and any information contained therein shall be used solely for the prosecution of this litigation.

6. Counsel of record for the party or parties receiving Protected Documents may create an index of the Protected Documents and furnish it to attorneys of record representing or having represented parties involved in litigation involving the claims alleged in this suit against the party or parties disclosing or producing the Protected Documents. The index may only identify the document, date, author, and general subject matter of any Protected Document, but may not reveal the substance of any such document. Counsel for the party or parties receiving Protected Documents shall maintain a current log of the names and addresses of persons to whom the index was furnished.

7. The term "copy" as used herein means any photographic, mechanical or computerized copy or reproduction of any document or thing, or any verbatim transcript, in whole or in part, of such document or thing.

8. To the extent that Protected Documents or information contained therein are used in depositions, at hearings, or at trial, such documents or information shall remain subject to the provisions of this Order, along with

the transcript pages of the deposition testimony and/or trial testimony referring to the Protected Documents or information contained therein.

9. Any court reporter or transcriber who reports or transcribes testimony in this action shall agree that all "confidential" information designated as such under this Order shall remain "confidential" and shall not be disclosed by them, except pursuant to the terms of this Order, and that any notes or transcriptions of such testimony (and any accompanying exhibits) will be retained by the reporter or delivered to counsel of record.

10. Inadvertent or unintentional production of documents or information containing Confidential Information which are not designated "confidential" shall not be deemed a waiver in whole or in part of a claim for confidential treatment.

11. The party or parties receiving Protected Documents shall not under any circumstances sell, offer for sale, advertise, or publicize Protected Documents or any information contained therein.

12. After termination of this litigation, the provisions of this Order shall continue to be binding, except with respect to those documents and information that become a matter of public record. This Court retains and shall have continuing jurisdiction over the parties and recipients of the Protected Documents for enforcement of the provisions of this Order following termination of this litigation.

13. Upon termination of this action by dismissal, judgment, or settlement, counsel for the party or parties receiving Protected Documents shall return the Protected Documents to the counsel for the party or parties disclosing or producing the Protected Documents. The party or parties receiving the Protected Documents shall keep their attorney work product which refers or relates to any Protected Documents. Attorney work product may be used in subsequent litigation provided that such use does not disclose Protected Documents or any information contained therein.

14. This Order shall be binding upon the parties and their attorneys, successors, executors, personal representatives, administrators, heirs, legal representatives, assigns, subsidiaries, divisions, employees, agents, independent contractors, or other persons or organizations over which they have control.

15. The Court anticipates and encourages the parties to file a motion to modify the terms hereof with respect to the sharing of Protected Documents with experts and consultants; shifting the cost burden of production equitably; and other terms that may be reasonably required to protect a party as provided in Rule 26(b) or (c) of the Federal Rules of Civil Procedure.

**[End of Document. Court will add ordered signature block for Judge's signature.]**

6. Even though a protective order might be in place, a court nevertheless has the discretion to deny discovery where a sufficient showing is not made that the requested information is both relevant and necessary. This happened in *Sybase, Inc. v. ANTS Software, Inc.*, No. A132541, 2011 Cal. App. Unpub. LEXIS 8248 (Cal.Ct.App.Oct. 28, 2011), excerpted below, where the appellate court refused to remand the case to the trial court to allow the defendant "a second bite at the apple" to present additional evidence:

## SYBASE, INC. v. ANTS SOFTWARE, INC.

No. A132541, 2011 Cal. App. Unpub. LEXIS 8248
(Cal. Ct. App. Oct. 28, 2011)

Petitioner Sybase, Inc. (Sybase), challenges a trial court order compelling production of the source code for its Aries software product in litigation against real party in interest, ANTs Software Inc. (ANTs). ANTs concedes this source code is a trade secret, and Sybase contends the trial court erred in ordering its disclosure because ANTs failed to make the requisite showing. (Evid. Code, § 1060.) We agree with Sybase and grant the petition.

BACKGROUND

Sybase is a developer of data management software whose flagship database product is its Adaptive Server Enterprise (ASE) software. In April 2008, Sybase entered into a licensing agreement for the ANTs Data Server (ADS) software, seeking to develop an ASE product, code named "Pegasus," that would incorporate the in-memory database technology of ADS. Sybase later filed a civil action against ANTs for alleged violations of this licensing agreement and a related nondisclosure agreement.

Sybase's Claims

The operative complaint includes the following allegations:

In 2007, the parties signed a nondisclosure agreement to facilitate negotiations for Sybase to license ADS. Patrick Moore, ANTs's vice-president of global alliances and government sector, participated in these negotiations. While negotiating with Sybase, ANTs was also negotiating with Sybase's competitor, Four J's Development Tools, Inc. (Four J's), for the sale of ADS. Moore passed confidential information about ANTs's negotiations with Sybase to Four J's and, in February 2008, joined Four J's as a vice-president.

In April 2008, the parties signed a license agreement under which Sybase paid $1.4 million for a license to use, modify, and distribute ADS, and the right to sublicense it (license agreement). The license agreement provided for Sybase to hire four key ANTs employees, who had specialized knowledge necessary to use ADS (key employees). ANTs agreed that for a period of five years, neither it, nor any of its successors or assigns, would solicit the key employees for employment.

A week later, ANTs e-mailed Four J's a copy of the license agreement, which contained the key employees' names. Shortly thereafter, ANTs and Four J's entered into an asset purchase agreement for ADS, but ANTs did not assign the license agreement to Four J's. Four J's immediately solicited two of the key employees, including Jacob Mathew (Mathew), who resigned his employment with Sybase and began working for Four J's in August 2008.

The complaint includes causes of action against ANTs for fraud in the inducement, negligent misrepresentation, breach of written contract, unfair competition (Bus. & Prof. Code, § 17200 et seq.), breach of the implied covenant of good faith and fair dealing, and negligence . . . .

Sybase's Alleged Damages

In late 2008, Sybase initially sought damages based on the reduction in value of the ADS license and its sublicensing rights, "including the possible complete loss of value to the software" due to Mathew's departure. Sybase also claimed "[c]osts and expenses incurred to cover work completed by . . . Mathew" and "to retain other employees," as well as the "[c]osts of lost market opportunity from delay to the project due to the loss of . . . Mathew as an employee." Sybase maintained that, as a result of Mathew's departure, "the release schedule of the ASE [in-memory database] option (product which contains the ANTs technology)," had been delayed approximately six months.

In January 2011, Sybase expanded its theory of damages and sought damages "based on the reduced functionality of its product due to the departure of its key engineer." Sybase explained that it initially expected only a delay in the release of Pegasus, but later realized it could "never" bring Pegasus to market without Mathew. Sybase said it developed a different ASE product, code named "Aries" and marketed as ASE 15.5, which was much less functional and drew less customer interest. Sybase sought damages resulting from "the less robust, less functionality of the Aries product versus the Pegasus product that was intended to be released."

Discovery

Request No. 11 of ANTs's fourth request for production of documents sought "All source code for 'Project Aries.' " Sybase objected and indicated it would not produce documents responsive to this request. ANTs moved to compel further responses to its requests for production, including request No. 11.

On February 10, 2011, the trial court granted the motion as to request No. 11 and request No. 17, which is not at issue in this petition. The trial court ordered: "[Sybase] shall fully respond to Request 11, but shall respond to Request 17 as narrowed herein: [¶] [Sybase] is to produce all documents related to reasons why [Sybase] faced delay and/or problems integrating the ANTs source code into ASE for the Pegasus project." The trial court ordered Sybase to prepare a detailed privilege log to the extent it contended "said documents" were privileged or private. Sybase subsequently identified the source code for Aries in a privilege log and asserted a privilege for "[c]onfidential/proprietary business information, trade secret."

In April 2011, ANTs moved to reopen discovery, contending it needed to conduct discovery regarding the new theories of damages Sybase asserted after the July 2010 discovery cut-off date and to file a motion to compel "the ASE Source Code and Other Court-Ordered Documents." ANTs maintained that, in addition to the January 2011 claim for damages based on an alleged loss of product functionality, Sybase had recently indicated it was seeking rescission of the licensing agreement. The trial court reopened discovery and allowed ANTs to file a motion to compel production of materials that Sybase had identified as privileged, including the Aries source code.

ANTs then moved to compel production of the Aries source code, Sybase's benchmark testing and performance analysis results between ADS and ASE, and other related documents. ANTs conceded that the Aries source code is a trade secret, but contended it needed the source code to defend against Sybase's claims. ANTs maintained it could not evaluate "whether or not . . . ADS source code was usable with [the] ASE code without the benefit of [Mathew]" unless it could review the ADS code and the ASE code into which it was supposed to be incorporated. In support of its motion, ANTs attached a declaration of counsel with excerpts from the deposition transcripts of two of Sybase's engineers, Sheshadri Ranganath and Sudipto Chowdhuri, who testified that the ADS code differed so fundamentally from the ASE code that significant modifications to ASE would be necessary to integrate the two; and that Sybase had opted to "organically develop" an in-memory database product because ADS did not offer anything more than ASE did, and it was easier to expand the ASE code than to integrate ADS into ASE. ANTs also included pages from a due diligence summary package that Sybase prepared before entering the licensing agreement, which discussed weaknesses in ADS. ANTs argued: "As Sybase witness testimony indicates that Sybase's reasons for not using the ADS code are unrelated to. Mathew's departure, ANTs needs to review the source code to (i) determine why the ADS code could not be integrated, (ii) determine whether or not the failure to integrate had anything to do with the loss of . . . Mathew[,] (iii) determine what portions of ADS were incorporated into ASE, [and] (iv) determine how ASE technically differs from ADS making the integration of four of five technologies difficult . . . ." To the extent Sybase asserted a claim for rescission, ANTs maintained the source code was necessary to determine whether Sybase had received the benefit of its bargain.

Sybase argued that there were "other, better ways for ANTs to obtain such information," including depositions and written discovery, and attached a declaration from Chowdhuri indicating that the source code for Aries was the result of years of engineering efforts; that the software industry is highly competitive; that Sybase vies to engineer databases that either offer new or superior functionality in the marketplace; and that if the source code were disclosed, Sybase's competitors could unfairly leverage its efforts to enhance their own offerings or to competitively position their products.

### The Trial Court's Order

On May 27, 2011, the trial court entered an order granting ANTs's motion, concluding that ANTs had made the showing required for the disclosure of trade secrets under *Bridgestone/Firestone, Inc. v. Superior Court* (1992) 7 Cal.App.4th 1384 (*Bridgestone*), and stating "access to the ASE source code and related documents is both relevant and necessary. [ANTs] cannot among other things, adequately defend the case without such access, given [Sybase's] claims that [ANTs's] source code was defective when delivered or alternatively that [ANTs's] source code could not be successfully integrated into [Sybase's] source code. Thus, these documents appear to be directly relevant to [ANTs's] defense, and [ANTs] would be unfairly disadvantaged in defending this lawsuit absent production of the source code." The trial court ordered Sybase "to produce its ASE source code as well as the documents related to the source code, including any benchmark testing results, performance analysis results or any related documents comparing ADS and ASE programs."

On June 22, 2011, the trial court entered a protective order for information designated " 'HIGHLY CONFIDENTIAL — OUTSIDE ATTORNEYS' EYES ONLY,' " limiting the persons with access to this information, setting forth specific procedures to protect the Aries source code during ANTs's inspection, and putting other safeguards in place to prevent and punish disclosure of confidential information both during and after the litigation, including the imposition of civil penalties.

On July 8, 2011, Sybase filed the instant petition for writ of mandate, contending the trial court erred in ordering disclosure of the Aries source code. After reviewing preliminary briefing from the parties, we issued an order to show cause and granted a temporary stay of the trial court's order to the extent it compels production of the Aries source code.

## DISCUSSION

### I. Writ Review of the Trial Court's Order

"Despite the general rule disfavoring writ review of discovery matters, writ review is appropriate when petitioner seeks relief from an order which may undermine a privilege. [citations.] . . . [I]nterlocutory review by writ is the only adequate remedy in such cases, since once privileged matter has been disclosed there is no way to undo the harm which consists in the very disclosure. [citation.]" (*Raytheon Co. v. Superior Court* (1989) 208 Cal.App.3d 683, 686 [attorney-client privilege]; accord, *People ex rel. Lockyer v. Superior Court* (2004) 122 Cal.App.4th 1060, 1071.) Writ review of an order compelling disclosure of a trade secret is therefore proper. (Evid. Code, § 1060 [trade secret privilege].)

We review a trial court's determination of a motion to compel discovery for abuse of discretion. (*Costco Wholesale Corp. v. Superior Court* (2009) 47 Cal.4th 725, 733.) "An abuse of discretion is shown when the trial court applies the wrong legal standard. [citation.] However, when the facts asserted in support of and in opposition to the motion are in conflict, the trial court's factual findings will be upheld if they are supported by substantial evidence. [citations.]." (*Ibid.*) " 'The scope of discretion always resides in the particular law being applied, i.e., in the "legal principles governing the subject of [the] action . . . ." Action that transgresses the confines of the applicable principles of law is outside the scope of discretion and we call such action an "abuse" of discretion.' [citation.]" (*Horsford v. Board of Trustees of California State University* (2005) 132 Cal.App.4th 359, 393.)

### II. The Standard for Obtaining Discovery of a Trade Secret

"[T]he owner of a trade secret has a privilege to refuse to disclose the secret, and to prevent another from disclosing it, if the allowance of the privilege will not tend to conceal fraud or otherwise work injustice." (Evid. Code, § 1060.) *Bridgestone* sets forth the standard for determining whether a trade secret must be disclosed in litigation: Once a party claiming the trade secret privilege has shown that it applies, the party seeking discovery must make "a prima facie, particularized showing that the information sought is relevant and necessary to the proof of, or defense against, a material element of one or more causes of action presented in the case, and that it is reasonable to conclude that the information sought is essential to a fair resolution of the lawsuit. It is then up to the holder of the privilege to demonstrate any claimed disadvantages of a protective order. Either party may propose or oppose less intrusive alternatives to disclosure of the trade secret, but the burden is upon the trade secret claimant to demonstrate that an alternative to disclosure will not be unduly burdensome to the opposing side and that it will maintain the same fair balance in the litigation that would have been achieved by disclosure." (*Bridgestone, supra*, 7 Cal.App.4th at p. 1393.)

*Bridgestone* involved a wrongful death suit against a tire manufacturer for negligent design and manufacture, strict liability, breach of warranty, and failure to warn in connection with a tire failure that caused a car accident. (*Bridgestone, supra*, 7 Cal.App.4th at p. 1388.) The plaintiffs sought the manufacturing specifications for the tire at issue, which included formulas necessary to translate and describe the rubber compound components in the tire. (*Id.* at pp. 1388-1389.) The court found the declaration of the plaintiffs' expert insufficient because it did not show "the necessity of the formula information to [the plaintiffs'] ability to carry their burden of proof." (*Id.* at p. 1397.) The declaration plainly established that the trade secret formulas would be helpful to the analysis of the case and to the expert's ability to reach conclusions and render opinions regarding the tire's failure and the defendant's knowledge of problems with it. Nonetheless, the expert did not "describe with any precision how or why the formulas were a predicate to his ability to reach conclusions in the case" and did not "explain why the formulas themselves (in addition to the specification information) were necessary." (*Id.* at pp. 1396-1397.) Significantly, the expert acknowledged that he was able to draw conclusions about a design defect in another case based on the specifications alone, without the formulas. (*Id.* at p. 1397.)

### III. ANTs Failed to Make the Requisite Showing in This Case

Sybase's primary contention is that ANTs "failed to make a prima facie, particularized showing of how or why the production of Sybase's trade secret information is not simply relevant, but necessary to its defense." In evaluating ANTs's claim of necessity, we begin by clarifying the trade secret at issue — the source code for Aries. Contrary to ANTs's assertions below, Aries is not "the product on which the lost engineer was working" or the version of ASE into which ADS "was supposed to be incorporated." The undisputed evidence establishes that Aries is the engineering code name for the product that Sybase brought to market after abandoning its efforts to develop an integrated product, Pegasus. According to Sybase, Aries is "a completely different [ASE] product." The question is whether ANTs has shown that the source code for the *Aries* version of ASE is necessary to its defense and a fair resolution of the proceedings. ANTs presents several arguments to establish necessity.

A. Purported Necessity to Determine Why ADS Was Not Integrated

ANTs contends it needs the Aries source code to evaluate Sybase's claims that Mathew's departure prevented integration of the ADS code, causing delay in the release of "ASE15.5" and resulting in a product with less robust features. Specifically, ANTs seeks to determine whether Sybase's product was delayed by Mathew's departure, whether ADS could be integrated without him, and why the ADS code could not be integrated. ANTs maintains that "the source code will unequivocally show how the ASE product operates in comparison to ADS," and "[its] experts will be able to tell if indeed the decreased functionality and product delay were caused by some issues other than the lost engineer." ANTs contends the Aries source code also will allow it to evaluate the engineers' deposition testimony regarding the differences between ADS and ASE that precluded integration.

The fundamental flaw in these contentions is ANTs's failure to demonstrate that the source code for Aries will provide the information it seeks. In its motion below, and in opposing Sybase's petition, ANTs identifies the source code it seeks only vaguely as "the ASE product," and "the ASE source code," without distinguishing Aries from other versions of ASE. Nothing in the record clarifies how the Aries version of ASE is relevant, let alone necessary, to why ADS was not integrated into an earlier version of ASE. To the extent a comparison of ADS with an ASE product's source code would reveal differences precluding integration, the relevant version of the ASE code is the earlier version into which ADS was to be incorporated.

This argument also fails because ANTs's own evidence shows that it was able to obtain testimony at a deposition regarding the decision not to incorporate the ADS code into ASE. ANTs contends, without citation to the record, that the key employees were not extensively involved in integration of ADS or related decisions and that none of the deponents recalled being told that Mathew's departure would affect product development. ANTs acknowledges, however, that it deposed Chowdhuri and Ranganath, who were responsible for making decisions regarding integration, and Chowdhuri testified: "We could not follow our original intent, which was to do the integration of [ADS] into . . . ASE, and that integration was not possible because . . . we didn't have . . . Mathew, who was really the key component for us to move forward with this strategy[, in-memory database functionality]." ANTs also claims that Mathew could not provide the information it seeks because he only worked for Sybase a short time and had no input regarding integration. We are unpersuaded by this contention, as ANTs fails to support it with citation to the record, and, although the record demonstrates that Mathew may have information relevant to whether the ADS code could be integrated, ANTs has not shown it could not obtain this information, either by contacting him directly or by deposing him.

Finally, the trial court ordered Sybase to produce documents regarding the reasons for the decision not to integrate the ADS code, and ANTs acknowledges that it does not know whether these documents are an "adequate substitute" for the Aries source code because Sybase has not produced them. ANTs argues: "Certainly ANTs cannot be expected to rely solely on documents it does not have?" Sybase claims it has not produced the documents as ordered by the trial court because proceedings have been stayed pending resolution of Sybase's petition. Presumably,

Sybase will produce these documents promptly upon issuance of this court's decision, and, if it fails to do so, ANTs's remedy lies in the trial court.

B. Purported Necessity to Determine Whether Sybase Used ADS

ANTs also contends it needs to review the Aries source code to determine which aspects of ADS were incorporated into ASE. ANTs presented deposition testimony below from Sybase's engineer, Chowdhuri, who stated: "[T]here were interesting IPs that ANTs had that we were definitely influenced by, and that is on the actual storage strategies, indexing strategies, query compilation strategies, locking strategies, recovery strategies." He said "[a] very, very preliminary version of [the storage strategy]" was incorporated into ASE, but to adopt that strategy would have required too great a change in the ASE store code; and that the indexing, query compilation, and locking strategies were not incorporated because they would require "[t]oo big of a modification" to the ASE code, "[t]oo great of an architectural change." Chowdhuri testified, however: "[T]here was one form of recovery that we partially were able to adopt into the ASE code" — a "little bit" of the recovery strategy was incorporated. He agreed that the in-memory database functionality that was included with Aries did not include anything from ADS other than "maybe some high level storage strategy and maybe a little bit of the recovery strategy[.]"

Sybase characterizes this argument as a contention "that [ANTs] needs [the Aries] source code to determine whether [Sybase] is lying when it says it did not use the ADS source code in this later version of its software." Sybase contends that ANTs did not assert this argument below and, relying on certain deposition testimony, maintains it would easily have overcome the argument if ANTs had raised it. The record demonstrates, however, that ANTs asserted this argument below, and that Sybase did not refute it. As the deposition testimony on which Sybase relies was not before the trial court, we do not consider it. (See *Butler v. Superior Court* (2000) 78 Cal.App.4th 1171, 1181.)

Nevertheless, ANTs's argument and evidence on this point falls short of the *Bridgestone* showing. Sybase's use of ADS in developing Aries is directly relevant to the extent of Sybase's damages, which stem from its alleged inability to incorporate the ADS technology into its product. ANTs's evidence indicates that Sybase was influenced by the ADS code and incorporated "a little bit" of one ADS strategy. ANTs is not required to rely on the testimony of Sybase's own engineers and is entitled to test Sybase's alleged inability to incorporate ADS. But, although ANTs has established its need to determine the extent to which Sybase used ADS in developing Aries, ANTs has failed to demonstrate that review of the Aries source code would permit such a determination. Indeed, ANTs has not presented any evidence showing that it is *possible* to determine from a review of the Aries source code whether the ADS source code, IPs, and strategies were incorporated into the Aries product and the extent to which Sybase was influenced by it. We conclude that, without such evidence, the record does not permit a finding of necessity.

ANTs contends no expert declaration was necessary, noting: "Software coding language is no different than French or Spanish; it is simply another form of language which can be read by someone who has . . . learn[ed] its grammar and syntax. ANTs will have experts proficient in software development who will be able to read and understand the ASE source code." The question here, however, is not whether an expert will be able to understand the Aries source code, but rather, what information would be obtained by an expert's review of this code and what conclusions might reasonably be drawn from it. The record contains nothing showing that an expert examining the Aries source code could determine the extent to which it was influenced by ADS.

ANTs maintains: "No ANTs expert could yet opine concerning *what* the ASE code might reveal because neither it nor any related documents have been produced," so an expert declaration would have offered only speculation. (Italics added.) An expert could explain, however, *whether* the source code for a software product such as Aries would reflect the extent to which it incorporates or was influenced by another software product and how that determination would be made. (*Bridgestone*, *supra*, 7 Cal.App.4th at p. 1397 [noting expert's failure to describe with precision how or why the trade secret was a predicate to his ability to reach conclusions].) ANTs has not provided evidence addressing this threshold question. In addition, an expert could explain Chowdhuri's testimony regarding the aspects of ADS that were incorporated into Aries, specifically, the terms "IP" and "strategy" and whether they are distinct from the source code itself.

Finally, for the first time in its return to the petition, ANTs contends it could not retain an expert to provide this information because it does not know in what computer language the Aries source code is written. We observe that ANTs had an opportunity in the discovery process to seek the information necessary to justify its request for Sybase's trade secret. We are not aware of any exception to the *Bridgestone* requirement based on a party's failure to use the discovery process to obtain the evidence necessary to make the requisite showing.

### C. Purported Necessity to Determine If Aries Is Less Functional and Robust

For the first time in the proceedings before this court, ANTs contends that the Aries source code is necessary to evaluate Sybase's claims that the product it ultimately brought to market lacks robust features and is less functional than an integrated product would have been. ANTs claims Aries is the "very item Sybase claims was damaged." On first glance, this argument seems compelling: How can one defend against a claim that a product is less functional without being allowed to examine the product? In this analysis, however, it is important to distinguish the product from the product's *source code*. ANTs has not shown whether and how the Aries source code would show that Aries itself is a less robust and functional product than Pegasus would have been, and, in any case, that the source code is necessary to such a determination. Indeed, it would seem that an expert could reach any necessary conclusions about the Aries product's functionality and feature set by examining the Aries product itself.

Accordingly, ANTs has failed to demonstrate the source code for the Aries version of ASE is necessary to its defense against Sybase's claims. For the same reasons, ANTs's showing does not reasonably permit a finding that the Aries source code is essential to a fair resolution of this action. The trial court therefore abused its discretion in compelling disclosure of the Aries source code, and writ relief setting aside this portion of its order is appropriate.

In granting Sybase's petition, we decline ANTs's request to "remand to the trial court with directions to allow ANTs to present specific declaration evidence from software programming experts as to how the ASE source code is necessary to [its] defense of Sybase's causes of action against [it] and how the ASE source code will be used." Existing law reasonably identified the standard ANTs was required to meet to obtain discovery of a trade secret, and we are not inclined to grant a second bite at the apple in these circumstances. Nonetheless, to the extent the related documents the trial court ordered Sybase to produce in May 2011 provide evidence that satisfies the *Bridgestone* standard, our holding should not be construed to preclude ANTs from renewing its motion based on that evidence. We leave such matters to the discretion of the trial court.

DISPOSITION

The order to show cause, having served its purpose, is discharged. Let a peremptory writ of mandate issue directing respondent court to vacate the portion of its May 27, 2011 order granting ANTs's motion to compel disclosure of the Aries source code and to issue a new and different order denying this portion of ANTs's motion. The stay previously issued will dissolve upon issuance of the remittitur. (Cal. Rules of Court, rules 8.490(c), 8.272.) Each party shall bear its own costs incurred in litigating this petition. (Cal. Rules of Court, rule 8.493(a)(1)(B).)

7. Another issue that frequently arises in trade secret litigation is whether the plaintiff must produce the trade secret information it claims was misappropriated or stolen, before the defendant is required to produce documents and witnesses relevant to what it is currently doing, even though a protective order is already in place. As a federal judge told the author in a hotly contested hearing on this matter, "Isn't this simply a question of who shows first?" Because the facts are different in each case, this issue is usually much more complicated. However, the weight of authority seems to be that the plaintiff's disclosure of its trade secrets should precede discovery of the defendant. *See* R. MILGRIM ON TRADE SECRETS § 16.0[5], n.26. A plaintiff/trade secret owner will typically argue that because it has so much information that it considers to be a trade secret, it would be burdensome to require it to produce all of its trade secrets until it knows what the defendant is actually doing. The defendant usually responds by arguing that the plaintiff is doing nothing more than conducting a fishing expedition and unless the plaintiff specifies what trade secrets are allegedly taken, the plaintiff has not met the requirement of pleading its case which specific particularity. These issues are discussed in the following thoughtful and well-reasoned opinion by a Colorado Federal Magistrate Judge, who sided with the defendant and ordered the plaintiff to produce its trade secrets first. Was this a fair result? Can you think of situations where it would be more equitable to order the defendant to "show first?" How about a gradual, step-by-step procedure where the plaintiff first produces categories of trade secrets it believes were taken, then the defendant produces its information, and then the plaintiff produces all the details of its trade secrets that it wants to assert?

## L-3 COMMUNICATIONS CORP. v. JAXON ENGINEERING & MAINTENANCE, INC.

Civ. Action No. 10-cv-02868-MSK-KMT (C. Col. Oct. 12, 2011)

ORDER

This matter is before the court on the Motions Hearing held on October 3, 2011 (hereinafter "Motions Hearing"). (*See* Doc.No. 118, filed Oct. 3, 2011.) At the Motions Hearing, the court found that Plaintiffs had sufficiently disclosed the trade secrets that they allege Defendants misappropriated to require that Defendants respond to Plaintiffs' trade secret-related discovery requests. However, the court also noted that it would inform the parties if it was persuaded otherwise by the cases submitted by the parties regarding this issue. The court has now considered those cases in light of the record before it and reverses its conclusion that Plaintiffs have sufficiently disclosed their trade secrets at issue in this case.

The parties do not dispute the relevant standard governing this issue. In a trade secret case, "[t]here is no privilege excepting trade secrets from discovery, but 'courts must exercise discretion to avoid unnecessary disclosures of such information.' " *Dura Global Techs., Inc. v. Magna Donnelly, Corp.* (*"Dura Global Techs. I"*), No. 07-cv-10945, 2007 U.S. Dist. LEXIS 89650 (E.D. Mich. Dec. 6, 2007) (quoting *Automeds Techs., Inc. v. Eller*, 160 F. Supp.2d 915, 925 (N.D. Ill. 1974)). As such, a "[p]laintiff will normally be required first to identify with reasonable particularity the matter which it claims constitutes a trade secret, before it will be allowed . . . to compel discovery of its adversary's trade secrets." *Id.* (quoting *Automeds*, 160 F. Supp at 926); *see also Gentex Corp. v. Sutter*, No. 3:07-cv-1269, 2008 U.S. Dist. LEXIS 96188 (M.D. Pa. Nov. 25, 2008).

This threshold disclosure requirement for discovery in trade secret cases serves several purposes. First, describing a trade secret with specificity puts the defendant on notice of what it has allegedly misappropriated. *See Sit-Up, Ltd. v. IAC/Interactive Corp.*, No. 05-cv-9292, 2008 U.S. Dist. LEXIS 12017 (S.D.N.Y. Feb. 20, 2008); *see also Leucadia, Inc. v. Applied Extrusion Technologies, Inc.*, 755 F. Supp. 635, 637 (D. Del. 1991) ("disclosure of Plaintiff's trade secrets prior to discovery of defendant may be necessary to enable the defendant and ultimately the Court to ascertain the relevance of plaintiff's discovery.") Second, this requirement prevents disclosure of trade secrets that were not misappropriated by the defendant, thereby giving the plaintiff access to trade secret information that it would otherwise be illegal for the plaintiff to misappropriate. *Gentex Corp.*, 2008 U.S. Dist. LEXIS 96188, at *1. Finally, "requiring the plaintiff to state its claimed trade secrets prior to engaging in discovery ensures that it will not mold its cause of action around the discovery it receives." *DeRubeis v. Witten Techs., Inc.*, 244 F. R.D. 676, 681 (N.D. Ga. 2007). In this case, the court notes that the fact that the individual defendants were former employees of the plaintiffs does not ameliorate the concerns underlying the last two purposes; in fact, that they were former employees actually increases these dangers.

To ensure that plaintiffs adequately disclose their trade secrets, courts commonly order a list of trade secrets at the outset of the litigation. *Dura Global Techs*

*I*, 2007 U.S. Dist. LEXIS 89650, at *2. Ultimately, whether a plaintiff has sufficiently disclosed its trade secrets is "a fact-specific question to be decided on a case-by-case basis." *Gentex Corp.*, 2008 U.S. Dist. LEXIS 96188, at *1 (quoting *DeRubeis*, 244 F.R.D. at 681).

Unfortunately, beyond the more general standard of "reasonable particularity," the case law does not provide clear guidance as how detailed a plaintiff's trade secret disclosures must be. This is because trade secrets are necessarily confidential. As a consequence, courts are very reluctant to discuss a plaintiff's trade secret disclosures in a court order or opinion. *See, e.g., d.* at *4 (declining to discuss the defendant's interrogatories or the plaintiff's answers to those interrogatories because they were designated confidential and filed under seal).

Nevertheless, what is clear is that general allegations and generic references to products or information are insufficient to satisfy the reasonable particularity standard. *Hill v. Best Med. Int'l*, No. 09-1184, 2010 WL 2546023, at *4 (W.D. Pa. June 24, 2010); *see also Dura Global Techs I*, at *4 (interrogatory response providing a list of general categories and types of information alleged to comprise their trade secret insufficient); *Automed Techs.*, 160 F. Supp. at 925 (general allegations of "software, designs, and research" and generic references to three research projects by name insufficient to identify trade secrets in question).

Here, after reviewing the entire record, including the audio recording of the Motions Hearing, the court now finds that Plaintiffs have not identified their trade secrets with sufficient particularity. First, Plaintiffs' disclosures of their trade secrets in their Amended Complaint (Doc. No. 33, filed Feb. 11, 2011 [Am. Compl.]) are mere general, categorical references to the equipment, methods, and software Plaintiffs use to conduct shielding effectiveness, pulse current injection, and continuous wave immersion testing. (Am. Compl. ¶¶ 40–55.) Thereafter, Plaintiffs only generally allege that Defendants misappropriated their trade secret customer lists; pricing templates and labor rates; vendor lists; drawings, designs, and processes of constructing its electromagnetic enclosures; and "other information." (*Id.* ¶ 58a.-e.) At no point in their Amended Complaint do Plaintiffs describe the actual equipment, methods, software or other information they claim as trade secrets. *See Dura Global Techs I*, at *4 (a list of general categories and types of information deemed insufficient). Indeed, it appears that Plaintiffs acknowledge that their Amended Complaint does not sufficiently disclose their trade secrets. (Doc. No. 48 [Scheduling Conf. Tr.] at 38:6-9, filed) ("[T]his is very complicated information. It doesn't belong in a complaint . . . . We would have given up our trade secrets, which is why parties enter into a protective order.")

At the Motions Hearing, Plaintiff's counsel, Ms. Parker, engaged in a lengthy discussion of the technology at issue and Plaintiffs' claimed trade secrets. However, Plaintiffs' counsel's description of its trade secrets as Plaintiffs' selection of parts, and of vendors; their methods of using the test equipment; and software that helps generate and assimilate raw data also amounts to a general, categorical description. Thus, Ms. Parker's discussion of Plaintiffs' trade secrets in open court is similarly insufficient. *Automed Techs.*, 160 F. Supp. at 925 (general allegations of "software, designs, and research" insufficient). Again, at no point in the Motions Hearing did Plaintiffs describe their actual selection of parts and vendors, the actual methods by which they use their equipment, or the actual software they use to process the generated raw data.

Finally, the court notes that Plaintiffs have not filed or served any disclosures of their trade secrets under seal, nor have they moved to seal either their Amended Complaint or the Motions Hearing. Although there is certainly no hard and fast rule that trade secrets described with the requisite reasonable particularity be filed under seal, they typically are, "[i]n order to preserve the secrecy required for such material." *See, e.g., Dura Global Techs. Inc. v. Magna Donnelly Corp.* (*"Dura Global Techs. II"*), No. 07-cv-10945-DT, 2011 U.S. Dist. LEXIS 112408, at *2 (E.D.

Mich. May 14, 2008) (where the court limited its discussion of the plaintiffs' List of Trade Secrets because it was filed under seal, but nevertheless found that the plaintiffs failed to describe their trade secrets with reasonable particularity.) Although not essential to the court's finding, the fact that all of Plaintiffs' discussions of its trade secrets have occurred in the public portions of the record further suggests that Plaintiffs have failed to disclose their trade secrets with reasonable particularity.

Finally, the court notes that Plaintiffs have not filed or served any disclosures of their trade secrets under seal, nor have they moved to seal either their Amended Complaint or the Motions Hearing. Although there is certainly no hard and fast rule that trade secrets described with the requisite reasonable particularity be filed under seal, they typically are, "[i]n order to preserve the secrecy required for such material." *See, e.g., Dura Global Techs., Inc. v. Magna Donnelly Corp.* (*"Dura Global Techs. II"*), No. 07-cv-10945-DT, 2011 U.S. Dist. LEXIS 112408, at *2 (E.D. Mich. May 14, 2008) (where the court limited its discussion of the plaintiffs' List of Trade Secrets because it was filed under seal, but nevertheless found that the plaintiffs failed to describe their trade secrets with reasonable particularity.) Although not essential to the court's finding, the fact that all of Plaintiffs' discussions of its trade secrets have occurred in the public portions of the record further suggests that Plaintiffs have failed to disclose their trade secrets with reasonable particularity.

Altogether, the court finds that Plaintiffs have failed to describe their trade secrets with reasonable particularity as required for Plaintiffs to discover Defendants' trade secrets. Accordingly, the court will order Plaintiffs to file a List of Trade Secrets which they claim have been misappropriated. Because this will affect certain discovery-related deadlines imposed by the court at the Motions Hearing (*See* Doc. No. 118, filed Oct. 3, 2011), those dates will also be adjusted accordingly as outlined below.

Wherefore, it is

ORDERED that Plaintiffs shall file a List of Trade Secrets, under seal, no later than October 24, 2011.

8. The risk that secret information might be inadvertently disclosed during trade secret litigation is high. Protective orders issued by the courts specify restrictions and procedures for handling secret information. Documents and information in court documents are typically filed "under seal" to maintain the secrecy of information belonging to both parties. The term of art "under seal"

means that the documents containing confidential information are placed in a sealed envelope that is deposited with the clerk. Unlike other public court documents, these documents are not available for review. Section 5 of the UTSA specifically requires secrets to be preserved during a lawsuit:

> In an action under this [Act], a court shall preserve the secrecy of an alleged trade secret by reasonable means, which may include granting protective orders in connection with discovery proceedings, holding in-camera hearings, sealing the records of the action, and ordering any person involved in the litigation not to disclose an alleged trade secret without prior court approval.

Other precautions the court may take to preserve the confidentiality of trade secrets include closing the trial to the public. For example, the trial in *Standard Brands*, as discussed in Chapt. 2 (B)(1), was held *in camera*.

9. Lawyers live in constant fear of an occasional lapse in which documents covered by a protective order accidentally become publicly available. Because court records are increasingly accessible online, inadvertent disclosure has become a much more significant problem than it was in the past. Cases are mixed on whether these types of inadvertent disclosures result in a loss of secrecy for the information. *Compare Plastic & Metal Fabricators, Inc. v. Roy*, 303 A.2d 725, 731 (Conn.1972) (description of a trade secret attached to an unsealed affidavit did not *per se* destroy the trade secret); *and Hoechst Diafoil Co. v. Nan Ya Plastics Corp.*, 174 F.3d 411, 417 (4th Cir. 1999) (accidently leaving a 28-page document in unsealed court records for several months did not result in a loss of trade secrets in the document).

## D. RELATIONSHIP BETWEEN THE PARTIES

### (1) Agreements

#### (a) Covenants Not To Compete

### LEARNING CURVE TOYS, INC. v. PLAYWOOD TOYS, INC.

342 F.3d 714 (7th Cir. 2003)

In 1992, Robert Clausi and his brother-in-law, Scott Moore, began creating prototypes of wooden toys under the name PlayWood Toys, Inc., a Canadian corporation. Clausi was the sole toy designer and Moore was the sole officer and director of PlayWood. Neither Clausi nor Moore had prior experience in the toy industry, but Clausi had "always been a bit of a doodler and designer," Trial Tr. at 58, and the two men desired to "create high-quality hard-wood maple toys for the independent toy market," *id.* at 241. As a newly formed corporation, PlayWood did not own a facility in which it could produce toys. Instead, it worked in conjunction with Mario Borsato, who owned a wood-working facility. Subject to a written confidentiality agreement with PlayWood, Borsato manufactured prototypes for PlayWood based on Clausi's design specifications.

PlayWood's first attempt to market publicly its toys was at the Toronto Toy Fair on January 31, 1992. PlayWood received favorable reviews from many of the toy retailers in attendance; PlayWood also learned that the best way to get recognition for its toys was to attend the New York Toy Fair ("Toy Fair") the following month. Based on this information, Clausi and Moore secured a position at the Toy Fair in order to display PlayWood's prototypes. It was during this Toy Fair that Clausi and Moore first encountered Learning Curve representatives Roy Wilson, Harry Abraham and John Lee.

On the morning of February 12, 1993, the first day of the Toy Fair, Roy Wilson stopped at PlayWood's booth and engaged Clausi and Moore in conversation. Wilson identified himself as Learning Curve's toy designer and explained that his company had a license from the Britt Allcroft Company to develop Thomas the Tank Engine & Friends™ (hereinafter "Thomas") trains and accessories. Wilson commented that he was impressed with the look and quality of PlayWood's prototypes and raised the possibility of working together under a custom manufacturing contract to produce Learning Curve's line of Thomas products. Clausi and Moore responded that such an arrangement would be of great interest to PlayWood. Later that same day, Harry Abraham, Learning Curve's vice president, and John Lee, Learning Curve's president, also stopped by PlayWood's booth. They too commented on the quality of PlayWood's prototypes and indicated that PlayWood might be a good candidate for a manufacturing contract with Learning Curve.

Clausi and Moore continued to have discussions with Learning Curve's representatives over the remaining days of the Toy Fair, which ended on February 14. During these discussions, Lee indicated that he would like two of his people, Abraham and Wilson, to visit PlayWood in Toronto the day after the Toy Fair ended in order to determine whether the two parties could work out a manufacturing arrangement for some or all of Learning Curve's wooden toys. Clausi, feeling a little overwhelmed by the suggestion, requested that their visit be postponed a few days so that he could better acquaint himself with Learning Curve's products. The parties ultimately agreed that Abraham and Wilson would visit PlayWood at Borsato's facility on February 18, 1993, four days after the conclusion of the Toy Fair. Clausi spent the next several days after the Toy Fair researching Learning Curve's products and considering how PlayWood could produce Learning Curve's trains and track.

On February 18, 1993, Abraham and Wilson visited PlayWood in Toronto as planned. The meeting began with a tour of Borsato's woodworking facility, where the prototypes on display at the Toy Fair had been made. After the tour, the parties went to the conference room at Borsato's facility. At this point, according to Clausi and Moore, the parties agreed to make their ensuing discussion confidential. Clausi testified:

> After we sat down in the board room, Harry [Abraham of Learning Curve] immediately said: "Look, we're going to disclose confidential information to you guys, and we're going to disclose some designs that Roy [Wilson of Learning Curve] has that are pretty confidential. If Brio were to get their hands on them, then we wouldn't like that. And we're going to do it under the basis of a confidential understanding."
>
> And I said: "I also have some things, some ideas on how to produce the track and

produce the trains now that I've had a chance to look at them for the last couple of days, and I think they're confidential as well. So if we're both okay with that, we should continue." So we did.

Immediately after the parties agreed to keep their discussion confidential, Wilson, at Abraham's direction, showed Clausi and Moore drawings of various Thomas characters and provided information on the projected volume of each of the products. Clausi testified that he considered the documents disclosed by Learning Curve during the meeting confidential because they included information on products not yet released to the public, as well as Learning Curve's projected volumes, costs and profit margins for various products. After viewing Wilson's various drawings, the parties discussed PlayWood's ideas on how to manufacture Learning Curve's trains. Clausi suggested that they might use a CNC machine, which he defined as a computer numerically controlled drill that carves in three dimensions, to create Learning Curve's trains out of a single piece of wood (as opposed to piecing together separate pieces of wood).

The parties' discussion eventually moved away from train production and focused on track design. Wilson showed Clausi and Moore drawings of Learning Curve's track and provided samples of their current product. At this point, Abraham confided to Clausi and Moore that track had posed "a bit of a problem for Learning Curve." Trial Tr. at 85. Abraham explained that sales were terrific for Learning Curve's Thomas trains, but that sales were abysmal for its track. Abraham attributed the lack of sales to the fact that Learning Curve's track was virtually identical to that of its competitor, Brio, which had the lion's share of the track market. Because there was "no differentiation" between the two brands of track, Learning Curve's track was not even displayed in many of the toy stores that carried Learning Curve's products. *Id.* Learning Curve had worked unsuccessfully for several months attempting to differentiate its track from that of Brio.

After detailing the problems with Learning Curve's existing track, Abraham inquired of Clausi whether "there was a way to differentiate" its track from Brio's track. Trial Tr. at 86. Clausi immediately responded that he "had had a chance to look at the track and get a feel for it [over] the last few days" and that his "thoughts were that if the track were more realistic and more functional, that kids would enjoy playing with it more and it would give the retailer a reason to carry the product, especially if it looked different than the Brio track." *Id.* at 87. Clausi further explained that, if the track "made noise and [ ] looked like real train tracks, that the stores wouldn't have any problem, and the Thomas the Tank line, product line would have [ ] its own different track" and could "effectively compete with Brio." *Id.* Abraham and Wilson indicated that they were "intrigued" by Clausi's idea and asked him what he meant by "making noise." *Id.*

Clausi decided to show Abraham and Wilson exactly what he meant. Clausi took a piece of Learning Curve's existing track from the table, drew some lines across the track (about every three-quarters of an inch), and stated: "We can go ahead and machine grooves right across the upper section . . . , which would look like railway tracks, and down below machine little indentations as well so that it would look more like or sound more like real track. You would roll along and bumpity-bumpity as you go along." Trial Tr. at 255. Clausi then called Borsato into the conference room and asked him to cut grooves into the wood "about a quarter of an inch deep from the top surface." *Id.* at 88. Borsato left the room, complied with Clausi's request, and returned with the cut track three or four minutes later. Clausi ran a train back and forth over the cut piece of track. The track looked more realistic than before, but it did not make noise because the grooves were not deep enough. Accordingly, Clausi instructed Borsato to cut the grooves "just a little bit deeper so that they go through the rails." *Id.* Borsato complied with Clausi's request once again and returned a few minutes later with the cut piece of track. Clausi proceeded to run a train back and forth over the track. This time the track made a "clickety-clack" sound, but the train did not run smoothly over the track because the grooves were cut "a little bit too deep." *Id.* at 258. Based on the sound produced by the track, Clausi told Abraham and Moore that if PlayWood procured a contract with Learning Curve to produce the track, they could call it "Clickety-Clack Track." *Id.* at 89.

Both Abraham and Wilson indicated that Clausi's concept of cutting grooves into the track to produce a clacking sound was a novel concept. Thereafter, Wilson and Clausi began to discuss how they could improve the idea to make the train run more smoothly on the track, but Abraham interrupted them and stated: "No, focus. You guys have to get the contract for the basic product first, and then we can talk about new products, because . . . it takes [our licensor] a long time to approve new products and new designs." Trial Tr. at 89.

The meeting ended shortly thereafter without further discussion about Clausi's concept for the noise-producing track. Before he left, Wilson asked Clausi if he could take the piece of track that Borsato had cut with him while the parties continued their discussions. Clausi gave Wilson the piece of track without hesitation. The piece of track was the only item that Abraham and Wilson took from the meeting. Clausi and Moore did not ask Wilson for a receipt for the cut track, nor did they seek a written confidentiality agreement to protect PlayWood's alleged trade secret. After the meeting, Clausi amended PlayWood's confidentiality agreement with Borsato to ensure that materials discussed during the meeting would remain confidential. Clausi also stamped many of the documents that he received from Learning Curve during the meeting as confidential because they included information on products not yet released to the public. PlayWood never disclosed the contents of Learning Curve's documents to anyone.

During March of 1993, PlayWood and Learning Curve met on three separate occasions to discuss further the possibility of PlayWood manufacturing Learning Curve's Thomas products. At one of the meetings, and at Learning Curve's request, PlayWood submitted a manufacturing proposal for the Thomas products. Learning Curve rejected PlayWood's proposal. Learning Curve told Clausi that its licensor wanted the Thomas products to be made in the United States.

Thereafter, PlayWood had no contact with Learning Curve until late October of 1993, when Abraham contacted Clausi to discuss another possible manufacturing contract because Learning Curve's secondary supplier was not providing enough product. Again, PlayWood submitted a manufacturing proposal at Learning Curve's request, but it too was rejected. Learning Curve later stated that its new business partner had decided to manufacture the product in China.

Clausi and Moore continued to work on PlayWood's toy concepts. After the 1994

New York Toy Fair, which was not particularly successful for PlayWood, Clausi and Moore began to focus their efforts on refining PlayWood's concept for the noise-producing track. During this time, Clausi and Moore made no attempt to license or sell the concept to other toy companies because they believed that PlayWood still had "an opportunity to get in the door" with Learning Curve if they could perfect the concept and also because they believed that they were bound by a confidentiality agreement. Trial Tr. at 267.

In December of 1994, while shopping for additional track with which to experiment, Moore discovered that Learning Curve was selling noise-producing track under the name "Clickety-Clack Track." Like the piece of track that Clausi had Borsato cut during PlayWood's February 18, 1993, meeting with Learning Curve, Clickety-Clack Track™ has parallel grooves cut into the wood, which cause a "clacking" sound as train wheels roll over the grooves. Learning Curve was promoting the new track as the first significant innovation in track design since the inception of wooden train systems . . . . It is quite simply the newest and most exciting development to come along recently in the wooden train industry, and it's sure to cause a sensation in the marketplace . . . . [I]t brings that sound and feel of the real thing to a child's world of make-believe without bells, whistles, electronic sound chips or moving parts.

PlayWood's Tr. Ex.71.

Moore was "stunned" when he saw the track because he believed that Learning Curve had stolen PlayWood's concept. Trial Tr. at 268. He testified: "This was our idea. This is what we've been working on even up to that day to go back to [Learning Curve] as an opportunity to get in the door, and there it is on the shelf." *Id.* Moore purchased a package of Clickety-Clack Track™ and showed it to Clausi. Clausi testified that he was disappointed when he saw the track because he believed that Learning Curve had taken PlayWood's name and design concept "almost exactly as per [their] conversation" on February 18, 1993. Trial Tr. at 103.

PlayWood promptly wrote a cease and desist letter to Learning Curve. The letter accused Learning Curve of stealing PlayWood's concept for the noise-producing track that it disclosed to Learning Curve "in confidence in the context of a manufacturing proposal." PlayWood's Tr. Ex.66 at 1. Learning Curve responded by seeking a declaratory judgment that it owned the concept.

Previously, on March 16, 1994, Learning Curve had applied for a patent on the noise-producing track. The patent, which was obtained on October 3, 1995, claims the addition of parallel impressions or grooves in the rails, which cause a "clacking" sound to be emitted as train wheels roll over them. The patent identifies Roy Wilson of Learning Curve as the inventor.

Clickety-Clack Track™ provided an enormous boost to Learning Curve's sales. Learning Curve had $20 million in track sales by the first quarter of 2000, and $40 million for combined track and accessory sales.

* * *

The parties agree that their dispute is governed by the Illinois Trade Secrets Act ("Act"), 765 ILCS 1065/1 *et seq.* To prevail on a claim for misappropriation of a trade secret under the Act, the plaintiff must demonstrate that the information at issue was a trade secret, that it was misappropriated and that it was used in the defendant's business. (citations omitted) The issue currently before us is whether there was legally sufficient evidence for the jury to find that PlayWood had a trade secret in its concept for the noise-producing toy railroad track that it revealed to Learning Curve on February 18, 1993.

The Act defines a trade secret as:

[I]nformation, including but not limited to, technical or non-technical data, a formula, pattern, compilation, program, device, method, technique, drawing, process, financial data, or list of actual or potential customers or suppliers, that:

(1) is sufficiently secret to derive economic value, actual or potential, from not being generally known to other persons who can obtain economic value from its disclosure or use; and

(2) is the subject of efforts that are reasonable under the circumstances to maintain its secrecy or confidentiality.

765 ILCS 1065/2(d). Both of the Act's statutory requirements focus fundamentally on the secrecy of the information sought to be protected. [Citations omitted.] However, the requirements emphasize different aspects of secrecy. The first requirement, that the information be sufficiently secret to impart economic value because of its relative secrecy, "precludes trade secret protection for information generally known or understood within an industry even if not to the public at large." *Pope*, 230 Ill.Dec. 646, 694 N.E.2d at 617. The second requirement, that the plaintiff take reasonable efforts to maintain the secrecy of the information, prevents a plaintiff who takes no affirmative measures to prevent others from using its proprietary information from obtaining trade secret protection. *See Jackson v. Hammer*, 274 Ill.App.3d 59, 210 Ill.Dec. 614, 653 N.E.2d 809, 816 (1995) ("[T]he Act requires a plaintiff to take 'affirmative measures' to prevent others from using information.").

Although the Act explicitly defines a trade secret in terms of these two requirements, Illinois courts frequently refer to six common law factors (which are derived from § 757 of the Restatement (First) of Torts) in determining whether a trade secret exists: (1) the extent to which the information is known outside of the plaintiff's business; (2) the extent to which the information is known by employees and others involved in the plaintiff's business; (3) the extent of measures taken by the plaintiff to guard the secrecy of the information; (4) the value of the information to the plaintiff's business and to its competitors; (5) the amount of time, effort and money expended by the plaintiff in developing the information; and (6) the ease or difficulty with which the information could be properly acquired or duplicated by others. [Citations omitted.]

Contrary to Learning Curve's contention, we do not construe the foregoing factors as a six-part test, in which the absence of evidence on any single factor necessarily precludes a finding of trade secret protection. Instead, we interpret the common law factors as instructive guidelines for ascertaining whether a trade secret exists under the Act. The language of the Act itself makes no reference to these factors as independent requirements for trade secret status, and Illinois case law imposes no such requirement that each factor weigh in favor of the plaintiff. *See ILG Indus., Inc. v. Scott*, 49 Ill.2d 88, 273 N.E.2d 393, 396 (1971) ("An exact definition of a trade secret, applicable to all situations, is not possible. Some factors to be considered in determining whether given information is one's trade secret are [the six factors enumerated in the Restatement].") (internal quotation marks omitted). In this respect, Illinois law is compatible with the approach in other states. Courts from other jurisdictions, as well as legal scholars, have noted that the Restatement factors are not to be applied as a list of requisite elements. [Citations omitted.]

The existence of a trade secret ordinarily is a question of fact. As aptly observed by our colleagues on the Fifth Circuit, a trade secret "is one of the most elusive and difficult concepts in the law to define." *Lear Siegler, Inc. v. Ark-Ell Springs, Inc.*, 569 F.2d 286, 288 (5th Cir.1978). In many cases, the existence of a trade secret is not obvious; it requires an ad hoc evaluation of all the surrounding circumstances. For this reason, the question of whether certain information constitutes a trade secret ordinarily is best "resolved by a fact finder after full presentation of evidence from each side." *Id.* at 289. We do not believe that the district court was sufficiently mindful of these principles. The district court, in effect, treated the Restatement factors as requisite elements and substituted its judgment for that of the jury. PlayWood presented sufficient evidence for the jury reasonably to conclude that the Restatement factors weighed in PlayWood's favor.

1. Extent to which PlayWood's concept for noise-producing toy railroad track was known outside of PlayWood's business

PlayWood presented substantial evidence from which the jury could have determined that PlayWood's concept for noise-producing toy railroad track was not generally known outside of Playwood's business. It was undisputed at trial that no similar track was on the market until Learning Curve launched Clickety-Clack Track™ in late 1994, more than a year after PlayWood first conceived of the concept. Of course, as Learning Curve correctly points out, "[m]erely being the first or only one to use particular information does not in and of itself transform otherwise general knowledge into a trade secret." *George S. May Int'l*, 195 Ill.Dec. 183, 628 N.E.2d at 654. "If it did, the first person to use the information, no matter how ordinary or well known, would be able to appropriate it to his own use under the guise of a trade secret." *Serv. Ctrs.*, 129 Ill.Dec. 367, 535 N.E.2d at 1137. However, in this case, there was additional evidence from which the jury could have determined that PlayWood's concept was not generally known within the industry.

First, there was substantial testimony that Learning Curve had attempted to differentiate its track from that of its competitors for several months, but that it had been unable to do so successfully.

Furthermore, PlayWood's expert witness, Michael Kennedy, testified that PlayWood's concept, as embodied in Clickety-Clack Track™, was unique and permitted "its seller to differentiate itself from a host of competitors who [were] making a generic product." Trial Tr. at 518. Kennedy explained that the look, sound and feel of the track made it distinct from other toy railroad track: "[W]hen a child runs a train across this track, he can feel it hitting those little impressions. And when you're talking about young children [,] having the idea that they can see something that they couldn't see before, feel something that they couldn't feel before, hear something that they couldn't hear before, that is what differentiates this toy from its other competitors." *Id.* at 489.

Finally, PlayWood presented evidence that Learning Curve sought and obtained a patent on the noise-producing track. It goes without saying that the requirements for patent and trade secret protection are not synonymous. Unlike "a patentable invention, a trade secret need not be novel or unobvious." 2 Rudolf Callmann, *The Law of Unfair Competition, Trademarks and Monopolies* § 14.15, at 14-124 (4th ed.2003). "The idea need not be complicated; it may be intrinsically simple and nevertheless qualify as a secret, unless it is common knowledge and, therefore, within the public domain." *Forest Labs., Inc. v. Pillsbury Co.*, 452 F.2d 621, 624 (7th Cir.1971) (internal quotation marks omitted). However, it is commonly understood that "[i]f an invention has sufficient novelty to be entitled to patent protection, it may be said a *fortiori* to be entitled to protection as a trade secret." 1 Roger M. Milgrim, *Milgrim on Trade Secrets* § 1.08[1], at 1-353 (2002) (internal footnotes omitted). In light of this evidence, we cannot accept Learning Curve's argument that no rational jury could have found that PlayWood's concept was unknown outside of its business.

2. Extent to which PlayWood's concept was known to employees and others involved in PlayWood's business

The district court did not address the extent to which PlayWood's concept was known to employees and others involved in PlayWood's business. However, we agree with PlayWood that the evidence was sufficient to establish that its concept for noise-producing track was known only by key individuals in its business.

At the outset, we note briefly that PlayWood was a small business, consisting only of Clausi and Moore. Illinois courts have recognized on several occasions that the expectations for ensuring secrecy are different for small companies than for large companies. *See Jackson*, 210 Ill.Dec. 614, 653 N.E.2d at 815 ("[T]he determination of what steps are reasonably necessary to protect information is different for a large company than for a small one."); *Elmer Miller, Inc. v. Landis*, 253 Ill.App.3d 129, 192 Ill.Dec. 378, 625 N.E.2d 338, 342 (1993) ("[R]easonable steps for a two or three person shop may be different from reasonable steps for a larger company."). Apart from Clausi (PlayWood's sole toy designer and the person who conceived of the concept for noise-producing track) and Moore (PlayWood's sole officer and director), the only person who knew about the concept was Borsato, the person who physically produced PlayWood's prototype at Clausi's direction. The concept was disclosed to Borsato in order for PlayWood to develop fully its trade secret. *See* 1 Roger M. Milgrim, *Milgrim on Trade Secrets* § 1.04, at 1-173 (2002) ("A trade secret does not lose its character by being confidentially disclosed to agents or servants, without whose assistance it could not be made of any value.") (internal quotation marks omitted). Moreover, Borsato's actions were governed by a written confidentiality agreement with PlayWood. Indeed, as an extra precaution, Clausi even amended PlayWood's confidentiality agreement with Borsato immediately after the February 18, 1993, meeting to ensure that materials discussed during the meeting would remain confidential. From this evidence, the jury reasonably could have determined that this factor also weighed in favor of PlayWood.

3. Measures taken by PlayWood to guard the secrecy of its concept

There also was sufficient evidence for the jury to determine that PlayWood took reasonable precautions to guard the secrecy of its concept. The Act requires the trade secret owner to take actions that are "reasonable under the circumstances to maintain [the] secrecy or confidentiality" of its trade secret; it does not require perfection. 765 ILCS 1065/2(d)(2). Whether the measures taken by a trade secret owner are sufficient to satisfy the Act's reasonableness standard ordinarily is a question of fact for the jury. Indeed, we previously have recognized that "only in an extreme case can what is a 'reasonable' precaution be determined [as a matter of law], because the answer depends on a balancing of costs and benefits that will vary from case to case." *Rockwell Graphic Sys., Inc. v. DEV Indus., Inc.*, 925 F.2d 174, 179 (7th Cir.1991).

Here, the jury was instructed that it must find "by a preponderance of the evidence that PlayWood's trade secrets were given to Learning Curve as a result of a confidential relationship between the parties." Trial Tr. at 1449. By returning a verdict in favor of PlayWood, the jury necessarily found that Learning Curve was bound to PlayWood by a pledge of confidentiality. The jury's determination is amply supported by the evidence. Both Clausi and Moore testified that they entered into an oral confidentiality agreement with Abraham and Wilson before beginning their discussion on February 18, 1993. In particular, Clausi testified that he told Abraham and Wilson: "I also have some things, some ideas on how to produce the track and produce the trains now that I've had a chance to look at them for the last couple of days, and I think they're confidential as well. So if we're both okay with that, we should continue." Trial Tr. at 77. In addition to this testimony, the jury heard that Learning Curve had disclosed substantial information to PlayWood during the February 18th meeting, including projected volumes, costs and profit margins for various products, as well as drawings for toys not yet released to the public. The jury could have inferred that Learning Curve would not have disclosed such information in the absence of a confidentiality agreement. Finally, the jury also heard (from several of Learning Curve's former business associates) that Learning Curve routinely entered into oral confidentiality agreements like the one with PlayWood.

PlayWood might have done more to protect its secret. As Learning Curve points out, PlayWood gave its only prototype of the noise-producing track to Wilson without first obtaining a receipt or written confidentiality agreement from Learning Curve-a decision that proved unwise in hindsight. Nevertheless, we believe that the jury was entitled to conclude that PlayWood's reliance on the oral confidentiality agreement was reasonable under the circumstances of this case. First, it is well established that "[t]he formation of a confidential relationship imposes upon the disclosee the duty to maintain the information received in the utmost secrecy" and that "the unprivileged use or disclosure of another's trade secret becomes the basis for an action in tort." *Burten v. Milton Bradley Co.*, 763 F.2d 461, 463 (1st Cir.1985). Second, both Clausi and Moore testified that they believed PlayWood had a realistic chance to "get in the door" with Learning Curve and to produce the concept as part of Learning Curve's line of Thomas products. Clausi and Moore did not anticipate that Learning Curve would violate the oral confidentiality agreement and utilize PlayWood's concept without permission; rather, they believed in good faith that they "were going to do business one day again with Learning Curve with respect to the design concept." Trial Tr. at 236-37. Finally, we believe that, as part of the reasonableness inquiry, the jury could have considered the size and sophistication of the parties, as well as the relevant industry. Both PlayWood and Learning Curve were small toy companies, and PlayWood was the smaller and less experienced of the two. Viewing the evidence in the light most favorable to PlayWood, as we must, we conclude that there was sufficient evidence for the jury to determine that PlayWood took reasonable measures to protect the secrecy of its concept.

4. Value of the concept to PlayWood and to its competitors

There was substantial evidence from which the jury could have determined that PlayWood's concept had value both to PlayWood and to its competitors. It was undisputed at trial that Learning Curve's sales skyrocketed after it began to sell Clickety-Clack Track™ In addition, PlayWood's expert witness, Michael Kennedy, testified that PlayWood's concept for noise-producing track had tremendous value. Kennedy testified that the "cross-cuts and changes in the [track's] surface" imparted value to its seller by causing the track to "look different, feel different and sound different than generic track." Trial Tr. at 504. Kennedy further testified that, in his opinion, the track would have commanded a premium royalty under a negotiated license agreement because the "invention allows its seller to differentiate itself from a host of competitors who are making a generic product with whom it is competing in a way that is proprietary and exclusive, and it gives [the seller] a significant edge over [its] competition." *Id.* at 518-19.

Despite this evidence, the district court concluded that PlayWood's concept had no economic value. The court's conclusion was based, in part, on the fact that PlayWood's prototype did not work perfectly; as noted by the court, the first set of cuts were too shallow to produce sound and the second set of cuts were too deep to permit the train to roll smoothly across the track. In the district court's view, even if the concept of cutting grooves into the wooden track in order to produce noise originated with Clausi, the concept lacked value until it was refined, developed and manufactured by Learning Curve.

We cannot accept the district court's conclusion because it is belied by the evidence. At trial, Kennedy was asked whether, in his opinion, the fact that PlayWood's prototype did not work perfectly affected the value of PlayWood's concept, and he testified that it did not. *See* Trial Tr. at 578. Kennedy testified that he would assign the same value to PlayWood's concept as it was conceived on February 18, 1993, as he would the finished product that became known as Clickety-Clack Track™ because, at that time, he would have known "that most of the design [had] already been done and that [he] just need[ed] to go a little bit further to make it really lovely." *Id.* at 578. Kennedy further testified that it was standard practice in the industry for a license to be negotiated based on a prototype (much like the one PlayWood disclosed to Learning Curve) rather than a finished product and that the license generally would cover the prototypical design, as well as any enhancements or improvements of that design. *See* Trial Tr. at 500-01. Based on this testimony, we cannot accept the district court's conclusion that PlayWood's concept possessed no economic value.

It is irrelevant under Illinois law that PlayWood did not actually use the concept

does not need to actually use in business—just value

in its business. "[T]he proper criterion is not 'actual use' but whether the trade secret is 'of value' to the company." *Syntex Ophthalmics, Inc. v. Tsuetaki*, 701 F.2d 677, 683 (7th Cir.1983). Kennedy's testimony was more than sufficient to permit the jury to conclude that the concept was "of value" to PlayWood. It is equally irrelevant that PlayWood did not seek to patent its concept. So long as the concept remains a secret, *i.e.*, outside of the public domain, there is no need for patent protection. Professor Milgrim makes this point well: "Since every inventor has the right to keep his invention secret, one who has made a patentable invention has the option to maintain it in secrecy, relying upon protection accorded to a trade secret rather than upon the rights which accrue by a patent grant." 1 Roger M. Milgrim, *Milgrim on Trade Secrets* § 1.08[1], at 1-353 (2002). It was up to PlayWood, not the district court, to determine when and how the concept should have been disclosed to the public.

5. Amount of time, effort and money expended by PlayWood in developing its concept

PlayWood expended very little time and money developing its concept; by Clausi's own account, the cost to PlayWood was less than one dollar and the time spent was less than one-half hour. The district court determined that "[s]uch an insignificant investment is . . . insufficient as a matter of Illinois law to establish the status of a 'trade secret.' " R.202 at 16. We believe that the district court gave too much weight to the time, effort and expense of developing the track.

Although Illinois courts commonly look to the Restatement factors for guidance in determining whether a trade secret exists, as we have noted earlier, the requisite statutory inquiries under Illinois law are (1) whether the information "is sufficiently secret to derive economic value, actual or potential, from not being generally known to other persons who can obtain economic value from its disclosure or use;" and (2) whether the information "is the subject of efforts that are reasonable under the circumstances to maintain its secrecy or confidentiality." 765 ILCS 1065/2(d). A significant expenditure of time and/or money in the production of information may provide evidence of value, which is relevant to the first inquiry above. However, we do not understand Illinois law to require such an expenditure in all cases.

As pointed out by the district court, several Illinois cases have emphasized the importance of developmental costs. However, notably, none of those cases concerned the sort of innovative and creative concept that we have in this case. Indeed, several of the cases in Illinois that emphasize developmental costs concern compilations of data, such as customer lists. In that context, it makes sense to require the expenditure of significant time and money because there is nothing original or creative about the alleged trade secret. Given enough time and money, we presume that the plaintiff's competitors could compile a similar list.

Here, by contrast, we are dealing with a new toy design that has been promoted as "the first significant innovation in track design since the inception of wooden train systems." PlayWood's Tr. Ex.71. Toy designers, like many artistic individuals, have intuitive flashes of creativity. Often, that intuitive flash is, in reality, the product of earlier thought and practice in an artistic craft. We fail to see how the value of PlayWood's concept would differ in any respect had Clausi spent several months and several thousand dollars creating the noise-producing track. Accordingly, we conclude that PlayWood's lack of proof on this factor does not preclude the existence of a trade secret.

6. Ease or difficulty with which PlayWood's concept could have been properly acquired or duplicated by others

Finally, we also believe that there was sufficient evidence for the jury to determine that PlayWood's concept could not have been easily acquired or duplicated through proper means. PlayWood's expert witness, Michael Kennedy, testified: "This is a fairly simple product if you look at it. But the truth is that because it delivers feeling and sound as well as appearance, it isn't so simple as it first appears. It's a little more elegant, actually, than you might think." Trial Tr. at 504. In addition to Kennedy's testimony, the jury heard that Learning Curve had spent months attempting to differentiate its track from Brio's before Clausi disclosed PlayWood's concept of noise-producing track. From this evidence, the jury could have inferred that, if PlayWood's concept really was obvious, Learning Curve would have thought of it earlier.

Despite this evidence, the district court concluded that PlayWood's concept was not a trade secret because it could have been easily duplicated, stating that "[h]ad PlayWood succeeded in producing and marketing [the] notched track, the appearance of the track product itself would have fully revealed the concept PlayWood now claims as a secret." R.202 at 5-6. Of course, the district court was correct in one sense; PlayWood's own expert recognized that, in the absence of patent or copyright protection, the track could have been reverse engineered just by looking at it. *See* Trial Tr. at 562. However, the district court failed to appreciate the fact that PlayWood's concept was not publicly available. As Professor Milgrim states: "A potent distinction exists between a trade secret which *will be* disclosed if and when the product in which it is embodied is placed on sale, and a 'trade secret' embodied in a product which has been placed on sale, which product admits of discovery of the 'secret' upon inspection, analysis, or reverse engineering." 1 Roger M. Milgrim, *Milgrim on Trade Secrets* § 1.05[4], at 1-228 (2002). "Until disclosed by sale the trade secret should be entitled to protection." *Id.; see also* 2 Rudolf Callmann, *The Law of Unfair Competition, Trademarks and Monopolies* § 14.15, at 14-123 (4th ed. 2003) ("The fact that a secret is easy to duplicate after it becomes known does not militate against its being a trade secret prior to that time."). Reverse engineering can defeat a trade secret claim, but only if the product could have been properly acquired by others, as is the case when the product is publicly sold. Here, PlayWood disclosed its concept to Learning Curve (and Learning Curve alone) in the context of a confidential relationship; Learning Curve had no legal authority to reverse engineer the prototype that it received in confidence. *See Laff v. John O. Butler Co.*, 64 Ill.App.3d 603, 21 Ill.Dec. 314, 381 N.E.2d 423, 433 (1978) ("[A] trade secret is open to anyone, not bound by a confidential relationship or a contract with the secret's owner, who can discover the secret through lawful means."). Accordingly, we must conclude that the jury was entitled to determine that PlayWood's concept could not easily have been acquired or duplicated through proper means.

* * *

### (b) Business Agreement

## B.F. GLADDING & CO. v. SCIENTIFIC ANGLERS, INC.

245 F.2d 722 (6th Cir. 1957)

This is an action originally brought by B. F. Gladding & Co., Inc., a New York corporation, an old, established fishing line manufacturer, against Scientific Anglers, Inc., a Michigan corporation, for specific performance of a contract, violation of trade secrets and for unfair competition. Scientific Anglers, Inc., was incorporated in 1946 with Leon P. Martuch as president and Clare S. Harris, vice-president, secretary and treasurer. Sometime in 1947 Gladding became the sole distributor of certain fishing line coating products then being made and sold by Scientific. On December 1, 1950, a written contract was entered into between Scientific and Gladding, and the issues of this case revolve around that contract. It will be sufficient to quote therefrom paragraphs 2, 8, 9, 10 and 13 which we cite in the margin.

During the operative existence of the contract (December 1, 1950 to December 31, 1953), a fishing line was developed chiefly by Scientific which has been and is being marketed by Gladding under the trade name of 'Aerofloat.' The 'Aerofloat' line is unusual in that because of the presence of numerous gas bubbles beneath the line coating, it will float; and for that reason is especially suitable for dry fly fishing. Some time after the contract had expired, Scientific began to make and sell an 'Air Cel' fishing line which is similar, if not the same, as Gladding's 'Aerofloat' line. Mr. Martuch, president of Scientific, after the contract terminated, filed two patent applications which cover the 'Aerofloat' line development. One application (Serial No. 403,823), filed January 13, 1954, disclosed the precise combination of variable orifice die and automatic timing mechanism that has been used by both parties in the manufacture of their respective 'Aerofloat' and 'Air Cel' lines. The other application (Serial No. 447,068) covers the 'Aerofloat' and 'Air Cel' lines as articles of manufacture. These applications were assigned to Scientific.

Gladding, acting under assumed rights by virtue of the contract, indicated to Scientific that it was interested in securing exclusive rights under the patent applications, and differences of opinion arose as to such assumed rights. After a series of letters had failed to compose the differences, Gladding brought the instant action in the District Court on January 19, 1955. Various hearings, motions, etc., were made and heard before the District Court, and on May 2, 1955, upon Gladding's petition, that Court granted a preliminary injunction against Scientific effective June 15, 1955. Gladding was required to post $2,000 bond. Trial of the case was held in August, 1955.

March 9, 1956, the District Court filed an opinion (*B. F. Gladding & Co., Inc., v. Scientific Anglers, Inc.*, 139 F.Supp. 236) in which it was stated that proper negotiations still had not been held pursuant to Article 10 of the contract and that unless Gladding was willing on or before April 14, 1956 (later extended by order of the Court), to meet a royalty charge up to five per cent (5%) on its net sales of the bubble or float line, that it no longer would have any rights in the patents applied for or to in any way interfere with the obtaining of the patents applied for by Scientific. In the opinion it was specifically held that Scientific had no right to condition negotiations on the guarantee by Gladding to pay minimum royalty on the basis of the sales of a certain number of the bubble lines. Other findings in the opinion we will later discuss.

Scientific and Gladding further negotiated. But Scientific insisted upon conditions which Gladding was unwilling to accept. The trial judge, in order to assist the parties, wrote several letters to their attorneys. Gladding by letter dated March 20, 1956, expressly agreed to pay 5% royalty and also agreed to include a so-called 'anti-shelving provision' in the license whereby Gladding would be required to make 'substantial use' of the inventions covered by the patent applications, and further that if 'substantial use' was not made, Scientific would have the right, upon sixty days notice, to cancel the license. Scientific again refused to accept Gladding's offer and insisted upon certain provisions to which we shall later advert.

Upon April 17, 1956, the trial judge, in a letter to the attorneys for the parties, again attempted to suggest possible solutions of their differences. The District Judge, in this letter and contrary to his former expressed view, stated that a minimum royalty should be included in any licensing agreement and suggested a minimum annual figure of $12,2500.00. It was further stated in the letter that, in the event Gladding's business was insufficient to meet such minimum royalty, Scientific could, in thirty days, cancel the exclusive license and Gladding would then 'have no license at all.' Gladding was unwilling to agree to these conditions, and in a subsequent letter to the trial judge attempted to explain that the Judge's position as to the requirements of a minimum royalty was inconsistent with his earlier position and in law was unsound. Gladding also wrote that if the Judge insisted on a minimum royalty provision in the compromise agreement, it would acquiesce up to the minimum amount of $3,500, stating that it was customary to set the minimum annual royalty at not more than one-half of the expected royalty income for an average good year, and that their expected yearly sales would amount to $7,000.

Scientific was unwilling to accept $3,500 as a minimum royalty, but following the Judge's suggestion, demanded $12,500; and in addition demanded that should Gladding lose the exclusive license from failure to pay the minimum royalty so demanded, then Gladding would also lose its non-exclusive license or shop right it already possessed.

Later, at the suggestion of Judge Picard, Scientific consented to a minimum royalty of $8,500. But, significantly, Scientific still insisted by letter, dated May 14, 1956, that Gladding would lose both its non-exclusive license or shop right and exclusive license if Gladding should fail to meet the minimum royalty which might be agreed upon.

On May 18, 1956, the District Court filed an amended opinion in which it was stated that Gladding refused to enter into an exclusive license on reasonable terms with Scientific and that the only course open to the Court was to dismiss Gladding's bill of complaint and dismiss the injunction it had issued upon Gladding's petition *See B. F. Gladding & Co., Inc., v. Scientific Anglers, Inc., 141 F.Supp. 630, 631.*

Judgment was entered on June 4, 1956, dismissing Gladding's bill of complaint and quashing the injunction. Scientific was awarded damages arising out of the loss of business during the period of the temporary injunction, and Scientific was held to be entitled to reasonable attorney's fees, disbursements and costs. Gladding appealed.

The Appeal

Appellant Gladding initially argues that, under the contract entered into by the parties, Scientific was obligated to grant to Gladding an exclusive license if Gladding was willing to pay the top royalty rate of five per cent stipulated in the contract and that no other negotiations or terms were to be considered. Appellant cites our decision in *Cold Metal Process Co. v. Republic Steel Corp.*, 6 Cir., 233 F.2d 828, 829, 844, in support of this position. While the Cold Metal case is similar, it is not on all fours with the instant case. In the Cold Metal case, Cold Metal agreed '3. When and if such claim or claims to common subject-matter are granted in any patent issued on Cold Metal's applications, Cold Metal shall grant to United a license to make, use and sell rolling mills under such claim or claims, which license shall be exclusive to United . . . .' Cold Metal in addition reserved the right to use the same patents in its own plant or plants. In the Cold Metal case negotiations were to take place as to the payment to be made by United to Cold Metal. *Cold Metal Process Co. v. United Engineering & Foundry Co.*, 3 Cir., 107 F.2d 27, 28. In the instant case the agreement provided that Gladding 'shall have the first refusal of exclusive rights thereunder.'

We are of the opinion that under the terms of the contract Gladding had an inchoate right to an exclusive license under any patent application filed by Scientific. All terms and conditions of any proposed licensing agreement were not and probably could not have been set forth clearly in the contract. The basis of the right was set out, while conditions, terms and provisions were left to agreement appropriate in the circumstances. In *De Stubner v. United Carbon Co.*, D.C., 67 F.Supp. 884, affirmed 4 Cir., 163 F.2d 735, a licensing agreement was construed in which no minimum royalty of any kind was provided for, but in which royalties were to be paid on products made under the license according to a rate which was not fixed therein, but which was to be later determined in the light of market conditions. The Court state (67 F.Supp. page 893):' The Court cannot go beyond the agreement of the parties and establish a minimum royalty where none was provided for by the parties themselves.' We are in accord with the above statement.

Gladding was fully aware that Scientific should not protected against non-use of the patents by Gladding, and was willing to include in the licensing agreement a so-called 'anti-shelving' provision whereby Gladding would be required to make 'substantial use' of the patents in order to continue in possession of the exclusive license.

When Gladding asked for an exclusive license, Scientific insisted upon one condition which Gladding was under no obligation to accept. Under Article 10 of the original contract, Gladding was granted a non-exclusive license or shop right in any invention, discovery or improvement made by Scientific during the term of the agreement and arising out of work done by Scientific for Gladding. It was clearly stated in Article 13 that should the agreement terminate, the termination would not 'affect any licenses or shop rights acquired by either party hereunder.' Scientific had no right to insist as a condition to granting an exclusive license that, should

Gladding fail to pay the requisite royalties, the exclusive license would and together with the previously acquired non-exclusive license or shop right.

The contract secures to Gladding an inchoate right to receive an exclusive license providing Gladding was willing to pay up to a 5% royalty and to abide by reasonable working terms and conditions. But such working terms do not, of course, authorize Scientific to insist on a minimum royalty or to insist on the loss of the non-exclusive license or shop right should be exclusive license fail. To hold otherwise would be to destroy the value of Gladding's right of 'first refusal' in any patent application filed by Scientific.

We have carefully read the exchange of correspondence between Scientific, Gladding and the District Judge and can reach no other conclusion that that the trial judge's finding that Gladding was unwilling to enter into an exclusive license on reasonable terms is clearly erroneous. *United States v. Gypsum Co.*, 333 U.S. 364, 68 S.Ct. 525, 92 L.Ed. 746. Scientific was insisting on unreasonable conditions, which, under the contract, Gladding was not obliged to accept. The evidence strongly indicates that Scientific was trying to avoid granting an exclusive license. On the other hand, Gladding made concessions which it was not obliged to make. Gladding is thus entitled to specific performance of the contract, without concessions outside its terms, the principal provision of the contract being that Gladding is to pay, as it has agreed, 5% royalty; and the minor provisions being reasonable working terms and conditions, which the trial court may provide in its decree.

Trade Secrets

Gladding next argues that Scientific is not entitled to use the trade secrets that constitute unpatentable contributions to the 'Aerofloat' line development prior to public disclosure. Gladding alleges that some of the unpatentable trade secrets are described in explicit detail in the bubble line patent application and others are not covered by either patent application. Gladding claims sole ownership of these trade secrets by virtue of the employment provided for in Article 2 of the contract in suit. The District Court held that no trade secrets exclusively belonging to Gladding were included in the bubble line as manufactured in the finished product or through the patents applied for, and that any trade secrets existing were either those developed by Scientific alone or by both Scientific and Gladding. The Court also held that the contract was designed to cover unpatentable as well as patentable processes and that it was contemplated by the parties that both were to enjoy the fruits of their efforts. The Court further held that the contract was not one to 'invent' and that Scientific was an independent contractor and not an employee within the meaning of the patent law.

A trade secret may be defined as any formula, pattern, device or compilation of information which is used in one's business, and which gives him an opportunity to obtain an advantage over competitors who do not know or use it. RESTATEMENT OF TORTS, Vol. IV, § 757(b). The protection given to trade secrets is against breach of faith and reprehensible means of learning another's secrets. In order for one to secure such protection it is necessary to show that (1) the subject matter of the designated trade secret is in fact secret, (2) that one is the owner or possessor of such secret, (3) and that the person who is using or disclosing or attempting to disclose the trade secret acquired it in such a manner that a disclosure by him would amount to a breach of confidence as to the person who disclosed it to him.

The usual trade secret case arises out of the employer-employee relationship whereby an employee acquires knowledge of the trade secret of his employer because of a confidential relationship. The instant case is somewhat unusual in that the alleged trade secrets of appellant here sought to be protected were not in existence when Scientific entered into the contract with Gladding. They were developed after the contract was executed and were either jointly developed by Scientific and Gladding or by Scientific alone. Gladding here makes no complaint of the finding of the trial court that the 'Aerofloat' line was a joint development. But Gladding says even though the secrets may have been jointly developed, they are still the exclusive secrets of Gladding because of the contract entered into by the parties. Gladding cites *Fairchild Engine and Airplane Corp. v. Cox*, Sup., 50 N.Y.S.2d 643, for the proposition that a process or development need not be patentable to get protection against disclosure as a trade secret. With this we agree. But the Fairchild case is distinguishable from the instant case and does not aid in the determination as to ownership of the trade secrets in the instant case. In the Fairchild case, a process of bonding aluminum to steel was developed by two employees of Fairchild who were employed to 'invent' and advance the process. A former vice-president and director of Fairchild, who had acquired knowledge of the process while so employed, was disclosing, or about to disclose, the process to another company. But, significantly, in the Fairchild case, the process or trade secret clearly belonged to Fairchild because of the fact that the two employees were employed by Fairchild for the specific purpose of inventing and developing the process. That is not the situation in the instant case. The contract clearly covered patentable developments or inventions made by Scientific. It provided that Scientific had the right to file patent applications on such inventions and Gladding was to have a shop right or non-exclusive license with the right of 'first refusal' as to securing an exclusive license. Gladding argues that Scientific was limited to patentable contributions or developments it made and that the unpatentable processes were to be the exclusive trade secrets of Gladding.

Article 8 of the agreement provides in part:

'. . . Each of the parties agrees that, during the term of this agreement, it will not disclose or divulge to any unauthorized person, any of the formulas, processes, machines, or apparatus (secret or otherwise), pertaining to the business in which the other party is or may become engaged during the term of this agreement. Each of the parties further agree (sic) that at no time, either during the term of this agreement or thereafter, will it disclose or divulge to any unauthorized person any trade secrets of the other party, or any confidential information relating to the other party's business of which it may gain knowledge during the term of this agreement, unless and until such time as said other party shall make public such trade secrets or confidential information.'

From a careful reading of Article 8 it can be seen that it was primarily placed in the contract to protect the trade secrets 'of the other party' and does not necessarily cover trade secrets which might be jointly owned and/or developed by both of the parties after the agreement. Even without any specific mention in the contract joint trade secrets would be protected against unlawful disclosure by one of the parties.

After careful consideration of the provisions of the contract, we do not feel constrained to upset the findings of the District Court that the parties contemplated that both would enjoy and control the fruits of their efforts and that no exclusive trade secrets of Gladding are being used by Scientific. [Citations omitted.]

Appellant further argues that Scientific is not entitled to use the trade secrets that may constitute patentable contributions to the 'Aerofloat' line prior to the issuance of letters patent on the applications. We find this claim without merit and for two reasons. First, we have previously affirmed the findings of the trial court that no exclusive trade secrets of Gladding are involved, and therefore Scientific should enjoy their use as well as Gladding. Furthermore, Article 10 of the contract does not so limit the rights of Scientific to such secrets. It is not necessary for the validity of a licensing agreement that letters patent be first issued. [Citations omitted.]

Article 10 speaks of Scientific's furnishing Gladding a copy of any patent application and Gladding having 'the first refusal of exclusive rights thereunder.' Clearly this implies that the rights are in the application and any resulting patent, but it does not mean that a patent must first issue.

Other contentions raised by appellant as to the identity of the inventor of the variable die application and bubble line application, we hold that we need not consider.

Finally appellant argues that Scientific should not be entitled to describe, in its bubble line application, the unpatentable contributions to the 'Aerofloat' line development solely in support of an effort to obtain patent protection on the use of a blowing agent which is a separate and subsidiary feature not included in the 'Aerofloat' line development. Gladding argues that claims 1 and 2 of the bubble line application are such that they will not be allowed by the Patent Office and thus only claims 3 to 8 will remain. Gladding says claims 3 to 8 are directed to the use of a blowing agent, which is a commercially worthless idea that has been abandoned by Scientific itself. But Gladding argues that the issuance of such a limited patent, even if granted, would effectively destroy some of the most valuable trade secrets relating to primer and plastisol coating and the process of applying the line coating, and thus make them available for use by competitors of Gladding. The District Court did not consider this aspect of the case, although the point was raised in appellant's complaint.

As previously said, we are of the opinion that the unpatentable secrets are not solely owned by Gladding but are joint trade secrets of the parties. But even if they are joint trade secrets, they are still entitled to protection against unlawful and unreasonable disclosure. [Citation omitted.] We are of the opinion that the trial judge should consider this aspect of the case and determine whether or not Scientific is unlawfully and unreasonably describing these secrets in the bubble line application. If Scientific is guilty of such conduct, then it should be enjoined.

Based on what we have heretofore said, the judgment is reversed and the cause is remanded to the District Court for appropriate action in accordance with this opinion. It appears that the proposed licensing agreement drawn by Gladding and enclosed in a letter to Scientific dated April 23, 1956, will be a proper licensing agreement.

Article 14 of the proposed licensing agreement dealing with a minimum royalty amounting to $3,500 can be eliminated at the option of Gladding if Gladding wishes to substitute the 'anti-shelving' or 'substantial use' provision previously suggested.

We add that the royalty should not be held to commence only upon the granting of a patent under the applications. In the licensing agreement submitted by Gladding to Scientific on April 23, 1956, Gladding agreed to pay royalties from and after July 8, 1955. Gladding now argues that this was an erroneous concession on its part, and the royalties should start to accrue only when patents are issued. We hold that under the original contract it was contemplated that royalties were to be paid when the exclusive license was granted, regardless of whether or not a patent had been actually granted or issued. [Citations omitted.] The royalties should commence upon the grant to Gladding by Scientific of an exclusive license. An accounting should be had to determine an award to Gladding for damages caused by reason of Scientific's manufacture and slae of its 'Air Cel' line in competition with Gladding's 'Aerofloat' line. Gladding is to recover the $2,000 bound deposited in the District Court in connection with the preliminary injunction originally granted by the District Court; the $250 bond in connection with this appeal; reasonable attorney's fees and costs.

### (c) Covenants Not to Compete

## MILWAUKEE LINEN SUPPLY CO. v. RING

246 N.W. 567 (Wis. 1933)

Action commenced May 6, 1932, to enjoin a discharged employee from violating his agreement not to solicit or divert the employer's customers or its business or patronage within a stated time and territory. Judgment for defendant entered June 20, 1932. The plaintiff appeals.

The defendant had been for eleven years in the employ of plaintiff as a driver of a wagon collecting and delivering towels and linen in the prosecution of its business of furnishing customers with towels and shop and office linen. On May 14, 1930, the defendant was promoted to the position of route foreman. A contract in writing was then signed by the parties whereby the plaintiff agreed to pay the defendant a stated wage of $42.50 per week, and the defendant agreed that he would not within two years after leaving plaintiff's employment call for or deliver laundered linen to persons who should have been customers of plaintiff and supplied by the defendant during any time he might have been employed under the contract, would not solicit or divert plaintiff's customers or its business or patronage within said period, and would not within said period engage in the supply business, or call for or deliver laundered or unlaundered towels or linens for himself or any other persons within the limits of Milwaukee and specified suburbs.

The contract was not to run for any specified term, but might be terminated by either party on two weeks' notice. The defendant continued to work under said contract until March 7, 1932, when the plaintiff terminated his service by giving the specified notice. The defendant thereafter endeavored to procure employment outside the towel and linen supply business, but was unable to do so. In April, 1932, he was employed as a solicitor by a competitor of plaintiff. The only work he could procure up to this time was peddling soap from door to door, at which he earned about $4 per week. He was partially disabled physically, and the disability so affected his appearance as to handicap him seriously in procuring employment in most lines, and he lacked experience and familiarity with lines of business other than that in which he had been so long employed.

The trial court found as above stated and many other evidentiary facts well supporting its conclusions of ultimate fact: "(17) That the restrictions against defendant's employment sought in this action to be enforced by the plaintiff are not reasonably necessary for the fair protection of the plaintiff's business or rights; (18) that said restrictions unreasonably restrict the rights of the defendant, giving due consideration to the existing circumstances; (19) that the interests of the public would be adversely affected under present conditions by the granting of the injunction prayed for and the keeping of the defendant out of employment, without any appreciable benefit to the plaintiff; (20) that the plaintiff has failed to prove that irreparable injury will result to it if the injunction asked for in this action is not granted; (21) that the granting of the injunction to plaintiff would do more injustice than justice and would result in greater damage to the defendant and the public than corresponding benefit to the plaintiff." Judgment was entered dismissing the complaint on the merits.

Robert B. Ells, of Milwaukee, for appellant.

Alfred C. Rudolph, of Milwaukee, for respondent.

FOWLER, J.

The contract in suit is one in restraint of trade, which is tersely defined as one whose "performance would limit competition in any business or restrict a promisor in the exercise of a gainful occupation." Such a contract "is illegal if the restraint is unreasonable," and such a contract "is unreasonable . . . if . . . it (a) is greater than is required for the protection of the person for whose benefit the restraint is imposed, or (b) imposes undue hardship upon the person restricted." RESTATEMENT OF THE LAW OF CONTRACTS, §§ 513, 514, 515. It will be observed that the findings of the learned trial judge designated above as (17) and (18) find as facts that the contract in suit is unreasonable as violating (a) above, and in effect for violating (b). Finding (17) appears to us to be amply supported by the evidence as does (18) when other evidentiary facts found are considered in connection with it.

The appellant contends that the decision of the trial court is in direct conflict with the decision of this court in *Eureka Laundry Co. v. Long*, 146 Wis. 205, 131 N. W. 412, 35 L. R. A. (N. S.) 119. It might so seem at first blush. The contracts involved are practically alike in their terms. But a contract in restraint of trade may be valid as applied to one set of circumstances and invalid as applied to another set. The circumstances involved in the two cases are dissimilar in many respects. There the defendant was a driver of a wagon collecting and delivering laundry, and the injunction issued only restrained him from operating in violation of his contract upon the route on which he had served the plaintiff; here the plaintiff seeks to enjoin the defendant from soliciting in the entire city of Milwaukee and its suburbs, and the employee was not a driver, but a route manager only and had no contacts with the customers except as he saw them while collecting overdue accounts, adjusting complaints, or soliciting resumption of patronage where customers had discontinued the plaintiff's business. There the defendant left plaintiff's employment and entered that of a rival concern; here the defendant was discharged by the plaintiff.

There it does not appear that the defendant was not fit for and might not procure other employment and he was not prevented from entering employment of the same nature in other portions of the city; here he is enjoined from following anywhere in the city or practically in the whole county of Milwaukee the only occupation he is fit or qualified to follow. There, there was no intimation or indication that the defendant would be likely to become a public charge if the injunction were granted; here such likelihood is quite apparent, in view of the prevailing conditions of unemployment of which the court should take judicial notice. There the relations between the driver and the customer were direct and intimate; here direct contacts were limited and comparatively few. There the defendant had personal acquaintance with all of the customers in the territory in which he was enjoined from operating; here the defendant had such acquaintance with only 100 out of 2,500 customers of plaintiff. There the defendant had been operating as a driver in the entire district in which his operation was enjoined up to the immediate time; here the defendant was not a driver at the immediate time, and his service as driver had terminated two years previous and had been limited to one route of the five maintained by the plaintiff and to another route which he had served several years prior. There the injunction ran against soliciting, contrary to the contract in suit, customers whom the defendant had served by delivering and collecting laundry; here the provision of the contract in suit respecting calling for or delivering does not apply because limited to calling for and delivering *under the contract*, and the defendant's calling for and delivering was not done under the contract, but before his contract as route manager was entered into when he was employed as a driver.

The differences between the facts in the two cases justify the difference in the judgments, when we consider the reasons that have governed and should govern courts in determining the validity of contracts in restraint of employment and in denying injunctional relief upon them. Formerly the sole reason for holding contracts in restraint of trade void was that they were contrary to public policy because the public should have the benefit of the services and business ability of everybody everywhere. With change of conditions, this in time came to be modified so that such contracts were considered valid if reasonable for the protection of the business for which the restraints of the contract were imposed. This has again been modified so that the interests not only of the public and the business for which the restraint is imposed, but also of the party restrained, are considered, and, if the restraint is reasonable upon consideration of all these interests, it is valid. This view was expressed by Lord MacNaghten in 1895 in *Nordenfelt v. Maxim-Nordenfelt*, on appeal to the House of Lords, 11 Rep. 27, as follows: "The public have an interest in every person's carrying on his trade freely; so has the individual. All interference with individual liberty of action in trading, and all restraints of trade of themselves, if there is nothing more, are contrary to public policy, and therefore void. That is the general rule. But there are exceptions; restraints of trade and interference with individual liberty of action may be justified by the special circumstances of a particular case. It is a sufficient justification, and, indeed it is the only justification, if the restriction is reasonable — reasonable that is in reference to the interests of the parties concerned, and reasonable in reference to the interests of the public, so framed and so guarded as to afford adequate protection to the party in whose favor it is imposed, while at the same time it is in no wise injurious to the public."

The question always resolves itself into "what is a reasonable restraint with reference to the particular case." Id., 11 Rep. 32. "Any restraint is unreasonable" which is more extensive "than the interests of the party with whom the contract is made can possibly require." Id. 11 Rep. 34. There is greater scope of restraint in contracts between vendor and vendee than betweeen employer and employee. In the latter class of cases, there is "small scope for the restraint of the right to labor and trade and a correspondingly small freedom of contract." In such cases, "in order that the court may uphold and enforce the restriction, . . . the court must find that the facts alleged disclose a restriction on the employee 'reasonably necessary for the fair protection of the employer's business or rights, and not unreasonably restricting the rights of the employee, due regard being had to the interests of the public and the circumstances and conditions under which the contract is to be performed.' " *Samuel Stores v. Abrams*, 94 Conn. 248, 108 A. 541, 543, 9 A. L. R. 1450, 1454, and cases there cited. If the reasonable and fair protection of plaintiff's business does not require such extended restriction of the defendant's field of employment as the contract provides, the restraint is unreasonable. "Public policy requires that the defendant's liberty of action in trading or employment shall not be unduly restricted." *Samuel Stores v. Abrams*, 94 Conn. 248, 108 A. 541, 544, 9 A. L. R. 1455. "The test which the law prescribes in all such cases is this: The restraint, in order to be valid, must be only such as is necessary to afford a fair protection to the party in favor of whom it is given, and not so large as to interfere with the interest of the public." *Sternberg v. O'Brien*, 48 N. J. Eq. 370, 22 A. 348, 349. A restraint that is unreasonable as to the defendant is prejudicial to the public, and is therefore not enforceable. Morris v. Saxelby, [1916] A. C. 688, Ann.Cas. 1916D, 537, 538. These rules are stated generally in 3 Williston on Contracts, § 1643. The learned trial judge had them clearly in mind in deciding the case, and his findings clearly throw the case outside the field of injunctional relief.

The judgment of the circuit court is affirmed.

## NOTES AND QUESTIONS:

1. The most effective way to protect a trade secret is to have the recipient of the secret or confidential information sign a nondisclosure agreement. This is a common practice in employment agreements, vendor or supplier contracts, consulting agreements, and non-disclosure agreements for allowing a prospective buyer to evaluate technology. Problems arise when the holder of the information becomes overzealous and tries to extend the agreement to cover information that is not really secret. This type of overreaching can result in the entire agreement being held to be unenforceable. As noted in Restatement (Third) of Unfair Competition, "[a]

promise to refrain from use or disclosure of information is ordinarily unenforceable unless the information is sufficiently secret to justify the restraint. RESTATEMENT (THIRD) OF UNFAIR COMPETITION § 41 reporters' note, cmt. d.

2. The Seventh Circuit's decision in *Learning Curve Toys, Inc. v. PlayWood Toys, Inc.*, 342 F.3d 714 (7th Cir.2003), demonstrates the advantage of having a confidential disclosure agreement in place before disclosing the details of a business opportunity. After reading the cases in the next section on creating a fiduciary relationship, consider what other hurdles the plaintiff in *Learning Curve* would have had to overcome in order to prevail if there had been no agreement. *Learning Curve* also demonstrates the potential difficulties of enforcing such an agreement when an unauthorized use of the trade secrets takes place.

3. Although in *B.F. Gladding & Co. v. Scientific Anglers, Inc.*, 245 F.2d 722 (6th Cir.1957), the agreement provided for Gladding to obtain exclusive rights under any patent application filed by Scientific, a dispute arose because the parties could not agree on the details of the licensing agreement. Could the parties have anticipated some of these issues and resolved them in the agreement so they did not have be negotiated after Gladding opted to exercise his option to obtain exclusive rights? Was the court correct in its observation that "[a]ll terms and conditions of any proposed licensing agreement . . . probably could not have been set forth in the contract?" *Id.* at 726. If so, why? If not, why not?

4. Many companies use covenants not to compete to prevent the unauthorized disclosure and use of confidential information. All such agreements are restraints on trade and must be reasonable in order to be enforced. The quote in *Milwaukee Linen Supply Co. v. Ring*, 246 N.W. 567, 569 (Wis.1933), from Lord MacNaghten in 1895 is particularily aprt: "It is a sufficient justification, and, indeed it is the only justification, if the restriction is reasonable — reasonable that is in reference to the interests of the parties concerned, and reasonable in reference to the interests of the public, so framed and so guarded as to afford adequate protection to the party in whose favor it is imposed, while at the same time it is in no wise injurious to the public." In most modern-day cases, the question of reasonableness usually centers on whether the scope of prohibited activity, length of the restraint, or geographical scope of the agreement, is unduly burdensome. Generally, if a court finds that an agreement is not reasonable, it has the power to revise or reform such agreements by a process called "blue-lining" or "blue-penciling." There are cases in which no amount of reformation can save the covenant. *See Fidelity Union Life Ins. Co. v. Protective Life Ins. Co.*, 356 F.Supp. 1199 (N.D.Tex.1972) (former employee working in a territory in which its former employer was not doing business).

5. States have taken different approaches to the issue of reasonableness for covenants not to compete from that taken by federal courts. California is one of the most difficult states in which to enforce a covenant not to compete. *See* CALIFORNIA BUSINESS AND PROFESSIONS CODE § 16600 ("Except as provided in this chapter, every contract by which anyone is restrained from engaging in a lawful profession, trade, or business of any kind is to that extent void.") California case law also indicates that noncompete provisions in employment contracts are invalid unless enforcement is necessary to protect the employer's trade secrets. *See also Metro Traffic Control, Inc. v. Shadow Traffic Network*, 22 Cal.App.4th 853 (Cal.Ct.App.1994).

Texas, on the other hand, is slightly more relaxed in that a former employer's confidential information is not the only basis for justifying covenants not to compete. THE TEXAS BUSINESS AND COMMERCE CODE indicates that:

> [a] covenant not to compete is enforceable if it is ancillary to or part of an otherwise enforceable agreement at the time the agreement is made to the extent it contains limitations as to time, geographical area, and scope of activity to be restrained that are reasonable and do not impose a greater restraint than is necessary to protect the goodwill or other business interest of the promisee." TEX. BUS. & COM. CODE § 15.50 (a).

This approach is discussed in the Texas Supreme Court's decision in *Alex Sheshunoff Management Services, L.P. v. Johnson*, 209 S.W.3d 644, 657 (Tex.2006) (an agreement not to disclose confidential information by a former employer is an otherwise enforceable ancillary agreement under § 15.50).

## (2) By "Special" Relationship

### (a) Employees

## PRINCE MANUFACTURING, INC. v. AUTOMATIC PARTNER, INC.

191 U.S.P.Q. 450 (N.J. Sup. Ct. 1976)

* * *

Plaintiff's claim against these three defendants is described in the pretrial order as "a claim based upon wrongful appropriation of plaintiff's intellectual property by defendants Nielsen, Church and Automatic Partner, Inc., in that while Nielsen was a director of the corporate plaintiff and Church was a director of and consultant for the corporate plaintiff they invented an automatic tennis machine with unique design features which by express agreement, implied agreement and common law became the property of plaintiff and gave rise to a duty by said defendants to convey all of their interests therein to plaintiff, and in that they violated their duty and refused to convey their interest in the invention to plaintiff, but instead fraudulently concealed the existence thereof, applied for and obtained a patent on the same, refused to convey their interest to plaintiff and wrongfully caused defendant Automatic Partner, Inc. to be incorporated for the purpose of manufacturing and selling a machine incorporating the design features aforesaid in competition with plaintiff . . .".

On the basis of the aforesaid allegations plaintiff seeks judgment against the defendants Automatic Partner, Inc., Church and Nielsen for the following relief as set forth in paragraph 1 of the pretrial order:

"A. Enjoining defendants from the manufacture or sale of a tennis machine incorporating any invention, product, process or procedure constituting plaintiff's intellectual right as aforesaid."

"B. Directing the corporate defendant to account to plaintiff for such profits as it has made on the sale of its tennis machine until the date of the injunction aforesaid."

"C. Directing all defendants to transfer to plaintiff or cause to be transferred to plaintiff all rights in its patents or other applications therefore, which they have in any invention, product, process or procedure wrongfully appropriate from plaintiff."

"D. For compensatory damages."

* * *

It might be said that this case had its genesis in 1968 or 1969 when Gerard Sweeton met Joseph Church at a meeting with R. H.McClure, since they are the three parties to the original partnership agreement Exhibit P-1. At that time they discussed the development and marketing of a compressed-air tennis machine, which was a concept not yet developed or marketed. Sweeton was shown plans of a tennis machine which Church had designed. A prototype was constructed by Sweeton in the Spring of 1969 similar to a type developed previously by his brother. The machine was not functionally effective and Sweeton and his brother redesigned a low-pressure machine and constructed another prototype. On the basis of this the three men formed a partnership to develop this prototype and enter the manufacturing business. This partnership agreement was in part oral and in part reduced to writing in Exhibit P-1. Under this agreement McClure and Church each obtained a one-third interest, and Sweeton Industries consisting of Sweeton and his brother obtained the other one-third interest. The partnership agreement specifically provided that the partners intended to "organize a company to further the financing and manufacture and sale of such devices when and if they prove successful and have commercial value". And it further provided that all developments by each party toward this end which had presently matured "will become a part of the assets of the partnership", and with reference to Church provided that this included "prior work done by J.H.Church." In furtherance of the provision in the partnership agreement regarding the formation of a company, plaintiff, Prince Manufacturing, Inc., was incorporated in August of 1970 for the stated purpose of manufacturing tennis machines which discharge tennis balls by means of compressed air. To this corporation was contributed the assets of the partnership, the partners became the owners of one-third each of the stock of the corporation, and McClure became president, Sweeton vice president and Church treasurer. Plaintiff was then to become the only company manufacturing a compressed air tennis machine.

In 1971 Nielsen entered the corporation. He was a plastics expert and was obtained by plaintiff to assist in the design of parts for the machine and to act as a consultant and director. At a meeting of the Board of Directors on April 21, 1972, evidenced by the minutes thereof Exhibit P-2, Nielsen was issued 5,000 shares of capital stock of plaintiff as compensation for past services and given an option to purchase an additional 5,000 shares at $1.00 per share within one year from the date thereof. A further resolution provided that he was to be paid $100 weekly for his services including consultation.

The plaintiff corporation has since shortly after its inception manufactured and retailed a compressed air tennis machine known as "The Prince" and referred to in this case as "Big Prince". The current production model is in evidence as Exhibit

P-13. It retails for $595 F.O.B. Princeton, weighs 80 lbs. and has no induced air flow in its design features. It differs from the machine described in the patent Exhibit P-6, which is part of the subject of this litigation, essentially in its size, weight, cost and the inclusion in the patent machine of an air induction system.

The "Big Prince" machine was the subject of a patent application by Sweeton and his brother, dated April 13, 1973, and the patent itself, Exhibit DN-2 did not actually issue until December 24, 1974. This patent does not include an air induction system nor could it be classified as a small tennis machine. The detent utilized in the patented machine is a spring-operated one rather than a rubber detent.

On or about April 28, 1972, defendant Nielsen became a director of plaintiff and served in that capacity until September 8, 1972, and on or about August 17, 1970, defendant Church became a director of plaintiff and served in that capacity until September 22, 1972. Both Nielsen and Church were also consultants to the plaintiff corporation and members of its technical committee. While in the employ of plaintiff Nielsen and Church both worked in the field of tennis machine research and development.

Both Church and Nielsen, by reason of their executive and employment capacities with plaintiff owed to plaintiff corporation a fiduciary obligation. As paid consultants on technical matters and members of the technical committee they were charged with the responsibility for tennis machine research and development.

In addition, by express contract found in a provision in the partnership agreement Exhibit P-1, the benefits of which became assets of the corporation when the same was founded pursuant to the agreement, Church conveyed to the partnership, and thus to the corporation his prior work in developing tennis machines.

The central document in this case is Exhibit P-5, a memorandum of May 10, 1972 from defendant Church to the Board of Directors of Plaintiff. The memorandum attached to the letter of transmittal is entitled "Notes on airflow pneumatic ball machines" and discusses at length with diagrams and text a number of technical subjects, principally the use of air induction and a venturi-shaped detent. In his letter of transmittal Church recognized that Prince had "under consideration the expenditure of substantial Corporate funds" on a research and development program relating to air flow problems existing in the "Big Prince" machine and presented his memorandum on the subject of the solution of such problems by the corporation. In other words, the memorandum itself is not directed to the development of a new machine, or a small machine, but to solving of problems in the then existing machine being manufactured by plaintiff.

During the employment of defendants Church and Nielsen by plaintiff they conceived the design features of a small backyard tennis machine incorporating an air induction system and a rubber venturi-shaped detent, to be manufactured inexpensively and profitably in part by the use of a mass-produced six gallon can as an air chamber rather than the theretofore utilized expensive hand-fabricated chamber. This conception was definitive, was disclosed to plaintiff, was a trade secret, and became the property of plaintiff by reason of the aforementioned fiduciary duty and express contracts.

In the summer of 1972, Church and Nielsen, pursuant to arrangements made by Sweeton, traveled to Baltimore, Maryland for a conference with Howard Head, then and now Chairman of the Board of Directors of the corporate plaintiff. There then existed considerable animosity between Church and Nielsen on the one hand and McClure on the other, and because of this antagonism Church and Nielsen preferred to conduct their business without McClure and his alleged interference. They were enthusiastic about the idea of a profitable production and marketing of a small tennis machine and wanted to ascertain whether Head would provide support therefor, financial or otherwise. They suggested to Head the formation of a separate corporation without McClure, with the corporate plaintiff to be a minor shareholder only and the other shares to be held by Head, Church and Nielsen. Head was not particularly enthusiastic because he was satisfied with the existing "Big Prince" machine being marketed by plaintiff, and felt that the time had not yet come to market a small tennis machine. However, he also recognized that in view of the existing fiduciary duties which they all owed to the corporation, the matter should be placed in writing and considered by the Board of Directors. He so suggested to Church and Nielsen, and they agreed, but they never did so. They were suspicious and fearful of McClure and did not want him to share in the concept of a small tennis machine which, unknown to them at that time, was already under the law a concept constituting a property right of plaintiff. Thus they did not present their proposal to the corporation at the Board of Directors meeting on August 25, 1972. Being unable to eliminate McClure from their plans to market a small tennis machine they then continued to consider how they alone could do so. The obvious answer was the formation of a new company for this purpose. Whether they terminated their affiliation with plaintiff for the purpose and design of forming a new business or not is immaterial. However, there is strong evidence to indicate that they did so for that reason. At the August 25th corporate meeting Church made a demand for a substantial amount of alleged back wages owed to him, raised a technicality about the validity of the meeting being conducted and otherwise created such dissension between himself and McClure that it became apparent to Howard Head that the corporation would benefit by the termination of their affiliation. Accordingly, he made to Church and Nielsen an offer to purchase their stock in the corporation and eventually such a sale was consumated and the fiduciary duty of Church and Nielsen was prospectively eliminated. They apparently failed to consider the facts upon which plaintiff's claim is now based and felt they were free of any obligation to plaintiff with respect to the development and marketing of a small tennis machine containing an air induction system with or without a rubber detent. There can be no doubt of their intention to do so since Nielsen admits that at that time he then intended to and did immediately proceed to work toward this end.

On or about September 22, 1972, defendants Church and Nielsen sold their shares of stock in plaintiff corporation to Head, and as a part of the contract, Exhibit DC-4, each entered into the following agreement with Head as purchaser:

"As additional consideration herefor, Seller for himself, his heirs, executors and administrators, hereby agrees to execute any and all instruments, papers, documents and forms which may be necessary to implement or complete any transaction entered into while associated with the said Prince Manufacturing Inc., its successors and assigns, which transaction shall include but not be limited to the assignment and transfer of any patents or other rights originally owned by Seller."

Defendant Nielsen, but not defendant Church, also entered into an agreement collateral to the agreement aforesaid stating the following:

"I, John Nielsen hereby agree that any invention, development or idea conceived by me relating to Tennis Ball Throwing Machines during the period of my association and its prior Partnership, are the sole ownership and possessions of Prince Manufacturing Corporation, Inc., and I disclaim any rights or claims to such."

The sale by defendants Church and Nielsen of their shares of stock in plaintiff corporation terminated their relationship with plaintiff.

Thereafter, in violation of their express contractual and fiduciary duties they proceeded to develop a small tennis machine incorporating certain trade secrets then the exclusive right and property of plaintiff.

* * *

### (b) Licensor/Licensee

## HYDE CORP. v. HUFFINES

314 S.W.2d 763 (Tex. 1958)

Petitioner, Hyde Corporation, presents the case here upon eighteen assignments of error; some of which are closely related and grouped for purposes of argument. It is unnecessary to discuss these assignments or points seriatim in order to dispose of the case. When the writ was granted, we had some doubt of the propriety as to the injunctive relief granted and one of the justices of the Court of Civil Appeals was of the opinion that the injunction was erroneously issued. However, upon further consideration, we have reached the conclusion that none of petitioner's assignments point out an error in the judgment of the Court of Civil Appeals. Such judgment will accordingly be affirmed.

Petitioner's assignments in the main present three major contentions: (a) That the pleadings, the evidence and the jury's findings do not support a recovery for Huffines upon the theory that Hyde Corporation had through violation of a confidential relationship, secured and wrongfully exploited Huffines' 'trade secrets.' (b) That Huffines' remedy, if any, lay in the federal courts as the suit is essentially one of patent infringement. (c) That the injunction was wrongfully issued, particularly in view of the fact that a patent had been issued to Huffines covering a part of the claims contended in his patent application.

Certain other assignments raise contentions that various portions of the jury's findings are without support in the evidence, buy we find that these matters were correctly decided in the lower appellate court and hence need not be discussed here.

The statement of the Court of Civil Appeals is essentially correct. However, in view of petitioner's first major contention, we will enlarge thereon by quoting from the patent application made by Huffines and the licensing agreement executed by the contending parties.

The respondent Huffines (plaintiff below) is the director of the Sanitation Department of the City of Wichita Falls, Texas. He constructed a mechanism which compressed the trash and garbage collected by the Sanitation Department so that the garbage trucks employed in hauling this refuse could carry substantially larger loads. He applied for a patent upon this device and in his application described it as a 'Compressor Mechanism for Refuse Truck.' It was stated in the application that:

> 'This invention relates to improvements in garbage and trash hauling trucks and more particularly to garbage or trash hauling trucks that utilize a compressor mechanism to compress the refuse for transportation.
>
> 'Various trucks of this character have been proposed heretofore, but these for the most part, were complex in construction, relatively easy to get out of order, and presented certain difficulties in loading and unloading the refuse, once it had been compressed into the carrying body of the truck.
>
> 'An object of this invention is to provide a garbage truck unit wherein the compressor will compact the refuse to enable a greater load to be transported to the place of disposal.
>
> 'Another object of this invention is to provide a compressor mechanism for a garbage or trash hauling truck that has a minimum of working parts to perform the compressing operation.
>
> 'A still further object of the invention is to provide a compressing mechanism for a truck of the character specified that is hydraulically operated, both to compress the refuse and to elevate the body of the truck into dumping position.
>
> 'Yet another object of the invention is to provide a truck body of the character specified, that is simple in construction, efficient in operation, the compressing and dumping mechanism of which is simple to operate, and which is relatively inexpensive to manufacture.'

The application contained seventeen claims of novelty and invention and it conclusively appears that the mechanism was of a type that is subject to protection in equity as a trade secret. [Citation omitted.]

It appears that E. E. Maxson, Vice President of Hyde Corporation, became interested in the device through the offices of a friend of Huffines. Maxson originally talked with Huffines about manufacturing the device for Huffines. Eventually, however, it was agreed that Hyde Corporation should manufacture and sell the device and pay a royalty to Huffines. On January 8, 1954 a licensing agreement was executed which became effective three months later, that is, on April 8, 1954.

This agreement refers to Huffines as 'Licensor' and to Hyde Corporation as 'Licensee.' It recites the fact that Licensor had invented certain new and useful improvements in a refuse compressor mechanism for vehicles and had made application for letters patent in the United States Patent Office, bearing Serial No. 400,236 and filing date of December 24, 1953 covering such device, and that

Licensee was desirous of acquiring an exclusive license to make, use and sell the said invention in the territory of the United States of America and its possessions, and in all foreign countries.

The contract then provided that:

> 'The Licensor hereby grants to the Licensee, under the terms and conditions hereinafter set forth, an Exclusive License to make, use and sell said aforementioned device in accordance with said patent application, or under any patent or patents that may issue therefrom, or any application or applications filed on improvements on said device conveyed to the Licensor by the Licensee, and under any patent or patents that may issue therefrom. Licensor agrees to use due diligence in protecting such improvements and to continue the agreement under the present application and applications for improvements that may be filed thereon, as long as such agreements and conditions set forth herein are fulfilled. . . .
>
> 'The Licensee agrees to pay Licensor the sum of one hundred twenty dollars ($120.00) per unit, and warrants and binds itself and its assigns to produce, sell and pay Licensor for a minimum of one hundred (100) units the first years. . . .
>
> 'Any litigation for infringements involving said application for patent, or involving an application or applications for patent on any improvements on said device, on involving any patents that may issue therefrom, whether offensive or defensive, but not connected with any Patent Office proceedings, shall be paid for by the parties hereto in proportion to the monies received from the manufacture and sale of said devices. However, if either of the parties hereto fails to bear his proportionate part of any such litigation, as aforesaid, the other party shall have the right, upon the expiration of thirty (30) days written notice to the party in default of his intention to bear the full expense of such litigation, but the party bearing such expense shall receive in full any damages that may be collected as a result of such litigation, otherwise monies collected as damages, or any expenses thereof, shall be shared proportionately.
>
> 'The effective date of this contract shall be the date on which the Licensee presents a finished pilot model of said device manufactured in accordance with the disclosure of said patent application, and when such pilot model is accepted by Licensor as a proper and salable article of munufacture within the scope of the claims of said application Licensee warrants and binds itself and its assigns to build and complete said pilot model within Ninety (90) days from date of this contract.
>
> 'The Licensee agrees not to question the validity of any application or applications, or any patent or patents issued as result of said application, or applications filed on improvements on said device, relative to the said Refuse Compressor Mechanism for Vehicles.
>
> 'This agreement may be automatically renewed at the end of the first year, so long as the agreements and conditions set forth herein are being fulfilled, and the same may apply to each succeeding year for the pendency

> of said patent application or applications, and for the life of any patent or patents that may issue therefrom. Failure to fulfill the conditions herein set out shall be considered as terminating this contract agreement, but either party hereto who considers such conditions are not being met, shall notify the other party in writing to that effect, setting out the particular deficiencies, and the party receiving such notice shall have thirty (30) days in which to remedy such deficiencies, before the contract agreement shall become null and void. Sixty (60) days notice to terminate this contract shall be given by Licensee. If more than one hundred (100) units are manufactured and sold in any one year, the additional amount so sold that year shall be credited to the amount to be sold the next ensuing year.
>
> 'The expense of the prosecution of said application or applications for patent or patents shall be at the expense of the Licensor, and he agrees to use due diligence in prosecuting said application or applications for patent or patents in an effort to bring same to a successful conclusion.
>
> 'Licensee agrees to convey to Licensor any improvements made by Licensee or its employees upon the machine involved herein, and agrees that such assignment may be made to Licensor or to any designated agent, at Licensor's expense, and Licensee may use the improvement during the term of this contract, without additional royalty.'

It conclusively appears that as a result of this agreement and the negotiations preceding its execution, Hyde Corporation gained full knowledge of the Huffines device not only from the application for patent but from scale models, blue prints, and actual construction of the device. On May 31, 1955, when the parties were in the second year of operations under the contract, Hyde Corporation repudiated the licensing agreement by giving the sixty-day notice provided for in the contract. However, according to the jury's findings, said defendant did not cease to manufacture the Huffines' device but on the contrary continued to produce the same substantially in accordance with the description of the mechanism contained in Huffines' patent application.

Shortly before the trial was concluded a patent was received by Huffines and introduced in evidence. Some ten claims are listed in the patent instead of seventeen as set out in the original application. In the course of the prosecution of the patent application it appears that certain claims were cancelled by Huffines, others amended and additional ones added before the patent was finally issued.

Against this factual background Hyde Corporation contends that it cannot be held in damages or restrained in equity from further manufacturing the mechanism because they did not gain knowledge of the device through fraud, deceit or any inequitable practice.

Special Issues Nos. 1 and 2 and the jury's answers thereto bear upon this contention and are as follows:

> 'Special Issue No. 1: Do you find from a preponderance of the evidence that J. D. Huffines disclosed his refuse compressor mechanism to Hyde Corporation because some officer or agent of Hyde Corporation represented to him that they were interested in manufacturing and selling said

refuse compressor mechanism? Answer: Yes.

'Special Issue No. 2: Do you find from a preponderance of the evidence that the defendant, Hyde Corporation, acted in good faith in acquiring knowledge of the design and novel features, if any, of the garbage disposal body in question? Answer: Yes.'

Petitioner contends that there is no evidence supporting the jury's answer to Special Issue No. 1 and insists that if any issue of breach of confidence be raised by the evidence, the trial court should have submitted its requested special issue inquiring if the details, plans and specifications of Huffines' refuse compressor mechanism were disclosed by Huffines to Hyde Corporation or its representative in confidence.

Petitioner's arguments as to the pleadings and evidence seem to run counter to the realities of the case as fixed by the written licensing agreement. It is true that there is no explicit written covenant contained in the contract which precludes petitioner from making use of information granted as a result of contract negotiations and disclosures by Huffines after the cancellation of the licensing agreement. It is also true that respondent's pleadings do not use the words 'in confidence' by way of stating a conclusion. The picture presented by the pleadings and the evidence both undisputed and as interpreted by the jury is that of a licensee after contracting with an inventor (in good faith according to the jury's answer to Special Issue No. 2) for the use of an invention upon which an application for patent was pending, repudiating the licensing agreement and insisting upon utilizing the device despite the fact that he secured information which enabled him to manufacture the device through the licensing agreement and the negotiations relating thereto. To say that petitioner did not gain knowledge of the device in this manner is to deny the stated purpose of the licensing agreement. While in the briefs and oral argument some concern was expressed that the Court of Civil Appeals' opinion would permit unscrupulous claimants to delve into the pockets of business firms through spurious claims for compensation for the use of ideas, *Matarese v. Moore-McCormack Lines, Inc.*, 2 Cir., 158 F.2d 631, 170 A.L.R. 440, that danger is hardly presented here. We are not called upon to consider at what period in the course of negotiations petitioner's actions may have ceased to be ethically permissible. We here have business relations culminating in a licensing agreement. The case seems to come squarely within the rule of the American Law Institute's Restatement of the Law that:

'One who discloses or uses another's trade secrets, without a privilege to do so, is liable to the other if (a) he discovers the secret by improper means, or (b) his disclosure or use constitutes a breach of confidence reposed in him by the other in disclosing the secret to him. . . . .' 4 Restatement of Torts, § 757.

The jury evidently believed that at the time the licensing agreement was entered into, Hyde Corporation was acting in good faith, but thereafter decided to use respondent's device without accounting to him. If so, it might be absolved under clause (a) of the rule but would be held liable under clause (b) thereof. In the present case, the parties occupied the position of licensor and licensee. They were in a sense coadventurers. There existed between them a confidential relationship as a matter of law and there was no need to submit these incidents of legal status to a jury for its determination. In commenting upon clause (b) of the rule above stated, it is said in the Restatement that:

> 'A breach of confidence under the rule stated in this Clause may also be a breach of contract which subjects the actor to liability under the rules stated in the Restatement of Contracts. But whether or not there is a breach of contract, the rule stated in this Section subjects the actor to liability if his disclosure or use of another's trade secret is a breach of the confidence reposed in him by the other in disclosing the secret to him. The chief example of a confidential relationship under this rule is the relationship of principal and agent (see Restatement of Agency, ss 395 and 396). Such is also the relationship between partners or other joint adventurers. But this confidence may exist also in other situations. For example, A has a trade secret which he wishes to sell with or without his business. B is a prospective purchaser. In the course of negotiations, A discloses the secret to B solely for the purpose of enabling him to appraise its value. Or, A requests a loan from B, a banker, for the purpose of aiding the manufacture of a product by A's secret process. In order to assure B about the soundness of the loan, A discloses the secret to him in confidence. In both cases B is under a duty not to disclose the secret or use it adversely to A. . . . ' 4 Restatement of Torts, § 757, Comment on Clause (b) p. 13.

While there may be some distinction in the theory of recovery under clauses (a) and (b), that is whether in tort or contract, *Aktiebolaget Bofors v. United States*, 194 F.2d 145, 90 U.S.App.D.C. 92, that point is not involved here. In the area of confidential relationships between partners, employers and employees, licensors and licensees, and the like, the injured party is not required to rely upon an express agreement to hold the trade secret in confidence, *Schreyer v. Casco Products Corp.*, 2 Cir., 190 F.2d 921, Smith v. Dravo Corporation, 7 Cir., 203 F.2d 369, nor should he be deprived of all relief because the offending person may have originally entered into the particular relationship unaffected by a then existing ulterior or improper motive.

Petitioner's contention that respondent's remedy, if any, rests in the federal courts is founded upon the premise that this is essentially a patent infringement suit. After petitioner had entered into the licensing contract with respondent, it purchased Patent No. 2,487,412 issued to Valentine O. Balbi covering a compressing device and instituted suit against Huffines in the United States District Court for the Northern District of Texas asserting the priority of the Balbi patent over that issued to Huffines and contending that the latter patent was invalid for a number of reasons.

We agree with the holding of the Court of Civil Appeals that this is not a 'patent case', although 'patent questions' may be involved herein. The gravamen of the present suit is breach of confidence. Trade secrets as distinguished from patents are subject to protection under the equitable jurisdiction of the state courts. In *E. I. Du Pont de Nemours Powder Co. v. Masland*, 244 U.S. 100, 37 S.Ct. 575, 576, 61 L.Ed. 1016, Mr. Justice Holmes stated the basis of the 'trade secret' case, viz.:

> 'The word 'property' as applied to trademarks and trade secrets is an unanalyzed expression of certain secondary consequences of the primary fact that the law makes some rudimentary requirements of good faith. Whether the plaintiffs have any valuable secret or not the defendant knows the facts, whatever they are, through a special confidence that he accepted. The property may be denied, but the confidence cannot be. Therefore the starting point for the present matter is not property or due process of law, but that the defendant stood in confidential relations with the plaintiffs, or one of them. These have given place to hostility, and the first thing to be made sure of is that the defendant shall not fraudulently abuse the trust reposed in him. It is the usual incident of confidential relations. If there is any disadvantage in the fact that he knew the plaintiffs' secrets, he must take the burden with the good.'

In the later case of *Becher v. Contoure Laboratories*, 279 U.S. 388, 49 S.Ct. 356, 357, 73 L.Ed. 752, Mr. Justice Holmes in distinguishing between the patent and trade secret suits said:

> 'It is not denied that the jurisdiction of the Courts of the United States is exclusive in the case of suits arising under the patent laws, but it was held below that the suit in the State Court did not arise under those laws. It is plain that that suit had for its cause of action the breach of a contract or wrongful disregard of confidential relations, both matters independent of the patent law, and that the subject matter of Oppenheimer's claim was an undisclosed invention which did not need a patent to protect it from disclosure by breach of trust. Irving Iron Works v. Kerlow Steel Flooring Co., 96 N.J.Eq. 702, 126 A. 291; E. I. Du Pont de Nemours Powder Co. v. Masland, 244 U.S. 100, 37 S.Ct. 575, 61 L.Ed. 1016, Oppenheimer's right was independent of and prior to any arising out of the patent law, and it seems a strange suggestion that the assertion of that right can be removed from the cognizance of the tribunals established to protect it by its opponent going into the patent office for a later title. It is said that to establish Oppenheimer's claim is to invalidate Becher's patent. But, even if mistakenly, the attempt was not to invalidate that patent but to get an assignment of it, and an assignment was decreed. Suits against one who has received a patent of land to make him a trustee for the plaintiff on the ground of some paramount equity are well known. Again, even if the logical conclusion from the establishing of Oppenheimer's claim is that Becher's patent is void, that is not the effect of the judgment.'

* * *

On Motion for Rehearing

While petitioner's motion for rehearing presents nothing that was not passed upon in the original opinion, there are certain matters which may be clarified by further statement.

Petitioner seems to have some objection to the use of the term 'trade secrets' in describing this case. The generally accepted definition of a 'trade secret' is that contained in the Restatement of Torts. In *Extrin Foods, Inc., v. Leighton*, 202 Misc.

592, 115 N.Y.S.2d 429, 433, the Court said:

> 'In resolving this issue the Court is first required to define the term 'secret' as applied to a formula. The term 'trade secret' is defined in the Restatement of Torts, § 757, p. 5, as follows:
>
> "b. Definition of trade secret. A trade secret may consist of any formula, pattern, device or compilation of information which is used in one's business, and which gives him an opportunity to obtain an advantage over competitors who do not know or use it. It may be a formula for a chemical compound, a process of manufacturing, treating or preserving materials, a pattern for a machine or other device, or a list of customers. . . . A trade secret is a process or device for continuous use in the operation of the business. Generally it relates to the production of goods, as, for example, a machine or formula for the production of an article.'

* * *

## NOTES AND QUESTIONS:

1. The opinion in *Prince Manufacturing* illustrates the limits of protection that employment agreements can provide in trade secret litigation. In this case, Church, a former director of and consultant for Prince, had a confidentiality agreement, but Nielsen, a former director of Prince, did not. Because Church and Nielson brought the technology to Prince, the two defendants denied receiving any confidential information from Prince. The court's opinion sidestepped the defendants' arguments by finding that, as directors and members of Prince's technical committee, both men had a fiduciary duty to Prince. What other positions at a company would create a fiduciary relationship?

2. In *Hyde Corp.*, the court struggled to find a rationale to support its holding that, if the defendant continued to make trucks incorporating Mr. Huffines' design, it had to pay royalties. Despite Hyde Corporation following the termination clause set out in the licensing agreement, the company could not terminate the agreement and avoid paying royalties to Huffines. The court found the parties "were in a sense coadventures," and in a business relationship that created a fiduciary duty under RESTATEMENT (FIRST) OF TORTS § 757. *See Hyde Corp. v. Huffines*, 314 S.W.2d 763, 775-76 (Tex. 1958). Would the outcome have been different if the compressor mechanism for the refuse truck had been known to the public at the time Mr. Huffines approached Hyde Corporation? What would have happened in the case if Mr. Huffines' patent had issued before Hyde terminated the agreement?

3. *Hyde Corp.* also raises an interesting question about when a fiduciary relationship is created between two parties to an arm's length agreement. Not all agreements that are negotiated at arm's length give rise to a fiduciary duty to the degree found in *Hyde.* The Texas Supreme Court addressed this issue in a subsequent case involving a franchise agreement. *See Crim Truck & Tractor Co. v. Navistar Int'l Transp. Corp.*, 823 S.W.2d 591 (Tex.1992). In that case, the court held that:

> Although a fiduciary duty encompasses at the very minimum a duty of good faith and fair dealing, the converse is not true. The duty of good faith and fair dealing merely requires the parties to "deal fairly" with one another and does not encompass the often more onerous burden which requires a party to place the interest of the other party before his own, often attributed to a fiduciary duty.

*Id.* at 594. The court then found that there was no duty under the agreement requiring the "more onerous burden," commenting that "although one businessman trusts another, and relies upon his promise to perform a contract, does not give a confidential relationship giving rise to an informal fiduciary relationship." *Id.* at 594.

### (c) Fiduciary Relationship Through Conduct

## PHILLIPS v. FREY

20 F.3d 623 (5th Cir. 1994)

This is an appeal from a jury verdict in a trade secret misappropriation case. The jury found that the defendants had misappropriated a trade secret connected with the manufacture and/or marketing of the plaintiffs' hunting stand. For the following reasons, we AFFIRM.

STATEMENT OF FACTS

Plaintiffs-appellees, W.C. Phillips and his wife Mary Phillips, are owners and operators of Ambusher, Inc. Ambusher's main line of business is the manufacture and distribution of single pole deer stands to be used by hunters. Ambusher's stand is collapsible and consists of four main parts: the upper seat section and three ladder pole sections that enable the seat to be elevated approximately fourteen feet above the ground It has a unique design in that it has a single pole that a hunter can climb instead of having to climb the tree. For further safety and security, it locks to the tree from the ground before a hunter climbs into it.

W.C.Phillips began developing single pole tree stands in 1967. He worked on their design, off and on, for three years. He has developed a number of different models over the years culminating in the "V-Lok" tree stand which is the subject of this suit. Ambusher also sold accessories to be used with the deer stands, including a gun/bow rest, a camo blind, a camo awning, a security cable, and an ATV "Piggy Back Bar." Ambusher and Buck Pro, Inc. are the only manufacturers of single pole tree stands in the United States. Buck Pro's tree stand is an exact copy of appellees' "V-Lok" tree stand.

Defendant John Collins was a customer who had bought products from appellees for a number of years. The events which form the basis of this suit began in the summer of 1990, when Collins and Phillips had a telephone conversation wherein Phillips mentioned his desire to sell the business, including all equipment, jigs, logos, and the spec book, for $140,000. Two weeks after that initial telephone call, Collins called Phillips back to inform him that he and two associates, Claude Frey and Gary Arnold, were interested in purchasing the business and wanted some information to look at. Collins informed Phillips that coming up with his asking price would not present a problem since he had $50,000 in savings, that Arnold already had a metal fabricating ship, and that Frey owned land. These facts led Phillips to believe that the defendants were legitimate prospective purchasers of Ambusher, Inc.

A couple of weeks later, on July 6, 1990, Phillips sent some information for Collins and his two associates to look over. This package included both a financial statement, and an inventory of his equipment and tools by make and model. He also included a video tape. Phillips wrote that he had a specification book that is referred to each time a component is made that is kept up to date and put away for safekeeping. He also stated that he had made a videotape of the component manufacturing the previous year, adding "[w]ithout the specs this information is no secret, and if you and your associate would like to view this for a detailed insight of the manufacturing procedures, I can send a copy to you . . . . This tape does not cover recent developments and the V-Lok stand." Because he felt the tape did not make sense without the "spec. book," Phillips made a different tape on July 7, 1990 demonstrating Ambusher's manufacturing process for tree stands and accessories. The video tape gave appellants the knowledge necessary to manufacture tree stands, and was intended to bypass the spec book. Phillips did this in order to allow appellants to evaluate the business as prospective purchasers.

In the latter part of July 1990, Collins called to arrange a tour of appellees' shop in Texarkana. The tour lasted about three hours. During the tour, Phillips and his employee showed the defendants first hand how to manufacture the "V-Lok" deer stand.

Two weeks later, some time in August 1990, Collins and appellants returned to Texarkana for a second visit. Collins purchased seven V-Lok stands and returned to Louisiana. On September 10, 1990, Phillips sent a more recent financial statement and a copy of the current inventory.

Shortly thereafter, Collins informed Phillips that he and appellants were having problems securing financing. Collins then made a counteroffer for the business for $30,000 down, a $10 royalty per stand and that Phillips was to help set up shop in Wisner, Louisiana. On September 14, 1990, Phillips refused this counteroffer. On September 15, 1990, Phillips offered to sell the business for $45,000 down and $20,000 per year at 10% interest for seven years. On October 1, 1990, Collins informed Phillips that he and appellants would be unable to purchase the business.

Collins returned the information Phillips had sent him, except for the video. However, none of the information Collins sent to Frey or Arnold was returned. Moreover, it was later discovered that appellants never attempted to secure a loan for the purchase of Ambusher, despite having sufficient assets to do so.

By the end of March, 1991, appellants were manufacturing and marketing a tree stand known as the "BP91" under the name Buck-Pro, Inc. The tree stand and accessories were identical to plaintiffs' "V-Lok" tree stand and accessories. The plaintiffs filed an action against appellants and John Collins in district court alleging misappropriation of both the design of the product and Ambusher's manufacturing process; that the appellants deceived the Phillips into disclosing confidential trade secrets under the guise of purchasing the business. Appellants denied these allegations, stating that the BP91 deer stand was designed by permissible reverse engineering, and counterclaimed against appellees for malicious prosecution. The jury verdict awarded appellees $56,500.13 in actual damages, $75,000 in punitive damages, and $7,000 in attorneys' fees. The jury found against the appellants on the malicious prosecution claim. On the same day that the judgment was entered, the trial court signed a permanent injunction enjoining appellants from manufacturing, selling, or marketing deer stands and assorted accessories. Appellants have timely appealed.

## DISCUSSION

The jury returned a verdict finding by a preponderance of the evidence that the defendants had misappropriated a trade secret of W.C. Phillips and Mary Phillips connected with the manufacture and/or marketing of a single pole V-Lok tree stand, T-Bar awning, or Piggy back bars for all terrain vehicles.[4]

* * *

### Did a Trade Secret Exist?

Primarily, appellants assert that the only trade secret involved in this case was the specification book, and that was never given to the appellants. Any information other than the spec book would not rise to the specter of a "trade secret." Appellants point out that Phillips stated in his letter that "[w]ithout the specs this information is no secret . . . ." Moreover, appellants claim that no admonitions against disclosure accompanied the videotape.

A trade secret is any formula, pattern, device or compilation of information used in a business, which gives the owner an opportunity to obtain an advantage over his competitors who do not know or use it. [Citations omitted.] "It may be a formula for a chemical compound, *a process of manufacturing*, treating or preserving materials, a pattern for a machine or other device, or a list of customers." Restatement of Torts § 757 comment b (1939) (emphasis added). [Citations omitted.]

Appellees contend, and we find that the evidence supports, that it was Ambusher's manufacturing process that was the trade secret misappropriated, not the design of the tree stand.

The method of manufacturing must be a trade secret to be protected, in other words, it must give the owner a competitive advantage. [Citation omitted.] The record before us indicates that the Phillips's manufacturing process took years to develop and allowed Ambusher to manufacture the tree stands in a cost efficient manner, giving Ambusher a competitive advantage over anyone who would not know or use this method.[5] [Citation omitted.] The manufacturing process itself was

---

[4] [5] The jury was instructed that in order to find that the defendants misappropriated the plaintiffs' trade secret, they must find each of the following elements by a preponderance of the evidence:

1. that a trade secret exists;
2. that it was acquired through a confidential relationship; and
3. that the defendants used the trade secret without authorization from the plaintiffs.

[5] [7] When Phillips informed the appellants that his tree stand and accessories were not patented,

divulged in both the video tape and the personal tours given to appellants during the course of negotiations for purchase of the business.[6]

Gary Arnold admitted at trial that prior to seeing the video tape sent to them by Phillips, he was unaware of how to mass produce deer stands. Additionally, the manufacturing equipment and tools used in Buck-Pro's manufacturing process were identical to those employed by Ambusher. This is some evidence that the manufacturing process came from improperly acquired trade secrets.

Secondly, appellants contend that the concept of a single-pole deer stand was not invented by Phillips, but was in fact the subject of a previous patent, thus rendering the trade secret public property through general disclosure. [Citation omitted.] Appellants argue that any property rights in a trade secret cease to exist prospectively once the matter has become public property through a general disclosure by the discoverer or by the legitimate discovery of and/or rightful disclosure to another. [Citation omitted.] On October 16, 1984, Lynn Thomas filed a patent for a "Portable Hunter Tree Stand." That patent provides:

A pair of spike-equipped jaw members which are pivotally coupled to the seat frame extended rearwardly therefrom and are normally biased apart to a fully open, tree-engaging position. The jaw members include integral, outwardly diverging locking arm portions which are adapted to be drawn together by the hunter with a rope during stand installation to forcibly compress the jaw members in binding, substantially circumferential engagement with the selected tree.

Whether the patented tree stand and the V-Lok stand are the same is irrelevant to our inquiry. We find that the jury's verdict can be supported by the misappropriation of the manufacturing process itself, which evidence in the record reveals gave Ambusher a competitive advantage over anyone who does not know or use it. Nowhere do appellants allege that they used the patent instead of the plaintiffs' trade secret to formulate their manufacturing process. The patent referred to merely describes a product, admittedly similar to the V-Lok Tree Stand, yet is devoid of detailed information of a manufacturing process or specifications.

In the same vein of argument, the appellants assert that they designed and manufactured their products by reverse engineering. Under Texas law, it is permissible to use a competitor's secret process if the process is discovered by

---

Frey asked Phillips what he would do if someone started building them. Phillips replied that it would be cost prohibitive to do so without knowledge of his manufacturing process.

[6] [8] Phillips trial testimony states that the video disclosed the manufacturing process to appellants:

> Q: Now what was on the tape that you actually sent?
>
> A: Well, first I took a walk through the shop so they could get an overview of all the equipment. I showed each individual piece of equipment, and I showed the bender and told the name. I showed the hydraulic presses. I even showed how they worked.
>
> I showed the saw, and the drills and the painting department, the assembly department, and just a tour through the entire facility. And then I wanted to show them how the equipment was used, and I went back and edited on some videotape showing people at work, showing the hydraulic press extruding or expanding the metal.
>
> I showed them how to put foam on the gun rest. I showed them how to form the base pole for the flange. I showed them how to crimp the metal. I showed them how to cut the foot stand and fold it up. And just — just about everything that we did in production was included on this tape.

reverse engineering applied to the finished product. [Citation omitted.] Since they never had access to the spec book, it was necessary to compile their own specification for the deer stands and accessories. Appellants claim that Phillips admitted that they utilized reverse engineering to design their products when he testified:

A: They manufactured without my book, yes.

Q: And how did they do that?

A: They laid the stand down and measured it and copied it, and built some specs to match.

Q: Not from your book but from the stand itself?

A: From the stand itself, yes, sir.

Although it is likely appellants used reverse engineering for the design of the BP91, there was no evidence that the appellants used this method to acquire the manufacturing process employed by Ambusher. A process or device may be a trade secret even where others can gain knowledge of the process from studying the manufacturer's marketed product. [Citation omitted.] Although trade secret law does not offer protection against discovery by fair and honest means such as independent invention, accidental disclosure, or "reverse engineering," protection will be awarded to a trade secret holder against the disclosure or unauthorized use by those to whom the secret has been confided under either express or implied restriction of nondisclosure or by one who has gained knowledge by improper means. [Citations omitted.] Therefore, this argument does not further their position on appeal.

(2) Breach of Confidential Relationship and Improper Discovery

One is liable for disclosure of trade secrets if (a) he discovers the secret by improper means, or (b) his disclosure or use constitutes a breach of confidence reposed in one who is in a confidential relationship with another who discloses protected information to him. [Citations omitted.]

The appellants assert that, even if the information disclosed was a trade secret, the information was not discovered through improper means. E.I. duPont deNemours & Co. v. Christopher, 431 F.2d 1012, 1014 (5th Cir.1970), cert. denied, 400 U.S. 1024, 91 S.Ct. 581, 27 L.Ed.2d 637 (1971), involved trade secret misappropriation through aerial photography of the construction of a chemical plant. In condemning this action and explicitly finding misappropriation of trade secrets through improper means, this court noted that industrial espionage of this type "has become a popular sport in some segments of our industrial community. However, our devotion to free wheeling industrial competition must not force us into accepting the law of the jungle as the standard of morality expected in our commercial relations." *Id.* at 1016. We find that there is evidence to support the finding that appellants acquired the confidential information through improper means.

The facts before us indicate that Collins induced Phillips to reveal information by assuring him that accumulating the purchase price would be easy because providing collateral for a business loan would present no obstacle. Arnold testified that he owned a home, a business known as Arnold's Service Center which is a metal fabricating facility, and a 40 acre farm in Wisner, Louisiana. Frey testified that he owns farm land in both Mississippi and Louisiana. Frey also stated that they never made any effort to borrow money or even apply for a loan. In the face of such evidence, it does not amount to a miscarriage of justice for the jury to believe that the defendants improperly discovered the trade secret and breached their confidential relationship.

Appellants' next claim is that Phillips should not recover since he completely disregarded all prohibitions that would afford his legal protection on any trade secrets by voluntarily disclosing the manufacturing process through the videotape and the on-cite tours. At no time did Phillips inform the appellants that the information was secret or in any way place them under a duty not to disclose.

It was this court that stated that it is not improper to obtain knowledge of a process where the holder of the alleged trade secret voluntarily discloses it or fails to take reasonable precautions to ensure its secrecy. [Citations omitted.] However, an owner of a trade secret will not lose the secret by disclosure if he creates a duty in some manner and places that duty upon another not to disclose or use the secret. [Citation omitted.] Therefore, while it is true that outside any confidential relationship, one who voluntarily discloses secret information or who fails to take reasonable precautions to secure its secrecy cannot properly claim that information constitutes a trade secret. [Citations omitted.]

The record does contain evidence that Phillips did take steps to protect his secret by not disclosing the process to anyone until the sales negotiations commenced. By this precaution, Phillips disclosed within a confidence that placed the appellants under a duty to keep the secret.

However, appellants deny that there was ever any confidential relationship established that would prevent them from using the information given to them. Appellants assert that the fact that a sale of Ambusher was contemplated does not create a per se confidential relationship between the parties.

They cite to a 1st circuit case which holds that although a confidential relationship will typically be implied if the disclosure was made in a business relationship between a purchaser and supplier, the implied confidential relationship may be defeated if the disclosing party voluntarily conveys a trade secret to another without limitation upon its use. [Citation omitted.] Appellants find similarity in the instant case, where Phillips took no steps to protect himself and never indicated that he was giving confidential information to Collins or appellants.

In Hyde Corp. v. Huffines, 158 Tex. 566, 314 S.W.2d 763, cert. denied, 358 U.S. 898, 79 S.Ct. 223, 3 L.Ed.2d 148 (1958), the Supreme Court of Texas held that an express agreement was not necessary where the actions of the parties and the nature of their relationship, taken as a whole, established the existence of a confidential relationship.

The chief example of a confidential relationship under this rule is the relationship of a principal and agent (See Restatement of Agency, Section 395 and 396). Such is also the relationship between partners or other joint adventurers. But this confidence may exist also in other situations. For example, A has a trade secret which he wishes to sell with or without his business. B is a prospective purchaser. In the course of negotiations, A discloses the secret to B solely for the purpose of enabling him to appraise its value . . . . In [that] case B is under a duty not to disclose the secret or use it adversely to A.

*Hyde*, 314 S.W.2d at 769; *Mercer*, 570 F.2d at 1238. The injured party is not required to rely on an express agreement to hold the trade secret in confidence, nor is he to be denied relief where the offending party originally entered into the relationship without an improper motive. *Id.* at 770.

In *Smith v. Snap-On Tools Corp.*, 833 F.2d 578, 581 (5th Cir.1988), Basil Smith invented a ratchet by combining parts of two existing tools and submitted a tool suggestion form to Snap-On Tools' corporate headquarters. A short time later, Snap-On began manufacturing and selling the ratchet without paying any proceeds to Smith who brought a diversity action claiming trade secret misappropriation. *Id.* at 579. The district court found that Snap-On had misappropriated the trade secret. This court then reversed, holding that the record reflected that there was no confidential relationship existing at the time of disclosure between Smith and the corporation since Smith never explicitly requested that his disclosure be held in confidence, he had submitted the trade secret on his own initiative without any solicitation from Snap-On Tools, and disclosure was not intended as part of the business negotiations. *Id.* at 580. We cited to the Restatement of Torts § 757(b) (1939) which states, "[o]ne who discloses or uses another's trade secret, without a privilege to do so, is liable to the other if . . . his disclosure or use constitutes a breach of confidence reposed in him by the other in disclosing the secret to *632 him." The proprietor of a trade secret may not unilaterally create a confidential relationship without the knowledge or consent of the party to whom he discloses the secret. *Snap — On Tools*, 833 F.2d at 579–80 (citing Restatement of Torts, comment j (1939)). However, no particular form of notice is needed; the question raised is whether the recipient of the information knew or should have known that the information was a trade secret and the disclosure was made in confidence. *Id.* at 580 (citing Restatement of Torts § 757 comment j (1939)).

The case before us is strikingly distinguishable. Even in *Snap-On* we implied that a manufacturer who has actively solicited disclosure from an inventor, and then used the disclosed material, would be liable for misappropriation of trade secrets even where the disclosure was made in the absence of any expressed understanding about confidentiality. *Id.* at 580. Although Phillips never explicitly requested that the secret of his manufacturing process, which gave him a competitive advantage over competitors, be held in confidence, both parties mutually came to the negotiation table, and the disclosure was made within the course of negotiations for the sale of a business. The jury could validly accept such evidence that the defendants knew or should have known that the information was a trade secret and the disclosure was made in confidence.

## CONCLUSION

Although the appellants' evidentiary attacks are couched in terms of "no evidence," they all appear to be nothing more than a sufficiency of the evidence assault. As previously mentioned, this vein of argument is waived by appellants since their trial counsel failed to move for a directed verdict at the close of the evidence.

The essence of this action is not infringement, but breach of faith, for it is clear that the plaintiffs could not assert a property right against one who would acquire the secret of their manufacturing process through reverse engineering of the plaintiffs' publicly marketed product, a study of the expired Thomas patent, or any variety of permissible means including the limited access to a company's trade secrets obtained during the evaluation of a potential purchase. As Judge King points out in *Omnitech Intern., Inc. v. Clorox Co.*, 11 F.3d 1316, 1325 (5th Cir.1994), [t]o hold otherwise would lead to one of two unacceptable results: (i) every time a company entered into preliminary negotiations for a possible purchase of another company's assets in which the acquiring company was given limited access to the target's trade secrets, the acquiring party would effectively be precluded from evaluating other potential targets; or (ii) the acquiring company would, as a practical matter, be forced to make a purchase decision without the benefit of examination of the target company's most important assets — its trade secrets.

The fact is that they did not. Instead, the jury found, they gained it from the plaintiffs via their confidential relationship, and in so doing incurred a duty not to use it to plaintiffs' detriment. This duty they have breached. [Citation omitted.] There was ample evidence available for the jury to conclude appellants were not sincere in their decision to buy the business, and procured the manufacturing process under the guise of purchasing the business. [Citation omitted.] Moreover, the record supports the conclusion that the appellants acquired the manufacturing process through improper means.

None of the appellants' arguments convince us that plain error exists that would require reversal. [Citations omitted.] We therefore conclude that the jury's verdict does not constitute a manifest miscarriage of justice.

AFFIRMED.

* * *

## WALTON v. MORGAN STANLEY & CO.

623 F.2d 796 (2d Cir. 1980)

Kathryn R. Walton and Irmgart Van Daell Heckel appeal from an order entered by Judge Morris Lasker in the District Court for the Southern District of New York on October 10, 1979. The district court dismissed appellants' complaint, which they had filed derivatively on behalf of Olinkraft, Inc. and which alleged that Morgan Stanley & Co., Inc. had breached a fiduciary duty it owed to Olinkraft, because appellants had not alleged any injury to Olinkraft and therefore, according to the district court, they lacked standing. We affirm the district court's order on a different ground: that appellants had failed to state a claim upon which relief may be granted.

The allegations of appellants' complaint, which we must accept as true in testing the propriety of the dismissal of the complaint, state the following:

In 1977, Kennecott Copper Corporation engaged Morgan Stanley, the investment banking and financial advisory concern, to find a company that Kennecott could acquire. One company Morgan Stanley considered was Olinkraft, which manufactures paper and other forest products. Olinkraft's management "cooperated" with Morgan Stanley's Mergers and Acquisitions Department, "supplied it with highly favorable confidential internal earnings projections," and "instructed (it) that the Confidential Inside Information was to be used in connection with the Kennecott Bid and was to be returned to Olinkraft if such bid did not go through."

Kennecott did not make a bid for Olinkraft, but two other companies did. The first, Texas Eastern Corporation, announced an offer on July 17, 1978, to acquire Olinkraft by paying $51 for Olinkraft shares, which had been selling for approximately $31 to approximately $39. After the announcement, Morgan Stanley's Arbitrage Department purchased, for Morgan Stanley's own account, 149,200 shares of Olinkraft common stock "upon the informed conviction that a competing offer at a higher price than $51 per share would be made for Olinkraft stock"; and after these purchases, Morgan Stanley's Mergers and Acquisitions Department, which knew of the Arbitrage Department's purchases, disclosed to Johns-Manville, which it was advising financially, the confidential Olinkraft information "in an effort to induce (Johns-Manville) to make a substantially higher offer than $51 per share."

On September 25, 1978, a Johns-Manville subsidiary created for the purpose of acquiring Olinkraft, JM Capital, announced an offer to pay $57 per Olinkraft share. On October 10, Texas Eastern announced an improved offer of $60 per Olinkraft share. Johns-Manville responded by increasing its offer to $65 per share on October 18. Texas Eastern then withdrew from the bidding, and Olinkraft and Johns-Manville agreed in principle to a merger at $65 per share.

On October 30, appellant Walton demanded that Olinkraft's board of directors commence proceedings to require Morgan Stanley to account for profits it made from its purchase of Olinkraft stock. Having been informed that the board would not act upon her demand, Walton filed her complaint on November 3.

The district court, citing *Warth v. Seldin*, 442 U.S. 490, 499, 95 S.Ct. 2197, 2205, 45 L.Ed.2d 343 (1975), dismissed the complaint on the ground that the appellants, not having alleged that Morgan Stanley's actions injured Olinkraft, had not established standing. The appellants, citing *Brophy v. Cities Service Co.*, 31 Del.Ch. 241, 70 A.2d 5 (1949), argue that injury is not a prerequisite of standing in this case because Delaware law, which governs in this diversity suit, makes a breach of fiduciary duty actionable irrespective of injury. The appellants are correct, for Brophy, which the Delaware courts have consistently followed, states that a plaintiff need not allege injury to the corporation when claiming a breach of fiduciary duty and seeking an accounting of profits. 70 A.2d at 8.

Morgan Stanley has not defended the district court's rationale for dismissing appellants' complaint. Instead, Morgan Stanley argues that, far from a standing in a fiduciary relationship to Olinkraft, it represented first Kennecott and then Johns-Manville "under circumstances that clearly placed it in an arm's length position regarding Olinkraft," that it therefore breached no duty by disclosing the Olinkraft information to Johns-Manville, and that, accordingly, the appellants have failed to state a claim upon which relief may be granted. We agree.

Because this appeal acquaints us only with the complaint and the appellee's motion to dismiss, we do not have the benefit of findings of fact about whatever communication occurred between Olinkraft, the potential target, and Morgan Stanley, the financial advisor to the potential acquirer: how the communication proceeded, what understandings were reached, what assumptions or expectations the trade's practice would justify. But the only logical conclusion to be drawn from the complaint is that Olinkraft and Morgan Stanley dealt at arm's length. Morgan Stanley's client was Kennecott, and its task was to obtain information with which to advise Kennecott. Morgan Stanley was never hired by Olinkraft, nor was Morgan Stanley's task ever to act on Olinkraft's behalf. On the other hand, the constituents of Olinkraft's management were Olinkraft's shareholders, and the duty of its management was to act on the shareholders' behalf. In short, Morgan Stanley and Olinkraft's management were at all times responsible to different interests, and they had no relationship to each other before or other than in the acquisition discussions. Morgan Stanley and Olinkraft's management must be presumed to have dealt, absent evidence of an extraordinary relationship, at arm's length.

Appellants contend that Morgan Stanley became a fiduciary of Olinkraft by virtue of the receipt of the confidential information. However, the fact that the information was confidential did nothing, in and of itself, to change the relationship between Morgan Stanley and Olinkraft's management. Put bluntly, although, according to the complaint, Olinkraft's management placed its confidence in Morgan Stanley not to disclose the information, Morgan Stanley owed no duty to observe that confidence. To be sure, in some instances the management of a potential target, such as Olinkraft, might be required by its responsibility to the shareholders' interest to cooperate, and even to disclose confidential information, to a potential acquirer or a financial advisor who, as did Morgan Stanley, stands at arm's length. But that obligation, while it burdens management, which might therefore reasonably insist upon an agreement of confidentiality, does not change the relationship between the target and the acquirer or its advisor. Appellants' complaint alleges no such agreement or understanding.

Given the different constituents and responsibilities of Morgan Stanley and Olinkraft's management, appellants' reliance on Brophy and on *Diamond v. Oreamuno*, 24 N.Y.2d 494, 301 N.Y.S.2d 78, 248 N.E.2d 910 (1969), a New York case which adopted Brophy's reasoning, is misplaced. Those cases predicate an accounting of profits without an allegation and showing of injury upon the fiduciary relationship of the officer, director, or employee to his corporation. Beyond corporate officers, directors, and in some instances employees, Delaware law has found a fiduciary relationship between a corporation's majority shareholders and its minority shareholders [Citation omitted.], but appellants have failed to cite any case from Delaware or elsewhere, and we have not found any, that considers one in Morgan Stanley's position to stand in a fiduciary relationship to one in Olinkraft's. Without some indication that the Delaware courts would accept appellants' theory of liability, we see no reason to extend Brophy beyond the established notion of a fiduciary, especially since Brophy represents an exception to the principle that standing requires injury. [Citation omitted.]

In sum, the appellants have failed to state a claim upon which relief may be granted, for the complaint, although it alleges a breach of fiduciary duty, fails to state facts from which a fiduciary relationship arises under Delaware law between Olinkraft and Morgan Stanley.

Affirmed.

OAKES, CIRCUIT JUDGE (Dissenting):

* * *

The question presented very briefly is whether the complaint, broadly construed, states a sufficient relation between Morgan Stanley and Olinkraft so as to prevent the former from utilizing nonpublic material information obtained from the latter for its own profit. I think it does. True, Morgan Stanley was hired and presumably paid by Kennecott for its services, and it was not hired by Olinkraft. Thus, at least during the initial approaches on Kennecott's behalf made by Morgan Stanley, it was surely not an agent of, and owed no especial duty to, Olinkraft or Olinkraft's stockholders. But after Olinkraft began to cooperate in the deal by turning over the "Confidential Inside Information" as to favorable earnings prospects, I think the acceptance of such information by Morgan Stanley, on the confidential terms, along with its understood role as intermediary in a cooperative takeover, imposed a duty on the investment banker under well-established common law principles not to use that information for its own profit. As Professor Scott stated in his treatise, "The same principles (that prevent a fiduciary from taking personal advantage of confidential information obtained as such, as against the beneficiary) are applicable even though the parties are not technically in a fiduciary relation, if one of them acquires confidential information from the other." [Citation omitted.]

While ordinarily this doctrine has been applied in the employee context, where an employee already had a duty as agent to his employer [citation omitted], or where an employee acquired secret information relating to a portion of his employer's business with respect to which he was not an agent [citation omitted], I see no logical reason why it should not extend to the case of a corporate marriage-broker where the parties are cooperative, absent agreements to the contrary. The fact that Morgan Stanley had no inherent pre-existing duty to Olinkraft should not prevent us from constructing a fiduciary relationship once the banker presumably agreed to use the information only for the Kennecott bid. Indeed, in Brophy, only after the employee acquired the confidential information did he become a fiduciary, thereby creating a duty and trust relationship. Id. at 7. As Judge Learned Hand noted when this court upheld for a third time the constitutionality of Section 16(b) of the Securities Exchange Act of 1934, 15 U.S.C. § 78p(b) (dealing with a sale by a director or corporate officer of stock in his company to an outsider based on inside information):

> When they sold shares, it could indeed be argued that they were not dealing with a beneficiary, but with one whom his purchase made a beneficiary. That should not, however, have obscured the fact that the director or officer assumed a fiduciary relation to the buyer by the very sale; for it would be a sorry distinction to allow him to use the advantage of his position to induce the buyer into the position of a beneficiary, although he was forbidden to do so, once the buyer had become one. [Citations omitted.]

To my mind, the need to police this sort of use of confidentially revealed information inheres in the role of the investment banker during merger/acquisition activity. As was pointed out by Morgan Stanley's own Robert F. Greenhill in an ABA Symposium, discussing the responsibilities of the investment banker in the tender offer context:

In terms of establishing and maintaining communications between both sides, he has an invaluable role. The ability to be recognized as advisor and yet not bind the principals permits confidential negotiations to progress while the public stance of the two companies is apparently that of adversaries. Secrecy is vital. Each side in the dialogue must trust the conduit through which the discussions take place. The investment banker maintains the dialogue.

Greenhill, Structuring an Offer, 32 Bus.Law. 1305, 1309 (1977). In this posture of a "dialogue," with confidential information changing hands and secrecy vital, it appears to me improper for the corporate marriage-broker, a potential insider to both acquiring and target companies, consciously and intentionally to profit from the dialogue. For me, this case is distinguishable from the late Judge Gurfein's *Frigitemp Corp. v. Financial Dynamics Fund, Inc.*, 524 F.2d 275 (2d Cir. 1975), which refused to hold an investment-company debenture buyer accountable for profits realized in connection with the debenture acquisition, even though it had been previously furnished with confidential information. There the information was, as the court's opinion pointed out, "required" to be disclosed to the investment company for the purpose of selling the debenture to it in an arm's length transaction. *Id.* at 279. Here, Olinkraft furnished its projections to Kennecott through Morgan Stanley, only in connection with Kennecott's contemplated acquisition, and not because it was required to do so but because it evidently wanted to cooperate. Olinkraft instructed Morgan Stanley to return the "Confidential Inside Information" if it was not used for the Kennecott bid. Unlike the defendants in Frigitemp, Morgan Stanley was not a party to the acquisition and received the information strictly as a result of its brokering efforts to bring the parties together.

Nor is this case like those holding that a commercial bank has no fiduciary duty to refrain from financing the takeover of a borrower and that the bank is not precluded from using information from one borrower to evaluate a loan to another. [Citations omitted.] The investment bank's role as broker in a friendly takeover and Morgan Stanley's purchase of Olinkraft stock distinguish this case from the commercial bank situation, even assuming arguendo the correctness of the bank cases' holdings.

This is not to say that plaintiffs below should be entitled to summary judgment; quite to the contrary, because serious factual issues are presented even reading the complaint in the most favorable light as I have done above. In the first place I wonder how the confidential information here favorable earnings projections could be "returned" as the complaint alleges. Surely the pieces of paper on which the projections are written could be returned, but one would have to be very naive to think that an experienced analyst would not be able to retain in his memory such favorable projections. I would assume that the highly capable people at Morgan Stanley or any other investment bank have facts and figures floating around in their heads that would on paper constitute the contents of many corporate annual reports.

Moreover, the precise role of Morgan Stanley in the instant transaction may be overstated in the complaint. One gathers that Olinkraft had employed the investment banking firm of Blyth Eastman Dillon & Co., Incorporated (Blyth), to render an opinion in connection with the merger proposals of both Texas Eastern and Johns-Manville. The joint proxy statement does not indicate when Blyth was engaged or whether it was employed in connection with the previous Kennecott tender offer possibility. I would be less inclined to find a fiduciary duty on the basis of Morgan Stanley's relation as broker to both parties, and the receipt of confidential information, were Olinkraft to have had its own broker on whom it relied for advice in the transaction. Olinkraft's use of its own broker would lessen the exclusivity and dependence the complaint implicitly alleges in the instant case. The usual other defenses of immateriality, lack of causation and the like are, of course, always open.

Finally, I do not think that considering the complaint to state a claim for relief would overly inhibit investment bankers in a takeover situation. While they surely want to acquire all the information they can, see McAtee, The Role of the Dealer Manager in the Disclosure Process, 32 Bus.Law. 1331, 1332 (1977), perhaps they should acquire confidential information only on the express understanding that it may be utilized in their Arbitrage Department, or that they may turn it over to other clients. Or perhaps they should erect a "Chinese wall" between their Mergers and Acquisitions Department and their Arbitrage Department. While there may be no "general duty between all participants in market transactions to forgo actions based on material, nonpublic information," *Chiarella v. United States, supra*, 100 S.Ct. at 1117, the duty here arises from a specific relation and agreement between the parties, at least in my view.

* * *

## NOTES AND QUESTIONS:

1. The court in *Phillips* had little difficulty in finding liability because of the evidence of clear deception by the recipient of the information. *See also Dravo Corp.*, discussed above in Chapt. 2(C)(1) and the Notes and Questions following that section as to the effect egregious conduct by the defendant might have on the outcome of a case.

2. The *Walton* case deals with the tough issue of how to protect confidential information when a company is in the process of being sold and potential investors want to receive confidential information as part of their due diligence. What was the harm to Olinkraft's shareholders? How persuasive is Judge Oakes's dissent? What effect do you think the lack of any financial loss to the plaintiff had on the outcome of the case?

### (d) Unsolicited Disclosures

## MOORE v. FORD MOTOR CO.

28 F.2d 529 (S.D.N.Y. 1928)

GODDARD, DISTRICT JUDGE.

This is a suit by the plaintiff to enjoin the defendant from using its 'Ford weekly purchase plan,' and for an accounting, on the ground that the plaintiff conceived and devised an original and novel invention and trade secret, to be used in connection with the sale of automobiles and tractors, which had never been used in the sale of automobiles or in the sale of other commodities; that plaintiff communicated this plan to the defendant by letter, and that the defendant appropriated his plan and copied his letter, and made use of them to its profit.

The claims of the plaintiff are based upon letters which passed between the plaintiff and the defendant, and upon the circular letter sent out by the defendant to the dealers in Ford automobiles and tractors, and put into effect March 30, 1923. These, exclusive of instructions to the dealers as to the placing of advertising, etc., and which were included with the circular letter, but which are not here material, are as follows:

* * *

Mr. DeForest, who had the correspondence with Mr. Moore, stated that his duties with the Ford Company, in 1922, consisted of handling the general correspondence which came to the sales department; that he had nothing whatever to do with the preparation of the 'Ford Weekly Purchase Plan'; that he first learned of it when a typewritten copy of it was given to him, to have mimeographed and sent out with advertising material to the branches of the Ford Motor Company; that he never showed the correspondence which passed between Mr. Moore and himself to any one in the Ford Company organization until Mr. Ryan, some time after March, 1923, inquired for it.

Mr. Davis testified that he joined the sales department of the Ford Motor Company in 1919, and that in 1922 he was acting as assistant to Mr. Ryan in the sales department; that he worked with Mr. Ryan in the preparation of the 'Ford Weekly Purchase Plan'; that prior to March 30, 1923, he had never seen plaintiff's letter of October 25, 1922, or any of the correspondence.

* * *

Aside from the alleged infringement of the plaintiff's literary rights in the letter, which have been discussed above, plaintiff bases his right to recovery on the ground that the defendant has, in violation of the common law, appropriated plaintiff's idea, namely, his sales plan, and that this, like trade secrets or other valuable trade information, belongs to the plaintiff until it is publicly disclosed, and plaintiff contends that, in his communication of his plan to the defendant in his letter of October 25, 1922, there was merely a restrictive publication or a confidential disclosure, and that a court of equity, therefore, should protect the plaintiff, by requiring the defendant, if it used his plan, to account to him for the benefits it received.

* * *

I do not think that, upon the facts, it could be held that there was a restricted disclosure of his plan by Mr. Moore, or a situation where a court of equity should attempt to extend defendant's obligation when plaintiff himself said none existed. I think it extremely doubtful whether the Ford Motor Company would have ever agreed to have permitted Mr. Moore to impart to it a plan in the nature of the one he advocated, with any limitation of its right to put into effect the 'Ford Weekly Purchase Plan. 'The parties were dealing at arm's length, though, of course, the defendant owed to the plaintiff the duty of not violating plaintiff's common-law literary rights in his communication discussed above. It is frequently not merely the idea, but it is the ability to carry it out successfully, that produces results. The plaintiff need not have disclosed his plan, except under such conditions as he himself imposed. The question of unfair competition is not involved. I think it would be going further than the courts have gone or should go, in the absence of some agreement, or a fiduciary relationship, to hold that, where one imparts a mere idea to another, and that one acts upon it and profits thereby, he is liable for the profits derived. Obviously, a contrary rule would place a serious limitation upon industry, and would be impractical, and, of course, no one need disclose his idea, except upon his terms.

* * *

Practically all of the elements in Mr. Moore's plan and in the 'Ford Weekly Purchase Plan' are found in sales plans which had been put into effect by others prior to the time the Ford plan went into effect. The sales plans used at an earlier date by the Radders Motor Company, Francis & Badger Motor Company, and L. G. Peed (Willys-Overland, Inc.) are similar to both Mr. Moore's plan and to the 'Ford Weekly Purchase Plan. 'Even if Mr. Moore's arguments were so convincing that they did lead the Ford Motor Company to adopt an installment plan for the sale of its automobiles and tractors, Mr. Moore cannot recover for that. Moreover, while it is possible that the germ of the 'Ford Weekly Purchase Plan' was obtained by the defendant from Mr. Moore's letter, the plaintiff, in my judgment, has not sustained the burden of proof that the defendant did get its idea of the 'Ford Weekly Purchase Plan' from Mr. Moore.

* * *

## DOWNEY v. GENERAL FOODS CORP.

286 N.E.2d 257 (N.Y. 1972)

The plaintiff, an airline pilot, brought this action against the defendant General Foods Corporation to recover damages for the alleged misappropriation of an idea. It is his claim that he suggested that the defendant's own gelatin product, 'Jell-O,' be named 'Wiggley' or a variation of that word, including 'Mr. Wiggle,' and that the product be directed towards the children's market; that, although the defendant disclaimed interest in the suggestion, it later offered its product for sale under the name 'Mr. Wiggle.' The defendant urges-by way of affirmative defense-that the plaintiff's 'alleged 'product concept and name' was independently created and developed' by it. The plaintiff moved for partial summary judgment 'on the question of liability' on 5 of its 14 causes of action and the defendant cross-moved for summary judgment dismissing the complaint. The court at Special Term denied both motions, and the Appellate Division affirmed [citation omitted], granting leave to appeal to this court on a certified question.

The plaintiff relies chiefly on correspondence between himself and the defendant, or, more precisely, on letters over the signature of a Miss Dunham, vice-president in charge of one of its departments. On February 15, 1965, the plaintiff wrote to the defendant, stating that he had an 'excellent idea to increase the sale of your product JELL-O * * * making it available for children'. Several days later, the defendant sent the plaintiff an 'Idea Submittal Form' (ISF) which included a form letter and a space for explaining the idea. In that form, the plaintiff suggested, in essence, that the produce 'be packaged & distributed to children under the name 'WIG-L-E' (meaning wiggly or wiggley) or 'WIGGLE-E' or 'WIGGLE-EEE' or 'WIGLEY.'' He explained that, although his children did not 'get especially excited about the Name JELL-O, or wish to eat it', when referred to by that name, 'the kids really took to it fast' when his wife 'called it 'wiggle-y,'' noting that they then 'associate(d) the name to the 'wiggleing' dessert.' Although this is the only recorded proof of his idea, the plaintiff maintains that he sent Miss Dunham two handwritten letters in which he set forth other variations of 'Wiggiley,' including 'Mr. Wiggley, Wiggle, Wiggle-e.'

A letter, dated March 8, 1965, over the signature of Miss Dunham, acknowledged the submission of the ISF and informed the plaintiff that it had no interest in promoting his suggestion. However, in July, the defendant introduced into the market a Jell-O product which it called 'Mr. Wiggle.' The plaintiff instituted the present action some months later. In addition to general denials, the answer contains several affirmative defenses, one of which, as indicated above, recites that the defendant independently created the product's concept and name before the plaintiff's submission to it.

In support of its position, the defendant pointed to depositions taken by the plaintiff from its employees and from employees of Young & Rubicam, the firm which did its advertising. From these it appears that the defendant first began work on a children's gelatin product in May, 1965-three months after the plaintiff had submitted his suggestion-in response to a threat by Pillsbury Company to enter the children's market with a product named 'Jiggly.' Those employees of the defendant in charge of the project enlisted the aid of Young & Rubicam which, solely on its own initiative, 'came up with the name 'Mr. Wiggle. ''In point of fact, Miss Dunham swore in her deposition that she had had no knowledge whatever of the plaintiff's idea until late in 1966, shortly before commencement of his suit; that ideas submitted by the general public were kept in a file by an assistant of hers 'under lock and key'; and that no one from any other of the defendant's departments ever asked to research those files. The assistant, who had alone handled the correspondence with the plaintiff over Miss Dunham's signature-reproduced by means of a signature duplicating machine-deposed that she had no contact whatsoever with Young & Rubicam and had never discussed the name 'Wiggle' or 'Mr. Wiggle' with any one from that firm.

In addition to the depositions of its employees and the employees of its advertising agency, the defendant submitted documentary proof of its prior use of some form of the word 'wiggle' in connection with its endeavor to sell Jell-O to children. Thus, it submitted (1) a copy of a report which Young & Rubicam furnished it in June of 1959 proposing 'an advertising program directed at children as a means of securing additional sales volume'; (2) a copy of a single dimensional reproduction of a television commercial, prepared in 1959 and used thereafter by the defendant in national and local television broadcasts, which contained the phrase, 'ALL THAT WIGGLES IS NOT JELL-O'; and (3) a copy of a newspaper advertisement that appeared in 1960, depicting an Indian 'squaw' puppet and her 'papoose' preparing Jell-O-the 'top favorite in every American tepee'-and suggesting to mothers that they '(m)ake a wigglewam of Jell-O for your tribe tonight!'

The critical issue in this case turns on whether the idea suggested by the plaintiff was original or novel. An idea may be a property right. But, when one submits an idea to another, no promise to pay for its use may be implied, and no asserted agreement enforced, if the elements of novelty and originality are absent, since the property right in an idea is based upon these two elements. [Citations omitted.] The Bram case [*Bram v. Dannon Milk Prods.*, 33 A.D.2d 1010, 307 N.Y.S.2d 571] is illustrative; in reversing Special Term and granting summary judgment dismissing the complaint, the Appellate Division made it clear that, despite the asserted existence of an agreement, the plaintiff could not recover for his idea if it was not original and had been used before (33 A.D.2d, at p. 1010, 307 N.Y.S.2d 571): 'The idea submitted by the plaintiff to the defendants, the concept of depicting an infant in a highchair eating and enjoying yogurt, was lacking in novelty and had been utilized by the defendants . . . prior to its submission. Lack of novelty in an idea is fatal to any cause of action for its unlawful use. In the circumstances a question of fact as to whether there existed an oral agreement between the parties would not preclude summary judgment.'

In the case before us, the record indisputably establishes, first, that the idea submitted-use of a word ('wiggley' or 'wiggle') descriptive of the most obvious characteristic of Jell-O, with the prefix 'Mr.' added-was lacking in novelty and originality and, second, that the defendant had envisaged the idea, indeed had utilized it, years before the plaintiff submitted it. As already noted, it had made use of the word 'wiggles' in a 1959 television commercial and the word 'wigglewam' in a 1960 newspaper advertisement. It was but natural, then, for the defendant to employ some variation of it to combat Pillsbury's entry into the children's market with its 'Jiggly.' Having relied on its own previous experience, the defendant was free to make use of 'Mr. Wiggle' without being obligated to compensate the plaintiff.

It is only necessary to add that, in light of the complete pretrial disclosure in this case of every one who had any possible connection with the creation of the name, the circumstance, adverted to by the courts below, that the facts surrounding the defendant's development of the name were within the knowledge of the defendant and its advertising agency does not preclude a grant of summary judgment. In the present case, it was shown beyond peradventure that there was no connection between Miss Dunham's department and the defendant's other employees or the employees of the advertising outfit who took part in the creation of 'Mr. Wiggle.' In exhaustive discovery proceedings-which included examinations of all parties concerned either with that name or the defendant's idea files-the plaintiff was furnished with every conceivable item of information in the defendant's possession bearing on the privacy and confidentiality of such files and on the absence of access to them by those outside of Miss Dunham's department. The hope, expressed by the plaintiff that he may be able to prove that the witnesses who gave testimony in examinations before trial lied, is clearly insufficient to create an issue of fact requiring a trial or defeat the defendant's motion for summary judgment. [Citations omitted.]

The order appealed from should be reversed, without costs, the question certified answered in the negative and the defendant's motion for summary judgment dismissing the complaint granted.

* * *

## SMITH v. SNAP-ON TOOLS CORP.

833 F.2d 578 (5th Cir. 1988)

Basil Smith, a resident of Mississippi, made a ratchet by combining parts of two existing tools. Hoping to see his ratchet made available for sale, he brought it to the attention of Snap-On Tools, Inc., a corporation with its principal place of business in Wisconsin, by showing the ratchet to an independent dealer, then submitting a tool suggestion form to corporate headquarters. Snap-On began manufacturing and selling the ratchet without paying any part of the proceeds to Smith. Smith brought a diversity action against Snap-On, claiming that the ratchet was a trade secret, that he submitted the ratchet in confidence to Snap-On, that Snap-On misappropriated the trade secret, and that Snap-On was liable in damages to him for the misappropriation. The district court, applying Wisconsin law, held that Snap-On had misappropriated Smith's trade secret and awarded Smith damages in the amount of two and one-half percent of Snap-On's gross sales from the ratchet plus pre-judgment interest. Smith appealed the damage award, seeking to recover Snap-On's profits rather than a reasonable royalty. Snap-On cross-appealed, contending that the district court erred 1) in holding that the device was a trade secret; 2) in holding that a confidential relationship existed between Smith and Snap-On; 3) in holding that Smith's claim was not barred by laches or the statute of limitations; 4) in awarding pre-judgment interest; 5) in awarding a reasonable royalty measure of damages for as long as Snap-On manufactured and marketed the tool rather than merely for the period during which Snap-On enjoyed a competitive advantage because it was able to produce the tool before its competitors could duplicate the model they saw on the market. Because the record does not support the finding that there was a confidential relationship between Smith and Snap-On, we reverse.

Wisconsin law prescribes two essential elements in a cause of action for misappropriation of trade secrets: an actual trade secret and a breach of confidence. The essence of the tort of trade secret misappropriation is the inequitable use of the secret. Even when a trade secret exists, a person who learns the secret legitimately, without any duty of confidentiality, is free to use it.

Wisconsin therefore follows trade secrets law as set out in § 757 of the Restatement of Torts. Under the Restatement, "[o]ne who discloses or uses another's trade secret, without a privilege to do so, is liable to the other if . . . his disclosure or use constitutes a breach of confidence reposed in him by the other in disclosing the secret to him." As the comment to this provision states, the proprietor of a trade secret may not unilaterally create a confidential relationship without the knowledge or consent of the party to whom he discloses the secret. No particular form of notice is necessary, however; the question is whether the recipient of the information knew or should have known that the disclosure was made in confidence.

Smith concedes that he never explicitly requested that his disclosure to Snap-On be held in confidence. Nonetheless, he argues, Snap-On knew or should have known that the disclosure was confidential. According to Smith, a "special relationship" existed between himself and Snap-On, based on the fact that he, as a relatively unsophisticated individual, submitted his invention to Snap-On, a large corporation. Under the circumstances, Smith contends, the manufacturer should have known that he, as the inventor, expected compensation even if he did not request it.

The district court accepted this argument, and found that Snap-On had clothed its independent dealer, Jackie Clark, to whom the disclosure was actually made, with apparent authority to accept tool submission suggestions from people like Smith. Pointing out the discrepancy in the circumstances of Smith, a mechanic with little education, and Snap-On, a large corporation, the court concluded that a special relationship between Smith and Snap-On existed from the time of the initial disclosure to Clark and that Snap-On knew or should have known that an inventor does not submit his invention to a manufacturer to appropriate without compensating the inventor.

This does not reflect Wisconsin law. The Supreme Court of Wisconsin has held that, when parties are dealing at arm's length, one party's disclosure of an alleged trade secret to another does not automatically create a confidential relationship. Although the case in which the Supreme Court of Wisconsin announced this holding involved two corporations, we see no reason to believe that it would have applied a different rule if the inventor had been an individual rather than a corporation.

Under certain circumstances, courts have found liability for misappropriation of trade secrets in cases involving implied confidentiality between an inventor and a manufacturer. When a manufacturer has actively solicited disclosure from an inventor, then made use of the disclosed material, the manufacturer may be liable for use or disclosure of the secret in the absence of any expressed understanding as to confidentiality. In this case, however, Smith disclosed the invention on his own initiative, without any prompting from Snap-On. Alternatively, courts have imposed liability when the disclosing inventor did not specifically request confidentiality from the manufacturer, but did make clear that the disclosure was intended as part of a course of negotiations aimed at creating a licensing agreement or entering into a similar business transaction. These cases are also distinguishable because Smith did not indicate that he wanted any pecuniary recompense for his suggestion. In fact, Smith testified that he did not mention compensation to Jackie Clark because he did not believe Clark was authorized to discuss such matters. When Smith sent Snap-On a tool suggestion report describing the ratchet shortly after the initial disclosure to Clark, he did not in any way indicate that he wanted compensation, and indeed wrote on the suggestion form, "I would like to be able to buy a nice new shiney [sic] one from the Snap-On truck." In none of his dealings with Snap-On over the next two years did Smith ever request confidentiality or indicate that he expected or desired any commercial arrangement based on his submission of the ratchet suggestion to Snap-On.

In February, 1978, more than two years after Smith showed the ratchet to Clark, Smith's lawyer sent a letter to the supervisor of Snap-On's Product Management Division in which he asked that Smith receive compensation. Reliance on confidentiality, however, must exist at the time the disclosure is made. An attempt to establish a special relationship long after an initial disclosure comes too late.

Because there was no confidential relationship between Smith and Snap-On, Snap-On violated no obligation to Smith by manufacturing the ratchet. We therefore REVERSE.

* * *

## NOTES AND QUESTIONS:

1. For many companies, especially those in high-tech areas, unsolicited disclosures are a difficult problem that has no easy (or inexpensive) solution. As *Moore v. Ford Motor Co.*, 28 F.2d 529 (S.D.N.Y.1928), illustrates, this predicament has been around for years. Fortunately for the defendant, its "Ford weekly purchase plan" was not much different from other purchase plans that were known at the time. Furthermore, Ford presented evidence that its plan was developed independently by individuals who did not have access to Mr. Moore's correspondence. General Foods, the defendant in *Downey v. General Foods Corp.*, 286 N.E.2d 257 (N.Y.1972), was faced with a more problematic situation because the employee who signed the correspondence with Mr. Downey was actually involved in the "Mr. Wiggle campaign." Were you convinced that summary judgment was appropriate because there was no genuine issue of material fact?

2. Many companies have a policy, sometimes called an NIH policy, of refusing to consider outside proposals. In other words, the company will not develop any product that was "**N**ot **I**nvented **H**ere." Other procedures to shield research and technical personnel from unsolicited proposals include requiring a sender to sign a waiver form designed to limit liability to a pre-stated condition, such as whether the sender can get a patent on the proposed idea. In many industries, the problem is much more difficult to control because many ideas come from customers who are in close contact with sales and product development personnel. As a practical matter, these company representatives cannot cut themselves off from their customers. This problem occurs often in the medical device industry, which works closely with physician clients. *See Goldberg v. Medtronic, Inc.*, 209 U.S.P.Q. 259 (N.D.Ill.1980), discussed in Chapter 4(D) *infra.* Lax procedures for screening unsolicited product ideas have spawned numerous lawsuits. So far, the best solution to this problem is twofold: (1) the company should institute formal internal procedures to deal with receiving and reviewing unsolicited proposals, and (2) establish a comprehensive continuing education program to train personnel in the procedures and familiarize them with the pitfalls and consequences of not following procedures.

### (e) By Operation of Law

## E.I. DuPONT DeNEMOURS & CO. v. CHRISTOPHER

431 F.2d 1012 (5th Cir. 1970)

This is a case of industrial espionage in which an airplane is the cloak and a camera the dagger. The defendants-appellants, Rolfe and Gary Christopher, are photographers in Beaumont, Texas. The Christophers were hired by an unknown third party to take aerial photographs of new construction at the Beaumont plant of E. I. duPont deNemours & Company, Inc. Sixteen photographs of the DuPont facility were taken from the air on March 19, 1969, and these photographs were later developed and delivered to the third party.

DuPont employees apparently noticed the airplane on March 19 and immediately began an investigation to determine why the craft was circling over the plant. By that afternoon the investigation had disclosed that the craft was involved in a photographic expedition and that the Christophers were the photographers. DuPont contacted the Christophers that same afternoon and asked them to reveal the name of the person or corporation requesting the photographs. The Christophers refused to disclose this information, giving as their reason the client's desire to remain anonymous.

Having reached a dead end in the investigation, DuPont subsequently filed suit against the Christophers, alleging that the Christophers had wrongfully obtained photographs revealing DuPont's trade secrets which they then sold to the undisclosed third party. DuPont contended that it had developed a highly secret but unpatented process for producing methanol, a process which gave DuPont a competitive advantage over other producers. This process, DuPont alleged, was a trade secret developed after much expensive and time-consuming research, and a secret which the company had taken special precautions to safeguard. The area photographed by the Christophers was the plant designed to produce methanol by this secret process, and because the plant was still under construction parts of the process were exposed to view from directly above the construction area. Photographs of that area, DuPont alleged, would enable a skilled person to deduce the secret process for making methanol. DuPont thus contended that the Christophers had wrongfully appropriated DuPont trade secrets by taking the photographs and delivering them to the undisclosed third party. In its suit DuPont asked for damages to cover the loss it had already sustained as a result of the wrongful disclosure of the trade secret and sought temporary and permanent injunctions prohibiting any further circulation of the photographs already taken and prohibiting any additional photographing of the methanol plant.

The Christophers answered with motions to dismiss for lack of jurisdiction and failure to state a claim upon which relief could be granted. Depositions were taken during which the Christophers again refused to disclose the name of the person to whom they had delivered the photographs. DuPont then filed a motion to compel an answer to this question and all related questions.

On June 5, 1969, the trial court held a hearing on all pending motions and an additional motion by the Christophers for summary judgment. The court denied the

Christophers' motions to dismiss for want of jurisdiction and failure to state a claim and also denied their motion for summary judgment. The court granted DuPont's motion to compel the Christophers to divulge the name of their client. Having made these rulings, the court then granted the Christophers' motion for an interlocutory appeal under 28 U.S.C.A. § 1292(b) to allow the Christophers to obtain immediate appellate review of the court's finding that DuPont had stated a claim upon which relief could be granted. Agreeing with the trial court's determination that DuPont had stated a valid claim, we affirm the decision of that court.

This is a case of first impression, for the Texas courts have not faced this precise factual issue, and sitting as a diversity court we must sensitize our Erie antennae to divine what the Texas courts would do if such a situation were presented to them. The only question involved in this interlocutory appeal is whether DuPont has asserted a claim upon which relief can be granted. The Christophers argued both at trial and before this court that they committed no 'actionable wrong' in photographing the DuPont facility and passing these photographs on to their client because they conducted all of their activities in public airspace, violated no government aviation standard, did not breach any confidential relation, and did not engage in any fraudulent or illegal conduct. In short, the Christophers argue that for an appropriation of trade secrets to be wrongful there must be a trespass, other illegal conduct, or breach of a confidential relationship. We disagree.

It is true, as the Christophers assert, that the previous trade secret cases have contained one or more of these elements. However, we do not think that the Texas courts would limit the trade secret protection exclusively to these elements. On the contrary, in *Hyde Corporation v. Huffines*, 1958, 158 Tex. 566, 314 S.W.2d 763, the Texas Supreme Court specifically adopted the rule found in the Restatement of Torts which provides:

'One who discloses or uses another's trade secret, without a privilege to do so, is liable to the other if (a) he discovered the secret by improper means, or (b) his disclosure or use constitutes a breach of confidence reposed in him by the other in disclosing the secret to him . . . .'

Restatement of Torts § 757 (1939).

Thus, although the previous cases have dealt with a breach of a confidential relationship, a trespass, or other illegal conduct, the rule is much broader than the cases heretofore encountered. Not limiting itself to specific wrongs, Texas adopted subsection (a) of the Restatement which recognizes a cause of action for the discovery of a trade secret by any 'improper' means.

The defendants, however, read Furr's Inc. v. United Specialty Advertising Co., Tex.Civ.App.1960, 338 S.W.2d 762, writ ref'd n.r.e., as limiting the Texas rule to breach of a confidential relationship. The court in Furr's did make the statement that

'The use of someone else's idea is not automatically a violation of the law. It must be something that meets the requirements of a 'trade secret' and has been obtained through a breach of confidence in order to entitle the injured party to damages and/or injunction. 338 S.W.2d at 766.

We think, however, that the exclusive rule which defendants have extracted from this statement is unwarranted. In the first place, in Furr's the court specifically found that there was no trade secret involved because the entire advertising scheme claimed to be the trade secret had been completely divulged to the public. Secondly, the court found that the plaintiff in the course of selling the scheme to the defendant had voluntarily divulged the entire scheme. Thus the court was dealing only with a possible breach of confidence concerning a properly discovered secret; there was never a question of any impropriety in the discovery or any other improper conduct on the part of the defendant. The court merely held that under those circumstances the defendant had not acted improperly if no breach of confidence occurred. We do not read Furr's as limiting the trade secret protection to a breach of confidential relationship when the facts of the case do raise the issue of some other wrongful conduct on the part of one discovering the trade secrets of another. If breach of confidence were meant to encompass the entire panoply of commercial improprieties, subsection (a) of the Restatement would be either surplus age or persiflage, an interpretation abhorrent to the traditional precision of the Restatement. We therefore find meaning in subsection (a) and think that the Texas Supreme Court clearly indicated by its adoption that there is a cause of action for the discovery of a trade secret by any 'improper means.' Hyde Corporation v. Huffines, supra.

The question remaining, therefore, is whether aerial photography of plant construction is an improper means of obtaining another's trade secret. We conclude that it is and that the Texas courts would so hold. The Supreme Court of that state has declared that 'the undoubted tendency of the law has been to recognize and enforce higher standards of commercial morality in the business world.' [Citation omitted.] That court has quoted with approval articles indicating that the proper means of gaining possession of a competitor's secret process is 'through inspection and analysis' of the product in order to create a duplicate. [Citation omitted.] Later another Texas court explained:

'The means by which the discovery is made may be obvious, and the experimentation leading from known factors to presently unknown results may be simple and lying in the public domain. But these facts do not destroy the value of the discovery and will not advantage a competitor who by unfair means obtains the knowledge without paying the price expended by the discoverer.' [Citation omitted.]

We think, therefore, that the Texas rule is clear. One may use his competitor's secret process if he discovers the process by reverse engineering applied to the finished product; one may use a competitor's process if he discovers it by his own independent research; but one may not avoid these labors by taking the process from the discoverer without his permission at a time when he is taking reasonable precautions to maintain its secrecy. To obtain knowledge of a process without spending the time and money to discover it independently is improper unless the holder voluntarily discloses it or fails to take reasonable precautions to ensure its secrecy.

In the instant case the Christophers deliberately flew over the DuPont plant to get pictures of a process which DuPont had attempted to keep secret. The Christophers delivered their pictures to a third party who was certainly aware of the means by which they had been acquired and who may be planning to use the information contained therein to manufacture methanol by the DuPont process. The third party has a right to use this process only if he obtains this knowledge through his own research efforts, but thus far all information indicates that the third party has gained this knowledge solely by taking it from DuPont at a time when DuPont was making reasonable efforts to preserve its secrecy. In such a situation DuPont has a valid cause of action to prohibit the Christophers from improperly discovering its trade secret and to prohibit the undisclosed third party from using the improperly obtained information.

We note that this view is in perfect accord with the position taken by the authors of the Restatement. In commenting on improper means of discovery the savants of the Restatement said:

> 'f. Improper means of discovery. The discovery of another's trade secret by improper means subjects the actor to liability independently of the harm to the interest in the secret. Thus, if one uses physical force to take a secret formula from another's pocket, or breaks into another's office to steal the formula, his conduct is wrongful and subjects him to liability apart from the rule stated in this Section. Such conduct is also an improper means of procuring the secret under this rule. But means may be improper under this rule even though they do not cause any other harm than that to the interest in the trade secret. Examples of such means are fraudulent misrepresentations to induce disclosure, tapping of telephone wires, eavesdropping or other espionage. A complete catalogue of improper means is not possible. In general they are means which fall below the generally accepted standards of commercial morality and reasonable conduct.' Restatement of Torts § 757, comment f at 10 (1939).

In taking this position we realize that industrial espionage of the sort here perpetrated has become a popular sport in some segments of our industrial community. However, our devotion to free wheeling industrial competition must not force us into accepting the law of the jungle as the standard of morality expected in our commercial relations. Our tolerance of the espionage game must cease when the protections required to prevent another's spying cost so much that the spirit of inventiveness is dampened. Commercial privacy must be protected from espionage which could not have been reasonably anticipated or prevented. We do not mean to imply, however, that everything not in plain view is within the protected vale, nor that all information obtained through every extra optical extension is forbidden. Indeed, for our industrial competition to remain healthy there must be breathing room for observing a competing industrialist. A competitor can and must shop his competition for pricing and examine his products for quality, components, and methods of manufacture. Perhaps ordinary fences and roofs must be built to shut out incursive eyes, but we need not require the discoverer of a trade secret to guard against the unanticipated, the undetectable, or the unpreventable methods of espionage now available.

In the instant case DuPont was in the midst of constructing a plant. Although after construction the finished plant would have protected much of the process from view, during the period of construction the trade secret was exposed to view from the air. To require DuPont to put a roof over the unfinished plant to guard its secret would impose an enormous expense to prevent nothing more than a school boy's trick. We introduce here no new or radical ethic since our ethos has never given moral sanction to piracy. The market place must not deviate far from our mores. We should not require a person or corporation to take unreasonable precautions to prevent another from doing that which he ought not do in the first place. Reasonable precautions against predatory eyes we may require, but an impenetrable fortress is an unreasonable requirement, and we are not disposed to burden industrial inventors with such a duty in order to protect the fruits of their efforts. 'Improper' will always be a word of many nuances, determined by time, place, and circumstances. We therefore need not proclaim a catalogue of commercial improprieties. Clearly, however, one of its commandments does say 'thou shall not appropriate a trade secret through deviousness under circumstances in which countervailing defenses are not reasonably available.'

Having concluded that aerial photography, from whatever altitude, is an improper method of discovering the trade secrets exposed during construction of the DuPont plant, we need not worry about whether the flight pattern chosen by the Christophers violated any federal aviation regulations. Regardless of whether the flight was legal or illegal in that sense, the espionage was an improper means of discovering DuPont's trade secret.

The decision of the trial court is affirmed and the case remanded to that court for proceedings on the merits.

* * *

## CHICAGO LOCK CO. v. FANBERG

676 F.2d 400 (9th Cir. 1982)

Since 1933 the Chicago Lock Company, a manufacturer of various types of locks, has sold a tubular lock, marketed under the registered trademark "Ace," which provides greater security than other lock designs. Tubular Ace locks, millions of which have been sold, are frequently used on vending and bill changing machines and in other maximum security uses, such as burglar alarms. The distinctive feature of Ace locks (and the feature that apparently makes the locks attractive to institutional and large-scale commercial purchasers) is the secrecy and difficulty of reproduction associated with their keys.

The District Court found that the Company "has a fixed policy that it will only sell a duplicate key for the registered series 'Ace' lock to the owner of record of the lock and on request of a bona fide purchase order, letterhead or some other identifying means of the actual recorded lock owner." Finding of Fact No. 14, Excerpt of Record at 89. In addition, the serial number-key code correlations are maintained by the Company indefinitely and in secrecy, the Company does not sell tubular key "blanks" to locksmiths or others, and keys to Ace locks are stamped "Do Not Duplicate." See Excerpt at 86-91.

If the owner of an Ace lock loses his key, he may obtain a duplicate from the Company. Alternatively, he may have a proficient locksmith "pick" the lock, decipher the tumbler configuration, and grind a duplicate tubular key. The latter procedure is quicker than the former, though more costly. The locksmith will, to avoid the need to "pick" the lock each time a key is lost, record the key code (i.e., the tumbler configuration) along with the serial number of the customer's lock. See Excerpt at 92. Enough duplicate keys have been made by locksmiths that substantial key code data have been compiled, albeit noncommercially and on an ad hoc basis.

Appellant Victor Fanberg, the son of locksmith Morris Fanberg and a locksmith in his own right, has published a number of locksmith manuals for conventional locks. Realizing that no compilation had been made of tubular lock key codes, in 1975 Fanberg advertised in a locksmith journal, Locksmith Ledger, requesting that individual locksmiths transmit to him serial number-key code correlations in their possession in exchange for a copy of a complete compilation when finished. A number of locksmiths complied, and in late 1976 Fanberg and his father began to sell a two-volume publication of tubular lock codes, including those of Ace locks, entitled "A-Advanced Locksmith's Tubular Lock Codes." In 1976 and 1977 Fanberg advertised the manuals in the Locksmith Ledger for $49.95 and indicated that it would be supplemented as new correlations became known. See Excerpt at 95-98. About 350 manuals had been sold at the time of trial. The District Court found that Fanberg "had lost or surrendered control over persons who could purchase the books," id. at 98, meaning that nonlocksmiths could acquire the code manuals.

The books contain correlations which would allow a person equipped with a tubular key grinding machine to make duplicate keys for any listed Ace lock if the serial number of the lock was known. On some models, the serial numbers appear on the exterior of the lock face. Thus, Fanberg's manuals would make it considerably easier (and less expensive) for a person to obtain (legitimately or illegitimately) duplicate keys to Ace locks without going through the Company's screening process. This is what caused consternation to the Company and some of its customers. At no time did Fanberg seek, or the Company grant, permission to compile and sell the key codes. Nor did the individual locksmiths seek authorization from the Company or their customers before transmitting their key code data to Fanberg.

The Company filed a three-count complaint against the Fanbergs, alleging federal question jurisdiction and diversity of citizenship, on December 2, 1976. The complaint, see Excerpt at 1-12, was predicated on theories of trademark infringement under 15 U.S.C. ss 1051 et seq., federal unfair competition under 15 U.S.C. ss 1125(a), and California common law unfair competition under former Cal.Civ.Code § 3369. On November 17, 1977, Judge Enright granted summary judgment for the Fanbergs on the federal claims, but left intact the state law claim. See Excerpt at 32-34. The complaint was amended, see Excerpt at 38-46, and a four-day bench trial was held before Judge Kerr on January 23-26, 1979. On November 28, 1979, Judge Kerr entered judgment in favor of the Company and filed findings of fact and conclusions of law. See Excerpt at 75-121.

The court found that the Company's high security policy for its Ace tubular locks, of which the confidential key code data were a part, was a "valuable business or trade secret-type asset" of the Company, and that the Fanbergs' publication of their compilation of these codes so undermined the Company's policy as to constitute "common law unfair competition in the form of an unfair business practice within the meaning of Section 3369 of the Civil Code of the State of California," as broadly interpreted in *Barquis v. Merchants Collection Association*, 7 Cal.3d 94, 101 Cal.Rptr. 745, 496 P.2d 817 (1972). Excerpt at 118-120. The court enjoined the Fanbergs from publishing or distributing any lists of key code correlations for the Company's registered series Ace tubular locks. See Excerpt at 121.

On this appeal the Fanbergs argue that the District Court erred on three grounds: (1) that the injunction against publication of their book constitutes a prior restraint prohibited by the First Amendment to the United States Constitution; (2) that the statute under which the injunction issued, former Cal.Civ.Code § 3369, is unconstitutionally vague; and (3) that the District Court applied erroneously the common law doctrine of trade secrets in concluding that the Fanbergs had committed an "unfair business practice" under Section 3369.

## THE TRADE SECRETS CLAIM

Appellants argue that the District Court erroneously concluded that they are liable under Section 3369 for acquiring appellee's trade secret through improper means. We agree, and on this basis we reverse the District Court.

Although the District Court's Findings of Fact and Conclusions of Law are lengthy, the thrust of its holding may be fairly summarized as follows: appellants' acquisition of appellee's serial number-key code correlations through improper means, and the subsequent publication thereof, constituted an "unfair business practice" within the meaning of Section 3369. See Excerpt at 119-20. Even though the court did not make an explicit finding that appellee's serial number-key code correlations were protectable trade secrets, both appellants and appellee premise their appeal on such an "implicit" finding. See Brief of Appellee at 13-14. We think it clear that the District Court based its decision on a theory of improper acquisition of trade secrets, and in the following discussion we assume arguendo that appellee's listing of serial number-key code correlations constituted a trade secret.

California courts have adopted the theory of trade secret protection set out in the Restatement (First) of Torts, § 757, and the comments thereto, in resolving disputes involving trade secrets. [Citations omitted.] Commission of this common law tort is enjoinable under the purview of "unfair competition" and "unlawful" or "unfair business practice" under Section 3369. [Citations omitted.]

The pertinent portion of Section 757 of the Restatement provides:

One who discloses or uses another's trade secret, without a privilege to do so, is liable to the other if

(a) he discovered the secret by improper means, or

* * *

(c) he learned the secret from a third person with notice of the facts that it was a secret and that the third person discovered it by improper means . . .

* * *

Trade secrets are protected, therefore, in a manner akin to private property, but only when they are disclosed or used through improper means. Trade secrets do not enjoy the absolute monopoly protection afforded patented processes, for example, and trade secrets will lose their character as private property when the owner divulges them or when they are discovered through proper means. "It is well recognized that a trade secret does not offer protection against discovery by fair and honest means such as by independent invention, accidental disclosure or by so-called reverse engineering, that is, starting with the known product and working backward to divine the process." [Citation omitted.]

Thus, it is the employment of improper means to procure the trade secret, rather than mere copying or use, which is the basis of liability. Restatement (First) of Torts, § 757, comment a (1939). The Company concedes, as it must, that had the Fanbergs bought and examined a number of locks on their own, their reverse engineering (or deciphering) of the key codes and publication thereof would not have been use of "improper means." Similarly, the Fanbergs' claimed use of computer programs in generating a portion of the key code-serial number correlations here at issue must also be characterized as proper reverse engineering. Excerpt at 96, 100-01; Brief of Appellee at 29-30. The trial court found that appellants obtained the serial number-key code correlations from a "comparatively small" number of locksmiths, who themselves had reverse-engineered the locks of their customers. See Excerpt at 96-97. The narrow legal issue presented here, therefore, is whether the Fanbergs' procurement of these individual locksmiths' reverse engineering data is an "improper means" with respect to appellee Chicago Lock Company.

The concept of "improper means," as embodied in the Restatement, and as expressed by the Supreme Court, connotes the existence of a duty to the trade secret owner not to disclose the secret to others. See Restatement (First) of Torts, § 757, comment h (1939). "The protection accorded the trade secret holder (i.e., in this case the Company) is against the disclosure or unauthorized use of the trade secret by those to whom the secret has been confided under the express or implied restriction of disclosure or nonuse." [Citation omitted.]

Thus, under Restatement § 757(c), appellants may be held liable if they intentionally procured the locksmiths to disclose the trade secrets in breach of the locksmiths' duty to the Company of nondisclosure. See Restatement (First) of Torts, § 757, comment h (1939). Critical to the District Court's holding, therefore, was its conclusion that the individual locksmiths, from whom the Fanbergs acquired the serial number-key code correlations, owed an implied duty to the Company not to make the disclosures. See Excerpt at 116.

We find untenable the basis upon which the District Court concluded that the individual locksmiths owe a duty of nondisclosure to the Company. The court predicated this implied duty upon a "chain" of duties: first, that the locksmiths are in such a fiduciary relationship with their customers as to give rise to a duty not to disclose their customers' key codes without permission, see Excerpt at 116; and second, that the lock owners are in turn under an "implied obligation (to the Company) to maintain inviolate" the serial number-key code correlations for their own locks, see id.

The court's former conclusion is sound enough: in their fiduciary relationship with lock owners, individual locksmiths are reposed with a confidence and trust by their customers, of which disclosure of the customers' key codes would certainly be a breach. This duty, however, could give rise only to an action by "injured" lock owners against the individual locksmiths, not by the Company against the locksmiths or against the Fanbergs.

The court's latter conclusion, that lock owners owe a duty to the Company, is contrary to law and to the Company's own admissions. A lock purchaser's own reverse-engineering of his own lock, and subsequent publication of the serial number-key code correlation, is an example of the independent invention and reverse engineering expressly allowed by trade secret doctrine. *See Sinclair, 42 Cal.App.3d at 226, 116 Cal.Rptr. at 661.* Imposing an obligation of nondisclosure on lock owners here would frustrate the intent of California courts to disallow protection to trade secrets discovered through "fair and honest means." *See Id.* Further, such an implied obligation upon the lock owners in this case would, in effect, convert the Company's trade secret into a state-conferred monopoly akin to the absolute protection that a federal patent affords. Such an extension of California trade secrets law would certainly be preempted by the federal scheme of patent regulation. [Citations omitted.]

Appellants, therefore, cannot be said to have procured the individual locksmiths to breach a duty of nondisclosure they owed to the Company, for the locksmiths owed no such duty. The Company's serial number-key code correlations are not subject to protection under Restatement § 757, as adopted by the California courts, because the Company has not shown a breach of any confidence reposed by it in the Fanbergs, the locksmiths, or the lock purchasers-i.e., it has failed to show the use of "improper means" by the Fanbergs required by the Restatement.

The District Court's conclusion that the Fanbergs committed an "unfair business practice" under Section 3369, therefore, must be reversed, and judgment should be entered in favor of appellants. In view of the foregoing we find it unnecessary to reach appellants' First Amendment and vagueness claims.

* * *

## NOTES AND QUESTIONS:

1. *E.I. duPont deNemours & Co. v. Christopher*, 431 F.2d 1012 (5th Cir.1970), reflects how liability can be found when efforts to discover another's trade secret involve "improper means" but are not per se illegal. Following the standards outlined in Restatement (First) of Torts § 757 (1939), the court had no trouble in finding that the Christophers' actions violated the "higher standards of commercial morality in the business world" and amounted to economic espionage. *Id.* at 1015 (citation and internal quotation marks omitted). Would the outcome have been different if DuPont's plant was at the base of a mountain, and the Christophers were able to discover the trade secrets simply by standing on the mountaintop and looking through a telescope? Would there be liability if the plant's layout could be determined using technology that was not available in 1970 — such as studying Internet satellite images from Google Earth? If not, why not?

2. Did *Chicago Lock* involve what is typically understood to be "reverse engineering?" For a good definition of "reverse engineering," see, McGraw-Hill, DICTIONARY OF SCIENTIFIC AND TECHNICAL TERMS 1704 (5th ed. 1994) ("The analysis of a completed system in order to isolate its individual components or building blocks."). The Fanbergs' conduct compromised the security of many of the Ace tubular locks that were already in the marketplace and had the potential of damaging Chicago Lock's business. If the Fanbergs' conduct did not involve traditional reverse engineering, how can their conduct be justified and the Christophers' conduct in *DuPont* not be justified?

3. Reverse engineering, a typical method used to determine details of a competitor's product, is the subject of some interesting cases. *See Mineral Deposits Ltd. v. Zigan*, 773 P.2d 606 (Colo.App.1988) (holding reverse engineering improper when the product was loaned in confidence); *Elle v. Babbitt*, 488 P.2d 440 (Or.1971) (holding reverse engineering was permissible because it was done on a leased machine that was not subject to a confidential relationship).

## (3) Shop Right

### RENTROP v. SPECTRANETICS CORP.

514 F. Supp. 2d 511 (S.D.N.Y. 2007)

* * *

II. Implied-in-Law License

Spectranetics claims that it owns an implied-in-law license in the form of a "shop right" to use the invention claimed in the' 064 Patent without liability for infringement. [Citation omitted.] While shop rights have been characterized by some courts in some cases as an implied license, other cases describe shop rights as a species of equitable estoppel. *Id.* at 1580-81. The Federal Circuit has noted that despite these competing theoretical bases for shop rights, the analysis is often the same irrespective of the theory because "the underlying analysis in each case is driven by principles of equity and fairness . . . ." *Id.* at 1581. Consistent with the Federal Circuit's emphasis on equity and fairness, the Circuit has embraced a "totality of the circumstances" approach to analyzing shop rights:

> the proper methodology for determining whether an employer has acquired a 'shop right' in a patented invention is to look to the totality of the circumstances on a case by case basis and determine whether the facts of a particular case demand, under principles of equity and fairness, a finding that a 'shop right' exists. In such an analysis, one should look to such factors as the circumstances surrounding the development of the patented invention and the inventor's activities respecting that invention, once developed, to determine whether equity and fairness demand that the employer be allowed to use that invention in his business.

*Id.* at 1581-82. While most cases addressing shop rights concern the employer/ employee relationship, the existence of an employment relationship is not a strict prerequisite to finding a shop right. *Id.* at 1583 n. 15. "Because broad equitable principles are involved in determining whether shop rights in an invention arise, '[t]he full nature of the parties' relationship must be examined to determine whether a shop right exists.' " *Id.* at 1582 (quoting Rosenberg, *Patent Law Fundamentals*, § 11.04, 11-20 (1991)).

The Federal Circuit has endorsed the consideration of the following factors for analyzing claims to shop rights:

The contractual nature of the relationship between employer and employee, whether the employee consented to the employer's use of the invention, and whether the employee induced, acquiesced in, or assisted the employer in the use of the invention . . . .

An employer will have shop rights in an invention in situations where the employer has financed an employee's invention by providing wages, materials, tools and a work place. Other factors creating shop rights include an employee's consent, acquiescence, inducement, or assistance to the employer in using the invention without demanding compensation. [Citations omitted.]

While shop rights are a common-law doctrine, the seminal cases elaborating on these equitable rights come from the United State Supreme Court in decisions that predate *Erie Railroad Co. v. Tompkins*, 304 U.S. 64, 58 S.Ct. 817, 82 L.Ed. 1188 (1938). The courts of both Colorado and New York have embraced and applied that precedent. [Citation omitted.] The federal common law of shop rights is also generally followed by other jurisdictions. In light of this widespread acceptance by state courts of the federal common law of shop rights, the Federal Circuit has stated that its most recent explication of shop rights in *McElmurry* governs shop right analyses in patent cases. *McElmurry*, 995 F.2d at 1580 n. 8.

Analysis

This is not a case in which equity and fairness require finding that Spectranetics possesses a shop right to use the invention claimed in the' 064 Patent without liability for infringement. Looking to the first factor approved by the Federal Circuit and the Supreme Court-the contractual nature of the relationship-the parties were never able to formalize their relationship and come to financial terms in a contractual agreement. The only agreement that the parties reached and abided by was a confidentiality agreement, which was established to mutually protect both Spectranetics and Dr. Rentrop. Because the parties did not agree to financial terms, Spectranetics has not paid any wages or fees to Dr. Rentrop for his invention of.9 laser catheter, and did not compensate him for the extensive work he conducted on his own time in New York to inspect prototypes and designs and direct changes to the product. The only fee Dr. Rentrop received was compensation to perform an animal test in California, for which Dr. Rentrop received $2,000.

The failure to come to financial terms did not result from Dr. Rentrop's failure to impress upon Spectranetics that he viewed the.9 laser catheter as his invention for which he expected a royalty. As Mr. Taylor corroborated, Dr. Rentrop stated his interest in a royalty during their first telephone conversation. Dr. Rentrop was thereafter persistent in his expectation of remuneration, and rejected as inadequate several consulting arrangements offered by Spectranetics that would have compensated him up to $50,000.

Spectranetics cannot, therefore, claim an equitable license to use the fruits of Dr. Rentrop's labor and inventive efforts. While it is true that Spectranetics invested substantial sums to develop a prototype under Dr. Rentrop's instruction, and its salaried employees worked to accomplish that goal at Spectranetics' facilities in Colorado, those contributions are not alone sufficient to establish shop rights. The totality of the circumstances based on the facts of this case support the conclusion that Spectranetics does not have a shop right in the form of an implied license to use the invention claimed in the '064 Patent. Spectranetics cannot claim to own any part of Dr. Rentrop's time, labor or inventive efforts, all of which occurred on Dr. Rentrop's own time and in New York. Dr. Rentrop has not been compensated by Spectranetics aside from $2,000 to perform an animal study in California; by contrast, Spectranetics' sales of the accused devices have brought in over $10 million dollars in revenue. Principles of equity and fairness do not weigh in Spectranetics' favor on these facts.

Although Spectranetics does not explicitly invoke an estoppel theory for its claimed shop right, I note that such a theory is also without support in the record. Dr. Rentrop did not induce, acquiesce or assist Spectranetics in using the.9 laser catheter in a manner that suggested his consent that Spectranetics use the.9 laser catheter without compensating Dr. Rentrop. Dr. Rentrop made it clear at all times that he expected remuneration. Furthermore, he did not delay in seeking patent protection once it was apparent to him that a suitable agreement would not be reached. Dr. Rentrop's first patent application for a.9 laser catheter was filed on January 4, 2000; the record reflects that Spectranetics proposed various consulting arrangements to Dr. Rentrop as late as August 1999 (DX N1) and November 1999 (PX 62).

Therefore, there is no basis on which to conclude that Spectranetics has a shop right or implied license to use Dr. Rentrop's patented invention without liability for infringement.

* * *

## NOTES AND QUESTIONS:

1. Even when there is no obligation for an employee to assign an invention to his employer, the common law doctrine of "shop right" typically allows the employer a royalty-free license to use the employee's patented invention. Although Dr. Rentrop was not an employee, the court nevertheless considered the shop right defense, "[b]ecause broad equitable principles are involved in determining whether shop rights in an invention arise." *Rentrop v. Spectranetics Corp.*, 514 F.Supp.2d 511, 530 (S.D.N.Y.2007). The court found no shop right existed in this case even though there was a confidentiality agreement between the parties. The court reasoned that the confidentiality agreement "was established to mutually protect" both parties. *Id.* at 531. Could Spectranetics' use of the invention after the consulting relationship ended also have provided the basis for a claim of trade secret misappropriation?

## (4) Liability of Successor in Interest

### FOREST LABORATORIES, INC. v. PILLSBURY CO.

452 F.2d 621 (7th Cir. 1971)

* * *

After hearing the testimony of various witnesses and considering the exhibits, the district court agreed with plaintiff that it had successfully developed a process for packing effervescent sweetener tablets so as to lengthen their shelf life. [Citation omitted.] One step of this packaging procedure was adjudged to be plaintiff's confidential trade secret. That step was described as follows: "Before packaging, the tablets are to be tempered in a room having 40% or less relative humidity for a period of between 24 to 48 hours."

* * *

Pillsbury purchased the assets of Tidy House Corporation on June 1, 1960. The district court found that the trade secret had been divulged by Forest to Tidy House on a confidential basis and that as Tidy House's successor, Pillsbury was bound by the confidential disclosure to Tidy House. On the state of this record we cannot sustain the district court's conclusion. The well settled rule of American jurisdictions, including Wisconsin, is that a corporation which purchases the assets of another corporation does not, by reason of succeeding to the ownership of property, assume the obligations of the transferor corporation. [Citations omitted.] Exceptions to this rule exist where (a) the purchasing corporation expressly or impliedly agrees to assume the liabilities of the seller, (b) the transaction amounts to a consolidation or merger of the two companies, (c) the purchasing corporation is merely a continuation of the selling corporation, or (d) the transaction is entered into fraudulently to escape liability. {citations omitted]

There is no evidence that Pillsbury expressly agreed to assume all the liabilities and obligations of Tidy House, and in the absence of the purchase agreement or any evidence of conduct or representations by Pillsbury that could support it, we cannot find an implied assumption of liabilities. [Citation omitted.] Since no new corporation emerged from the transaction, a consolidation did not occur. [Citation omitted.] Contrary to the district court's statement, what evidence there was indicated that not all the assets of Tidy House were sold to Pillsbury. Apparently Tidy House, Inc. continued its corporate existence after the sale and leased to Pillsbury the buildings housing the facilities it had sold. There is no indication of the financial situation or the extent of the corporate activity of Tidy House following the transaction. Consequently, again on the strength of this record, we cannot conclude that the sale of assets amounted to a merger. [Citations omitted.] Pillsbury can hardly be said to be a mere continuation of Tidy House since the transfer of assets was not a part of a reorganization. [Citations omitted.] And finally there is no suggestion whatever that Pillsbury was acting in bad faith when it purchased the Tidy House business. In sum, we are not convinced that Pillsbury subjected itself to the obligation of secrecy as Tidy House's "successor." Moreover, the knowledge of Tidy House's employees cannot properly be imputed to Pillsbury just because they went to work for Pillsbury. [Citations omitted.]

Section 757(b) of the Restatement of Torts provides:

"One who discloses or uses another's trade secret, without a privilege to do so, is liable to the other if

* * *

"(b) his disclosure or use constitutes a breach of confidence reposed in him by the other in disclosing the secret to him . . . ."

Since Pillsbury does not stand in the shoes of Tidy House, plaintiff's confidant, Pillsbury's use of the secret does not come within the confines of § 757 (b).

Nevertheless, even though Pillsbury is not liable under § 757(b) of the Restatement of Torts for using Forest's trade secret as Tidy House's successor, the evidence shows that Pillsbury acquired actual knowledge of the confidentiality of the disclosure made by Forest to Tidy House. Thus Mr. Richard Egan, a former employee of Tidy House and of Pillsbury, and considered by the trial judge to be a credible witness, testified that he communicated the trade secret to Dr. Julian Stein, Fred McCarne, and possibly others employed by Pillsbury at a meeting in the middle of 1962. He also told them that the Forest process had been received in confidence by Tidy House.

Section 758(b) of the Restatement states:

"One who learns another's trade secret from a third person without notice that it is secret and that the third person's disclosure is a breach of his duty to the other, or who learns the secret through a mistake without notice of the secrecy and the mistake,

* * *

"(b) is liable to the other for a disclosure or use of the secret after the receipt of such notice unless prior thereto he has in good faith paid value for the secret or has so changed his position that to subject him to liability would be inequitable."

Thus under § 758(b) of the Restatement of Torts, Pillsbury would be liable for its use of the secret after receipt of the notice unless prior thereto it had in good faith paid value for the secret. To satisfy this exception, Pillsbury argues that it purchased the trade secret when it acquired Tidy House's assets, and that Mr. Egan's communications did not occur until well after the acquisition. However, the record does not show that Pillsbury paid anything specifically for the trade secret. For all that appears on the record, Pillsbury's purchase of Tidy House assets at most involved only the purchase of its packaging facilities as part of the existing marketing structure, which included plaintiff as supplier. Nothing has been brought to our attention which would show that Pillsbury actually gave value for Tidy House's tempering expertise with a view toward independently exploiting that know-how for its intrinsic value. Comment (e) to § 758(b) of the Restatement states that "not every change of position prevents the recipient of a trade secret from being subjected to the duty not to disclose or use the secret after notice. The issue is whether the imposition of the duty would be inequitable under the circumstances." The mere possibility that some arbitrary portion of the purchase price could *ex post facto* be ascribed to the potential of the trade secret for Pillsbury's later independent use does not demonstrate a change of position which it would be inequitable not to protect under the circumstances. The purpose of Restatement § 758(b) is to protect bona fide purchasers and reasonable reliance, but it may operate harshly on those who have expended substantial sums in development of their trade secrets. [Citation omitted.] For this reason, we require a specific showing that Pillsbury in good faith paid value for Forest's trade secret at that time, and since there is a dearth of such proof, under § 758(b) of the Restatement, it remained liable to Forest for using the trade secret after the receipt of notice.

## NOTES AND QUESTIONS:

1. *Forest Laboratories, Inc. v. Pillsbury Co.*, 452 F.2d 621 (7th Cir.1971), illustrates how tricky acquisitions can be if the subject of the acquisition has improperly used another party's trade secrets. An asset acquisition, as opposed to a stock purchase, is generally considered to be an effective way to insulate the acquirer from such liability. But, as shown in *Forest Laboratories*, even then the acquisition agreement must be carefully drafted to avoid liability for potential misappropriation claims against all of the acquired assets. The *Forest Laboratories* case provides a cautionary tale for any attorney drafting an asset purchase agreement.

2. The Restatement (Third) of Unfair Competition notes that if an "actor has in good faith paid value for the trade secret, undertaken significant investment in equipment or research relating to the trade secret, or otherwise substantially changed its position in reliance on the information," before it received knowledge that the trade secret had been improperly acquired, "the imposition of particular remedies for subsequent disclosure may be inappropriate." *Id.* § 40 cmt. *d.* This position is a departure from § 758(b) of the Restatement (Second) of Torts, which conferred absolute immunity on third parties who paid value in good faith for a trade secret that happened to be misappropriated by another.

3. The UTSA provides that "[i]n exceptional circumstances, an injunction may condition future use upon payment of a reasonable royalty for no longer than the period of time for which use could have been prohibited." UTSA § 2(b). One of the "exceptional circumstances" is "a material and prejudicial change of position prior to acquiring knowledge . . . that renders a prohibitive injunction inequitable." *Id.* The Comment for that section regarding "innocent acquirers of misappropriated trade secrets" rejected the Restatement of Torts' "conferral of absolute immunity upon all third parties who have paid value in good faith for a trade secret misappropriated by another" found in Section 758(b). Instead, the UTSA adopted the rule in *Forest.* Does this language impose an unreasonable burden on a company that acquires a broad range of assets from another to make sure the acquisition agreement covers every possible detail in the acquired assets?

4. How do these discussions square with the following comment in the UTSA on calculating damages for trade secret misappropriation?

> If a person charged with misappropriation has materially and prejudicially changed position in reliance upon knowledge of a trade secret acquired in good faith and without reason to know of its misappropriation by another,

> however, the same considerations that can justify denial of all injunctive relief also can justify denial of all monetary relief."

UTSA, § 3 cmt.

## E. TORT OF MISAPPROPRIATION

### INTERNATIONAL NEWS SERVICE v. ASSOCIATED PRESS
248 U.S. 215 (1918)

The parties are competitors in the gathering and distribution of news and its publication for profit in newspapers throughout the United States. The Associated Press, which was complainant in the District Court, is a co-operative organization, incorporated under the Membership Corporations Law of the state of New York, its members being individuals who are either proprietors or representatives of about 950 daily newspapers published in all parts of the United States. That a corporation may be organized under that act for the purpose of gathering news for the use and benefit of its members and for publication in newspapers owned or represented by them, is recognized by an amendment enacted in 1901 (Laws N. Y. 1901, c. 436). Complainant gathers I n all parts of the world, by means of various instrumentalities of its own, by exchange with its members, and by other appropriate means, news and intelligence of current and recent events of interest to newspaper readers and distributes it daily to its members for publication in their newspapers. The cost of the service, amounting approximately to $3,500,000 per annum, is assessed upon the members and becomes a part of their costs of operation, to be recouped, presumably with profit, through the publication of their several newspapers. Under complainant's by-laws each member agrees upon assuming membership that news received through complainant's service is received exclusively for publication in a particular newspaper, language, and place specified in the certificate of membership, that no other use of it shall be permitted, and that no member shall furnish or permit any one in his employ or connected with his newspaper to furnish any of complainant's news in advance of publication to any person not a member. And each member is required to gather the local news of his district and supply it to the Associated Press and to no one else.

Defendant is a corporation organized under the laws of the state of New Jersey, whose business is the gathering and selling of news to its customers and clients, consisting of newspapers published throughout the United States, under contracts by which they pay certain amounts at stated times for defendant's service. It has widespread news-gathering agencies; the cost of its operations amounts, it is said, to more than $2,000,000 per annum; and it serves about 400 newspapers located in the various cities of the United States and abroad, a few of which are represented, also, in the membership of the Associated Press.

The parties are in the keenest competition between themselves in the distribution of news throughout the United States; and so, as a rule, are the newspapers that they serve, in their several districts.

Complainant in its bill, defendant in its answer, have set forth in almost identical terms the rather obvious circumstances and conditions under which their business is conducted. The value of the service, and of the news furnished, depends upon the promptness of transmission, as well as upon the accuracy and impartiality of the news; it being essential that the news be transmitted to members or subscribers as early or earlier than similar information can be furnished to competing newspapers by other news services, and that the news furnished by each agency shall not be furnished to newspapers which do not contribute to the expense of gathering it. And further, to quote from the answer:

> Prompt knowledge and publication of worldwide news is essential to the conduct of a modern newspaper, and by reason of the enormous expense incident to the gathering and distribution of such news, the only practical way in which a proprietor of a newspaper can obtain the same is, either through co-operation with a considerable number of other newspaper proprietors in the work of collecting and distributing such news, and the equitable division with them of the expenses thereof, or by the purchase of such news from some existing agency engaged in that business.

The bill was filed to restrain the pirating of complainant's news by defendant in three ways: First, by bribing employees of newspapers published by complainant's members to furnish Associated Press news to defendant before publication, for transmission by telegraph and telephone to defendant's clients for publication by them; second, by inducing Associated Press members to violate its by-laws and permit defendant to obtain news before publication; and, third, by copying news from bulletin boards and from early editions of complainant's newspapers and selling this, either bodily or after rewriting it, to defendant's customers.

The District Court, upon consideration of the bill and answer, with voluminous affidavits on both sides, granted a preliminary injunction under the first and second heads, but refused at that stage to restrain the systematic practice admittedly pursued by defendant, of taking news bodily from the bulletin boards and early editions of complainant's newspapers and selling it as its own. The court expressed itself as satisfied that this practice amounted to unfair trade, but as the legal question was one of first impression it considered that the allowance of an injunction should await the outcome of an appeal. [Citation omitted.] Both parties having appealed, the Circuit Court of Appeals sustained the injunction order so far as it went, and upon complainant's appeal modified it and remanded the cause, with directions to issue an injunction also against any bodily taking of the words or substance of complainant's news until its commercial value as news had passed away. [Citation omitted.] The present writ of certiorari was then allowed. [Citation omitted.]

The only matter that has been argued before us is whether defendant may lawfully be restrained from appropriating news taken from bulletins issued by complainant or any of its members, or from newspapers published by them, for the purpose of selling it to defendant's clients. Complainant asserts that defendant's admitted course of conduct in this regard both violates complainant's property right in the news and constitutes unfair competition in business. And notwithstanding the case has proceeded only to the stage of a preliminary injunction, we have deemed it proper to consider the underlying questions, since they go to the very merits of the action and are presented upon facts that are not in dispute. As presented in argument, these questions are: (1) Whether there is any property in news; (2) Whether, if there be property in news collected for the purpose of being published, it survives the instant of its publication in the first newspaper to which it is communicated by the news-gatherer; and (3) whether defendant's admitted course of conduct in appropriating for commercial use matter taken from bulletins or early editions of Associated Press publications constitutes unfair competition in trade.

The federal jurisdiction was invoked because of diversity of citizenship, not upon the ground that the suit arose under the copyright or other laws of the United States. Complainant's news matter is not copyrighted. It is said that it could not, in practice, be copyrighted, because of the large number of dispatches that are sent daily; and, according to complainant's contention, news is not within the operation of the copyright act. Defendant, while apparently conceding this, nevertheless invokes the analogies of the law of literary property and copyright, insisting as its principal contention that, assuming complainant has a right of property in its news, it can be maintained (unless the copyright act by complied with) only by being kept secret and confidential, and that upon the publication with complainant's consent of uncopyrighted news of any of complainant's members in a newspaper or upon a bulletin board, the right of property is lost, and the subsequent use of the news by the public or by defendant for any purpose whatever becomes lawful.

A preliminary objection to the form in which the suit is brought may be disposed of at the outset. It is said that the Circuit Court of Appeals granted relief upon considerations applicable to particular members of the Associated Press, and that this was erroneous because the suit was brought by complainant as a corporate entity, and not by its members; the argument being that their interests cannot be protected in this proceeding any more than the individual rights of a stockholder can be enforced in an action brought by the corporation. From the averments of the bill, however, it is plain that the suit in substance was brought for the benefit of complainant's members, and that they would be proper parties, and, except for their numbers, perhaps necessary parties. Complainant is a proper party to conduct the suit as representing their interest; and since no specific objection, based upon the want of parties, appears to have been made below, we will treat the objection as waived. [Citation omitted.].

In considering the general question of property in news matter, it is necessary to recognize its dual character, distinguishing between the substance of the information and the particular form or collocation of words in which the writer has communicated it.

No doubt news articles often possess a literary quality, and are the subject of literary property at the common law; nor do we question that such an article, as a literary production, is the subject of copyright by the terms of the act as it now stands. In an early case at the circuit Mr. Justice Thompson held in effect that a newspaper was not within the protection of the copyright acts of 1790 (1 Stat. 124) and 1802 (2 Stat. 171). [Citation omitted.] But the present act is broader; it provides that the works for which copyright may be secured shall include 'all the writings of an author,' and specifically mentions 'periodicals, including newspapers.' [Citation omitted.] Evidently this admits to copyright a contribution to a newspaper, notwithstanding it also may convey news; and such is the practice of the copyright office, as the newspapers of the day bear witness. [Citation omitted.]

But the news element-the information respecting current events contained in the literary production-is not the creation of the writer, but is a report of matters that ordinarily are publici juris; it is the history of the day. It is not to be supposed that the framers of the Constitution, when they empowered Congress 'to promote the progress of science and useful arts, by securing for limited times to authors and inventors the exclusive right to their respective writings and discoveries' (Const. art. 1, § 8, par. 8), intended to confer upon one who might happen to be the first to report a historic event the exclusive right for any period to spread the knowledge of it.

We need spend no time, however, upon the general question of property in news matter at common law, or the application of the copyright act, since it seems to us the case must turn upon the question of unfair competition in business. And, in our opinion, this does not depend upon any general right of property analogous to the common-law right of the proprietor of an unpublished work to prevent its publication without his consent; nor is it foreclosed by showing that the benefits of the copyright act have been waived. We are dealing here not with restrictions upon publication but with the very facilities and processes of publication. The peculiar value of news is in the spreading of it while it is fresh; and it is evident that a valuable property interest in the news, as news, cannot be maintained by keeping it secret. Besides, except for matters improperly disclosed, or published in breach of trust or confidence, or in violation of law, none of which is involved in this brance of the case, the news of current events may be regarded as common property. What we are concerned with is the business of making it known to the world, in which both parties to the present suit are engaged. That business consists in maintaining a prompt, sure, steady, and reliable service designed to place the daily events of the world at the breakfast table of the millions at a price that, while of trifling moment to each reader, is sufficient in the aggregate to afford compensation for the cost of gathering and distributing it, with the added profit so necessary as an incentive to effective action in the commercial world. The service thus performed for newspaper readers is not only innocent but extremely useful in itself, and indubitably constitutes a legitimate business. The parties are competitors in this field; and, on fundamental principles, applicable here as elsewhere, when the rights or privileges of the one are liable to conflict with those of the other, each party is under a duty so to conduct its own business as not unnecessarily or unfairly to injure that of the other. [Citations omitted.]

Obviously, the question of what is unfair competition in business must be determined with particular reference to the character and circumstances of the business. The question here is not so much the rights of either party as against the public but their rights as between themselves. [Citation omitted.] And, although we may and do assume that neither party has any remaining property interest as against the public in uncopyrighted news matter after the moment of its first publication, it by no means follows that there is no remaining property interest in it as between themselves. For, to both of them alike, news matter, however little susceptible of ownership or dominion in the absolute sense, is stock in trade, to be gathered at the cost of enterprise, organization, skill, labor, and money, and to be distributed and sold to those who will pay money for it, as for any other merchandise. Regarding the news, therefore, as but the material out of which both parties are seeking to make profits at the same time and in the same field, we hardly can fail to recognize that for this purpose, and as between them, it must be regarded as quasi property, irrespective of the rights of either as against the public.

In order to sustain the jurisdiction of equity over the controversy, we need not affirm any general and absolute property in the news as such. The rule that a court of equity concerns itself only in the protection of property rights treats any civil right of a pecuniary nature as a property right [Citations omitted.]; and the right to acquire property by honest labor or the conduct of a lawful business is as much entitled to protection as the right to guard property already acquired [Citations omitted.]. It is this right that furnishes the basis of the jurisdiction in the ordinary case of unfair competition.

The question, whether one who has gathered general information or news at pains and expense for the purpose of subsequent publication through the press has such an interest in its publication as may be protected from interference, has been raised many times, although never, perhaps, in the precise form in which it is now presented.

*Board of Trade v. Christie Grain & Stock Co.*, 198 U. S. 236, 250, 25 Sup. Ct. 637, 49 L. Ed. 1031, related to the distribution of quotations of prices on dealings upon a board of trade, which were collected by plaintiff and communicated on confidential terms to numerous persons under a contract not to make them public. This court held that, apart from certain special objections that were overruled, plaintiff's collection of quotations was entitled to the protection of the law; that, like a trade secret, plaintiff might keep to itself the work done at its expense, and did not lose its right by communicating the result to persons, even if many, in confidential relations to itself, under a contract not to make it public; and that strangers should be restrained from getting at the knowledge by inducing a breach of trust.

In *National Tel. News Co. v. Western Union Tel. Co.*, 119 Fed. 294, 56 C. C. A. 198, 60 L. R. A. 805, the Circuit Court of Appeals for the Seventh Circuit dealt with news matter gathered and transmitted by a telegraph company, and consisting merely of a notation of current events having but a transient value due to quick transmission and distribution; and, while declaring that this was not copyrightable although printed on a tape by tickers in the offices of the recipients, and that it was a commercial not a literary product, nevertheless held that the business of gathering and communicating the news-the service of purveying it-was a legitimate business, meeting a distinctive commercial want and adding to the facilities of the business world, and partaking of the nature of property in a sense that entitled it to the protection of a court of equity against piracy.

* * *

Not only do the acquisition and transmission of news require elaborate organization and a large expenditure of money, skill, and effort; not only has it an exchange value to the gatherer, dependent chiefly upon its novelty and freshness, the regularity of the service, its reputed reliability and thoroughness, and its adaptability to the public needs; but also, as is evident, the news has an exchange value to one who can misappropriate it.

The peculiar features of the case arise from the fact that, while novelty and freshness form so important an element in the success of the business, the very processes of distribution and publication necessarily occupy a good deal of time. Complainant's service, as well as defendant's, is a daily service to daily newspapers; most of the foreign news reaches this country at the Atlantic seaboard, principally at the city of New York, and because of this, and of time differentials due to the earth's rotation, the distribution of news matter throughout the country is principally from east to west; and, since in speed the telegraph and telephone easily outstrip the rotation of the earth, it is a simple matter for defendant to take complainant's news from bulletins or early editions of complainant's members in the eastern cities and at the mere cost of telegraphic transmission cause it to be published in western papers issued at least as early as those served by complainant. Besides this, and irrespective of time differentials, irregularities in telegraphic transmission on different lines, and the normal consumption of time in printing and distributing the newspaper, result in permitting pirated news to be placed in the hands of defendant's readers sometimes simultaneously with the service of competing Associated Press papers, occasionally even earlier.

Defendant insists that when, with the sanction and approval of complainant, and as the result of the use of its news for the very purpose for which it is distributed, a portion of complainant's members communicate it to the general public by posting it upon bulletin boards so that all may read, or by issuing it to newspapers and distributing it indiscriminately, complainant no longer has the right to control the use to be made of it; that when it thus reaches the light of day it becomes the common possession of all to whom it is accessible; and that any purchaser of a newspaper has the right to communicate the intelligence which it contains to anybody and for any purpose, even for the purpose of selling it for profit to newspapers published for profit in competition with complainant's members.

The fault in the reasoning lies in applying as a test the right of the complainant as against the public, instead of considering the rights of complainant and defendant, competitors in business, as between themselves. The right of the purchaser of a single newspaper to spread knowledge of its contents gratuitously, for any legitimate purpose not unreasonably interfering with complainant's right to make merchandise of it, may be admitted; but to transmit that news for commercial use, in competition with complainant-which is what defendant has done and seeks to justify-is a very different matter. In doing this defendant, by its very act, admits that it is taking material that has been acquired by complainant as the result of organization and the expenditure of labor, skill, and money, and which is salable by complainant for money, and that defendant in appropriating it and selling it as its own is endeavoring to reap where it has not sown, and by disposing of it to newspapers that are competitors of complainant's members is appropriating to itself the harvest of those who have sown. Stripped of all disguises, the process amounts to an unauthorized interference with the normal operation of complainant's legitimate business precisely at the point where the profit is to be reaped, in order to divert a material portion of the profit from those who have earned it to those who have not; with special advantage to defendant in the competition because of the fact that it is not burdened with any part of the expense of gathering the news. The transaction speaks for itself and a court of equity ought not to hesitate long in characterizing it as unfair competition in business.

The underlying principle is much the same as that which lies at the base of the equitable theory of consideration in the law of trusts-that he who has fairly paid the price should have the beneficial use of the property. Pom. Eq. Jur. § 981. It is no answer to say that complainant spends its money for that which is too fugitive or evanescent to be the subject of property. That might, and for the purposes of the discussion we are assuming that it would furnish an answer in a common-law controversy. But in a court of equity, where the question is one of unfair competition, if that which complainant has acquired fairly at substantial cost may be sold fairly at substantial profit, a competitor who is misappropriating it for the purpose of disposing of it to his own profit and to the disadvantage of complainant cannot be heard to say that it is too fugitive or evanescent to be regarded as property. It has all the attributes of property necessary for determining that a misappropriation of it by a competitor is unfair competition because contrary to good conscience.

The contention that the news is abandoned to the public for all purposes when published in the first newspaper is untenable. Abandonment is a question of intent, and the entire organization of the Associated Press negatives such a purpose. The cost of the service would be prohibited if the reward were to be so limited. No single newspaper, no small group of newspapers, could sustain the expenditure. Indeed, it is one of the most obvious results of defendant's theory that, by permitting indiscriminate publication by anybody and everybody for purposes of profit in competition with the news-gatherer, it would render publication profitless, or so little profitable as in effect to cut off the service by rendering the cost prohibitive in comparison with the return. The practical needs and requirements of the business are reflected in complainant's by-laws which have been referred to. Their effect is that publication by each member must be deemed not by any means an abandonment of the news to the world for any and all purposes, but a publication for limited purposes; for the benefit of the readers of the bulletin or the newspaper as such; not for the purpose of making merchandise of it as news, with the result of depriving complainant's other members of their reasonable opportunity to obtain just returns for their expenditures.

It is to be observed that the view we adopt does not result in giving to complainant the right to monopolize either the gathering or the distribution of the news, or, without complying with the copyright act, to prevent the reproduction of its news articles, but only postpones participation by complainant's competitor in the processes of distribution and reproduction of news that it has not gathered, and only to the extent necessary to prevent that competitor from reaping the fruits of complainant's efforts and expenditure, to the partial exclusion of complainant. and in violation of the principle that underlies the maxim 'sic utere tuo,' etc.

It is said that the elements of unfair competition are lacking because there is no attempt by defendant to palm off its goods as those of the complainant, characteristic of the most familiar, if not the most typical, cases of unfair competition. [Citation omitted.] But we cannot concede that the right to equitable relief is confined to that class of cases. In the present case the fraud upon complainant's rights is more direct and obvious. Regarding news matter as the mere material from which these two competing parties are endeavoring to make money, and treating it, therefore, as quasi property for the purposes of their business because they are both selling it as such, defendant's conduct differs from the ordinary case of unfair competition in trade principally in this that, instead of selling its own goods as those of complainant, it substitutes misappropriation in the place of misrepresentation, and sells complainant's goods as its own.

Besides the misappropriation, there are elements of imitation, of false pretense, in defendant's practices. The device of rewriting complainant's news articles, frequently resorted to, carries its own comment. The habitual failure to give credit to complainant for that which is taken is significant. Indeed, the entire system of appropriating complainant's news and transmitting it as a commercial product to defendant's clients and patrons amounts to a false representation to them and to their newspaper readers that the news transmitted is the result of defendant's own investigation in the field. But these elements, although accentuating the wrong, are not the essence of it. It is something more than the advantage of celebrity of which complainant is being deprived.

The doctrine of unclean hands is invoked as a bar to relief; it being insisted that defendant's practices against which complainant seeks an injunction are not different from the practice attributed to complainant, of utilizing defendant's news published by its subscribers. At this point it becomes necessary to consider a distinction that is drawn by complainant, and, as we understand it, was recognized by defendant also in the submission of proofs in the District Court, between two kinds of use that may be made by one news agency of news taken from the bulletins and newspapers of the other. The first is the bodily appropriation of a statement of fact or a news article, with or without rewriting, but without independent investigation or other expense. This form of pirating was found by both courts to have been pursued by defendant systematically with respect to complainant's news, and against it the Circuit Court of Appeals granted an injunction. This practice complainant denies having pursued and the denial was sustained by the finding of the District Court. It is not contended by defendant that the finding can be set aside, upon the proofs as they now stand. The other use is to take the news of a rival agency as a 'tip' to be investigated, and if verified by independent investigation the news thus gathered is sold. This practice complainant admits that it has pursued and still is willing that defendant shall employ.

Both courts held that complainant could not be debarred on the ground of unclean hands upon the score of pirating defendant's news, because not shown to be guilty of sanctioning this practice.

As to securing 'tips' from a competing news agency the District Court (240 Fed. 991, 995), while not sanctioning the practice, found that both parties had adopted it in accordance with common business usage, in the belief that their conduct was technically lawful, and hence did not find in it any sufficient ground for attributing unclean hands to complainant. The Circuit Court of Appeals (245 Fed. 247, 157 C. C. A. 436) found that the tip habit, though discouraged by complainant, was 'incurably journalistic,' and that there was 'no difficulty in discriminating between the utilization of tips and the bodily appropriation of another's labor in accumulating and stating information.'

We are inclined to think a distinction may be drawn between the utilization of tips and the bodily appropriation of news matter, either in its original form or after rewriting and without independent investigation and verification; whatever may appear at the final hearing, the proofs as they now stand recognize such a distinction; both parties avowedly recognize the practice of taking tips, and neither party alleges it to be unlawful or to amount to unfair competition in business. In a line of English cases a somewhat analogous practice has been held not to amount to an infringement of the copyright of a directory or other book containing compiled information. In Kelly v. Morris, L. R. 1 Eq. 697, 701, 702, Vice Chancellor Sir William Page Wood (afterwards Lord Hatherly), dealing with such a case, said that defendant was

'not entitled to take one word of the information previously published without independently working out the matter for himself, so as to arrive at the same result from the same common sources of information, and the only use that he can legitimately make of a previous publication is to verify his own calculations and results when obtained.'

This was followed by Vice Chancellor Giffard in Morris v. Ashbee, L. R. 7 Eq. 34, where he said:

'In a case such as this no one has a right to take the results of the labour and expense incurred by another for the purposes of a rival publication, and thereby save himself the expense and labour of working out and arriving at these results by some independent road.'

A similar view was adopted by Lord Chancellor Hatherly and the former Vice Chancellor, then Giffard, L.J., in *Pike v. Nicholas*, L. R. 5 Ch. App.Cas. 251, and shortly afterwards by the latter judge in *Morris v. Wright*, L. R. 5 Ch. App.Cas. 279, 287, where he said, commenting upon *Pike v. Nicholas*:

'It was a perfectly legitimate course for the defendant to refer to the plaintiff's book, and if, taking that book as his guide, he went to the original authorities and compiled his book from them, he made no unfair or improper use of the plaintiff's book; and so here, if the fact be that Mr. Wright used the plaintiff's book in order to guide himself to the persons on whom it would be worth his while to call, and for no other purpose, he made a perfectly legitimate use of the plaintiff's book.'

A like distinction was recognized by the Circuit Court of Appeals for the Second Circuit. [Citations omitted.]

In the case before us, in the present state of the pleadings and proofs, we need go no further than to hold, as we do, that the admitted pursuit by complainant of the practice of taking news items published by defendant's subscribers as tips to be investigated, and, if verified, the result of the investigation to be sold-the practice having been followed by defendant also, and by news agencies generally-is not shown to be such as to constitute an unconscientious or inequitable attitude towards its adversary so as to fix upon complainant the taint of unclean hands, and debar it on this ground from the relief to which it is otherwise entitled.

There is some criticism of the injunction that was directed by the District Court upon the going down of the mandate from the Circuit Court of Appeals. In brief, it restrains any taking or gainfully using of the complainant's news, either bodily or in substance from bulletins issued by the complainant or any of its members, or from editions of their newspapers, '*until its commercial value as news to the complainant and all of its members has passed away.*' The part complained of is the clause we have italicized; but if this be indefinite, it is no more so than the criticism. Perhaps it would be better that the terms of the injunction be made specific, and so framed as to confine the restraint to an extent consistent with the reasonable protection of complainant's newspapers, each in its own area and for a specified time after its publication, against the competitive use of pirated news by defendant's customers. But the case presents practical difficulities; and we have not the materials, either in the way of a definite suggestion of amendment, or in the way of proofs, upon which to frame a specific injunction; hence, while not expressing approval of the form adopted by the District Court, we decline to modify it at this preliminary stage of the case, and will leave that court to deal with the matter upon appropriate application made to it for the purpose.

The decree of the Circuit court of Appeals will be

Affirmed.

MR. JUSTICE CLARKE took no part in the consideration or decision of this case.

MR. JUSTICE HOLMES, Dissenting.

When an uncopyrighted combination of words is published there is no general right to forbid other people repeating them-in other words there is no property in the combination or in the thoughts or facts that the words express. Property, a creation of law, does not arise from value, although exchangeable-a matter of fact. Many exchangeable values may be destroyed intentionally without compensation. Property depends upon exclusion by law from interference, and a person is not excluded from using any combination of words merely because some one has used it before, even if it took labor and genius to make it. If a given person is to be prohibited from making the use of words that his neighbors are free to make some other ground must be found. One such ground is vaguely expressed in the phrase unfair trade. This means that the words are repeated by a competitor in business in such a way as to convey a misrepresentation that materially injures the person who first used them, by appropriating credit of some kind which the first user has earned. The ordinary case is a representation by device, appearance, or other indirection that the defendant's goods come from the plaintiff. But the only reason why it is actionable to make such a representation is that it tends to give the defendant an advantage in his competition with the plaintiff and that it is thought undesirable that an advantage should be gained in that way. Apart from that the defendant may use such unpatented devices and uncopyrighted combinations of words as he likes. The ordinary case, I say, is palming off the defendant's product as the plaintiff's but the same evil may follow from the opposite falsehood-from saying whether in words or by implication that the plaintiff's product is the defendant's, and that, it seems to me, is what has happened here.

Fresh news is got only by enterprise and expense. To produce such news as it is produced by the defendant represents by implication that it has been acquired by the defendant's enterprise and at its expense. When it comes from one of the great news collecting agencies like the Associated Press, the source generally is indicated, plainly importing that credit; and that such a representation is implied may be inferred with some confidence from the unwillingness of the defendant to give the credit and tell the truth. If the plaintiff produces the news at the same time that the defendant does, the defendant's presentation impliedly denies to the plaintiff the credit of collecting the facts and assumes that credit to the defendant. If the plaintiff is later in Western cities it naturally will be supposed to have obtained its information from the defendant. The falsehood is a little more subtle, the injury, a little more indirect, than in ordinary cases of unfair trade, but I think that the principle that condemns the one condemns the other. It is a question of how strong an infusion of fraud is necessary to turn a flavor into a poison. The dose seems to me strong enough here to need a remedy from the law. But as, in my view, the only ground of complaint that can be recognized without legislation is the implied misstatement, it can be corrected by stating the truth; and a suitable acknowledgment of the source is all that the plaintiff can require. I think that within the limits recognized by the decision of the Court the defendant should be enjoined from publishing news obtained from the Associated Press for ___ hours after publication by the plaintiff unless it gives express credit to the Associated Press; the number of hours and the form of acknowledgment to be settled by the District Court.

MR. JUSTICE MCKENNA concurs in this opinion. MR. JUSTICE BRANDEIS, dissenting.

* * *

A Legislature, urged to enact a law by which one news agency or newspaper may prevent appropriation of the fruits of its labors by another, would consider such facts and possibilities and others which appropriate inquiry might disclose. Legislators might conclude that it was impossible to put an end to the obvious injustice involved in such appropriation of news, without opening the door to other evils, greater than that sought to be remedied. Such appears to have been the opinion of our Senate which reported unfavorably a bill to give news a few hours' protection; and which ratified, on February 15, 1911, the convention adopted at the Fourth International American Conference; and such was evidently the view also of the signatories to the International Copyright Union of November 13, 1908, as both these conventions expressly exclude news from copyright protection.

Or legislators dealing with the subject might conclude, that the right to news values should be protected to the extent of permitting recovery of damages for any unauthorized use, but that protection by injunction should be denied, just as courts of equity ordinarily refuse (perhaps in the interest of free speech) to restrain actionable libels, and for other reasons decline to protect by injunction mere political rights; and as Congress has prohibited courts from enjoining the illegal assessment or collection of federal taxes. If a Legislature concluded to recognize property in published news to the extent of permitting recovery at law, it might, with a view to making the remedy more certain and adequate, provide a fixed measure of damages, as in the case of copyright infringement.

Or again, a Legislature might conclude that it was unwise to recognize even so limited a property right in published news as that above indicated; but that a news agency should, on some conditions, be given full protection of its business; and to that end a remedy by injunction as well as one for damages should be granted, where news collected by it is gainfully used without permission. If a Legislature concluded (as at least one court has held, *New York and Chicago Grain and Stock Exchange v. Board of Trade*, 127 Ill. 153, 19 N. E. 855, 11 Am. St. Rep. 107, 2 L. R. A. 411) that under certain circumstances news-gathering is a business affected with a public interest; it might declare that, in such cases, news should be protected against appropriation, only if the gatherer assumed the obligation of supplying it at reasonable rates and without discrimination, to all papers which applied therefor. If legislators reached that conclusion, they would probably go further, and prescribe the conditions under which and the extent to which the protection should be afforded; and they might also provide the administrative machinery necessary for insuring to the public, the press, and the news agencies, full enjoyment of the rights so conferred.

Courts are ill-equipped to make the investigations which should precede a determination of the limitations which should be set upon any property right in news or of the circumstances under which news gathered by a private agency should be deemed affected with a public interest. Courts would be powerless to prescribe the detailed regulations essential to full enjoyment of the rights conferred or to introduce the machinery required for enforcement of such regulations. Considerations such as these should lead us to decline to establish a new rule of law in the effort to redress a newly disclosed wrong, although the propriety of some remedy appears to be clear.

## SYNERCOM TECHNOLOGY, INC. v. UNIVERSITY COMPUTING CO.

474 F. Supp. 37 (N.D. Tex. 1979)

First, this court found that, in developing new input formats, instruction manuals and related services to provide more simplified access to a computer program for structural analysis (STRAN), Synercom expended "approximately four man years at a cost in the range of $100,000." Moreover, by the time EDI entered the computerized structural analysis market with its SACS II program, Synercom had incurred costs approaching $500,000. Thus "without the cost of developing the input formats or of training customers in their usage, EDI was in position to simply pluck the fruits of Synercom's labors and risks, if SACS II was as good or better than STRAN."

This court found further that EDI's marketing strategy was to make its SACS II program compatible with the STRAN format so that STRAN users could switch to SACS II with minimum expense, and to capture the market aided in its pricing by lower cost. Additionally, the court found that in 1976, when the relationship between UCC and Synercom was deteriorating, UCC and EDI embarked upon a marketing effort that "if not aimed squarely at the old Synercom accounts included them in its sights." Finally, this court found that EDI and UCC willfully infringed Synercom's copyrights in its User's Manuals and that EDI's original counsel "conducted this litigation in a manner calculated to delay hearing on the merits and to increase the costs of litigation to Synercom as much as possible."

Analysis

The question for decision is whether EDI and UCC engaged in unfair competition by creating a structural analysis package designed specifically to be adaptable to an input methodology developed at great expense by Synercom and by directing its marketing program in significant part at Synercom's accounts.

The central legal doctrine upon which Synercom premises its claim of unfair competition is the doctrine of misappropriation. That doctrine was born into widespread acceptance in 1918 with the decision of the United States Supreme Court in *International News Service v. Associated Press* [citation omitted], a case decided under the pre-Erie federal common law. In that case the court enjoined I.N.S. from copying from A.P. bulletin boards uncopyrighted news gathered by A.P. correspondents and then selling the stories to I.N.S. member papers. The effect of the decision was not to grant A.P. a monopoly in the news stories gathered by its reporters, but to postpone reproduction and dissemination by I.N.S. until the immediate commercial value of the news was gone. The court emphasized the peculiarly short-lived value of news, and found that A.P. had a "quasi-property" right in freshly gathered news.

From this rather spectacular beginning there emerged a widely accepted action for the business tort of misappropriation, classified by several states under the general heading of unfair competition. The courts of Texas have embraced the doctrine. [Citations omitted.] In its typical formulation, the doctrine of misappropriation is said to require proof of three elements: "(i) the creation of plaintiff's product through extensive time, labor, skill and money, (ii) the defendant's use of that product in competition with the plaintiff, thereby gaining a special advantage in that competition (I. e., a 'free ride') because defendant is burdened with little or none of the expense incurred by the plaintiff, and (iii) commercial damage to the plaintiff." [Citation omitted.]

Even casual analysis will reveal, however, that the doctrine's reach cannot be as broad as is indicated by this formulation of elements. Literally applied, for instance, the doctrine as set out would encompass the manufacture by a non-patentee of a product upon which a patent had expired. Obviously, then, the doctrine of misappropriation has limits, both inherent to the doctrine itself and externally imposed by the United States Constitution and the federal patent and copyright laws. The analysis here will proceed upon the assumption that the activity involved in this case is unlawful under the common law doctrine of misappropriation, whatever may be the inherent limits of that doctrine. The initial inquiry, then, will be whether the states, here the State of Texas, may legitimately punish the conduct engaged in by EDI and UCC, or whether Texas is foreclosed from regulating that conduct by federal law. More succinctly, the question, as it is so often in cases of this nature, is one of preemption.

The starting point for the effort to measure the permissible scope of state regulation of intellectual property is the analysis of the Supreme Court in two cases decided the same day, *Sears, Roebuck & Co. v. Stiffel Co.*, 376 U.S. 225, 84 S.Ct. 784, 11 L.Ed.2d 661 (1964) and *Compco Corp. v. Day-Brite Lighting, Inc.*, 376 U.S. 234, 84 S.Ct. 779, 11 L.Ed.2d 669 (1964). Both cases involved mechanical devices (a pole-lamp in Sears and a lighting fixture in Compco) created and patented (both cases involved design patents) by the plaintiff and copied by the defendant. In both cases the lower court had held the design patent invalid but had granted the plaintiffs relief under the state law of unfair competition. The Supreme Court reversed the lower court decisions, finding the state laws preempted under the Supremacy Clause of the Constitution, U.S.Const. Art. VI, the Patent-Copyright Clause, U.S.Const. Art. I, § 8, cl. 8, and the patent and copyright laws enacted by Congress. The court reasoned that one of the essential goals of the patent laws was to ensure that all inventions and discoveries were freely available to the public except those that were found to merit the temporary (17 years) reward of protection from competition by meeting the stringent requirements of patentability. Devices that did not meet those standards, the court reasoned, were intended by Congress to be freely available to the public, and state laws that effectively removed such devices from the public domain conflicted with the Congressional purpose and, consequently, were preempted.

The language of the decisions is broad, giving a wide reading to the preemptive sweep of patent and copyright legislation:

> (W)hen an article is unprotected by a patent or a copyright, state law may not forbid others to copy that article. To forbid copying would interfere with the federal policy, found in article I, § 8, cl. 8, of the Constitution and in the implementing federal statutes, of allowing free access to copy whatever the federal patent and copyright laws leave in the public domain. [Citation omitted.]

Despite the broad language of the decisions, it is important to note the precise factual context in which the cases arose. The devices in question were clearly the Type of things to which the patent laws applied; these devices had simply been found not to meet the requirements of patentability. Thus if state law protection had been accorded to the plaintiffs in these cases, state law would have operated essentially as an extension of the patent system and, in fact, would have effectively subsumed the scheme of patent legislation by granting protection for a presumably unlimited period of time to devices that failed to meet the tests for federal patent protection. Thus the holdings of Sears and Compco are unremarkable; a contrary holding would have significantly eviscerated the purposes of federal patent legislation.

Nonetheless, were these decisions the last word on the subject of preemption in the patent and copyright fields, this court would be constrained to hold state protection of the activity complained of here preempted, simply because of the broad language of Sears and Compco. But since those cases the Supreme Court has issued several decisions that have cut back on at least the language of Sears and Compco and have attempted to fashion some sort of workable interplay between state and federal law in the field of intellectual property. The result of these more recent decisions is that the precise dimensions of the preemptive sweep of federal law, and, consequently, the permissible reach of state law in this area has become a matter of difficulty and confusion that requires careful analysis of each case in the light of the relevant case law. The line between the permissible and the impermissible exercise of state power has become difficult to discern.

The first significant step back from the sweeping language of Sears and Compco was taken in *Goldstein v. California*, 412 U.S. 546, 93 S.Ct. 2303, 37 L.Ed.2d 163

(1973). Involved in that case was a California penal statute outlawing tape piracy. Goldstein and others who had been convicted under the statute challenged the power of California to punish tape piracy, arguing that state regulation of the activity was preempted by the federal copyright laws. The Supreme Court found, however, that the California law was not preempted and it upheld the convictions, reasoning that Congress, which until 1971 did not legislate with respect to copyright in musical recordings, had not determined that recordings were unworthy of any protection but had simply left the area "unattended." Hence the states were free to regulate with respect to musical recordings.

In a narrow sense, the Goldstein decision is as unremarkable as the Sears and Compco decisions. The case involved a penal statute regulating conduct that might be termed "culpable" in a sense that the conduct involved in Sears and Compco was not. Thus the statute in question was more an exercise of the state police power than were the laws found preempted in Sears and Compco; enforcement of the California law could not be said to conflict with the scheme of federal copyright regulation. In a sense, then, the Goldstein decision did not appear to work a significant departure from Sears and Compco.

On the other hand, the tone and language of the Goldstein decision altered at least the angle of approach to preemption problems. That is, whereas the court in Sears and Compco appeared to start with the presumption that intellectual property not specifically given protection by federal law was not a legitimate subject for state law protection, the court in Goldstein began with the premise that state regulation is permissible absent a Congressional intention to occupy the field. Still, the analysis in the three cases is along the same lines. In each case the court's central concern was whether the state law conflicted unacceptably with the goals of federal legislation.

That analysis was further elucidated by the Supreme Court in *Kewanee Oil Co. v. Bicron Corp.*, 416 U.S. 470, 94 S.Ct. 1879, 40 L.Ed.2d 315 (1974), a decision that represents the most significant departure from Sears and Compco. The plaintiff in Kewanee was a corporation that, after more than a decade of work, had succeeded in growing a valuable 17-inch crystal useful in the detection of ionizing radiation. Several employees, all of whom had signed trade secret agreements, joined the defendant Bicron Corporation, which then succeeded in growing a 17-inch crystal in only nine months. While the trial court permanently enjoined the defendant from making use of the crystal on the basis of Ohio trade secret law, the Sixth Circuit reversed that decision, finding state protection preempted under Sears and Compco. The Supreme Court, however, reinstated the trial court's decision, finding Ohio's trade secret law not preempted. Before considering the court's analysis, it is important to consider the facts of Kewanee and their relation to those in Sears and Compco.

First, Kewanee involved an invention clearly subject to the reach of the patent laws. No patent was applied for because the requirement of novelty could not be satisfied the crystal had been in commercial use for more than one year prior to its development by the plaintiff. Yet the effect of the court's decision was to permanently prevent its use by the defendant unless the defendant could discover the process through its own independent efforts or through "working backwards" from the plaintiff's product. At least in a temporal sense, then, enforcement of the Ohio trade secrets law afforded the plaintiff greater protection against the defendant than a patent would have. On the other hand, Kewanee, unlike Sears and Compco, involved an element of culpable conduct the breach of trade secret agreements so that the enforcement of the state law was in the nature of an exercise of the state's police power.

In reaching its decision, the court closely examined the effect of the trade secret law in order to determine if its enforcement would conflict with either of the dual purposes of the patent laws namely, the policies of encouraging invention and of ensuring disclosure of invention. First, the court set out the standard for determining whether state law is preempted:

> The only limitation on the States is that in regulating the area of patents and copyrights they do not conflict with the operation of the laws in this area passed by Congress . . . .
>
> The question of whether the trade secret law of Ohio is void under the Supremacy Clause involves a consideration of whether that law "stands as an obstacle to the accomplishment of the full purposes and objectives of Congress." [Citation omitted.]

Applying this test, the court found that enforcement of the Ohio trade secret law did not conflict with the purposes of the federal patent laws.

It is in the context of these decisions, then, that this court must determine whether the state law doctrine of misappropriation may properly be applied to the activities of UCC and EDI, or whether application of the doctrine would "stand as an obstacle to the accomplishment of the full purposes and objectives of Congress." That standard, of course, does not draw a clearly defined boundary around the preemptive scope of federal law. In a literal sense, any state regulation of writings and inventions conflicts in some way with the goals of the federal patent and copyright laws. The question, then, is how much state interference with federal goals can be tolerated. In that regard, the cases suggest several lines of inquiry.

First, and perhaps most important, is the concept of federalism. Preemption analysis involves by its very nature the problem of federalism, and a state law is far more likely to avoid preemption if it is an exercise of the traditional state power to provide for the health and welfare of its citizens. In both Goldstein and Kewanee, where state law was found not to be preempted, the activity in question was the type of culpable conduct traditionally governed by state law. Thus in discussing trade secret laws in Kewanee, Justice Burger wrote as follows:

> (t)here is the inevitable cost to the basic decency of society when one firm steals from another. A most fundamental human right, that of privacy, is threatened when industrial espionage is condoned or is made profitable; the state interest in denying profit to such illegal ventures is unchallengeable.416 U.S. at 487, 94 S.Ct. at 1889.

Thus the state interest in enforcing its law is far more compelling where theft of secrets or "industrial espionage" is involved.

A second line of inquiry suggested by the cases is whether there is a need for uniformity of legislation; that is, whether enforcement of state law would create a risk of conflicting legal standards governing a given type of conduct. This was a concern of the court in Sears and Compco.

In addition, it is important to determine whether Congress has expressed an intention to leave a matter free of protection, or whether it has simply left the matter "unattended." Kewanee may have stripped much of the force from this inquiry but it should be remembered that each of these inquiries is but an avenue of approach to the fundamental question of whether enforcement of a state law would interfere unacceptably with the purposes of federal legislation.

In this case there was no theft of trade secrets by EDI or UCC, no breach of contract, and no breach of a confidential relationship. In that sense application of the state misappropriation doctrine here would not be an exercise of the state police power, at least not to the extent of the state laws involved in Goldstein and Kewanee.

The input formats appropriated by the defendants here are not matters left "unattended" by Congress. They are writings within the meaning of the federal copyright laws, and this court found in its order of August 24, 1978 that the formats embody only an idea not an expression, and hence are not copyrightable. Thus the formats are the Type of things covered by the copyright laws, but they simply do not qualify for protection under those laws; alternatively, if they do, the protection is very narrow. Nor would the format qualify for patent protection. [Citations omitted.] These determinations, however, are not dispositive of the question of preemption in the light of Kewanee.

In addition, there is some risk that permitting states to limit the availability of the type of material involved here would result in substantial confusion as to whether use of such formats in a particular state was legal. This is hardly a compelling factor, though, as the Kewanee result produced the possibility of an equally nonuniform level of protection for trade secrets.

The overriding question is whether enforcement of the misappropriation doctrine here would conflict unacceptably with the goals of the federal patent and copyright laws. Enforcement of the state law would certainly not interfere with the federal policy of encouraging invention and creativity. On the contrary, that policy would be advanced by permitting the states to protect the input formats involved here. The more difficult question is whether application of the misappropriation doctrine here interferes unacceptably with the federal policy of full disclosure and free use of discoveries except where, in carefully limited circumstances, federal law grants temporary protection.

It is clear, first of all, that application of the misappropriation doctrine here would conflict with the federal policy of disclosure of and free access to discoveries. The result would be that no one could copy Synercom's input formats, and so Synercom would have a favored access to customers using its program, unless a competing package were devised with costs so much lower than Synercom's as to justify the expense of retraining users and of starting anew in the creation of stored data input. Thus the more precise question is whether this conflict with federal law would be so great as to require preemption of the state law.

It is this court's conclusion that the conflict with federal policy would be unacceptable, and that, consequently, the state law doctrine of misappropriation may not be applied to limit the use of Synercom's input format by EDI and UCC. To begin with, this court has found that the input format embodied is an idea and not an expression. None of the cases discussed has permitted a state to regulate the use of ideas. In fact, the court in Goldstein was careful to point out that "(n)o restraint has been placed on the use of an idea or concept." [Citation omitted.] Furthermore, the consequences of applying the misappropriation doctrine here would be significantly greater than the application of the state laws involved in Goldstein or Kewanee. The tape piracy statute in Goldstein did not prevent competition from recording "the same composition in precisely the same manner and with the same personnel as appeared on the original recording." Id. The trade secrets law enforced in Kewanee did not prevent others from growing a crystal identical to the plaintiff's by independent effort or by working backwards from the plaintiff's product. Application of the misappropriation doctrine here, however, would have a greater competitive impact, for Synercom's competitors would have to produce a package of substantially lower cost in order to attract any of Synercom's customers. Moreover, the focus of the misappropriation doctrine is much closer to the focus of the federal patent and copyright laws than either a tape piracy statute or a trade secret law, which are more concerned with ethical conduct than with the use of concepts and ideas. Thus the state interest here is not so great as it was in either Kewanee or Goldstein, where "industrial espionage" was involved. Finally, whereas the misappropriation doctrine typically extends protection for a limited period of time to matters with time value, as in I.N.S., here permanent protection is sought under the statute. Thus enforcement of the doctrine here would work a more significant interference with federal policy than it would in the typical misappropriation case. In sum, assuming that the state law doctrine of misappropriation would prevent the defendants from copying Synercom's input format, the operation of the doctrine here is preempted.

* * *

## NATIONAL BASKETBALL ASSOCIATION v. MOTOROLA, INC.

105 F.3d 841 (2d Cir. 1997)

Motorola, Inc. and Sports Team Analysis and Tracking Systems ("STATS") appeal from a permanent injunction entered by Judge Preska. The injunction concerns a handheld pager sold by Motorola and marketed under the name "Sports Trax," which displays updated information of professional basketball games in progress. The injunction prohibits appellants, absent authorization from the National Basketball Association and NBA Properties, Inc. (collectively the "NBA"), from transmitting scores or other data about NBA games in progress via the pagers, STATS's site on America On-Line's computer dial-up service, or "any equivalent means."

The crux of the dispute concerns the extent to which a state law "hot-news" misappropriation claim based on *International News Service v. Associated Press* [citation omitted] (*"INS"*), survives preemption by the federal Copyright Act and whether the NBA's claim fits within the surviving *INS*-type claims. We hold that a narrow "hot-news" exception does survive preemption. However, we also hold that appellants' transmission of "real-time" NBA game scores and information tabulated from television and radio broadcasts of games in progress does not constitute a misappropriation of "hot news" that is the property of the NBA.

The NBA cross-appeals from the dismissal of its Lanham Act claim. We hold that any misstatements by Motorola in advertising its pager were not material and affirm.

1. BACKGROUND

The facts are largely undisputed. Motorola manufactures and markets the Sports Trax paging device while STATS supplies the game information that is transmitted to the pagers. The product became available to the public in January 1996, at a retail price of about $200. Sports Trax's pager has an inch-and-a-half by inch-and-a-half screen and operates in four basic modes: "current," "statistics," "final scores" and "demonstration." It is the "current" mode that gives rise to the present dispute. In that mode, Sports Trax displays the following information on NBA games in progress: (i) the teams playing; (ii) score changes; (iii) the team in possession of the ball; (iv) whether the team is in the free-throw bonus; (v) the quarter of the game; and (vi) time remaining in the quarter. The information is updated every two to three minutes, with more frequent updates near the end of the first half and the end of the game. There is a lag of approximately two or three minutes between events in the game itself and when the information appears on the pager screen.

Sports Trax's operation relies on a "data feed" supplied by STATS reporters who watch the games on television or listen to them on the radio. The reporters key into a personal computer changes in the score and other information such as successful and missed shots, fouls, and clock updates. The information is relayed by modem to STATS's host computer, which compiles, analyzes, and formats the data for retransmission. The information is then sent to a common carrier, which then sends it via satellite to various local FM radio networks that in turn emit the signal received by the individual Sports Trax pagers.

Although the NBA's complaint concerned only the Sports Trax device, the NBA offered evidence at trial concerning STATS's America On-Line ("AOL") site. Starting in January, 1996, users who accessed STATS's AOL site, typically via a modem attached to a home computer, were provided with slightly more comprehensive and detailed real-time game information than is displayed on a Sports Trax pager. On the AOL site, game scores are updated every 15 seconds to a minute, and the player and team statistics are updated each minute. The district court's original decision and judgment [citation omitted], did not address the AOL site, because "NBA's complaint and the evidence proffered at trial were devoted largely to Sports Trax." [Citation omitted.] Upon motion by the NBA, however, the district court amended its decision and judgment and enjoined use of the real-time game information on STATS's AOL site. [Citation omitted.] Because the record on appeal, the briefs of the parties, and oral argument primarily addressed the Sports Trax device, we similarly focus on that product. However, we regard the legal issues as identical with respect to both products, and our holding applies equally to Sports Trax and STATS's AOL site.

* * *

We hold that the surviving "hot-news" *INS*-like claim is limited to cases where: (i) a plaintiff generates or gathers information at a cost; (ii) the information is time-sensitive; (iii) a defendant's use of the information constitutes free riding on the plaintiff's efforts; (iv) the defendant is in direct competition with a product or service offered by the plaintiffs; and (v) the ability of other parties to free-ride on the efforts of the plaintiff or others would so reduce the incentive to produce the product or service that its existence or quality would be substantially threatened. We conclude that Sports Trax does not meet that test.

* * *

C. The State-Law Misappropriation Claim

The district court's injunction was based on its conclusion that, under New York law, defendants had unlawfully misappropriated the NBA's property rights in its games. The district court reached this conclusion by holding: (i) that the NBA's misappropriation claim relating to the underlying games was not preempted by Section 301 of the Copyright Act; and (ii) that, under New York common law, defendants had engaged in unlawful misappropriation. *Id.* At 1094–1107. We disagree.

1. Preemption Under the Copyright Act

Summary

When Congress amended the Copyright Act in 1976, it provided for the preemption of state law claims that are interrelated with copyright claims in certain ways. Under 17 U.S.C. § 301, a state law claim is preempted when: (i) the state law claim seeks to vindicate "legal or equitable rights that are equivalent" to one of the bundle of exclusive rights already protected by copyright law under 17 U.S.C. § 106 — styled the "general scope requirement"; and (ii) the particular work to which the state law claim is being applied falls within the type of works protected by the Copyright Act under Sections 102 and 103 — styled the "subject matter requirement."

The district court concluded that the NBA's misappropriation claim was not preempted because, with respect to the underlying games, as opposed to the broadcasts, the subject matter requirement was not met. 939 F.Supp. at 1097. The court dubbed as "partial preemption" its separate analysis of misappropriation claims relating to the underlying games and misappropriation claims relating to broadcasts of those games. *Id.* At 1098, n. 24. The district court then relied on a series of older New York misappropriation cases involving radio broadcasts that considerably broadened *INS*. We hold that where the challenged copying or misappropriation relates in part to the copyrighted broadcasts of the games, the subject matter requirement is met as to both the broadcasts and the games. We therefore reject the partial preemption doctrine and its anomalous consequence that "it is possible for a plaintiff to assert claims both for infringement of its copyright in a broadcast and misappropriation of its rights in the underlying event." *Id.* We do find that a properly-narrowed *INS* "hot-news" misappropriation claim survives preemption because it fails the general scope requirement, but that the broader theory of the radio broadcast cases relied upon by the district court were preempted when Congress extended copyright protection to simultaneously-recorded broadcasts.

b) "Partial Preemption" and the Subject Matter Requirement

The subject matter requirement is met when the work of authorship being copied or misappropriated "fall[s] within the ambit of copyright protection." [Citation omitted.] We believe that the subject matter requirement is met in the instant matter and that the concept of "partial preemption" is not consistent with Section 301 of the Copyright Act. Although game broadcasts are copyrightable while the underlying games are not, the Copyright Act should not be read to distinguish between the two when analyzing the preemption of a misappropriation claim based on copying or taking from the copyrightable work. We believe that:

> [O]nce a performance is reduced to tangible form, there is no distinction between the performance and the recording of the performance for the purposes of preemption under § 301(a). Thus, if a baseball game were not broadcast or were telecast without being recorded, the Players' performances similarly would not be fixed in tangible form and their rights of publicity would not be subject to preemption. By virtue of being videotaped, however, the Players' performances are fixed in tangible form, and any rights of publicity in their performances that are equivalent to the rights contained in the copyright of the telecast are preempted.
>
> *Baltimore Orioles*, 805 F.2d at 675 [citation omitted].

Copyrightable material often contains uncopyrightable elements within it, but Section 301 preemption bars state law misappropriation claims with respect to uncopyrightable as well as copyrightable elements. In *Harper & Row*, for example, we held that state law claims based on the copying of excerpts from President Ford's memoirs were preempted even with respect to information that was purely factual and not copyrightable. We stated:

> [T]he [Copyright] Act clearly embraces "works of authorship," including "literary works," as within its subject matter. The fact that portions of the Ford memoirs may consist of uncopyrightable material . . . does not take the work as a whole outside the subject matter protected by the Act. Were this not so, states would be free to expand the perimeters of copyright protection to their own liking, on the theory that preemption would be no bar to state protection of material not meeting federal statutory standards. [Citation omitted.].

The legislative history supports this understanding of Section 301(a)'s subject matter requirement. The House Report stated:

> As long as a work fits within one of the general subject matter categories of sections 102 and 103, the bill prevents the States from protecting it even

> if it fails to achieve Federal statutory copyright because it is too minimal or lacking in originality to qualify, or because it has fallen into the public domain. [Citation omitted.]

Adoption of a partial preemption doctrine — preemption of claims based on misappropriation of broadcasts but no preemption of claims based on misappropriation of underlying facts — would expand significantly the reach of state law claims and render the preemption intended by Congress unworkable. It is often difficult or impossible to separate the fixed copyrightable work from the underlying uncopyrightable events or facts. Moreover, Congress, in extending copyright protection only to the broadcasts and not to the underlying events, intended that the latter be in the public domain. Partial preemption turns that intent on its head by allowing state law to vest exclusive rights in material that Congress intended to be in the public domain and to make unlawful conduct that Congress intended to allow. This concern was recently expressed in *ProCD, Inc. v. Zeidenberg* [citation omitted], a case in which the defendants reproduced non-copyrightable facts (telephone listings) from plaintiffs' copyrighted software. In discussing preemption under Section 301(a), Judge Easterbrook held that the subject matter requirement was met and noted:

> ProCD's software and data are "fixed in a tangible medium of expression", and the district judge held that they are "within the subject matter of copyright". The latter conclusion is plainly right for the copyrighted application program, and the judge thought that the data likewise are "within the subject matter of copyright" even if, after *Feist*, they are not sufficiently original to be copyrighted. [*ProCD, Inc. v. Zeidenberg,*] 908 F.Supp. [640] at 656–57 [(W.D.Wis. 1996)]. *Baltimore Orioles, Inc. v. Major League Baseball Players Ass'n*, 805 F.2d 663, 676 (7th Cir.1986), supports that conclusion, with which commentators agree . . . . One function of § 301(a) is to prevent states from giving special protection to works of authorship that Congress has decided should be in the public domain, which it can accomplish only if "subject matter of copyright" includes all works of a *type* covered by sections 102 and 103, even if federal law does not afford protection to them. [Citation omitted.]. We agree with Judge Easterbrook and reject the separate analysis of the underlying games and broadcasts of those games for purposes of preemption.

c) The General Scope Requirement

Under the general scope requirement, Section 301 "preempts only those state law rights that 'may be abridged by an act which, in and of itself, would infringe one of the exclusive rights' provided by federal copyright law." [Citation omitted.] However, certain forms of commercial misappropriation otherwise within the general scope requirement will survive preemption if an "extra-element" test is met. As stated in *Altai:*

> But if an "extra element" is "required instead of or in addition to the acts of reproduction, performance, distribution or display, in order to constitute a state-created cause of action, then the right does not lie 'within the general scope of copyright,' and there is no preemption." [Citation omitted.]

*ProCD* was in part an application of the extra-element test. Having held the misappropriation claims to be preempted, Judge Easterbrook went on to hold that the plaintiffs could bring a state law contract claim. The court held that the defendants were bound by the software's shrink-wrap licenses as a matter of contract law and that the private contract rights were not preempted because they were not equivalent to the exclusive rights granted by copyright law. In other words, the contract right claims were not preempted because the general scope requirement was not met. *ProCD*, 86 F.3d at 1455.

We turn, therefore, to the question of the extent to which a "hot-news" misappropriation claim based on *INS* involves extra elements and is not the equivalent of exclusive rights under a copyright. Courts are generally agreed that some form of such a claim survives preemption. [Citation omitted.] This conclusion is based in part on the legislative history of the 1976 amendments. The House Report stated:

"Misappropriation" is not necessarily synonymous with copyright infringement, and thus a cause of action labeled as "misappropriation" is not preempted if it is in fact based neither on a right within the general scope of copyright as specified by section 106 nor on a right equivalent thereto. For example, state law should have the flexibility to afford a remedy (under traditional principles of equity) against a consistent pattern of unauthorized appropriation by a competitor of the facts (i.e., not the literary expression) constituting "hot" news, whether in the traditional mold of *International News Service v. Associated Press*, 248 U.S. 215 [39 S.Ct. 68, 63 L.Ed. 211] (1918), or in the newer form of data updates from scientific, business, or financial data bases. [Citation omitted.] The crucial question, therefore, is the *breadth* of the "hot-news" claim that survives preemption.

In *INS*, the plaintiff AP and defendant INS were "wire services" that sold news items to client newspapers. AP brought suit to prevent INS from selling facts and information lifted from AP sources to INS-affiliated newspapers. One method by which INS was able to use AP's news was to lift facts from AP news bulletins. *INS*, 248 U.S. at 231, 39 S.Ct. at 69–70. Another method was to sell facts taken from just-published east coast AP newspapers to west coast INS newspapers whose editions had yet to appear. *Id.* At 238, 39 S.Ct. at 72. The Supreme Court held (prior to *Erie R. Co. v. Tompkins*, 304 U.S. 64, 58 S.Ct. 817, 82 L.Ed. 1188 (1938)), that INS's use of AP's information was unlawful under federal common law. It characterized INS's conduct as

amount[ing] to an unauthorized interference with the normal operation of complainant's legitimate business precisely at the point where the profit is to be reaped, in order to divert a material portion of the profit from those who have earned it to those who have not; with special advantage to defendant in the competition because of the fact that it is not burdened with any part of the expense of gathering the news. [Citation omitted.]

The theory of the New York misappropriation cases relied upon by the district court is considerably broader than that of *INS*. For example, the district court quoted at length from *Metropolitan Opera Ass'n v. Wagner-Nichols Recorder Corp.* [Citation omitted.] *Metropolitan Opera* described New York misappropriation law as standing for the "broader principle that property rights of commercial value are to be and will be protected from any form of commercial immorality"; that misappropriation law developed "to deal with business malpractices offensive to the ethics of [ ] society"; and that the doctrine is "broad and flexible.' " [Citation omitted.]

However, we believe that *Metropolitan Opera* 's broad misappropriation doctrine based on amorphous concepts such as "commercial immorality" or society's "ethics" is preempted. Such concepts are virtually synonymous for wrongful copying and are in no meaningful fashion distinguishable from infringement of a copyright. The broad misappropriation doctrine relied upon by the district court is, therefore, the equivalent of exclusive rights in copyright law.

Indeed, we said as much in *FII*. That decision involved the copying of financial information by a rival financial reporting service and specifically repudiated the broad misappropriation doctrine of *Metropolitan Opera*. We explained:

We are not persuaded by FII's argument that misappropriation is not "equivalent" to the exclusive rights provided by the Copyright Act . . . . Nor do we believe that a possible exception to the general rule of preemption in the misappropriation area — for claims involving "any form of commercial immorality," . . . quoting *Metropolitan Opera Ass'n v. Wagner-Nichols Recorder Corp.*, 199 Misc. 786, 101 N.Y.S.2d 483, . . . — should be applied here. We believe that no such exception exists and reject its use here. Whether or not reproduction of another's work is "immoral" depends on whether such use of the work is wrongful. If, for example, the work is in the public domain, then its use would not be wrongful. Likewise, if, as here, the work is unprotected by federal law because of lack of originality, then its use is neither unfair nor unjustified. [Citation omitted.] In fact, *FII* only begrudgingly concedes that even narrow "hot news" *INS*-type claims survive preemption. *Id.* At 209.

Moreover, *Computer Associates Intern., Inc. v. Altai Inc.* indicated that the "extra element" test should not be applied so as to allow state claims to survive preemption easily. [Citation omitted.] "An action will not be saved from preemption by elements such as awareness or intent, which alter 'the action's scope but not its nature' . . . . Following this 'extra element' test, we have held that unfair competition and misappropriation claims grounded solely in the copying of a plaintiff's protected expression are preempted by section 301." [Citation omitted.].

In light of cases such as *FII* and *Altai* that emphasize the narrowness of state misappropriation claims that survive preemption, most of the broadcast cases relied upon by the NBA are simply not good law. Those cases were decided at a time when simultaneously-recorded broadcasts were not protected under the Copyright Act and when the state law claims they fashioned were not subject to federal preemption. For example, *Metropolitan Opera* [Citation omitted.], involved the unauthorized copying, marketing, and sale of opera radio broadcasts. As another example, in *Mutual Broadcasting System v. Muzak Corp.* [citation omitted], the defendant simultaneously retransmitted the plaintiff's baseball radio broadcasts onto telephone lines. As discussed above, the 1976 amendments to the Copyright Act were specifically designed to afford copyright protection to simultaneously-recorded broadcasts, and *Metropolitan Opera* and *Muzak* could today be brought as copyright infringement cases. Moreover, we believe that they would *have* to be brought as copyright cases because the amendments affording broadcasts copyright protection also preempted the state law misappropriation claims under which they were decided.

Our conclusion, therefore, is that only a narrow "hot-news" misappropriation claim survives preemption for actions concerning material within the realm of copyright. *See also 1 McCarthy on Trademarks and Unfair Competition* (4th ed. 1996), § 10:69, at 10–134 (discussing *National Exhibition Co. v. Fass*, 133 N.Y.S.2d 379 (Sup.Ct.1954), *Muzak*, 30 N.Y.S.2d 419, and other cases relied upon by NBA that pre-date the 1976 amendment to the Copyright Act and concluding that after the amendment, "state misappropriation law would be unnecessary and would be preempted: protection is solely under federal copyright").

In our view, the elements central to an *INS* claim are: (i) the plaintiff generates or collects information at some cost or expense, *see FII*, 808 F.2d at 206; *INS*, 248 U.S. at 240, 39 S.Ct. at 72–73; (ii) the value of the information is highly time-sensitive, *see FII*, 808 F.2d at 209; *INS*, 248 U.S. at 231, 39 S.Ct. at 69–70; *Restatement (Third) Unfair Competition*, § 38 cmt. C.; (iii) the defendant's use of the information constitutes free-riding on the plaintiff's costly efforts to generate or collect it, *see FII*, 808 F.2d at 207; *INS*, 248 U.S. at 239–40, 39 S.Ct. at 72–73; *Restatement* § 38 at cmt. C.; *McCarthy*, § 10:73 at 10–139; (iv) the defendant's use of the information is in direct competition with a product or service offered by the plaintiff, *FII*, 808 F.2d at 209, *INS*, 248 U.S. at 240, 39 S.Ct. at 72–73; (v) the ability of other parties to free-ride on the efforts of the plaintiff would so reduce the incentive to produce the product or service that its existence or quality would be substantially threatened, *FII*, 808 F.2d at 209; *Restatement*, § 38 at cmt. C.; *INS*, 248 U.S. at 241, 39 S.Ct. at 73 ("[INS's conduct] would render [AP's] publication profitless, or so little profitable as in effect to cut off the service by rendering the cost prohibitive in comparison with the return).

*INS* is not about ethics; it is about the protection of property rights in time-sensitive information so that the information will be made available to the public by profit seeking entrepreneurs. If services like AP were not assured of property rights in the news they pay to collect, they would cease to collect it. The ability of their competitors to appropriate their product at only nominal cost and thereby to disseminate a competing product at a lower price would destroy the incentive to collect news in the first place. The newspaper-reading public would suffer because no one would have an incentive to collect "hot news."

We therefore find the extra elements — those in addition to the elements of copyright infringement — that allow a "hotnews" claim to survive preemption are: (i) the time-sensitive value of factual information, (ii) the free-riding by a defendant, and (iii) the threat to the very existence of the product or service provided by the plaintiff.

2. The Legality of Sports Trax

We conclude that Motorola and STATS have not engaged in unlawful misappropriation under the "hot-news" test set out above. To be sure, some of the elements of a "hot-news" *INS* claim are met. The information transmitted to Sports Trax is not precisely contemporaneous, but it is nevertheless time-sensitive. Also, the NBA does provide, or will shortly do so, information like that available through Sports Trax. It now offers a service called "Gamestats" that provides official play-by-play game sheets and half-time and final box scores within each arena. It also provides such information to the media in each arena. In the future, the NBA plans to enhance Gamestats so that it will be networked between the various arenas and will support a pager product analogous to Sports Trax. Sports Trax will of course directly compete with an enhanced Gamestats.

However, there are critical elements missing in the NBA's attempt to assert a "hot-news" *INS*-type claim. As framed by the NBA, their claim compresses and confuses three different informational products. The first product is generating the information by playing the games; the second product is transmitting live, full descriptions of those games; and the third product is collecting and retransmitting strictly factual information about the games. The first and second products are the NBA's primary business: producing basketball games for live attendance and licensing copyrighted broadcasts of those games. The collection and retransmission of strictly factual material about the games is a different product: e.g., box-scores in newspapers, summaries of statistics on television sports news, and real-time facts to be transmitted to pagers. In our view, the NBA has failed to show any competitive effect whatsoever from Sports Trax on the first and second products and a lack of any free-riding by Sports Trax on the third.

With regard to the NBA's primary products — producing basketball games with live attendance and licensing copyrighted broadcasts of those games — there is no evidence that anyone regards Sports Trax or the AOL site as a substitute for attending NBA games or watching them on television. In fact, Motorola markets Sports Trax as being designed "for those times when you cannot be at the arena, watch the game on TV, or listen to the radio . . ."

The NBA argues that the pager market is also relevant to a "hot-news" *INS*-type claim and that Sports Trax's future competition with Gamestats satisfies any missing element. We agree that there is a separate market for the real-time transmission of factual information to pagers or similar devices, such as STATS's AOL site. However, we disagree that Sports Trax is in any sense free-riding off Gamestats.

An indispensable element of an *INS* "hot-news" claim is free riding by a defendant on a plaintiff's product, enabling the defendant to produce a directly competitive product for less money because it has lower costs. Sports Trax is not such a product. The use of pagers to transmit real-time information about NBA games requires: (i) the collecting of facts about the games; (ii) the transmission of these facts on a network; (iii) the assembling of them by the particular service; and (iv) the transmission of them to pagers or an on-line computer site. Appellants are in no way free-riding on Gamestats. Motorola and STATS expend their own resources to collect purely factual information generated in NBA games to transmit to Sports Trax pagers. They have their own network and assemble and transmit data themselves.

To be sure, if appellants in the future were to collect facts from an enhanced Gamestats pager to retransmit them to Sports Trax pagers, that would constitute free-riding and might well cause Gamestats to be unprofitable because it had to bear costs to collect facts that Sports Trax did not. If the appropriation of facts from one pager to another pager service were allowed, transmission of current information on NBA games to pagers or similar devices would be substantially deterred because any potential transmitter would know that the first entrant would quickly encounter a lower cost competitor free-riding on the originator's transmissions.

However, that is not the case in the instant matter. Sports Trax and Gamestats are each bearing their own costs of collecting factual information on NBA games, and, if one produces a product that is cheaper or otherwise superior to the other, that producer will prevail in the marketplace. This is obviously not the situation against which *INS* was intended to prevent: the potential lack of any such product or service because of the anticipation of free-riding.

For the foregoing reasons, the NBA has not shown any damage to any of its products based on free-riding by Motorola and STATS, and the NBA's misappropriation claim based on New York law is preempted.

* * *

## BARCLAYS CAPITAL, INC. v. THEFLYONTHEWALL.COM, INC.

650 F.3d 876 (2d Cir. 2011)

SACK, CIRCUIT JUDGE:

The parties, the district court, and amici have raised a wide variety of interesting legal and policy issues during the course of this litigation. We need not address most of them. We conclude that under principles that are well established in this Circuit, the plaintiffs' claim against the defendant for "hot news" misappropriation of the plaintiff financial firms' recommendations to clients and prospective clients as to trading in corporate securities is preempted by federal copyright law. Based upon principles explained and applied in *National Basketball Association v. Motorola, Inc.*, 105 F.3d 841 (2d Cir. 1997) (sometimes hereinafter "NBA"), we conclude that because the plaintiffs' claim falls within the "general scope" of copyright, 17 U.S.C. § 106, and involves the type of works protected by the Copyright Act, 17 U.S.C. §§ 102 and 103, and because the defendant's acts at issue do not meet the exceptions for a "hot news" misappropriation claim as recognized by NBA, the claim is preempted. We therefore reverse the judgment of the district court with respect to that claim.

The plaintiffs-appellees — *Barclays Capital Inc.* ("Barclays"); Merrill Lynch, Pierce, Fenner & Smith Inc. ("Merrill Lynch"); and Morgan Stanley & Co. Inc. ("Morgan Stanley") (collectively, the "Firms") — are major financial institutions that, among many other things, provide securities brokerage services to members of the public. Largely in that connection, they engage in extensive research about the business and prospects of publicly traded companies, the securities of those companies, and the industries in which those companies are engaged. The results of the research are summarized by the Firms in reports, which customarily contain recommendations as to the wisdom of purchasing, holding, or selling securities of the subject companies. Although the recommendations and the research underlying them in the reports are inextricably related, it is the alleged misappropriation of the recommendations, each typically contained in a single sentence, that is at the heart of the district court's decision and the appeal here.

Each morning before the principal U.S. securities markets open, each Firm circulates its reports and recommendations for that day to clients and prospective clients. The recipients thus gain an informational advantage over non-recipients with respect to possible trading in the securities of the subject companies both by learning before the world at large does the contents of the reports and, crucially for present purposes, the fact that the recommendations are being made by the Firm. The existence of that fact alone is likely to result in purchases or sales of the securities in question by client and non-client alike, and a corresponding short-term increase or decrease in the securities' market prices. The Firms and similar businesses, under their historic and present business models, profit from the preparation and circulation of the reports and recommendations principally insofar as they earn brokerage commissions when a recipient of a report and recommendation turns to the firm to execute a trade in the shares of the company being reported upon.

The defendant-appellant is the proprietor of a news service distributed electronically, for a price, to subscribers. In recent years and by various means, the defendant has obtained information about the Firms' recommendations before the Firms have purposely made them available to the general public and before exchanges for trading in those shares open for the day. Doing so tends to remove the informational and attendant trading advantage of the Firms' clients and prospective clients who are authorized recipients of the reports and recommendations. The recipients of the information are, in turn, less likely to buy or sell the securities using the brokerage services of the reporting and recommending Firms, thereby reducing the incentive for the Firms to create such reports and recommendations in the first place. This, the Firms assert, will destroy their business models and have a severely deleterious impact on their ability to engage in further research and to create further reports and recommendations.

In an attempt to preserve their business models, the Firms have increasingly taken measures to seek to prevent or curtail such pre-market — and therefore, from their point of view, premature — public dissemination of their recommendations. As the district court reported in *Barclays Capital Inc. v. Theflyonthewall.com* ("Fly I"), 700 F. Supp. 2d 310 (S.D.N.Y. 2010), the Firms have, for example: "communicated to their employees that the unauthorized dissemination of their equity research or its contents is a breach of loyalty to the Firm, undermines the Firm's creation of revenue, and can result in discipline, including firing," *id.* at 319-20; included in their licensing agreements with third-party distributors and in the reports themselves provisions prohibiting redistribution of their content, id. at 320; adopted policies limiting public dissemination of the reports and the information they contain, id.; and employed emerging Internet technology by which the Firms can seek to find the source of such "leaks" and to "plug" them, id. It is not clear from the record the extent to which these efforts are currently effective, but no concern has been expressed to us as to their legality or legitimacy.

The Firms instituted this litigation as part of the same endeavor. The first of their two sets of claims against the defendant sounds in copyright and is based on allegations of verbatim copying and dissemination of portions of the Firms' reports by the defendant. The Firms have been entirely successful on these copyright claims. *See* Fly I, 700 F. Supp.2d at 328 ("Fly no longer disputes . . . that it infringed the copyrights in [seventeen of the Firms' reports] . . . . [J]udgment shall [therefore] be entered for the [Firms] on their claims of copyright infringement."). Although the extent to which the Firms' success on the copyright claims has alleviated their overall concerns is not clear, their victory on these claims is secure: Fly has not challenged the resulting injunction on appeal. Appellant's Br. at 61.

What remains before us, then, is the second set of claims by the Firms, alleging that Fly's early republication of the securities recommendations that the Firms create — their "hot news" — is tortious under the New York State law of misappropriation. The district court agreed and granted carefully measured injunctive relief. It is to the misappropriation cause of action that this appeal and therefore this opinion is devoted.

## BACKGROUND

We find little to take issue with in the district court's careful findings of facts, to which we must in any event defer. We therefore borrow freely from them.

### The Firms and their Research Reports

The Firms are multinational financial entities that provide a variety of asset management, sales and trading, investment banking, and brokerage services to institutional investors, businesses of various sizes, and individuals. Among their many activities, the Firms compile research reports on specific companies whose securities are publicly traded, on industries, and on economic conditions generally. They disseminate such reports and accompanying trading recommendations to clients, such as hedge funds, private equity firms, pension funds, endowments, and individual investors. The reports, which vary in format, range from a single page to hundreds of pages in length. They typically include data analysis, qualitative discussion, and the recommendation. In the process of producing and disseminating the reports, the Firms employ hundreds of research analysts and spend hundreds of millions of dollars annually.

In preparing a company report, an analyst will gather data related to its business, and may visit its physical facilities, converse with industry experts or company executives, and construct financial or operational models. The analyst then uses that information in light of his or her expertise, experience, and judgment to arrive at formal projections and recommendations regarding the value of the company's securities.

This litigation concerns the trading "Recommendations," a term which the district court defined as "actionable reports," i.e., Firm research reports "likely to spur any investor into making an immediate trading decision. Recommendations upgrade or downgrade a security; begin research coverage of a company's security (an event known as an 'initiation'); or predict a change in the security's target price." Fly I, 700 F. Supp.2d at 316. The better known and more respected an analyst is, the more likely that a recommendation for which he or she is primarily responsible will significantly affect the market price of a security.

Most Recommendations are issued sometime between midnight and 7 a.m. Eastern Time, allowing stock purchases to be made on the market based on the reports and Recommendations upon the market opening at 9:30 a.m. Timely receipt of a Recommendation affords an investor the opportunity to execute a trade in the subject security before the market has absorbed and responded to it.

The Firms typically provide complimentary copies of the reports and Recommendations to their institutional and individual clients using a variety of methods. The Firms then conduct an orchestrated sales campaign in which members of their sales forces contact the clients the Firms think most likely to execute a trade based upon the Recommendation, with the understanding that continued receipt of reports and Recommendations may be made contingent on the generation of a certain level of trading commissions paid to the Firm.

The Firms contend that clients are much more likely to place a trade with a Firm if they learn of the Recommendation directly from that Firm rather than elsewhere, and estimate that more than sixty percent of all trades result from Firm solicitations, including those highlighting Recommendations. It is from the commissions on those trades that Firms profit from the creation and dissemination of their reports and Recommendations. They assert that the timely, exclusive delivery of research and Recommendations therefore is a key to what they frequently refer to as their "business model."

Theflyonthewall.com

The defendant — appellant Theflyonthewall.com, Inc. ("Fly") is, among other things, a news "aggregator." For present purposes, "[a]n aggregator is a website that collects headlines and snippets of news stories from other websites. Examples include Google News and the Huffington Post." Tony Rogers, "Aggregator," About.com Guide, available at http://journalism.about.com/od/journalismglossary/g/aggregatordefinition.htm (latest visit Jan. 4, 2011).

Understanding that investors not authorized by the Firms to receive the reports and Recommendations are interested in and willing to pay for early access to the information contained in them — especially the Recommendations, which are particularly likely to affect securities prices — several aggregators compile securities-firm recommendations, including the Recommendations of the Firms, sometimes with the associated reports or summaries thereof, and timely provide the information to their own subscribers for a fee. Fly is one such company. It employs twenty-eight persons, about half of whom are devoted to content production. It does not itself provide brokerage, trading, or investment-advisory services beyond supplying that information.

Typical clients of the Firms are hedge funds, private equity firms, pension funds, endowments, and wealthy individual investors. By contrast, Fly's subscribers are predominately individual investors, institutional investors, brokers, and day traders. These customers purchase one of three content packages on Fly's website, paying between $25 and $50 monthly for unlimited access to the site.

In addition to maintaining its website, Fly distributes its content through third-party distributors and trading platforms, including some, such as Bloomberg and Thomson Reuters, that also separately provide authorized dissemination of the Firms' Recommendations. Fly has about 3,300 direct subscribers through its website, and another 2,000 subscribers who use third-party platforms to receive the service.

Fly characterizes itself as a source for breaking financial news, claiming to be the "fastest news feed on the web." Fly I, 700 F. Supp.2d at 322 (internal quotation marks omitted). It advertises that its "quick to the point news is a valuable resource for any investment decision." Id. Fly has emphasized its access to analyst research, saying that its newsfeed is a "one-stop solution for accessing analyst comments," and brags that it posts "breaking analyst comments as they are being disseminated by Wall Street trading desks, consistently beating the news wires." Id. at 322–23 (internal quotation marks omitted).

The cornerstone of Fly's offerings is its online newsfeed, which it continually updates between 5:00 a.m. and 7:00 p.m. during days on which the New York Stock Exchange is open. The newsfeed typically streams more than 600 headlines a day in ten different categories, including "hot stocks," "rumors," "technical analysis," and "earnings." One such category is "recommendations." There, Fly posts the recommendations (but not the underlying research reports or supporting analysis) produced by sixty-five investment firms' analysts, including those at the plaintiff Firms. A typical Recommendation headline from 2009, for example, reads "EQIX: Equinox initiated with a Buy at BofA/Merrill. Target $110." Id. at 323.

Fly's headlines, including those in the "recommendations" category, are searchable and sortable. Users can also subscribe to receive automated e-mail, pop-up, or audio alerts whenever Fly posts content relevant to preselected companies' securities.

Fly publishes most of its recommendation headlines before the New York Stock Exchange opens each business day at 9:30 a.m. Fly estimates that the Firms' Recommendation headlines currently comprise approximately 2.5% of Fly's total content, down from 7% in 2005.

According to Fly, over time it has changed the way in which it obtains information about recommendations. Some investment firms, such as Wells Fargo's investment services, will send Fly research reports directly as soon as they are released. Others, including the plaintiff Firms, do not. Until 2005, for recommendations of firms that do not, including the plaintiff Firms, Fly relied on employees at the investment firms (without the firms' authorization) to e-mail the research reports to Fly as they were released. Fly staff would summarize a recommendation as a headline (e.g., "EQIX initiated with a Buy at BofA/Merrill. Target $110."). Sometimes Fly would include in a published item an extended passage taken verbatim from the underlying report.

Fly maintains that because of threats of litigation in 2005, it no longer obtains recommendations directly from such investment firms. Instead, it gathers them using a combination of other news outlets, chat rooms, "blast IMs" sent by people in the investment community to hundreds of recipients, and conversations with traders, money managers, and its other contacts involved in the securities markets. Fly also represents that it no longer publishes excerpts from the research reports themselves, and now disseminates only the Recommendations, typically summarizing only the rating and price target for a particular stock.

The Firms' Response to The Threat Posed by Fly and Other Aggregators

Because the value of the reports and Recommendations to an investor with early access to a Recommendation is in significant part derived from the informational advantage an early recipient may have over others in the marketplace, most of the trading the Firms generate based on their reports and Recommendations occurs in the initial hours of trading after the principal U.S. securities markets have opened. Such sales activity typically slackens by midday. The Firms' ability to generate revenue from the reports and Recommendations therefore directly relates to the informational advantage they can provide to their clients. This in turn is related to the Firms' ability to control the distribution of the reports and Recommendations so that the Firms' clients have access to and can take action on the reports and Recommendations before the general public can.

The Firms have employed a variety of measures in an attempt to stem the early dissemination of Recommendations to non-clients. Most of them have either been instituted or augmented relatively recently in response to the increasing availability of Recommendations from Fly and competing aggregators and news services. The Firms describe these steps as follows:

> The Firms have made a "very substantial and costly effort to study the unauthorized dissemination of their research reports and . . . to plug the leaks they have found." Merrill Lynch, for example, has: (a) worked with third-party vendors to limit access to Merrill Lynch clients; (b) employed an internal security program to detect breaches of security; (c) investigated Merrill Lynch employees, including a review of cell phones, for leaks to third parties; (d) internalized Merrill Lynch's email subscription system; (e) identified and blacklisted websites that seek to post links to Merrill Lynch content; and (f) created unique signature URLs when links to research are sent to clients so that clients' usage can be monitored and abuse tracked. [citation to record] (describing breach control as an "all-consuming task"). Barclays and Morgan Stanley have undertaken comparable measures to protect their research.
>
> Firm has a restrictive media and communications policy intended to preserve the time-sensitive value of Recommendations for their clients. The policies provide that any disclosure of equity research to the press occurs only after expiration of a prescribed period of time, and even then it is limited to entities that use the research as part of contextual news reporting and analysis.

Appellees' Br. at 13 [Citations omitted.]. As outlined above, the district court also cataloged these efforts, emphasizing their increasing intensity "in recent years." It is not clear from the record, however, the extent to which these efforts increased in response to the actions of Fly and others similarly disseminating the Recommendations on Internet-borne services, nor does the record disclose how successful the measures have been. Fly has not challenged the legality of the Firms' anti-dissemination efforts in these proceedings.

The Complaint and Pre-Trial District Court Proceedings

In 2004, the Firms identified Fly as one of several entities systematically publishing the Recommendations without the Firms' permission. Others doing the same included larger and better-known news outlets with far broader audiences, such as Bloomberg, Dow Jones, and Thomson Reuters. All of them regularly post short headlines reporting Recommendations soon after they become available.1 The Firms nonetheless focused their legal actions in this regard on Fly.

In March and April 2005, the Firms complained to Fly that its publication of the Firms' Recommendations in February and March of that year infringed the Firms' copyrights and was tortious under New York State's "hot news" misappropriation doctrine. The Firms demanded that Fly cease and desist. Fly's counsel responded in April and May 2005, representing that Fly had altered its reporting practices so that it no longer obtained the Recommendations from research reports sent by employees of the Firms, instead gathering the information from independent, public sources. Fly continued posting the Firms' Recommendations. On June 26, 2006, the Firms filed this suit naming Fly as the sole defendant.

The Firms assert two causes of action in their complaint: copyright infringement based on Fly's extensive excerpting of 17 research reports released in February and March 2005, and "hot news" misappropriation based on Fly's continual electronic publication of the Firms' Recommendations. The gravamen of the latter claim is that the aggregate widespread, unauthorized reporting of Recommendations by Fly and other financial news providers — including better known, better financed, more broadly accessed outlets — has threatened the viability of the Firms' equity research operations. The Firms allege that this unauthorized distribution allows clients and prospective clients to learn of Recommendations from sources other than the Firms before the Firms' sales staff can reach out to them to solicit their business, thereby reducing the ability of research to drive commission revenue. This, they assert, seriously threatens their ability to justify the expense of maintaining their extensive research operations.

On August 16, 2006, Fly answered, raising several affirmative defenses, including "fair use" and protections purportedly afforded to it and its dissemination of news by the First Amendment.

On May 18, 2009, after completion of discovery, the Firms and Fly cross-moved for summary judgement. The district court (Denise L. Cote, Judge) denied the summary judgment motions on November 6, 2009. The Firms then waived their claims for actual damages, and the court set the case for a bench trial.

The Trial and The District Court Decision

In a joint pre-trial order dated February 12, 2010, the parties stipulated to, among other things, the district court's jurisdiction and the identification of the issues presented for trial. Joint Pre-Trial Order (Dkt. No. 167), Barclays Capital Inc. v. Theflyonthewall.com, No. 06-cv-4908 (S.D.N.Y. April 21, 2010) (the "Joint Pre-trial Order"). The parties also agreed that:

> The following affirmative defenses previously asserted by Defendant are not to be tried:
>
> . . .
>
> Defendant's publication of daily news from firms in the financial industry, including Plaintiffs, is constitutionally protected by the First Amendment to the U.S. Constitution.

Joint Pre-trial Order at 5 (emphasis in original). The district court read this to mean that Fly had waived any First Amendment defenses to the Firms' "hot news" misappropriation claim. See Barclays Capital Inc. v. Theflyonthewall.com ("Fly II"), 700 F. Supp.2d 310, 352-54 (S.D.N.Y. 2010) (Opinion and Order Denying Stay).

Fly also abandoned the "fair use" copyright-infringement defense, thereby effectively conceding liability on the copyright claim. An injunction "which restrains Fly from further infringement of 'any portion of the copyrighted elements of any research reports' generated by Barclays Capital or Morgan Stanley," Fly I, 700 F. Supp.2d at 331, was entered and, so far as we know, remains in effect.

In the pre-trial order, the Firms contended that they satisfied all five "elements" of the tort purportedly identified in NBA, 105 F.3d at 845, although the Firms did not explicitly refer to that case. Joint Pre-Trial Order at 3. Fly appeared to concede that the Firms generate their Recommendations at great expense and that the Recommendations are time-sensitive, but disputed the other three "elements" of the misappropriation claim. Id. at 4.

At a four-day bench trial in early March of last year, the witnesses for the plaintiffs were primarily Firm executives responsible for or familiar with a Firm's research activities. The defendant called, inter alios, Fly employees to testify, including Fly's President and majority owner, Ron Etergino. Inasmuch as Fly had effectively conceded liability for copyright infringement, the primary issues at trial were (1) the scope of remedies for copyright infringement, (2) whether Fly was liable for "hot news" misappropriation and, if so, (3) the appropriate remedy.

On March 18, 2010, the district court issued its Opinion and Order, deciding for the plaintiffs on both the copyright-infringement and the "hot news" misappropriation claims. It awarded the plaintiffs statutory damages and attorney's fees related to the copyright infringement claim. As part of its judgment in favor of the plaintiffs on the misappropriation claim, the court entered an order, inter alia, enjoining Fly from reporting Recommendations for a period ranging from thirty minutes to several hours after they are released by the plaintiffs. See Fly I, 700 F. Supp.2d at 348; Permanent Injunction (Dkt. No 138), Barclays Capital v. Theflyonthewall.com, 700 F. Supp.2d 310 (S.D.N.Y. 2010) (the "Permanent Injunction").

Relying upon one of two — or arguably three — iterations of NBA's multi-factor "test," the district court concluded that for a misappropriation claim under New York law to survive federal copyright law preemption, and for the plaintiff to succeed on the claim, the plaintiff is required to demonstrate that:

> (i) [it] generates or gathers information at a cost; (ii) the information is time-sensitive; (iii) a defendant's use of the information constitutes free

> riding on the plaintiff's efforts; (iv) the defendant is in direct competition with a product or service offered by the plaintiffs; and (v) the ability of other parties to free-ride on the efforts of the plaintiff or others would so reduce the incentive to produce the product or service that its existence or quality would be substantially threatened.

Fly I, 700 F. Supp.2d at 334-35 (quoting NBA, 105 F.3d at 845). The district court concluded that the first two "elements" — the cost of generating information and time-sensitivity — were not disputed by Fly and in any case were easily met. Id. at 335-36.

The district court decided with respect to the third factor, "free riding," that, "[i]n essence, [it] exists where a defendant invests little in order to profit from information generated or collected by the plaintiff at great cost." Id. at 336. According to the court, "Fly does no equity research of its own, nor does it undertake any original reporting or analysis." Id. at 336.

In deciding in the Firms' favor on this issue, the district court rejected Fly's argument that its efforts in the collection, aggregation, and dissemination of information were sufficient to avoid a finding of free-riding, on the ground that efforts contributed nothing to the actual Recommendations that Fly provided to its subscribers. Id. at 336-37. The court also disagreed with Fly's argument that its gathering of the Recommendations from public sources renders that information freely available for all: "[T]he fact that others also engage in unlawful behavior does not excuse a party's own illegal conduct." Id. at 337.

In concluding that the fourth factor, direct competition, was present, the district court relied on its finding that both Fly and the Firms were engaged in "disseminating Recommendations to investors for their use in making investment decisions," that production and distribution of the reports was among the Firms' "primary businesses," and that the companies used similar distribution channels. Id. at 339-40. The court also thought significant Fly's then-recent attempts to link its subscribers to discount brokerage services, which in the district court's view had the potential to further draw commission revenue away from the Firms.

The district court rejected Fly's contention that our decision in NBA required the court to find "head-to-head competition in a primary market," concluding that neither Fly's lack of brokerage and investment-advisory services nor its role as a news aggregator was inconsistent with a finding of direct competition. Id. at 340. The court appeared to conclude that Fly's other activities were immaterial, so long as Fly, like the Firms, was engaged in the business of disseminating Recommendations.

Finally, the district court concluded that the fifth factor, sufficiently reduced economic incentives, was present. The court found that "common sense and the circumstantial evidence about the plaintiffs' business model make the Firms' contentions about [their] reduced incentives utterly credible." Id. at 342. The Firms had asserted that they had been forced to cut their analyst staffs and budgets significantly during the previous five years, in significant measure although by no means exclusively because of competition from unauthorized redistributions of their Recommendations. They acknowledged, as did the court, that there were unrelated substantial causes for the contraction during this period, including the then-recent recession and accompanying stock-market collapse, and the April 2003 Global Research Analyst Settlement.

Fly sought to portray the Firms' evidence of reduced economic incentives, which was based almost entirely on the testimony of the Firms' own research executives, as speculative and self-serving. The district court concluded to the contrary (1) that the executives' testimony was credible despite their employment by the Firms, (2) that the Firms did not need to demonstrate actual harm, but rather merely show that harm would occur if Fly and others were allowed to continue their conduct, and (3) that the precise impact of the recent recession and the Global Research Analyst Settlement was irrelevant, because the mere showing that Fly and others like it significantly affected the Firms' incentives was sufficient to establish the fifth factor, even if other events also contributed to the reduction in incentives. Id. at 342-43.

Having concluded that the Firms had established the tort of "hot news" misappropriation, the district court entered a permanent injunction barring Fly from reporting a Recommendation until either (a) half an hour after the market opens, if the report containing the recommendation was released before 9:30 a.m., or (b) two hours after release, if the report was released after 9:30 a.m. This time period represented roughly the midpoint between what Fly and the Firms, respectively, requested.

Perhaps because Fly purported to waive its First Amendment defenses, the district court's opinion contains no explicit discussion of First Amendment doctrine beyond the court's reference, in consideration of the propriety of injunctive relief, to "public policy considerations," and the balancing of "the public interest in unrestrained access to information." Id. at 344. Similarly, although in the court's thorough recitation of the history of the law of "hot news" misappropriation, it explained in some detail the role of Copyright Act preemption of state tort law, it did not expressly consider whether "hot news" misappropriation was preempted by federal copyright law in this case. Instead, it adopted as determinative NBA's ruling that a narrow form of the "hot news" misappropriation tort survives preemption, and it applied language from that decision indicating the tort's limitations by virtue of preemption doctrine.

Post-Trial Procedural History

Fly filed a notice of appeal on April 9, 2010. Four days later, it moved before the district court to stay or modify the injunction pending that appeal. In support of its motion, Fly argued (1) that it was likely to succeed on the merits on appeal, specifically with regard to the direct competition and reduced incentive elements of the misappropriation claim; (2) that it would suffer irreparable harm from the operation of the injunction as customers cancelled their subscriptions; and (3) that the injunction's curtailment of First Amendment protected speech required a finding of irreparable harm. On May 7, 2010, the district court denied Fly's motion on the grounds (1) that Fly was not likely to succeed on the merits of its appeal; (2) that Fly had shown evidence of only two instances of customers cancelling their subscriptions because of the injunction; and (3) that Fly had waived its First Amendment arguments prior to trial. See Fly II, 700 F. Supp.2d at 349-56.

Fly thereupon moved in this Court for a stay of the injunction and an expedited appeal. On May 19, 2010, a panel of this Court granted the motion.

On appeal, Fly argues principally that (1) the district court erred in finding that the plaintiffs established "hot news" misappropriation under New York law, specifically in that the plaintiffs failed to prove time-sensitivity, free-riding, direct competition, and reduced incentives; (2) that the district court's injunction violates Fly's free-speech rights under the First Amendment; (3) that the district court's finding of "hot news" misappropriation violates the Copyright Clause of the Constitution and the Copyright Act; (4) that the district court failed to apply the proper standard in granting injunctive relief; and (5) that the injunction is unreasonably overbroad.

## DISCUSSION

### I. Standard of Review

"When reviewing a judgment following a bench trial in the district court, we review the court's findings of fact for clear error and its conclusions of law de novo." Tiffany (NJ) Inc. v. eBay Inc., 600 F.3d 93, 96 (2d Cir.), cert. denied, 131 S. Ct. 647, 178 L. Ed.2d 513 (2010).

### II. Viability of the "Hot News" Misappropriation Tort

Amici Google, Inc. and Twitter, Inc., referring to the "hot news" misappropriation tort as an "end-run" around the Constitution's Copyright Clause and Supreme Court precedent, and arguing that their position is supported by "[i]mportant public policy concerns," urge us to "repudiate the tort." Brief for Google, Inc. and Twitter, Inc. as Amici Curiae Supporting Reversal at 3, Barclays Capital Inc. v. Theflyonthewall.com, No. 10-1372-cv (2d Cir. June 22, 2010).

We need not address the viability vel non of a "hot news" misappropriation tort under New York law. Were we to do so, though, plainly we would be bound by the conclusion of the previous Second Circuit panel in NBA that the tort survives. See, e.g., United States v. Jass, 569 F.3d 47, 58 (2d Cir. 2009) (explaining the binding nature of one panel opinion on a subsequent panel of the same circuit); Meacham v. Knolls Atomic Power Lab., 461 F.3d 134, 141 (2d Cir. 2006) (similar), rev'd on other grounds, 554 U.S. 84, 128 S. Ct. 2395, 171 L. Ed.2d 283 (2008). We are therefore without the authority to "repudiate" that view.

Were we indeed called upon to consider the continued viability of the tort under New York law, perhaps we would certify that issue to the New York Court of Appeals. The issue we address, however, is federal preemption. As a federal court, we answer that question ourselves.

### III. Copyright Act Preemption

#### A. National Basketball Association v. Motorola, Inc.

National Basketball Association v. Motorola, Inc., 105 F.3d 841 (2d Cir. 1997), appears to be the only judicial decision — surely the only decision binding upon us — that addresses directly the preemption issue raised in this appeal.

There, defendant Motorola, Inc. produced and sold (or otherwise provided) to members of the public a telephonic pager called Sports Trax. Motorola's co-defendant, STATS, Inc., supplied statistical information about National Basketball Association ("NBA") professional basketball games. The information was transmitted to Sports Trax pagers owned or leased by Motorola and STATS customers roughly simultaneously with the playing of the games. NBA, 105 F.3d at 843. "The information included "(i) the teams playing; (ii) score changes; (iii) the team in possession of the ball; (iv) whether the team is in the free-throw bonus; (v) the quarter of the game; and (vi) time remaining in the quarter." Id. at 844.

> The information [was] updated every two to three minutes, with more frequent updates near the end of the first half and the end of the game. There [was] a lag of approximately two or three minutes between events in the game itself and when the information appear[ed] on the pager screen.

Id.

Sports Trax gathered the information for the service by employing persons who would watch the games on television or listen to accounts of them on the radio and supply the information to STATS's host computer. The computer compiled, analyzed, and formatted the data for retransmission. The information was then sent to FM radio stations which retransmitted them to the subscribers' individual Sports Trax pagers. Id.

The NBA itself also publicly disseminated similar, and therefore to some extent competitive, information. As Judge Winter wrote for the NBA panel:

> [T]he NBA does provide, or will shortly do so, information like that available through Sports Trax. It now offers a service called "Gamestats" that provides official play-by-play game sheets and half-time and final box cores within each arena. It also provides such information to the media in each arena. In the future, the NBA plans to enhance Gamestats so that it will be networked between the various arenas and will support a pager product analogous to Sports Trax. Sports Trax will of course directly compete with an enhanced Gamestats.

Id. at 853.

The district court whose decision was on appeal in NBA had found for the plaintiff on its New York-law "hot news" misappropriation claim arising out of the defendants' taking, redistributing, and profiting from the facts generated by the NBA in the course of the playing of NBA games. The district court therefore had entered a permanent injunction against the defendants, but stayed that injunction pending appeal. Id.

1. NBA Preemption Analysis.

a. Copyright Act

The NBA panel began its analysis by noting that prior to the 1976 amendments to the Copyright Act, the Act contained no express provisions as to the circumstances under which the federal copyright law preempted state law. The 1976 Amendments changed that.

Title 17 U.S.C. § 301, enacted in 1976, sets forth a two-part test to determine whether a state-law claim is preempted by the Copyright Act, with a further "extra elements" exception we discuss below. Such a claim is preempted (i) if it seeks to vindicate "legal or equitable rights that are equivalent" to one of the bundle of exclusive rights already protected by copyright law under 17 U.S.C. § 106 — the "general scope requirement"; and (ii) if the work in question is of the type of works protected by the Copyright Act under 17 U.S.C. §§ 102 and 103 — the "subject matter requirement." 25 NBA, 105 F.3d at 848 (quoting 17 U.S.C. § 301).

The NBA panel observed that "[t]he subject matter requirement" — the second factor in a preemption analysis — "is met when the work of authorship being copied or misappropriated 'falls within the ambit of copyright protection.' " Id. at 849 (quoting Harper & Row, Inc. v. Nation Enters., 723 F.2d 195, 200 (1983) (brackets omitted), rev'd on other grounds, 471 U.S. 539, 105 S. Ct. 2218, 85 L. Ed.2d 588 (1985)). In deciding whether a state-law claim is preempted by the Copyright Act, then, it is not determinative that the plaintiff seeks redress with respect to a defendant's alleged misappropriation of uncopyrightable material — e.g., facts — contained in a copyrightable work. "Copyrightable material often contains uncopyrightable elements within it, but Section 301 preemption bars state law misappropriation claims with respect to uncopyrightable as well as copyrightable elements," if the work as a whole satisfies the subject matter requirement. NBA, 105 F.3d at 849; see also id. at 850 (quoting ProCD, Inc. v. Zeidenberg, 86 F.3d 1447, 1453 (7th Cir. 1996)).

In NBA, facts about what transpired during broadcasted NBA basketball games thus fell within the subject matter of copyright for the purpose of the court's preemption analysis, even though the games themselves were not copyrightable. Id. at 848-49 ("Although game broadcasts are copyrightable while the underlying games are not, the Copyright Act should not be read to distinguish between the two when analyzing the preemption of a misappropriation claim based on copying or taking from the copyrightable work.").

Turning to the other preemption element, the NBA panel thought it clear that what the NBA was seeking to protect fell within the "general scope of copyright." Title 17 U.S.C. § 106, which states that the general scope of copyright, "affords a copyright owner the exclusive right to: (1) reproduce the copyrighted work; (2) prepare derivative works; (3) distribute copies of the work by sale or otherwise; and, with respect to certain artistic works, (4) perform the work publicly; and (5) display the work publicly. See 17 U.S.C. 106(1)-(5)." Computer Assocs. Int'l, Inc. v. Altai, Inc., 982 F.2d 693, 716 (2d Cir. 1992). "Section 301 [of the Copyright Act] thus preempts only those state law rights that 'may be abridged by an act which, in and of itself, would infringe one of the exclusive rights' provided by federal copyright law," id. (quoting Harper & Row, 723 F.2d at 200), i.e., "acts of reproduction, performance, distribution or display," id. (internal quotation marks omitted). The claim of tortious behavior in NBA was indeed for the acts of reproduction, distribution, and display of facts by the defendants of material taken from the copyrighted broadcasts. The NBA panel therefore concluded that the plaintiff's tort claim was within the general scope of copyright.

The court was thus satisfied that both preemption factors were met.

b. Extra-Element Test

Having decided that the two preliminary factors counseled in favor of preemption, the NBA panel observed:

> [C]ertain forms of commercial misappropriation otherwise within the general scope requirement will survive preemption if an "extra-element" test is met. As stated in Altai:
>
> > But if an "extra element" is "required instead of or in addition to the acts of reproduction, performance, distribution or display, in order to constitute a state-created cause of action, then the right does not lie 'within the general scope of copyright,' and there is no preemption."
>
> Altai, 982 F.2d at 716 (quoting 1 Melville B. Nimmer & David Nimmer, Nimmer on Copyright § 1.01[B] at 1-14-15 (1991)).

NBA, 105 F.3d at 850; see also Harper & Row, 723 F.2d at 200 ("[W]hen a state law violation is predicated upon an act incorporating elements beyond mere reproduction or the like, the rights involved are not equivalent and preemption will not occur."). It is with respect to the "extra elements" that the NBA Court proffered a three-factor analysis: "We . . . find the extra elements — those in addition to the elements of copyright infringement — that allow a 'hotnews' claim to survive preemption are: (i) the time-sensitive value of factual information, (ii) the free-riding by a defendant, and (iii) the threat to the very existence of the product or service provided by the plaintiff." Id. at 853 (emphasis added).

i. International News Service v. Associated Press

The NBA Court briefly summarized the Supreme Court's seminal 1918 "hot news" decision, International News Service v. Associated Press, 248 U.S. 215, 39 S. Ct. 68, 63 L. Ed. 211 (1918) ("INS"):

> INS involved two wire services, the Associated Press ("AP") and International News Service ("INS"), that transmitted news stories by wire to member newspapers. Id. INS would lift factual stories from AP bulletins and send them by wire to INS papers. Id. at 231. INS would also take factual stories from east coast AP papers and wire them to INS papers on the west coast that had yet to publish because of time differentials. Id. at 238. The Supreme Court held that INS's conduct was a common-law misappropriation of AP's property. Id. at 242.

NBA, 105 F.3d at 845.

INS itself is no longer good law. Purporting to establish a principal of federal common law, the law established by INS was abolished by Erie Railroad Co. v. Tompkins, 304 U.S. 64, 58 S. Ct. 817, 82 L. Ed. 1188 (1938), which largely abandoned federal common law. But, as the NBA panel pointed out, "[b]ased on legislative history of the 1976 [Copyright Act amendments], it is generally agreed that a 'hot-news' INS-like claim survives preemption." NBA, 105 F.3d at 845 (citing H.R. Rep. No. 94-1476 at 132).

The House of Representatives Report with respect to the preemption provisions of the 1976 Copyright Act amendments commented in this regard:

> "Misappropriation" is not necessarily synonymous with copyright infringement, and thus a cause of action labeled as "misappropriation" is not preempted if it is in fact based neither on a right within the general scope of copyright as specified by [17 U.S.C. §] 106 [specifying the general scope of copyright] nor on a right equivalent thereto. For example, state law should have the flexibility to afford a remedy (under traditional principles of equity) against a consistent pattern of unauthorized appropriation by a competitor of the facts (i.e., not the literary expression) constituting "hot" news, whether in the traditional mold of [INS], or in the newer form of data updates from scientific, business, or financial data bases.

H.R.No. 94-1476 at 132, reprinted in 1976 U.S.C.C.A.N. at 5748 (footnote omitted), quoted in NBA, 105 F.3d at 850. The House Report thus anticipated that INS-like state-law torts would survive preemption. It did not itself create such a cause of action or recognize the existence of one under federal law. It allowed instead for the survival of such a state-law claim.

The NBA Court thus used INS as a description of the type of claims — "INS-like" — that, Congress has said, are not necessarily preempted by federal copyright law. Some seventy-five years after its death under Erie, INS thus maintains a ghostly presence as a description of a tort theory, not as precedential establishment of a tort cause of action.

ii. Moral Dimensions

One source of confusion in addressing these misappropriation cases is that INS itself was a case brought in equity to enjoin INS from copying AP's uncopyrightable news. In that context, the INS Court emphasized the unfairness of INS's practice of pirating AP's stories. It condemned, in what sounded biblical in tone, the defendant's "reap[ing] where it ha[d] not sown." INS, 248 U.S. at 239. The Court said:

> This defendant . . . admits that it is taking material that has been acquired by complainant as the result of organization and the expenditure of labor, skill, and money, and which is salable by complainant for money, and that defendant in appropriating it and selling it as its own is endeavoring to reap where it has not sown, and by disposing of it to newspapers that are competitors of complainant's members is appropriating to itself the harvest

> of those who have sown. Stripped of all disguises, the process amounts to an unauthorized interference with the normal operation of complainant's legitimate business precisely at the point where the profit is to be reaped, in order to divert a material portion of the profit from those who have earned it to those who have not; with special advantage to defendant in the competition because of the fact that it is not burdened with any part of the expense of gathering the news. The transaction speaks for itself, and a court of equity ought not to hesitate long in characterizing it as unfair competition in business.

Id. at 239-40 (emphasis added). This dicta has been absorbed by New York misappropriation law:

New York courts have noted the incalculable variety of illegal practices falling within the unfair competition rubric, calling it a broad and flexible doctrine that depends more upon the facts set forth than in most causes of action. It has been broadly described as encompassing any form of commercial immorality, or simply as endeavoring to reap where one has not sown; it is taking the skill, expenditures and labors of a competitor, and misappropriating for the commercial advantage of one person a benefit or property right belonging to another. The tort is adaptable and capacious.

Roy Exp. Co. Establishment of Vaduz, Liech. v. Columbia Broad. Sys., Inc., 672 F.2d 1095, 1105 (2d Cir. 1982) (citation and alteration omitted). And it has been reflected in the rhetoric of federal district courts applying New York law. See, e.g., Fly I, 700 F. Supp.2d at 336 (quoting INS); NBA v. Sports Team Analysis & Tracking Sys. ("NBASDNY"), 939 F. Supp. 1071, 1075 (S.D.N.Y. 1996) (quoting INS), rev'd, NBA, 105 F.3d 841.

The NBA Court also noted that the district court whose decision it was reviewing had "described New York misappropriation law as standing for the 'broader principle that property rights of commercial value are to be and will be protected from any form of commercial immorality'; that misappropriation law developed 'to deal with business malpractices offensive to the ethics of [] society'; and that the doctrine is 'broad and flexible.' " NBA, 105 F. 3d at 851 (brackets in original) (quoting NBASDNY, 939 F. Supp. at 1098-1110) (internal citation omitted). But Judge Winter explicitly rejected the notion that "hot news" misappropriation cases based on the disapproval of the perceived unethical nature of a defendant's ostensibly piratical acts survive preemption. The Court concluded that "such concepts are virtually synonymous [with] wrongful copying and are in no meaningful fashion distinguishable from infringement of a copyright. The broad misappropriation doctrine relied upon by the district court is, therefore, the equivalent of exclusive rights in copyright law." NBA, 105 F.3d at 851 (deeming preempted the broad theory of misappropriation embodied in Metropolitan Opera Ass'n v. Wagner-Nichols Recorder Corp., 199 Misc. 786, 101 N.Y.S.2d 483 (N.Y. County Sup. Ct. 1950), aff'd, 279 A.D. 632, 107 N.Y.S.2d 795 (1st Dep't 1951)).

No matter how "unfair" Motorola's use of NBA facts and statistics may have been to the NBA — or Fly's use of the fact of the Firms' Recommendations may be to the Firms — then, such unfairness alone is immaterial to a determination whether a cause of action for misappropriation has been preempted by the

Copyright Act. The adoption of new technology that injures or destroys present business models is commonplace. Whether fair or not, that cannot, without more, be prevented by application of the misappropriation tort. Indeed, because the Copyright Act itself provides a remedy for wrongful copying, such unfairness may be seen as supporting a finding that the Act preempts the tort. *See id.*

iii. Narrowness of the Preemption Exception

The NBA panel repeatedly emphasized the "narrowness" of the "hot news" tort exception from preemption. See id. at 843, 848, 851, 852 (using the word "narrow" or "narrowness" five times). Although our discussion of preemption in NBA did not focus on the importance of maintaining the uniform nationwide scheme that the Copyright Act, with its 1976 preemption amendment, 17 U.S.C. § 301, provides, we later underscored it. In Krause v. Titleserv, Inc., 402 F.3d 119, 123 (2d Cir. 2005), we declined to limit protection for copyrights held by "owners" of computer programs to those with formal title to such programs. The first reason we gave was that title may depend on state law that differs from one state to another.

> The result would be to undermine some of the uniformity achieved by the Copyright Act. . . . If [the relevant section of the Copyright Act] required formal title, two software users, engaged in substantively identical transactions might find that one is liable for copyright infringement while the other is protected by [the section], depending solely on the state in which the conduct occurred. Such a result would contradict the Copyright Act's "express objective of creating national, uniform copyright law by broadly preempting state statutory and common-law copyright regulation." Community for Creative Non-Violence v. Reid, 490 U.S. 730, 740, 109 S. Ct. 2166, 104 L. Ed.2d 811 (1989); see also 17 U.S.C. § 301(a).

Id. at 123 (emphasis added).

Indeed, central to the principle of preemption generally is the value of providing for legal uniformity where Congress has acted nationally. See, e.g., Paneccasio v. Unisource Worldwide, Inc., 532 F.3d 101, 113 (2d Cir. 2008) ("The purpose of ERISA preemption is to ensure that all covered benefit plans will be governed by unified federal law, thus simplifying life for employers administering plans in several states, because a patchwork scheme of regulation would introduce considerable inefficiencies in benefit program operation." (internal quotation marks and brackets omitted)).

This is a pressing concern when considering the "narrow" "hot news" misappropriation exemption from preemption. The broader the exemption, the greater the likelihood that protection of works within the "general scope" of the copyright and of the type of works protected by the Act will receive disparate treatment depending on where the alleged tort occurs and which state's law is found to be applicable.

The problem may be illustrated by reference to a recent case in the Southern District of New York. In Associated Press v. All Headline News Corp., 608 F. Supp. 2d 454 (S.D.N.Y. 2009), the court sought to determine whether there was a difference between New York and Florida "hot news" misappropriation law in order for it to analyze, under choice-of-law principles, which state's law applied. Judge Castel observed that "[n]o authority has been cited to show that Florida recognizes a cause of action for hot news misappropriation. Then again, defendants have not persuasively demonstrated that Florida would not recognize such a claim." Id. at 459-60.

It appears, then, that the alleged "hot news" misappropriation in All Headline News Corp. might have been permissible in New York but not in Florida. The same could have been said for the aggregation and publication of basketball statistics in NBA, and the same may be said as to the aggregation and publication of Recommendations in the case at bar. To the extent that "hot news" misappropriation causes of action are not preempted, the aggregators' actions may have different legal significance from state to state — permitted, at least to some extent, in some; prohibited, at least to some extent, in others. It is this sort of patchwork protection that the drafters of the Copyright Act preemption provisions sought to minimize, and that counsels in favor of locating only a "narrow" exception to Copyright Act preemption.

c. Three- and Five-Part "Tests"

Before concluding that the NBA's claim was preempted, the NBA panel set forth in its opinion — twice — a five-part "test" for identifying a non-preempted "hot news" misappropriation claim. The district court in this case, when applying NBA, structured its conclusions-of-law analysis around NBA's first iteration of the "test":

> We hold that the surviving "hot-news" INS-like claim is limited to cases where: (i) a plaintiff generates or gathers information at a cost; (ii) the information is time-sensitive; (iii) a defendant's use of the information constitutes free-riding on the plaintiff's efforts; (iv) the defendant is in direct competition with a product or service offered by the plaintiffs; and (v) the ability of other parties to free-ride on the efforts of the plaintiff or others would so reduce the incentive to produce the product or service that its existence or quality would be substantially threatened. We conclude that Sports Trax does not meet that test.

NBA, 105 F.3d at 845; see Fly I, 700 F. Supp.2d at 334-35 (quoting the passage but omitting the first fifteen prefatory words). But the panel restated the five-part inquiry later in its opinion:

> In our view, the elements central to an INS claim are: (i) the plaintiff generates or collects information at some cost or expense, see [Financial Information, Inc. v. Moody's Investors Serv., 808 F.2d 204, 206 (2d Cir. 1996) ("FII")]; INS, 248 U.S. at 240; (ii) the value of the information is highly time-sensitive, see FII, 808 F.2d at 209; INS, 248 U.S. at 231; Restatement (Third) Unfair Competition, § 38 cmt. c.; (iii) the defendant's use of the information constitutes free-riding on the plaintiff's costly efforts to generate or collect it, see FII, 808 F.2d at 207; INS, 248 U.S. at 239-40; Restatement § 38 at cmt. c.; McCarthy, § 10:73 at 10-139; (iv) the defendant's use of the information is in direct competition with a product or service offered by the plaintiff, FII, 808 F.2d at 209, INS, 248 U.S. at 240;

> (v) the ability of other parties to free-ride on the efforts of the plaintiff would so reduce the incentive to produce the product or service that its existence or quality would be substantially threatened, FII, 808 F.2d at 209; Restatement, § 38 at cmt. c.; INS, 248 U.S. at 241 ("[INS's conduct] would render [AP's] publication profitless, or so little profitable as in effect to cut off the service by rendering the cost prohibitive in comparison with the return.").

NBA, 105 F.3d at 852.

Throughout this litigation the parties seem to have been in general agreement that the district court and we should employ a five-part analysis taken from the NBA opinion. It is understandable, of course, that counsel and the district court did in this case, and do in other comparable circumstances, attempt to follow our statements in precedential opinions as to what the law is — which we often state in terms of what we "hold." But that reading is not always either easy to make or technically correct. As Judge Friendly put it in colorful terms: "A judge's power to bind is limited to the issue that is before him; he cannot transmute dictum into decision by waving a wand and uttering the word 'hold.' " United States v. Rubin, 609 F.2d 51, 69 (2d Cir. 1979) (Friendly, J., concurring), quoted in Pierre N. Leval, Judging Under the Constitution: Dicta about Dicta, 81 N.Y.U. L. Rev. 1249, 1249 (2006). See also generally Leval, supra (containing seminal discussion of judicial use of the term "holding"); id. at 1256 ("A dictum [i.e., a conclusion or point of view in an opinion that is not a holding] is an assertion in a court's opinion of a proposition of law [that] does not explain why the court's judgment goes in favor of the winner."); Judith M. Stinson, Why Dicta Becomes Holding and Why it Matters, 76 Brook. L. Rev. 219, 219 n.2 (2010) (collecting authorities addressing difficulties with judicial use of the term "hold").

It is axiomatic that appellate judges cannot make law except insofar as they reach a conclusion based on the specific facts and circumstances presented to the court in a particular appeal. Subordinate courts and subsequent appellate panels are required to follow only these previous appellate legal "holdings." The NBA panel decided the case before it, and we think that the law it thus made regarding "hot news" preemption is, as we have tried to explain, determinative here. But the Court's various explanations of its five-part approach are not. Indeed, we do not see how they can be: The two five-part "tests" are not entirely consistent, and are less consistent still with the three-" extra element" test, which also appears later in the opinion:

> We therefore find the extra elements — those in addition to the elements of copyright infringement — that allow a "hotnews" claim to survive preemption are: (i) the time-sensitive value of factual information, (ii) the free-riding by a defendant, and (iii) the threat to the very existence of the product or service provided by the plaintiff."

Id. at 853.

For example, the fifth of the five factors in the first iteration of the test is that "the ability of other parties to free-ride on the efforts of the plaintiff or others would so reduce the incentive to produce the product or service that its existence or quality would be substantially threatened." NBA, 105 F.3d at 845 (emphasis added). The second iteration is similar, but adds a quotation from INS which can be read to make the factor far more difficult to demonstrate: that the conduct "would render [the plaintiff's] publication profitless, or so little profitable as in effect to cut off the service by rendering the cost prohibitive in comparison with the return.' " Id. at 852 (emphasis added) (quoting INS, 248 U.S. at 241). Then, in rehearsing the "extra elements" that may avoid preemption, the panel referred to "the threat to the very existence of the product or service provided by the plaintiff." Id. at 853 (emphasis added).

The distinctions between these various statements of a multi-part test are substantial. Were we required to rule on the district court's findings of fact ourselves in light of these various versions of elements, we might well perceive no clear error in a finding that the existence or quality, id. at 845, of the Firms' reports were placed in jeopardy by what the district court found to be "free riding." By contrast, we might otherwise conclude that there is insufficient record evidence to sustain a finding either that the alleged free-riding by Fly and similar aggregators "in effect . . . cut off the [Firms'] service by rendering the cost prohibitive in comparison with the return," id. at 852, or were a "threat to the very existence of the product or service provided by the plaintiff[s]," id. at 853.

It seems to us that each of NBA's three multi-element statements serves a somewhat different purpose. The first is a general introduction, by way of summary, of what the decision concludes. The second may be described as "stating the elements of the tort." Confold Pac., Inc. v. Polaris Indus., 433 F.3d 952, 960 (7th Cir. 2006) (Posner, J.). And the third focuses on what "extra elements" are necessary to avoid preemption despite the conclusion that the "general scope requirement" and the "subject matter requirement," NBA, 105 F.3d at 848, have been met.

In our view, the several NBA statements were sophisticated observations in aid of the Court's analysis of the difficult preemption issues presented to it. See Leval, supra, at 1254. Inconsistent as they were, they could not all be equivalent to a statutory command to which we or the district court are expected to adhere.

We engage in this somewhat extended discussion because the parties agreed that the district court should employ the five-part analysis derived NBA, and the district court did so. But we cannot supplant this Court's view of the law with the view of the parties. See, e.g., Kamen v. Kemper Fin. Servs. Inc., 500 U.S. 90, 99, 111 S. Ct. 1711, 114 L. Ed.2d 152 (1991); Hankins v. Lyght, 441 F.3d 96, 104 (2d Cir. 2006); Becker v. Poling Transp. Corp., 356 F.3d 381, 390 (2d Cir. 2004).

2. NBA Preemption Analysis Applied to The NBA Facts

Applying the principles of preemption it had identified, the NBA Court concluded that the tort claim that the NBA sought to assert against Motorola and STATS was preempted by the Copyright Act because, the "general scope requirement" and the "subject matter requirement" having been satisfied, the "extra elements" necessary for such a claim nonetheless to survive preemption were absent. This was so despite the fact that Motorola and STATS were indeed disseminating, on a timely basis, information about NBA games that the NBA was also circulating. The Court concluded that:

> An indispensable element of an INS "hot news" claim is free-riding by a defendant on a plaintiff's product, enabling the defendant to produce a directly competitive product for less money because it has lower costs . . . . Appellants are in no way free-riding on [the NBA service that provided game statistics to the public]. Motorola and STATS expend their own resources to collect purely factual information generated in NBA games to transmit to [Motorola] pagers. They have their own network and assemble and transmit data themselves.
>
> To be sure, if appellants in the future were to collect facts from an enhanced [NBA] pager to retransmit them to [Motorola's] pagers, that would constitute free-riding and might well cause [the NBA service] to be unprofitable because it had to bear costs to collect facts that [Motorola] did not. If the appropriation of facts from one pager to another pager service were allowed, transmission of current information on NBA games to pagers or similar devices would be substantially deterred because any potential transmitter would know that the first entrant would quickly encounter a lower cost competitor free-riding on the originator's transmissions.
>
> However, that is not the case in the instant matter. [Motorola] and [the NBA] are each bearing [its] own costs of collecting factual information on NBA games, and, if one produces a product that is cheaper or otherwise superior to the other, that producer will prevail in the marketplace. This is obviously not the situation against which INS was intended to prevent: the potential lack of any such product or service because of the anticipation of free-riding.

NBA, 105 F.3d at 854 (footnote omitted).

B. Preemption and This Appeal

We conclude that applying NBA and copyright preemption principles to the facts of this case, the Firms' claim for "hot news" misappropriation fails because it is preempted by the Copyright Act. First, the Firms' reports culminating with the Recommendations satisfy the "subject matter" requirement because they are all works "of a type covered by section[] 102," i.e., "original works of authorship fixed in a[] tangible medium of expression." 17 U.S.C. § 102. As discussed above, it is not determinative for the Copyright Act preemption analysis that the facts of the Recommendations themselves are not copyrightable. See NBA, 105 F.3d at 850. Second, the reports together with the Recommendations fulfill the "general scope" requirement because the rights "may be abridged by an act which, in and of itself, would infringe one of the exclusive rights' provided by federal copyright law," Altai, Inc., 982 F.2d at 716 (citing Harper & Row, 723 F.2d at 200), i.e., "acts of reproduction, performance, distribution or display," id. (internal quotation marks omitted).

Third and finally, the Firms' claim is not a so-called INS-type non-preempted claim because Fly is not, under NBA's analysis, "free-riding." It is collecting, collating and disseminating factual information — the facts that Firms and others in the securities business have made recommendations with respect to the value of and the wisdom of purchasing or selling securities — and attributing the information to its source. The Firms are making the news; Fly, despite the Firms' understandable desire to protect their business model, is breaking it. As the INS Court explained, long before it would have occurred to the Court to cite the First Amendment for the proposition:

> [T]he news element — the information respecting current events contained in the literary production — is not the creation of the writer, but is a report of matters that ordinarily are publici juris; it is the history of the day. It is not to be supposed that the framers of the Constitution, when they empowered Congress "to promote the progress of science and useful arts, by securing for limited times to authors and inventors the exclusive right to their respective writings and discoveries" (Const., Art I, § 8, par. 8), intended to confer upon one who might happen to be the first to report a historic event the exclusive right for any period to spread the knowledge of it.

INS, 248 U.S. at 234.

The use of the term "free-riding" in recent "hot news" misappropriation jurisprudence exacerbates difficulties in addressing these issues. Unfair use of another's "labor, skill, and money, and which is salable by complainant for money," INS, 248 U.S. at 239, sounds like the very essence of "free-riding," and, the term "free-riding" in turn seems clearly to connote acts that are quintessentially unfair.

It must be recalled, however, that the term free-riding refers explicitly to a requirement for a cause of action as described by INS. As explained by the NBA Court, "[a]n indispensable element of an INS 'hot news' claim is free-riding by a defendant on a plaintiff's product." NBA, 105 F.3d at 854.

The practice of what NBA referred to as "free-riding" was further described by INS. The INS Court defined the "hot news" tort in part as "taking material that has been acquired by complainant as the result of organization and the expenditure of labor, skill, and money, and which is salable by complainant for money, and . . . appropriating it and selling it as [the defendant's] own . . . ." INS, 248 U.S. at 239. That definition fits the facts of INS: The defendant was taking news gathered and in the process of dissemination by the Associated Press and selling that news as though the defendant itself had gathered it. But it does not describe the practices of Fly. The Firms here may be "acquiring material" in the course of preparing their reports, but that is not the focus of this lawsuit. In pressing a "hot news" claim against Fly, the Firms seek only to protect their Recommendations, something they create using their expertise and experience rather than acquire through efforts akin to reporting.

Moreover, Fly, having obtained news of a Recommendation, is hardly selling the Recommendation "as its own," INS, 248 U.S. at 239. It is selling the information with specific attribution to the issuing Firm. Indeed, for Fly to sell, for example, a Morgan Stanley Recommendation "as its own," as INS sold the news it cribbed from AP to INS subscribers, would be of little value to either Fly or its customers. If, for example, Morgan Stanley were to issue a Recommendation of Boeing common stock changing it from a "hold" to a "sell," it hardly seems likely that Fly would profit significantly from disseminating an item reporting that "Fly has changed its rating of Boeing from a hold to a sell." It is not the identity of Fly and its reputation as a financial analyst that carries the authority and weight sufficient to affect the market. It is Fly's accurate attribution of the Recommendation to the creator that gives this news its value.

We do not perceive a meaningful difference between (a) Fly's taking material that a Firm has created (not "acquired") as the result of organization and the expenditure of labor, skill, and money, and which is (presumably) salable by a Firm for money, and selling it by ascribing the material to its creator Firm and author (not selling it as Fly's own), and (b) what appears to be unexceptional and easily recognized behavior by members of the traditional news media — to report on, say, winners of Tony Awards or, indeed, scores of NBA games with proper attribution of the material to its creator. INS did not purport to address either.

It is also noteworthy, if not determinative, that INS referred to INS's tortious behavior as "amount[ing] to an unauthorized interference with the normal operation of complainant's legitimate business precisely at the point where the profit is to be reaped, in order to divert a material portion of the profit from those who have earned it to those who have not . . . ." Id. at 240 (emphases added). As we have seen, the point at which the Firms principally reap their profit is upon the execution of sales or purchases of securities. It is at least arguable that Fly's interference with the "normal operation" of the Firms' business is indeed at a "point" where the Firms' profits are reaped. But it is not at all clear that that profit is being in any substantial sense "diverted" to Fly by its publication of Recommendations news. The lost commissions are, we would think, diverted to whatever broker happens to execute a trade placed by the recipient of news of the Recommendation from Fly.

To be sure, as the district court pointed out, "Fly [has made efforts], which have met with some success, to link its subscribers to discount brokerage services." Fly I, 700 F. Supp.2d at 340 (emphasis added). The court viewed these steps as "reflect[ing] the final stage in [Fly's] direct competition with the Firms by leveraging its access to their Recommendations and driving away their commission revenue[s]." Fly I, 700 F. Supp.2d at 340.

But we see nothing in the district court's opinion or in the record to indicate that the so-called "final stage" has in fact matured to a point where a significant portion of the diversion of profits to which the Firms object is lost to brokers in league with Fly or its competitors. Firm clients are, moreover, free to employ their authorized knowledge of a Recommendation to make a trade with a discount broker for a smaller fee. And, as we understand the record, the Firms channel fees to their brokerage operations using a good deal more than their Recommendations alone. A non-public Firm report, quite apart from the attached Recommendation — by virtue of the otherwise non-public information the report contains, including general news about the state of the markets, securities, and economic conditions — seems likely to play a substantial part in the Firms' ability to obtain trading business through their research efforts. It is difficult on this record for us to characterize Fly's publication of Recommendations as an unauthorized interference with the normal operation of Firms' legitimate business precisely at the point where the profit is to be reaped which, directly or indirectly, diverts a material portion of the Firms' profits from the Firms to Fly and others engaged in similar practices. See INS, 248 U.S. at 240.

We do not mean to be parsing the language of INS as though it were a statement of law the applicability of which determines the outcome of this appeal. As we have explained, the law that INS itself established was overruled many years ago. But in talking about a " 'hot-news' INS-like claim," as we did in NBA, 105 F.3d at 845, or "the INS tort," as the district court did in this case, Fly I, 700 F. Supp. 2d at 336, we are mindful that the INS Court's concern was tightly focused on the practices of the parties to the suit before it: news, data, and the like, gathered and disseminated by one organization as a significant part of its business, taken by another entity and published as the latter's own in competition with the former. The language chosen by the INS Court seems to us to make clear the substantial distance between that case and this one.

Here, like the defendants in NBA and unlike the defendant in INS, Fly "[has its] own network and assemble[s] and transmit[s] data [it]sel[f]." NBA, 105 F.3d at 854. In NBA, Motorola and STATS employees watched basketball games, compiled the statistics, scores, and other information from the games, and sold the resulting package of data to their subscribers. We could perceive no non-preempted "hot news" tort. Here, analogous to the defendant's in NBA, Fly's employees are engaged in the financial-industry equivalent of observing and summarizing facts about basketball games and selling those packaged facts to consumers; it is simply the content of the facts at issue that is different.

And, according to our decision in NBA: "An indispensable element of a[non-preempted] INS 'hot-news' claim is free-riding by a defendant on a plaintiff's product, enabling the defendant to produce a directly competitive product for less money because it has lower costs." See id. In NBA, we concluded that the defendant's Sports Trax service was not such a product, in part because it was "bearing [its] own costs of collecting factual information on NBA games." Id. In this case, as the district court found, approximately half of Fly's twenty-eight employees are involved on the collection of the Firms' Recommendations and production of the newsfeed on which summaries of the Recommendations are posted. Fly I, 700 F. Supp.2d at 325. Fly is reporting financial news — factual information on Firm Recommendations — through a substantial organizational effort. Therefore, Fly's service — which collects, summarizes, and disseminates the news of the Firms' Recommendations — is not the "INS-like" product that could support a non-preempted cause of action for misappropriation.

By way of comparison, we might, as the NBA Court did, see id., 105 F.3d at 854, speculate about a product a Firm might produce which might indeed give rise to an non-preempted "hot-news" misappropriation claim. If a Firm were to collect and disseminate to some portion of the public facts about securities recommendations in the brokerage industry (including, perhaps, such facts it generated itself — its own Recommendations), and were Fly to copy the facts contained in the Firm's hypothetical service, it might be liable to the Firm on a "hot-news" misappropriation theory. That would appear to be an INS-type claim and might survive preemption.40 See also, e.g., All Headline News Corp., 608 F. Supp. 2d at 454 (suggesting, in a case presenting facts more closely analogous to INS, that the plaintiff may have had a non-preempted "hot news" cause of action). See generally Complaint (Dkt. No. 1), AP v. All Headline News Corp., No. 08-cv-323 (S.D.N.Y. Jan. 14, 2008). But the Firms have no such product and make no such claim. On the facts of this case, they do not have an "INS-like" non-preempted "hot news" misappropriation cause of action against Fly.

C. Judge Raggi's Concurrence

Judge Raggi would reach the same outcome as do we, but "would apply the NBA test to this case and reverse on the ground that the Firms failed to satisfy its direct competition requirement for a non-preempted claim." Post, at [12]. We express no opinion as to whether there is or was direct competition between the Firms and Fly with regard to the Recommendations because we are bound by the holding of NBA. On the facts of that case, the plaintiff's cause of action was preempted by the copyright law because the defendants did not "free ride" on the plaintiff's work product. The NBA panel did not decide the case before it on the basis of the presence or absence of direct competition, which it thought to be an element of the preemption inquiry but did not depend upon in its analysis. We think that the NBA panel's decision that the absence of "free riding" was fatal to the plaintiff's claim in that case is binding upon us on the facts presented here. In other words, even were we to conclude, hypothetically and contrary to Judge Raggi's views, that there was indeed direct competition between the Firms and Fly with respect to the Recommendations, we would nonetheless be bound to reverse the judgment of the district court based on our reading of NBA. The presence or absence of direct competition is thus not determinative and is therefore a matter we are not called upon to decide here.

CONCLUSION

We conclude that in this case, a Firm's ability to make news — by issuing a Recommendation that is likely to affect the market price of a security — does not give rise to a right for it to control who breaks that news and how. We therefore reverse the judgment of the district court to that extent and remand with instructions to dismiss the Firms' misappropriation claim.

## NOTES AND QUESTIONS:

1. In *Synercom Technology, Inc. v. University Computing Co*, 474 F.Supp. 37, 39 (N.D.Tex.1979), Judge Higginbotham sets forth the following a test for the tort of misappropriation that does not necessarily exclude trade secrets:

> (i) the creation of plaintiff's product through extensive time, labor, skill and money, (ii) the defendant's use of that product in competition with the plaintiff, thereby gaining a special advantage in that competition (i.e., a 'free ride') because defendant is burdened with little or none of the expense incurred by the plaintiff, and (iii) commercial damage to the plaintiff.

(Citation omitted.)

Does the way the Supreme Court approached misappropriation in *International News Service v. Associated Press*, 248 U.S. 215 (1918) ("*INS*"), preclude the application of the doctrine of misappropriation to trade secrets? What exactly was the Supreme Court protecting in *INS*? Was it the "quasi property" in the fresh news or the rights of the plaintiff against the defendant's unfair competition? Compare the reasoning in Justice Holmes' dissent in *INS* with his decision in *Masland*, discussed above in Chapter 2, for whether there was a property right that should be protected, or a prohibition of improper acts by a defendant.

2. The majority in *INS* directed the discussion away from the public interest by noting that "[t]he fault in the [defendant's] reasoning lies in applying as a test the right of the complainant as against the public, instead of considering the rights of complainant and defendant, competitors in business, as between themselves." *Compare* the Court's reasoning that the defendant took "material that has been acquired by the complainant as the result of organization and the expenditure of labor, skill, and money, and which is salable by complainant for money, and that defendant in appropriating it and selling it as its own is endeavoring to reap where it has not sown," (248 U.S. at 239) *with* the federal statute against unfair competition that was passed several years ago. *See* 15 U.S.C. § 1125(a).

3. *Synercom Technology* presents a detailed discussion of cases that define the limits of the patent and copyright laws. How can the input formulas in *Synercom*, which are *not* protectable under the copyright laws, provide the basis for the court's holding that since such formulas are "not unattended" by the copyright laws, application of state law to find misappropriation of the formulas is preempted? In other words, how can something that is not copyrightable be attended by copyright laws?

4. What are the outer limits of protection under the misappropriation doctrine in modern jurisprudence? Are you convinced that the court in *Barclays Capital, Inc. v. Theflyonthewall.com, Inc.*, 650 F.3d 876 (2d Cir.2011), was correct in analogizing the facts to those in *NBA*?

5. When different courts attempt to apply the misappropriation doctrine, the outcomes can be inconsistent. *Compare U.S. Golf Ass'n v. St. Andrew Systems, DataMax, Inc.*, 749 F.2d 1028 (3d Cir.1984) with *U.S. Golf Ass'n v. Arroyo Software Corp.*, 49 U.S.P.Q.2d 1979 (Cal.Ct.App.1999). The *St. Andrews* court found that, since the maker of a handicapping computer that used the USGA formula was not a direct competitor of the USGA, there was no misappropriation. Under essentially the same facts, the *Arroyo* court found liability where the applicable state law did not require direct competition in order to find liability. Should such economically important decisions turn on peculiarities in state law? Should there be a federal law against misappropriation?

6. Every once in a while a case comes along that causes a severe scratching of the head. The court in *U.S. Sporting Products, Inc. v. Johnny Stewart Game Calls, Inc.*, 865 S.W.2d 214 (Tex.App.1993) affirmed the trial court's finding of misappropriation under Texas law for copying taped animal and bird sounds and selling them in competition with the plaintiff. Whether there was preemption under the copyright laws was not discussed.

# Chapter 3

# ENFORCEMENT OF RIGHTS

This Chapter will explore various types of civil actions that are available under Federal Law, which include § 43(a) of the Lanham Act, 15 U.S.C. § 1125 (a), and § 337 of the Tariff Act of 1930, 19 U.S.C. § 1337; and civil remedies in several criminal statutes, such as the Racketeer Influenced & Corrupt Organization Act, 18 U.S.C. §§ 1961-1963 (i.e., RICO), and the Computer Fraud and Abuse Act, 18 U.S.C. § 1030. This chapter also deals with litigation issues such as traditional affirmative defenses, including laches and statutes of limitations, which are oftentimes raised in state and federal trade secret cases, and the potential for indemnification by a liability insurance carrier for having to defend against a trade secret misappropriation claim.

As discussed above, more than 40 states have adopted a version of the Uniform Trade Secrets Act, and the others have recognized common law actions for enforcing trade secret rights, such as for breach of contract, breach of a fiduciary duty, unjust enrichment, trade secret misappropriation, tortious interference with contract, etc. These types of enforcement actions are illustrated in many of the cases in previous chapters and will not be repeated here.

## A. FEDERAL CAUSE OF ACTION UNDER LANHAM ACT

### REPAP ENTERPRISES INC. v. KAMYR INC.

27 U.S.P.Q.2d 1685 (E.D. Pa. 1993)

Kamyr has violated Section 43(a) of the Lanham Act, 15 United States Code, Section 1125(a). Section 43(a) proscribes not only acts that would technically qualify as trademark infringement, but also unfair competitive practices involving actual or potential deception.

The credible evidence demonstrates that Kamyr has engaged in such practices. The credible evidence unquestionably establishes that Defendant Kamyr has made false or misleading statements as to the creation or ownership of intellectual property. That such statements have a tendency to deceive or create confusion in a substantial portion of the intended audience. That the deception or confusion is material, that is, it's likely to influence investment or purchasing decisions. That the misrepresentations affect or likely will affect commerce and that there is injury or a likelihood of injury to plaintiff in terms of its loss of clearly understood title to its own intellectual property. And a resulting loss of the value thereof, including loss of goodwill.

With respect to the actual or likely effect on commerce, I find and conclude that this requirement has been met because Kamyr's applications have had the effect of creating a cloud, thereby discouraging investments by American companies in the commercialization of the Alcell process.

The filing of the applications themselves were activities in commerce and the potential injury to the value of Repap's intellectual property, because of Kamyr's patent applications, amounts to an effect upon commerce. Accordingly, Repap has proved its claim under Section 43(a) of the Lanham Act.

Kamyr had taken trade secrets of Repap, concerning the Alcell process and technology and incorporated those trade secrets into its United States patent application, its European patent application and the other patent applications described above.

Kamyr has thus represented to the world that Repap's trade secrets originated with Kamyr. This is a false and misleading description and representation of fact. Under the law, an entity which obtains trade secrets in confidence, may not use such secrets to the prejudice of the giver as here occurred.

Repap is likely to be damaged. The South African patent has already issued and the patent applications, except for the United States patent applications, either have been or will be published for the world to see within some 18 months after filing. Once patent applications owned by Kamyr are published, as occurs automatically, in virtually all countries of the world except the United States or any patent is issued to Kamyr in the United States or elsewhere, the world considers the claims contained therein to be the exclusive property of Kamyr.

Thus the rights of Repap to the information disclosed and the claims in the Kamyr patent concerning Repap's trade secrets, is and will continue to be under a cloud. And is causing and will continue to cause serious and irreparable harm to Repap's business, absent relief by this Court.

. . .

## NOTES AND QUESTIONS:

1. What facts in *Repap Enterprises Inc. v. Kamyr Inc.*, 27 U.S.P.Q.2d 1685 (E.D. Pa. 1993), provided the plaintiff with a basis for a cause of action under § 43(a) of the Lanham Act, 15 U.S.C. § 1125(a), which provides:

> Any person who, on or in connection with any goods or services, or any container for goods, uses in commerce any . . . false designation of origin, false or misleading description of fact or misleading representation of fact, which, (A) is likely to cause confusion, or to cause mistake, or to deceive as to the affiliation, connection, or association of such person with another person, or as to the origin, sponsorship, or approval of his or her goods, services, or commercial activities by another person, or (B) in commercial advertising or promotion, misrepresents the nature, characteristics, qualities, or geographic origin of his or her or another person's goods, services, or commercial activities, shall be liable in a civil action by any person who believes that he or she is or is likely to be damaged by such act.

What are the critical elements of a trade secret action that can be brought under § 43(a)?

2. Rather than bringing suit in federal court under diversity jurisdiction or in state court under UTSA, breach of contract, or as a tort action, would the availability of treble damages and the award of attorney's fees make filing suit under the Lanham Act a more attractive alternative?

## B. TARIFF ACT ACTION

### TIANRUI GROUP CO. v. INTERNATIONAL TRADE COMMISSION

100 U.S.P.Q.2d 1401 (Fed. Cir. 2011)

BRYSON, J. CIRCUIT JUDGE

This appeal arises from a determination by the International Trade Commission that the importation of certain cast steel railway wheels violated section 337 of the Tariff Act of 1930, 19 U.S.C. § 1337. The Commission found that the wheels were manufactured using a process that was developed in the United States, protected under domestic trade secret law, and misappropriated abroad. We are asked to decide whether the Commission's statutory authority over "[u]nfair methods of competition and unfair acts in the importation of articles . . . into the United States," as provided by section 337(a)(1)(A), allows the Commission to look to conduct occurring in China in the course of a trade secret misappropriation investigation. We conclude that the Commission has authority to investigate and grant relief based in part on extraterritorial conduct insofar as it is necessary to protect domestic industries from injuries arising out of unfair competition in the domestic marketplace.

We are also asked to decide whether the Commission erred by finding that the imported wheels would injure a domestic industry when no domestic manufacturer is currently practicing the protected process. In light of the evidence before the Commission regarding the marketplace for cast steel railway wheels, we affirm the Commission's determination that the wheel imports threaten to destroy or substantially injure an industry in the United States, in violation of section 337.

Amsted Industries Inc. is a domestic manufacturer of cast steel railway wheels. It owns two secret processes for manufacturing such wheels, the "ABC process" and the "Griffin process." Amsted previously practiced the ABC process at its foundry in Calera, Alabama, but it no longer uses that process in the United States. Instead, Amsted uses the Griffin process at three of its domestic foundries. Amsted has licensed the ABC process to several firms with foundries in China.

TianRui Group Company Limited and TianRui Group Foundry Company Limited (collectively, "TianRui") manufacture cast steel railway wheels in China. In 2005, TianRui sought to license Amsted's wheel manufacturing technology, but the parties could not agree on the terms of a license. After the failed negotiations, TianRui hired nine employees away from one of Amsted's Chinese licensees, Datong

ABC Castings Company Limited. Some of those employees had been trained in the ABC process at the Calera plant in Alabama, and others had received training in that process at the Datong foundry in China.

Datong had previously notified those employees through a written employee code of conduct that information pertaining to the ABC process was proprietary and confidential. Each employee had been advised that he had a duty not to disclose confidential information. Eight of the nine employees had also signed confidentiality agreements before leaving Datong to begin working for TianRui. In the proceedings brought by Amsted before the International Trade Commission, Amsted alleged that the former Datong employees disclosed information and documents to TianRui that revealed the details of the ABC process and thereby misappropriated Amsted's trade secrets. TianRui partnered with Standard Car Truck Company, Inc., ("SCT") to form the joint venture Barber TianRui Railway Supply, LLC. SCT and Barber have marketed TianRui wheels to United States customers and have imported TianRui wheels into the United States. Other than Amsted, SCT and Barber are the only companies selling or attempting to sell cast steel railway wheels in the United States.

Amsted filed a complaint with the Commission alleging a violation of section 337 based on TianRui's misappropriation of trade secrets. Section 337(a)(1)(A) prohibits "[u]nfair methods of competition and unfair acts in the importation of articles . . . into the United States, . . . the threat or effect of which is . . . to destroy or substantially injure an industry in the United States."

TianRui moved to terminate the proceedings on the ground that the alleged misappropriation occurred in China and that Congress did not intend for section 337 to be applied extraterritorially. An administrative law judge at the Commission denied that motion based on his view that section 337 focuses not on where the misappropriation occurs but rather on the nexus between the imported articles and the unfair methods of competition. The administrative law judge also rejected TianRui's argument that Chinese courts would provide a better forum for Amsted's complaint.

At the merits stage, the administrative law judge analyzed the alleged misappropriation under Illinois trade secret law. After noting that the Commission has looked to general principles of tort or commercial law in past investigations involving trade secret misappropriation, the administrative law judge cited this court's statement in *Leggett & Platt, Inc. v. Hickory Springs Manufacturing Co.* [citation omitted], that "[t]rade secret misappropriation is a matter of state law," as the basis for applying state law to this section 337 investigation. He applied Illinois law because Amsted, SCT, and Barber all have their principal place of business in Illinois. He noted, however, that "the Illinois law relating to trade secrets does not differ substantially from the law applied in previous Commission trade secret investigations," and he then applied general principles of trade secret law, including the six factors defining a trade secret set forth in the comments to section 757 of the Restatement (First) of Torts.

Following a 10-day evidentiary hearing, the administrative law judge found that TianRui had misappropriated 128 trade secrets relating to the ABC process from Datong. That conclusion was based on evidence that included an admission by

TianRui's expert that TianRui's foundry used the asserted trade secrets; his only contention was that the trade secrets were not actually secret. In addition, the administrative law judge compared TianRui's manufacturing specifications with secret Datong documents outlining the ABC process and found them essentially identical. In fact, some of the TianRui specifications contained the same typographical errors that were found in the Datong documents. The administrative law judge also relied on similarities in foundry layout between the Datong and TianRui plants. The administrative law judge summarized the evidence as to the appropriation of the trade secrets by saying that "there is overwhelming direct and circumstantial evidence that TianRui obtained its manufacturing process for cast steel railway wheel[s] through the misappropriation of [Amsted's] ABC Trade Secrets."

Besides contesting the Commission's authority to apply section 337 extraterritorially, TianRui contended that Amsted did not satisfy the domestic industry requirement of section 337 based on the fact that Amsted no longer practiced the ABC process in the United States. Because none of Amsted's domestic operations used the ABC process, TianRui argued that there was no "domestic industry" that could be injured by the misappropriation of trade secrets relating to that process.

The administrative law judge rejected that argument, holding that it was not essential that the domestic industry use the proprietary process, as long as the misappropriation of that process caused injury to the complainant's domestic industry. Applying that standard, the administrative law judge concluded that Amsted's domestic industry would be substantially injured by the importation of TianRui wheels.

The Commission decided not to review the administrative law judge's initial determination and issued a limited exclusion order. TianRui then appealed to this court.

The main issue in this case is whether section 337 authorizes the Commission to apply domestic trade secret law to conduct that occurs in part in a foreign country.

Section 337 authorizes the Commission to exclude articles from entry into the United States when it has found "[u]nfair methods of competition [or] unfair acts in the importation of [those] articles." 19 U.S.C. § 1337(a)(1)(A). The Commission has long interpreted section 337 to apply to trade secret misappropriation. [Citations omitted.] TianRui does not challenge that interpretation. Nor does it dispute the Commission's factual finding that proprietary information belonging to Amsted was disclosed to TianRui in breach of obligations of confidentiality imposed on the former Datong employees or the finding that the information was used in manufacturing the imported railway wheels. Instead, TianRui focuses on the fact that the disclosure of the trade secret information occurred in China. According to TianRui, section 337 cannot apply to extraterritorial conduct and therefore does not reach trade secret misappropriation that occurs outside the United States.

Amsted argues that the Commission did not apply section 337 extraterritorially, because trade secrets were misappropriated in the United States as a legal matter when railway wheels made by exploiting those trade secrets were imported into the United States and sold to customers or disclosed to the Association of American Railroads for certification purposes. Amsted argues that Illinois law defines trade secret misappropriation very broadly and that under Illinois law any unauthorized "use" of an article embodying a trade secret constitutes misappropriation. That definition of misappropriation, according to Amsted, is broad enough to encompass any use of articles produced by the misappropriated process, not simply the acts that constitute a direct breach of the duty of confidentiality. Amsted concludes that the administrative law judge therefore had sufficient evidence to find trade secret misappropriation based on TianRui's importation of the wheels and its disclosure of those wheels for certification purposes. Like Amsted, the Commission argues that it applied section 337 based on TianRui's conduct in the United States and did not apply the statute extraterritorially to conduct occurring in China. In the alternative, the Commission contends that section 337 applies to imported articles produced with misappropriated trade secrets, even if the disclosure of the proprietary information occurred outside the United States.

At the outset, we reject Amsted's argument that Illinois trade secret law governs the section 337 inquiry in this case. The question of what law applies in a section 337 proceeding involving trade secrets is a matter of first impression for this court. We hold that a single federal standard, rather than the law of a particular state, should determine what constitutes a misappropriation of trade secrets sufficient to establish an "unfair method of competition" under section 337.

The administrative law judge acknowledged that in previous section 337 proceedings involving trade secret misappropriation, the Commission has applied general principles of trade secret law, not the law of any particular state. The administrative judge, however, felt bound to apply state law because of a statement by this court that issues of trade secret misappropriation are ordinarily matters of state law. [Citation omitted.] That statement is, of course, true as a general matter and was true of the trade secret issue in the *Leggett & Platt* case, which addressed state law trade secret claims that were before this court under supplemental jurisdiction. But where the question is whether particular conduct constitutes "unfair methods of competition" and "unfair acts" in importation, in violation of section 337, the issue is one of federal law and should be decided under a uniform federal standard, rather than by reference to a particular state's tort law.

The question under section 337 is not whether the policy choices of a particular state's legislature or those reflected in a particular state's common law rules should be vindicated, but whether goods imported from abroad should be excluded because of a violation of the congressional policy of protecting domestic industries from unfair competition, which is a distinctly federal concern as to which Congress has created a federal remedy. In light of the fact that section 337 deals with international commerce, a field of special federal concern, the case for applying a federal rule of decision is particularly strong. In fact, the nonstatutory unfair competition provision of section 337 falls comfortably into both of the categories that have been described as calling for the application of federal common law — instances in which "a federal rule of decision is 'necessary to protect uniquely federal interests,' . . . and those in which Congress has given the courts the power to develop substantive law." [Citations omitted.]

Fortunately, trade secret law varies little from state to state and is generally governed by widely recognized authorities such as the Restatement of Unfair

Competition and the Uniform Trade Secrets Act. Moreover, the federal criminal statute governing theft of trade secrets bases its definition of trade secrets on the Uniform Trade Secrets Act, so there is no indication of congressional intent to depart from the general law in that regard. [Citation omitted.] In any event, there is no dispute in this case pertaining to the substantive law of trade secrets. The administrative law judge's findings establish that TianRui obtained access to Amsted's confidential information through former Datong employees, who were subject to duties of confidentiality imposed by the Datong code of employee conduct, and that TianRui exploited that information in producing the subject goods. TianRui does not take issue with those findings, which are sufficient to establish the elements of trade secret misappropriation under either Illinois law or the generally understood law of trade secrets, as reflected in the Restatement, the Uniform Trade Secrets Act, and previous Commission decisions under section 337. Therefore, the choice of law issue, although it could be important in other cases, does not affect the outcome of this case.

In this case, TianRui argues that section 337 is inapplicable because Amsted's confidential information was disclosed in China. The legal issue for us to decide is thus whether section 337 applies to imported goods produced through the exploitation of trade secrets in which the act of misappropriation occurs abroad.[1] To answer that question, we must review the principles that apply to federal statutes that create causes of action based in part on conduct that occurs overseas.

It is a "longstanding principle of American law 'that legislation of Congress, unless a contrary intent appears, is meant to apply only within the territorial jurisdiction of the United States.' " [Citation omitted.] That presumption expresses a canon of construction that is rooted in the "commonsense notion that Congress generally legislates with domestic concerns in mind." [Citation omitted.] The canon "serves to protect against unintended clashes between our laws and those of other nations which could result in international discord," [citation omitted], and "preserv[es] a stable background against which Congress can legislate with predictable effects." [Citation omitted.] The presumption is not an end in itself, but functions as a tool for ascertaining congressional intent.

The presumption against extraterritoriality does not govern this case, for three reasons. First, section 337 is expressly directed at unfair methods of competition and unfair acts "in the importation of articles" into the United States. As such, "this is surely not a statute in which Congress had only 'domestic concerns in mind.' " [Citation omitted.] The focus of section 337 is on an inherently international transaction — importation. In that respect, section 337 is analogous to immigration statutes that bar the admission of an alien who has engaged in particular conduct or who makes false statements in connection with his entry into this country. [Citation omitted.] In such cases, the focus is not on punishing the conduct or the false statements, but on preventing the admission of the alien, so it is reasonable to assume that Congress was aware, and intended, that the statute would apply to conduct (or statements) that may have occurred abroad. [Citations omitted.]

Second, in this case the Commission has not applied section 337 to sanction purely extraterritorial conduct; the foreign "unfair" activity at issue in this case is relevant only to the extent that it results in the importation of goods into this country causing domestic injury. In light of the statute's focus on the act of importation and the resulting domestic injury, the Commission's order does not purport to regulate purely foreign conduct. [Citation omitted.] Because foreign conduct is used only to establish an element of a claim alleging a domestic injury and seeking a wholly domestic remedy, the presumption against extraterritorial application does not apply. [Citations omitted.]

The dissent disregards the domestic elements of the cause of action under section 337 and characterizes this case as involving "conduct which *entirely* occurs in a foreign country." That characterization accurately describes most of the events constituting the misappropriation, but the determination of misappropriation was merely a predicate to the charge that TianRui committed unfair acts in importing its wheels into the United States. In other words, the Commission's interpretation of section 337 does not, as the dissent contends, give it the authority to "police Chinese business practices Under the dissent's construction of section 337, the importation of goods produced as a result of trade secret misappropriation would be immune from scrutiny if the act of misappropriation occurred overseas. That is, as long as the misappropriating party was careful to ensure that the actual act of conveying the trade secret occurred outside the United States, the Commission would be powerless to provide a remedy even if the trade secret were used to produce products that were subsequently imported into the United States to the detriment of the trade secret owner. We think it highly unlikely that Congress, which clearly intended to create a remedy for the importation of goods resulting from unfair methods of competition, would have intended to create such a conspicuous loophole for misappropriators

Third, the legislative history of section 337 supports the Commission's interpretation of the statute as permitting the Commission to consider conduct that occurs abroad. Congress first enacted a prohibition against "unfair methods of competition" in the Federal Trade Commission Act, Pub. L. No. 63-203, § 5, 38 Stat. 717, 719 (1914), codified as amended at 15 U.S.C. § 45. Congress chose that phrase because it was "broader and more flexible" than the traditional phrase "unfair competition," which had acquired a narrow meaning in its common law usages. [Citation omitted.]

Congress intended a similarly broad and flexible meaning when it used the same language to prohibit "unfair methods of competition" in importation. That provision was added to the law in the Tariff Act of 1922, Pub. L. No. 67-318, § 316(a), 42 Stat. 858, 943, pursuant to a recommendation of the Tariff Commission (the former name of the International Trade Commission) in a 1919 report. [Citation omitted.] In its report, the Commission identified several deficiencies in U.S. trade laws, including the absence of any remedy for unfair competition other than dumping [citation omitted], and the lack of any adequate "governmental machinery" for investigating allegations of dumping, "one element of which must be found abroad". [Citation omitted.] In a subsequent annual report, issued while the bill that was to become the 1922 Tariff Act was pending before Congress, the Commission renewed the recommendations from the 1919 report relating to unfair competition. [Citation omitted.]

In section 316 of the Tariff Act of 1922, Congress responded to the Commission's recommendation by declaring "unfair methods of competition and unfair acts in the importation of articles into the United States" to be unlawful. That Act authorized the Tariff Commission to investigate allegations of such conduct in accordance with rules that the Commission would promulgate, and it gave the President the authority to impose additional duties or to exclude articles that the Commission found to be in violation of that provision. The Senate report on the 1922 Act explained that "[t]he provision relating to unfair methods of competition in the importation of goods is broad enough to prevent every type and form of unfair practice and is, therefore, a more adequate protection to American industry than any antidumping statute the country has ever had." [Citation omitted.]

After the enactment of the Tariff Act of 1922, the Commission advised Congress that the new provisions "make it possible for the President to prevent unfair practices, even when engaged in by individuals residing outside the jurisdiction of the United States." [Citation omitted.] When Congress subsequently enacted the Tariff Act of 1930, section 316 of the 1922 Act became section 337 of the new Act with some modifications to the provisions regarding remedies and judicial review. Congress did not, however, disagree with the Commission's characterization of the prohibition on "unfair methods of competition" in the importation of articles into the United States, even though opponents criticized the Commission's broad authority to investigate acts of unfair competition with respect to goods imported into this country. [Citation omitted.] In light of the legislative background, and in particular in view of the close working relationship between the Commission and the relevant congressional committees, it is fair to conclude that Congress contemplated that, in exercising its new authority over unfair competition, the Commission would consider conduct abroad in determining whether imports that were the products of, or otherwise related to, that conduct were unfairly competing in the domestic market.

The Commission's interpretation of section 337 as reaching acts of trade secret misappropriation that occur abroad is consistent with the position it has taken regarding overseas acts of unfair competition since the enactment of section 337's predecessor. [Citations omitted.] Thus, even if we were to conclude that section 337 is ambiguous with respect to its application to trade secret misappropriation occurring abroad, we would uphold the Commission's interpretation of the scope of the statute. As it is, we conclude that the Commission's longstanding interpretation is consistent with the purpose and the legislative background of the statute, and we therefore hold that it was proper for the Commission to find a section 337 violation based in part on acts of trade secret misappropriation occurring overseas.

TianRui argues that the Commission should not be allowed to apply domestic trade secret law to conduct occurring in China because doing so would cause improper interference with Chinese law. We disagree. In the first place, as we have noted, the Commission's exercise of authority is limited to goods imported into this country, and thus the Commission has no authority to regulate conduct that is purely extraterritorial. The Commission does not purport to enforce principles of trade secret law in other countries generally, but only as that conduct affects the U.S. market. That is, the Commission's investigations, findings, and remedies affect foreign conduct only insofar as that conduct relates to the importation of articles into the United States. The Commission's activities have not hindered TianRui's ability to sell its wheels in China or any other country.

Second, TianRui has failed to identify a conflict between the principles of misappropriation that the Commission applied and Chinese trade secret law. Indeed, in its forum non conveniens motion TianRui argued that Chinese trade secret law would provide a "more than adequate" remedy for any alleged misappropriation. In addition, China has acceded to the Agreement on Trade-Related Aspects of Intellectual Property Rights ("TRIPS"), Apr. 15, 1994, Marrakesh Agreement Establishing the World Trade Organization, Annex 1C. We cannot discern any relevant difference between the misappropriation requirements of TRIPS article 39 and the principles of trade secret law applied by the administrative law judge in this case. We therefore detect no conflict between the Commission's actions and Chinese law that would counsel denying relief based on extraterritorial acts of trade secret misappropriation relating to the importation of goods affecting a domestic industry.

Finally, even apart from the acts of importation, the conduct at issue in this case is not the result of the imposition of legal duties created by American law on persons for whom there was no basis to impose such duties. The former Datong employees had a duty not to disclose Amsted's trade secrets arising from express provisions in the Datong employee code and, in the case of most of the employees, from confidentiality agreements that they signed during their employment with Datong.[7] Thus, the question in this case is whether the disclosure of protected information in breach of that duty is beyond the reach of section 337 simply because the breach itself took place outside the United States. To answer that question in the affirmative would invite evasion of section 337 and significantly undermine the effectiveness of the congressionally designed remedy.

Our conclusion that section 337 authorized the Commission's actions in this case is not inconsistent with court decisions that have accorded a narrow construction to the extraterritorial application of U.S. patent law, in particular *Microsoft Corp. v. AT&T Corp.* [citation omitted]; *Amgen, Inc. v. U.S. International Trade Commission* [citation omitted]; and *In re Amtorg Trading Corp.* [Citation omitted.]. Those decisions focused on statutory provisions specific to patent law, especially the territorial limitations in the patent-granting clause. The import of those decisions is that the Commission's broad and flexible authority to exclude from entry articles produced using "unfair methods of competition" cannot be used to circumvent express congressional limitations on the scope of substantive U.S. patent law. Because there is no parallel federal civil statute regulating trade secret protection, there is no statutory basis for limiting the Commission's flexible authority under section 337(a)(1)(A)with respect to trade secret misappropriation.

In *Amtorg*, our predecessor court considered whether the Commission's authority to investigate "[u]nfair methods of competition and unfair acts in the importation of articles into the United States" authorized the Commission to enjoin imports of products made by a patented process. It did not, the court concluded, because section 337 did not enlarge the substantive scope of patent law. At the time, the protections of a United States patent were expressly limited to United States territories. [Citation omitted.] And the use or sale of a product made by a patented process did not constitute infringement of the process patent. [Citation omitted.] The court reasoned that the sale of products made abroad by a patented process must therefore be lawful unless "it was the purpose of Congress in enacting section

337 . . . to broaden the field of substantive patent rights, and create rights in process patents extending far beyond any point to which the courts have heretofore gone in construing the patent statutes." [Citation omitted.] After reviewing the legislative history, the court concluded that Congress did not intend to expand the scope of substantive patent law when it enacted section 337.

The court's analysis in *Amtorg* primarily addressed the scope of patent law and only secondarily considered the Commission's authority over "unfair methods of competition." To the extent *Amtorg* construed the scope of the Commission's jurisdiction over unfair methods of competition, Congress has subsequently rejected that construction in response to criticism by the Tariff Commission. In its next annual report to Congress after *Amtorg* was decided, the Commission criticized the decision for holding that "the importation for use or sale of products made abroad by a process patented in the United States was not an unfair method of competition." [Citation omitted.] In response to the Commission's report, Congress amended the law to declare that the importation of products made by a process patented in the United States "shall have the same status for the purposes of section [337]" as the importation of a patented product. [Citations omitted.] *Amtorg* thus has no effect on the scope of the Commission's authority to regulate trade secret misappropriation relating to the production of goods imported into this country.

*Amgen* and *Microsoft* are inapposite for similar reasons. In *Amgen*, the complainant asserted a product patent covering recombinant DNA and host cells against a different imported product, rEPO. [Citation omitted.]. Because the imported rEPO was produced abroad using the patented recombinant DNA and host cells, the complainant argued that the Commission had jurisdiction to bar its importation under 19 U.S.C. § 1337(a)(1)(B)(ii), the successor to section 1337a. We rejected that argument because section 1337(a)(1)(B)(ii) is limited to articles made abroad by a process patented in the United States, and the asserted patent covered products instead of processes. Because that decision did not address the Commission's section 337(a)(1)(A) jurisdiction over unfair practices, it is not relevant to the question in this case.

In *Microsoft*, the Supreme Court addressed the scope of an exception to "the general rule under United States patent law that no infringement occurs when a patented product is made and sold in another country." [Citation omitted.] That exception, 35 U.S.C. § 271(f), allows infringement to be found when the "components" of a patented invention are supplied from the United States and combined abroad. The Court narrowly construed the term "component" to exclude the "intangible code" of an operating system because, inter alia, the presumption against extraterritorial application of United States law "applies with particular force in patent law." [Citation omitted.] Consequently, the Court held, the substantive patent right did not reach the sale of computers in foreign countries.

By contrast, as we have noted, the statutory prohibition on "unfair methods of competition and unfair acts in the importation of articles . . . into the United States" naturally contemplates that the unfair methods of competition and unfair acts leading to the prohibited importation will include conduct that takes place abroad. Because the statute applies to goods that are presented for importation, it would be a strained reading of the statute to bar the Commission from considering acts of trade secret misappropriation that occur abroad. In cases in which misappropriated trade secrets are used in the manufacture of the imported goods, the misappropriation will frequently occur overseas, where the imported goods are made. To bar the Commission from considering such acts because they occur outside the United States would thus be inconsistent with the congressional purpose of protecting domestic commerce from unfair methods of competition in importation such as trade secret misappropriation.

TianRui's second ground for appeal focuses on the requirement of section 337 that the acts of unfair competition threaten "to destroy or substantially injure an industry in the United States." [Citation omitted.] TianRui contends that in trade secret cases, the domestic industry must practice the misappropriated trade secret in order for the Commission to be authorized to grant relief. Because Amsted has no domestic operations practicing the misappropriated ABC process, TianRui argues that its imported wheels cannot be held to injure or threaten injury to any domestic industry within the meaning of section 337.

Section 337 contains different requirements for statutory intellectual property (such as patents, copyrights, and registered trademarks) than for other, nonstatutory unfair practices in importation (such as trade secret misappropriation). The provisions that apply to statutory intellectual property require that an industry relating to the protected articles exists or is in the process of being established. [Citation omitted.] Such an industry will be deemed to exist if there is significant domestic investment or employment relating to the protected articles. [Citation omitted.] In contrast, the general provision relating to unfair practices is not satisfied by evidence showing only that a domestic industry exists; it requires that the unfair practices threaten to "destroy or substantially injure" a domestic industry. [Citation omitted.] On the other hand, there is no express requirement in the general provision that the domestic industry relate to the intellectual property involved in the investigation. Notwithstanding that textual distinction, TianRui contends that investigations involving intellectual property under the unfair practices provision require the existence of a domestic industry that relates to the asserted intellectual property in the same manner that is required for statutory intellectual property.

In support of its argument, TianRui cites the legislative history of the Omnibus Trade and Competitiveness Act of 1988, Pub. L. No. 100-418, § 1342, 102 Stat. 1107, 1212, which created the separate requirements for statutory intellectual property. Before that Act, section 337 of the Tariff Act of 1930 set forth the same requirements for all unfair practices in import trade, including the injury requirement. [Citation omitted.] The 1988 Act removed the injury requirement for statutory intellectual property and instead simply required evidence that "an industry in the United States, relating to the articles protected by the [statutory intellectual property], exists or is in the process of being established." [Citation omitted.] The Senate report noted that "[a]lthough the injury test has been eliminated for certain intellectual property rights cases, a complainant must still establish that a U.S. industry relating to the articles or intellectual property right concerned 'exists or is in the process of being established.' " [Citation omitted.] According to TianRui, that legislative history demonstrates that Congress removed the injury requirement only for statutory intellectual property, but retained the requirement that a domestic industry exists that relates to the asserted rights for *all* intellectual property, including trade secrets.

We disagree with TianRui's interpretation of the legislative history. Congress recognized that prior to the 1988 Act section 337 did not define "industry." [Citation omitted.] Both the Senate and the House of Representatives agreed that an "industry" would exist for intellectual property investigations if there was significant domestic investment or employment relating to the articles protected by the intellectual property. [Citations omitted.] They disagreed, however, as to whether that definition should apply to common law trademarks and trade secrets. [Citations omitted.] The Senate proposed that the definition apply to common law trademarks and trade secrets, and the language from the Senate report cited by TianRui is consistent with that proposal. But the Senate receded from its proposal after conference, and the new definition of "industry" was limited to statutory intellectual property. Because the Senate's proposal did not become law, we cannot rely on the legislative history discussing that proposal to read a strict definition of "industry" into section 337(a)(1)(A), when the statute itself contains no such definition.

TianRui next contends that its construction is required by the reenactment doctrine. TianRui argues that the Commission had a longstanding interpretation that defined "industry" for trade secret investigations as the portion of "complainant's domestic operations devoted to utilization of the confidential and proprietary technology at issue" in the investigation. [Citation omitted.] Because Congress substantially reenacted the Commission's jurisdiction over unfair practices without disapproving of that interpretation, according to TianRui, Congress effectively adopted the Commission's interpretation.

The Commission disagrees with TianRui's characterization of its prior decisions. The Commission contends that it has applied that definition in some trade secret investigations, but that in other investigations it has relied on a more flexible "realities of the marketplace" test. We have reviewed the investigations cited by the parties and conclude that there was not a consistent interpretation, as TianRui contends. [Citations omitted.] TianRui's argument based on the reenactment doctrine therefore falls with its premise.

In sum, we conclude that the Commission did not err in defining the domestic industry in this case. The parties submitted evidence indicating that the imported TianRui wheels could directly compete with wheels domestically produced by the trade secret owner. That type of competition, the Commission concluded, is sufficiently related to the investigation to constitute an injury to an "industry" within the meaning of section 337(a)(1)(A). We hold that the Commission's conclusion in that regard is based on a proper construction of the statute and that its factual analysis of the effect of TianRui's imports on the domestic industry is supported by substantial evidence.

AFFIRMED

## NOTES AND QUESTIONS:

1. Section 337 actions are primarily used to bar imports of products that infringe U.S. patents. The court in *TianRui* held that the importation of goods in which the misappropriated trade secrets were used violated § 337, even though all the acts of misappropriation occurred in China. A dissent to the *TianRui Group Co. v. International Trade Commission*, 100 U.S.P.Q.2d 1401 (Fed. Cir. 2011), decision argued that the Tariff Act does not extend to the importation of products that used misappropriated trade secrets because there is nothing unfair about the importation of the products, and the unfair act was only the misappropriation, which occurred wholly outside the U.S. How did the majority address this argument? Are you convinced that the majority decision was on solid ground in finding a § 337 violation based on the act of importation?

2. In countries such as China where trade secret law is still developing, it is extremely difficult to enforce trade secret rights. Some lawyers have suggested that agreements with Chinese companies should be subject to Hong Kong law, which still retains the English-based law system that was in place before England returned Hong Kong to China. The *TianRui* decision provides a powerful tool for at least preventing imports from China, which use misappropriated trade secrets, provided that the critical factual evidence can be developed.

3. Note that the court did not apply Illinois trade secret law, but federal law, which it found was a combination of the principles described in RESTATEMENT (THIRD) UNFAIR COMPETITION and the UTSA. Does this decision create a new federal trade secret law? Recall that the Supreme Court in *Ruckelshaus*, discussed above in Chapt. 1(C), applied Missouri law in determining whether there was a property interest in trade secrets under the Fifth Amendment's Taking Clause. This was a determination based on *Monsanto*'s state law rights, as opposed to an application of federal law.

4. Section 337 also requires that the acts in question threaten to "destroy or substantially injure a domestic industry in the United States." How did the Federal Circuit find that there was a threatened injury to a domestic industry when the complainant was not even using the misappropriated trade secrets?

## C. CIVIL RICO ACTION

### CONTINENTAL DATA SYSTEMS, INC. v. EXXON CORP.

638 F. Supp. 432 (E.D. Pa. 1986)

Before discussing the substance and merits of defendant Exxon's RICO claim, it is necessary to outline the structure of the statute in the civil context. Plaintiff is proceeding under Section 1962(c), which provides:

It shall be unlawful for any person employed by or associated with any enterprise engaged in, or the activities of which affect, interstate or foreign commerce, to conduct or participate, directly or indirectly, in the conduct of such enterprise's affairs through a pattern of racketeering activity or collection of unlawful debt.

Section 1964(c) provides for a private right of action for "[a]ny person injured in his business or property by reason of a violation of section 1962," and allows treble damages when a violation is shown.

Section 1961 defines some of the terms in Section 1962(c) which are elements of a violation:

(4) "enterprise" includes any individual, partnership, corporation, association, or other legal entity and any union or group of individuals associated in fact although not a legal entity; (5) "pattern of racketeering activity" requires at least two acts of racketeering . . . the last of which occurred within ten years . . . after the commission of a prior act of racketeering activity;

"Racketeering activity" consists of specified state law offenses punishable by imprisonment for more than one year, or various federal offenses. 28 U.S.C. § 1961(1).

Plaintiff's position is that Morris, Geddes, Halpern and Raybuck, all employees of Exxon Office Systems, constituted an enterprise through which Exxon engaged in a pattern of racketeering activity. Plaintiff's First Supplemental Memorandum at 17. Plaintiff argues that defendant Exxon used Geddes' "team" at Exxon Office Systems, an "association in fact to misappropriate Continental's information about its software so that Exxon could profit therefrom." Plaintiff's First Supplemental Memorandum at 18.

I do believe, however, that summary judgment as to Exxon on the RICO claim is appropriate in this case. Having concluded that the Geddes "team" constitutes for the purpose of this motion an association in fact, and therefore an enterprise within the meaning of the statute, it remains for plaintiff to show facts that establish Exxon violated section 1962(c). To establish this violation, plaintiff must show that Exxon, employed by or associated with the enterprise, the Geddes "team", conducted or participated, directly or indirectly, in the conduct of such enterprise's affairs through a pattern of racketeering activity, paraphrasing Section 1962(c). In other words, the facts read in the light most favorable to plaintiff must establish that Exxon was associated with or employed by the Geddes "team," and engaged in a pattern of racketeering activity through the Geddes "team."

As a preliminary observation, the language of RICO, and section 1962(c) in particular, envision a particular relationship between the "person" performing the wrongful conduct and the "enterprise." The RICO "person" is the active wrongdoer, while the RICO "enterprise" is a passive instrumentality or mechanism through which the "person" performs the predicate acts. This understanding comports with the Congress' expressed desire to use RICO to attack the infiltration of "legitimate" business by organized crime, while not restricting the reach of the statute to the organized crime context. *See, Sedima, S.P.R.L. v. Imrex Co., Inc.* [citation omitted]; *B.F. Hirsch v. Enright Refining Co., Inc.* [citation omitted].

In the instant case, Continental has failed to adduce facts which demonstrate that Exxon, rather than the Geddes team — which comprises the RICO "enterprise," according to Continental — has engaged actively in the performance of racketeering activities. Plaintiff has not shown that Exxon's policy, either formal or informal, required or encouraged performance of the predicate acts. Nor has plaintiff established that Exxon directed this conduct, or knowingly adopted it during its course. To be sure, Exxon acted indirectly through its employees, including the Geddes "team," even in the performance of the wrongful conduct upon which plaintiff bases this lawsuit. This is necessarily the case because of the nature of the corporate form. But to recast the facts to attribute to Exxon the active role in the commission of the predicate acts belies any reasonable interpretation of the facts. The mere fact that the "team" functioned as a unit and was given sales quotas is inadequate to establish that Exxon conducted the Geddes team's affairs through a pattern of racketeering activity. It turns the facts on their head.

The only sense in which one may colorably attribute to Exxon a violation of section 1962(c) is through the principles of agency and *respondeat superior.* Under ordinary principles of agency, an employer is liable for the wrongs of its employee if the employee acted within the scope of his employment, or if he acted with apparent authority. [Citation omitted.]

The losses caused by the torts of employees, which as a practical matter are sure to occur in the conduct of the employer's enterprise, are placed upon that enterprise itself, as a required cost of doing business. *They are placed upon the employer because, having engaged in an enterprise, which will on the basis of all past experience involve harm to others through the torts of employees, and sought to profit by it, it is just that he, rather than the innocent injured plaintiff, should bear them;* and because he is better able to absorb them, and to distribute them, through prices, rates or liability insurance, to the public and so to shift them to society, to the community at large. [Citation omitted.] Thus, when an employer seeks to profit from a business, and in the course of conducting that business torts will occur from time to time, it has been deemed just for the employer to bear the consequences of those wrongs. These principles apply both to common law torts, [citation omitted] and to a wide range of federal statutory wrongs. [Citation omitted.].

Whether *respondeat superior* liability attaches under RICO has been the subject of substantial controversy, in both the courts and the literature. [Citations omitted.] The statute does not explicitly address the issue. Such silence could be understood to imply that ordinary agency principles attach, and hence *respondeat superior* liability as well. [Citation omitted.] Also, the fact that RICO provides for treble damages does not necessarily bar application of respondeat superior within its rubric. [Citation omitted.] I believe, however, that the application of ordinary agency principles runs counter to the intended structure and operation of RICO civil liability.

In *B.F. Hirsch v. Enright Refining Co., Inc.* [citation omitted], the Third Circuit Court of Appeals held that the corporate person charged with the RICO violation cannot be the same entity as the "enterprise" under section 1962(c). The court explained: "It is in keeping with that Congressional scheme to orient section 1962(c) toward punishing the infiltrating criminals rather than the legitimate corporation which might be an innocent victim of the racketeering activity in some circumstances." [Citation omitted.] To allow liability to be attributed to the "enterprise" because it employed the RICO "person" would place the onus of the RICO violation on the "enterprise." It would place the corporate "enterprise" in the same position, subject to the same liability, as the employee "person." It makes little sense to require that the "enterprise" and the "person" be distinct, but then to impute liability from the "person" to the "enterprise" as a matter of course when the "enterprise" employs the "person." Such a result is simply inconsistent with the framework of the statute and the intent of Congress.

*American Society of Mechanical Engineers, supra,* does not mandate a contrary result. [Citation omitted.] That case holds that the policy of *respondeat superior* liability attaching when an agent acting with apparent authority violates the antitrust laws is consistent with the liberal remedial goals of the antitrust laws. It does not hold that an agent acting with apparent authority necessarily causes *respondeat superior* liability to attach under all federal statutes with remedial goals.

The Supreme Court stated in *Sedima* [citation omitted], "RICO is to be read broadly. This is the lesson not only of Congress' self-consciously expansive language and overall approach, . . . but also of its express admonition that RICO is to 'be liberally construed to effectuate its remedial purpose.' " In this instance, too broad a construction of the statute's remedial provisions would operate to defeat the structure established in the statute and to convert it into a blunt instrument, contrary to the intent of Congress. For that reason, I conclude that defendant Exxon cannot be held liable on the RICO count in this action on the basis of *respondeat superior.* Because I concluded previously that the evidence presented by plaintiff does not support a finding of RICO liability against Exxon as the active participant in racketeering activity, I will grant summary judgment in favor of Exxon on that claim.

. . .

## NOTES AND QUESTIONS:

1. The *Continental Data* opinion reflects how courts applied RICO in trade secret litigation. Originally designed to curtail "racketeering" and combat organized criminal groups such as the Mafia, the Racketeer Influenced and Corrupt Organizations (RICO) Act provides for criminal penalties and civil causes of action for acts performed as part of an ongoing criminal operation. In 1985, the U.S. Supreme Court held that, when criminal activities such as mail and wire fraud are involved, a party could, even in the absence of a criminal conviction, bring a private cause of action under RICO. *See Sedima, S.P.R.L. v. Imrex Co.*, 473 U.S. 479 (1985). If trade secret owners prevail in a RICO action, they may recover treble damages and attorneys' fees.

## D. THE COMPUTER FRAUD AND ABUSE ACT

### SHURGARD STORAGE CENTERS, INC. v. SAFEGUARD SELF STORAGE, INC.

119 F. Supp. 2d 1121 (W.D. Wash. 2000)

INTRODUCTION

Shurgard Storage Centers, Inc. (plaintiff) and Safeguard Self Storage, Inc. (defendant) are competitors in the self-storage business. The plaintiff alleges that the defendant embarked on a systematic scheme to hire away key employees from the plaintiff for the purpose of obtaining the plaintiff's trade secrets. The plaintiff also alleges that some of these employees, while still working for the plaintiff, used the plaintiff's computers to send trade secrets to the defendant via e-mail. The plaintiff's complaint alleges misappropriation of trade secrets, conversion, unfair competition, violations of the Computer Fraud and Abuse Act (CFAA), tortious interference with a business expectancy, and seeks injunctive relief and damages. The defendant has moved to dismiss the CFAA claim pursuant to Fed.R.Civ.P. 12(b)(6), docket no. 7 no. 7. The Court now DENIES the defendant's motion to dismiss the CFAA claim for the reasons set forth in this order.

MOTION TO DISMISS STANDARD

When considering a motion to dismiss under 12(b)(6), a court must accept all allegations in the complaint as true and make all reasonable inferences in favor of the plaintiff. [Citation omitted.] A motion to dismiss may be granted when "it appears beyond a doubt that the plaintiff can prove no set of facts in support of his claim which would entitle him to relief." Conley v. Gibson [Citation omitted.]. "Nonetheless, conclusory allegations without more are insufficient to defeat a motion to dismiss for failure to state a claim." Pillsbury, Madison & Sutro v. Lerner [Citation omitted.]. [Citations omitted.].

FACTS

The plaintiff alleges the following facts which the Court accepts as true for the purposes of this motion. The plaintiff is the industry leader in full and self-service storage facilities in both the United States and Europe. The plaintiff's growth in the last 25 years is primarily due to the development and construction of top-quality storage centers in "high barrier to entry" markets. Pursuant to this strategy, the plaintiff has developed a sophisticated system of creating market plans, identifying appropriate development sites, and evaluating whether a site will provide a high return on an investment. The plaintiff invests significant resources in creating a marketing team to carry out these tasks for each potential market. These teams become familiar with the market, identify potential acquisition sites, and develop relationships with brokers and sellers in the market so that the plaintiff has the best opportunity to acquire a preferred site.

The defendant began self-storage operations in 1997. The defendant is a direct competitor of the plaintiff and develops self-storage facilities in the United States and abroad.

In late 1999, the defendant approached Eric Leland, a Regional Development Manager for the plaintiff, and offered him employment with the defendant. Because of his position with the plaintiff, Mr. Leland had full access to the plaintiff's confidential business plans, expansion plans, and other trade secrets. While still employed by the plaintiff, but acting as an agent for the defendant, Mr. Leland sent e-mails to the defendant containing various trade secrets and proprietary information belonging to the plaintiff. Mr. Leland did this without the plaintiff's knowledge or approval. Mr. Leland was later hired by the defendant in October 1999, and he has continued to give the defendant proprietary information belonging to the plaintiff. The defendant has hired away other employees of the plaintiff who have intimate knowledge of the plaintiff's business models and practices, and the defendant continues to recruit employees of the plaintiff.

DISCUSSION

The motion to dismiss raises challenging issues regarding the scope of a civil claim under a criminal statute, the Computer Fraud and Abuse Act, 18 U.S.C. § 1030. In its complaint, the plaintiff asserts that it is entitled to relief under the CFAA. In its opposition to the motion to dismiss, the plaintiff specifies that its claim is sufficient under 18 U.S.C. §§ 1030(a)(2)(C), 1030(a)(4), and 1030(a)(5)(C).

Statutory Interpretation

As a preliminary matter, the Court must determine the appropriate method by which to interpret the statute. The defendant, citing United States v. Flores-Garcia, 198 F.3d 1119, 1121 (9th Cir.2000), asserts that a court should ascertain a statute's plain meaning by examining the statute's language as well as its object and policy. The plaintiff, however, proposes a different standard: "In interpreting a statute we must examine its language. If the statute is clear and unambiguous, that is the end of the matter. There is no need to look beyond the plain meaning in order to derive the standard articulated in Flores-Garcia, the case cited by the defendant, only applies when the statute is ambiguous. In Flores-Garcia, the court construed the meaning of a statute; in that case whether "knowingly" in the phrase "knowingly aided and assisted any alien" applied to the term "alien." See Flores-Garcia [Citation omitted.]. The court attempted to find the meaning because the statute was unclear. [Citation omitted.] The Burton standard is the correct standard for statutory interpretation, and the unambiguous meaning of a statute should be the first and final inquiry unless it would lead to an absurd result. [Citation omitted.]

B. Does the plaintiff state a claim under 18 U.S.C. § 1030(a)(2)(C)?

Under § 1030(a)(2)(C), "[w]hoever . . . intentionally accesses a computer without authorization or exceeds authorized access, and thereby obtains . . . information from any protected computer if the conduct involved an interstate or foreign communication . . . shall be punished" as provided in section (c) of the statute. 18 U.S.C. § 1030(a)(2)(C). Additionally, § 1030(g) provides that "[a]ny person who suffers damage or loss by reason of a violation of this section may maintain a civil action against the violator to obtain compensatory damages and injunctive relief or other equitable relief." 18 U.S.C. § 1030(g). A "protected computer" means a computer "which is used in interstate or foreign commerce or communication." 18 U.S.C. § 1030(e)(2)(B). "The term 'exceeds authorized access' means to access a computer with authorization and to use such access to obtain or alter information in the computer that the accesser is not entitled so to obtain or alter." 18 U.S.C. § 1030(e)(6).

The defendant contends the plaintiff's complaint does not state a claim for relief under 18 U.S.C. § 1030(a)(2)(C) for two reasons. First, the defendant asserts that the plaintiff has not alleged that the employees in question accessed the trade secrets without authorization. Second, the defendant argues that the plaintiff has not alleged facts showing that the alleged behavior by the defendant impacts the national economy.

i. Did Plaintiff allege that its former employees were without authorization or that they exceeded authorized access?

The defendant's first ground for challenging the plaintiff's claim under § 1030(a)(2)(C) is that the plaintiff has not alleged that its former employees did not have authorized access to the information in question. The defendant notes that the plaintiff alleged that Mr. Leland had full access to all the information allegedly transferred to the defendant. Accordingly, the defendant argues that the plaintiff cannot maintain an action under § 1030(a)(2)(C) because it has not alleged that anyone accessed its computers without authorization or exceeded authorized access to those computers.

The plaintiff responds by arguing that the authorization for its former employees ended when the employees began acting as agents for the defendant. The plaintiff cites to the Restatement (Second) of Agency § 112 (1958) and argues that when Mr. Leland or other former employees used the plaintiff's computers and information on those computers in an improper way they were "without authorization."

In United States v. Galindo, 871 F.2d 99 (9th Cir.1989), an employee of a jewelry store was authorized to pick up mail for the store. See Galindo, 871 F.2d at 100. The employee was convicted of stealing the mail. See id. In a possible attempt to conceal her actual receipt of the mail, the employee forged a signature when she received the mail. See id. at 101. The court held that the employee was not an agent of the jewelry store when the employee used fraud to obtain the mail. See id. Relying on Galindo, the plaintiff argues that its former employees were not its agents when they accessed the computers to send the trade secrets to the defendant.

Under the Restatement (Second) of Agency, relied upon by the Galindo court:

Unless otherwise agreed, the authority of an agent terminates if, without knowledge of the principal, he acquires adverse interests or if he is otherwise guilty of a serious breach of loyalty to the principal.

Restatement (Second) of Agency § 112 (1958). Under this rule, the authority of the plaintiff's former employees ended when they allegedly became agents of the defendant. Therefore, for the purposes of this 12(b)(6) motion, they lost their authorization and were "without authorization" when they allegedly obtained and sent the proprietary information to the defendant via e-mail. The plaintiff has stated a claim under 18 U.S.C. § 1030(a)(2)(C). [Citation omitted.]

ii. Did the plaintiff have to allege that the violation of 18 U.S.C. § 1030(a)(2)(C) affected the national economy?

The defendant's second argument challenging the plaintiff's claim under § 1030(a)(2)(C), as well as its other claims under the CFAA, is that the CFAA was only intended to protect information in large businesses where information, if released or stolen, could affect the public. The defendant maintains that since information from the storage business is not of the type that the CFAA was intended to protect (as opposed to the transportation or power-supply industries), the CFAA does not apply.

Nowhere in language of § 1030(a)(2)(C) is the scope limited to entities with broad privacy repercussions. The statute simply prohibits the obtaining of information from "any protected computer if the conduct involved an interstate or foreign communication." 18 U.S.C. § 1030(a)(2)(C) (emphasis added). According to the statute, a protected computer is a computer used in interstate or foreign commerce. See 18 U.S.C. § 1030(e)(2)(B). This language is unambiguous. There is no reasonable implication in any of these terms that suggests only the computers of certain industries are protected. Therefore, the defendant's argument on this issue is unpersuasive.

C. Does the plaintiff state a claim under 18 U.S.C. § 1030(a)(4)?

A person violates 18 U.S.C. § 1030(a)(4) if he or she:

> . . . knowingly and with intent to defraud, accesses a protected computer without authorization, or exceeds authorized access, and by means of such conduct furthers the intended fraud and obtains anything of value, unless the object of the fraud and the thing obtained consists only of the use of the computer and the value of such use is not more than $5, 000 in any 1-year period.

18 U.S.C. § 1030(a)(4). The only element disputed by the defendant under § 1030(a)(4) that is not present under § 1030(a)(2)(C) is the intent to defraud. The plaintiff argues for a broad definition of "defraud" in this context, stating fraud is simply "wronging one in his property rights by dishonest methods or schemes." Plaintiff's Memorandum in Opposition, docket no. 11. [Citation omitted.] Moreover, the plaintiff relies on United States v. Czubinski, 106 F.3d 1069, 1078 (1st Cir. 1997), for the proposition that this section of the CFAA's use of "fraud" simply means wrongdoing and not proof of the common law elements of fraud. This is the proper standard for fraud in this context, and construing the complaint in the light most favorable to the plaintiff, the complaint alleges that the defendant participated in dishonest methods to obtain the plaintiff's secret information. Therefore, the plaintiff has stated a claim upon which relief can be granted under 18 U.S.C. § 1030(a)(4).

D. Does the plaintiff state a claim under 18 U.S.C. § 1030(a)(5)(C)?

Under 18 U.S.C. § 1030(a)(5)(C), "[w]hoever . . . intentionally accesses a protected computer without authorization, and as a result of such conduct, causes damage" violates the CFAA. 18 U.S.C. § 1030(a)(5)(C). The only new issue under this portion of the statute is whether the plaintiff has alleged that "damage" occurred. "The term 'damage' means any impairment to the integrity or availability of data, a program, a system, or information, that . . . causes loss aggregating at least $5,000 in value during any 1-year period to one or more individuals . . . ." 18 U.S.C. § 1030(e)(8)(A).

The defendant raises two objections to this claim. First, the defendant asserts that the legislative history of this section of the CFAA shows that it is only intended to apply to "outsiders," and thus would not apply to employees. However, there is no ambiguity in the statute as to when a party is liable, ("Whoever . . . intentionally accesses . . . .") so this argument lacks merit. See 18 U.S.C. § 1030(a)(5)(C). Second, the defendant argues that the plaintiff has not pled that it incurred "damage" as defined in the statute. Specifically, the defendant argues that the alleged loss of information by the plaintiff is not "damage" under the statute. The statute says damage is "any impairment to the integrity . . . of data . . . or information." 18 U.S.C. § 1030(e)(8)(A) (emphasis added). The unambiguous meaning of "any" clearly demonstrates that the statute is meant to apply to "any" impairment to the integrity of data. However, the word "integrity" is ambiguous in this context. Webster's New International Dictionary (3d ed. 1993), defines "integrity" as, "an unimpaired or unmarred condition." This necessarily contemplates maintaining the data in a protected state. Because the term may be ambiguous, the court examines the legislative history to determine if "integrity" and thus "damage" could include the alleged access and disclosure of trade secrets in this case.

The term "damage" was addressed in the Senate Report regarding the 1996 amendments to the CFAA:

The 1994 amendment required both "damage" and "loss," but it is not always clear what constitutes "damage." For example, intruders often alter existing log-on programs so that user passwords are copied to a file which the hackers can retrieve later. After retrieving the newly created password file, the intruder restores the altered log-on file to its original condition. Arguably, in such a situation, neither the computer nor its information is damaged. Nonetheless, this conduct allows the intruder to accumulate valid user passwords to the system, requires all system users to change their passwords, and requires the system administrator to devote resources to resecuring the system. Thus, although there is arguably no "damage," the victim does suffer "loss." If the loss to the victim meets the required monetary threshold, the conduct should be criminal, and the victim should be entitled to relief. The bill therefore defines "damage" in new subsection 1030(e)(8), with a focus on the harm that the law seeks to prevent.

S.Rep. No. 104-357, at 11 (1996). This example given in the report is analogous to the case before the Court. The "damage" and thus violation to the "integrity" that was caused in the example is the accumulation of passwords and subsequent corrective measures the rightful computer owner must take to prevent the infiltration and gathering of confidential information. Similarly, in this case, the defendant allegedly infiltrated the plaintiff's computer network, albeit through different means than in the example, and collected and disseminated confidential information. In both cases no data was physically changed or erased, but in both cases an impairment of its integrity occurred. From the legislative history it is clear that the meaning of "integrity" and thus "damage" apply to the alleged acts of the defendant in this case and thus the plaintiff has stated a claim under 18 U.S.C. § 1030(a)(5)(C).

E. The Legislative History of the CFAA Supports the Plaintiff's Claim in This Case.

Although the Court concludes that the plaintiff has stated a claim under the CFAA, this Court is mindful of its obligation to construe statutes so as to avoid "absurd" results. [Citation omitted.] Though the defendant's arguments about the legislative history and intent of the CFAA go to the meaning of what this Court finds to be unambiguous language, save for "integrity," those same arguments can be construed as relevant to, for lack of a better term, an "absurdity inquiry." Thus, considering the novelty of the legal issues presented to the Court, an in-depth analysis of the legislative history of the CFAA is appropriate.

The core of the defendant's arguments concerning legislative intent is that the CFAA was not meant to apply to the kind of factual situation presented in this case. Instead, the defendant maintains the CFAA is limited to those industries whose computers contain vast amounts of information, which if released, could significantly affect privacy interests in the public at large. The defendant also maintains the CFAA is limited to "outsiders" or "hackers," and not "insiders" (employees). Though the original scope of the CFAA was limited to the concerns addressed by the defendant, its subsequent amendments have broadened the scope sufficiently to cover the behavior alleged in this case.

The first version of the CFAA was passed in 1984. See S.Rep. No. 99-432, at 3 (1986). This first bill was directed at protecting classified information on government computers as well as protecting financial records and credit information on government and financial institution computers. See id. In 1986, the CFAA was amended to "provide additional penalties for fraud and related activities in connection with access devices and computers." Id. At 1. Specifically, the 1986 amendments added protection for "federal interest computers:"

> Throughout its consideration of computer crime, the Committee has been especially concerned about the appropriate scope of Federal jurisdiction in this area. It has been suggested that, because some States lack comprehensive computer crime statutes of their own, the Congress should enact as sweeping a Federal statute as possible so that no computer crime is left uncovered. The Committee rejects this approach and prefers instead to limit Federal jurisdiction over computer crime to those cases in which there is a compelling Federal interest, i.e., where computers of the Federal Government or certain financial institutions are involved, or where the crime itself is interstate in nature.

The CFAA was amended in 1996, and the phrase "protected computer" was added in place of "federal interest computer." The Senate Report on these amendments demonstrates the broad scope of this phrase. See S.Rep. No. 104-357, at 3 (1996) ("[The CFAA is strengthened] by closing gaps in the law to protect better the confidentiality, integrity, and security of computer data and networks."); Id. at 4; ("The privacy protection coverage of the statute has two significant gaps. First, omitted from the statute's coverage is information on any civilian or State and local government computers, since the prohibition on unauthorized computer access to obtain non classified information extends only to the Federal Government when the perpetrator is an outsider.") (emphasis added); Id. at 5; ("[The CFAA] facilitates addressing in a single statute the problem of computer crime, rather than identifying and amending every potentially applicable statute affected by advances in computer technology. As computers continue to proliferate in businesses and homes, and new forms of computer crimes emerge, Congress must remain vigilant to ensure that the [CFAA] is up-to-date and provides law enforcement with the necessary legal framework to fight computer crime.") Id.

Finally, in what is dispositive of the scope of the CFAA, the report states:

> The proposed subsection 1030(a)(2)(C) is intended to protect against the interstate or foreign theft of information by computer . . . . This subsection would ensure that the theft of intangible information by the unauthorized use of a computer is prohibited in the same way theft of physical items are protected. In instances where the information stolen is also copyrighted, the theft may implicate certain rights under the copyright laws. The crux of the offense under subsection 1030(a)(2)(C), however, is the abuse of a computer to obtain the information.

* * *

Those who improperly use computers to obtain other types of information-such as financial records, nonclassified Government information, and information of nominal value from private individuals or companies face only misdemeanor penalties, unless the information is used for commercial advantage, private financial gain or to commit any criminal or tortious act.

For example, individuals who intentionally break into, or abuse their authority to use, a computer and thereby obtain information of minimal value of $5,000 or less, would be subject to a misdemeanor penalty. The crime becomes a felony if the offense was committed for purposes of commercial advantage or private financial gain, for the purposes of committing any criminal or tortious act in violation . . . of the laws of the United States or of any State, or if the value of the information obtained exceeds $5,000.

Id. at 7-8 (emphasis added). This legislative history, although in reference § 1030(a)(2), demonstrates the broad meaning and intended scope of the terms "protected computer" and "without authorization" that are also used in the other relevant sections. The report recognizes that someone could be liable under § 1030(a)(2)(C) where intellectual property rights are involved. Finally, the report states the statute is intended to punish those who illegally use computers for commercial advantage. In sum, this passage makes clear that the CFAA was intended to encompass actions such as those allegedly undertaken by the present defendant. The legislative history of the CFAA comports with the plain meaning of the statute.

CONCLUSION

For the reasons stated above, the defendant's motion to dismiss the Computer Fraud and Abuse Act claim is DENIED.

IT IS SO ORDERED.

## FACEBOOK, INC. v. MAXBOUNTY, INC.

No. 5:10-cv-04712-JF(HRL), 2011 U.S. Dist. LEXIS 104055 (N.D. Cal. Sept. 14, 2011)

Pursuant to Fed. R. Civ. Pro. 12(b)(6), Defendant MaxBounty Inc. ("MaxBounty") moves to dismiss Claims One through Three asserted by Plaintiff Facebook, Inc. ("Facebook") for failure to state a claim upon which relief may be granted. The First Amended Complaint ("FAC") includes claims for: (1) violation of 15 U.S.C. § 7701 ("CAN-SPAM Act"); (2) violation of 18 U.S.C. § 1030 ("Computer Fraud and Abuse Act"); (3) fraud; (4)khl,yuj tortious interference with contract; (5) breach of contract; (6) violation of 15 U.S.C. § 1125(c) (federal trademark dilution); and (7) violation of 15 U.S.C. § 1125(a) (false designation of origin). Facebook seeks compensatory, statutory, and punitive damages.

### I. BACKGROUND

Facebook is a popular social networking website with more than 500 million active users. (FAC ¶ 10) It is designed to be "a network that helps people communicate more efficiently and effectively with their friends, family, and co-workers." (Id.) To become a Facebook user an individual must provide his or her real identity. (Id. at ¶¶ 11–12) Commercial, political, and charitable organizations also may establish a presence on Facebook by creating "pages" to which users can connect their profiles. (Id. at ¶ 14) All users must agree to Facebook's statement of rights and responsibilities. Facebook's advertising guidelines prohibit false, misleading, fraudulent, and deceptive advertisements. (Id. at ¶ 38(c)) They also prohibit advertisements that are "deceptive or fraudulent about any offer made," (Id. at ¶ 38(d)), and any advertisement that includes a "discount or free offer . . . must link to a page that clearly and accurately offers the exact deal the advertisement has displayed . . . ." (Id. at ¶ 38(h)) Moreover, advertisements that contain, facilitate or promote spam are prohibited, (Id. at ¶ 3 8(j)), and if obtaining the promoted benefit requires user enrollment in a third-party subscription service then that requirement must be stated both in the advertisement and on the Facebook page. (Id. at ¶ 38(k))

MaxBounty is an advertising and marketing company that uses a network of publishers to drive traffic to its customers' websites. Its marketing program is based on a cost-per-action model ("CPA"). As explained on MaxBounty's website, "an advertiser under the CPA model pays only when a specific action is taken on their website. The advertiser defines the action in advance and only pays when the action is taken . . . [g]enerally speaking, the more involved the action, the higher a publisher would expect to be paid for generating it." MaxBounty acts as an intermediary between its network of publishers (advertisement content creators) and its customers (third-party advertisers). MaxBounty appears to generate revenue for its CPA program through a shared compensation agreement with its network of publishers.

Facebook alleges that MaxBounty engaged and continues to engage in impermissible advertising and commercial activity on Facebook.com. (FAC ¶¶ 41–42) It asserts that MaxBounty misleads its affiliates "into believing that Defendant's campaigns are approved by Facebook . . . ." (Id. at ¶ 51) It claims that MaxBounty facilitates traffic to its contracting advertiser websites by "provid[ing] instruction and support on how to design these unauthorized Facebook campaigns, and [by] provid[ing] substantial advance payments to its affiliates that agree to participate in these campaigns." (Id.) Facebook also claims that MaxBounty's conduct has caused it economic damage, has "tainted the Facebook experience," has resulted in users' "real economic loss in the form of undisclosed subscription fees," and has caused and continues to cause significant harm to Facebook's reputation and goodwill. (Id. at ¶¶ 58–59)

A. The Alleged Fraudulent Scheme

Facebook alleges that MaxBounty, through its network of affiliates, creates Facebook pages that are intended to re-direct unsuspecting Facebook users away from Facebook.com to third-party commercial sites. (FAC ¶¶ 42–57) It provides examples of two such pages in the complaint. (Id. at ¶¶ 44–48) Both pages utilize a similarly structured, multi-step scheme: in the first step, MaxBounty establishes a network of affiliates; in the second step, MaxBounty's affiliates create numerous Facebook pages that function like (and in effect are) advertisements; in the third step, the page displays a message indicating that upon registration a user will be able to take advantage of a "limited time offer," such as receiving a gift card or becoming a product tester for a high-end product (e.g. an Apple iPad); in the fourth step, the Facebook user is induced by the page and begins the registration process. (Id.) The registration process requires three discrete user actions: (1) to become a "fan" of the page, (2) to invite all of his or her Facebook friends to join to the page, and (3) to complete additional administrative registration requirements. (Id. at ¶¶ 44, 47) Upon completion of these requirements, Facebook users are not sent the promised item but instead are directed "to a domain registered to and managed by the Defendant that then redirected the user to a third-party commercial website . . ." (Id. at ¶¶ 45, 50) The third-party commercial site informs the user that he or she must complete still more steps in order to obtain the promised item. (Id. at ¶¶ 46) Such additional steps include signing up for numerous "sponsor offers," which typically are offers for memberships in subscription services. (Id.) Facebook asserts that "[MaxBounty] received payment for the traffic it delivered to [the third-party commercial sites] based on the [number of] users who successfully completed the steps to receive a free gift." (Id. at ¶¶ 46, 48)

B. MaxBounty's Motion to Dismiss

In a previous motion to dismiss (dkt. entry 11), MaxBounty argued that Facebook's claim under the CAN-SPAM Act was insufficient as a matter of law because the "customer advertisements Facebook complains about. . . are not email and therefore cannot give rise to a claim under the CAN-SPAM Act." (Mot. to Dismiss, 1:9–11). MaxBounty also contended that Facebook's claim under the Computer Fraud and Abuse Act ("CFAA") failed to satisfy the heightened pleading standard of Fed. R. Civ. Pro. 9(b), pointing out that a plaintiff must plead with particularity "conduct which furthers the intended fraud." (Reply to Pl.'s Opp., 5:3–15). Finally, MaxBounty argued that Facebook failed to plead adequately the elements of its state law claims for fraud, aiding and abetting, and conspiracy. (MTD, 1:18–23; 6:23–7:13). On March 28, 2011, this Court denied MaxBounty's motion to dismiss Facebook's CAN-SPAM and CFAA claims, concluding that Facebook had pled both claims sufficiently. (Order Granting in Part and Denying in Part Motion to Dismiss, at 8, 9) The Court granted MaxBounty's motion with respect to Facebook's common law fraud claim, finding that the claim needed additional specificity. (Order at 10, 11) Facebook filed the operative FAC on April 19, 2011.

MaxBounty filed the instant motion on May 13, 2011, asserting that Facebook still has failed to plead MaxBounty's role in the alleged fraud with sufficient particularity, and that in light of Facebook's amended allegations the Court no longer may draw any reasonable inference that would allow Facebook to prevail on its CAN-SPAM and CFAA claims.

II. LEGAL STANDARD

"Dismissal under Rule 12(b)(6) is appropriate only where the complaint lacks a cognizable legal theory or sufficient facts to support a cognizable legal theory." Mendiondo v. Centinela Hosp. Center, 521 F.3d 1097, 1104 (9th Cir.2008). For purposes of a motion to dismiss, "all allegations of material fact are taken as true and construed in the light most favorable to the nonmoving party." Cahill v. Liberty Mutual Ins. Co., 80 F.3d 336, 337–338 (9th Cir.1996). However, "[w]hile a complaint attacked by a Rule 12(b)(6) motion to dismiss does not need detailed factual allegations, a plaintiff's obligation to provide the 'grounds' of his 'entitle [ment] to relief' requires more than labels and conclusions, and a formulaic recitation of the elements of a cause of action will not do." Bell Atlantic Corp. v. Twombly, 550 U.S. 544, 127 S.Ct. 1955, 167 L.Ed.2d 929 (2007) (internal citations omitted). Leave to amend must be granted unless it is clear that the complaint's deficiencies cannot be cured by amendment. Lucas v. Department of Corrections, 66 F.3d 245, 248 (9th Cir.1995).

## III. DISCUSSION

### A. Fraud

#### 1. Rule 9(b) Standard

Under Fed. R. Civ. Pro. 9(b), "[i]n all averments of fraud or mistake, the circumstances constituting fraud or mistake shall be stated with particularity." However, intent, knowledge, and other conditions of the mind may be averred generally. Fed. R. Civ. Pro. 9(b). A complaint meets this standard if it alleges " 'the time, place, and content of the alleged fraudulent misrepresentation or omission; the identity of the person engaged in the fraud; and the circumstances indicating falseness' or 'the manner in which [the] representations [or omissions] were false and misleading.' " Genna v. Digital Link Corp., 25 F.Supp.2d 1038 (N.D.Cal.1997) (brackets in original) (quoting In re GlenFed Sec. Litig., 42 F.3d 1541, 1547–58 n. 7 (9th Cir.1994)). Conclusory allegations that a defendant's conduct was fraudulent is insufficient. In re Worlds of Wonder Securities Litigation, 694 F.Supp. 1427, 1432 (N.D.Cal.1988).

#### 2. Common law fraud

The elements of a claim for fraud under California law are: (1) a misrepresentation; (2) knowledge of falsity (or scienter); (3) intent to defraud, i.e. to induce reliance; (4) justifiable reliance; and (5) resulting damage. Lazar v. Superior Ct., 12 Cal.4th 631, 638, 49 Cal.Rptr.2d 377, 909 P.2d 981 (1996). Generally, fraud allegations may not be based solely on information and belief. McFarland v. Memorex Corp., 493 F.Supp. 631, 638–39 (N.D.Cal.1980). This general rule may be relaxed when facts are peculiarly within the knowledge of the other party. Fong v. United States, 300 F.2d 400, 409 (9th Cir.1962) (holding that plaintiff's allegations were sufficiently pled because they stated facts primarily within the defendant's knowledge); see also Russell v. Epic Healthcare Mgmt. Group, 193 F.3d 304, 308 (5th Cir.1999) (finding the 9(b) standard may be relaxed when facts "relating to the alleged fraud are peculiarly within the perpetrator's knowledge . . . ."). Even under a more relaxed standard, a plaintiff "must still set forth the factual basis for his belief," and mere speculation and conclusory allegations are insufficient to state a claim. Russell, 193 F.3d at 308.

This Court directed Facebook to plead facts identifying who at MaxBounty had knowledge of the alleged fraud, what those individuals knew, how MaxBounty contributed to the alleged fraud, and which of MaxBounty's affiliates were responsible for creating the Facebook pages at issue. (Order at 7, 8) The FAC alleges that Adam Harrison identifies himself as MaxBounty's Facebook Affiliate Manager and encourages and directs affiliates to make specific changes to their promotional Facebook Pages. (FAC at ¶ 49) These actions allegedly encourage affiliates to generate traffic for MaxBounty's advertisers through fraudulent and deceptive means. (Id. at ¶ 50) The FAC further alleges that MaxBounty affiliate Mitchell Fillmore created Facebook pages that offered a free IKEA gift card in conformity with the scheme described above, and that Fillmore was contacted by

Harrison, who then provided technical assistance. (Id. at ¶ 52) When Fillmore raised concerns as to whether Facebook permitted his activities, Harrison allegedly reassured him and offered him $30,000 to continue creating similar pages. (Id. at ¶ 53) These allegations contain sufficient factual detail to make Facebook's claim plausible.

3. Aiding and abetting the alleged fraud

"A claim for aiding and abetting requires (1) the existence of an independent primary wrong, (2) actual knowledge by the alleged aider and abettor of the wrong and his or her role in furthering it, and (3) substantial assistance in the wrong." In re 3 Com Securities Litigation, 761 F.Supp. 1411, 1418 (N.D.Cal.1990) (citing Harmsen v. Smith, 693 F.2d 932, 943 (9th Cir.1982)). "Substantial assistance requires that the defendant's actions be a 'substantial factor' in causing the plaintiff's injury." Impac Warehouse Lending Group v. Credit Sussie First Boston LLC, 270 Fed. Appx. 570, 572 (9th Cir.2008) (internal citation omitted).

This Court directed Facebook to plead facts tending to show that MaxBounty had actual knowledge of the wrongful activity, describing MaxBounty's role in furthering the fraud, and explaining how MaxBounty provided substantial assistance in the wrongful activity. (Order at 8) The FAC alleges specifically that Harrison assured an affiliate that MaxBounty approved of the specific techniques the affiliate used. (Id. at ¶¶ 49–53) This is sufficient to satisfy Rule 9(b).

4. Conspiracy

To state a claim for conspiracy, Facebook must plead "an agreement to participate in an unlawful overt act that is performed in furtherance of an agreement. The existence of this agreement may be either express or inferred from a defendant's conduct. However, a conspiracy to commit fraud must satisfy the particularity requirement of Rule 9(b)." In re 3 Com Securities Litigation, 761 F.Supp. 1411, 1418 (N.D.Cal.1990).

The FAC alleges that MaxBounty's "Facebook Affiliate Manager" was aware of the deceptive campaigns that MaxBounty's affiliates promoted on Facebook and offered an advance payment to induce an affiliate to continue creating allegedly fraudulent pages. Again, this is sufficient for purposes of Rule 9(b).

B. CAN-SPAM Act and Computer Fraud and Abuse Act

1. CAN-SPAM and CFAA Claims

The CAN-SPAM Act makes it unlawful for any person to "initiate the transmission" of a "commercial electronic mail message" that is "materially false or materially misleading." 15 U.S.C. § 7704(a)(1). In this context, "initiate" means "to originate or transmit such message or to procure the origination or transmission of such message." 15 U.S.C. § 7702(9). To "procure" the initiation of an electronic mail message means "intentionally to pay or provide other consideration to, or induce, another person to initiate such a message on one's behalf." 15 U.S.C. § 7702(12).

Using "materially" misleading header information in an electronic mail message includes "the alteration or concealment of header information" that would "impair . . . the ability of a recipient of the message to respond to a person who initiated the electronic message." 15 U.S.C. § 7704(a)(6).

MaxBounty claims that Facebook has failed to show that MaxBounty is liable for procurement or inducement of the messages at issue. (Mot. To Dismiss at 2) MaxBounty also claims that Facebook fails to allege factual details necessary to its claim that the messages contain materially misleading header information. (Id. at 3) The FAC alleges that Fillmore, a MaxBounty affiliate, sent the messages at issue and duped Facebook users into sending additional messages. (FAC ¶¶ 50–53) Facebook also alleges that none of the messages associated with MaxBounty's campaigns identify MaxBounty as the initiator despite the fact that MaxBounty initiated the messages by inducing Facebook users to execute malicious computer code that causes messages to be sent automatically to all of their Facebook "friends." (FAC ¶ 54) These allegations are sufficient at the pleading stage.

2. Computer Fraud and Abuse Act ("CFAA")

The CFAA makes it unlawful for anyone knowingly and with intent to defraud to access a protected computer without authorization or exceeding authorization and through such conduct to further the intended fraud. 18 U.S.C. § 1030(a)(4). Under the CFAA, "an employee accesses a computer in excess of his or her authorization when that access violates the employer's access restrictions, which may include restrictions on the employee's use of the computer or of the information contained in that computer." *U.S. v. Nosal*, 642 F.3d 781 (9th Cir. Apr. 28, 2011). Nosal also held that "an individual who is authorized to use a computer for certain purposes but goes beyond those limitations is considered by the CFAA as someone who has 'exceed [ed] authorized access.' " *Id.*

MaxBounty argues that because Facebook granted it access to the Facebook site, it could not have exceeded its "authorized access" within the meaning of the CFAA. (Mot. to Dismiss at 3–4) However, Facebook alleges that MaxBounty and its affiliates registered for Facebook accounts and accepted Facebook's terms of use, which places restrictions on their use of the Facebook site. (FAC ¶¶ 12, 31–40) In this light, Facebook's allegations are sufficient to state a claim under the CFAA.

## NOTES AND QUESTIONS:

1. The CFAA does not create a broad basis for a federal civil action against trade secret theft because of the requirement that a computer be used. Additionally, not all courts recognize the applicability of the CFAA for a pure civil action. *See Garelli Wong & Assocs., Inc. v. Nichols*, 551 F. Supp. 2d 704 (N.D. Ill. 2008) (refusing to extend the private action provisions of the CFAA to a pure civil claim). Thus, as shown in this section and the previous sections in this chapter, there is no single federal trade secret law. Most litigants are forced to rely on state laws, but can use various federal laws, such as the Lanham Act, the Tariff Act, RICO and CFAA, when the facts lend themselves to such actions.

2. The decision in *Facebook, Inc. v. MaxBounty, Inc.*, No. 5:10-cv-04712-JF (HRL), 2011 U.S. Dist. LEXIS 104055 (N.D. Cal. Sept. 14, 2011), illustrates how civil plaintiffs are testing the outer boundaries of the CFAA. However, in view of the 9th Circuit *en banc* decision in *United States v. Nosal*, 676 F.3d 854 (9th Cir. Apr. 10, 2012), in which it disagreed with decisions in other circuits as to what "authorized access" means and limited the Act to individuals who had no authority at all to use the computer, these boundaries will remain in a state of flux for awhile. *See* case discussion in Chapt. 5(D).

3. *Nosal* is also important reading for employers (more specifically, lawyers for employers) so that restrictions on access and use of computers are specified in detail in employment agreements. New employees should also be aware of any restrictions on computer access and use so that she or he does not run afoul of the CFAA. How should employment agreements be drafted in order to make sure they can be used against rogue employees?

4. The lack of a broad federal law against trade secret theft has prompted a call for a Federal Trade Secrets Act. *See* R. Mark Halligan, *Protection of U.S. Trade Secret Assets: Critical Amendments to the Economic Espionage Act of 1996*, 7 J MARSHALL REV. INTELL. PROP. L. 656 (2008); Christopher Rebel J. Pace, *The Case for a Federal Trade Secrets Act*, 8 HARV. J.L. & TECH 427 (1995); David S. Almeling, *Four Reasons to Enact a Federal Trade Secrets Act*, 19 FORDHAM INTELL. PROP. & MEDIA ENT. L.J. 769 (2009). Amendments were proposed to the Economic Espionage Act in October 2011 to provide such federal protection, but did not pass. Other attempts will surely be made, which will likely result in a federal trade secrets law at some time in the future.

## E. AFFIRMATIVE DEFENSES

Federal Rule of Civil Procedure 8, lists estoppel, fraud, illegality, laches, license, statute of limitations, and a number of others, as defenses that must be pleaded affirmatively. State procedural rules have similar provisions. Although many practitioners allege a number of other "affirmative defenses" in their answers, most of them, such as lack of novelty, lack of secrecy, etc., have been dealt with in previous chapters. Of those specifically mentioned in the Federal Rules of Civil Procedure, laches, estoppel and statute of limitation issues are the ones that are most frequently dealt with in published decisions. It is always a good idea for the attorney drafting an answer to check this provision of the rules to make sure that all affirmative defenses are included in order to avoid a waiver.

## (1) Laches

### ANACONDA CO. v. METRIC TOOL & DIE CO.

485 F. Supp. 410 (E.D. Pa. 1980)

. . .

D. Is Anaconda's Suit Barred by Laches?

Metric argues that Anaconda is not entitled to relief because of laches. The essential elements of laches are inexcusable delay in instituting suit and prejudice resulting to the defendant from such delay. [Citation omitted.] Laches is an equitable defense; its existence depends on the particular equitable circumstances of each case, and is a question primarily addressed to the discretion of the trial court. [Citation omitted.] In recognition of the equitable nature of the defense of laches, courts have also considered whether the party asserting the defense is a conscious wrongdoer. [Citations omitted.] If laches is invoked by a defendant who is a conscious wrongdoer, he can prevail only if the plaintiff's delay "is so prolonged and inexcusable that it amounts to a virtual abandonment of the right by the plaintiff for a long period of time." John Wright, supra, quoting Tisch Hotels, supra.

1. Burden of Proof of Laches

The allocation of the burden of proof of laches depends on the length of the plaintiff's delay. If the delay is shorter than the applicable statute of limitations, then the defendant has the burden of proving laches. If, on the other hand, the delay is longer than the applicable statute of limitations, then the defendant is entitled to a rebuttable presumption of both elements of laches. In that case, the plaintiff has the burden of disproving laches. [Citation omitted.]

The relevant statute of limitations here is six years, as we have previously noted. In order to allocate the burden of proof of laches, we must determine whether the plaintiff has slept on its rights for more than six years. [Citation omitted.] We note that a plaintiff against whom laches is invoked is chargeable with knowledge not only of facts which were actually known to him at the time, but also of facts which he could have learned by means of an inquiry pursued with reasonable diligence.

"[T]he law is well settled that where the question of laches is in issue the plaintiff is chargeable with such knowledge as he might have obtained upon inquiry provided the facts already known by him were such as to put upon a man of ordinary intelligence the duty of inquiry." Johnston v. Standard Mining Co., 148 U.S. 360, 370, 13 S.Ct. 585, 589, 37 L.Ed. 480 (1893). [Citations omitted.]

Six years before filing this suit, Anaconda knew that Hussian had paid an unauthorized visit to its Mattoon plant; that he had advertised in the Mattoon newspapers for tool and die makers to work in his plant in the Philadelphia area, about 1000 miles away; that he sought to hire present or former Anaconda employees at high salaries to design and build a P&W machine for the manufacture of flexible metal hose; that he had in fact hired Ames and Van Meter, who had built a P&W machine; that Metric had sold TCA to Western Electric; and that Metric's production was improving so that it would be a serious competitive threat. This knowledge was plainly sufficient to put a reasonably prudent person on inquiry to determine whether Metric had designed its P&W machine by misappropriating Anaconda's trade secrets. However, Anaconda made no such inquiry; nor did it take any action to assert its rights in its trade secrets. In fact, by April 15, 1969, more than seven years before it initiated legal action, Anaconda had actual knowledge of all the essential elements of Metric's misappropriation. Since its delay exceeded six years, Anaconda must rebut the presumption of laches by negating one or both of the essential elements of laches. In addition, plaintiff may avoid or diminish the effect of laches by showing that defendant was a conscious wrongdoer.

2. Inexcusability of Anaconda's Delay in Instituting Suit

Anaconda argues that its delay in bringing suit was reasonable or excusable because it did not know of the misappropriation until 1976, when Sauers provided it with photographs showing that Metric's machine was nearly identical to Anaconda's. It contends that while Anaconda executives may have had some relevant information in 1968 and 1969, they had no "hard evidence" of misappropriation. Although Hogan, the Mattoon plant manager, testified that he suspected at the time that Metric was receiving technical information from former employees of Anaconda, the plaintiff argues that "suspicion is not knowledge," quoting Kraft v. Cohen, 32 F.Supp. 821, 825 (E.D.Pa.1940), rev'd on other grounds, 117 F.2d 579 (3d Cir. 1941).

While Anaconda did not have access in 1969 to all the evidence of misappropriation which it has presented here, it did have knowledge of all the essential elements of Hussian's campaign to gain access to its trade secrets. That knowledge was sufficient to make Hogan suspicious, and it was sufficient to put a reasonably diligent person on inquiry. As we have noted, a plaintiff against whom laches is invoked, who knows facts sufficient to put a reasonably prudent person on inquiry, is chargeable with knowledge of facts which he could have discovered by an inquiry pursued with reasonable diligence. While an estimation of what Anaconda could have learned by means of an inquiry into the misappropriation of its trade secrets is necessarily speculative, as it is based on a hypothetical inquiry which never took place, we are confident that an inquiry reasonably pursued would have disclosed further details of the misappropriation. For example, it would not have been unreasonable, given the extent of its knowledge in 1969, for Anaconda to have hired a private investigator to find out, by lawful means, whether Ames and Van Meter were revealing confidential information. We do not think that a reasonable person would have waited until photographs which virtually proved misappropriation came into his possession fortuitously. We note also that the liberal discovery procedures of the federal courts would have been available to Anaconda in any legal action it initiated, as they have been in this action.

Anaconda also contends that its delay was reasonable or excusable because it was not actually damaged by Metric's adverse use of its trade secret until late in 1970 when Metric began to supplant it as Western Electric's supplier of TCA. We do not find that argument persuasive. And in any event, it provides an excuse for delay until the early 1970's, and not until August, 1976.

We conclude that Anaconda has failed to rebut the presumption that its delay in instituting suit was unreasonable and inexcusable. We add only that the result on this point would be the same even if there were no presumption.

3. Prejudice to the Defendant

Anaconda contends that Metric has not been prejudiced by the delay in bringing suit. It notes that no prejudice has resulted to defendant's ability to defend this action, as might have occurred if, for instance, a witness had died or records had been destroyed. While the defendant claims that he was prejudiced in that he built five P&W machines and invested much of his capital in TCA manufacture, Anaconda points out that Metric received considerable profits on this investment, and argues that Metric cannot have been prejudiced by carrying on a lucrative activity.

The prejudice which is an essential element of laches must be more than the mere continued use of a misappropriated trade secret. [Citation omitted.] However, the expansion of one's business and the expenditure of capital to undertake an activity which is later subjected to legal challenge is the kind of change of position which will support the defense of laches. [Citations omitted.] By investing more and more of its resources in TCA manufacture, Metric exposed itself to greater damage liability and increased the cost to its business which is likely to result from injunctive relief. Anaconda's prompt action would have made it possible for Metric to devote its resources to other equally profitable business operations, instead of increasing its exposure to liability. Thus the mere fact that Metric's TCA operation was profitable does not preclude a finding of prejudice sufficient to support the defense of laches. While Metric has produced no evidence to show that it ever contemplated expanding its business in other areas, it is entitled to a rebuttable presumption of prejudice because Anaconda's delay exceeded the six-year period of the statute of limitations. Anaconda has failed to rebut that presumption.

4. Conscious Wrongdoing

In balancing the equities to determine whether plaintiff's suit is barred by laches, a court may consider whether the defendant "has engaged in particularly egregious conduct which would change the equities significantly in plaintiff's favor." TWM Manufacturing, supra, 592 F.2d at 349. Such egregious conduct may be shown by demonstrating, for example, that the defendant to a claim of patent infringement participated in "deliberate, calculated plagiarism," id., or that the defendant to a claim of trademark infringement "was fully aware of the plaintiff's mark and reputation," Alfred Dunhill, supra, 350 F.Supp. at 1368.

We have no difficulty in concluding that Metric was a conscious wrongdoer. The only inference that can be drawn from Hussian's conduct is that after his initial attempts to buy or build a P&W machine failed, he deliberately set out to construct a duplicate of Anaconda's machine. He knew that Anaconda had the only machine in the United States then capable of manufacturing TCA, and he knew or should have known that the machine, and the manufacturing process, were confidential. As we have noted, Hussian treated Metric's P&W machine as confidential, thereby evincing his awareness that the machine was not a matter of public knowledge, and also perhaps demonstrating some fear of apprehension.

5. Anaconda's Apparent Acquiescence in Metric's Misconduct; The Effect of Anaconda's Conduct on Relief

Although we have labeled Metric a "conscious wrongdoer," we view the effect of this categorization as mitigated somewhat by Anaconda's apparent acquiescence in its misconduct. Anaconda's inaction was not "so prolonged and inexcusable that it amounts to a virtual abandonment of the right," John Wright, supra, quoting Tisch Hotels, supra, so as to give the laches defense its full effect. However, Hussian had every reason to believe that Anaconda was aware of his intentions, since he had been discovered in the Mattoon plant, and had offered jobs to or sought information from Anaconda employees. Anaconda's failure to protest or even to investigate his activities could justifiably have given Hussian the impression that he had the right to pursue the course of action he was following. Although Hussian's original scheme did amount to conscious wrongdoing, Anaconda's seeming acquiescence in his activities makes the continuation of his wrongful conduct less egregious. We turn now to the impact of this state of affairs on relief.

While Anaconda has failed to rebut the presumption of laches by disproving the existence of inexcusable delay or of prejudice, it has, as we have seen, succeeded in demonstrating that Metric was a conscious wrongdoer. There is some authority to the effect that laches will bar the award of damages against even a conscious wrongdoer, but will not bar injunctive relief. [Citations omitted.] On the other hand, most recent decisions discussing the conscious wrongdoer doctrine as a bar to laches assume that conscious wrongdoing, if proved, would totally negate the defense of laches permitting both damages and injunctive relief. E.g., TWM Manufacturing, supra.

We do not find it necessary to subscribe to one rule or the other. The essential nature of laches lies in the balancing of equities in light of the particular circumstances of each case. [Citation omitted.] Because the egregiousness of Metric's conduct is offset by the unreasonableness of Anaconda's inaction, particularly its inaction after Hussian was aware that Anaconda was aware of his activities, we do not believe that it would be fair either to permit laches to bar the action totally, or to permit the conscious wrongdoer doctrine completely to counteract the laches defense. Given the rather unique facts of this case, the result which we deem appropriate is to bar the plaintiff's damage claim because of laches, but to permit its claim for injunctive relief. This result is in accordance with Hanover Star, supra, and is also based on our recognition that the showing of conscious wrongdoing here is not as strong as that contemplated in decisions like TWM Manufacturing, supra.

We are confident that it is within our power to limit the effect of the laches defense in this manner, since the invocation of laches is an appeal to the equitable side of the court. [Citation omitted.] "Whether laches bars an action in a given case depends upon the circumstances of that case and 'is a question primarily addressed to the discretion of the trial court.' " Burnett v. New York Central Railroad Co., 380 U.S. 424, 435, 85 S.Ct. 1050, 1058, 13 L.Ed.2d 941 (1965), quoting Gardner v. Panama Railroad Co., 342 U.S. 29, 30, 72 S.Ct. 12, 13, 96 L.Ed. 31 (1951). The equities of this case, as we perceive them, require that we deny the laches defense its full effect of barring all relief, but give it partial effect. Consequently, we will grant equitable relief, but will not award damages because of the plaintiff's laches. The remaining question is how long injunctive relief should be effective.

. . . .

## NOTES AND QUESTIONS:

1. The traditional elements of laches are: (a) inexcusable delay in instituting suit and (b) prejudice to the defendant resulting from the delay. The court in *Anaconda* applied these traditional elements in reaching its decision. Can you think of any special considerations as to why a plaintiff should act quickly in bringing a suit when trade secrets are involved, as compared to other types of torts?

2. In *Anaconda*, the court made a determination as to whether the plaintiff delayed too long before asserting its rights. Why should a court simply not rely on the statute of limitations in a trade secret action for determining the timeliness of a lawsuit?

### (2) Statute of Limitations Issues

## VON BRIMER v. WHIRLPOOL CORP.

367 F. Supp. 740 (N.D. Cal. 1973)

Defendant also contends that, even if plaintiffs were able to establish all of the substantive elements of their claim, summary judgment must be entered against plaintiffs on the first claim because the action is barred by the applicable statute of limitations. The parties agree that in an action in which jurisdiction is based on diversity of citizenship, the Court must apply the appropriate California statute as construed by that state's courts. They disagree, however, on the specific statute to be applied. Relying on Monolith Portland Midwest Co. v. Kaiser Aluminum & C. Corp., 407 F.2d 288 (9 Cir. 1969), defendant contends that the applicable statute is § 339(1) of California Code of Civil Procedure which imposes a two-year limitation upon actions "upon a contract, obligation or liability not founded upon an instrument of writing ***." The holding in the Monolith case was based upon an express and unchallenged finding of the district court that " 'no conduct of the defendants *** was shown to constitute any variety of fraud ***.' " 407 F.2d at 293, n. 4. Plaintiffs' specific allegations of fraud, which are assumed to be true for the purposes of this motion, clearly distinguish the instant case from the Monolith ruling.

Given this assumption of fraud, the applicable limitation period is three years with the action accruing when the aggrieved party discovers facts constituting the fraud. § 338(4), California Code of Civil Procedure. Interpreting this section, the California Supreme Court has held:

> The statute commences to run only after one has knowledge of facts sufficient to make a reasonably prudent person suspicious of fraud, thus putting him on inquiry.

Hobart v. Hobart Estate Co., 26 Cal.2d 412, 437, 159 P.2d 958, 972 (1945). [Citation omitted.]

The aggrieved person must, of course, have available to him the means of inquiry into the facts constituting the fraud before he will be charged with constructive knowledge of those facts. [Citation omitted.]

The complaint was filed on May 13, 1969. More than three years earlier, von Brimer had received a notice dated April 26, 1966, from the Patent Office advising him that Interference Number 95,373 had been declared with regard to his Patent Number 3,194,032 on a "Washing Machine and Electromagnetic Drive System Therefor." This notice specified the claims of von Brimer's patent which were involved in the interference and identified the opposing parties as Robert E. Lake and his assignee, Whirlpool Corporation. Finally, the two-page notice specified the precise claims which conflicted.

While this question of knowledge can be a factual one, "when [the] knowledge had by or imputed to plaintiff is such as to compel the conclusion that a prudent man would have suspected the fraud, the court may determine as a matter of law that there has been 'discovery.' " Helfer v. Hubert, 208 Cal.App.2d at 26-27, 24 Cal.Rptr. at 902. Under all of the circumstances, including von Brimer's firsthand knowledge of the disclosures made to Whirlpool in August, 1962, the April 26, 1966, notice of interference was clearly sufficient to have made a reasonably prudent man suspicious of fraud and thus to have commenced the running of the period of limitation as a matter of law.

Plaintiffs argue that von Brimer did not actually discover the fraud until July 13, 1966, when he received Robert E. Lake's Preliminary Statement with regard to Interference Number 95,373. This contention is unpersuasive. Actual knowledge of Whirlpool's defense of priority as revealed in Lake's Preliminary Statement was not necessary to make von Brimer suspicious of the alleged fraudulent appropriation. The April 26, 1966, notice to von Brimer was enough to put him on inquiry. Under the Patent Office rules and practice then in effect, no interference would have been declared unless the Lake application and the von Brimer patent claimed a common subject matter and until the conflicting claims were expressed in exactly the same language, excluding immaterial limitations or variations. Moreover, the parties listed on the interference notice, Lake and Whirlpool, were the very parties to whom von Brimer had disclosed his invention during the 1962 negotiations. Unlike the defendants in Sime v. Malouf, 95 Cal.App.2d 82, 212 P.2d 946, supra, Whirlpool did not close off von Brimer's avenues of inquiry by intentionally concealing its identity and filing the interfering patent application in the name of a dummy agent. In fact, counsel for plaintiffs conceded at oral argument that the April 26, 1966, notice would have made von Brimer realize that " 'there's something fishy here' ***." These facts and this suspicion clearly compel the conclusion that, as a matter of law, "discovery" under § 338(4), California Code of Civil Procedure, occurred upon receipt of the April 26, 1966, notice and, therefore, the three-year limitation period of that section began to run at that time.

Plaintiffs also contend that the statute of limitations was tolled under § 356, California Code of Civil Procedure, by the interference action. Section 356 is operative when a "plaintiff is legally prevented from taking action to protect his rights." Hoover v. Galbraith, 7 Cal.3d 519, 526, 102 Cal.Rptr. 733, 737, 498 P.2d 981, 985 (1972) (statute tolled during pendency of appeal); Dillon v. Board of Pension Com'rs., 18 Cal.2d 427, 431, 116 P.2d 37, 39 (1941) (city charter required Board action before court proceedings permitted); see also Eistrat v. Cekada, 50 Cal.2d 289, 291-292, 324 P.2d 881, 882 (1958) (federal restraining order prohibits action against bankrupt or his property).

The facts disclose no injunction or statutory bar which legally prevented von Brimer from filing and prosecuting his claim for fraudulent appropriation. The mere declaration of an interference by the Patent Office has no such effect. Interference actions in the Patent Office do not prevent a federal court from exercising jurisdiction over a patent infringement action. [Citation omitted.] A fortiori an interference action would not prevent prosecution of an unfair competition suit which is based on activities predating the issuance of the patent. Section 356 had no effect on the running of the statute of limitations in this action. Therefore, von Brimer's first claim was time-barred three years after the receipt of the April 26, 1966, notice.

. . . .

## COMPUTER ASSOCIATES INTERNATIONAL, INC. v. ALTAI, INC.

918 S.W.2d 435 (Tex. 1996)

This case comes to us on certified questions from the United States Court of Appeals for the Second Circuit. Computer Assocs. Int'l, Inc. v. Altai, Inc., 22 F.3d 32 (2d Cir. 1994). We are asked to decide two issues: (1) whether the discovery rule exception to section 16.003(a) of the Texas Civil Practice and Remedies Code applies to claims for misappropriation of trade secrets; and if not, (2) whether the application to such claims of the two-year limitations period provided by section 16.003(a) contravenes the "open courts" provision of Article I, Section 13 of the Texas Constitution. We hold that the discovery rule exception does not apply to the claim for misappropriation of trade secrets and that application of section 16.003(a) does not violate the Texas Constitution.

1. The certified questions are included as an appendix to the Court's opinion.

I

Claude Arney, a developer of computer software, was employed by Computer Associates International, Inc., in its Dallas office from 1978 until January 1984. During his employment, Arney signed an employment agreement which prohibited him from retaining or divulging Computer Associates' trade secrets. In January 1984, Arney left Computer Associates to accept employment at Altai, Inc. In an exit interview, Arney represented that he retained no proprietary information of

Computer Associates and would not divulge Computer Associates' trade secrets to any third party. However, when Arney left Computer Associates he took copies of the computer source code for two versions of ADAPTER. ADAPTER is an operating system compatibility component of CA-SCHEDULER, which is a job scheduling program for IBM mainframe computers. ADAPTER connects CA-SCHEDULER with the three different operating systems used on IBM mainframe computers and enables CA-SCHEDULER to run on any of the IBM operating systems. ADAPTER was also used with a group of Computer Associates' programs called the DYNAM line. However, ADAPTER is not a separate product and is not capable of operating as an independent product. Before Arney left Computer Associates, Altai developed ZEKE, a job scheduling program for IBM mainframe computers which was similar to CA-SCHEDULER. In early 1984, Arney copied approximately thirty percent of the ADAPTER source code to write OSCAR 3.4 for Altai. It is undisputed that no one at Altai (other than Arney) knew that Arney possessed the ADAPTER source code or that Arney had copied portions of the source code when he created OSCAR 3.4. OSCAR 3.4 is Altai's operating system compatibility component which was used in several of Altai's programs, including ZEKE. Like ADAPTER, OSCAR 3.4 is not a separate product and is not capable of operating as an independent product. From 1985 to August 1988, Altai used OSCAR 3.4 as a component of several of its computer programs that competed with several of Computer Associates' programs.

In July 1988, Computer Associates first discovered that Altai had copied and used the ADAPTER source code in several of its computer programs. In August 1988, Computer Associates sued Altai in federal district court for misappropriation of trade secrets and copyright infringement. Among other things, the federal district court determined that Computer Associates' action for misappropriation of trade secrets under Texas law was preempted by the federal copyright act. Computer Assocs. Int'l, Inc. v. Altai, Inc., 775 F. Supp. 544, 563-66 (E.D.N.Y. 1991). The United States Court of Appeals reversed and remanded for further consideration of Computer Associates' misappropriation claims. Computer Assocs. Int'l, Inc. v. Altai, Inc., 982 F.2d 693, 720-21 (2d Cir. 1992). On remand, the district court determined that the discovery rule exception did not apply and that Computer Associates' action for misappropriation of trade secrets was barred by section 16.003(a) of the Texas Civil Practice and Remedies Code. Computer Assocs. Int'l, Inc. v. Altai, Inc., 832 F. Supp. 50, 51-52 (E.D.N.Y. 1993). Subsequently, the United States Court of Appeals certified the questions to this Court. Computer Assocs. Int'l, Inc. v. Altai, Inc., 22 F.3d 32 (2d Cir. 1994).

II

Computer Associates argues that the discovery rule exception to the two-year statute of limitations should apply to a claim of misappropriation of trade secrets. A trade secret is any formula, pattern, device or compilation of information which is used in one's business and presents an opportunity to obtain an advantage over competitors who do not know or use it. [Citation omitted.] A cause of action for misappropriation of trade secrets accrues when the trade secret is actually used. [Citation omitted.] The parties do not contest that, upon accrual, section 16.003(a) of the Texas Civil Practice and Remedies Code establishes a two-year statute of limitations for injury to the property of another or conversion of the property of another. In this case, Altai first used the source code in 1985. Not until 1988 did Computer Associates file its suit. Altai concedes that Computer Associates did not know about the use of the source code until 1988. The question is whether we should permit the discovery rule exception in these circumstances.

To answer this question, we must understand the objective of statutes of limitations. The purpose of statutes of limitations is to compel the assertion of claims within a reasonable period while the evidence is fresh in the minds of the parties and witnesses. [Citation omitted.] "Society's interest in repose is to have disputes either settled or barred within a reasonable time. It is based on the theory that the uncertainty and insecurity caused by unsettled claims hinder the flow of commerce." Safeway Stores, Inc. v. Certainteed Corp., 710 S.W.2d 544, 545 (Tex. 1986). The discovery rule exception defers accrual of a cause of action until the plaintiff knew or, exercising reasonable diligence, should have known of the facts giving rise to the cause of action. [Citation omitted.] The discovery rule, in application, proves to be a very limited exception to statutes of limitations.

Similar to the discovery rule exception, where fraud is alleged, we have granted the claimant the benefit of deferring the cause of action until the claimant discovered or should have discovered the fraud. [Citation omitted.] We have also permitted claimants to receive the benefit of deferring the accrual of a cause of action in cases where the facts forming the basis of an injury were concealed. [Citation omitted.] In short, we have said: "Fraud vitiates whatever it touches, Morris v. House, 32 Tex. 492 (1870), and . . . limitations begin to run from the time the fraud is discovered or could have been discovered by the defrauded party by exercise of reasonable diligence." Estate of Stonecipher, 591 S.W.2d at 809. Although similar in effect, the discovery rule exception and deferral based on fraud or concealment exist for different reasons. Unlike the discovery rule exception, deferral in the context of fraud or concealment resembles equitable estoppel. "Fraudulent concealment estops the defendant from relying on the statute of limitations as an affirmative defense to [the] plaintiff's claim." Borderlon v. Peck, 661 S.W.2d 907, 908 (Tex. 1983).

Unrelated to fraud or concealment, this Court has permitted the discovery rule exception in certain limited circumstances. From these cases, we can glean a unifying principle which facilitates balancing those factors that are considered before this Court has permitted application of the discovery rule exception to the statute of limitations. [HN7] Generally, application has been permitted in those cases where the nature of the injury incurred is inherently undiscoverable and the evidence of injury is objectively verifiable. The requirement of inherent undiscoverability recognizes that the discovery rule exception should be permitted only in circumstances where "it is difficult for the injured party to learn of the negligent act or omission." Willis v. Maverick, 760 S.W.2d 642, 645 (Tex. 1988); see Kelley v. Rinkle, 532 S.W.2d 947, 949 (Tex. 1976) ("A person will not ordinarily have any reason to suspect that he has been defamed by the publication of a false credit report to a credit agency until he makes application for credit . . . ."); Hays v. Hall, 488 S.W.2d 412, 414 (Tex. 1972) ("One who undergoes a vasectomy operation, and then after tests is told that he is sterile, cannot know that he is still fertile, if that be the case, until either his wife becomes pregnant or he is shown to be fertile by further testing."); Gaddis, 417 S.W.2d at 580 ("It is a virtual certainty that the patient has no knowledge on the day following surgery — nor for a long time thereafter — that a foreign object was left in the incision.").

We note that, in Willis, we also relied on the fiduciary relationship obligating an attorney to "render a full and fair disclosure of facts material to the client's representation." 760 S.W.2d at 645. We stated that "facts which might ordinarily require investigation likely may not excite suspicion where a fiduciary relationship is involved," and that absent the discovery rule exception the client "would have to hire a second attorney to observe the work of the first." 760 S.W.2d at 645-46. But the fiduciary rationale is, in reality, a variation on the inherently undiscoverable element. Fiduciaries are presumed to possess superior knowledge, meaning the injured party, the client, is presumed to possess less information than the fiduciary. Consequently, in the fiduciary context, it may be said that the nature of the injury is presumed to be inherently undiscoverable, although a person owed a fiduciary duty has some responsibility to ascertain when an injury occurs. [Citation omitted.]

We now consider whether to permit the application of the discovery rule exception to the statute of limitations in misappropriation of trade secret cases in light of the unifying principle: (1) whether the injury is inherently undiscoverable; and (2) whether evidence of the injury is objectively verifiable. Computer Associates asserts that it could not have reasonably discovered the theft of its trade secret within two years after Altai's first actual use. Therefore, Computer Associates argues that its cause of action was inherently undiscoverable. It bolsters its contention by focusing on Altai's oral stipulation which states that Computer Associates did not know or have reason to know of Altai's alleged misappropriation within the two-year statute of limitations. Computer Associates misconstrues the meaning of "inherently undiscoverable." [HN8] Inherently undiscoverable encompasses the requirement that the existence of the injury is not ordinarily discoverable, even though due diligence has been used.

In this age of technological innovation, intellectual property, including trade secrets, is a jealously guarded commodity. Extensive precautions are taken to prevent and eliminate trade secret misappropriations, the intention being to promote the rapid detection of misappropriation. See generally 3 MILGRIM ON TRADE SECRETS § 13.04[2] (1993)(identifying only forty-three out of a reported six-thousand trade secret misappropriation cases — less than one percent — that implicated the statute of limitations). While some trade secret misappropriations might not be quickly discovered, this isolated fact does not alter the reality that, in most cases, trade secret misappropriation generally is capable of detection within the time allotted for bringing such suits. Id. In the present case, Arney misappropriated Computer Associates' source code by absconding with a stack of "greenbar" computer paper upon which the code was printed when he left the company. As Altai points out, Computer Associates could have detected Arney's theft by using document control logs — a common practice among high technology companies dependent upon trade secrets. [Citations omitted.]

Additionally, we live in a world of high employee mobility and easy transportability of information. Under these circumstances, it is not unexpected that a former employee will go to work for a competitor and that the competitor might thereby acquire trade secrets. [Citations omitted.] This reality is reflected in the confidentiality agreement requested of and exit interview given to Arney by Computer Associates. Vigilance in the area of trade secrets is required, particularly because once a trade secret is made public all ownership is lost. See, e.g., Luccous v. J.C. Kinley Co., 376 S.W.2d 336, 338 (Tex. 1964) ("It is self-evident that the subject matter of a trade secret must be kept secret."); see also Schalk v. State, 823 S.W.2d 633, 638-44 (Tex. Crim. App. 1991), cert. denied, 503 U.S. 1006, 112 S. Ct. 1763, 118 L. Ed. 2d 425 (1992) (discussing various measures taken to insure secrecy). High employee mobility and critical interest in maintaining a proprietary interest in a trade secret are endemic to the computer software industry. [HN12] Suspicions should abound when a competitor markets a product similar to that previously developed by a former employer after one of the former employer's employees begins work for the competitor.

In the past, this Court has noted the "shocking results" of barring a plaintiff's suit before the injury has even been discovered. See Gaddis, 417 S.W.2d at 581; Hays, 488 S.W.2d at 414. This rationale offers no principled basis for distinguishing between cases in which the rule applies and those in which it does not. If carried to its logical conclusion, the rationale mandates applying the discovery rule exception to every case, thus eviscerating the whole notion of an absolute time bar to litigation. It is clear that "preclusion of a legal remedy alone is not enough to justify a judicial exception to the statute. The primary purpose of limitations, to prevent litigation of stale or fraudulent claims, must be kept in mind." Robinson v. Weaver, 550 S.W.2d 18, 20 (Tex. 1977). The discovery rule is a limited exception to strict compliance with the statute of limitations. [Citation omitted.] Because misappropriation of trade secrets is not a cause of action that is inherently undiscoverable, permitting application of the discovery rule exception in these cases would do no more than permit the litigation of stale claims.

Before concluding, we note that the principle we have applied has two elements. The second element is that the alleged injury be objectively verifiable. See e.g., Gaddis, 417 S.W.2d at 581 ("This is a peculiar type of case [leaving sponge in patient] which is not particularly susceptible to fraudulent prosecution."). Requiring objective verifiability assures that the policy underpinnings of statutes of limitations are met — balancing the possibility of stale or fraudulent claims against individual injustice. We relied heavily on this element in deciding not to extend the discovery rule exception to cases of medical misdiagnoses: "Unlike Gaddis v. Smith there exists in the present case no physical evidence which in-and-of-itself establishes the negligence of some person." Robinson, 550 S.W.2d at 21. And we considered this element in at least one other case. [Citation omitted.] Because trade secret misappropriation claims are not inherently undiscoverable, it is not necessary for us to reach the question of whether such misappropriations may be verified by objective evidence.

Finally, we recognize that thirty-nine states and the District of Columbia have adopted the Uniform Trade Secrets Act, which provides a discovery rule exception that tolls the statute of limitations in misappropriation of trade secret cases. See UNIF. TRADE SECRETS ACT § 6, 14 U.L.A. 462 (1990) (citing laws of Alabama, Alaska, Arizona, Arkansas, California, Colorado, Connecticut, Delaware, District of Columbia, Florida, Georgia, Hawaii, Idaho, Illinois, Indiana, Iowa, Kansas, Kentucky, Louisiana, Maine, Maryland, Minnesota, Mississippi, Montana, Nebraska, Nevada, New Hampshire, New Mexico, North Carolina, North Dakota, Oklahoma, Oregon, Rhode Island, South Carolina, South Dakota, Utah, Virginia, Washington, West Virginia and Wisconsin). No state supreme court, however, has yet adopted the discovery rule exception for trade secret cases as an exercise of its common law jurisdiction. [Citations omitted.] We decline to be the first. We will not overlay section 16.003(a) with the discovery rule exception for misappropriation of trade secret causes of action.

III

Having determined that the discovery rule exception does not apply in this case, we must address Computer Associates' challenge to the two-year statute of limitations period provided by section 16.003(a) as violating the "open courts" provision of Article I, Section 13 of the Texas Constitution. It does not. The "open courts" provision guarantees that "meaningful remedies must be afforded, 'so that the legislature may not abrogate the right to assert a well-established common law cause of action unless the reason for its action outweighs the litigants' constitutional right of redress.' " Trinity River Auth., 889 S.W.2d at 261 (quoting Texas Ass'n of Business v. Texas Air Control Bd., 852 S.W.2d 440, 448 (Tex. 1993)). Therefore, a litigant alleging a violation of this guarantee must first show the abrogation of a cognizable common law cause of action and second, that the restriction is unreasonable or arbitrary when balanced against the purpose and basis of the statute. Sax v. Votteler, 648 S.W.2d 661, 666 (Tex. 1983).

The traditional rule in Texas is that a cause of action accrues and the two-year limitations period begins to run as soon as the owner suffers some injury, regardless of when the injury becomes discoverable. [Citation omitted.] Failure to permit a discovery rule exception to this traditional rule does not abrogate a common law right. Id. Even assuming that section 16.003(a) is legislative action which affects a common law cause of action for purposes of "open courts" analysis, application of a two-year statute of limitations without a discovery rule exception is not unreasonable or arbitrary when balanced against the purpose of the statute. As we explained above, a significant purpose of statutes of limitations is to prevent the litigation of stale and fraudulent claims. This policy, combined with the nature of trade secret property rights, which requires an owner to vigilantly guard the secret from the world in order to preserve its rights, makes application of the two-year statute of limitations reasonable under the circumstances.

## NOTES AND QUESTIONS:

1. In *Von Brimer v. Whirlpool Corp.*, 367 F. Supp. 740 (N.D. Cal. 1973), the court dealt extensively with the question of whether the plaintiff's cause of action sounded in tort or contract. Eliminating the need to determine whether trade secret litigation is a contract or tort action, the statute of limitations provision of the UTSA states that:

> An action for misappropriation must be brought within 3 years after the misappropriation is discovered or by the exercise of reasonable diligence

> should have been discovered. For the purposes of this section, a continuing misappropriation constitutes a single claim.

Uniform Trade Secrets Act § 6. This section of the UTSA also eliminates the need to ensure that an action is pled correctly when the limitations period might be an issue. This question is still an issue for states that have not adopted the UTSA.

2. By adopting the discovery rule, the UTSA also eliminated the question of whether it applies in trade secret cases, which was at issue in *Computer Associates International, Inc. v. Altai, Inc.*, 918 S.W.2d 453 (Tex. 1996). Why is the rule applied in *Computer Associates* manifestly unfair to trade secret owners? Texas came to its senses after *Computer Associates* was decided, by passing legislation adopting the discovery rule for trade secret cases. *See* TEX. CIV. PRAC. & REM. CODE ANN. § 10.010(b)(Vernon 2002).

3. As explained in the Comment to § 6 of the UTSA, "[t]here presently is a conflict of authority as to whether trade secret misappropriation is a continuing wrong." If the continuing tort doctrine is applied to trade secrets, a new limitations period starts each time a trade secret is used. The Comment clarifies that:

> This Act rejects a continuing wrong approach to the statute of limitations but delays the commencement of the limitation period until an aggrieved person discovers or reasonably should have discovered the existence of misappropriation. If objectively reasonable notice of misappropriation exists, three years is sufficient time to vindicate one's legal rights.

Do you agree?

## F. INSURANCE COMPANY INDEMNIFICATION

### CONTINENTAL CASUALTY CO. v. CONSOLIDATED GRAPHICS INC.

646 F.3d 210 (5th Cir. 2011)

Consolidated Graphics Inc., Thousand Oaks Printing & Specialties, Inc., and Daniel Chambers (collectively, the Consolidated Graphics defendants) seek to recover the cost of defending a suit against them and indemnity for an adverse judgment entered against them in that suit from two insurers, Continental Casualty Company (Continental) and Sentry Insurance (Sentry). The Consolidated Graphics defendants appeal the district court's grant of summary judgment in favor of the insurers. We affirm.

I

This case concerns whether either Sentry, the primary insurer, or Continental, an excess insurer, has a duty to defend and indemnify the Consolidated Graphics defendants in an underlying tort suit. We begin with the facts of that underlying litigation.

Thousand Oaks Printing & Specialties, Inc. (Thousand Oaks), a California corporation, is a subsidiary of Consolidated Graphics, a large printing and graphics corporation. Rudamac, Inc. (Rudamac) is a family-owned printing company in California. Daniel Chambers, the nephew of Rudamac's owner and president, was employed by Rudamac for approximately nine years. When Chambers's aunt refused to give him an ownership interest in the company, he devised a scheme to direct a substantial portion of Rudamac's business to Thousand Oaks and to become an employee of one of the Consolidated Graphics defendants. He allegedly misappropriated trade secrets, including price information, private data regarding product prices, profit margins, and information about promotions given, to three of Rudamac's customers: Dacor, AIG and Tiger Woods Foundation. Thousand Oaks and Consolidated Graphics were allegedly actively complicit in this scheme.

Rudamac sued Consolidated Graphics, Thousand Oaks, and Chambers in California state court for misappropriation of trade secrets, unfair business practices, intentional interference with prospective economic advantage, breach of fiduciary duty, constructive trust, unjust enrichment, a demand for an accounting, and intentional interference with at-will employment relations. Rudamac alleged that Chambers acted for himself and as the undisclosed agent of Consolidated Graphics and Thousand Oaks. The case was tried to a jury on theories of misappropriation, interference, and breach of fiduciary duty, and the jury found against the Consolidated Graphics defendants on all counts. The jury awarded Rudamac $5,698,000 in compensatory damages. The jury also awarded $1,500,000 in punitive damages against Thousand Oaks and $6,647,000 in punitive damages against Consolidated Graphics. The judgment rendered in the California trial court was affirmed on appeal.

Consolidated Graphics and its subsidiaries were insured under two primary liability insurance policies issued by Sentry and an excess liability insurance policy issued by Continental. Each of the policies provided liability coverage for "advertising injury." While the Rudamac litigation was pending, Continental brought a declaratory judgment action against the Consolidated Graphics defendants in federal court, which had diversity jurisdiction. Sentry intervened. Both Continental and Sentry sought a declaratory judgment that they had no duty to defend or indemnify the Consolidated Graphics defendants in the Rudamac litigation, contending that no "advertising injury" had been alleged in that underlying suit or had occurred within the meaning of the policies. The parties filed cross motions for summary judgment, and the district court granted summary judgment in favor of Continental and Sentry. The Consolidated Graphics defendants now appeal.

## II

We first consider Sentry's policies and its duty to defend. The parties agree that Texas law governs, and Texas law instructs that an insurer's duty to defend is determined under the eight-corners doctrine. The court considers only the factual allegations in the pleadings and the terms of the insurance policy. "If a petition does not allege facts within the scope of coverage, an insurer is not legally required to defend a suit against its insured.

In applying the eight-corners rule, the court construes the pleadings liberally. The liability insurer has a duty to defend "if the facts alleged in the pleadings would give rise to any claim within the coverage of the policy."

The Sentry policies included liability coverage for "advertising injury" and provided:

> a. We will pay those sums that the insured becomes legally obligated to pay as damages because of "personal injury" or "advertising injury" to which this insurance applies. We will have the right and duty to defend any "suit" seeking those damages.
>
> . . .
>
> [ ]b[.] This insurance applies to:
>
> . . .
>
> (2) "Advertising injury" caused by an offense committed in the course of advertising your goods, products or services . . .
>
> "Advertising injury" is defined as:
>
> injury arising out of one or more of the following offenses:
>
> a. Oral or written publication of material that slanders or libels a person or organization or disparages a person's or organization's goods, products or services;
>
> b. Oral or written publication of material that violates a person's right of privacy;
>
> c. Misappropriation of advertising ideas or style of doing business; or
>
> d. Infringement of copyright, title or slogan.
>
> The policy does not define the term "advertising" or "advertisement."
>
> The Consolidated Graphics defendants rely on only one of the foregoing offenses, "[m]isappropriation of advertising ideas or style of doing business," in support of their claim in this court that Sentry had a duty to defend them. They point to four paragraphs in the complaint filed by Rudamac in the underlying tort litigation, which alleged:
>
> 19. Plaintiff's customer and supplier lists are compilations of detailed information about each of its customers and suppliers . . . . [T]his information typically included specialized information, including a list of key personnel and decision-makers with the customer or supplier's company as well as specific contract information . . .
>
> . . .
>
> 21. Plaintiff's trade secret/financial information includes price information, including private data regarding the competitive pricing of the products, profit margin, particularized pricing information such as mark ups, discounts, or other promotions given . . .
>
> 22. Plaintiff's marketing strategies include Plaintiff's long and short-term plans for developing new and existing suppliers for various orders and products.

. . .

> 42. Plaintiff alleges . . . that [Defendants] utilized [Rudamac's] successful business history and pricing strategy to solicit and misappropriate customers . . . of [Rudamac] . . .

The district court concluded that the allegations regarding "pricing . . . promotions" alleged "[m]isappropriation of [an] advertising idea[ ]" within the meaning of Sentry's policy. We will assume, without deciding, that this is a correct construction of the policy under Texas law. We need not reach that issue because the district court further held, and we agree, that there were no facts alleged in the Rudamac litigation that would support a finding that an "advertising injury" was "committed in the course of advertising [the Consolidated Graphics defendants'] goods, products or services" as required under the Sentry policy.

The Consolidated Graphics defendants assert that the term "advertising" must be construed broadly under Texas law. However, decisions of the Texas courts and of this court applying Texas law lead us to conclude that the concept of "advertising" cannot be stretched to encompass the allegations in the Rudamac suit.

The Supreme Court of Texas was called upon to construe the meaning of "advertising" in Smith v. Baldwin. The plaintiff in that case had asserted a claim under provisions of the Texas Deceptive Trade Practices Act that declared " 'advertising goods or services with intent not to sell them as advertised' " to be a deceptive or misleading practice. The Texas court turned to Black's Law Dictionary for a definition of "advertise," citing with approval the following definition:

> Advertise. To advise, announce, apprise, command, give notice of, inform, make known, publish. On call to the public attention by any means whatsoever. Any oral, written, or graphic statement made by the seller in any manner in connection with the solicitation of business and includes, without limitation because of enumeration, statements and representations made in a newspaper or other publication or on radio or television or contained in any notice, handbill, sign, catalog, or letter, or printed on or contained in any tag or label attached to or accompanying any merchandise.

The misrepresentations at issue in Smith v. Baldwin included a builder's statement in a contract to build a home that, when completed, would meet the requirements for a final Veterans Administration inspection compliance report. The Supreme Court of Texas indicated that "advertising" connotes public notice of some sort, and that the representations at issue were not "advertising." The court reasoned that "[t]he representations concerning compliance with V.A. standards and regulations and the ability to complete the house as scheduled were not marketing devices designed to induce the public to patronize Alan Baldwin, Builder. Smith was not enticed to enter into a contractual relationship because of a public notice drawing attention to Baldwin's capabilities as a contractor."

A Texas intermediate court of appeals has held that "advertising injury," when used in an insurance policy, contemplates dissemination to the public. In ANR Production Co. v. American Guarantee & Liability Insurance Co., a Texas court of appeals considered whether an insurer had a duty to defend, pursuant to an insurance policy covering "advertising injury," against claims alleging breach of contract, fraud, negligent misrepresentation, and violations of the Texas Deceptive Trade Practices Act. In holding that the insurer had no duty to defend, the court explained that " '[a]dvertising' is defined as advising, announcing, or publishing a matter to the public. It is distinguished from other forms of communication in that it calls a matter to the public's attention." The court further noted that if it accepted the insured's broad definition of advertising, "any time parties negotiated any kind of contract, there would be a potential for coverage under advertising injury for representations or omissions made during the negotiations."

In Sport Supply Group, Inc. v. Columbia Casualty Co., we considered and applied Texas law in construing the meaning of "misappropriation of advertising ideas" in an insurance policy. We concluded that "[u]nder Texas law, it appears that the term 'advertising' in an insurance policy is used in a conventional sense: to refer to a public announcement (such as on a billboard, in a newspaper, on a signpost, or in a television or radio commercial) that 'induce[s] the public to patronize' a particular establishment or to buy a particular product."

The Consolidated Graphics defendants cite cases from other jurisdictions, including the Minnesota Supreme Court's decision in General Casualty Co. of Wisconsin v. Wozniak Travel, Inc., in which that court defined "advertising" broadly as "any oral, written, or graphic statement made by the seller in any manner in connection with the solicitation of business." The Consolidated Graphics defendants also cite the Wisconsin Supreme Court's decision in Acuity v. Bagadia, in which that court observed that "advertising" is "susceptible to multiple reasonable interpretations," including a broad definition encompassing customer solicitation. There are additional decisions in jurisdictions other than Texas that ascribe a broad meaning to the term "advertising."

But Texas is not alone in its view that "advertising," in the context of an insurance policy, requires a measure of public dissemination. For example, the California Supreme Court, in Hameid v. National Fire Insurance of Hartford, considered whether an insurer had a duty to defend under the "advertising injury" coverage of its policy when the underlying complaint alleged that the insured took a competitor's customer list and solicited customers from the competitor. In concluding that the insurer owed no duty to defend, the court interpreted the term "advertising" as used in the policies to mean "widespread promotional activities usually directed to the public at large." The court noted that adopting a broader definition of advertising that would include one-on-one solicitation of customers "would encourage litigation" and "eliminate the clarity and certainty that is essential to the insurance industry." The court further explained that "defin[ing] 'advertising' to mean the widespread distribution of promotional materials to the public at large . . . interprets the contractual term under its ordinary and popular meaning. It allows uniformity in interpretation under different factual circumstances that may or may not lead to coverage." Other courts have expressed similar views.

Our responsibility, however, is to discern and apply Texas law. Texas law and our precedent make clear that in the Rudamac litigation against the Consolidated Graphics defendants, it was never alleged that the defendants caused an injury "in the course of advertising your goods, products or services" within the meaning of Sentry's policy. The contacts Chambers had with the three customers were not through public dissemination of any kind. They were direct dealings. The district court did not err in holding that Sentry had no duty to defend the Consolidated Graphics defendants.

## III

With good reason, the Consolidated Graphics defendants do not contend that they have inflicted an "advertising injury" within the meaning of Continental's excess liability policy. That policy defines advertising injury in pertinent part to include "[t]he use of another's advertising idea in your 'advertisement,' " and the policy expressly defines "advertisement" as "notice that is broadcast or published to the general public or specific market segments about your goods, products or services for the purpose of attracting customers or supporters." The Consolidated Graphics defendants do not assert that any conduct of this nature was alleged in the underlying tort litigation.

The Consolidated Graphics defendants argue only that if Sentry had a duty to defend, then Continental had a duty to defend if Sentry's policy limits were exhausted. We do not consider that argument because, as we have held, Sentry was not obligated to defend the Consolidated Graphics defendants.

## IV

A remaining issue is whether either of the insurers is obligated to indemnify the Consolidated Graphics defendants. The district court disposed of this issue in a single sentence, concluding, "Based on the court's finding of no duty to defend, it also follows from this judgment that neither party has a duty to indemnify," citing the Supreme Court of Texas's decision in Farmers Texas County Mutual Insurance Co. v. Griffin. The Consolidated Graphics defendants contend that the duty to indemnify cannot be resolved on the basis of the summary judgment record.

The Supreme Court of Texas did not hold in Griffin that there can be no duty to indemnify if there is no duty to defend, and we do not read the district court's opinion to so construe Griffin. The decision in Griffin observed that the Texas courts have long recognized that "[a]n insurer's duty to defend and duty to indemnify are distinct and separate duties." "It may sometimes be necessary to defer resolution of indemnity issues until the liability litigation is resolved. In some cases, coverage may turn on facts actually proven in the underlying lawsuit." "In many cases, however, the court may appropriately decide the rights of the parties before judgment is rendered in the underlying tort suit." In Griffin the insurer had no duty to defend, "and the same reasons that negate the duty to defend likewise negate any possibility the insurer will ever have a duty to indemnify." The Supreme Court of Texas therefore was able to determine that there was no duty to indemnify even though the underlying litigation had not concluded. The Supreme Court of Texas further explained the interplay between and independence of the duty to defend and the duty to indemnify in D.R. Horton-Texas, Ltd. v. Markel International Insurance Co.

At the time that the district court determined the insurers had no duty to indemnify the Consolidated Graphics defendants, the trial in the underlying tort litigation had concluded. Sentry moved for summary judgment based on the charge to the jury and its verdict in that case. The Consolidated Graphics defendants assert that the charge and verdict do not prove that the claims in that litigation were not covered. They cite a Fifth Circuit decision, National Union Fire Insurance Co. of Pittsburgh, Pennsylvania v. Puget Plastics Corp., for the proposition that evidence may be admitted in coverage litigation if the underlying case does not resolve the factual issues necessary to determine coverage. The Consolidated Graphics defendants misapprehend the respective burdens of proof.

Sentry is not relying on an exclusion in its policy in asserting that there is no coverage. It is relying on the insuring clauses. Under these circumstances, the Consolidated Graphics defendants have the burden of establishing that the claims for which they seek defense costs and indemnification come within their policy's coverage. Since the insurers did not have the burden on this issue, they could satisfy their summary judgment burden by pointing to the absence of evidence to support the Consolidated Graphics defendants' case. Sentry did this by pointing to the jury charge and verdict form. The Consolidated Graphics defendants then had the burden of "identify[ing] specific evidence in the record and articulat[ing] the manner in which that evidence" showed that they were entitled to coverage. The Consolidated Graphics defendants did not respond with any evidence that would establish a basis for coverage. Without any evidence suggesting that the Consolidated Graphics defendants disseminated Rudamac's trade secrets in a public manner, the Consolidated Graphics defendants cannot survive summary judgment. Accordingly, Continental and Sentry were entitled to summary judgment on this issue.

V

Lastly, the Consolidated Graphics defendants argue that the district court committed error by granting a motion by Sentry to amend its pleadings on the same day the court entered a final judgment in the case. They contend that they should have been allowed ten days to respond to the amended pleading. Sentry and Continental argue that any error in this regard was harmless. We agree. The district court did not grant judgment on the pleadings but rather based on Sentry's and Continental's summary judgment motions. The amended pleadings did not alter the summary judgment evidence in the record or the arguments in the motions. Accordingly, any error in this regard was harmless.

. . .

For the foregoing reasons, we AFFIRM the district court's judgment.

## NOTES AND QUESTIONS:

1. One of the first actions taken by attorneys retained to defend against a trade secret misappropriation claim is to check whether the defendant's general liability insurance policy might provide indemnification against the claim. As discussed in *Continental Casualty Co. v. Consolidated Graphics Inc.*, 646 F.3d 210 (5th Cir. 2011), coverage typically depends on whether the defendant can show that the claim resulted from an "advertising injury," as that term is defined in the policy. Even

though the court in *Continental Casualty* found that "it was never alleged that the defendants caused an injury 'in the course of advertising your goods, products or services,' " *id.* at 216, can you think of a situation where coverage would be granted in this case?

2. Would an action brought under § 43(a) of the Lanham Act, 15 U.S.C. § 1125(a), discussed above in Chapt. 3(A), be more likely to result in coverage than a state court action based on breach of the nondisclosure provisions in an employment agreement, where liability is based on "false designation of origin, false or misleading description of fact, or false or misleading representation of fact"? If so, why? If not, why not?

3. Can you think of any reason(s) why an attorney drafting a complaint for a trade secret case might want to avoid alleging an advertising-type of injury that would trigger coverage for the defendant?

# Chapter 4

# REMEDIES

## A. PRELIMINARY INJUNCTION

### UNIVERSITY OF TEXAS v. CAMENISCH
451 U.S. 390 (1981)

The purpose of a preliminary injunction is merely to preserve the relative positions of the parties until a trial on the merits can be held. Given this limited purpose, and given the haste that is often necessary if those positions are to be preserved, a preliminary injunction is customarily granted on the basis of procedures that are less formal and evidence that is less complete than in a trial on the merits. A party thus is not required to prove his case in full at a preliminary-injunction hearing [citation omitted], and the findings of fact and conclusions of law made by a court granting a preliminary injunction are not binding at trial on the merits [Citations omitted.]. In light of these considerations, it is generally inappropriate for a federal court at the preliminary-injunction stage to give a final judgment on the merits. [Citations omitted.]

Should an expedited decision on the merits be appropriate, Rule 65(a)(2) of the Federal Rules of Civil Procedure provides a means of securing one. That Rule permits a court to "order the trial of the action on the merits to be advanced and consolidated with the hearing of the application." Before such an order may issue, however, the courts have commonly required that "the parties should normally receive clear and unambiguous notice [of the court's intent to consolidate the trial and the hearing] either before the hearing commences or at a time which will still afford the parties a full opportunity to present their respective cases." Pughsley v. 3750 Lake Shore Drive Cooperative Bldg., 463 F.2d 1055, 1057 (C.A.7 1972); Nationwide Amusements, Inc. v. Nattin, 452 F.2d 651 (C.A.4 1971). This procedure was not followed here.

In short, where a federal district court has granted a preliminary injunction, the parties generally will have had the benefit neither of a full opportunity to present their cases nor of a final judicial decision based on the actual merits of the controversy. Thus when the injunctive aspects of a case become moot on appeal of a preliminary injunction, any issue preserved by an injunction bond can generally not be resolved on appeal, but must be resolved in a trial on the merits. Where, by contrast, a federal district court has granted a permanent injunction, the parties will already have had their trial on the merits, and, even if the case would otherwise be moot, a determination can be had on appeal of the correctness of the trial court's decision on the merits, since the case has been saved from mootness by the injunction bond.

The principle underlying this basic distinction, although sometimes honored in the breach, is reflected in the relevant precedents. For instance, in this Court's decision in Liner v. Jafco, Inc., 375 U.S. 301, 84 S.Ct. 391, 11 L.Ed.2d 347, a decision often cited for the proposition that an injunction bond prevents a case from becoming moot, the injunction was permanent, not preliminary. The District Court there had thus reached a final decision on the merits.

American Bible Society v. Blount, 446 F.2d 588 (C.A.3 1971), illuminates the distinction from a different angle. In that case, the plaintiffs had secured a preliminary injunction and had posted an injunction bond. When the issue of injunctive relief became moot, the Court of Appeals held that the case as a whole was not moot, since the defendant would "in all likelihood institute suit against the sureties at some future time and, in any such action, the court [would] be faced with deciding the same issues that are in contention here." Id., at 594. The appellate court ruled that liability on the injunction bond could not arise until there was a final judgment in favor of the defendant: "This rule is consistent with the policy considerations behind the injunction bond. The requirement of security is rooted in the belief that a defendant deserves protection against a court order granted without the full deliberation a trial offers." Id., at 595, n. 12. The court therefore remanded the case to the trial court, where such "full deliberation" could take place.

In Klein v. Califano, 586 F.2d 250 (C.A.3 1978), the same United States Court of Appeals, sitting en banc, was confronted with a different situation involving a moot injunction which was survived by a possible claim for recoupment on a bond. The court "recognize[d] that part of the rationale of American Bible Society was the policy of the Rule 65 security bond to protect defendants from the consequences of temporary restraining orders granted without opportunity for full deliberation of the merits of a dispute." Id., at 256. Because the District Court in Klein had "had such an opportunity to assess the merits of the complaint and [had] granted summary judgment and a permanent injunction," ibid., the Court of Appeals reached the merits of the case.

The present case is replete with circumstances indicating the necessity for a full trial on the merits in the nisi prius court, where a preliminary injunction has become moot and an injunction bond has been issued. The proceedings here bear the marks of the haste characteristic of a request for a preliminary injunction: the parties have relied on a short stipulation of facts, and even the legal theories on which the University has relied have seemed to change from one level of the proceeding to another. The District Court and the Court of Appeals both properly based their decisions not on the ultimate merits of Camenisch's case but rather on the balance of the Canal Authority factors. While it is true that some of the Court of Appeals' language suggests a conclusion that Camenisch would win on the merits, the court certainly did not hold that the standards for a summary judgment had been met.

In sum, the question whether a preliminary injunction should have been issued here is moot, because the terms of the injunction, as modified by the Court of Appeals, have been fully and irrevocably carried out. The question whether the University must pay for the interpreter remains for trial on the merits. Until such a trial has taken place, it would be inappropriate for this Court to intimate any view on the merits of the lawsuit.

## NOTES AND QUESTIONS:

1. Since time is often of the essence in trade secret litigation, the equitable remedy of preliminary relief is a valuable tool in enforcing trade secret rights. The UTSA does not specifically provide for preliminary relief, but states that "[a]ctual or threatened misappropriation may be enjoined." *See* UTSA § 2(a). Such injunctive relief may be sought under the Federal Rules of Civil Procedure or comparable state statues in the form of temporary restraining orders, preliminary stay orders, or temporary injunctions.

2. The Federal Rules of Civil Procedure permit courts to issue temporary restraining orders without notice to the defendant. *See* Fed. R. Civ. P. 65(b). In the absence of specific authority, such as that provided in the trademark anticounterfeiting law, courts are reluctant to grant such *ex parte* relief. *See* 15 U.S.C. § 1116(d). This reluctance, however, can often be overcome in trade secret cases involving misappropriated copyrightable materials such as engineering drawings and blueprints. If faced with such a situation, the plaintiff's attorney could include a cause of action under copyright laws for infringement and request an *ex parte* temporary restraining and seizure order, where such *ex parte* relief is sanctioned. *See* 17 U.S.C. §§ 502(a), 503(a). Seizure and impoundment of misappropriated materials without notice has proven to be extremely effective in preventing spoliation of evidence. A temporary restraining order regarding information stored in a computer would, for example, allow the plaintiff to download the computer's hard drive before it could be purged of misappropriated material. What potential problems could arise from using copyright laws in this way?

3. Under the Federal Rules of Civil Procedure, a temporary restraining order (TRO) lasts only 14 days unless it is renewed. *See* Fed. R. Civ. P. 65(b)(2). Even if a court grants a TRO, it is obligated to schedule a hearing for a preliminary injunction at the earliest possible time. *See* Fed. R. Civ. P. 65(b)(3). It is not uncommon for a court to accelerate the trial date and consolidate the preliminary injunction hearing with a trial on the merits. *See* Fed. R. Civ. P. 65(a)(2). A plaintiff who decides to pursue a preliminary injunction would be wise to be prepared for trial before filing the lawsuit.

4. The U.S. Supreme Court has summarized the essential elements a movant must establish before a court may grant a preliminary injunction as follows:

> A plaintiff seeking a preliminary injunction must establish that he is likely to succeed on the merits, that he is likely to suffer irreparable harm in the absence of preliminary relief, that the balance of equities tips in his favor, and that an injunction is in the public interest.

*Winter v. Nat. Res. Def. Council*, 555 U.S. 7, 20 (2008). What evidence would be relevant to show that the injunction would be in the public interest or the possibility of irreparable harm?

5. Although the court in *University of Texas v. Camenisch*, 451 U.S. 390, 395 (1981), held that "the findings of fact and conclusions of law made by a court granting a preliminary injunction are not binding at trial on the merits," there can be limited exceptions. (Citation omitted.) *See Am Gen. Corp. v. Daimler Chrysler Corp.*, 246 F. Supp. 2d 1030 (N.D. Ind. 2003). In *Am General*, the court held that its

earlier interpretation of the agreement in question "deserv[ed] preclusive effect." *Id.* at 1035-36.

## B. INEVITABLE DISCLOSURE DOCTRINE

### MAXXIM MEDICAL, INC. v. MICHAELSON

51 F. Supp. 2d 773 (S.D. Tex. 1999)

This case involves the scope of a covenant not to compete agreement, confidentiality agreement, and non-solicitation agreement entered into by Maxim and its prior employee, Michelson. It also involves whether Michelson is liable for conversion, breach of fiduciary duty, and misappropriation of trade secrets. Maxim is a Texas corporation with, until 1997, its corporate headquarters located in Sugarland, Texas. Maxim, among other things, provides doctors sterile prepackaged trays of medical utensils. Michelson was employed by Maxim and its predecessors in interest for several years as a salesman and a supervisor. Michelson lives in California, but in his most recent capacity for Maxim, he supervised ten salesmen that served clients not only in California, but also Nevada, and for a time, Arizona, and El Paso, Texas.

During his employment at Maxim, Michelson signed at least two stock option agreements. In consideration for receiving stock options. Michelson agreed not to compete with Maxim for a one year period and to keep Maxim's confidential information secret.

In January 1999, Michelson began to negotiate employment with another company, PHS. The day before Michelson resigned from Maxim, he exercised some of his stock options. He also requested a large batch of client information printed. The individual who received this request forwarded it to another office employee. Michelson contacted this office employee later and requested additional information. Because the request was so large, she started the printing job, but it would not be completed until later that evening. She left the list of requested information on her desk with a stapler on top of it. Before leaving, she noticed that Michelson was the last front office employee remaining.

The next day, the list was gone. After informing Michelson of such, Michelson told her that he had taken it. He also lied to her and told her that the client information she had printed was useless because the printing was off line. That same day, Michelson resigned from Maxim and started employment at PHS. After Maxim employees checked Michelson's laptop, they discovered that he had deleted a great deal of confidential company information from his hard drive.

* * *

California has adopted the Uniform Trade Secret Act ("UTSA"). Under the UTSA, a court may enjoin actual or threatened misappropriation. CAL. CIVIL CODE § 3426.2. In the landmark case of PepsiCo, Inc. v. Redmond, 54 F.3d 1262 (7th Cir. 1995), the court applied this provision of the UTSA to create what is now considered the "inevitable disclosure" doctrine.

Defendant William Redmond was a ten-year veteran sales employee of Pepsi. Id.

at 1264. By 1994, he had become General Manager of Pepsi's California Business Unit, having revenues of more than $ 500 million and representing 20% of Pepsi's North American profits. Id. Because Redmond's position was relatively high up in Pepsi's hierarchy, Redmond had access to significant inside information and Pepsi trade secrets, including sales and marketing plans and "pricing architecture." Id.

In the spring of 1994, a former Pepsi executive who had become the head of Quaker's Gatorade division began to solicit Redmond. Id. Quaker eventually offered Redmond the position of "Vice President-On Premises Sales." Id. For some time, Redmond negotiated with Quaker over the salary of the position. Id. Eventually, Quaker offered Redmond the position of "Vice President-Field Operations." Throughout this time, Redmond kept his Quaker negotiations secret from Pepsi. Id.

On November 10, 1994, Redmond finally announced to his superiors that he was leaving Pepsi to go to its fierce competitor, Quaker. Although Redmond had really only been offered the Gatorade "Vice President-Field Operations" position, Redmond told a number of Pepsi personnel that he was offered the chief operating officer position of the combined Quaker-Snapple company. Id. Apparently, Redmond hoped to further negotiate with Pepsi on salary. Id.

On November 16, 1994, Pepsi sought an injunction preventing Redmond from working for Quaker. The district court issued an injunction barring Redmond from assuming his new job through May of 1995 and permanently barred his use of Pepsi trade secrets. Redmond appealed the injunction, and the Seventh Circuit affirmed the district court.

In its decision, the court held that a plaintiff may prove a claim of trade secret misappropriation by demonstrating that defendant's new employment will inevitably lead him to rely on the plaintiff's trade secrets. Id. at 1269. A number of factors in that case convinced the court that Redmond would inevitably rely on Pepsi's trade secrets. First, Pepsi had established beyond question that Redmond possessed extensive Pepsi trade secrets. Redmond had more than just general skills and knowledge. Instead, he had "particularized plans or processes developed by [Pepsi] and disclosed to him while the employer-employee relationship existed, which are unknown to others in the industry and which give the employer an advantage over his competitors" Id. These included Pepsi's annual Strategic Plan containing its competitive plans, financial goals, and three-year manufacturing, production, marketing, packaging and distribution strategies; its Annual Operating Plan, including its so-called "pricing architecture" for the coming year; its "attack plans" for specific markets; and its innovations in selling and delivery systems. Id. at 1265. Moreover, Redmond had signed a confidentiality agreement with Pepsi agreeing not to disclose confidential information relating to Pepsi's business not generally known or available to the public or recognized as standard practice. Id. at 1266.

Second, Redmond's responsibilities in his new position with Quaker were parallel to his old job so that he would have to refer to and use Pepsi's secrets. "Unless Redmond possessed an uncanny ability to compartmentalize information, he would necessarily be making decisions about Gatorade and Snapple by relying on his knowledge of [Pepsi's] trade secrets."[14] The court rejected defendants' arguments that Redmond's new agreement with Quaker required him to refrain from using

Pepsi's trade secrets, and their claims that Pepsi's secrets would be completely useless to Redmond in any event as he executed his responsibilities to integrate the Gatorade and Snapple business lines. Id. at 1270. In this fiercely competitive field, "PepsiCo finds itself in the position of a coach, one of whose players has left, playbook in hand, to join the opposing team before the big game. Id.

Third, Redmond's deceit played a part in the court's decision that he would inevitably disclose Pepsi's trade secrets. In this regard, the court relied on the district court's findings:

Redmond's lack of forthrightness on some occasions, and out and out lies on others, in the period between the time he accepted the position with defendant Quaker and when he informed plaintiff that he had accepted that position leads the court to conclude that defendant Redmond could not be trusted to act with the necessary sensitivity and good faith under the circumstances in which the only practical verification that he was not using plaintiff's secrets would be defendant Redmond's word to that effect.

Id. In other words, having shown himself to be untrustworthy in one context, the court doubted he would honor the non-disclosure obligation were he allowed to assume his new position. For these reasons, the district court's limited injunction, preventing Redmond from assuming his new position for six months, i.e., until the Pepsi trade secrets he possessed were stale, was affirmed.

Redmond has been widely followed. The only reported case that did not follow Redmond did so on a factual basis. Bridgestone/Firestone, Inc. v. Lockhart, 5 F. Supp. 2d 667, 682 (S.D. Ind. 1998) ("Because misappropriation does not appear to be inevitable, or even seriously threatened, this case is different from PepsiCo v. Redmond."). Although only a California Superior Court has had the opportunity to determine whether to follow Redmond, this Court believes that the California Supreme Court would follow the overwhelming majority of other jurisdictions to do so. See also Johanna L. Edelstein, Note, Intellectual Slavery?: The Doctrine of Inevitable Disclosure of Trade Secrets, 26 GOLDEN GATE U. L. REV. 717, 719 (Spring 1996) ("Because California has adopted the U.T.S.A. and because PepsiCo was a fact intensive analysis, this decision will affect California law.").

One commentator has delineated the factors that courts have relied upon in determining whether disclosure is inevitable. D. Peter Harvey. "Inevitable" Trade Secret Misappropriation after PepsiCo, Inc. v. Redmond, 537 PLI/PAT 199, 226 (1998). These factors include: (1) Is the new employer a competitor? (2) What is the scope of the defendant's new job? (3) Has the employee been less than candid about his new position? (4) Has plaintiff clearly identified the trade secrets which are at risk? (5) Has actual trade secret misappropriation already occurred? (6) Did the employee sign a non-disclosure and/or non-competition agreement? (7) Does the new employer have a policy against use of others' trade secrets? (8) Is it possible to "sanitize" the employee's new position? Id. at 226-27.

In the case sub judice, all of the factors espoused in Redmond and above weigh heavily in favor of a finding of inevitable disclosure. It is undisputed that Michelson was in possession of a great deal of Maxim's proprietary information and trade secrets. As in Redmond, Michelson was a relatively high level manager who had a great deal of Maxim's confidential information and trade secrets in his possession. Michelson was directly involved in Maxim's pricing scheme and in its marketing strategy. Over a period of time, Michelson developed significant relationships with many of Maxim's clients. Michelson also signed a confidentiality agreement in which he agreed not to disclose confidential information relating to Maxim's business not generally known or available to the public. Like Redmond, Michelson left Maxim to go to his company's direct competitor.

Michelson's position at PHS is also sufficiently parallel to the position he held at Maxim. Although the vice-president of PHS tried to distinguish Michelson's position at PHS, there is no dispute that Michelson will inevitably be in direct competition with Maxim armed with Maxim's trade secrets. "Unless [Michelson] possessed an uncanny ability to compartmentalize information, he would necessarily be making decisions about [PHS] by relying on his knowledge of [Maxim's] trade secrets." Redmond, 54 F.3d at 1270. It is difficult not to conclude that PHS, entering the sterile tray assembly business, hired Michelson at a substantial raise in salary in order to utilize Maxim's trade secrets.

The Court also notes that PHS does not even have an agreement with PHS that would require him to refrain from using Maxim's trade secrets. Furthermore, Michelson's and PHS's vice-president's contentions that Maxim's secrets would be completely useless to Michelson as he executed his responsibilities were directly rejected by the Redmond court. Id. In this fiercely competitive field, the point is that Maxim "finds itself in the position of a coach, one of whose players has left, playbook in hand, to join the opposing team before the big game." Id.

Michelson was also not candid regarding his new position; like Redmond, he negotiated for some time with PHS without telling Maxim. During these negotiations, Michelson divulged Maxim's confidential stock option agreement to PHS. Michelson also destroyed confidential information on his laptop hard drive and ordered a large batch of confidential client information printed the day before his departure. Michelson then lied to the staff member who printed the information by stating that the print out was off-line, thereby rendering it useless. Michelson, in an attempt to explain his suspicious actions, testified that these actions were a huge mistake and that he "will regret them for the rest of his life." The explanation was less than credible. Furthermore, his open hostility to Maxim and dissatisfaction with the company was palpable. There was also some evidence that Michelson might have backed up the deleted confidential information from his laptop hard drive. Michelson asserts that he did not do so, and that he threw away the printouts of the client information. In any event, his "lack of forthrightness on some occasions, and out and out lies on others, in the period between the time he accepted the position with [PHS] and when he informed plaintiff that he had accepted that position leads the court to conclude that defendant [Michelson] could not be trusted to act with the necessary sensitivity and good faith under the circumstances in which the only practical verification that he was not using plaintiff's secrets would be defendant [Michelson's] word to that effect." Id.

As a result, the Court concludes that, if Michelson has not already, he will inevitably disclose Maxim's trade secrets to PHS. Therefore, Maxim has a substantial likelihood of prevailing on the merits of its trade secret misappropriation claim.

b. Breach of fiduciary duty and conversion claims

Agents are considered to be fiduciaries of their principal. [Citation omitted.] It is clear that through Michelson's actions, outlined supra, he put himself and his interests above that of his principal, thus, breaching his fiduciary duties. Accordingly, Maxim has a substantial likelihood of prevailing on the merits of its breach of fiduciary duty claim.

c. Conversion claim

The elements of a conversion claim are: (1) the plaintiff's ownership or right to possession of the property; (2) the defendant's conversion by a wrongful act or disposition of property rights; and (3) damages. Moore v. Regents of Univ. of Cal., 51 Cal. 3d 120, 144 & n. 38, 271 Cal. Rptr. 146, 793 P.2d 479 (Cal. 1990); Burlesci v. Petersen, 68 Cal. App. 4th 1062, 1065, 80 Cal. Rptr. 2d 704, 706 (Cal.App. 1st Dist. 1998) (citing Moore).

It is undisputed that Maxim owned the material on the hard drive of Michelson's laptop, as well as the computer printouts of the client information Michelson ordered. It is also undisputed that Michelson, at a minimum, destroyed this property. It is also without question, that Maxim has spent monies on recovering the information from the laptop hard drive. Therefore, there is a substantial likelihood that Maxim will prevail on the merits of its conversion claim.

B. The rest of the preliminary injunction prerequisites

This Court has found that Maxim has a substantial likelihood of prevailing on its breach of the confidentiality agreement, misappropriation, breach of fiduciary duty, and conversion claims. Thus, the Court must next determine the remaining three prerequisites to obtaining injunctive relief, i.e., (1) whether there is a substantial threat that the movant will suffer irreparable injury if the injunction is denied; (2) whether the threatened injury outweighs any damage that the injunction might cause the defendant; and (3) whether the injunction will not disserve the public interest. Morales, 164 F.3d at 224.

It is beyond dispute that Maxim will suffer irreparable harm if Michelson is permitted to work for PHS until the information he has becomes stale. As discussed supra, absent injunctive relief, Maxim will find itself in the big game competing against one of its own using its own playbook against it. Although Michelson will be without the PHS job until the information he has is stale, i.e., one year, by all accounts, he is a very talented salesman and manager. It is for this very reason that we are here today. Michelson's burden of finding another position is dwarfed by the impact on Maxim of Michelson competing with it. This injunction, which is to ensure that Michelson is not to benefit from his breach of contract, fiduciary duties, conversion, and misappropriation of trade secrets, is solely in the public's interest. If the Court did not enjoin such, Michelson would be permitted to benefit from his own wrongdoing. As a result, the Court determines that Maxim's application for preliminary injunction should be granted. Accordingly, the Court

ORDERS that Maxim's application for preliminary injunction is GRANTED; and further

ORDERS that Defendant Mark Michelson is enjoined for one year from his resignation date from working as or for a direct competitor of Maxim in any of the product lines he was associated with at Maxim during the last two years. Maxim is not required to post security. The trial date for this cause will issue by separate order.

## WHYTE v. SCHLAGE LOCK CO.

101 Cal. App. 4th 1443 (2002)

The doctrine of inevitable disclosure permits a trade secret owner to prevent a former employee from working for a competitor despite the owner's failure to prove the employee has taken or threatens to use trade secrets. Under that doctrine, the employee may be enjoined by demonstrating the employee's new job duties will inevitably cause the employee to rely upon knowledge of the former employer's trade secrets. No published California decision has accepted or rejected the inevitable disclosure doctrine.

In this opinion, we reject the inevitable disclosure doctrine. We hold this doctrine is contrary to California law and policy because it creates an after-the-fact covenant not to compete restricting employee mobility.

This holding leads us to affirm the trial court's order denying the application of Schlage Lock Company (Schlage) for a preliminary injunction and granting the motion of J. Douglas Whyte (Whyte) and Kwikset Corporation (Kwikset) to dissolve a temporary restraining order. We reach the issue of inevitable disclosure because we conclude certain information Schlage seeks to protect does constitute trade secret, but the evidence presented below, viewed (as it must be) through the lens of the applicable standard of review, fails to establish actual or threatened misappropriation.

### FACTS

Schlage is a subsidiary of defendant Ingersoll-Rand Company (Ingersoll-Rand). Kwikset and Schlage manufacture and sell locks and related products. They are fierce competitors and vie intensely for shelf space at The Home Depot, which is the major seller of locks and alone accounts for 38 percent of Schlage's sales.

Whyte worked as Schlage's vice-president of sales and was responsible for sales to The Home Depot and other "big box" retailers such as HomeBase, Lowe's, Menard's, and Sears. Whyte signed a confidentiality agreement to protect Schlage's proprietary information and agreed to abide by Schlage's code of ethics, which forbids disclosure of confidential information for personal or noncompany uses. Whyte did not sign a covenant not to compete.

The Home Depot periodically conducts a review of its suppliers' product lines, prices, pricing and marketing concessions, and ability to deliver product. The Home Depot uses this "line review" to determine which products it will sell and which products to remove from its shelves. As part of the line review, The Home Depot usually asks vendors, such as Kwikset and Schlage, to submit proposals for pricing and marketing concessions and for the amount of promotional discounts and advertising funds, and to present information about product changes and new products.

The Home Depot conducted a line review with Schlage in February 2000. The Home Depot followed Schlage's recommendation to remove Kwikset's Titan brand of locks and to expand Schlage's presence on its shelves. Whyte participated in the line review and in drafting the line review agreement confirming the business relationship between Schlage and The Home Depot.

Whyte's sales abilities impressed Kwikset's president, Christopher Metz. Metz realized Whyte "was killing my team," and asked him "what it would take to get him to leave Ingersoll-Rand . . . ." Whyte apparently got what it took, for he accepted a position with Kwikset on June 3, 2000. He did not resign from Schlage, however, until June 14 — after participating on behalf of Schlage in confidential meetings with The Home Depot on June 5.

Whyte departed Schlage on June 16, 2000. Schlage was not pleased with Whyte, and the parting was not amicable. Schlage contends Whyte left to revenge belittling comments made by Schlage's president, Robert Steinman, and contends Whyte disavowed a confidentiality agreement, stole trade secret information (including a copy on computer disk of the line review agreement with The Home Depot), and lied about returning company information. Whyte denies taking any trade secrets, claims he reaffirmed the confidentiality agreement, and contends that in the exit interview on June 16 Steinman vowed to destroy his career.

On June 25, 2000, Whyte became Kwikset's vice-president of sales for national accounts. His job duties at Kwikset are substantially similar to those at Schlage: handling the lock products account for The Home Depot and other "big box retailers."

* * *

As an alternative to proof of actual or threatened misappropriation, Schlage urges us to reverse and enjoin Whyte from working for the lock division of Kwikset under the doctrine of inevitable disclosure. Under the doctrine of inevitable disclosure, "a plaintiff may prove a claim of trade secret misappropriation by demonstrating that defendant's new employment will inevitably lead him to rely on the plaintiff's trade secrets." (PepsiCo, Inc. v. Redmond (7th Cir. 1995) 54 F.3d 1262, 1269 (PepsiCo).) The inevitable disclosure doctrine results in an injunction prohibiting employment, not just use of trade secrets. The doctrine's justification is that unless the employee has "an uncanny ability to compartmentalize information" the employee will necessarily rely — consciously or subconsciously — upon knowledge of the former employer's trade secrets in performing his or her new job duties. (Id. at p. 1269.)

Courts applying the doctrine of inevitable disclosure have considered the degree of similarity between the employee's former and current positions, the degree of competition between the former and current employers, the current employer's efforts to safeguard the former employer's trade secrets, and the former employee's "lack of forthrightness both in his activities before accepting his job . . . and in his testimony." (PepsiCo, supra, 54 F.3d at p. 1267; see also Merck & Co. Inc. v. Lyon (M.D.N.C. 1996) 941 F. Supp. 1443, 1460.)

PepsiCo is the leading case on inevitable disclosure. There, PepsiCo sought to enjoin its former employee, William Redmond, from working for a competitor, the Quaker Oats Company. PepsiCo and Quaker Oats were fierce competitors, particularly in "sports drinks" and "new age drinks." (PepsiCo, supra, 54 F.3d at pp. 1263-1264.) Redmond's high position at PepsiCo gave him access to its trade secrets regarding these products, including strategic plans, product innovations, "pricing architecture," selling and delivery innovations, and marketing " 'attack plans.' " (Id. at pp. 1264-1265.) To protect these trade secrets, PepsiCo had Redmond sign a confidentiality agreement. Quaker Oats courted Redmond, and he ultimately accepted a high-level position in that company. (Id. at p. 1264.) When Redmond resigned from PepsiCo, it immediately sought and obtained an injunction preventing him from assuming his duties at Quaker Oats. (Id. at p. 1265.)

PepsiCo did not contend Quaker Oats actually stole trade secrets, but asserted Redmond "cannot help but rely on [PepsiCo's] trade secrets as he helps plot [Quaker Oats'] new course." (PepsiCo, supra, 54 F.3d at p. 1270.) The Seventh Circuit Court of Appeals agreed and applied the Illinois Trade Secrets Act to affirm an injunction preventing Redmond from working for Quaker Oats. (Id. at pp. 1270-1271.) The Seventh Circuit first concluded that Illinois law permits a court to enjoin employment based upon inevitable disclosure of trade secrets. (Id. at p. 1269.) The Seventh Circuit then agreed with the district court finding that "unless Redmond possessed an uncanny ability to compartmentalize information, he would necessarily be making decisions about [Quaker Oats' products] by relying on his knowledge of [PepsiCo's] trade secrets." (Ibid.) Such inevitability of disclosure, coupled with Redmond's and Quaker Oats' "lack of candor on their part and proof of their willingness to misuse [PepsiCo's] trade secrets," led the Seventh Circuit to affirm the injunction barring Redmond from working for Quaker Oats. (Id. at pp. 1270-1271.)

Schlage asserts the facts here are "strikingly similar" to PepsiCo's, and we are inclined to agree. Schlage and Kwikset are fierce competitors; Whyte's job duties at Kwikset are virtually identical to those he had at Schlage; Whyte knew of Schlage's trade secrets (in particular, those important to The Home Depot account); Whyte signed a confidentiality agreement; and, if we are to believe Schlage's evidence, Whyte was not "forthright" with Schlage. Whyte's evidence did show Kwikset made efforts to safeguard Schlage's trade secrets. Nonetheless, the similarity between this case and PepsiCo and other inevitable disclosure cases means we cannot distinguish those cases on the facts.

No published California decision has accepted or rejected the doctrine of inevitable disclosure. Two federal district courts in California recently concluded inevitable disclosure is not the law of this state. (Globespan, Inc. v. O'Neill (C.D.Cal. 2001) 151 F. Supp. 2d 1229, 1235 (order by Baird, J.) ["The Central District of California has considered and rejected the inevitable disclosure doctrine"]; Bayer

Corp. v. Roche Molecular Systems, Inc. (N.D.Cal. 1999) 72 F. Supp. 2d 1111, 1120 (order by Alsup, J.) ["California trade-secrets law does not recognize the theory of inevitable disclosure"]; but see Note, Intellectual Slavery?: The Doctrine of Inevitable Disclosure of Trade Secrets (1996) 26 Golden Gate U. L.Rev. 717, 719 ["Because California has adopted the [Uniform Trade Secrets Act] and because PepsiCo was a fact intensive analysis, this decision will affect California law"].)

These federal decisions do not, of course, establish the law of the State of California or bind its courts. We are free to consider the inevitable disclosure doctrine, and we reject it.

Our survey confirms the majority of jurisdictions addressing the issue have adopted some form of the inevitable disclosure doctrine. (E.g., RKI, Inc. v. Grimes (N.D.Ill. 2001) 177 F. Supp. 2d 859; H & R Block Eastern Tax Services, Inc. v. Enchura (W.D.Mo. 2000) 122 F. Supp. 2d 1067; Maxxim Medical, Inc. v. Michelson (S.D.Tex. 1999) 51 F. Supp. 2d 773, revd. without reported opn. (5th Cir. 1999) 182 F.3d 915; Lexis-Nexis v. Beer (D.Minn. 1999) 41 F. Supp. 2d 950, 959 [dictum because no finding of trade secrets]; Novell Inc. v. Timpanogos Research Group Inc. (D. Utah 1998) 46 U.S.P.Q.2D (BNA) 1197, 1215 [adopting inevitable disclosure but noting "[n]o Utah appellate court has considered . . . the application of this doctrine"]; Merck & Co. Inc. v. Lyon, supra, 941 F. Supp. 1443; Branson Ultrasonics Corp. v. Stratman (D.Conn. 1996) 921 F. Supp. 909 [invoking inevitable disclosure to enforce covenant not to compete]; Surgidev Corp. v. Eye Technology, Inc., supra, 648 F. Supp. 661; Bendinger v. Marshalltown Trowell Co. (Ark. 1999) 338 Ark. 410 [994 S.W.2d 468]; E.I. duPont de Nemours [*1461] & Co. v. American Potash & Chemical Corp. (Del.Ch. 1964) 41 Del. Ch. 533 [200 A.2d 428]; Strata Marketing, Inc. v. Murphy (Ill.App.Ct. 2000) 317 Ill. App. 3d 1054 [251 Ill. Dec. 595, 740 N.E.2d 1166]; National Starch and Chemical Corp. v. Parker Chemical Corp. (N.J.Super-.Ct.App.Div. 1987) 219 N.J. Super. 158 [530 A.2d 31]; Procter & Gamble Co. v. Stoneham (Ohio Ct.App. 2000) 140 Ohio App. 3d 260 [747 N.E.2d 268]; see also Comment, An Overview of Individual States' Application of Inevitable Disclosure: Concrete Doctrine or Equitable Tool? (2002) 55 SMU L. Rev. 621.)

Some other courts, though agreeing with the doctrine, have distinguished it or decided their cases on other grounds. (E.g., Padco Advisors, Inc. v. Omdahl (D.Md. 2002) 179 F. Supp. 2d 600, 611 ["inappropriate" to adopt the doctrine because no tangible trade secrets were taken]; Hoskins Mfg. Co. v. PMC Corp. (E.D.Mich. 1999) 47 F. Supp. 2d 852 [disclosure not inevitable because parties' differing technology made trade secrets useless]; Bridgestone/Firestone, Inc. v. Lockhart (S.D.Ind. 1998) 5 F. Supp. 2d 667, 682 [finding PepsiCo is "instructive" but does not warrant finding of inevitable disclosure because there was no evidence the employee took confidential information]; Lumex, Inc. v. Highsmith, supra, 919 F. Supp. 624 [deciding case based upon noncompete covenant rather than inevitable disclosure]; Northwest Bec-Corp v. Home Living Service (Idaho 2002) 136 Idaho 835 [41 P.3d 263] [distinguishing PepsiCo on ground plaintiff failed to submit evidence supporting claim of misappropriation]; Travenol Laboratories, Inc. v. Turner (N.C.Ct.App. 1976) 30 N.C. App. 686 [228 S.E.2d 478] [suggesting inevitable disclosure limited to situation where employee has highly technical information]; see also Comment, An Overview of Individual States' Application of Inevitable Disclosure: Concrete Doctrine or Equitable Tool?, supra, 55 SMU L.Rev. 621.)

A smaller but growing band of cases rejects the inevitable disclosure doctrine. (Globespan, Inc. v. O'Neill, supra, 151 F. Supp. 2d 1229; Del Monte Fresh Produce Co. v. Dole Food Co., Inc. (S.D.Fla. 2001) 148 F. Supp. 2d 1326, 1337; PSC, Inc. v. Reiss (W.D.N.Y. 2000) 111 F. Supp. 2d 252; Bayer Corp. v. Roche Molecular Systems, Inc., supra, 72 F. Supp. 2d at p. 1120; Earth Web, Inc. v. Schlack (S.D.N.Y. 1999) 71 F. Supp. 2d 299; Government Technology Services, Inc. v. IntelliSys Technology Corp. (Va.Cir.Ct., Oct. 20, 1999, No. 160265), 51 Va. Cir. 55, 1999 Va. Cir. LEXIS 502, 1999 WL 1499548.)

The decisions rejecting the inevitable disclosure doctrine correctly balance competing public policies of employee mobility and protection of trade secrets. The inevitable disclosure doctrine permits an employer to enjoin the former employee without proof of the employee's actual or threatened use of trade secrets based upon an inference (based in turn upon circumstantial evidence) that the employee inevitably will use his or her knowledge of those trade secrets in the new employment. The result is not merely an injunction against the use of trade secrets, but an injunction restricting employment.

Business and Professions Code section 16600 generally prohibits covenants not to compete, and California public policy strongly favors employee mobility. (Application Group, Inc. v. Hunter Group, Inc. (1998) 61 Cal. App. 4th 881, 900 [72 Cal. Rptr. 2d 73].) Business and Professions Code section 16600 protects a person's right to "follow any of the common occupations of life" (Continental Car-Na-Var Corp. v. Moseley (1944) 24 Cal. 2d 104, 110 [148 P.2d 9]) and to pursue the " 'business or profession he may choose' " (American Credit Indemnity Co. v. Sacks (1989) 213 Cal. App. 3d 622, 633 [262 Cal. Rptr. 92]). We agree the doctrine of inevitable disclosure "creates a de facto covenant not to compete" and "runs[s] counter to the strong public policy in California favoring employee mobility." (Bayer Corp. v. Roche Molecular Systems, Inc., supra, 72 F. Supp. 2d at p. 1120; accord, Globespan, Inc. v. O'Neill, supra, 151 F. Supp. 2d at p. 1234; PSC, Inc. v. Reiss, supra, 111 F. Supp. 2d at p. 256 [inevitable disclosure doctrine binds employee to implied-in-fact restrictive covenant that "runs counter to New York's strong public policy against such agreements"].)

The policy favoring employee mobility does not in itself, however, require rejection of the inevitable disclosure doctrine, for California law also protects trade secrets. (Civ. Code, § 3426 et seq.(8)) Nearly 40 years ago, the California Supreme Court recognized covenants not to compete are enforceable notwithstanding Business and Professions Code section 16600 if "necessary to protect the employer's trade secrets." (Muggill v. Reuben H. Donnelley Corp. (1965) 62 Cal. 2d 239, 242 [42 Cal. Rptr. 107, 398 P.2d 147] (opn. of Traynor, J.); see also Metro Traffic Control, Inc. v. Shadow Traffic Network, supra, 22 Cal. App. 4th at p. 859.) Further,[HN24] Business and Professions Code section 16600 generally does not invalidate a noncompetition agreement that merely prohibits solicitation of the former employer's customers. (John F. Matull & Associates, Inc. v. Cloutier (1987) 194 Cal. App. 3d 1049, 1054 [240 Cal. Rptr. 211].) (5d)) The injunction proposed by Schlage — which only would proscribe Whyte from selling door locks to The Home Depot — appears narrowly tailored to protect Schlage's trade secrets.

The chief ill in the covenant not to compete imposed by the inevitable disclosure doctrine is its after-the-fact nature: The covenant is imposed after the employment contract is made and therefore alters the employment relationship without the employee's consent. When, as here, a confidentiality agreement is in place, the inevitable disclosure doctrine "in effect convert[s] the confidentiality agreement into such a covenant [not to compete]." (PSC, Inc. v. Reiss, supra, 111 F. Supp. 2d at p. 257.) Or, as another federal court put it, "a court should not allow a plaintiff to use inevitable disclosure as an after-the-fact noncompete agreement to enjoin an employee from working for the employer of his or her choice." (Del Monte Fresh Produce Co. v. Dole Food Co., Inc., supra, 148 F. Supp. 2d at p. 1337; see also Matheson, Employee Beware: The Irreparable Damage of the Inevitable Disclosure Doctrine (1998) 10 Loyola Consumer L.Rev. 145, 162 ["the inevitable disclosure doctrine transforms employee access to trade secrets into a de facto non-competition agreement"].)

The doctrine of inevitable disclosure thus rewrites the employment agreement and "such retroactive alterations distort the terms of the employment relationship and upset the balance which courts have attempted to achieve in construing non-compete agreements." (Earth Web, Inc. v. Schlack, supra, 71 F. Supp. 2d at p. 311.) The result, as the Earth Web court explained, is "the imperceptible shift in bargaining power that necessarily occurs upon the commencement of an employment relationship marked by the execution of a confidentiality agreement. When that relationship eventually ends, the parties' confidentiality agreement may be wielded as a restrictive covenant, depending on how the employer views the new job its former employee has accepted. This can be a powerful weapon in the hands of an employer; the risk of litigation alone may have a chilling effect on the employee." (Id. at p. 310.) As a result of the inevitable disclosure doctrine, the employer obtains the benefit of a contractual provision it did not pay for, while the employee is bound by a court-imposed contract provision with no opportunity to negotiate terms or consideration. (Matheson, Employee Beware: The Irreparable Damage of the Inevitable Disclosure Doctrine, supra, 10 Loyola Consumer L.Rev. at p. 160.)

Schlage and Whyte did not agree upon a covenant not to compete. We decline to impose one, however restricted in scope, by adopting the inevitable disclosure doctrine.

Lest there be any doubt about our holding, our rejection of the inevitable disclosure doctrine is complete. If a covenant not to compete (which would include, for example, a nonsolicitation clause), is part of the employment agreement, the inevitable disclosure doctrine cannot be invoked to supplement the covenant, alter its meaning, or make an otherwise unenforceable covenant enforceable. California law concerning enforcement of noncompetition agreements, not the inevitable disclosure doctrine, would measure the covenant's scope, meaning, and validity. Our opinion does not change that law. Under the circumstances presented in this case, an employer might prevent disclosure of trade secrets through, for example, an agreed-upon and reasonable nonsolicitation clause that is narrowly drafted for the purpose of protecting trade secrets. Thus, regardless whether a covenant not to compete is part of the employment agreement, the inevitable disclosure doctrine cannot be used as a substitute for proving actual or threatened misappropriation of trade secrets.

Because we reject the inevitable disclosure doctrine and the evidence failed to prove actual or threatened misappropriation of trade secrets, we do not address Schlage's contention the balance of hardships weighs in favor of issuing an injunction. (King v. Meese (1987) 43 Cal. 3d 1217, 1227 [240 Cal. Rptr. 829, 743 P.2d 889]; Hart v. Cult Awareness Network, supra, 13 Cal. App. 4th at p. 785.)

## NOTES AND QUESTIONS:

1. Does the "inevitable disclosure doctrine" make sense from an evidentiary point of view? According to *Maxxim*, what kind of evidence of "inevitable disclosure" is needed to avoid being thrown out as being based on speculation? *See Maxxim Med., Inc. v. Michaelson*, 51 F. Supp. 2d 773, 784 (S.D. Tex. 1999); *Pepsico, Inc. v. Redmond*, 54 F.3d 1262, 1268 (7th Cir. 1995).

2. Despite rejecting the "inevitable disclosure doctrine," California courts have granted injunctions based on "threatened misappropriation" or threatened disclosure. *See Cent. Valley Gen. Hosp. v. Smith*, 162 Cal. App. 4th 501, 524 (2008); *Flir Systems, Inc. v. Parrish*, 174 Cal. App. 4th 1270, 1279 (2009). Courts in Texas and Pennsylvania have taken a similar approach where there is a "possibility of disclosure" or disclosure is "likely." *See Rugen v. Interactive Bus. Sys., Inc.*, 864 S.W.2d 548, 552-53 (Tex. App. 1993); *Bimbo Bakeries USA, Inc. v. Botticella*, 613 F.3d 102, 111 (3d Cir. 2010).

3. Would it be more accurate to say that "inevitable disclosure" is not really a "doctrine," but "is just one way of showing a threatened disclosure" in the absence of an actual disclosure? *See Interbake Foods, L.L.C. v. Tomasiello*, 461 F. Supp. 2d 943, 970-75, (N.D. Iowa 2006).

4. For an in-depth discussion of this doctrine, *see Applicability of Inevitable Disclosure Doctrine Barring Employment of Competitor's Former Employee*, 36 A.L.R. 6th 537 (2008). States rejecting the "inevitable disclosure doctrine" include California, Kentucky, Louisiana, Maryland, Massachusetts, and Virginia. The following states accept the doctrine: Connecticut, Delaware, Illinois, Indiana, Iowa, Minnesota, New Jersey, North Carolina, Ohio, Pennsylvania, Texas, Utah, Washington, and New York.

## C. LIMITED OR PERMANENT INJUNCTIONS

### STANDARD BRANDS, INC. v. ZUMPE

264 F. Supp. 254 (E.D. La. 1967)

* * *

It is hornbook law that injunctive relief is an unusual remedy, available only in those instances in which the rights of the parties cannot be otherwise adequately protected. The issuance of an injunction is not justified by the mere fact that irreparable harm may possibly ensue if restraint is not imposed. The plaintiff must make out a case for the issuance of the injunction by demonstrating that there is a clear present need for it. Injunctions will not be issued merely to allay the fears and apprehensions or to soothe the anxieties of the parties. Nor will an injunction be issued 'to restrain one from doing what he is not attempting and does not intend to do.

These rules, applicable generally to injunctive relief have been applied to the issuance of injunctions sought to prevent the disclosure of confidential information and trade secrets. It has been frequently held that damages are not an adequate remedy for the improper disclosure of confidential information. When Louisiana courts have been presented with questions relating to improper disclosure of confidential information and when it was not necessary to enjoin working for a competitor, they have followed the same principles apparently followed generally in this area in other states. Therefore it is appropriate to refer to the principles that have been generally applied in the United States with respect to the propriety of issuance of an injunction.

What is entitled to protection is 'knowledge confidentially gained' but 'an employer cannot prevent his employee from using the skill and intelligence acquired through experience received in the course of the employment. The employee may achieve superiority by every lawful means and upon the rightful termination of his contract use that superiority for the benefit of rivals in business of his former employer. 'In Sarkes Tarzian Inc. v. Audio Devices Inc., 166 F.Supp. 250, 262, 278-79 (S.D.Cal.1958), the Court said:

> Of necessity, whenever a change of employment of this type occurs and former employees enter into the employ of another with whom they engage in a competitive business, it is inevitable that some of the knowledge acquired while in the employ of the other should be made available to the new employer. But, as already appears, the courts will not deprive the employee of the rights to use the skill he developed through the years. . . .

This has never been interpreted to prevent the employee from using the knowledge he has acquired while in one man's employ after he leaves that employ. The law does not require the employee to make a tabula rasa of his mind, by erasing from it the knowledge he has acquired." *See also Midland-Ross Corporation v. Yokana*, 293 F.2d 411 (3rd Cir. 1961).

On the other hand, the employer is entitled to injunctive relief to protect the disclosure of trade secrets or confidential information after an ex-employee has disclosed them or threatened to do so. However, it is obvious that an injunction issued only after an actual disclosure has occurred locks the door after the horse is out. May an injunction be issued if, as here, the ex-employee is by the testimony of his ex-employer an honest and honorable man who performs his obligations, has not yet disclosed any confidential information, has not threatened to do so, and has asserted that he will carefully maintain the confidence reposed in him?

An employer seeking injunctive protection for his trade secrets prior to their disclosure generally alleges either that the ex-employee actually intends to divulge the secrets, or that he will inevitably do so, whether consciously or not, because of the type of work in which he will be involved, or that there is a substantial probability of disclosure. Here, the claim of intention to disclose is not made and the facts do not support the claim that disclosure is inevitable. An injunction could be issued only on the basis of the possibility or probability of disclosure and the irreparable injury that would result if there were such disclosure.

Even after full consideration of the irreparable harm that may result from disclosure of confidential information, there appears to be no reason to depart in such cases from the rules applicable to the issuance of injunctions generally.

Nor is the case put in a different light because of the existence here of an express agreement not to reveal trade secrets or confidential information. A duty not to disclose trade secrets will usually be implied from the employment relationship. The existence of the covenant not to disclose merely makes enforcement by injunction available upon a showing that if the employee accepts his intended position he will break the covenant. In other states, the difficulties implicit in employer enforcement have led to the use of a covenant not to compete. But this device is not of course available in Louisiana — either directly or, as set forth above, by necessary inference.

Two recent cases have involved the problems implicit in enjoining disclosure prospectively. Such suits have been comparatively rare and it has been usually considered that, 'if there has been no actual disclosure, the employer must prove that there is a substantial*270 threat of imminent disclosure.' Ellis, Trade Secrets, puts it this way: 'Opportunity to do wrong and a suspicion that wrong will be done is not enough to warrant action by a court to prevent such wrong. Actual or threatened invasion of rights must be shown.

In *B. F. Goodrich Co. v. Wohlgemuth*, 117 Ohio App. 493, 192 N.E.2d 99 (1963), Goodrich sought to enjoin Wohlgemuth from performing any work on high altitude pressure suits for any of its competitors. The state appellate court, reversing the trial court in part, enjoined prospective disclosure of trade secrets relying however on a 'substantial threat of disclosure' found in Wohlgemuth's statements indicating that he intended to use his secret knowledge to assist his new employer. Although Standard relies upon the decision, it should be noted that the court refused to enjoin Wohlgemuth from working for the new employer even on the project that involved space suit work and that it supported its issuance of an injunction by the ex-employee's statements indicating his intention to disclose trade secrets.

The second recent decision, also relied upon by Standard, is *E. I. duPont de Nemours & Co. v. American Potash & Chemical Corp.*, 200 A.2d 428 (Del.Ch.1964). An injunction was there sought to prevent a former employee, Hirsch, from disclosing trade secrets relative to manufacturing titanium dioxide pigments. The case was before the court on a motion for summary judgment. The Chancellor found that 'At least at this stage it is impossible to say that all of plaintiff's trade secrets in these areas are susceptible of consciously being so isolated by Hirsch,' and that at the trial a 'reasonable probability of disclosure' might be shown. The evidence might warrant 'a possible finding after final hearing of a threat of unlawful disclosure sufficiently imminent to justify injunctive relief.' The court therefore denied the motion for summary judgment. It did not determine the merits of the controversy nor indeed finally decide exactly what evidence would be required to support an injunction.

These decisions do not therefore alter materially, if indeed they alter at all, the legal principles already stated. Absent imminence of disclosure, an injunction should not issue. Disclosure has not been shown to be either imminent or eventually inevitable.

If Zumpe is not fully aware of the areas in which confidential information and trade secrets exist, these reasons for judgment outline them fully to him. The evidence indicates that, should be violate his contract, Standard is likely to discover it soon. Enforcement measures can then be taken. While this may not be an absolute remedy, it is all that the principle of law regulating the use of the injunction affords.

With respect to the issuance of an injunction, there is one ultimate test. The suit for an injunction, in Louisiana, as at common law, seeks to invoke equitable relief. Here as in other trade secrets cases, the court should seek to enforce 'the difference between right and wrong, honesty and dishonesty. The evidence does not persuade that Zumpe, either alone or in concert with Reily, has violated his contract or has threatened to do so or that a violation is either imminent or inevitable. There is no evidence of wrongdoing or dishonesty on his part. Absent disclosure or imminent threat of disclosure, injunctive relief should not be granted.

## SHELLMAR PRODUCTS CO. v. ALLEN-QUALLEY CO.

87 F.2d 104 (7th Cir. 1937)

* * *

It is clear that appellant's claim for relief against the injunctive decree is based upon the well-recognized principle that equity will dissolve an injunction when there is no longer a basis for it; or expressed more narrowly, an injunction issued to protect a right will be dissolved upon the extinguishment of that right. These principles are not here denied, and the question presented for solution is whether the basis for the injunction lawfully issued still exists, or has the right once established been extinguished.

In support of its contention that Allen-Qualley's right to the injunction has been extinguished, appellant relies upon the general principle that the issuance of a patent extinguishes all rights of secrecy in the subject matter disclosed in the patent. Its theory is constructed upon the assumption that the original decree was based upon the conclusion that the wrap, process and machine were first invented by Allen-Qualley, and were secrets of which no one other than it had any knowledge. That assumption is erroneous. The findings upon which the original decree was based were that the wrap, process and machine were Allen-Qualley's trade secrets; that they had been disclosed to appellant in confidence; and that it had violated that confidence by manufacturing and selling the wrap without Allen-Qualley's authority, after negotiations for a co-operative arrangement had failed.

The District Court's opinion in the original case clearly and correctly set forth the distinction between the rights under unpatented secret processes and those under patents, as follows (31 F.(2d) 293, 296):

> The difference between secret processes and patents is that the owner of a patent has a monopoly against all the world, while the owner of a secret process has no right 'except against those who have contracted, expressly or by implication, not to disclose the secret, or who have obtained it by

> unfair means.' . . . The jurisdiction of equity to protect such trade secrets is founded upon trust or confidence. The court 'fastens the obligation upon the conscience of the party, and enforces it against him in the same manner as it enforces against a party to whom a benefit is given, the obligations of performing a promise on the faith of which the benefit has been conferred.' . . . Whether the subject-matter is patentable or not, if the designer discovers and keeps secret a process of manufacture, though he will not have an exclusive right to it as against the public, after he shall have published it, or against those who in good faith acquire knowledge of it, yet he has a property right, which a court of chancery will protect against one who in bad faith and breach of confidence undertakes to apply it to his own use. (Cases cited.)

The findings of the court in the original action placed appellant in the precise situation described in the quotation, and it was enjoined because of its bad faith in breaching the confidence which Allen-Qualley had placed in it. This was done notwithstanding the conceded and pleaded disclosures of Olsen, Royal's public practice, the Cameron machine of appellant, and the disclosure of Allen-Qualley to its licensee.

The Olsen United States patent was issued prior to Allen-Qualley's confidential disclosure to appellant, and its application was filed long before Allen-Qualley had designed its wrap or filed its application for a patent, and yet the court protected the confidential communication, because appellant by its inequitable conduct had taken itself outside the pale of the general public to which the disclosure of that patent was made. True, the Olsen patent was required to be and was assigned to Allen-Qualley by appellant because of appellant's inequity in purchasing it. That, however, did not add to the inviolability of the confidential communication, as between appellant and Allen-Qualley, nor did it detract from it. It merely gave to Allen-Qualley a monopoly against all the world. As between it and appellant, the effect was the same as if a patent had issued on the Olm and Mair application, which belonged to Allen-Qualley. In that event anyone, except appellant, could have infringed it if he desired to do so and thereby hazard an action for infringement at the hands of Allen-Qualley. But not so with appellant, for the consensus of authority is that by its inequitable conduct appellant has precluded itself from enjoying the patent disclosure, and will not be permitted to place upon Allen-Qualley the burden of suing for patent infringement, when its proprietary rights in the process have already been adjudicated against appellant. [Citations omitted.]

Appellant's reliance upon the Royal, Robinson and Novick patents as grounds for review, lies in the facts that they were issued since the decree was entered, and constitute disclosures by others than Allen-Qualley with which appellant was in no way connected. Hence, it argues that as a part of the general public, it is entitled, as against Allen-Qualley, to make use of that company's secret process, and that the injunction should be dissolved. In support of that contention, it relies upon John D. Park & Sons Co. v. Hartman (C.C.A.) 153 F. 24, 12 L.R.A.(N.S.) 135, and Thum Company v. Tloczynski, 114 Mich. 149, 72 N.W. 140, 142, 68 Am.St.Rep. 469, 38 L.R.A. 200. Generally, those cases merely reiterate the well-known principle that the public is free to make use of secret processes discovered by fair and honest means, and neither presents facts analogous to those presented here. Appellant quotes from the last cited case as follows:

> It should also be observed . . . that the word 'property,' as applied to trade secrets and trade inventions, has its limitations; for it is undoubtedly true that when an article manufactured by some secret process, which is not the subject of a patent, is thrown upon the market, the whole world is at liberty to discover, if it can by any fair means, what that process is, and, when the discovery is thus made, to employ it in the manufacture of similar articles. In such a case the manufacturer's or inventor's property in his process is gone.

Immediately following this quotation, however, the court said:

> But the authorities all hold that, while knowledge obtained in this manner is perfectly legitimate, that which is obtained by any breach of confidence cannot be sanctioned.

The facts before us now show that appellant discovered nothing from the Royal, Robinson and Novick patents. The word 'discover' means to get first sight or knowledge of; to get knowledge of what has existed but has not theretofore been known to the discoverer. The process disclosed by these patents had been discovered by appellant when it received the confidential communications from Allen-Qualley, and it will not be heard to say that it again discovered the process from the subsequent patents upon which it now relies. Furthermore, as a defense at the original trial, appellant relied upon the product and process subsequently patented by Royal, to show that Allen-Qualley had no secret, and it received an adverse ruling thereon. The same disclosure, so far as appellant is concerned, is not strengthened in any manner by the issuance of the patent to Royal, and lends no support for the relief now sought. The Royal patent is but a counterpart of the British Robinson patent, both being obtained by Royal, and what has been said applies to both. Neither they nor the Novick patent furnished any ground for relieving appellant from the injunction which resulted from its own misconduct. It is clear that a patent disclosure by Allen-Qualley would not entitle appellant to the relief sought, and we conceive of no reason why a stranger's disclosure would atone for the wrong. This, in effect, was decided in the original decree, and we affirm that decision. True, the Novick disclosure was not before that court, but the Olsen United States patent was considered, and Olsen was a stranger to Allen-Qualley so far as the disclosure was concerned.

* * *

## CONMAR PRODUCTS CORP. v. UNIVERSAL SLIDE FASTENER CO.

172 F.2d 150 (2d Cir. 1949)

Courts have been accustomed to speak of trade secrets as 'property,' and at times to deal with them as if they were. That may be permissible and to some extent desirable, when the question is whether the wrongdoer has got access to them by some wrongful means, like breaking into a factory, or copying formulae or blue prints. When, however, the dispute turns, as it does here, upon whether the wrongdoer has acquired a secret from the employee who has himself acquired it lawfully, the wrong consists in inducing him to break his contract, or to be disloyal to a confidence reposed in him; and in either case it is a species of the tore — recognized now for over a century — of inducing an obligor to default upon an obligation. Since the specifications of the patents in suit disclosed the first six secrets and part of the seventh, that much of the secrets upon issue of the patents fell into the public demesne; and, prima facie, the defendants were free to use them. The Seventh Circuit, and apparently the Sixth as well, have, however, held that if before issue one has unlawfully obtained and used information which the specifications later disclose, he will not be free to continue to do so after issue; his wrong deprives him of the right which he would otherwise have had as a member of the public. We have twice refused to follow this doctrine; and we adhere to our decisions. Conceivably an employer might exact from his employees a contract not to disclose the information even after the patent issued. Of what possible value such a contract could be, we find it hard to conceive; but, if an employer did exact it, others would perhaps be obliged to turn to the specifications, if they would use the information. Be that as it may, we should not so construe any secrecy contract unless the intent were put in the most inescapable terms; and the plaintiff's contract had none such. In their absence we do not see why a wrongful inducement to divulge the disclosure before issue should deprive the wrongdoer of his right to avail himself of the patentee's dedication; for, as we have just said, the contract is to be construed as imposing secrecy only until issue. The doctrine must rest upon the theory that it is a proper penalty for the original wrong to deny the wrongdoer resort to the patent; and for that we can find no support in principle. Thus, any possible liability for exploiting whatever the patents in suit disclosed, ended with their issue. Since the earliest notice was on November 16, 1940, it is not necessary to resort to this reasoning as to the first six secrets and as to part of the seventh, because the two patents in suit issued before November 16, 1940; but the doctrine does become important as to the remaining part of the seventh secret.

It is almost, if not quite, impossible to learn what was that part of the seventh secret which did remain undisclosed after the issue of the Ulrich patent in suit; but for argument we will assume that the plaintiff proved that some parts did so remain. Whatever these were, they were all disclosed in two later patents to Ulrich: No. 2,338,884, issued January 11, 1944, and No. 2,370,380, issued February 27, 1945; and in any event the right to an injunction against exploiting any secrets whatever had therefore expired before the judgment was entered in November, 1947. All that could remain was the right to an accounting for profits or to a claim for damages between November 16, 1940, and the date of issue of these patents. We think, however, that the defendants had an excuse for exploiting that secret over that period, if they did so. As we have said, by November 16, 1940, they had invested $40,000 in the offending machine; that is, they had either paid or committed themselves to pay that much. The Restatement of Torts makes it an excuse for continued exploitation of a secret that at the time when one, who has theretofore been innocently exploiting it, first learns that he has induced the breach of an obligation, he has substantially changed his position. The opinions which support this are not very satisfactory; so far as we have found, in all but one or two it is doubtful whether what the judges say is more than dictum. However, they do all point the same way, for they assume that the situation is proper for the application of the doctrine that a bona fide purchaser takes free from a trust. The act of inducing the breach is the wrong, and the inducer's ignorance is an excuse only because one is not ordinarily held liable for consequences which one could not have anticipated. Although it is proper to prevent any continued use of the secret after the inducer has learned of the breach, the remedies must not invade the inducer's immunity over the period while he was ignorant. They may invade it, if the inducer has changed his position on the faith of his ignorance. We agree with the Comment of the Restatement that each case must stand on its facts; the answer depends upon weighing the loss to the inducer against the benefit to the obligee. In the case at bar we have no hesitation in deciding that issue in favor of the defendants. On November 16, 1940, when the defendants were first charged with any duty to desist, they had become free to exploit the major part of the secrets-the first six and an undetermined part of the seventh. Their duty at most extended no further than to change their machines and their methods, so as not to continue to exploit the still protected vestiges of the seventh; and even these would become free when the two other patents issued. Certainly, to compel them to make that change was seriously to invade the immunity they had enjoyed to that time; it would have compelled a disruption of their business and a redesigning of their machines. Opposed to this was a benefit to the plaintiff, the importance of which no one could even guess; for it must be measured by the advantage of suppressing only the use of the yet undisclosed part of the seventh secret, while the defendants remained free to use all the rest. The plaintiff had the burden of showing that the balance was in its favor, and we should be wholly unwarranted in deducing that conclusion from the maze of verbiage which wraps the issue.

## WINSTON RESEARCH CORP. v. MINNESOTA MINING & MANUFACTURING CO.

350 F.2d 134 (9th Cir. 1965)

Mincom argues that in any event a two-year injunction from March 1, 1964, was not sufficient to overcome the wrongful advantage obtained by Winston. Mincom points out that four years were required to develop its machine, whereas Winston developed its machine in fourteen months. For this reason, and because the injunction was stayed for some time, Mincom argues that injunctive relief should be granted for at least three years from the completion of appellate review.

As we have noted, the appropriate injunctive period is that which competitors would require after public disclosure to develop a competitive machine. The time (fourteen months) which Winston in fact took with the aid of the very disclosure and use complained of by Mincom would seem to be a fair measure of the proper period. The district court granted an injunction for a somewhat longer period, presumably because the Mincom machine was built in such a way as to require some time for persons unfamiliar with it to determine the details of its construction, and to compensate for delay which Mincom encountered in the final stages of its development program because Winston had hired away Mincom's key personnel. Whether extension of the injunctive period for the latter reason was proper we need not decide, for Winston has not raised that question.

We think it was proper to make the injunctive period run from the date of judgment since public disclosure occurred at about that time. The stays subsequently granted by the district court and this court were limited in scope and do not justify an extension of the injunctive period.

Winston argues that injunctive was not appropriate because it obstructed and delayed further important research and development by Winston, and (somewhat inconsistently with its successful argument that no damages had been proved) because money damages would have afforded an adequate remedy. In deciding to grant injunctive relief, and in framing its decree, the district court evidenced a keen awareness of the impact of its decision upon the public interest. We think the court acted reasonably and within its discretion in granting a limited injunction, particularly in light of the stay granted by the district court (and subsequently extended by this court) to allow access by the interested government agencies to Winston's machine.

Winston contends that several provisions of the decree are not sufficiently 'specific in terms' to satisfy Fed.R.Civ.P. Rule 65(d). As we have said, references in the decree to the general approach adopted by Mincom are to be read as limited by the particular specifications of the basic mechanical elements of the Mincom machine and their relationship to each other which are subsequently detailed in the decree. Similarly, the reference in the decree to a 'shortened and widened' shaft derives the requisite specificity from a context which clearly related these generalized directions to a specific result to be achieved.

We agree with Winston that in one respect the district court's injunction was unenforceably broad. As we have noted, the district court found that 'knowledge of the reasons for' the particular specifications of the Mincom machine, and 'knowledge of what not to do . . . and how not to make the same mistakes' as Mincom made in arriving at these specifications were Mincom trade secrets. Disclosure or use of these 'trade secrets' was enjoined. Winston argues that these provisions of the decree are too broad and indefinite, prohibit use by former Mincom employees of their personal knowledge and skill, and render these employees substantially unemployable in the work for which their specialized training and experience have equipped them. Mincom responds that the provisions are to be read narrowly as applying only to knowledge of the reasons for the particular specifications of the Mincom machine which the court held to be protectable trade secrets, and of mistakes to be avoided in developing these specifications.

Even so read, the provisions cannot stand, for their necessary effect is to prohibit conduct by Tobias, Johnson, and the other former Mincom employees in which they have a right to engage. As we have said, the general approach adopted by Mincom in the development of its machine and the basic mechanical elements incorporated in that machine were not protectible 'trade secrets,' since they were generally known. Mincom's former employees-and Winston-are free to utilize both in their efforts to build a machine equal or superior to the Mincom machine, so long as they do not, within the time covered by the injunction, utilize the particular specifications of the Mincom machine or their substantial equivalents. Moreover, Mincom's former employees cannot be denied the right to use their general skill, knowledge, and experience, even though acquired in part during their employment by Mincom. But the only practical way of enforcing the broad injunctive provisions here challenged would be to prohibit former Mincom employees from engaging in any development work in this area at all. They simply could not exclude their knowledge 'of what not to do' and of why Mincom's machine was built as it was from any development work they might now attempt involving the general approach and basic mechanical elements of the Mincom machine.

Moreover, such broad injunctive provisions are unnecessary. The specific provisions of the decree are both sufficient and readily enforceable. If Mincom's former employees disclose or utilize the Mincom design features detailed in the district court's judgment, or their substantial equivalents, alert enforcement of the specific provisions of the decree will amply protect Mincom's rights without improperly restricting either its former employees or potential competitors.

* * *

## COMPUTEK COMPUTER & OFFICE SUPPLIES, INC. v. WALTON

156 S.W.3d 217 (Tex. App. 2005)

Daron Walton d/b/a OEM Supplies (OEM) sued Computek Computer & Office Supplies, Inc., and Michael Williams, Computek's owner, (collectively, Computek), alleging, among other claims, that Williams used trade secrets obtained during his employment with OEM to form a competing company. The trial court found in favor of OEM on this claim and awarded it actual and exemplary damages. In addition, the trial court entered a permanent injunction against Computek. In its first issue, Computek contends that the permanent injunction is improper because it lacks specificity and is overly broad. In its second issue, Computek contends the award of joint and several exemplary damages against two defendants is improper. For the reasons that follow, we (1) reverse the permanent injunction in part and remand it to the trial court for further proceedings, and (2) modify the permanent injunction in part. Further, we reverse the judgment of the trial court on the merits as to the joint and several award of exemplary damages and remand that issue to the trial court for further proceedings. In all other respects, the permanent injunction and judgment on the merits are affirmed.

### FACTUAL AND PROCEDURAL BACKGROUND

Daron Walton and Michael Williams worked as sales representatives at ABBA, which sold office supplies to businesses. Walton left ABBA and started OEM, a business that competed with ABBA. In November 2000, Walton hired Williams. Williams brought with him the contacts he established at ABBA. Williams testified that he and Walton orally agreed that Williams could take his ABBA clients with him when he left OEM. OEM used TeleMagic, a computer program, to keep track of its salespersons' contacts with clients. The information included clients' names, contact information, current and past purchase orders, quoted prices, and personal information. The TeleMagic documents were labeled as confidential and the property of OEM. In addition, Williams had purchase orders for his ABBA clients that included some of this information.

In May 2002, while he was still employed by OEM, Williams incorporated Computek to compete with OEM. In August 2002, Williams deleted all of the information from 300 to 400 client files in OEM's TeleMagic program, and removed paperwork regarding those clients, such as purchase orders, from OEM's office. Williams used some of the deleted information to start Computek. When Walton discovered the information had been deleted and that client files had been removed, he fired Williams. Subsequently, OEM sued Williams for breach of a covenant not to compete, misappropriation of trade secrets, unfair competition, violation of the Texas Theft Liability Act, and conversion, and sought actual and exemplary damages and attorney's fees. OEM obtained a temporary restraining order and then a temporary injunction, which restrained Williams from taking certain actions regarding OEM clients or the information on the records Williams deleted or removed, including "[c]anvassing, soliciting, or accepting any business . . . from any OEM clients" or "using OEM confidential and proprietary information or the records and files taken from OEM or that were in OEM's possession prior to [Williams] leaving employment with OEM to solicit OEM clients."

The case was tried to the court. At the close of the trial, the court orally found for OEM on the claim for misappropriation of trade secrets and awarded actual damages of $113,000, exemplary damages of $100,000, and offset these amounts by $1,500. Alternatively, the trial court found for OEM on the theft of property claim and awarded OEM $113,000 in actual damages, $1,000 additional damages pursuant to the statute, $60,000 attorney's fees, and costs of court. The court found in Computek's favor on all other claims. The trial court subsequently signed a "Judgment of the Trial on the Merits," which found for OEM on the claim for misappropriation of trade secrets and for Computek on the remainder of the claims and awarded OEM $113,000 in actual damages, $100,000 in exemplary damages, and offset these amounts by $1,500. The trial court also signed a permanent injunction. Computek filed a motion to clarify/modify injunction and judgment and for new trial, which was overruled by operation of law. This appeal timely followed.

## PERMANENT INJUNCTION

In its first issue, Computek contends the permanent injunction is improper because it lacks clarity. Computek argues the injunction fails to specify which OEM clients Computek may not contact and that it is overly broad because it prevents Computek from engaging in activities it has a lawful right to perform. Computek requests that this Court either modify the permanent injunction (citation omitted), or reverse and remand to the trial court for further proceedings. [Citation omitted.]

### Standard of Review and Applicable Law

Whether to grant a permanent or temporary injunction is ordinarily within the sound discretion of the trial court and, on appeal, review of the trial court's action is limited to the question of whether the action constituted a clear abuse of discretion. [Citation omitted.] Because an injunction is an equitable remedy, a trial court weighs the respective conveniences and hardships of the parties and balances the equities. [Citation omitted.]

However, "[e]very order granting an injunction . . . shall set forth the reasons for its issuance; shall be specific in terms; shall describe in reasonable detail and not by reference to the complaint or other document, the act or acts sought to be restrained . . . ." TEX.R. CIV. P. 683. An injunction must be as definite, clear, and precise as possible and when practicable it should inform the defendant of the acts he is restrained from doing, without calling on him for inferences or conclusions about which persons might well differ and without leaving anything for further hearing. [Citations omitted.] Persons seeking the extraordinary remedy of injunction must be specific in pleading the relief sought, and the courts are without authority to grant relief beyond that so specified. [Citation omitted.]

An injunction should be broad enough to prevent a repetition of the evil sought to be corrected. *Id.* However, an injunction must not be so broad as to enjoin a defendant from activities that are a lawful and proper exercise of his rights. *Id.* at 796. Moreover, where a party's acts are divisible, and some acts are permissible and some are not, an injunction should not issue to restrain actions that are legal or about which there is no asserted complaint. [Citation omitted.] Thus, the entry of an injunction that enjoins lawful as well as unlawful acts may constitute an abuse of discretion. *Id.*

Discussion

1. Whether the permanent injunction lacks specificity

Numbered paragraphs one and two of the permanent injunction enjoin Computek from doing business, or authorizing anyone else to do business, with any OEM client not listed on Attachment A or that was a new account set up while Williams worked for OEM. Attachment A is a list of 184 clients that Williams brought from ABBA to OEM that Computek may contact. However, the clients Computek may not contact, which is the purpose of paragraphs one and two, are not named or identified. Paragraph three enjoins Computek from advising OEM clients to cancel their business with OEM. It refers to those who were OEM clients as of October 16, 2002 (two days before the request for injunction was filed and the temporary restraining order was signed) and new accounts set up while Williams worked for OEM; however, it does not name or identify those clients. Paragraphs four and five enjoin Computek from disclosing or using the non-ABBA information and files Williams took from OEM or that OEM possessed before Williams left OEM's employment; those paragraphs do not specifically list the information and files Computek may not use or disclose.

Computek argues that the injunction lacks specificity because paragraphs one through five seek to prevent Computek from doing business with OEM clients, but the injunction does not include a list of OEM clients.[1] Rather, because it includes a

[1] [1] The permanent injunction provides that the defendants are jointly and severally restrained from:

1. Canvassing, soliciting, or accepting any business in his own name or for any other individual, partnership, corporation, or other business entity, with the exception of OEM, from any OEM clients that are not listed on Attachment A, attached hereto and incorporated by reference, or were new accounts set up while Defendants worked for Plaintiff; and

2. Giving any person, firm, partnership, or corporation or retaining for themselves the right to canvas, solicit, or accept any business for any other service agency, from any OEM

list of clients Computek may contact, but not a list of those it must not contact, Computek contends that it cannot know whether a contact is an OEM client.

OEM responds that the first paragraph clearly enjoins Computek from contacting those OEM clients existing at the time the injunction became effective. Further, OEM responds that the first paragraph should be reformed to add language that it refers to clients of OEM as of October 16, 2002, or that were new accounts set up while Williams worked for OEM. Although these dates narrow the scope of OEM clients included in the injunction, the dates alone do not identify the OEM clients who are off-limits to Computek. Accordingly, we agree with Computek that these paragraphs enjoin Computek from taking specific actions involving specific OEM clients who are not identified or listed in the permanent injunction, and from using or disclosing information and files that are not specifically identified in the permanent injunction. Because these OEM clients are not specifically named, we agree with Computek that it must ask every non-ABBA contact it makes whether it was an OEM client during the relevant times, and that question may be construed as "canvassing" or "soliciting," and thus a violation of the permanent injunction. We agree with Computek that the permanent injunction lacks specificity in this regard.

OEM argues that Computek has the information as to the clients it may not contact "as demonstrated by their repeated contacts of those clients." OEM's brief contains no record reference to support this statement, and no testimony at the trial referred to Computek's violation of substantially similar provisions of the temporary injunction. However, even if the trial court had expressly found Computek had such information, rule 683 provides that the order granting an injunction "shall set forth the reasons for its issuance; shall be specific in terms; shall describe in reasonable detail and *not by reference to the complaint or any other document*, the act or acts sought to be restrained." TEX.R. CIV. P. 683 (emphasis added). Thus, the injunction itself must provide the specific information as to the off-limits clients, without inferences or conclusions, or, in this case, implied references to other records Computek might have. [Citations omitted.] Thus, we cannot agree with

---

clients that are not listed on Attachment A or were new accounts set up while Defendants worked for Plaintiff; and

3. Directly or indirectly requesting or advising any OEM clients, as of 10/16/02, or were new accounts set up while Defendants worked for Plaintiff, to change, withdraw, curtail, or cancel their business with OEM; and

4. Directly or indirectly disclosing to any other person, firm, or corporation the contents of the information or files taken from OEM or that were in OEM's possession prior to Defendants leaving employment with OEM with the exception the Defendants may use the information contained in Defendants' paper work brought by Defendants from A[BBA]; and

5. Directly or indirectly using OEM confidential and proprietary information or the records and files taken from OEM or that were in OEM's possession prior to Defendants leaving employment with OEM to solicit OEM clients with the exception the Defendants may use the information contained in Defendants' paper work brought by Defendants from A[BBA] . . .

6. Inducing or attempting to influence any employee of OEM to wrongfully convert confidential and proprietary information from the client customer files belonging to OEM in selling products to OEM clients; and

7. Removing or destroying any files, or copies of files, including but not limited to Defendants' computer or computer files.

Attachment A is titled "Michael Williams ABBA Client List." It contains the names of 184 clients that the evidence shows Williams brought to OEM from ABBA.

OEM that the lack of specificity as to OEM clients is cured by any knowledge Computek may have outside the permanent injunction.

2. Whether the permanent injunction is overly broad

Computek argues that the permanent injunction is "overbroad" because it prevents lawful activities. Specifically, Computek argues that paragraph seven, which bars Computek from "[r]emoving or destroying any files, or copies of files, including but not limited to Defendants' computer or computer files," prevents Computek from removing or destroying any files on its computers, including those that were unrelated to OEM or the litigation. Computek argues that it has the legal right to dispose of its own records or files that are "routine," such as deleting computer files no longer in use or throwing away paper records of old sales leads. [Citation omitted.]

OEM replies that, although paragraph seven does not refer specifically to OEM, the context of the injunction shows clearly that it refers only to files specifically related to OEM. OEM refers to the preceding six paragraphs that clearly refer to activities or property of OEM. However, those paragraphs are quite detailed and specifically limit Computek's external business activities in relation to OEM. In contrast, paragraph seven refers to Computek's internal procedures, without any limit. We conclude that the injunction enjoins activities Computek has a legal right to perform, such as deleting records and files that have nothing to do with OEM, and thus that the injunction is too broad.

Because we agree that the trial court abused its discretion by entering a permanent injunction that lacks specificity and is overly broad, we resolve Computek's first issue in its favor.

. . .

## NOTES AND QUESTIONS:

1. In *Standard Brands*, the court refused to grant an injunction because it was not convinced that there was any threatened, imminent, or anticipated violation of Zumpe's employment agreement or Standard Brands' trade secret rights. Wasn't the fact that Zumpe had knowledge of a number of Standard Brands' valuable trade secrets and his employment with a direct competitor, sufficient evidence to justify granting an injunction even though there was no evidence he had actually communicated them to Luzianne or had used them? Was the inevitable disclosure doctrine not applied?

2. Wouldn't the prophylactic use of temporary injunctions promote judicial economy? If Luzianne had actually used Standard Brands' trade secrets, wouldn't a preemptive temporary injunction eliminate the need for Standard Brands to return to court and present the same proof of its trade secrets? What are the policy considerations against a court using its equitable powers to grant an injunction against a prospective violation of a trade secret owner's rights? Note that the reasoning in this case is similar to that articulated in the *Ashland* opinion discussed

in Chapt. 2(B)(1)(c). Although the *Ashland Oil* court found there had been "isolated instances of breached confidentiality in the past," it determined that those breaches were insufficient "to overcome the continuing presumption of Congressional propriety" and refused to grant an injunction. 409 F.Supp. at 308. Was the *Ashland Oil* court's decision the result of a strict application of the considerations for granting an injunction, or were there undertones of a separation of powers issue between Congress and the court?

3. The UTSA provides for termination of an injunction "when the trade secret has ceased to exist," although "the injunction may be continued for an additional reasonable period of time in order to eliminate commercial advantage that otherwise would be derived from the misappropriation." UTSA § 2(a). Accordingly, the issue discussed in *Shellmar Products Co. v. Allen-Qualley Co.*, 87 F.2d 104 (7th Cir. 1936), and *Conmar Products Corp. v. Universal Slide Fastener Co.*, 172 F.2d 150 (2d Cir. 1949), of whether an injunction should be perpetual regardless of whether the trade secret is in the public domain, is not applicable in states that have adopted the UTSA.

4. *Shellmar Products* and *Conmar Products* generated considerable discussion and controversy over the years about the proper duration of an injunction. Are these cases really inconsistent with each other? Can you come up a persuasive argument as to how they are factually distinguishable?

5. In determining the duration of an injunction, the court in *Winston Research Corp. v. Minnesota Mining & Manufacturing Co.*, 350 F.2d 134 (9th Cir. 1965), used the time advantage that a misappropriator acquires over good faith competitors of the plaintiff as a guideline. Is it a better argument that the duration of the injunction should be the time it would take for "independent development" of the information — that is, the time it would take the defendant to develop the information without misappropriation? Some commentators have suggested that in deciding this question, "[t]he court should ask whether and when the particular misappropriator, and not some third party or the trade secret holder, could and would legitimately have replicated the trade secret at issue." *See* D. Kirk Jamieson, *Just Deserts: A Model to Harmonize Trade Secret Injunctions*, 72 Neb. L. Rev. 515, 548 (1993).

6. In *Winston Research*, the duration of the injunction was based primarily upon an objective standard — that is, how long after public disclosure of the secret information it would take a legitimate competitor to develop a successful tape recorder. Section 44 of the Restatement (Third) of Unfair Competition recommends the following subjective standard:

> [I]njunctive relief should ordinarily continue only until the defendant could have acquired the information by proper means. . . . . An injunction also should not ordinarily extend beyond the time when the defendant could have properly acquired and implemented the information through reverse engineering or independent discovery."

Restatement (Third) of Unfair Competition § 44 cmt. *f* at 503-04. When appropriate, however, the Restatement recommends using the following objective approach:

In some cases this duration may be measured by the time it would take a person of ordinary skill in the industry to discover the trade secret by independent means or to obtain the trade secret through the reverse engineering of publicly marketed products."

*Id.* at 504. Which approach would provide the most equitable outcome for the plaintiff?

7. The two-year injunction in *Winston Research* began on the date of judgment, which the court determined would be about the length of time it would take for a public disclosure of the trade secrets to take place. The court could have started the injunction period on the date the trade secret was misappropriated. If using the date of misappropriation as the starting date, the trial court can issue a permanent injunction only for the period that has not expired prior to the entry of judgment. Considering that this latter option reduces the duration of the injunction, is this truly an effective equitable remedy? Taking into consideration that, unlike the objective standard, this approach allows a trial court the discretion to reduce the duration of the injunction, is this a more reasonable standard? *See Rockwell Graphic*, discussed above. Although the *Rockwell Graphic* court found it would have taken the defendant eight years to legitimately to replicate the misappropriated trade secrets, it ultimately enjoined the defendant from using the trade secrets for only two years.

8. It is axiomatic that injunctions must be specific and not overly broad. These issues were discussed by the court in *Computek Computer & Office Supplies, Inc. v. Walton*, 156 S.W.3d 217 (Tex. App. 2005), which illustrates the type of dispute that can happen after an injunction is entered by the trial court, which oftentimes happens when the court grants injunction terms requested by the winning party.

## D. DAMAGES AND ATTORNEYS' FEES

### UNIVERSITY COMPUTING CO. v. LYKES-YOUNGSTOWN CORP.

504 F.2d 518 (5th Cir. 1974)

Once having determined that the jury finding that AIMES III was a trade secret wrongfully appropriated by the defendants was proper, the problem remains as to what is the appropriate measure of damages. It seems generally accepted that 'the proper measure of damages in the case of a trade secret appropriation is to be determined by reference to the analogous line of cases involving patent infringement, just as patent infringement cases are used by analogy to determine the damages for copy-right infringement.' *International Industries, Inc. v. Warren Petroleum Corp.*, 248 F.2d 696, 699 (3d Cir. 1957). The case law is thus plentiful, but the standard for measuring damages which emerges is very flexible.

In some instances courts have attempted to measure the loss suffered by the plaintiff. While as a conceptual matter this seems to be a proper approach, in most cases the defendant has utilized the secret to his advantage with no obvious effect on the plaintiff save for the relative differences in their subsequent competitive positions. Largely as a result of this practical dilemma, normally the value of the secret to the plaintiff is an appropriate measure of damages only when the defendant has in some way destroyed the value of the secret. The most obvious way this is done is through publication, so that no secret remains. Where the plaintiff retains the use of the secret, as here, and where there has been no effective disclosure of the secret through publication the total value of the secret to the plaintiff is an inappropriate measure.

Further, unless some specific injury to the plaintiff can be established — such as lost sales — the loss to the plaintiff is not a particularly helpful approach in assessing damages.

The second approach is to measure the value of the secret to the defendant. This is usually the accepted approach where the secret has not been destroyed and where the plaintiff is unable to prove specific injury. In the case before us, then, the 'appropriate measure of damages, by analogy to patent infringement, is not what plaintiff lost, but rather the benefits, profits, or advantages gained by the defendant in the use of the trade secret.' *International Industries, Inc. v. Warren Petroleum, supra*, 248 F.2d at 699. The cases reveal, however, many variations in the way this benefit to the defendant can be measured.

Normally only the defendant's actual profits can be used as a measure of damages in cases where profits can be proved, and the defendant is normally not assessed damages on wholly speculative expectations of profits. [Citation omitted.] Had the defendants here been able to sell the AIMES III system at a profit, our task would be simplified. Because the defendants failed in their marketing efforts, no actual profits exist by which to value the worth to the defendants of what they misappropriated. However, the Supreme Court has held in a patent case that the lack of actual profits does not insulate the defendants from being obliged to pay for what they have wrongfully obtained in the mistaken belief their theft would benefit them. [Citation omitted.]

The rationale for this seems clearly to be that the risk of defendants' venture, using the misappropriated secret, should not be placed on the injured plaintiff, but rather the defendants must bear the risk of failure themselves. Accordingly the law looks to the time at which the misappropriation occurred to determine what the value of the misappropriated secret would be to a defendant who believes he can utilize it to his advantage, provided he does in fact put the idea to a commercial use.

This second technique frequently entails using what is called the 'reasonable royalty' standard: While the parties to this action agree this is the appropriate standard, they are unable to agree on what the measure entails. Originally this measure was intended to deal with the situation where the misappropriated idea is used either to improve the defendant's manufacturing process, or is used as part of a larger manufactured product. In the early case of *Egry Register Co. v. Standard Register Co.*, 23 F.2d 438 (6th Cir. 1928), a patent infringement case, the defendant manufactured and sold cash registers which in part used a device developed by the plaintiff to roll paper through the machine. The trial court had awarded the plaintiff the total profits the defendant had made on all sales of the machines using this device. The Sixth Circuit Court of Appeals held this measure of damages was inequitable, because the device was only a part of the larger product sold by the defendant. Because no actual apportionment of profits based on what percentage of the success of the marketing of the machines was due to the plaintiff's device could be shown, the court held the proper measure of damages would be a reasonable royalty on defendant's sales, thereby creating an apportionment of profits based on an approximation of the actual value of the infringed device to the defendant.

The Court explained its new measure in this way:

> To adopt a reasonable royalty as the measure of damages is to adopt and interpret, as well as may be, the fiction that a license was to be granted at the time of beginning the infringement, and them to determine what the license price should have been. In effect, the court assumes the existence ab initio of, and declares the equitable terms of, a supposititious license, and does this nunc pro tunc; it creates and applies retrospectively a compulsory license . . . .' The Court further held the proper standard would be a willing buyer-willing seller test: '. . . the primary inquiry . . . is what the parties would have agreed upon, if both were reasonably trying to reach agreement.

Egry Register, supra, at 443.

The language of the Egry decision has been often quoted, but the type of measure used by the Court, based on actual sales, has taken many different forms. As the term is presently understood, the 'reasonable royalty' measure of damages is taken to mean more than simply a percentage of actual profits. The measure now, very simply, means 'the actual value of what has been appropriated.' *Vitro Corporation of America v. Hall Chemical Co.*, 292 F.2d 678, 683 (6th Cir. 1961). When this is not subject to exact measurement, a reasonable estimate of value is used. Many different factors are now considered in arriving at the 'reasonable royalty' in any given case:

> As pointed out in many cases . . . in a case where no established royalty is shown it is for the Court to determine a reasonable royalty which represents the value of that which has been wrongfully taken by the infringer . . . it is sufficient to point out that in making such determination many factors were taken into consideration . . . . In fact, the reasonable royalty was based upon the advantages which would have accrued to (the infringer) had it negotiated a license . . .

*Union Carbide Corp. v. Graver Tank and Manufacturing Co.*, 282 F.2d 653, 674-675 (7th Cir. 1960), *cert. denied*, 365 U.S. 812, 81 S.Ct. 692, 5 L.Ed.2d 691 (1961).

On other important variation on this 'reasonable royalty' standard is the standard of comparison method, which also attempts to measure the value to the defendant to what he appropriated. As the Court in *International Industries, Inc. v. Warren Petroleum Corp.*, 248 F.2d 696, 699 (3d Cir. 1957) explained this method, relating it to the facts of the case in which the defendant had misappropriated a method of converting dry cargo vessels into ones equipped to transport liquefied petroleum gas, and had actually used the technique to convert one vessel:

> This method contemplates the comparison of the cost of transportation by means of the use of the trade secret with a method of accomplishing the same result which would have been open to defendant had he not appropriated the trade secret.

Occasionally this has been taken to mean the difference in costs to the defendant of developing the trade secret on his own, using the actual development costs of the plaintiff as the complete measure of damages. [Citation omitted.] This measure of damages simply uses the plaintiff's actual costs, and in our view is frequently inadequate in that it fails to take into account the commercial context in which the misappropriation occurred.

In certain cases, where the trade secret was used by the defendant in a limited number of situations, where the plaintiff was not in direct competition with the defendant, where the development of the secret did not require substantial improvements in existing trade practices but rather merely refined the existing practices, and where the defendant's use of the plaintiff's trade secret has ceased, such a limited measure might be appropriate. In the type of case which we now consider, when the parties were potentially in direct competition and the course of conduct of the defendant extended over a period of time and included a number of different uses of the plaintiff's trade secret, and where the process of developing a computer system was very difficult and required substantial technical and theoretical advances, we believe a broader measure of damages is needed.

This broader measure should take into consideration development costs, but as only one of a number of different factors. We believe this type of measure is appropriate despite the fact that the inclusion of other factors means the final damage figure 'need not be as precise as if the actual development costs for the trade secret were itself the measure of damages.' *Forest Laboratories, Inc. v. Pillsbury Co.*, 452 F.2d 621, 628 (7th Cir. 1971).

Our review of the caselaw leads us to the conclusion that every case requires a flexible and imaginative approach to the problem of damages. We agree with the Court of Appeals for the Sixth Circuit that 'each case is controlled by its own peculiar facts and circumstances,' *Enterprise Manufacturing Co. v. Shakespeare Co.*, 141 F.2d 916, 920 (6th Cir. 1944), and accordingly we believe that the cases reveal that most courts adjust the measure of damages to accord with the commercial setting of the injury, the likely future consequences of the misappropriation, and the nature and extent of the use the defendant put the trade secret to after misappropriation. Naturally in some cases the damages will be subject to exact measurement, either because the parties had previously agreed on a licensing price as in *Vitro Corp. v. Hall Chemical Co., supra*, or because some industry standard provides a clear measure. Where the damages are uncertain, however, we do not feel that that uncertainty should preclude recovery; the plaintiff should be afforded every opportunity to prove damages once the misappropriation is shown.

Certain standards do emerge from the cases. The defendant must have actually put the trade secret to some commercial use. The law governing protection of trade secrets essentially is designed to regulate unfair business competition, and is not a substitute for criminal laws against theft or other civil remedies for conversion. If the defendant enjoyed actual profits, a type of restitutionary remedy can be afforded the plaintiff-either recovering the full total of defendant's profits or some apportioned amount designed to correspond to the actual contribution the plaintiff's trade secret made to the defendant's commercial success. Because the primary concern in most cases is to measure the value to the defendant of what he actually obtained from the plaintiff, the proper measure is to calculate what the parties would have agreed to as a fair price for licensing the defendant to put the trade secret to the use the defendant intended at the time the misappropriation took place.

In calculating what a fair licensing price would have been had the parties agreed, the trier of fact should consider such factors as the resulting and foreseeable changes in the parties' competitive posture; that prices past purchasers or licensees may have paid; the total value of the secret to the plaintiff, including the plaintiff's development costs and the importance of the secret to the plaintiff's business; the nature and extent of the use the defendant intended for the secret; and finally whatever other unique factors in the particular case which might have affected the parties' agreement, such as the ready availability of alternative processes. [Citation omitted.]

* * *

## JET SPRAY COOLER, INC. v. CRAMPTON

385 N.E.2d 1349 (Mass. 1979)

The protection which we afford to trade secrets against one who wrongfully uses them is grounded on principles of public policy to which we have adhered since Peabody v. Norfolk, 98 Mass. 452, 457 (1868): "It is the policy of the law, for the advantage of the public, to encourage and protect invention and commercial enterprise." This encouragement and protection is afforded trade secrets because the public has a manifest interest not only in commercial innovation and development, but also in "(t)he maintenance of standards of commercial ethics." Kewanee Oil Co. v. Bicron Corp., 416 U.S. 470, 481, 94 S.Ct. 1879, 1886, 40 L.Ed.2d 315 (1974).

Early Federal decisions are remarkably similar. In Fowle v. Park, 131 U.S. 88, 97, 9 S.Ct. 658, 662, 33 L.Ed. 67 (1889), the Supreme Court held that "(t) he policy of the law is to encourage useful discoveries by securing their fruits to those who make them." In Board of Trade of Chicago v. Christie Grain & Stock Co., 198 U.S. 236, 250, 25 S.Ct. 637, 639, 49 L.Ed. 1031 (1905), Mr. Justice Holmes said that the board had "the right to keep the work which it has done, or paid for doing, to itself. The fact that others might do similar work, if they might, does not authorize them to steal the plaintiff's." Again in Dr. Miles Medical Co. v. John D. Park & Sons, 220 U.S. 373, 402, 31 S.Ct. 376, 382, 55 L.Ed. 502 (1911), the Court held that "(t)he complainant relies upon the ownership of its secret process and its rights are to be determined accordingly. Anyone may use it who fairly, by analysis and experiment, discovers it. But the complainant is entitled to be protected against invasion of its rights in the (secret) process by fraud or by breach of trust or contract." Further, in E. I. duPont de Nemours Powder Co. v. Masland, 244 U.S. 100, 102, 37 S.Ct. 575, 576, 61 L.Ed. 1016 (1917), the Supreme Court said that an employee "shall not fraudulently abuse the trust reposed in him." In Becher v. Contoure Laboratories, Inc., 279 U.S. 388, 391, 49 S.Ct. 356, 357, 73 L.Ed. 752 (1929), the Court recognized a cause of action against an employee for "breach of a contract or wrongful disregard of confidential relations." Finally, in United States v. Dubilier Condenser Corp., 289 U.S. 178, 186, 53 S.Ct. 554, 557, 77 L.Ed. 1114 (1933), the Court held that an inventor "may keep his invention secret and reap its fruits indefinitely." See generally Waters Servs., Inc. v. Tesco Chems., Inc., 410 F.2d 163, 171 (5th Cir. 1969); Hutter, Trade Secret Misappropriation: A Lawyer's Practical Approach to the Case

Law, 1 W. New England L. Rev. 1, 9 (1978).

Consistent with these principles, once information is demonstrated to be "of an appropriate nature to qualify" the information as a trade secret, any inquiry into the misuse of the trade secret must focus on the conduct of the defendant. Jet Spray Cooler, Inc. v. Crampton, supra 361 Mass. at 843, 282 N.E.2d 921. If the defendant has acquired the information as a result of a confidential relationship which he enjoyed with the plaintiff, and, if the defendant has used the information without the permission of the plaintiff, then the defendant's use of the information is wrongful, and the defendant is liable to the plaintiff in damages "for the wrongful use of the information." Id. at 845, 282 N.E.2d at 927.

The first damage master apparently did not focus on the facts found in the case on liability. The liability master found that "(s)ince their inception the plaintiffs have conducted an extensive research and development program in a constant effort to improve their products and have, on occasion, consulted with independent engineering firms to help develop new products as well as to improve their existing products." Jet Spray Cooler, Inc. v. Crampton, supra at 836, 282 N.E.2d at 923. Additionally, in Jet Spray Cooler the plaintiffs had maintained sufficient secrecy to protect the confidentiality of the information in the Foster-Miller report. Id. at 844, 282 N.E.2d 921.

The first damage master apparently attached no importance to either of these factors and concentrated on the lack of novelty rather than on the impropriety of the method used to procure the secret. The fact that a process is the combination and adaptation of old principles to new purposes does not prevent the process from being a trade secret if the process as distilled accomplishes a result which gives the holder a competitive advantage due to his own ingenuity, research and development. Moreover, "the fact that the secret was easy to duplicate does not militate against its being a trade secret. The important point is that the owner and those to whom it was necessary to reveal the secret knew of the trade secret." Maruchnics, Industrial Trade Secrets, Their Use and Protection, 4 Clev.-Mar.L.Rev. 69, 71-72 (1955). Thus, the first damage master erred as matter of law in failing to focus on the abuse of the confidential relationship and on the secrecy attached to the report which was designed to improve the plaintiffs' product and give it a competitive advantage. By not focusing on the defendants' conduct and on the secrecy attached to the Foster-Miller report, the first damage master erred in his assessment of damages.

The measure of damages in cases involving business torts such as the misappropriation of trade secrets entitles a plaintiff to recover full compensation for his lost profits and requires a defendant to surrender the profits which he realized from his tortious conduct. [Citations omitted.]

Of course, a plaintiff is not entitled to both the profits made by the defendant and his own lost profits. [Citations omitted.]

However, while a plaintiff is not entitled to a double recovery, "the plaintiff is entitled to the profit he would have made had his secret not been unlawfully used, but not less than the monetary gain which the defendant reaped from his improper acts" (footnotes omitted). 2 Callman, Unfair Competition, Trademarks and Monopolies § 59.3 at 496 (3d ed. 1968). Clark v. Bunker, 453 F.2d 1006, 1011 (9th Cir. 1972). Cf. Sperry Rand Corp. v. A-T-O, Inc., 447 F.2d 1387, 1392-1393 (4th Cir. 1971), cert. denied, 409 U.S. 892, 93 S.Ct. 117, 34 L.Ed.2d 150 (1972). Only in this way can we ensure that an unfair competitor will not be encouraged to proceed with his unfair methods in the hope "that his profits might exceed the injured party's losses." National Merchandising Corp. v. Leyden, supra 370 Mass. at ___, 348 N.E.2d 776. Therefore, a plaintiff in an action involving the misappropriation of trade secrets may proceed in the alternative to determine whether the defendant's wrongful profits exceed the plaintiff's losses caused by the misuse of the plaintiff's trade secrets. See Id. at 771 & n.16, 348 N.E.2d 771 & n.16.

We now consider the first damage master's method of assessing damages in light of traditional principles. The first damage master found that "(t)he plaintiffs introduced detailed evidence in relation to the period from the inception of Crathco . . . concerning alleged profits made by the defendants year by year on sale of their units, and concerning alleged plaintiffs' loss year by year of profits on sales by the defendants to plaintiffs' customers to the extent that the plaintiffs' profits would have exceeded the profits made by the defendants thereon." Nonetheless, the first damage master disregarded this information and refused to assess damages based on the defendants' profits or the plaintiffs' lost profits because he found that the only effect of the defendants' wrongful use of the Foster-Miller report was the fact that the defendants were able to enter the market in competition with the plaintiffs three months earlier than they could have done without the benefit of the information contained in the report.

To the extent that the first damage master's findings with regard to the three-month period of time may be interpreted as applying a "head start rule" in assessing damages in this action, such a measure of damages is improper. The application of a "head start" approach would limit damages to that period of time in which "others in the trade are likely, through legitimate business procedures, to have become aware of these secrets." Analogic Corp. v. Data Translation, Inc., 371 Mass. 643, ___, 358 N.E.2d 804, 808 (1976).

Generally, the "head start rule" has been applied in cases where the plaintiff's product, including the trade secret, has been marketed. The marketing of the product gives competitors a legitimate opportunity to study the product and to learn the principles of the trade secret through reverse engineering or similar procedures. [Citations omitted.]

In a petition for injunctive relief, we have indicated that the time necessary to engineer in reverse is one factor to be considered in determining the propriety of the duration of injunctive relief. [Citations omitted.] We have not applied this theory in an action for damages. The defendants contend that the actual marketing by the plaintiffs of a product incorporating the trade secrets in question is irrelevant to the application of a head start rule. In support of their argument, the defendants rely on National Rejectors, Inc. v. Trieman, 409 S.W.2d 1 (Mo.1966), and Structural Dynamics Research Corp. v. Engineering Mechanics Research Corp., 401 F.Supp. 1102 (E.D.Mich.1975). However, in National Rejectors, the Supreme Court of Missouri held that no trade secrets belonging to the plaintiffs had been misappropriated by the defendants. Id. at 34. In Structural Dynamics, not only was the remedy based on a "reasonable royalty" because the defendants had made no profits, Id. at 1119, but also the plaintiffs had marketed products containing the trade secrets. Id. at 1109.

But the Value of the misappropriated trade secrets to the defendants is not the basis of the defendants' liability, and the value of the misappropriated trade secrets should not form the basis of the plaintiffs' recovery. [Citation omitted.] Therefore, by focusing on the value of the misappropriated trade secrets, and not on the wrongful conduct of the defendants, the first damage master's assessment of damages was legally incorrect. The judge properly rejected the master's report and committed the case to a second damage master. [Citation omitted.]

II. The Report of the Second Damage Master.

The judge's order of reference to the second damage master instructed the master: "(1) to find the extent of the use made by the defendants of the trade secret (Foster Miller Report); (2) To find the amount of profits made by the defendants on the sale of units incorporating the trade secret; and (3) To find the amount of the plaintiffs' loss of profits due to the defendants' sales of such dispensers to plaintiffs' customers to the extent such loss exceeds the defendants' profits on these same sales." This order of reference is consistent with our traditional principles of damage assessment in cases involving business torts. The second damage master made specific findings with regard to each of the three issues which the judge had instructed him to examine.

First, the second damage master addressed the extent to which the trade secrets had been used by the defendants. He found that each visual display beverage dispenser unit sold by the corporate defendant from 1963 to September 30, 1975 (the accounting period) incorporated the trade secrets contained in the Foster-Miller report. The second damage master also found that during the accounting period the defendants sold 27,110 dispensers with gross sales of $6,322,357.18.

Second, the master computed the net profits of the defendants during the accounting period from sales incorporating the trade secrets. Since all the sales of the defendants incorporated the trade secrets, the second damage master computed the total net profits of the defendants. He found that the records submitted by the corporate defendant showed total net profits of $67,604.80 during the accounting period. He rejected a claim by the defendants that $15,422.20 in losses incurred during two of the years of the accounting period should be deducted from their total net profits. He also disallowed certain other deductions claimed by the defendants and added them to the defendants' net profits:

(a) $105,553.17 in legal fees and expenses in defending this action.

(b) $19,759.61 in Federal income taxes paid by the corporate defendant during the accounting period.

(c) $21,578.29 in Massachusetts excise taxes paid by the corporate defendant during the accounting period.

(d) $18,698.03 in bad debts incurred on sales by the corporate defendant during the accounting period.

(e) $681.575.80 in salaries and consultant's fees paid to the individual defendants by the corporate defendant during the accounting period.

(f) $22,508.40 for Key Life insurance premiums paid by the corporate defendant on the lives of the individual defendants during the accounting period.

(g) $17,110.52 for group insurance coverage on the lives of the individual defendants at various times during the accounting period.

The net profits of the defendants as recomputed by the second damage master totaled $954,388.62 during the accounting period.

Finally, the second damage master considered the question of the lost profits of the plaintiffs to the extent that they exceeded the profits of the defendants. The plaintiffs claimed that their profits on the sales made by the corporate defendant to the plaintiffs' customers would have totaled nearly $1,500,000 more than Crathco made on the same sales during the accounting period. The master rejected this claim, finding the plaintiffs' evidence on this aspect of damages "conjectural, speculative and theoretically unsound."

The second damage master also found that the individual defendants had made no "profits as such." Therefore, he found in favor of the individual defendants.

Both the plaintiffs and the defendants filed objections to the second master's report. On September 23, 1977, the judge modified and then adopted the report of the second damage master. See Mass.R.Civ.P. 53(e)(2). He accompanied his order with a comprehensive, well reasoned memorandum of decision.

The judge allowed the defendants' deductions for bad debts and for salaries and consultant's fees paid to the individual defendants. The judge then computed the total of the defendants' net profits at $282,100.83.

* * *

Because the plaintiffs' lost profits were a lesser amount than the defendants' profits as computed by the judge, he awarded damages to the plaintiffs in the amount of the defendants' net profits. Both the plaintiffs and the defendants appeal from certain of the judge's modifications of the second damage master's report.

* * *

In this action, the second damage master's subsidiary findings also reveal that during the accounting period the plaintiffs never marketed a product incorporating the recommendations contained in the Foster-Miller report. The master further found that the Crathco dispenser offered "serious competition" to the Jet Spray dispenser "because it was superior to the dispensers produced by other manufacturers and also that Crathco's dispenser was comparable to Jet's particularly since it contained the improvements recommended in the Foster-Miller Report."

In light of these findings, we cannot determine whether the plaintiffs' lost profits in this action were "due to" the defendants' sales of products utilizing the trade secrets, or whether the plaintiffs' lost profits were "due to" the plaintiffs' own business decision to refrain from marketing products containing the information in the report. See supra at ___ & n.12. Here, the uncertainty in the assessment of damages arises not from any action of the defendants, but from the inaction of the plaintiffs. Compare National Merchandising Corp. v. Leyden, supra 370 Mass. at ___, 348 N.E.2d 771. Therefore, we conclude that the plaintiffs have not proved their lost profits "due to" the defendants' sales to the plaintiffs' customers with sufficient certainty to allow the plaintiffs to recover damages based on lost profits.

* * *

An award to a plaintiff of the defendant's net profits is made primarily to ensure that the defendant is not unjustly enriched as a result of his wrongful acts. [Citation omitted.] Since the award of a defendant's net profits is made only where the defendant's net profits exceed the plaintiff's demonstrable losses, the plaintiff may actually recover far more than its actual loss. [Citations omitted.]

Here, the plaintiffs have been awarded the entirety of the defendants' net corporate profits from 1964 to 1975. This award is made because it is impossible for the defendants to segregate the portion of their profits which is attributable to the misappropriated trade secrets from the portion of their profits which may be attributable to other factors. [Citation omitted.] Thus it is likely that the "plaintiff may recover more than his exact loss." National Merchandising Corp. v. Leyden, supra.

In these circumstances, we do not think that the plaintiffs will be unfairly deprived of compensation or that the defendants will be "unjustly enriched if (they are) not required to pay interest on the total profits so awarded." Carter Prods., Inc. v. Colgate-Palmolive Co., supra at 417. The observation of the United States Court of Appeals for the Seventh Circuit in L. P. Larson, Jr., Co. v. William Wrigley, Jr., Co., 20 F.2d 830, 836 (7th Cir. 1927), rev'd on other grounds, 277 U.S. 97, 48 S.Ct. 449, 72 L.Ed. 800 (1928), is particularly apt here: "The award here in issue is so palpably and unquestionably ample to fully compensate (the plaintiff) for any and all invasion of its rights, as to suggest no circumstances which invoke the court's discretion to enlarge it by allowance of interest back of the date of the master's report. . . ." Therefore, the judge properly awarded interest only from the date on which the second damage master's report was filed. [Citations omitted.]

## GOLDBERG v. MEDTRONIC, INC.
209 U.S.P.Q. 259 (N.D. Ill. 1980)

* * *

In Count I, Goldberg alleges that in the period of 1965-66, he disclosed, in confidence, to officials of Medtronic responsible for the development and sale of pacemaker leads, the concept of a safe, sutureless, visually and remotely installable lead for heart pacemakers. He further alleges that he sought assistance in research and development of the lead and that these facts gave rise to a confidential, fiduciary relationship. Finally, Goldberg alleges that the misappropriated information was incorporated into Medtronic's popular "Model 6917 Sutureless Myocardial Lead."

Medtronic maintains that no confidential disclosures were made. Alternatively, if any such disclosures were made, Medtronic did not assume an obligation of confidence. In addition, Medtronic alleges that any duty of confidentiality was terminated by operation of law as a result of public disclosures by Dr. Goldberg and others concerning the screwin lead. Medtronic further alleges that no information gleaned from Dr. Goldberg was used to develop its Model 6917 lead.

The evidence demonstrates that Dr. Goldberg first contacted Medtronic in connection with his idea in the fall of 1964. Dr. Goldberg was interested in approaching the heart inferiorly as opposed to from the neck region. Using a mediastinoscope, he would screw a rigid, helically shaped lead tip into the ventricle with an insertion tool. Goldberg asked Charles Eddy, Medtronic's local sales representative, if they would provide material to conduct research and experiments. Medtronic agreed to do so.

In the next year, Goldberg conducted experiments on dogs at Michael Reese Hospital in Chicago. He worked with Arthur Rone, a research assistant. He was under the supervision of Dr. Joseph St. Ville, a cardiac surgeon. He also consulted with Dr. Falls Hersey, Chairman of the Department of Surgery at Michael Reese Hospital. The only other individuals to have seen Goldberg's apparatus were Dr. Norman Brill, a surgeon at the hospital and Goldberg's associate, Dr. Milton Weinberg, Jr., Chairman of the Department of Thoracic Surgery at Cook County Hospital.

In the summer of 1965, Goldberg and his associates submitted a paper at the Fifth Multidiscipline Research Forum of the American Medical Association ("AMA"). At the meeting, Dr. Goldberg discussed mediastinoscopy and indicated that he was able to approach the heart through the inferior mediastinum and place an electrical lead on the ventricle. He did not, however, disclose the screw-in lead concept at that meeting or the precise method of insertion and attachment.

Subsequently, Goldberg was contacted by Inga Haug, a Medtronic representative, who had heard of his presentation at the AMA meeting and his statement that he could attach a lead to the heart through a mediastinoscope through the inferior mediastinum. Haug invited Goldberg to Medtronic headquarters in Minneapolis to discuss his work. Medtronic paid Goldberg's expenses for this trip. In Minneapolis, Goldberg met briefly with Earl Bakken, President of Medtronic. Later, he explained and demonstrated his screw-in lead concept to Bakken and other Medtronic representatives. Bakken denies that these meetings took place but numerous other witnesses testified as to their existence. The court finds that Goldberg made this trip and discussed his concepts for insertion of pacemaker leads.

In December, 1965, Eddy first saw the screw-in lead Goldberg developed. Eddy communicated his information to Bakken. Bakken stated certain objections to the method of insertion, mediastinoscopy, but not to the screw-in lead concept. Bakken had received these objections from Dr. Chardack, who was advising Medtronic and who apparently was apprised of Goldberg's work.

In January, 1966, Goldberg made a presentation on the topic of mediastinoscopy at the Michael Reese Heart Institute. Eddy was present and immediately contacted Bakken as to what was discussed. Bakken continued to express his lack of interest in the procedure.

After further discussion with Eddy on the topic of Goldberg's screw-in leads, Bakken instructed Eddy to invite Goldberg to Medtronic's headquarters in Minneapolis in March, 1966. Medtronic once again paid Goldberg's expenses for the trip, yet Bakken has no record of any such meetings. Eddy, however, testified that he had made the arrangements for the trip and that his diary reflects that the meeting took place on March 16, 1966.

Goldberg again demonstrated his leads to Bakken who indicated that he would be interested in working with Goldberg on the project. Medtronic agreed to provide equipment for the research. Goldberg agreed not to publish the results of his work prematurely so as to protect, as Eddy testified, the proprietary interests of the parties. Eddy conceded that the leads would be improved through further research and that the research involved confidential proprietary information. Medtronic agreed to make for Goldberg his helically tipped screw-in lead.

In the ensuing months, Medtronic sent Goldberg many leads and other equipment for use in his research. Medtronic, again, kept no records of its transactions with Goldberg.

In April, 1966, Bakken called Goldberg and stated that Medtronic's advisor, Dr. Chardack, did not see the need for a new lead and opposed the procedure of mediastinoscopy. For these reasons, Medtronic would not actively participate in the research. Medtronic continued, however, to supply equipment.

At Bakken's request, Eddy contacted Herb Taus at General Electric Company and told him that Goldberg had an innovative technique for implanting pacemaker leads and was looking for assistance on the project. Bakken instructed Eddy to keep Medtronic advised of the research and of any progress achieved. He was instructed to maintain a rapport and relate to Medtronic anything he saw or was told.

While at General Electric, Goldberg disclosed his idea of a screw-in lead to Henry Tachick. The research which followed was successful in the development of a viable lead. General Electric, however, filed a patent application on behalf of Tachick, not Goldberg. Several years later, the U.S. Patent and Trademark Office put Goldberg's patent application and Tachick's patent into an interference to determine the actual inventor. Goldberg prevailed when General Electric filed a disclaimer under 35 U.S.C. § 253.

Shortly after Goldberg's first visit to Medtronic in the fall of 1965, Medtronic hired Lee Balduc to conduct research in and to manufacture leads. In April, 1966, just after Bakken told Goldberg he was not interested in actively assisting him in his research, Bolduc, working directly for Medtronic, made a special lead for Goldberg and was going to send it to him. Later, Eddy asked Bakken about the status of the electrode. Bakken stated that he had changed his mind and would not provide this electrode to Goldberg even though it incorporated Goldberg's designs. Eddy and Bolduc then met with Goldberg in June, 1966 at an AMA conference and discussed Goldberg's research.

In January, 1967, Goldberg met with Medtronic officials in Minneapolis. The progress of his research at General Electric was discussed. Again, Medtronic has no record of this meeting. Eddy's diary established the exact date of the meeting as January 7, 1967.

In May, 1967, Eddy and Manny Villafona from the Minneapolis office of Medtronic came to Chicago and observed Goldberg install his lead in a dog. Goldberg apprised them of the present and anticipated developments in the apparatus. Eddy immediately informed Bakken of what Goldberg had shown them.

On June 7, 1967, Eddy received a phone call from Jack Schwartz, Medtronic's national sales manager. Schwartz wanted Eddy to obtain technical data about Goldberg's lead for Wilson Greatbatch, a member of Medtronic's Board of Directors and its Design Review Board.

Some time prior to August, 1968, Bolduc showed Bakken a screw-in lead to be installed with a mediastinoscope.

By means of a letter dated October 28, 1968, General Electric offered to license its lead derived from Dr. Goldberg's work, under its Tachick application. The letter was sent to Bakken, who discussed it with Taus and Bolduc but not Eddy.

In 1969, Bolduc's work on screw-in leads resulted in Medtronic's Model 6917 lead. This lead embodied Goldberg's concepts of a rigid, helical tip screwed into the heart with a special tool. The coil was, however, mounted on a plastic platform similar to that in the Chardack model. Bakken instructed Bolduc to proceed with testing the lead without first seeking the approval of the Design Review Board so as to avoid Chardack's objection. There was testimony that Bolduc admitted that the idea behind the Model 6917 lead was derived from Goldberg.

In October, 1972, Medtronic began marketing its Model 6917 lead for use in humans. Goldberg became aware of the Model 6917 lead when, in 1973, Medtronic's representative in Chicago demonstrated it at Michael Reese Hospital. Goldberg informed him that the Model 6917 embodied ideas and designs that were rightfully his. Medtronic refused to discuss the matter.

Plaintiff has established by a preponderance of the evidence that there was a confidential relationship between Medtronic and Goldberg, that Goldberg disclosed his confidential, proprietary ideas to Medtronic, and that Medtronic misappropriated the confidential information.

Virtually concurrent with Goldberg's first disclosure to Medtronic and Bakken's seemingly feigned lack of interest, Medtronic hired Bolduc to conduct parallel research on the leads. Bolduc, however, had the benefit of Goldberg's work. Even though Medtronic directed Goldberg to General Electric, there followed consistent and concerted efforts to keep informed of the status of his research. Medtronic made certain that it was kept apprised of each and every development of Goldberg's work.

The fact that General Electric may have made certain disclosures to Medtronic is of no consequence. Medtronic knew or should have known that all of the work constituted confidential proprietary information. Besides, it had already received the information through its monitoring of Goldberg's work.

Medtronic used the confidential information in designing its Model 6917 lead, thus misappropriating the information. Forest Laboratories, Inc. v. Pillsbury Co., 452 F.2d 621, 171 USPQ 731 (7th Cir. 1971). An indication of this is reflected in Bakken's refusal to permit Bolduc to send to Goldberg the lead which Goldberg was having Bolduc make for him. In addition, the extremely close monitoring of Goldberg's every development indicates the extent of Medtronic's interest and the fact that it was more than a disinterested observer.

Medtronic alleges numerous defenses, none of which defeat plaintiff's tort claim. First, Medtronic maintains that Dr. Lillehei disclosed the concept of screw-in electrodes at a symposium attended by cardiac surgeons and Bakken, in Buffalo, New York in May, 1965. While this may be the case, the concept which was disclosed involved an emergency, short-term procedure which never resulted in a viable apparatus solving the problem Dr. Goldberg was addressing. Medtronic's Model 6917 lead was derived from Dr. Goldberg's work. Medtronic's argument that Goldberg disclosed nothing of value is belied by their manifest interest in the progress and content of his research and by the examination of Medtronic's lead incorporating it.

Medtronic also claims that Goldberg himself disclosed his ideas to the public thereby negating its duty of confidentiality. Goldberg did not make the progress of his research public so as to permit Medtronic to utilize his ideas in their Model 6917 lead. Most of the persons consulted by Goldberg were associates of his or others who could assist him in his work. There was no credible evidence that Goldberg published the content of his ideas and research and precise technique prior to Medtronic's misappropriation. Regardless of the knowledge of others and the extent of their experimentation in the field in which Goldberg was a leader, the ineluctible fact is that Medtronic misappropriated and utilized Goldberg's idea and design.

None of the concepts which Medtronic misappropriated were obtained from public information. The availability of lawful means of gaining the information is not a defense where those means were not utilized. [Citations omitted.]

While others may have been working in the field of electrical pacing of the heart and may have suggested the use of helically tipped electrode leads, Dr. Goldberg was the source of Medtronic's idea of using a rigid screw-in lead, remotely installed. While the idea may have originated with Dr. Goldberg and may have been refined by him, however, the work in actually manufacturing the Model 6917 lead was performed by Medtronic. This fact is relevant only to the issue of damages.

The question of damages is that which prompted plaintiff to waive his jury demand. The court ruled that this issue is equitable, within the province of the court not the jury. The court has determined that Goldberg's work provided the origin of the concept of and contributed to the production of Medtronic's Model 6917 lead. Medtronic's gross income from the sale of the Model 6917 lead prior to the issuance of Goldberg's patent which would terminate Medtronic's duty was $12,842,000.00. The costs incurred in the production of the leads were $4,086,000.00. Other elements of cost, if any there be, are not in the evidence. The value of the contribution of Goldberg to the development of the lead is not precisely ascertainable, nor can he be credited with the development, promotion and marketing of the product. However, after a consideration of the evidence, the court determines that Goldberg's contribution to the development of the Model 6917 lead was ten percent. As a result, Goldberg is entitled to ten percent of the net profits derived from its sale.

## NOTES AND QUESTIONS:

1. The opinion in *University Computing Co. v. Lykes-Youngstown Corp.*, 504 F.2d 518 (5th Cir. 1974), sets forth one of the more comprehensive discussions of measuring damages in trade secret cases and is most instructive as to the different approaches that can be employed in determining damages. The court analogizes damage assessment in trade secret cases to those in patent and copyright cases; however, this is not a perfect analogy. The specific statutory provisions regarding damages in patent and copyright infringement cases are not directly applicable to trade secret cases. The United States Code sets forth the measure of damages in patent infringement cases as follows:

> Upon finding for a claimant the court shall award the claimant damages adequate to compensate for the infringement, but in no event no less than a reasonable royalty for the use made by him of the invention by the infringer.

35 U.S.C. § 284. In case of copyright infringement, the Code states:

> The copyright owner is entitled to recover the actual damages suffered by him or her as a result of the infringement, and any profits of the infringer that are attributable to the infringement and are not taken into account in computing actual damages.

17 U.S.C. § 504(b). It is a truism to say that every case should be determined in accordance with the law, after careful consideration of the individual facts of the case. As the court in *University Computing* explained, "every case requires a flexible and imaginative approach to the problem of damages . . . each case is controlled by its own peculiar facts and circumstances." 504 F.2d at 538 (citation and internal quotation marks omitted).

2. *University Computing* also discusses three basic approaches for assessing damages: (1) "loss suffered by the plaintiff" when the value of the trade secret is destroyed; (2) "specific injury to the plaintiff . . . such as lost sales;" and (3) "measure the value of the secret to the defendant, . . . [i.e.,] the benefits, profits, or advantages gained by the defendant in the use of the trade secret" which "frequently entails using what is called the 'reasonable royalty' standard." *Id.* at 535-36.

3. The UTSA, which has been adopted in most, but not all states, uses a broad and flexible approach to the issue of damages:

> Damages can include both the actual loss caused by the misappropriation and the unjust enrichment caused by misappropriation that is not taken into account in computing actual loss. In lieu of damages measured by any other methods, the damages caused by misappropriation may be measured by imposition of liability for a reasonable royalty for a misappropriator's unauthorized disclosure or use of a trade secret.

UTSA § 3.

4. Section 45 of the RESTATEMENT (THIRD) OF UNFAIR COMPETITION calls for "the need for flexibility in formulating monetary remedies in order to achieve compen-

satory and restitutionary objectives." To that end, the RESTATEMENT formulated the following broad guidelines:

> (1) One who is liable to another for an appropriation of the other's trade secret under the rule stated in § 40 is liable for the pecuniary loss to the other caused by the appropriation or for the actor's own pecuniary gain resulting from the appropriation, whichever is greater, unless such relief is inappropriate under the rule stated in Subsection (2).

Subsection (2) lists the following "primary factors" for "whether monetary relief is appropriate and the method of measuring such relief":

> (a) the degree of certainty with which the plaintiff has established the fact and extent of the pecuniary loss or the actor's pecuniary gain resulting from the appropriation; (b) the nature and extent of the appropriation; (c) the relative adequacy to the plaintiff of other remedies; (d) the intent and knowledge of the actor and the nature and extent of any good faith reliance by the actor; (e) any unreasonable delay by the plaintiff in bringing suit or otherwise asserting its rights; and (f) any related misconduct on the part of the plaintiff.

5. In *Jet Spray Cooler, Inc. v. Crampton*, 385 N.E.2d 1349, 1356 (Mass. 1979), the court cautioned that "a plaintiff is not entitled to both the profits made by the defendant and his own lost profits," but held that "the plaintiff is entitled to the profit he would have made had his secret not been unlawfully used, but not less than the monetary gain which the defendant reaped from his improper acts." Proving a plaintiff's lost profits is tricky. The evidence presented often requires sales projections that are subject to attack as being unsubstantiated and mere speculation. If the defendant profited from the misappropriation, the plaintiff's safe harbor approach to proving up damages is to develop a damage model based on defendant's profits or gain. An alternative damage model can be developed if there is creditable evidence that plaintiff's lost profits would have been significantly greater than the defendant's ill-gotten profits. In a lost profits award case, is it fair for a court to award a plaintiff more damages than the evidence showed it lost? *See Jet Spray*, 385 N.E.2d at 1356.

6. Courts often award a "reasonable" royalty when the plaintiff's loss cannot be determined more directly. *See University Computing*, 504 F.2d at 535-36. In determining a "reasonable" royalty, courts have used the patent analogy and considered the 15 factors set forth in *Georgia-Pacific Corp. v. U.S. Plywood Corp.*, 318 F. Supp. 1116 (S.D.N.Y. 1979).

7. Courts have broad discretion in awarding damages. Based on its finding that, without the plaintiff's input, the defendant could not have marketed pacemakers without the helical lead, the *Goldberg v. Medtronic, Inc.*, 209 U.S.P.Q. 259 (N.D. Ill. 1980), court held that a 10% royalty was a reasonable damage award. The court's approach in *Goldberg* reflects the RESTATEMENT's comment that, "[t]he extent to which the actor's sales or other benefits are attributable to such independent improvements or modifications . . . can affect the computation of monetary relief." RESTATEMENT (THIRD) OF UNFAIR COMPETITION § 40 cmt. *b* at 456.

8. When the plaintiff cannot show a lost profit or other measurable damage, the court may use another approach to damages by determining the value of a trade secret that has been destroyed through public disclosure. *See University Computing*, 504 F.2d at 535-36. Less frequently, courts have allowed damages to be based on the trade secret's fair market value or on the plaintiff's capital investment in the trade secret. *See Precision Plating & Metal Finishing Inc. v. Martin-Marietta Corp.*, 435 F.2d 1262 (5th Cir. 1970), and *Dravo Corp.*, 208 F.2d at 388.

9. Punitive damages depend on the law in the particular state in which the case is tried. In states that have adopted the UTSA, courts may award punitive damages not exceeding twice the amount of actual damages in which "willful and malicious misappropriation has been found." UTSA § 3(b). As discussed earlier, one of the advantages of bringing a trade secret action under the Lanham Act is that the court can award damages "not exceeding three times" the amount of actual damages. *See* Lanham Act § 43 (15 U.S.C. § 1117(a)).

10. Although attorney's fees are not available at common law, the UTSA allows attorney's fees where misappropriation is found to be "willful and malicious." *See* UTSA § 4. The Lanham Act also allows for an award of "reasonable" attorney's fees "in exceptional cases." 15 U.S.C. § 1117(a).

# Chapter 5

# CRIMINAL ENFORCEMENT

Government enforcement of trade secret rights has evolved over the years. At the state level, before states passed criminal laws specifically directed to trade secrets, trade secret cases were prosecuted under the crime of theft. *See Hancock v. Texas*, 402 S.W.2d 906 (Tex.Crim.App.1966). Now, a number of states have laws specific to theft of trade secrets. Illustrative of enforcement of these laws is *Schalk v. Texas*, 823 S.W.2d 633 (Tex.Crim.App.1991) (*en banc*), dealt with in the first section below, which involved several Texas Instruments employees who left to form a new competing company. Because states do not have the resources to pursue large-scale espionage prosecutions, however, enforcement at the state level was largely left to civil suits.

As discussed in *United States v. Hsu*, 155 F.3d 189, 194 (3d Cir. 1998), excerpted below, after the Cold War ended there was a "rising tide of international and domestic economic espionage" which involved a substantial amount of intellectual property theft. As there were no federal laws directed specifically to trade secret theft, prosecutors had to use other laws to pursue these economic espionage criminals. Such laws included the NATIONAL STOLEN PROPERTY ACT, 18 U.S.C. § 2314, the federal mail and wire fraud statutes, 18 U.S.C. §§ 1341 and 1343, respectively, and conspiracy to transport stolen goods interstate, 18 U.S.C. § 2314 and 18 U.S.C. § 371. These laws could also be used as predicate offenses under RICO, 18 U.S.C. §§ 1961-1963, enacted in 1970.

In 1996, Congress passed the ECONOMIC ESPIONAGE ACT OF 1996, 18 U.S.C. § 1831, *et seq.* ("EEA"), which was the first federal law specifically directed to protecting commercially valuable trade secrets. As discussed above in Chapter 4, the EEA currently has no civil counterpart, although legislation was introduced in Congress in 2011, but not passed, to add a civil counterpart to the EEA to operate as a Federal Trade Secret Law.

Another federal law for prosecuting trade secret theft is the COMPUTER FRAUD AND ABUSE ACT, 18 U.S.C. §§ 1030, *et seq.* ("CFAA"), which was initially passed in 1984 for protecting classified information on government computers as well as protecting financial records and credit information on government and financial institution computers. The CFAA was amended in 1996 by changing the term "government computer" to "protected computer," which effectively broadened the CFAA to cover computer information theft in private business. By imposing criminal liability for the unauthorized use of computers, the CFAA was used to prosecute parties for fraud, trafficking in passwords, extortion, obtaining financial and credit card records, and securing information from "unauthorized computers."

This chapter provides an overview of these laws and how they can be used as an additional remedy beyond civil lawsuits for protecting against trade secret theft. For a more comprehensive treatment of criminal laws applicable to trade secrets, *see* Geraldine Szott Moohr, The Criminal Law of Intellectual Property and Information, Cases and Comments (Thomson-West 2008).

## A. STATE TRADE SECRET LAWS

### SCHALK v. TEXAS

823 S.W.2d 633 (Tex. Crim. App. 1991) (*en banc*)

Appellants were convicted of theft of trade secrets. V.T.C.A. Penal Code § 31.05. They pled not guilty to the indictments and were afforded a joint trial on the merits. A jury found both appellants guilty of the offenses as charged and assessed punishment at two years confinement in the Texas Department of Corrections and a $5,000 fine for each. Appellants raised six points of error in the court of appeals, alleging the evidence was insufficient to establish trade secret status and mental culpability for the act of theft thereof, additional points concerning the authorization of the search, and an allegation of jury misconduct. The court of appeals affirmed appellants' convictions in separate published opinions. Schalk v. State, 767 S.W.2d 441 (Tex.App. — Dallas 1988); Leonard v. State, 767 S.W.2d 171 (Tex.App. — Dallas 1988). Appellants petitioned this Court on six grounds for review, two of which we granted, to-wit: 1) "The court of appeals erred in holding that the evidence is sufficient to show that the so-called computer programs that were alleged in the indictment were trade secrets"; and 2) "The court of appeals erred in holding that the search warrant sufficiently described the magnetic tapes that were seized and that the magnetic tapes were not seized pursuant to a general exploratory search." We will affirm the court of appeals.

A brief recitation of the facts is necessary to set the background for the alleged commission of the instant offense. Appellants Schalk and Leonard are former employees of Texas Instruments (hereafter TI). Both men have doctoral degrees and specialized in the area of speech research at TI. Schalk resigned his position with TI in April 1983 to join a newly developed company, Voice Control Systems (hereafter VCS). In February 1985, Leonard resigned from TI and joined VCS. Several TI employees eventually joined the ranks of VCS. Speech research was the main thrust of the research and development performed by VCS. In fact, VCS was a competitor of TI in this field.

In April 1985 Sam Kuzbary, then employed with VCS and a former TI employee, noticed some information which he believed to be proprietary to TI stored in the memory of the computer he was using at VCS. Kuzbary contacted TI and agreed to serve as an "informant" for them. He then searched the premises of VCS and photographed materials which he recognized from his employment with TI. A TI internal investigation revealed that a few hours prior to Schalk's and Leonard's departures from TI, each appellant, utilizing TI computers, copied the entire contents of the directories respectively assigned to them. This information included computer programs which TI claimed to be its trade secrets.

* * *

To reiterate, we granted review to consider, first, whether the evidence was sufficient to establish that the computer programs named in the indictments were trade secrets, and second, to determine whether the items listed in the search warrant were sufficiently described so as to preclude a general exploratory search. We will first address the trade secrets issue and then examine the search warrant to determine the specificity of its scope.

Trade Secrets

We begin our discussion with the nature of the alleged trade secrets in the instant case, viz computer programs. Texas trade secret law has its origins in the civil law arena. See BPI Systems, Inc. v. Leith, 532 F.Supp. 208 (W.D.Tex.1981) (Fifth Circuit case applying Texas law utilizing the trade secrets definition from the Restatement of Torts, citing Hyde Corp. v. Huffines, 158 Tex. 566, 314 S.W.2d 763 (1958)). In BPI, the subject of the trade secret litigation was a computer software program, which the court found met the trade secrets definition under Texas civil law.

Prior to the enactment of § 31.05, theft of trade secrets was subject to criminal charges under theft of property statutes. See Hancock v. State, 402 S.W.2d 906, 908 (Tex.Cr.App.1966) (cites to theft statutes defining "property"). This Court's decision in Hancock, while not dispositive of the instant situation, does recognize computer programs as "property" subject to criminal jurisdiction.

Few cases have been decided under Penal Code § 31.05. See Falcone v. State, 682 S.W.2d 418 (Tex.App. — Houston [1st] 1984, no pet.) (in discussion of whether theft of trade secret computer programs was properly charged under the general theft statute, the court determined that the charge should have been made pursuant to the more specific theft of trade secrets statute). See also Atkins v. State, 667 S.W.2d 540 (Tex.App. — Dallas 1983, no pet.) (indictment for theft of trade secrets reading "architectural plans designed and drawn by Billy Joe Noles" held fatally defective because it did not effectively identify the property in question).

Having determined that computer programs are proper subjects for trade secret litigation under Texas civil and criminal law, we now look to the case sub judice to determine whether the programs which appellants copied and took with them to VCS are trade secrets as defined by § 31.05 of the Penal Code, to-wit:

§ 31.05 Theft of Trade Secrets

(a) For purposes of this section:

(1) "Article" means any object, material, device, or substance or any copy thereof, including a writing, recording, drawing, sample, specimen, prototype, model, photograph, micro-organism, blueprint, or map.

(2) "Copy" means a facsimile, replica, photograph, or other reproduction of an article or a note, drawing, or sketch made of or from an article.

(3) "Representing" means describing, depicting, containing, constituting, reflecting, or recording.

(4) "Trade secret" means the whole or any part of any scientific or technical information, design, process, procedure, formula, or improvement that has value and that the owner has taken measures to prevent from becoming available to persons other than those selected by the owner to have access for limited purposes.

(b) A person commits an offense if, without the owner's effective consent, he knowingly:

(1) steals a trade secret;

(2) makes a copy of an article representing a trade secret; or

(3) communicates or transmits a trade secret.

(c) An offense under this section is a felony of the third degree

Appellants claimed on appeal that the programs did not meet the statutory trade secrets criteria because they alleged their former employer TI failed to take "measures to prevent [the information] from becoming available to persons other than those selected by the owner." V.T.C.A. Penal Code, § 31.05(a)(4). We note, as did the court of appeals, that the statute sets no standards for degree or sufficiency of the "measures" taken. See Schalk, 767 S.W.2d at 447; Leonard, 767 S.W.2d at 176.

Specifically, appellants pointed to considerable disclosure of speech research information, citing the "academic environment" of the laboratory in which they worked as encouraging the sharing of information, rather than maintaining secrecy. Appellants also claimed that TI policy favored protection of its research and development efforts through the patent process, as opposed to trade secret designation. Further, appellants allege that the programs that are the subject of the instant case were not listed in the TI register of trade secrets and that TI was lax in implementing its standard procedures with regard to notifying employees of trade secrets within the company. The precise issue before us in the case sub judice is one of first impression in Texas, to-wit: what constitutes requisite "measures" to protect trade secret status? Appellants emphasize the degree or extent to which "measures" were taken, rather than whether "measures" were taken. We agree with the court of appeals that the issue in this case presents a question of factual insufficiency. [Citations omitted.]

We will analyze the court of appeals opinion in view of the "measures" which that court found sufficient to meet the definition of trade secrets under section 31.05 of the Texas Penal Code. The court of appeals listing included the following measures:

Non-disclosure Agreements

1) non-disclosure agreements signed by all new employees when hired;

2) exit interviews with terminating employees to emphasize non disclosure of confidential information;

Plant Security

3) identification badges to prevent unauthorized personnel from entering certain areas;

4) use of security guards and closed-circuit television monitors;

5) entry to speech lab limited to small number of total TI personnel; speech lab physically located in separate wing or building;

6) print-outs and hard copies of data were to be kept out of sight and nighttime security checks were conducted for data left out on desks; data found during such checks was subject to security report;

Computer Software Security

7) issuance of computer passwords or access codes so that data stored in restricted directories was not available to unauthorized personnel; all access required certain code clearance or password information before the computer would respond;

Other Measures

8) TI Trade Secret Register referred to "speech processing";

9) general reference to admonitions to lab personnel to protect software developed in the lab.

A literal reading of 31.05(a)(4) indicates that the above corporate actions and policies would qualify as "measures" under the statute, i.e., such that "the owner has taken measures to prevent from becoming available to persons other than those selected by the owner to have access for limited purposes." The statutory definition, without elaboration as to degree or type of measures, indicates that "some measures" would be sufficient, and we agree that the above listing does constitute "some measures" as the court of appeals determined. Schalk, 767 S.W.2d at 447; Leonard, 767 S.W.2d at 176. We believe, however, that elaboration of the term "measures," beyond the scope of the court of appeals discussion, is necessary from the standpoint of the remainder of the definition, to-wit: "to prevent from becoming available to persons other than those selected by the owner to have access for limited purposes."

Appellants' claims on appeal to the court of appeals and to this Court focus on the encouraged disclosure of speech research information to non-TI personnel engaged in similar research activities. We therefore next direct our attention to the disclosure issue to determine whether appellants' first ground for review has merit. Appellants argue, somewhat convincingly, that TI encouraged the sharing of speech research to others in the same field, thereby demonstrating to the speech research community that TI was on the leading edge of such research and fostered the free flow of information on the subject. In support of their position, appellants point to numerous published articles and papers in which their research was discussed, meetings during which TI speech laboratory activities were shared, and the giving of certain information and materials to schools and government agencies involved in similar research projects.

Returning to the list of "measures" adopted by TI and scrutinizing them in light of the appellants' allegations of extensive disclosure, it becomes apparent that because we have limited precedent to guide us in this analysis, we must look to other jurisdictions for assistance. To facilitate the interpretation of these issues, we will group certain of the "measures" which have similar characteristics.

Non-Disclosure Agreements

Appellants Schalk and Leonard each signed three separate types of non-disclosure agreements with TI. First, upon beginning employment with TI, each signed an "Employee Trade Secret Information Acknowledgement" agreement, which reads in pertinent part as follows:

* * *

Last, each appellant participated in an exit interview conducted by the legal department prior to or at the time of termination of employment. An integral part of the exit interview is the signing of another non-disclosure form entitled "Trade Secret Listing for Termination of Employment." In this agreement, appellants acknowledged that they had been advised of their obligations to the company concerning trade secrets and proprietary information to which they had access during their employment with TI. The agreement further states, "I have been advised that I cannot disclose to others, or use for my own benefit or the benefit of others, any proprietary information and trade secrets to which I have had access at TI . . . . I am free to use information in the public domain and my own skill, knowledge, know how, and experience to whatever extent and in whatever way I wish so long as such use does not involve such trade secrets or proprietary information."

* * *

Appellants unquestionably contracted with TI, giving rise to a fiduciary duty not to disclose TI trade secrets or TI proprietary information to anyone not so designated by the company.

We now determine whether the information disclosed with TI's permission or encouragement, such as published articles, seminar papers, speeches given at public meetings, information provided to government agencies, etc., was so extensive as to destroy any trade secret status that may have existed regarding the computer software which is the subject of the instant indictments. It is axiomatic that the core element of a trade secret must be that it remain a secret. [Citations omitted.] In the instant case appellants rely heavily on the facts detailing disclosure of the work performed in the speech research lab. Certainly, much information was disclosed to various sources through various means. The record reflects, however, from trial testimony by Dr. George Doddington, chief scientist and head of the speech research lab at TI, that the algorithms composing the actual software which is the subject of these indictments, were not disclosed, nor at any time was such disclosure encouraged or authorized.

* * *

In *Dickerman Associates, Inc. v. Tiverton Bottled Gas Co.*, 594 F.Supp. 30 (D.C.Mass.1984), the court held that although portions of the computer software system were disclosed during demonstrations to prospective purchasers, it represented but a small fraction of the whole system and this limited disclosure was insufficient to permit an understanding of the design and architecture of the program. Courts have also held that access to the computer software program by a few customers does not destroy trade secret status. *J & K Computer Systems, Inc. v. Parrish*, 642 P.2d 732 (Utah 1982). *See also* Annot., Computer Trade Secret, 53 A.L.R. 4th 1046, 1072, citing Ward v. Superior Court, 3 Computer L.Serv.Rep. 206 (Cal.Super.1972) (program held not generally available to public where owner did not sell details of program itself but only sold remote plotting service that the program made possible).

The instant situation is analogous to Dickerman and J & K. For example, in a letter transmitting computer software to the USAF Academy, Dr. Doddington stated the following:

Here is a tape containing the most significant software packages that we have in our laboratory that you desired to receive. I have enclosed both documentation and source listings for your use. I hope you find these data to be helpful in setting up your laboratory and structuring your software for maximum efficiency. Please understand that we can not [sic] support this software in any way other than to provide you with the listings as we are doing by sending you the tape.

With this in mind, and considering that the software is sensitive to the exact system configuration, the software that we are sending will probably find best use as a template or guide for helping you to define and develop your own software . . . .

This letter, ironically presented as defendant's exhibit, supports instead the State's position because it emphasizes the limited nature of the disclosure and is consistent with relevant caselaw on this topic. Q-CO Industries, 625 F.Supp. at 617, quoting Imperial Chemical Indus. Ltd. v. National Distillers & Chem. Corp., 342 F.2d 737, 742 (2d Cir.1965), to-wit: ". . . [A] trade secret can exist in a combination of characteristics and components, each of which, by itself, is in the public domain, but the unified process and operation of which, in unique combination, affords a competitive advantage and is a protectable secret." We find, based on the record in this case, that the limited disclosures made by TI in regard to the speech research lab activities merely described the application and configuration of the certain elements of the software but did not reveal the actual composition of the programs.

Doddington testified that disclosure of the programs named in the instant indictments was never authorized. We note that even if TI had authorized disclosure of such programs on a limited basis, trade secret status would not necessarily be destroyed because it could still meet that part of the statutory definition which reads "that the owner has taken measures to prevent from becoming available to persons other than those selected by the owner." (emphasis added). V.T.C.A. Penal Code § 31.05(a)(4).

Plant Security Measures

The measures used by TI to secure its premises to prevent unauthorized personnel from admission to or exposure to its proprietary research data were reasonable under the circumstances. The issuance of identification badges, use of security guards and closed-circuit television monitors, entry to the speech lab limited to small number of personnel, nighttime security checks, etc. are fairly common to research oriented industries. Although these measures relate to the TI plant and not specifically or uniquely to the speech lab, they do affect and serve to limit access to the speech lab, and therefore serve to protect the trade secret status of the information developed therein.

Computer Software Access

Testimony at trial enumerated detailed restricted user access basically utilizing a series of passwords and restrictive codes in order to access the desired software utilities. Trade secret caselaw dealing with computer software recognizes these types of measures as protective of trade secret status. See generally, Annot., 53 A.L.R. 1046, § 7[a] (cases supporting trade secret status for computer software).

Other Measures

The court of appeals listed as one of the preventive measures the fact that the TI Trade Secret Register referred to "speech processing." Conflicting testimony indicates that the register entry may relate to a different area of speech research than that conducted in the lab by appellants and therefore did not refer to the software programs under indictment. We find the evidence inconclusive to support the theory that the register entry refers to the specific software involved in the instant case. It was also brought out in testimony that the Trade Secret Register was not timely updated and distributed to TI employees in accordance with the company policy manual. Further, the "admonitions" to lab personnel to protect lab software are simply too general in nature to determine whether they should be considered a protective measure. In fact, such "admonitions" were tempered with memoranda and conversations that encouraged sharing of information with others outside TI.

Correlative to the above-mentioned Trade Secret Register and "admonitions" regarding non-disclosure, appellants also claimed that they were not informed by TI that the programs which they worked on at TI and later took with them to VCS were trade secrets. In support of this contention, they point out that the TI Trade Secret Register was not updated and distributed to employees in a timely manner as was required by the company policy manual. They further contend that the "speech processing" entry in the Register is not the speech research with which they were involved. In addition, they claim that extensive dissemination of certain information destroyed any secrecy that may have existed or been intended. Clearly, the contractual agreements that appellants made with TI gave appellants ample notice that their employment would be directed towards proprietary and trade secret information. Indeed the actual programs they developed were not in existence at the time they signed the initial agreements, so they could not have been named definitively. Granted, a stronger case for the State would have resulted from the naming of the subject programs in the exit interview agreements. Even so, if the programs were trade secrets at time of creation, there is insufficient evidence to suggest that trade secret status was destroyed prior to the exit interview. Because the exit interview agreement covers trade secrets, and the exit form itself states that it is non-exclusive, listing of the specific programs was not a requirement to maintain trade secret status.

Conclusion

We need not decide today whether any one of the preventive measures listed, standing alone, is factually sufficient to support trade secret status. We do find that the combination of employment agreements, strict plant security, restricted computer access, the non-authorization of disclosure of the subject programs and the general non-disclosure of those programs by TI and its employees served to support trade secret status of the computer programs that are the subject of the instant indictments. Appellants neither requested nor received permission to copy the files containing these programs. The unauthorized copying of an article representing a trade secret constitutes an offense under V.T.C.A. Penal Code § 31.05(b)(2). Therefore we affirm the court of appeals' ruling that the subject programs are trade secrets. Appellants' first ground for review is overruled.

## NOTES AND QUESTIONS:

1. In *Schalk*, the primary issue was whether Texas Instruments had "taken measures to prevent [the trade secret] from becoming available to persons other than those selected by the owner to have access for limited purposes." 823 S.W.2d at 637 (internal quotation marks omitted). Before the court could reach this issue, however, it had to resolve the question of whether the computer programs Schalk took were "property," which was a required element of the offense under the Texas Penal Code. The court resolved this issue handily by relying on "Texas civil and criminal law." *Id.* at 636. As demonstrated in the previous chapters in this book, trade secrets are indisputably intangible property and constitute valuable assets to the businesses that own them.

2. The Texas law at issue in *Schalk* required the state to prove the defendant "knowingly [made] a copy of an article representing [a] trade secret[]." Tex. Penal Code § 31.05(b). If the defendant used a trade secret only in performing his job, such as a method for manufacturing a product and did not make "a copy of an article," can the state prove the defendant committed an offense under the Penal Code? *Mens rea* is always a difficult element of proof; how can the state prove that the defendant "knowingly" copied a trade secret?

3. Can laws like the one in *Schalk* have a chilling effect on employees going to work for a competing company? Are these laws any more of a deterrent than the inevitable disclosure doctrine discussed earlier?

4. Not all attempts to enforce state criminal laws against trade secret theft succeed. For example, when a prototype of a new version of Apple's iPhone was left in a bar by an Apple employee, a search warrant, reproduced below, was issued

against a blogger who allegedly bought it from the person who found it. The search warrant, however, was ultimately dismissed and the property returned in the face of arguments that there was no misappropriation because the phone was not stolen, but lost. The search warrant is reproduced below to illustrate the information used as a basis for issuing the search warrant and the sweeping scope of such investigations.

SBSW 6643

**FILED**
**SAN MATEO COUNTY**

**IN THE SUPERIOR COURT OF THE COUNTY OF SAN MATEO** APR 29 2010

**STATE OF CALIFORNIA**

Clerk of the Superior Court
By ________ DEPUTY CLERK

**REQUEST FOR EX-PARTE ORDER TO SEAL DOCUMENTS**

San Mateo County Sheriff's Office Detective Matthew Broad, the affiant of the search warrant and affidavit for 40726 Greystone Terrace, Fremont, CA, requests that the search warrant, the affidavit in support of the search warrant, and the return of the search warrant when filed be sealed unless ordered unsealed by further order of this court.

Based on my experience and training it is my belief that release of the information to the media or to the public in general would hinder the progress of the investigation, as it may alert involved parties as to the direction of the investigation and the identity of witnesses and witness statements to investigators.

I declare, under penalty of perjury, that the above information is true and correct to the best of my knowledge.

Matthew Broad

**ORDER**

**IT IS ORDERED THAT:** The search warrant, the affidavit in support of the search warrant and the return to said search warrant described above be sealed unless ordered unsealed by further order of this court.

Dated: 4/28/10

JUDGE OF THE SUPERIOR COURT
County of San Mateo, State of California

SBSW 664-3

FILED
SAN MATEO COUNTY
APR 29 2010
Clerk of the Superior Court
By DEPUTY CLERK

## RETURN TO SEARCH WARRANT

**IN THE**
**SUPERIOR COURT FOR THE SAN MATEO COUNTY JUDICIAL DISTRICT**
**COUNTY OF SAN MATEO, STATE OF CALIFORNIA**

The property taken from the premises located at 40726 Greystone Terrace, Fremont, state of California, and occupied by Jason Chen, by virtue of the search warrant dated 4/23/2010, and signed by Judge Cretan, Judge of the Superior Court, San Mateo County Judicial District, county of San Mateo, state of California, is described in the attached "Search Warrant Inventory," attached hereto and by reference made a part hereof as fully as though set forth herein.

I, Matthew Broad, by whom this warrant was executed, do swear that the inventory set forth in the attached, "Search Warrant Inventory," contains a true and detailed account of all the property taken by me under the warrant.

Detective Matthew Broad

Subscribed and sworn before me
this April 28, 2010

Judge of the Superior Court

SBSW 6643

FILED
SAN MATEO COUNTY
APR 29 2010
Clerk of the Superior Court
By ______
DEPUTY CLERK

**IN THE SUPERIOR COURT OF THE COUNTY OF SAN MATEO**
**STATE OF CALIFORNIA**

# AFFIDAVIT FOR SEARCH WARRANT

The undersigned, being first duly sworn, deposes and says: That on or about 3/18/2010, in the County of San Mateo, State of California, the crime(s) of

496(a) PC – Buy or receive stolen property (a felony)

499c(b)(3) PC – Theft; Without authority make or cause to be made a copy (definition includes photograph) of any article representing a trade secret (a felony)

594(b)(1) – Maliciously damages property of another valued over $400 (a felony)

was/were committed by **Jason Shao Chen, DOB 2/16/1981, CDL B8607050, Male, 5-11, 150**

That there is probable cause to believe that certain articles and property, consisting of:

See Appendix B – attached hereto and incorporated herein

are now concealed on the person(s) of **Jason Shao Chen, DOB 2/16/1981, CDL B8607050, Male, 5-11, 150**

in the vehicle(s) described as any vehicle that is at the location of the search warrant and under the dominion and control of Jason Chen.

and in and upon the premises and building known and designated as, and commonly called,

40726 Greystone Terrace
Fremont, CA

in said county and state described as Alameda, CA

That the following facts established the existence of grounds for the issuance of a Search Warrant for the search of the person(s), vehicle(s), and premises above described:

I, Detective Matthew Broad, am your affiant. I have been a peace officer in the State of California since July of 1996 and am in possession of an Advanced POST Certificate. I have been employed by the San Mateo County Sheriff's Office since August of 2001 and I am currently assigned to the Rapid Enforcement Allied Computer Team (REACT) as of July 2005.

From 1999 through 2001, I held the position of Special Agent with the United States Secret Service (USSS). During my tenure with the USSS, I attended a 12-week Criminal Investigators Training Program at the Federal Law Enforcement Training Center in Glynco, Georgia. I also attended a 12-week training course at the John J. Rowley Training Center in Beltsville, Maryland. During my training, I received blocks of instruction concerning financial crimes investigations including (but not limited to) theft, internet fraud, identity theft, credit card fraud,

ar

check fraud, counterfeit currency, bank fraud, wire fraud, money laundering, access device fraud, cellular telephone fraud, and organized crime. During my tenure as a Special Agent assigned to the San Jose Resident Office, I conducted numerous investigations regarding the above-mentioned crimes.

From 1996 through 1998, I held the position of Police Officer with the San Carlos Police Department. During my tenure at the department, I attended an 18-week basic police academy that was sanctioned by the California Commission for Peace Officer Standards and Training (POST). Portions of the academy's curriculum included blocks of instruction concerning the investigation of theft, credit card fraud, burglary, identity theft, forged checks, cellular telephone fraud, and access device fraud. As a police officer and as a deputy, I have conducted numerous investigations in the areas of Internet fraud, credit card fraud, access device fraud, forged financial instruments, counterfeit software, and identity theft.

While assigned to the REACT Task Force, I have received approximately 480 hours of specialized training in the preservation and examination of digital and computer related evidence and I have conducted approximately 110 forensic examinations on criminal cases. I was also certified as an Encase Certified Examiner (EnCE) through Guidance Software in 2008.

I have learned the following information through my own investigative efforts and through official law enforcement channels:

**Summary:**

Suspect Brian Hogan found or stole a prototype iPhone 4G that was accidentally left at a restaurant by Apple employee Robert "Gray" Powell. Hogan identified the owner of the phone as Apple Engineer Gray Powell through the contents of the phone and through Internet searches. Rather than return the prototype phone to Powell and/or Apple, Hogan subsequently sold the iPhone Jason Chen in Fremont for $5000. Upon receiving the stolen property, Chen disassembled the iPhone, thereby causing it to be damaged. Chen created copies of the iPhone prototype in the form of digital images and video, which were subsequently published on the Internet based magazine Gizmodo.com.

This search warrant seeks authorization to search the residence of Jason Chen for evidence related to the purchase of the iPhone prototype, copying (photographic images and video), and publishing of the iPhone prototype by Jason Chen who is residing at 40726 Greystone Terrace in Fremont, CA.

**Facts:**

On 4/20/2010, I met with representatives from Apple regarding the theft and/or loss of an Apple iPhone 4G prototype iPhone. I met with Rick Orloff (Director, Information Security), Bruce Sewell (Senior Vice President, General Counsel and Secretary), and George Riley (O'Melveny and Myers, LLP) regarding the theft of an unreleased Apple iPhone 4G.

The above Apple representatives told me that on or about 3/25/2010, Apple employee Robert Gray Powell (known as Gray Powell) lost a prototype iPhone 4G cellular device while he was at the Gourmet Haus Staudt restaurant located at 2615 Broadway in Redwood City, San Mateo County, CA. At the time the phone was lost, it possessed a case that was intended to make it look like an Apple iPhone 3GS. At the time of the theft, the 3GS was a consumer product that was being sold by Apple at retail stores, unlike the unreleased prototype 4G iPhone which is a trade secret of Apple.

The missing iPhone prototype subsequently appeared in video and picture format on the Internet based web magazine Gizmodo.com. The internet site also posted pictures and/or copies of the iPhone. The pictures included images of the phone disassembled and they showed details of the phone's internal components. Per Penal Code section 499c(a)(7), the definition of "copy," includes "any facsimile, replica, photograph, or other reproduction."

Riley stated the publication of the device and its features is immensely damaging to Apple. By publishing details about the phone and its features, sales of current Apple products are hurt wherein people that would have otherwise purchased a currently existing Apple product would wait for the next item to be released, thereby hurting overall sales and negatively effecting Apple's earnings. Riley stated he could not currently provide an estimated loss, but he believed it was, "huge."

I asked Riley what the value of the missing iPhone was. He stated that it was invaluable and that he could not place an amount on it. We discussed the fact that the phone was sold by Suspect Hogan for $8500.00 (discussed below) and I asked if the phone was worth at least that amount. Riley said that it was.

Orloff (Director, Information Security) told me that on 4/19/2010, he received a telephone call from a female who identified herself as Katherine Martinson. Martinson reported to Orloff that her roommate, Brian Hogan, was previously in possession of the lost/stolen prototype iPhone and that Hogan sold the iPhone to the web based magazine Gizmodo.com.

Orloff showed me a photograph of a sticker that Martinson sent to him via email. The depicted sticker possessed serialized type number that Orloff said belonged to the prototype iPhone. Martinson told him the sticker was still inside of their (Martinson and Hogan's) residence as of 4/19/2010. The stickers were on what appeared to be a coffee table.

Orloff said that Witness Martinson contacted him due to the fact that Suspect Hogan connected the stolen iPhone to her computer and she believed that Apple would eventually trace the iPhone back to her via IP addresses. Therefore she contacted Apple in order to absolve herself of criminal responsibility. Orloff also stated that by attaching the iPhone to a computer, evidence of the connection will likely be found within the computer's "Library," folder. The "Library" folder is a directory that stores user settings, maintains system logs, stores application information, and other system information for the computer and/or particular user.

Sewell told me that after Gizmodo.com released its story regarding the iPhone prototype on or about 4/19/2010, Steve Jobs (Apple CEO) contacted the editor of Gizmodo.com, Brian Lam. Jobs requested that Lam return the phone to Apple. Lam responded via the email address blam@gizmodo.com that he would return the iPhone on the condition that Apple provided him with a letter stating the iPhone belonged to Apple. The letter stated the following:

**From:** brian lam <blam@brianlam.net>
**Date:** April 19, 2010 4:08:07 PM PDT
**To:** Steve Jobs <sjobs@apple.com>
**Subject: Let's see if this goes through.**

Hey Steve, this email chain is off record on my side.

I understand the position you're in, and I want to help, but it conflicts with my own responsibilities to give the phone back without any confirmation that its real, from apple, officially.

Something like that-- from you or apple legal--is a big story, that would make up for giving the phone back right away. If the phone disappears without a story to explain why it went away, and the proof it went to apple, it hurts our business. And our reputation. People will say this is a coordinated leak, etc

I get that it would hurt sales to say this is the next iphone. I have no interest in hurting sales. That does nothing to help Gizmodo or me.

Maybe Apple can say it's a lost phone, but not one that you've confirmed for production – that it is merely a test unit of sorts. Otherwise, it just falls to apple legal, which serves the same purpose of confirmation. I don't want that, either.

Gizmodo lives and dies like many small companies do. We don't have access, or when we do, we get it taken away. When we get a chance to break a story, we have to go with it, or we perish. I know you like walt and pogue, and like working with them, but I think Gizmodo has more in common with old Apple than those guys do. So I hope you understand where I'm coming from.

Right now, we have nothing to lose. The thing is, Apple PR has been cold to us lately. It affected my ability to do my job right at iPad launch. So we had to go outside and find our stories like this one, very aggressively.

I want to get this phone back to you ASAP. And I want to not hurt your sales when the products themselves deserve love. But I have to get this story of the missing prototype out, and how it was returned to apple, with some acknowledgement it is Apple's.

And I want to work closer with Apple, too. I'm not asking for more access--we can do our jobs with or without it--but again, this is the only way we can survive while being cut out of things. That's my position on things.

B

Sewell said that after the letter confirming the ownership of the phone was sent to Lam, Lam responded via email that the phone was in the possession of Jason Chen at 40726 Graystone Terrace in Fremont, CA. The contents of the email included the following:

Bruce, thanks.
Here's Jason Chen, who has the iPhone. And here's his address. You two should coordinate a time.

40726 Greystone Terrace
Fremont CA 94538

Happy to have you pick this thing up. Was burning a hole in our pockets. Just so you know, we didn't know this was stolen when we bought it. Now that we definitely know it's not some knockoff, and it really is Apple's, I'm happy to see it returned to its rightful owner.

P.S. I hope you take it easy on the kid who lost it. I don't think he loves anything more than Apple except, well, beer. Maybe some spankings.

Sewell subsequently communicated with Jason Chen via email to arrange the return of the phone. Chen utilized the email jchen@gizmodo.com and provided Sewell with an internet link showing the location of his residence. Sewell subsequently went to the above location, met with Chen and received the missing iPhone. Chen provided the phone to him with the SIM card removed and the case (3GS disguise) removed.

I asked Sewell if the male who returned the iPhone to him was the same male who appeared in the Gizmodo video with the stolen prototype iPhone. He said that it was.

Sewell said that upon returning to Apple, employees attempted to power the phone and found that it no longer functioned. Upon examining the phone, they found the following damage occurred to it as a result of the phone being disassembling:

1. Broken ribbon cable
2. One screw was inserted into the wrong location and caused an electrical short
3. Back plate snaps were broken.

Cr

4. Stripped screws.

Continuing on 4/20/2010, I accessed Gizmodo's website at Gizmodo.com and viewed pictures and video of the missing/stolen iPhone. The web pages include photographs of the phone in both assembled and disassembled forms, images and video of an Asian male who identifies himself as "Jason Chen" holding the phone, a copy of the letter sent by Apple confirming that the phone belongs to Apple, and a narrative about how the phone was found and bought by Gizmodo.

Riley (Attorney, O'Melveny and Myers, LLP) said the missing/stolen iPhone prototype was currently in the possession of Apple and they would provide the phone to me to be booked into evidence as soon as a transfer could be arranged.

On 4/21/2010, I met and interviewed Witness Katherine Martinson at the REACT San Mateo office. Martinson said she currently resides at 3615 Farm Hill Blvd., #14 in Redwood City with Brian Hogan and Thomas Warner. Hogan and Warner share a room while Martinson has her own bedroom.

Martinson said that on 3/26/2010 her housemate (identified as Brian Hogan, DOB: 1/9/1989) told her that he found an iPhone while he was visiting the Gourmet Haus Staudt restaurant located at 2615 Broadway in Redwood City. Hogan told her that he was drinking with friends when an intoxicated male tried to give him an iPhone that was left on a stool, incorrectly believing it belonged to Hogan. Hogan told Martinson he remained at the bar "a while longer," but no one claimed the phone.

Hogan told Martinson that upon his return home to 3615 Farm Hill Blvd #14, Redwood City, he removed the case (iPhone 3GS disguise) and saw that the phone was not a typical iPhone. From the applications on the phone, Hogan told Martinson he previously accessed a Facebook (social networking website) application and learned that the owner of the phone was Gray Powell. When Hogan first showed the phone to Martinson on the afternoon of 3/26/2010, the phone no longer worked and they believed that Apple remotely wiped the contents of the phone.

Martinson described Hogan as technically knowledgeable. She said that based upon the appearance of the phone, the new features that were present (like a forward facing camera), and statements he made to her, he knew that the phone was a prototype that belonged to Apple and/or Gray Powell. Martinson said that together, they conducted an Internet search for Gray Powell and located his Linked In (professional social networking site) profile that identified him as an engineer for Apple.

Martinson said Hogan understood that he possessed a valuable piece of technology and that people would be interested in buying it. He subsequently contacted the periodicals Gizmodo.com, PC World, and Engadget.com in an attempt to start bidding for the iPhone prototype. Martinson said Hogan communicated via email and that it is highly likely that evidence of those emails reside on Hogan's computer, which was located in a downstairs common area of their residence.

Martinson said that while Hogan possessed the phone, he attached it to his computer and to Martinson's computer without her permission. He attached the iPhone in an attempt to re-install the phone's operating system in order to make the phone functional again. Both attempts failed.

Martinson said that within approximately 10 days of obtaining the prototype iPhone, Hogan made contact with Jason Chen, who offered Hogan $10,000 for the iPhone. Martinson said she believes Hogan met with Chen on three occasions for unknown purposes. When Hogan told Martinson that he was offered $10,000 for the phone she asked him why they would pay that sum of money. Hogan told Martinson that Chen would pay that sum because, "They know it's valuable. They [Gizmodo.com] would receive millions and millions of hits." Martinson indicated "hits" meant the number of persons that would visit Gizmodo's website as a result of publishing information about the iPhone prototype.

Martinson said that Hogan is knowledgeable on the subjects of economics. From her conversations with Hogan, she believes he was aware that selling the phone to a magazine would hurt Apple sales and/or profits.

Martinson said she and other friends attempted to talk Hogan out of selling the iPhone prototype on the basis that the sale would ruin the career of Robert "Gray" Powell (Apple engineer who lost the phone). Hogan's response to her was that it, "Sucks for him. He lost his phone. Shouldn't have lost his phone."

Martinson said Hogan later showed her a camera box that contained $5000.00 in $100 US Treasury Notes. Hogan told her that the money was a result of selling the phone to Jason Chen. Martinson said Hogan told her he has received a total of $8500.00 the sale of the phone, but she is not sure of the source of the additional $2500.00. Martinson said Hogan also told her that he will receive a cash bonus from Gizmodo.com in July if and when Apple makes an official product announcement regarding the new iPhone.

Martinson said she believes Hogan took photographs of the iPhone for the purpose of selling the images to Internet based magazines. She said she saw Hogan in possession of an SLR (Single Lens Reflex) type camera in their residence during the time frame of the sale of the iPhone prototype.

Martinson said Hogan owns a desktop computer at her residence and it is the only computer he utilizes. Based upon the fact it is the only computer available to him and the fact that he told her he corresponded via email with Gizmodo.com and other magazines, she believes copies of the iPhone images and email communications will be found upon his computer at their residence.

Martinson said there is no hard telephone line to the residence and all three occupants utilize personal cellular telephones. She said Hogan has utilized the same cellular telephone with the number 650.454.0557 since he moved into the residence in December, 2009.

Martinson brought a camera with her to the interview and stated that Hogan removed two stickers from the iPhone prototype. She said the stickers were still on Hogan's desk located with his computer in a common area of the residence. Martinson said she took pictures of the stickers. I subsequently removed the storage card from the camera and downloaded the pictures as evidence.

I viewed the images and saw one visible sticker with a second possibly below the first. The visible sticker possessed the following numbers with a bar code:

N90_DVT_GEAX_0493
iPhone SWE + L200221

Cu

George Riley (Attorney, O'Melveny and Myers, LLP) provided me with a written statement that states the above numbers were unique to the missing/stolen prototype iPhone.

Continuing on 4/21/2010, I spoke with Witness/Victim Robert "Gray" Powell via telephone. He told me that on 3/25/2010, he left work at approximately 2030 hours and went home. He picked up his uncle (name unknown) and went to the Gourmet Haus Staudt located at 2615 Broadway in Redwood City, CA. Powell remained at the restaurant for approximately 2 hours until closing at approximately 2300 hours.

Powell said he sat at the bar with his uncle. He said the last memory he had of the prototype phone was placing it in his bag, which he then put on the floor by his feet. Powell said that his bag was knocked over at one point in time and it was possible the prototype iPhone fell out of the bag and onto the floor.

I asked Powell if it was possible that someone stole the prototype iPhone from his bag. He said he did leave his bag with his uncle at one point during the evening when he went to the bathroom and it was possible, although unlikely, that someone removed the prototype iPhone from his bag.

Powell said he left the restaurant when the restaurant started to close and believes the finder of the prototype iPhone could not have remained in the restaurant more than 15 minutes.

Powell said he did not give Brian Hogan, Jason Chen, and/or any other person permission to view, take, carry away, possess, sell, or otherwise use the Apple iPhone prototype that was lost and/or stolen from him while at the Gourmet Haus Staudt located at 2615 Broadway in Redwood City, CA

Continuing on 4/21/2010, I prepared a search warrant and affidavit for presentation on 4/22/2010 seeking authorization to search the residence of Brian Hogan. That evening and before the presentation of the warrant could be made, Witness Martinson telephoned me at approximately 2245 hours, and said that Hogan and Warner were aware of the investigation and were in the process of removing evidence from the residence. I subsequently responded to their residence at 3516 Farm Hill Blvd., #14 in Redwood City in an attempt to prevent the evidence from leaving the residence, however by the time San Mateo County Sheriff's Office units arrived at the scene, Hogan and Warner had departed with Hogan's computer, the iPhone 4G stickers, and other digital media.

I spoke with Witness Katherine Martinson and Witness Zackary Corbin who were present inside of the apartment. Corbin stated that Hogan and Warner departed in separate vehicles and based upon the direction they walked while removing evidence, that they did not load the items into the vehicle that Hogan departed in; a black VW Jetta.

Continuing on 4/21/2010 at approximately 2330 hours, REACT Det. Josh McFall went to 247 Hillview in Redwood City and he located a black VW Jetta bearing CA license plate 5CSB531 parked in front of the residence with a warm engine. Det. McFall also observed a skylight illuminate while he watched the house, thereby indicating the occupants were awake.

I responded to 247 Hillview in Redwood City and I knocked on the front door. A male (John Hogan, 11/21/1949) almost immediately answered the door. John Hogan identified himself as the father of Brian Hogan. John was aware of the investigation and I informed him that Brian

*cvr*

and/or Thomas Warner were attempting to conceal/destroy evidence. I then asked John if I could enter the house for the purpose of locating the missing evidence and speaking with Brian. John then allowed us to enter the residence and he led me to an upstairs bedroom where I found Christy Gilmore (3/10/1989, Brian Hogan's girlfriend) and Brian Hogan seated on a bed.

While in the residence, I told Brian that he was not under arrest, nor was I going to place him under arrest at this time for the sale of the missing iPhone Prototype. I indicated to Brian Hogan that the removal and/or destruction of evidence was a demonstration of his consciousness of guilt and that it was imperative that we recover any items that were removed and/or concealed by him or Warner. Hogan stated he wanted to cooperate with the investigation and he told me that he and Warner removed his computer, a thumb drive, a flash card, and the Apple iPhone prototype stickers from his residence. Hogan said that all of the items were in the possession of Warner and that Warner took the items in order to "protect" him (Hogan).

I subsequently observed Hogan telephone Thomas Warner and tell Warner to bring the computer and other evidence to the 247 Hillview. When Warner did not respond, Christy Gilmore (Hogan's girlfriend) and I both made phone calls to Warner in an attempt to locate him and the evidence. Gilmore subsequently received a call from Warner wherein Warner told her that he left Hogan's computer at the Sequoia Christian Church located on Topaz St, between Harding Avenue and Brewster Avenue in Redwood City.

While in the residence, I observed Hogan utilize a black LG cellular telephone (bearing SN 911KPFX363699) to make and receive telephone calls. Based upon my training and experience, I know that persons who buy and sell stolen property often use cellular devices to negotiate via telephone calls, email, and/or text message. I also know that the continued use of the phone would likely overwrite and destroy evidence that currently exists on the phone. Based upon the above facts and the fact that the cellular device was in plain view, I seized the phone as evidence and to prevent any further destruction of the digital evidence.

Sgt. Ken Taylor, Christy Gilmore, and I then drove to the above mentioned church and located a black desktop HP computer bearing SN MXX7120MY5 and a flat screen monitor on the church property and in front of an office door. Gilmore said the computer belonged to Hogan and I seized it as evidence.

I made additional telephone calls to Warner in an attempt to locate the other missing evidence items. Warner claimed that he did not know where the stickers were and he never possessed the thumb drive and/or the flash card. I subsequently obtained consent for the search of vehicles belonging to Brian Hogan and Christy Gilmore. During the searches, I located a Canon SLR digital camera with no memory card in the memory card slot. The camera was located in Hogan's white Acura bearing CA license plate 5GTN988. The car was parked behind Hogan's apartment on Farm Hill Blvd. I did not locate the stickers and/or storage devices during either search.

At approximately 0100 hours, I observed Thomas Warner arrive at 247 Hillview Ave in Redwood City while driving a white Ford bearing CA license plate 3CJJ702. Warner stated that he helped Hogan move out of the apartment by taking his computer. Warner claimed he lost the iPhone prototype sticker and he believed it fell out of his wallet when he paid for gas at a Chevron station located at Whipple Ave and Veterans Blvd in Redwood City. I asked Warner for consent to search his wallet and vehicle for evidence related to this case. He consented to both searches. During the search of the vehicle, I located a 1st generation iPhone in the front passenger's seat of the vehicle. Also on the front passenger's seat, I located a BlackBerry model 8310 cellular device bearing SN 359158027638348. Both cellular devices were powered on.

Based upon the fact that Warner directly assisted Hogan with the removal and concealment of evidence directly related to this case, I believe it is highly likely that Warner was involved and/or conspired with Hogan in the negotiation and subsequent sale of the prototype iPhone and that his efforts to conceal and/or destroy the evidence as an indication of his consciousness of guilt. I also know that cellular devices like BlackBerries and iPhones function as small computing devices and that they maintain large quantities of data which include, but are not limited to call logs, email communications, system logs, GPS logs, text messages, applications, and Internet browsing history. Additionally, based upon my training and experience, I know that continued use of the devices can result in the deletion of data and/or potential evidence on the phone. Therefore, I seized the items as evidence.

A records check through County Communications revealed two (2) outstanding misdemeanor warrants for Suspect Warner. Warner was subsequently arrested and handcuffed by Deputy Jim Goulart of the Sheriff's Office for the outstanding warrants only. While seated in the back of a patrol car, Warner made a spontaneous statement to Det. Josh McFall that he knew where the missing flash drive was located. Det. McFall read a Miranda Advisement to Warner and Warner waived his rights. Warner subsequently directed us to a bush located on the north side of Harding Ave at the intersection of Lancaster Way, Redwood City. In the bush, I located a 512 MB Memorex thumb drive and a 1GB Lexar Media compact flash card. The Lexar 1GB flash card appeared to be of the same type that would be utilized by the previously mentioned and seized Canon SLR camera.

Continuing on the 4/22/2010 at approximately 0230 hours, I went to the Chevron Gas Station located at 585 Whipple Avenue in Redwood City. I conducted a search of the premises and located the missing Apple prototype sticker in the parking lot near the entrance to the convenience store.

On 4/22/2010 at approximately 1245 hours, Apple employee Venkat Memula delivered the prototype iPhone to me at the REACT San Mateo Office to be retained as evidence in this case.

Continuing on 4/23/2010, I conducted a query on the address 40726 Greystone Terrace in Fremont. The address was the where Bruce Sewell of Apple reportedly retrieved the stolen iPhone from Suspect Jason Chen. The address was listed on the database Clear as being occupied by Jason Chen (2/16/1981) via a credit bureau source. The records produced by Clear also listed Chen as the owner of the residence. From my prior experience, I have found the Clear database to be accurate and reliable.

Det Josh McFall conducted a DMV search for Chen and located DMV CDL B8607050. The license's record possesses a photograph of a male that appears to be the same male who identified himself as Jason Chen while showing the stolen iPhone on one of the videos that was found on Gizmodo.com.

**Conclusions:**

Based upon fact that Witness Bruce Sewell met Jason Chen at 40726 Greystone Terrace in Fremont and Chen returned the stolen iPhone to Sewell at that location, the fact that the Clear

au

database lists Chen as the owner of the residence, the fact that Brian Lam identified Chen's address as the above listed residence, and upon the fact that the DMV photograph associated with Jason Chen appears to be the same person who appears on Gizmodo.com with the stole iPhone, I believe Suspect Chen is currently residing at 40726 Greystone Terrace in Fremont, Alameda County, CA.

Based upon my training and experience as well as the statements of Witness Katherine Martinson, Bruce Sewell, and upon the fact that digital evidence was posted on the website Gizmodo.com with Jason Chen's image, I believe that evidence of the theft of the iPhone prototype, the vandalism of the iPhone prototype, and the sale of its associated trade secrets will be found in and/or upon the items requested in Appendix A.

Based upon my training and experience, I know that computers, cameras, and other digital storage devices would likely have been utilized in this case to create copies of the iPhone prototype and to communicate with co-conspirators regarding the sale, transfer, and publication of the iPhone prototype. I therefore believe evidence in the form of digital images, email communications, instant message communications, internet files associated with searches for Gray Powell and/or iPhone prototypes, contact lists, address books, written notes, documents, telephone call records, text messages, and other information requested in Appendix A will be located in or upon the items sought in this search warrant.

Based upon my training and experience, I also know that information stored on digital storage devices can remain on said devices for an indefinite period of time and that even deleted data and/or files can often be recovered with the use of specialized forensic tools.

I therefore pray that a search warrant be issued so the items set forth in Appendix B can be recovered.

I also request that, upon adjudication of the case(s) against all defendant(s) in this action, including the resolution of any and all appeals, and the written concurrence of the District Attorney's Office, the property be disposed of in accordance with the procedures set forth in California Penal Code §1407 to 1422, without the necessity of a further Court Order issued pursuant to California Penal Code §1536.

**I declare under penalty of perjury under the laws of the State of California that the foregoing is true and correct to the best of my knowledge.**

Det. Matthew Broad
San Mateo County Sheriff's Office

Subscribed and sworn to before
me this 23 day of April, 2010

(SEAL)

JUDGE OF THE SUPERIOR COURT
County of San Mateo, State of California

**Appendix "A"**

**Description of Items to be searched:**

40726 Greystone Terrace, Fremont, Alameda County, California is a townhouse located in a three-story structure located at the intersection of Westerly Common and Greystone Terrace. The building has a green painted exterior with white trim. There is a gray concrete patio with three concrete steps leading to the front door. The door is a brown wooden door with two square glass windows in the upper portion. Black metal numerals depicting the number "40726" are affixed on the front of the building to the right of the brown wooden door. There is a two-pane sliding window in the front wall to the right of the metal numerals. The front door to 40726 Greystone Terrace is between 40734 Greystone Terrace and 40718 Greystone Terrace.

**Appendix "B"**

**Description of property to be seized:**

1. Computer systems, digital storage devices, computer hardware (including peripherals and cables), and data, including but not limited to central processing units (CPUs), hard disk drives, thumb drives, flash drives, digital cameras, digital video cameras, floppy disk drives, tape drives, removable media drives, optical/CD-ROM drives, servers, workstations, display screens, thumb drives, memory cards, cellular telephones, digital cameras, input devices (including but not limited to keyboards, mice, and trackballs), printers, modems, peripherals, floppy disks, magnetic tapes, cassette tapes, removable storage media, and/or optical CD-ROM disks or cartridges, found together or separately from one another. Such systems also commonly include cables linking computer systems to other systems or phone lines.

2. Documentation or other material describing the operation of any computer systems, computer hardware, software, and/or computer peripherals found at the premises, including instructions on how to access disks, files, or other material stored within same, including but not limited to computer manuals, printouts, passwords, file name lists, "readme" and/or "help files."

3. All records and data **located and/or stored on** any computers, hard drives, or memory storage devices, located at the listed location including digital photographs and/or video of the Apple prototype 4G iPhone, email communications pertaining to the sale of photographs of the prototype phone and/or the sale of the physical prototype 4G Apple iPhone, internet history, cache files, and/or Internet pages pertaining to searches and/or research conducted on Apple employee Gray Powell, call records, contact lists, text messages related to the sale of photographs of the prototype iPhone and/or physical prototype iPhone, and indicia that identifies the owner and/or operators of the computer or electronic device. I further request that the above items be allowed to be examined by a forensic computer examiner and that the examination be conducted at an offsite facility due to the need for special equipment to properly conduct the examination and preserve the evidence and

that said search may be continued beyond the ten-day period beginning upon issuance of this Search Warrant, to the extent necessary to complete the search on the computer systems.

4. Printed documents, images, and/or notations pertaining to the sale and/or purchase of the stolen iPhone prototype and/or the sale and/or transfer of trade secret information pertaining to the iPhone prototype.

5. Any article of personal property tending to establish the identity of persons who have dominion and control over the premises and vehicles to be searched, including all keys to the described location and vehicles, rent receipts, utility bills, telephone bills, addressed mail, purchase receipts, sales receipts, and articles of personal property tending to show ownership of vehicles including, but not limited to vehicle pink slips and vehicle registration. All personal property and documents used by the persons named as means of identification, including but not limited to driver's licenses, credit cards, passports, social security cards, and photographs relative to the person(s) described.

## B. MAIL AND WIRE FRAUD

### CARPENTER v. UNITED STATES
484 U.S. 19 (1987)

In 1981, Winans became a reporter for the Wall Street Journal (the Journal) and in the summer of 1982 became one of the two writers of a daily column, "Heard on the Street." That column discussed selected stocks or groups of stocks, giving positive and negative information about those stocks and taking "a point of view with respect to investment in the stocks that it reviews." 612 F.Supp., at 830. Winans regularly interviewed corporate executives to put together interesting perspectives on the stocks that would be highlighted in upcoming columns, but, at least for the columns at issue here, none contained corporate inside information or any "hold for release" information. Id., at 830, n. 2. Because of the "Heard" column's perceived quality and integrity, it had the potential of affecting the price of the stocks which it examined. The District Court concluded on the basis of testimony presented at trial that the "Heard" column "does have an impact on the market, difficult though it may be to quantify in any particular case." Id., at 830.

The official policy and practice at the Journal was that prior to publication, the contents of the column were the Journal's confidential information. Despite the rule, with which Winans was familiar, he entered into a scheme in October 1983 with Peter Brant and petitioner Felis, both connected with the Kidder Peabody brokerage firm in New York City, to give them advance information as to the timing and contents of the "Heard" column. This permitted Brant and Felis and another conspirator, David Clark, a client of Brant, to buy or sell based on the probable impact of the column on the market. Profits were to be shared. The conspirators agreed that the scheme would not affect the journalistic purity of the "Heard" column, and the District Court did not find that the contents of any of the articles were altered to further the profit potential of petitioners' stock-trading scheme. Id., at 832, 834-835. Over a 4-month period, the brokers made prepublication trades on the basis of information given them by Winans about the contents of some 27 "Heard" columns. The net profits from these trades were about $690,000.

In November 1983, correlations between the "Heard" articles and trading in the Clark and Felis accounts were noted at Kidder Peabody and inquiries began. Brant and Felis denied knowing anyone at the Journal and took steps to conceal the trades. Later, the Securities and Exchange Commission began an investigation. Questions were met by denials both by the brokers at Kidder Peabody and by Winans at the Journal. As the investigation progressed, the conspirators quarreled, and on March 29, 1984, Winans and Carpenter went to the SEC and revealed the entire scheme. This indictment and a bench trial followed. Brant, who had pleaded guilty under a plea agreement, was a witness for the Government.

The District Court found, and the Court of Appeals agreed, that Winans had knowingly breached a duty of confidentiality by misappropriating prepublication information regarding the timing and contents of the "Heard" column, information that had been gained in the course of his employment under the understanding that it would not be revealed in advance of publication and that if it were, he would report it to his employer. It was this appropriation of confidential information that underlay both the securities laws and mail and wire fraud counts. With respect to the § 10(b) charges, the courts below held that the deliberate breach of Winans' duty of confidentiality and concealment of the scheme was a fraud and deceit on the Journal. Although the victim of the fraud, the Journal, was not a buyer or seller of the stocks traded in or otherwise a market participant, the fraud was nevertheless considered to be "in connection with" a purchase or sale of securities within the meaning of the statute and the rule. The courts reasoned that the scheme's sole purpose was to buy and sell securities at a profit based on advance information of the column's contents. The courts below rejected petitioners' submission, which is one of the two questions presented here, that criminal liability could not be imposed on petitioners under Rule 10b-5 because "the newspaper is the only alleged victim of fraud and has no interest in the securities traded."

In affirming the mail and wire fraud convictions, the Court of Appeals ruled that Winans had fraudulently misappropriated "property" within the meaning of the mail and wire fraud statutes and that its revelation had harmed the Journal. It was held as well that the use of the mail and wire services had a sufficient nexus with the scheme to satisfy §§ 1341 and 1343. The petition for certiorari challenged these conclusions.

The Court is evenly divided with respect to the convictions under the securities laws and for that reason affirms the judgment below on those counts. For the reasons that follow, we also affirm the judgment with respect to the mail and wire fraud convictions.

II.

Petitioners assert that their activities were not a scheme to defraud the Journal within the meaning of the mail and wire fraud statutes; and that in any event, they did not obtain any "money or property" from the Journal, which is a necessary element of the crime under our decision last Term in McNally v. United States, 483 U.S. 350, 107 S.Ct. 2875, 97 L.Ed.2d 292 (1987). We are unpersuaded by either submission and address the latter first.

We held in McNally that the mail fraud statute does not reach "schemes to defraud citizens of their intangible rights to honest and impartial government," id., at 355, 107 S.Ct., at 2879, and that the statute is "limited in scope to the protection of property rights." Id., at 360, 107 S.Ct., at 2882. Petitioners argue that the Journal's interest in prepublication confidentiality for the "Heard" columns is no more than an intangible consideration outside the reach of § 1341; nor does that law, it is urged, protect against mere injury to reputation. This is not a case like McNally, however. The Journal, as Winans' employer, was defrauded of much more than its contractual right to his honest and faithful service, an interest too ethereal in itself to fall within the protection of the mail fraud statute, which "had its origin in the desire to protect individual property rights." McNally, supra, at 359, n. 8, 107 S.Ct., at 2881, n. 8. Here, the object of the scheme was to take the Journal's confidential business information-the publication schedule and contents of the "Heard" column-and its intangible nature does not make it any less "property" protected by the mail and wire fraud statutes. McNally did not limit the scope of § 1341 to tangible as distinguished from intangible property rights.

Both courts below expressly referred to the Journal's interest in the confidentiality of the contents and timing of the "Heard" column as a property right, 791 F.2d, at 1034-1035; 612 F.Supp., at 846, and we agree with that conclusion. Confidential business information has long been recognized as property. See Ruckelshaus v. Monsanto Co., 467 U.S. 986, 1001-1004, 104 S.Ct. 2862, 2874, 81 L.Ed.2d 815 (1984); Dirks v. SEC, 463 U.S. 646, 653, n. 10, 103 S.Ct. 3255, 3260, n. 10, 77 L.Ed.2d 911 (1983); Board of Trade of Chicago v. Christie Grain & Stock Co., 198 U.S. 236, 250-251, 25 S.Ct. 637, 639-40, 49 L.Ed. 1031 (1905); cf. 5 U.S.C. § 552(b)(4). "Confidential information acquired or compiled by a corporation in the course and conduct of its business is a species of property to which the corporation has the exclusive right and benefit, and which a court of equity will protect through the injunctive process or other appropriate remedy." 3 W. Fletcher, Cyclopedia of Law of Private Corporations § 857.1, p. 260 (rev. ed. 1986) (footnote omitted). The Journal had a property right in keeping confidential and making exclusive use, prior to publication, of the schedule and contents of the "Heard" column. Christie Grain, supra. As the Court has observed before:

"[N]ews matter, however little susceptible of ownership or dominion in the absolute sense, is stock in trade, to be gathered at the cost of enterprise, organization, skill, labor, and money, and to be distributed and sold to those who will pay money for it, as for any other merchandise." International News Service v. Associated Press, 248 U.S. 215, 236, 39 S.Ct. 68, 71, 63 L.Ed. 211 (1918).

Petitioners' arguments that they did not interfere with the Journal's use of the information or did not publicize it and deprive the Journal of the first public use of it, see Reply Brief for Petitioners 6, miss the point. The confidential information was generated from the business, and the business had a right to decide how to use it prior to disclosing it to the public. Petitioners cannot successfully contend based on Associated Press that a scheme to defraud requires a monetary loss, such as giving the information to a competitor; it is sufficient that the Journal has been deprived of its right to exclusive use of the information, for exclusivity is an important aspect of confidential business information and most private property for that matter.

We cannot accept petitioners' further argument that Winans' conduct in revealing prepublication information was no more than a violation of workplace rules and did not amount to fraudulent activity that is proscribed by the mail fraud statute. Sections 1341 and 1343 reach any scheme to deprive another of money or property by means of false or fraudulent pretenses, representations, or promises. As we observed last Term in McNally, the words "to defraud" in the mail fraud statute have the "common understanding" of " 'wronging one in his property rights by dishonest methods or schemes,' and 'usually signify the deprivation of something of value by trick, deceit, chicane or overreaching.' " 483 U.S., at 358, 107 S.Ct., at 2881 (quoting Hammerschmidt v. United States, 265 U.S. 182, 188, 44 S.Ct. 511, 512, 68 L.Ed. 968 (1924)). The concept of "fraud" includes the act of embezzlement, which is " 'the fraudulent appropriation to one's own use of the money or goods entrusted to one's care by another.' " Grin v. Shine, 187 U.S. 181, 189, 23 S.Ct. 98, 102, 47 L.Ed. 130 (1902).

The District Court found that Winans' undertaking at the Journal was not to reveal prepublication information about his column, a promise that became a sham when in violation of his duty he passed along to his co-conspirators confidential information belonging to the Journal, pursuant to an ongoing scheme to share profits from trading in anticipation of the "Heard" column's impact on the stock market. In Snepp v. United States, 444 U.S. 507, 515, n. 11, 100 S.Ct. 763, 768, n. 11, 62 L.Ed.2d 704 (1980) (per curiam), although a decision grounded in the provisions of a written trust agreement prohibiting the unapproved use of confidential Government information, we noted the similar prohibitions of the common law, that "even in the absence of a written contract, an employee has a fiduciary obligation to protect confidential information obtained during the course of his employment." As the New York courts have recognized: "It is well established, as a general proposition, that a person who acquires special knowledge or information by virtue of a confidential or fiduciary relationship with another is not free to exploit that knowledge or information for his own personal benefit but must account to his principal for any profits derived therefrom." Diamond v. Oreamuno, 24 N.Y.2d 494, 497, 301 N.Y.S.2d 78, 80, 248 N.E.2d 910, 912 (1969); see also Restatement (Second) of Agency §§ 388, Comment c, 396(c) (1958).

We have little trouble in holding that the conspiracy here to trade on the Journal's confidential information is not outside the reach of the mail and wire fraud statutes, provided the other elements of the offenses are satisfied. The Journal's business information that it intended to be kept confidential was its property; the declaration to that effect in the employee manual merely removed any doubts on that score and made the finding of specific intent to defraud that much easier. Winans continued in the employ of the Journal, appropriating its confidential business information for his own use, all the while pretending to perform his duty of safeguarding it. In fact, he told his editors twice about leaks of confidential information not related to the stock-trading scheme, 612 F.Supp., at 831, demonstrating both his knowledge that the Journal viewed information concerning the "Heard" column as confidential and his deceit as he played the role of a loyal employee. Furthermore, the District Court's conclusion that each of the petitioners acted with the required specific intent to defraud is strongly supported by the evidence. Id., at 847-850.

Lastly, we reject the submission that using the wires and the mail to print and send the Journal to its customers did not satisfy the requirement that those mediums be used to execute the scheme at issue. The courts below were quite right in observing that circulation of the "Heard" column was not only anticipated but an essential part of the scheme. Had the column not been made available to Journal customers, there would have been no effect on stock prices and no likelihood of profiting from the information leaked by Winans.

The judgment below is

Affirmed.

## UNITED STATES v. MARTIN

228 F.3d 1 (1st Cir. 2000)

This case arises out of an electronic mail "pen-pal" relationship between a dissatisfied Maine chemist, Caryn Camp, and a California scientist, Dr. Stephen Martin.

* * *

III. Conspiracy to Transport Stolen Property in Interstate Commerce

The jury also found Martin guilty of conspiracy to transport stolen goods interstate, in violation of 18 U.S.C. § 2314 and 18 U.S.C. § 371, as charged in count 14. Again, a conviction for conspiracy does not require that the defendant was successful in the underlying offense, see Giry, 818 F.2d at 126, but only that an agreement to commit the underlying offense existed, see Echeverri, 982 F.2d at 679, and that at least one co-conspirator committed an overt act in furtherance of the conspiracy, see United States v. Cassiere, 4 F.3d 1006, 1014 (1st Cir.1993). To be found guilty of a conspiracy to transport stolen goods interstate, Martin must have agreed to transport "goods, wares, [or] merchandise," with a "value of $5,000 or more," in interstate or foreign commerce, and "known the same to have been stolen, converted or taken by fraud." Dowling v. United States, 473 U.S. 207, 214, 105 S.Ct. 3127, 87 L.Ed.2d 152 (1985) (citing 18 U.S.C. § 2314). Although intangible, "purely intellectual" property does not fall within the auspices of § 2314, intangible components of tangible items may contribute to the $5,000 value requirement. See United States v. Brown, 925 F.2d 1301, 1307–08 & n. 14 (10th Cir.1991).

The indictment for conspiracy to transport stolen goods was based in part on Martin's July 21 request for a copy of x-Chek software and his July 22 acknowledgment that Camp would be sending him additional test kits. See Brief for Appellant 31 (admitting that the "evidence at trial established . . . two instances on which Dr. Martin requested 'property,' as opposed to 'information.' "). Martin received a large package from Camp in the mail after sending these two e-mails. However, Martin claims that (1) this evidence is insufficient to establish the existence of an agreement with Camp to transport stolen property; and (2) that the property in question did not meet the $5,000 value requirement of 18 U.S.C. § 2314.

Martin first challenges the sufficiency of the evidence to support the existence of an agreement between Camp and himself with respect to stolen property. For the same reasons that a rational jury could plausibly have found an agreement to steal trade secrets, we conclude that the same rational jury could have found an agreement between Camp and Martin by which she would send him property from IDEXX. However, the question remains whether that agreement (1) covered "stolen" property in violation of § 2314, and (2) covered property with a value of more than $5,000.

For property to be "stolen" under 18 U.S.C. § 2314, the defendant must have "known" it to be "stolen, converted or taken by fraud." Although the prosecution introduced testimony that IDEXX only provided x-Chek for "free" under a license agreement with its customers, Martin claimed that, based on Camp's previous e-mail communication, he believed the software was free. However, in a conviction challenged for sufficiency of the evidence, we must give the jury's finding great weight, asking only whether a "reasonable" or "rational" jury could have "plausibly" found guilt beyond a reasonable doubt. See Echeverri, 982 F.2d at 677; United States v. Ortiz, 966 F.2d 707, 711 (1st Cir.1992). In this case, given that three months had passed since Camp had described x-Chek as "free," that she had originally discussed it in connection with customer satisfaction, that the "free" label occurred at the end of a lengthy e-mail, and that Martin was a scientist who had surely dealt with companies such as IDEXX before, a jury could certainly have concluded that he knew that such companies did not provide major software packages for free to those who were neither customers nor potential customers, and that Martin knew the software had been stolen or converted from IDEXX.

Moreover, with respect to the "free" test kits, the evidence is much stronger that Martin knew that they had been "stolen, converted or taken by fraud." First, when Camp sent Martin the original set of kits, she told him not to "say where [he] got them," and not to mention them to her relatives, because "all rules are null-and-void now that IDEXX has been acquiring kits from its competitors by sneaky means." Even though Camp noted that it was part of her job to send free kits to potential customers, Martin was clearly not a potential customer, and could not plausibly have believed that this mandate applied to his "spy" sending free kits to him. Furthermore, Martin admitted that, in the future, he would have to buy the kits, suggesting that he did not really believe he was entitled to obtain them for free.

Finally, the jury could have plausibly concluded that Martin's July 21 request to Camp to "absorb as much information, physically and intellectually, as you can," included a request to send him physical goods such as test kits and software. Martin had already received items from Camp, and was at the time expecting further items, such as the x-Chek software. Although Martin is correct that § 2314 does not apply to purely "intangible information," the theft of which is punishable under copyright law and other intellectual property statutes, see United States v. Brown, 925 F.2d 1301, 1307 (10th Cir.1991), § 2314 does apply when there has been "some tangible item taken, however insignificant or valueless it may be, absent the intangible component," id. at 1308 n. 14. Given that at this time Camp had already sent Martin numerous tangible items, he would have been on notice that any request to "absorb information" might (and likely would) produce tangible material that he would receive.

As for Martin's claim that the value of his requests did not meet the $5,000 floor, there is evidence that the value of the x-Chek software approached $2,500, and that individual diagnostic kits ranged from $1,500 to $2,200. Furthermore, there is evidence that Martin was aware of the potential cost of test kits. Whether the actual items received exceeded the statutory value or not (and there is strong evidence that they in fact did), a jury could plausibly have concluded that Martin, with sufficient knowledge of the kit price, had requested items that would likely have exceeded $5,000 and thus satisfied the value prong of the conspiracy charge.

## IV. Wire Fraud and Mail Fraud

The remainder of defendant's convictions are based on four counts of wire fraud and two counts of mail fraud pursuant to 18 U.S.C. §§ 2 (aiding and abetting), 1341 (mail fraud), 1343 (wire fraud), and 1346 (honest services fraud). Because of the similarity of the operative language of the wire fraud and mail fraud statutes, we analyze the offenses together. See Carpenter v. United States, 484 U.S. 19, 25 n. 6, 108 S.Ct. 316, 98 L.Ed.2d 275 (1987); United States v. Boots, 80 F.3d 580, 586 n. 11 (1st Cir.1996). To prove wire or mail fraud, the government must show: (1) a scheme to defraud by means of false pretenses; (2) the defendant's knowing and willing participation in the scheme with the intent to defraud; and (3) the use of interstate wire or mail communications in furtherance of the scheme. See Cassiere, 4 F.3d at 1011 (citing United States v. Serrano, 870 F.2d 1, 6 (1st Cir.1989)) (elements of wire fraud); United States v. Montminy, 936 F.2d 626, 627 (1st Cir.1991) (elements of mail fraud).

Although the mail and wire fraud statutes originally required that the scheme to defraud aim to deprive the victim of property or some other item of economic value, see United States v. Sawyer, 85 F.3d 713, 723 (1st Cir.1996), congressional legislation aimed at overruling McNally v. United States, 483 U.S. 350, 107 S.Ct. 2875, 97 L.Ed.2d 292 (1987), expanded the definition to include "schemes intended to deprive another of the intangible right to honest services." Id. Despite concerns about the overreaching of the wire and mail fraud statutes into the employer-employee relationship, see, e.g., United States v. Lemire, 720 F.2d 1327, 1336 (D.C.Cir.1983), courts have upheld convictions based on employee misconduct, see, e.g., United States v. Frost, 125 F.3d 346 (6th Cir.1997). As a result of this expanded definition, in order to uphold Martin's conviction, sufficient evidence must exist to show his participation in either (1) a scheme to defraud IDEXX of property or other items of economic value by false pretenses, or (2) a scheme to defraud IDEXX of Camp's honest services by false pretenses. Note that Martin's success in the scheme is not relevant. See, e.g., Serrano, 870 F.2d at 6. We conclude that a rational jury could have found that such evidence had been proven under either theory.

### A. Property Theory

Confidential information may be considered property for the purposes of §§ 1341 and 1343. See United States v. Czubinski, 106 F.3d 1069, 1074 (1st Cir.1997). Where such information is obtained — thus depriving the rightful owner of its property rights — through dishonest or deceitful means, the wire and mail fraud statutes may be violated. See id. However, mere access to the confidential information is insufficient; rather, "either some articulable harm must befall the holder of the information as a result of the defendant's activities, or some gainful use must be intended by the person accessing the information, whether or not this use is profitable in the economic sense." Id. In other words, for Martin's convictions to stand under this prong of the wire and mail fraud statutes, sufficient evidence must exist for a reasonable jury to find that Martin knowingly and willingly participated in a scheme to defraud IDEXX of confidential information or other property via false pretenses, and in so doing either harmed IDEXX or intended to use the information for his own gain.

Martin claims that because, on their face, the e-mails on which counts 7–10 are based contained no misrepresentations, they cannot provide the basis for a scheme to defraud. However, the e-mails themselves need not be fraudulent; rather, it is the scheme itself that must rely on false pretenses. See United States v. Green, 786 F.2d 247, 249 (7th Cir.1986) ("The causal connection between the mailing and the success of the scheme, not the knavery in the mailings, is what matters.").

A reasonable jury could first have found that, as of July 12 (the date after which the four wire fraud and two mail fraud convictions stem), Camp had agreed with Martin to send him confidential information and tangible property. Camp had previously noted that her e-mails contained information that she should not have spread; Martin's repeated questions designed to elicit further information, including his acceptance of Camp as his "spy," provide further evidence of the scheme. A reasonable jury could have found that Martin intended to use such confidential information either to compete with IDEXX, thus harming IDEXX, or at the very least for his own pecuniary gain. For example, Martin and Camp engaged in a lengthy discussion of the best manner in which to design a test kit that would surpass IDEXX's in serving demanding customers in the veterinary profession. A reasonable jury could have found that Martin's requests, including to "absorb as much information, physically and intellectually as possible," indicate that his participation in the scheme was both willing and knowing. Finally, a reasonable jury could have found that Camp's actions — including requesting information beyond her job description without informing IDEXX of her conflicted interests, sending Martin information and property under the pretense that he was a customer who had a right to receive information and property free, and relaying confidential information in violation of both her fiduciary duty to IDEXX and her signed non-disclosure and non-compete agreements — constituted false pretenses.

B. Honest Services Theory

Alternatively, the jury could have found that Martin and Camp's e-mail communications and mail deposits constituted a scheme to deprive IDEXX of Camp's honest services. Although the honest services doctrine has mainly been used to punish fraud against the citizenry perpetrated by government officials, see, e.g., Czubinski at 1076–77, courts both before McNally v. United States, 483 U.S. 350, 107 S.Ct. 2875, 97 L.Ed.2d 292 (1987), and after the passage of § 1346 have been willing to expand the doctrine to the employer-employee relationship, see id. at 1077; United States v. Sun-Diamond Growers of California, 138 F.3d 961, 973 (D.C.Cir.1998) (§ 1346 "has also been used, as here, to prosecute private citizens who defraud private entities"). However, courts have been hesitant to impose federal mail and wire fraud liability upon every employee transgression, and have required "a failure to disclose something which in the knowledge or contemplation of the employee poses an independent business risk to the employer," or creates "reasonably foreseeable economic harm" to the employer. Sun-Diamond, 138 F.3d at 973 (quoting United States v. Lemire, 720 F.2d 1327, 1337 (D.C.Cir.1983)). While this Court has held that merely examining confidential information for one's own purposes does not rise to this level, see Czubinski at 1077, use of confidential information for "private purposes" may rise to the necessary level of self-dealing. See id.

A jury could reasonably have found that Camp's disclosure of confidential information was in knowing breach of her fiduciary duty to IDEXX. Moreover, the evidence supports a finding that Camp's failure to disclose her communication with Martin posed "an independent business risk" to IDEXX and created "reasonably foreseen economic harm" to IDEXX. By July 1998, Camp knew that Martin intended his company to compete with IDEXX — in fact, she was authoring proposals detailing how that competition would be most successful.

Under 18 U.S.C. § 2, Martin is guilty of aiding and abetting a crime if he "willfully participated in it," that is, wished it to occur and affirmatively participated in its successful outcome. See United States v. Indelicato, 611 F.2d 376, 385 (1st Cir.1979). The government has offered substantial evidence of Martin's willing participation in (in fact, sponsorship of) Camp's breach of fiduciary duty. A jury could have found that Martin's request for information about IDEXX's competitive stance, his willing receipt of IDEXX materials and inventory, and his request that Camp gather as much information as possible prior to leaving the company both encouraged and aided Camp in breaching her fiduciary duty to IDEXX. Moreover, in Martin's use of "spy" terminology, in his specific requests for information, and in his apparent willingness to use the information to compete directly with IDEXX, a reasonable jury could have found that his participation in the scheme to defraud IDEXX of Camp's honest services, i.e., to have Camp breach her fiduciary duties for personal gain and harm to IDEXX, was sufficient to maintain liability for aiding and abetting pursuant to 18 U.S.C. § 2.

C. The Individual Counts of Wire and Mail Fraud

The individual counts of wire and mail fraud then only need be communications designed to effect a scheme under either the property theory or the honest services theory. Again, the communications need not be fraudulent on their face. See United States v. Green, 786 F.2d 247, 249 (7th Cir.1986) (citing United States v. Sampson, 371 U.S. 75, 83 S.Ct. 173, 9 L.Ed.2d 136 (1962)). We examine each count in turn to determine if a rational jury might have plausibly concluded that they were used to effect one of the two possible schemes to defraud.

Martin claims that the e-mails on which counts 7 and 8 are based (Camp's offer to send him x-Chek software and his affirmative response) cannot be communications designed to effect a scheme to defraud because he had no knowledge that the software was not free. As previously pointed out, the record belies this claim. In any event, Camp certainly knew that she was only supposed to send x-Chek to customers; Martin was clearly not a customer. Thus her x-Chek offer could be construed as part of a scheme to defraud IDEXX of her honest services. In other words, a reasonable jury could conclude that Camp's offer to send x-Chek to Martin breached her fiduciary duty to IDEXX and caused IDEXX harm. As a reasonable jury could also find that Martin aided and abetted this breach, see supra, the evidence is sufficient to convict on counts 7 and 8. Furthermore, a jury could reasonably have found that Martin knew that he was not entitled to a free copy of x-Chek. If so, Martin would have obtained the software through false pretenses, and thus satisfied the alternative prong of the wire fraud test with his affirmative response.

Martin admits that his e-mail on which count 9 is based, asking Camp to "absorb as much physically and intellectually as you can," could be construed as "requesting . . . non-confidential public information," Appellant Brief 38, but only if read in isolation. Martin argues that as a non-competitor, he had no use for confidential information, and that the words "as you can" incorporated previous guidelines of confidentiality. Id. at 39. However, it is not our task to determine if alternate interpretations of the evidence were available to the jury, but rather if the evidence was sufficient for the jury to reach a reasonable interpretation upon which it could convict. See, e.g., United States v. Batista-Polanco, 927 F.2d 14, 17 (1st Cir.1991). Certainly the request made by Martin in this particular e-mail is highly suggestive of a request for information which he knew was confidential and would require Camp's "spying" to unearth. A reasonable jury could have interpreted his request in this manner, and thus found that this communication was made in furtherance of the scheme to defraud.

Martin claims that because Camp's July 21 e-mail (on which count 10 is based) denies any use of confidential information, that it could not be part of the scheme to defraud. However, this e-mail alerted Martin to the delivery of seven binders (which included information marked specifically as "confidential"), provided further information about IDEXX procedures and methods, and noted that Camp had "found a jackpot." Despite Camp's denial, we have found above that sufficient evidence existed for the jury to find that a scheme to defraud existed and that Martin received confidential information in connection with this scheme. Given that evidence, this communication — among other things, notifying Martin that she had sent documents to him — clearly furthered the scheme.

With respect to the mail fraud counts (11 and 12), Martin claims that, because Camp mailed items to Martin on her own initiative, Martin could not be guilty of aiding and abetting mail fraud on these counts. Again, defense counsel confuses what Martin is guilty of aiding and abetting — the scheme to defraud, not the individual mailing. Again, the jury had sufficient evidence to find Martin guilty of aiding and abetting the scheme to defraud, either through deprivation of property under false pretenses or via honest services fraud. Camp's mailing of the packages to Martin was in furtherance of the scheme: either because it finalized the property removal from IDEXX or provided the final pieces to Martin's future competition with IDEXX. Thus sufficient evidence existed to convict Martin on either count. Moreover, § 1341 itself criminalizes the act of "causing" another to deposit items in the mails that further a scheme to defraud. Especially with respect to the second mail fraud count, based on the package that included the IDEXX software, a reasonable jury could have found that Martin's request caused Camp to send him those materials, and found him guilty of violating § 1341 without relying on aiding and abetting liability.

## CONCLUSION

A careful reading of the seven-month e-mail communication between Dr. Stephen Martin and Caryn Camp could lead to the conclusion Martin and his counsel urge — that this is simply a pen-pal relationship between a lonely Maine lab technician and a reclusive California scientist. However, the evidence could also lead a reader to the conclusion that something far more sinister was afoot: that an originally harmless communication mushroomed into a conspiracy to steal trade secrets and transport stolen property interstate, and that the electronic mail and U.S. mails were used to further a scheme to defraud IDEXX. Because we find there was sufficient evidence for a reasonable jury to conclude the latter beyond any reasonable doubt, we AFFIRM the defendant's conviction on all counts.

## UNITED STATES v. NOSAL

No. CR 08-00237 MHP, 2010 U.S. Dist. LEXIS 24359
(N.D. Cal. Apr. 13, 2009)

Defendant David Nosal ("Nosal") has been indicted on theft of trade secrets, illegal computer intrusion, and mail fraud. Now before the court is Nosal's second motion to dismiss the Superceding Indictment against him, this time on the alleged basis that none of the twenty counts adequately states an offense. The court has considered the parties' arguments and submissions, and for the reasons stated below, the court issues the following memorandum and order. This order serves to memorialize and supplement the court's ruling on this motion in open court on March 2, 2009.

BACKGROUND

Nosal was a high level executive at an international executive search firm, Korn/Ferry International ("KFI"), from approximately April 1996 to October 2004. KFI was one of the leading providers of executive recruitment services, engaging in searches to fill executive, board-of-director, and similar high level positions, for businesses in the United States. Nosal terminated his employment with KFI in October 2004, with plans to start a competing executive search firm.

Upon his departure, Nosal voluntarily entered into a separation agreement and agreed to serve as an independent contractor to KFI from November 1, 2004 through October 15, 2005. Under the terms of that Separation and General Release Agreement and an Independent Contractor Agreement (collectively, "the Nosal-KFI Agreements"), Nosal agreed to cooperate with KFI on certain ongoing search assignments and agreed not to compete with KFI by not performing executive search, executive placement, management assessment, or management audit services on behalf of any other entity than KFI during the period the Nosal-KFI Agreements were in place. In exchange for his services, Nosal was to receive $25,000 per month during that year, as well as two lump-sum payments on July 31st and October 15, 2005.

Becky Christian was an employee of KFI from approximately September 1999 through January 2005. The individual identified in the Superceding Indictment as "J.F." was employed by KFI from approximately December 1997 to August 2005. J.F. was Nosal's executive assistant prior to Nosal's departure from KFI. According to the Superceding Indictment, both individuals helped Nosal set up his new executive search firm and assisted Nosal in obtaining trade secrets and other things of value from KFI's computer system, prior to and upon termination of their employment with KFI by using their own KFI password-protected user accounts. Specifically, the Superceding Indictment alleges that J.F. and Christian assisted Nosal in obtaining source lists and other custom reports of names and contact information from the KFI "Searcher" database, a highly confidential and proprietary database of executives and companies.

On April 10, 2008, Nosal and co-defendant Becky Christian were charged by indictment with federal statutory violations relating to their alleged involvement in stealing confidential and proprietary information from KFI for the purpose of assisting Nosal in his own executive search activities. On June 16, 2008, the court granted the defendant Christian's motion to sever.

* * *

Nosal brings this motion to dismiss the indictment against him, alleging that none of the twenty counts adequately states an offense. Generally, Nosal argues that KFI's allegations involve civil matters and matters of state law and are being improperly raised in the context of a federal criminal prosecution. More specifically, Nosal categorizes the charges into three sets and argues that each set fails to state an offense.

According to Nosal, the first set of charges allege theft and misappropriation of trade secrets in violation of the Economic Espionage Act, 18 U.S.C. section 1832 ("EEA"). Nosal argues that the counts are multiplicitous and neither alleges the required element of the knowledge of illegality of the offense. The government's next set of charges allege that Nosal accessed a computer without authorization in violation of the Computer Fraud and Abuse Act, 18 U.S.C. section 1030 ("CFAA"). Nosal argues that the government only alleges misappropriation and that act is not covered by the CFAA. The government's final set of charges allege that Nosal committed mail fraud by violating the Nosal-KFI Agreements, by failing to disclose that violation, and by continuing to receive monthly payments in the mail. Nosal argues that conduct does not amount to mail fraud because it constitutes an undisclosed breach of contract of an unenforceable contract provision.

The United States opposes Nosal's motion, arguing that Nosal mischaracterizes the charged offenses, all counts are adequately plead, and moreover dismissal of indictments is disfavored as a remedy. The court heard oral argument on the motion on March 2, 2009 and ruled from the bench, denying plaintiff's motion in part and indicating its intent to grant the motion with respect to the mail fraud counts. This memorandum and order provides written detail of that ruling.

## LEGAL STANDARD

Under Rule 12(b) of the Federal Rules of Criminal Procedure, a party may file a motion to dismiss based on "any defense, objection, or request that the court can determine without a trial of the general issue." Fed.R.Crim.P. 12(b); *United States v. Shortt Accountancy Corp.*, 785 F.2d 1448, 1452 (9th Cir.1986). In considering a motion to dismiss, the court is limited to the face of the indictment and must accept the facts alleged in that indictment as true. *Winslow v. United States*, 216 F.2d 912, 913 (9th Cir.1955); *United States v. Ruiz-Castro*, 125 F.Supp.2d 411, 413 (D.Haw.2000). A court must decide such a motion before trial "unless it finds good cause to defer a ruling." Fed.R.Crim.P. 12(d); *Shortt Accountancy*, 785 F.2d at 1452 (*citing* former Fed.R.Crim.P. 12(e)).

* * *

III. Mail Fraud Charges

Nosal argues the mail fraud conspiracy and substantive charges in counts twelve through twenty should be dismissed because they improperly seek to cover a civil matter-breach of contract. Nosal contends the government's mail fraud charges are based solely on Nosal having allegedly committed fraud by deceiving KFI about the fact that he was conducting his own executive-search-related activities during the period the Nosal-KFI Agreements were in place. Nosal argues that any alleged breach of his agreement not to compete with KFI by not performing executive search and other services on behalf of any other entity during the period the Nosal-KFI Agreements were in place is a breach of contract claim and not a federal crime. Nosal further argues the mail fraud charges should be dismissed because they rest on alleged fraud arising out of a contractual non-compete provision that is invalid under California law.

Nosal is charged with mail fraud and conspiracy to commit mail fraud under 18 U.S.C. sections 1341 and 1349, respectively. To prove a violation of the mail fraud statute, the government must show that (1) the defendant formed a scheme to defraud; (2) the defendant used the United States mails or caused a use of the United States mails in furtherance of the scheme; and (3) the defendants did so with the specific intent to deceive or defraud. *See Schreiber Distribut. Co. v. Serv-Well Furniture Co., Inc.*, 806 F.2d 1393, 1399-1400 (9th Cir.1986). The mail fraud statute has been broadly construed by the courts, given that the purpose of the statute is to proscribe the use of the mails "in any situation where it is closely entwined with fraudulent activity." *Id., citing United States v. Halbert*, 640 F.2d 1000, 1009 (9th Cir.1981).

Here, the Superceding Indictment alleges that Nosal committed mail fraud by engaging in a scheme to defraud KFI by means of false and fraudulent misrepresentations and promises. Specifically, Nosal is alleged to have provided materially false information to, and purposefully omitting and concealing material information from, KFI regarding Nosal's executive-search-related activities that were in violation of the Nosal-KFI Agreements. It was allegedly part of the scheme that Nosal and Christian directed others to take without authorization and in excess of authorized access confidential and proprietary information and trade secrets from KFI's computer system with the intent to defraud, and subsequently used that information to conduct executive searches and related activities. Also part of the alleged scheme was that Nosal misrepresented on numerous occasions to KFI executives that he was complying with the Nosal-KFI Agreements, so that he could both continue to receive his monthly independent contractor payments and remain eligible to receive his lump-sum payments under the agreements. The alleged use of the mails in furtherance of the scheme to defraud consists of eight monthly payment checks that were mailed by KFI to Nosal.

The government contends that because Nosal caused the checks to be mailed for the purpose of executing his scheme to defraud, this is sufficient to support the charges under examination here. On oral argument, the government asserted that evidence of the conspiracy to commit mail fraud charge is provided by the bi-weekly telephone calls between Nosal and KFI executive in which Nosal falsely told KFI he was complying with the Nosal-KFI agreements. The court disagrees that these allegations of Nosal having mislead KFI support the charges.

The government relies at least in part on the theory of deprivation of honest services, describing in its brief and on oral argument Nosal's alleged scheme to deprive KFI of his honest services as an independent contractor for the purpose of the charges at hand. However, the Superceding Indictment fails to make any such allegations, relying on the false and fraudulent pretenses theory instead. Furthermore, the honest services doctrine has mainly been used to punish fraud against citizens perpetrated by government officials. *See, e.g., U.S. v. Kincaid-Chauncey*, 556 F.3d 923, 939 (9th Cir.2009), *citing U.S. v. Silvano*, 812 F.2d 754, 759 (1st Cir.1987) ("the theory relies on the idea that 'a public official acts as 'trustee for the citizens and the State . . . and thus owes the normal fiduciary duties of a trustee, e.g., honesty and loyalty to them.' ") While honest services fraud can occur in the employer-employee relationship, courts have been hesitant to impose federal liability upon every private dispute involving an employee transgression that incurs no public deprivation of rights. *See, e.g., U.S. v. Czubinski*, 106 F.3d 1069, 1077 (1st Cir.1997) (holding that examining confidential information for one's own purposes dues not rise to the requisite level of a workplace violation to sustain a mail fraud charge under the honest services theory).

The government acknowledges that the mail fraud statute may not reach every private business practice that involves a deprivation of honest services through a breach of contract or of a fiduciary duty. On the state of the Superceding Indictment before this court, that acknowledgment is of no moment since the government has not alleged an honest services theory. What the government does argue is that the mail fraud statute reaches breaches of contract or of a fiduciary duty where there was a recognizable scheme to defraud and where the defendant made fraudulent representations reasonably calculated to deceive. This is nothing more than a false and fraudulent pretense theory and on this theory the allegations of the Superceding Indictment fall short. The fraudulent representations that are calculated to deceive must also be performed in specific furtherance of the scheme. Nosal's acquiescence in allowing KFI to mail the monthly payment checks to his home does not contain sufficient deception to bring it within the purview of the mail fraud statute. The Nosal-KFI Agreements were broad and while certain of Nosal's alleged actions may have been misleading, there is a dearth of allegations regarding intentional and specific misrepresentations of fact made to further the fraudulent scheme. Accordingly, the mail fraud charges cannot be sustained.

The court need not reach Nosal's argument regarding the validity of non-competition clauses under California law and whether an undisclosed breach of such a provision can constitute fraud. The court finds that the government has failed to allege a scheme to defraud that involves the use of the mails in furtherance of the scheme and the specific intent to defraud. Even accepting the allegations of the indictment as true, the government has insufficiently pled the elements of mail fraud to withstand a motion to dismiss. The mail fraud charges must be dismissed because the law is clear that the prosecution cannot cure defects in an indictment by providing more particularized notice subsequent to the indictment. *See Russell v. U.S.*, 369 U.S. 749, 770, 82 S.Ct. 1038, 8 L.Ed.2d 240 (1962) ("a bill of particulars cannot save an invalid indictment . . . [f]or a defendant could then be convicted on the basis of facts not found by, and perhaps not even presented to, the grand jury which indicted him.") Accordingly, the court GRANTS defendant's motion to dismiss counts twelve through twenty of the Superceding Indictment.

* * *

## NOTES AND QUESTIONS:

1. The *Carpenter v. United States*, 484 U.S. 19 (1987), court held that the prepublication stock information was "property" and that Carpenter's use of it over the telephone violated the wire fraud statute. What happens to that "property" once it is published in the WALL STREET JOURNAL? How does this use of the term "property" square with the definition of a trade secret in the RESTATEMENT (THIRD) OF UNFAIR COMPETITION and the TSUS? What was the property that was taken in *Carpenter*?

2. In *United States v. Martin*, 228 F.3d 1 (1st Cir. 2000), property rights were discussed as important issues under both conspiracy to transport stolen goods interstate and mail and wire fraud laws. How does the breach of Camp's employment agreement fit into this discussion?

3. The *Martin* court found Camp had improperly disclosed confidential information to Martin. If Camp had not signed a non-disclosure agreement, would she have had a fiduciary duty not to disclose the information to Martin? If it was Camp who improperly disclosed the trade secrets, what was Martin's crime? How did Martin "use" the trade secrets?

4. In response to a suggestion by the Supreme Court in *McNally v. United States*, 483 U.S. 350 (1987), Congress passed the "honest services" amendment to 18 U.S.C. § 1346, which added that "the term 'scheme or artifice to defraud' includes a scheme or artifice to deprive another of the intangible right of honest services." Is this comparable to any doctrine in trade secret law in civil cases? Questions have been raised about whether this wording is "void for vagueness." *See* Geraldine Szott Moohr, *Mail Fraud and the Intangible Rights Doctrine: Someone to Watch Over Us*, 31 HARV. J. ON LEGIS. 153, 187-99 (1994).

5. The court in *United States v. Nosal*, No. CR 08-00237 MHP, 2009 U.S. Dist. LEXIS 31423 (N.D. Cal. Apr. 13, 2009), dismissed the mail fraud charges, which were based on the defendant allowing checks to be mailed to him allegedly for the purpose of executing his fraudulent scheme because "Nosal's acquiescence in allowing KFI to mail the monthly payment checks to his home does not contain sufficient deception to bring it within the purview of the mail fraud statute." Other counts of the indictment based on the EEA were upheld. However, an *en banc* decision of the 9th Circuit Court of Appeals dismissed the CFAA counts in *United States v. Nosal*, 676 F.3d 854 (9th Cir. Apr. 10, 2012), which is excerpted below.

## C. FEDERAL ECONOMIC ESPIONAGE ACT OF 1996

### UNITED STATES v. HSU

155 F.3d 189 (3d Cir. 1998)

RENDELL, CIRCUIT JUDGE:

In this appeal we explore for the first time the relationship between the confidentiality provisions of the newly-enacted Economic Espionage Act of 1996, 18 U.S.C. § 1831, *et seq.*, and principles of criminal law regarding discovery and disclosure of material evidence. The district court ordered the government to disclose alleged corporate trade secrets based upon a theory that we find does not apply. It also held that the defense of legal impossibility does not pertain to the attempt and conspiracy crimes with which the defendants are charged. We will affirm the court's holding regarding the applicability of the defense of legal impossibility, but will reverse its discovery order and remand for a review of other asserted defenses to the crimes in the indictment.

#### I. FACTUAL AND PROCEDURAL BACKGROUND

##### A. The Government's Sting Operation

On July 10, 1997, a federal grand jury indicted Kai-Lo Hsu, Chester S. Ho, and Jessica Chou (collectively, "the defendants") for their involvement in an alleged conspiracy to steal corporate trade secrets from Bristol-Myers Squibb. The indictment alleges that the defendants sought to obtain the processes, methods, and formulas for manufacturing Taxol, an anti-cancer drug produced by Bristol-Myers and regarded by the company as a highly valuable trade secret.

According to the indictment, the defendants' conspiracy began on June 7, 1995, when Chou, the Manager of Business Development for Yuen Foong Paper Company in Taiwan ("YFP"), requested information about Taxol from John Hartmann, an undercover FBI agent whom Chou mistakenly believed to be a technological information broker in the United States. From August 28, 1995, until January 12, 1996, Chou allegedly contacted Hartmann repeatedly to obtain information about Taxol manufacturing techniques and distribution. These contacts led to a meeting in Los Angeles on February 27, 1996, between Hartmann and Hsu, the Technical Director for YFP's operations. Hsu purportedly told Hartmann at that meeting that YFP wanted to diversify into biotechnology and to introduce technology from advanced countries into Taiwan. When Hartmann responded that Bristol-Myers would be unlikely to share its secret technology with YFP, Hsu allegedly responded, "We'll get [it] another way," and told Hartmann to pursue paying Bristol-Myers employees for the confidential Taxol formulas.

The indictment asserts that Hsu and Chou then "communicated many times" with Hartmann over the next fourteen months to discuss the transfer of Taxol technology and to negotiate a specific price for the acquisition of Bristol-Myers's trade secrets. In response, Hartmann told the defendants that a corrupt Bristol-

Myers scientist would be willing to sell Taxol information to YFP. The "corrupt" scientist was actually a Bristol-Myers employee cooperating with the FBI. Intrigued by such a prospect, Chou allegedly sent an e-mail to Hartmann on March 13, 1997, outlining the "core technology" that YFP would need to complete a deal, including:

1. The design and assembly of bioreactor with an agreed scale
2. Light requirement
3. Media requirement for growth and production
4. Operating mode for the process, such as batch or continuous
5. Yield, such as cell density, titers, taxane constitution
6. Duration of culture to reach the maximal yield
7. Scientific names of yew species which are applicable to the bioreactor.
8. Cell lines excluded!!!

Chou also allegedly told Hartmann that she would offer $400,000 in cash, stock, and royalties to the Bristol-Myers scientist in exchange for his disclosure of the Taxol secrets. In addition, Chou and Hsu purportedly began making arrangements for a 1997 meeting between the parties, the purpose of which was for YFP to establish the authenticity of the "corrupt" scientist and to determine whether Hartmann really could produce the Taxol trade secrets that Chou and Hsu had requested.

Hartmann agreed to a meeting, and on June 14, 1997, he and the Bristol-Myers scientist met with three representatives from YFP, including Hsu, Ho, and another unidentified scientist, at the Four Seasons Hotel in Philadelphia. Ho was a professor of biotechnology and the Director of the Biotechnology Innovation Center at the National Chiao Tung University in Taiwan, and he had apparently been asked to evaluate the Taxol technology at the meeting as a favor to YFP.

The indictment alleges that the bulk of the June 14 meeting consisted of detailed discussions regarding the manufacturing processes for Taxol. The Bristol-Myers scientist explained the background and history of Taxol production, and displayed copies of Bristol-Myers documents outlining specific technological processes and scientific data pertaining to the manufacture of the drug. According to the indictment, these documents contained trade secrets and were "clearly marked with Bristol-Myers identification as well as the block stamped word 'CONFIDENTIAL.' " Hsu, Ho, and the other YFP employee reviewed the documents during the meeting and purportedly asked the Bristol-Myers scientist "numerous" questions regarding specific areas of Taxol technology. Finally, after Hartmann and the Bristol-Myers scientist left the room, the FBI rushed in and arrested Hsu and Ho at the hotel.

The indictment returned by the grand jury charged Hsu, Ho, and Chou with six counts of wire fraud in violation of 18 U.S.C. § 1343, one count of general federal conspiracy in violation of 18 U.S.C. § 371, two counts of foreign and interstate travel to facilitate commercial bribery in violation of 18 U.S.C. § 1952(a)(3), one count of aiding and abetting in violation of 18 U.S.C. § 2, and, most importantly for our purposes, two counts of criminal activity under the Economic Espionage Act of 1996 ("the EEA"), including attempted theft of trade secrets, and a conspiracy to steal trade secrets, in violation of 18 U.S.C. §§ 1832(a)(4) and (a)(5).

B. The Government's Motion to Maintain the Confidentiality of the Bristol-Myers Trade Secrets

Shortly after the indictment was returned, the defense requested in discovery a copy of the Bristol-Myers documents disclosed to Hsu and Ho at the June 14 meeting. However, on August 12, 1997, the government filed a motion pursuant to 18 U.S.C. § 1835 and Fed.R.Crim.P. 16(d)(1) for a protective order to prevent the disclosure of the Bristol-Myers trade secrets allegedly contained in those documents. The government proposed that the district court enter an order under which the trial judge would review the documents and the proposed redactions by Bristol-Myers *in camera*, and would then permit redactions of proprietary secret information. The documents as redacted would be used at trial. The gravamen of the government's contention was that the defendants had no need for the actual trade secrets themselves, because they had been charged only with attempt and conspiracy to steal trade secrets, rather than with the actual theft of trade secrets, under the EEA.

The defendants maintained, though, that unique constitutional and procedural requirements of criminal prosecutions dictated full access to the documents shown to them during the investigation. The defendants also contended that they needed the documents to establish the defense of legal impossibility, arguing that they could not be convicted of attempting to steal trade secrets if the documents did not actually contain trade secrets. Therefore, they proposed an order under which the proprietary information in the Bristol-Myers documents would be disclosed, but only to select members of the defense team, such as the defendants' attorneys and trial experts, and under which the documents would be filed under seal and returned or destroyed at the end of the case.

The district court agreed with the defendants and adopted their version of the proposed protective order. *See United States v. Hsu*, 982 F.Supp. 1022 (E.D.Pa.1997). The court held that legal impossibility is not a viable defense to the crime of attempted theft of trade secrets under the EEA, and it thus rejected the defendants' argument that they needed the documents to establish that claim. *Id.* at 1028-29. Nevertheless, it ordered the government to divulge the alleged trade secrets, because it found that the existence of a trade secret is an essential element of the crime of the *theft* of trade secrets, and that the existence of a trade secret in that prosecution is "a question of fact which the defendants have the right to have a jury decide." *Id.* at 1024. Believing the defendants to be charged both with actual theft and attempted theft of trade secrets, the court concluded that "if during discovery we deny to the defendants complete access to the Taxol technology, we inhibit their constitutional right to effective cross-examination as well as their right to have a jury, rather than a judge, determine whether a 'trade secret' exists." *Id.* at 1025. Therefore, the court held, the defendants "are entitled to review the June 14th documents to the extent of their constitutional rights." *Id.* at 1029.

The district court's opinion "encourage[d]" the government to file an interlocutory appeal to clarify the "unsettled and important questions of law" raised by this case. *Id.* at 1022 n. 1. Accordingly, the government appealed the district court's Order on November 25, 1997, pursuant to a section in the EEA providing that "[a]n interlocutory appeal by the United States shall lie from a decision or order of a district court authorizing or directing the disclosure of any trade secret." 18 U.S.C. § 1835. We now have jurisdiction under that section, and we exercise plenary review over the novel legal questions presented by the government's appeal. *In re Grand Jury*, 111 F.3d 1066, 1069 n. 4 (3d Cir.1997).

We note at the outset that we disagree with the district court as to the offenses charged. The indictment is limited to charging the defendants with attempt and conspiracy and contains no charge of actual theft of trade secrets. As we will discuss below, we believe this changes the analysis greatly. We begin, though, with an overview of the EEA and an analysis of the relevant statutory provisions.

## II. THE ECONOMIC ESPIONAGE ACT OF 1996

The EEA became law in October 1996 against a backdrop of increasing threats to corporate security and a rising tide of international and domestic economic espionage. The end of the Cold War sent government spies scurrying to the private sector to perform illicit work for businesses and corporations, S.Rep. No. 104-359, at 7 (1996), and by 1996, studies revealed that nearly $24 billion of corporate intellectual property was being stolen each year. Richard J. Heffernan & Dan T. Swartwood, *Trends in Intellectual Property Loss* 4, 15 (1996).

The problem was augmented by the absence of any comprehensive federal remedy targeting the theft of trade secrets, compelling prosecutors to shoehorn economic espionage crimes into statutes directed at other offenses.

For example, the government often sought convictions under the National Stolen Property Act ("NSPA"), 18 U.S.C. § 2314, or the mail and wire fraud statutes, 18 U.S.C. §§ 1341 and 1343. However, the NSPA "was drafted at a time when computers, biotechnology, and copy machines did not even exist," S.Rep. No. 104-359, at 10, and industrial espionage often occurred without the use of mail or wire. Consequently, it soon became clear to legislators and commentators alike that a new federal strategy was needed to combat the increasing prevalence of espionage in corporate America. Congress recognized "the importance of developing a systematic approach to the problem of economic espionage," H. Rep. No. 104-788, at 7 (1996), *reprinted in* 1996 U.S.C.C.A.N. 4021, 4025, and stressed that "[o]nly by adopting a national scheme to protect U.S. proprietary economic information can we hope to maintain our industrial and economic edge and thus safeguard our national security." S.Rep. No. 104-359, at 11. The House and Senate thus passed the Economic Espionage Act, and the President signed the bill into law on October 11, 1996.

The EEA consists of nine sections which protect proprietary information from misappropriation. Three sections are of particular import to our analysis: what acts are penalized by the statute, how the law defines a "trade secret," and when trade secrets are to remain confidential.

A. Criminal activities

The EEA criminalizes two principal categories of corporate espionage, including "Economic espionage" as defined by 18 U.S.C. § 1831, and the "Theft of trade secrets" as defined by § 1832. The former provision punishes those who knowingly misappropriate, or attempt or conspire to misappropriate, trade secrets with the intent or knowledge that their offense will benefit a foreign government, foreign instrumentality, or foreign agent. The legislative history indicates that § 1831 is designed to apply only when there is "evidence of foreign government sponsored or coordinated intelligence activity." 142 Cong. Rec. S12,212 (daily ed. Oct. 2, 1996) (Managers' Statement for H.R. 3723). By contrast, § 1832, the section under which the defendants are charged, is a general criminal trade secrets provision. It applies to anyone who knowingly engages in the theft of trade secrets, or an attempt or conspiracy to do so, "with intent to convert a trade secret, that is related to or included in a product that is produced for or placed in interstate or foreign commerce, to the economic benefit of anyone other than the owner thereof, and intending or knowing that the offense will, injure any owner of that trade secret." Section 1832(a) makes clear that attempt and conspiracy are distinct offenses, and it lists them separately from those acts that constitute completed crimes under the statute.

Section 1832 also contains at least three additional limitations not found in § 1831. First, a defendant charged under § 1832 must intend to convert a trade secret "to the economic benefit of anyone other than the owner thereof," including the defendant himself. This "economic benefit" requirement differs from § 1831, which states merely that the offense "benefit," in any manner, a foreign government, instrumentality, or agent. Therefore, prosecutions under § 1832 uniquely require that the defendant intend to confer an economic benefit on the defendant or another person or entity. Second, § 1832 states that the defendant must intend or know that the offense will injure an owner of the trade secret, a restriction not found in § 1831. The legislative history indicates that this requires "that the actor knew or was aware to a practical certainty that his conduct would cause such a result." S.Rep. No. 104-359, at 15. Finally, unlike § 1831, § 1832 also requires that the trade secret be "related to or included in a product that is produced for or placed in interstate or foreign commerce."

B. What constitutes a "trade secret"

The EEA defines a "trade secret" to expressly extend protection to the misappropriation of intangible information for the first time under federal law. 18 U.S.C. § 1839(3) provides that a "trade secret" means:

all forms and types of financial, business, scientific, technical, economic, or engineering information, including patterns, plans, compilations, program devices, formulas, designs, prototypes, methods, techniques, processes, procedures, programs, or codes, whether tangible or intangible, and whether or how stored, compiled, or memorialized physically, electronically, graphically, photographically, or in writing if-

(A) the owner thereof has taken reasonable measures to keep such information secret; and

(B) the information derives independent economic value, actual or potential, from not being generally known to, and not being readily ascertainable through proper means by, the public.

The EEA's definition of a "trade secret" is similar to that found in a number of state civil statutes and the Uniform Trade Secrets Act ("UTSA"), a model ordinance which permits civil actions for the misappropriation of trade secrets. There are, though, several critical differences which serve to broaden the EEA's scope. First, and most importantly, the EEA protects a wider variety of technological and intangible information than current civil laws. Trade secrets are no longer restricted to formulas, patterns, and compilations, but now include programs and codes, "whether tangible or intangible, and whether or how stored." Second, the EEA alters the relevant party from whom proprietary information must be kept confidential. Under the UTSA, information classified as a "trade secret" cannot be generally known by businesspersons or competitors of the trade secret owner. UTSA § 1(4). The EEA, however, indicates that a trade secret must not be generally known to, or readily ascertainable by, the general public, rather than simply those who can obtain economic value from the secret's disclosure or use. Finally, the EEA contains a definition crafted to reach only illicit behavior. Although legislators eliminated language providing that general knowledge, skills, and experience are not "trade secrets," 142 Cong. Rec. S12,213 (daily ed. Oct. 2, 1996) (Managers' Statement), it is clear that Congress did not intend the definition of a trade secret to be so broad as to prohibit lawful competition such as the use of general skills or parallel development of a similar product. *See, e.g., id.* at S12,212 (noting that "[t]his legislation does not in any way prohibit companies, manufacturers, or inventors from using their skills, knowledge and experience to solve a problem or invent a product that they know someone else is working on").

C. Preservation of confidentiality

The EEA also contains a provision designed to preserve the confidentiality of trade secrets during criminal prosecutions. 18 U.S.C. § 1835 states that a court:

*shall* enter such orders and take such other action as may be necessary and appropriate to preserve the confidentiality of trade secrets, consistent with the requirements of the Federal Rules of Criminal and Civil Procedure, the Federal Rules of Evidence, and all other applicable laws. An interlocutory appeal by the United States shall lie from a decision or order of a district court authorizing or directing the disclosure of any trade secret. (emphasis added).

This section does not, of course, abrogate existing constitutional and statutory protections for criminal defendants. It does, however, represent a clear indication from Congress that trade secrets are to be protected to the fullest extent during EEA litigation. Moreover, it further encourages enforcement actions by protecting owners who might otherwise "be reluctant to cooperate in prosecutions for fear of further exposing their trade secrets to public view, thus further devaluing or even destroying their worth." H.R. Rep. No. 104-788, at 13, 1996 U.S.C.C.A.N. at 4032. Therefore, as with the definition of trade secrets, the confidentiality provision aims to strike a balance between the protection of proprietary information and the unique considerations inherent in criminal prosecutions.

## III. DISCUSSION

With this statutory framework in mind, we turn our attention to determining whether the district court properly ordered the government to disclose the alleged trade secrets in this case. We begin by recognizing that the defendants are charged only with attempting to steal, and conspiring to steal, trade secrets under § 1832. The district court believed that the defendants were charged with both attempted theft of trade secrets as well as with "the *completed* offense of unauthorized conveyance of a trade secret under 18 U.S.C. § 1832(2)." 982 F.Supp. at 1023 (emphasis added). It thus found that the defendants' constitutional rights to cross-examination and a fair trial would be violated absent full disclosure of the Bristol-Myers documents.

However, the district court's analysis represents an incorrect reading of the indictment and a mistaken view of the charges lodged under the EEA. For one thing, there is no § 1832(2) in the statute. More importantly, the defendants are *not* charged with the completed offense of theft of trade secrets. They have been indicted only for *attempting* to steal, and *conspiring* to steal, trade secrets pursuant to §§ 1832(a)(4) and (a)(5). Therefore, our task is to examine the defendants' entitlement to the information they seek, as defending against the attempt and conspiracy provisions of the EEA, rather than the completed theft provisions. We need not decide, as the district court did, whether a failure to disclose trade secrets would undermine the constitutional rights of defendants charged with a completed offense under the statute.

The defendants argue that unfettered access to confidential documents is required even in EEA prosecutions for attempt and conspiracy. They assert that documents containing trade secrets are "material to the preparation of the defendant's defense," and therefore, that they must be disclosed consistent with the terms of Fed.R.Crim.P. 16(a)(1)(C). In particular, they contend that disclosure is warranted by (1) the availability of a legal impossibility defense, and (2) their need for access to the proprietary information as it relates to their defense of the allegations of the indictment and other defenses to the crimes charged.

### A. Legal Impossibility: The Relationship of the Existence of Trade Secrets to the Crimes Charged

As previously mentioned, the district court believed that the defendants had been charged with the substantive offense of theft of trade secrets, and, without addressing in any detail the EEA's concern for confidentiality of trade secrets in prosecutions under the statute, concluded that the defendants' constitutional rights required disclosure of the redacted material. The court premised its view on the fact that the existence of a trade secret was an element of the offense, and that the defendants thus had a constitutional right to access the alleged secrets based on the due process and fair trial guarantees of the Fifth and Sixth Amendments. We need not determine whether the district court was correct in its ruling, because the crimes actually charged do not include the substantive offense of theft of trade secrets. Rather, the crimes charged-attempt and conspiracy-do not require proof of the existence of an actual trade secret, but, rather, proof only of one's attempt or conspiracy with intent to steal a trade secret. 18 U.S.C. § 1832(a). We must determine how and to what extent this alters the analytic landscape, including statutory and policy considerations regarding confidentiality under the EEA, and principles of disclosure of material information under the federal criminal rules.

It should be noted at the outset that the confidentiality provision of the EEA does not exist in a vacuum. As the EEA provides in § 1835, confidentiality must coexist with or be tempered by other principles of the law, including a defendant's constitutional rights and the Federal Rules of Criminal Procedure. Therefore, we must first ask whether the non-disclosure of trade secret data does have implications if a defendant is defending against charges of attempt and conspiracy to steal trade secrets. The answer lies in the resolution of the question of whether the nonexistence of a trade secret matters in defense of an attempt or conspiracy crime. If the defense of legal impossibility is viable-that is, if the defendants are not guilty of attempt if the material is not truly a trade secret-then it could matter, and the defendants' constitutional or statutory rights could be implicated. If the defense of legal impossibility is not cognizable, then the existence or nonexistence of an actual trade secret is of little consequence for an attempt or conspiracy crime. Thus, we will first address the threshold question of whether legal impossibility is a defense to crimes of attempt and conspiracy, as this discussion frames the remainder of our analysis.

1. Attempt

The defendants' primary contention in the district court, and one of their principal arguments on appeal, is that they need to view the unredacted Taxol documents to prove their defense of legal impossibility. They assert that they can successfully defend against a charge of attempt to steal trade secrets if the documents used at the June 14, 1997, meeting did not actually contain trade secrets. Only by disclosure can they determine whether the materials did, in fact, contain proprietary information, and therefore mount their defense.

The law of impossible attempts has received much scholarly attention, but remains a murky area of the law. The common law distinguishes between two types of impossibilities-legal and factual-and provides that the former is a defense while the latter is not. In this regard, "[l]egal impossibility is said to occur where the intended acts, even if completed, would not amount to a crime." *United States v. Berrigan*, 482 F.2d 171, 188 (3d Cir.1973). By contrast, "factual impossibility is said to occur when extraneous circumstances unknown to the actor or beyond his control prevent consummation of the intended crime." *Id.* For example, legal impossibility occurs when A shoots a corpse believing it to be alive and intending to commit murder; the attempt does not amount to murder even if completed. Factual impossibility occurs when A fires a gun at a bed intending to kill V, and V is not on the bed; the crime cannot be completed because of extraneous factors beyond A's control.

The difficulty, of course, is that the distinction between factual and legal impossibility is essentially a matter of semantics, for *every* case of legal impossibility can reasonably be characterized as a factual impossibility. For instance, the fact that A shoots a corpse, rather than a person, is also a product of circumstances beyond A's control; A did not commit murder because the person he intended to kill was already dead. Likewise, in the case at bar, the defendants argue that their crimes would have been legally impossible if the redacted portions of the June 14 documents did not contain trade secrets. Yet this could just as easily be characterized as a factual impossibility, because extraneous circumstances unknown to the defendants, i.e., that documents they believed to contain trade secrets really did not, would have prevented the consummation of their crime.

As a result, the great majority of jurisdictions have now recognized that legal and factual impossibility are "logically indistinguishable," *United States v. Darnell*, 545 F.2d 595, 597 (8th Cir.1976), and have abolished impossibility as a defense. *See, e.g., United States v. Quijada*, 588 F.2d 1253, 1255 (9th Cir.1978) (eschewing any effort to distinguish between the two concepts); *United States v. Duran*, 884 F.Supp. 577, 580 n. 5 (D.D.C.1995) (noting that "categorizing a case as involving legal versus factual impossibility is difficult, if not pointless."), *aff'd*, 96 F.3d 1495 (D.C.Cir.1996).

In fact, we are the only circuit which continues to recognize a common law defense of legal impossibility. We established its validity in *United States v. Berrigan*, 482 F.2d at 190, where we held that legal impossibility is a defense to certain crimes of attempt. *Berrigan* involved a federal prisoner convicted of attempting to smuggle letters in and out of a federal prison without the knowledge and consent of the warden, in violation of 18 U.S.C. § 1791 and 28 C.F.R. § 6.1. The evidence showed that the defendant used another prisoner on study-release as a courier for his mail, believing all along that the warden was not aware of the duo's scheme. However, the warden had learned of the defendant's first correspondence, and, working with the police, he allowed the courier to carry all subsequent letters with his knowledge and consent. Thus, the defendant argued that his crime was legally impossible; he had been charged with attempt to smuggle letters without the warden's knowledge and consent, and yet the warden both knew and consented to the crime.

On appeal, we agreed with the defendant and held that his crime was legally impossible. We recognized that "elimination of impossibility as a defense . . . is consistent with the overwhelming modern view," 482 F.2d at 186 (quotation omitted), but we concluded that legal impossibility remains a valid defense to common law crimes of attempt in this circuit. Emphasizing that "[f]ederal criminal law is purely statutory," *id.* at 185, we wrote that we had no choice but to recognize a defense of legal impossibility in the absence of a federal statute providing otherwise. *Id.* at 190. Therefore, we stated, "attempting to do that which is not a crime is not attempting to commit a crime." *Id.*

In subsequent years, however, we have explored and defined *Berrigan*'s reach and have recognized exceptions to the *Berrigan* rule. In *United States v. Everett*, we held that legal impossibility was "no defense to the charge of attempted distribution of a controlled substance under 21 U.S.C. § 846 (1976)." 700 F.2d 900, 908 (3d Cir.1983). In that case, a jury convicted the defendant of attempting to distribute the drug phenyl-2-propanone in violation of the Comprehensive Drug Abuse

Prevention and Control Act ("the Drug Control Act"). However, the liquid Everett gave to an undercover agent was not, in fact, a controlled substance. Relying on *Berrigan*, Everett thus argued that his conviction should be set aside as having been legally impossible; he was convicted of an attempt to distribute drugs, but the substance he distributed was not actually a narcotic.

We rejected Everett's argument and held that *Berrigan* did not apply to the Drug Control Act. We noted that *Berrigan* was a case of statutory interpretation, and we found that we should limit its reasoning to the particular law in that case (18 U.S.C. § 1791). As our opinion stated, "[w]e cannot rest on *Berrigan*'s interpretation of what Congress meant by the word 'attempts' when it enacted 18 U.S.C. § 1791. Instead we must examine legislative intent anew. If Congress chose in enacting [the Drug Control Act] to define 'attempt' to punish efforts to [distribute narcotics] regardless of impossibility, that intent governs." 700 F.2d at 904. Therefore, we reviewed the legislative history of the Drug Control Act, and we concluded that "Congress intended to eliminate the defense of impossibility when it enacted section 846." *Id.*

We agree with *Everett*'s analysis and we believe it should be employed in this case. Consistent with *Everett*, we should resort to legislative intent to determine whether Congress meant to permit a defense of impossibility to an "attempt" crime under the EEA. When Congress uses a common law term such as "attempt," we generally presume that it intended to adopt the term's widely-accepted common law meaning, including any common law defenses such as impossibility. *United States v. Cicco*, 10 F.3d 980, 984 (3d Cir.1993). However, as *Everett* recognized, "the courts will not impose that meaning if there are 'grounds for inferring an affirmative instruction from Congress' to define it otherwise." 700 F.2d at 904 (quoting *Morissette v. United States*, 342 U.S. 246, 273, 72 S.Ct. 240, 96 L.Ed. 288 (1952)).

After reviewing the legislative history of the EEA, we conclude that Congress did not intend to allow legal impossibility to be asserted as a defense to attempt crimes created by its terms. Congress never spoke directly as to why it used the term "attempt," or as to the issue of legal impossibility, in any of the reports or debates on the statute. We find, however, that, as we held in *Everett*, the underlying purposes of the law provide substantial evidence of a congressional intent that the defense of legal impossibility should not apply.

One of the key findings in *Everett* was that the Drug Control Act was designed to offer a "comprehensive" solution to narcotics offenses. 700 F.2d at 906-07. We concluded from this that Congress could not have intended to adopt the impossibility defense, "whose viability at common law was questionable at best," because doing so would only "hamper federal efforts to enforce the drug laws." *Id.* at 907.

Here, the very same goals, and the very same language, appear throughout the legislative history of the EEA. Just as the Drug Control Act embraced a "comprehensive" solution for drug trafficking, so too does the EEA attempt to provide a "comprehensive" mechanism for curtailing the escalating threat of corporate espionage. The Senate Report includes an entire section entitled "Need for a Comprehensive Federal Law," and "underscore[s] the importance of developing a systematic approach to the problem of economic espionage." S.Rep. No. 104-359, at 11. The Report notes that "a Federal criminal statute will provide a comprehensive approach to [the theft of trade secrets]-with clear extraterritoriality, criminal forfeiture, and import-export sanction provisions." *Id.* at 12. Likewise, the House Report states that the EEA is designed to provide a "systematic approach" to trade secret theft, and asserts that "a comprehensive federal criminal statute will better facilitate the investigation and prosecution of this crime." H.R.Rep. No. 104-788, at 7, 1996 U.S.C.C.A.N. at 4025. The House also explained that the EEA was crafted to punish virtually every form of illegal industrial espionage, "from the foreign government that uses its classic espionage apparatus to spy on a company, to the two American companies that are attempting to uncover each other's bid proposals, or to the disgruntled former employee who walks out of his former company with a computer diskette full of engineering schematics." *Id.* at 5, 1996 U.S.C.C.A.N. at 4024.

In an effort to undermine this evidence of intent, the defendants offer the statement of Senator Herbert Kohl, a co-sponsor of the trade secrets legislation, who commented that the EEA should "only be used in flagrant and egregious cases of information theft." 142 Cong. Rec. S12,212 (daily ed. Oct. 2, 1996). The defendants contend that this demonstrates an intent to limit the statute's reach. However, the Senator's remarks are taken out of context. His entire statement reads, in pertinent part, as follows:

> [W]e have carefully drafted these measures to ensure that they can only be used in flagrant and egregious cases of information theft. Moreover, trade secrets are carefully defined so that the general knowledge and experience that a person gains from working at a job is not covered.
>
> Mr. President, we do not want this law used to stifle the free flow of information or of people from job to job. But we built in a number of safeguards to prevent exactly these problems.

*Id.* Senator Kohl did not intend to limit the statute's comprehensive scope. He meant merely to allay any fears that the government would use the EEA to police clearly innocuous and otherwise lawful behavior, such as occurs when employees change jobs or start their own companies using general knowledge that they have acquired through prior employment. *See, e.g.,* Sen. Rep. No. 104-359, at 12 (clarifying that the EEA "does not apply to innocent innovators or to individuals who seek to capitalize on their lawfully developed knowledge, skill or abilities"). We do not read Senator Kohl's comments a undermining the comprehensiveness of the statute as it pertains to the theft of trade secrets. We believe that the great weight of the EEA's legislative history evinces an intent to create a comprehensive solution to economic espionage, and we find it highly unlikely that Congress would have wanted the courts to thwart that solution by permitting defendants to assert the common law defense of legal impossibility.

We also find it significant, as *Everett* did, that the statute we are considering was drafted at a time when "the doctrine of impossibility had become mired in fine distinctions and had lost whatever acceptance at common law it may have possessed when the statute considered in *Berrigan* was first enacted in 1930." 700 F.2d at 905. The EEA was drafted in 1996, more than twenty-five years after the National Commission on Reform of the Federal Criminal Laws had concluded that the abolition of legal impossibility was already "the overwhelming modern position." *Id.*

(quotation omitted). In fact, to this day, "[a]side from the Third Circuit in *Berrigan*, *every* Circuit that has considered the defense of impossibility has rejected it." *Duran*, 884 F.Supp. at 580 (emphasis added). Thus, we doubt that Congress meant to permit legal impossibility to be asserted as a defense to EEA crimes.

Finally, we are mindful, as *Everett* was, 700 F.2d at 907 n. 16, of the potential damage that the defendants' position could work on law enforcement under the statute. If we were to hold that legal impossibility is a defense to the attempted theft of trade secrets, the government would be compelled to use actual trade secrets during undercover operations in order to obtain convictions under § 1832(a)(4). Aside from the logistical difficulties this would create, it would also have the bizarre effect of forcing the government to disclose trade secrets to the very persons suspected of trying to steal them, thus gutting enforcement efforts under the EEA. We believe Congress could not have intended such a result, inasmuch as it was striving to prevent economic espionage and to maintain the confidentiality of trade secrets. Therefore, given the strong indicia of legislative intent, and given the practical import of a contrary finding, we conclude that Congress could not have intended EEA attempt crimes to be subject to the somewhat obscure and rarely used common law defense of legal impossibility.

Accordingly, we hold that legal impossibility is not a defense to a charge of attempted misappropriation of trade secrets in violation of 18 U.S.C. § 1832(a)(4). We agree with the district court's conclusion that a charge of "attempt" under the EEA requires proof of the same elements used in other modern attempt statutes, including the Model Penal Code. A defendant is guilty of attempting to misappropriate trade secrets if, "acting with the kind of culpability otherwise required for commission of the crime, he . . . purposely does or omits to do anything that, under the circumstances as he believes them to be, is an act or omission constituting a substantial step in a course of conduct planned to culminate in his commission of the crime." Model Penal Code § 5.01(1)(c) (1985). Thus, the defendant must (1) have the intent needed to commit a crime defined by the EEA, and must (2) perform an act amounting to a "substantial step" toward the commission of that crime. *See Cicco*, 10 F.3d at 984-85 (attempt crimes require a showing of intent and "evidence of conduct constituting a substantial step toward commission of the crime in pursuit of the culpable intent"); *Everett*, 700 F.2d at 908 (conviction for attempt requires proof of intent and "some measure of objective evidence corroborating the attempted" crime).

It naturally follows that the government need not prove that an actual trade secret was used during an EEA investigation, because a defendant's culpability for a charge of attempt depends only on "the circumstances as he believes them to be," not as they really are. The government can satisfy its burden under § 1832(a)(4) by proving beyond a reasonable doubt that the defendant sought to acquire information which he or she believed to be a trade secret, regardless of whether the information actually qualified as such. Consequently, in the instant case, the defendants have no arguable constitutional or statutory right to view the unredacted portion of the Taxol documents in order to defend against charges of attempt on the basis of legal impossibility.

2. Conspiracy

We also hold that the defendants have no need for the Taxol documents to defend against the government's charges of conspiracy, because we conclude that legal impossibility is not a defense to conspiracy. Although we have stated that impossibility may be a valid defense to attempt crimes, *Berrigan*, 482 F.2d at 190, we have never recognized the defense for conspiracy charges, and we are persuaded by the views of our district courts, and by the decisions of our sister circuits, that the impossibility of achieving the goal of a conspiracy is irrelevant to the crime itself. [Citations omitted.]

It is well-settled that conspiracy and attempt serve different roles in the criminal law. The law of attempts was traditionally viewed as a way "to deal with conduct which create[d] a risk of immediate harmful consequences." Wayne R. LaFave & Austin W. Scott, Jr., *Substantive Criminal Law*, § 6.5(b), at 91 (2d ed.1986). Even under the modern view, attempt prosecutions generally proceed only against those who have taken a "substantial step" toward commission of a substantive crime. *See* Model Penal Code § 5.01(1)(c) (1985). However, the law of conspiracy is much more preventive, aiming to nip criminal conduct in the bud before it has the chance to flourish into more ominous behavior. *See Wallach*, 935 F.2d at 470 (noting that conspiracy serves to protect society and prevent criminal behavior "in its early stages"); LaFave & Scott, *supra*, § 6.5(b), at 91 (stating that "[c]ourts have generally taken a broader view of the purposes of conspiracy"). As the Supreme Court has written,

> [t]he law of conspiracy identifies the agreement to engage in a criminal venture as an event of sufficient threat to social order to permit the imposition of criminal sanctions for the agreement alone, plus an overt act in pursuit of it, regardless of whether the crime agreed upon actually is committed. Criminal intent has crystallized, and the likelihood of actual, fulfilled commission warrants preventive action. *United States v. Feola*, 420 U.S. 671, 694, 95 S.Ct. 1255, 43 L.Ed.2d 541 (1975) [Citations omitted.].

It is thus the conspiratorial agreement itself, and not the underlying substantive acts, that forms the basis for conspiracy charges. *United States v. Jannotti*, 673 F.2d 578, 591 (3d Cir.1982) (en banc). The "illegality of the agreement does not depend on the achievement of its ends," and it is "irrelevant that the ends of the conspiracy were from the very inception of the agreement objectively unattainable." *Id.; see also United States v. Olgin*, 745 F.2d 263, 273 (3d Cir.1984) (stating that "the objective impossibility of attaining the goals of a conspiracy is irrelevant to the guilt of those who conspire"). Consequently, it is equally irrelevant that the commission of a substantive offense may have been legally impossible for the conspiracy to achieve all along. We therefore join our sister circuits, and the district courts in our own circuit, in squarely holding that legal impossibility is not a defense to conspiracy.

Second, in *O'Kelley v. United States*, the Eighth Circuit held that several defendants could not be convicted of a conspiracy to steal goods in interstate commerce where the goods were not in interstate commerce. 116 F.2d 966, 968 (8th Cir.1941). However, this statement was also dicta, because there was no jurisdiction to prosecute the defendants absent proof of an effect on interstate commerce, and, as in *Ventimiglia*, there was no showing that the defendants possessed the requisite criminal intent.

Finally, in *Woo Wai v. United States*, the Ninth Circuit reversed a conviction for a conspiracy to smuggle aliens into the U.S., because, *inter alia*, the act would not have been a crime even if completed. 223 F. 412, 414-15 (9th Cir.1915). Yet *Woo Wai* was an entrapment case, and any references to the impossibility of the crime were wholly extraneous to the holding. Moreover, to the extent that *Woo Wai* states that impossibility is a defense to conspiracy in the Ninth Circuit, the Ninth Circuit has since rejected that claim expressly. *See, e.g., Everett*, 692 F.2d at 599; *United States v. Sanford*, 547 F.2d 1085, 1091 (9th Cir.1976).

As a result, the Taxol trade secrets in the Bristol-Myers documents are not "material" to the preparation of the defendants' impossibility defense, because proof that the defendants sought to steal actual trade secrets is not an element of the crimes of attempt or conspiracy under the EEA. A defendant can be convicted of attempt or conspiracy pursuant to 18 U.S.C. §§ 1832(a)(4) or (a)(5) even if his intended acts were legally impossible.

B. Relevance of Purported Secret Information to Other Aspects of the Defense Strategy

Having concluded that the defendants' right to access actual trade secrets is not required in order to defend against an element of the government's case, the question remains whether the defendants' right of access to the information as it relates to other defenses passes muster under the test of materiality. The defendants argue that the unredacted documents are also material to the preparation of the potential defenses of entrapment, outrageous government conduct, and jurisdiction, and contend that the documents are needed to defend against the elements of attempt and conspiracy, the allegations of the indictment, and the evidence that the government intends to introduce at trial.

As an initial matter, we note that we are skeptical of the materiality, let alone relevance, of the redacted trade secret information to these issues. For example, the defendants argue that they need the unredacted documents to disprove the intent and "substantial step" elements of attempt and the "overt act" requirement of conspiracy. However, proof of these factors is necessarily independent of any trade secrets contained in the Bristol-Myers documents, because the defendants can be guilty of attempt and conspiracy to steal trade secrets even if the documents contained no confidential information at all. *See* MPC § 5.01(1)(c) (attempt), § 5.02(1)(a) (conspiracy).

However, we will not address defendants' claim of need for the redactions as to any other defense or aspect of the case for two reasons. First, the defendants never raised the materiality of the redacted information as to any other defenses before the district court, and the court never addressed these other arguments in its opinion. The defendants' briefs to the district court argued only that the government must prove the existence of an actual trade secret in a prosecution for attempt and conspiracy and that legal impossibility remains a viable defense. We will not examine other contentions as to the materiality or relevance of trade secret information that are being raised for the first time on appeal. *See Harris v. City of Philadelphia*, 35 F.3d 840, 845 (3d Cir.1994) ("This court has consistently held that it will not consider issues that are raised for the first time on appeal.").

Further, no one-not this Court, not the district court, not even the parties themselves-knows the content of the redacted Bristol-Myers documents at issue in this case. It was stated at oral argument that the documents have been reviewed and edited for trade secrets by Bristol-Myers employees alone, without any oversight by the court, the government, or the defense. Thus, while we might be skeptical of the defendants' asserted need for this information, we will not decide whether they have a right to access documents that could conceivably reveal information needed to preserve their rights to a fair trial. Only defense counsel know the precise contours of the defendants' case, and we are not in a position to make judgments about the impact of the redacted material without having seen the material ourselves.

Accordingly, we will remand this action to the district court. If the defendants raise before the district court the additional arguments that they have urged on appeal, we would expect the district court to conduct an *in camera* review to determine whether the documents have been properly redacted to exclude only confidential information and to assess whether what was redacted is "material" to the defense.

In such event, because "public policy requires protection of portions of a document, . . . *in camera* inspection by the trial judge or magistrate is unavoidable." *Bogosian v. Gulf Oil Corp.*, 738 F.2d 587, 596 (3d Cir.1984). Even if proof of an actual trade secret is not an element of §§ 1832(a)(4) and (a)(5), an independent assessment of whether materials are nonetheless discoverable is anticipated in the language of § 1835, which provides that the district court "shall enter such orders and take such other action as may be necessary and appropriate to preserve the confidentiality of trade secrets, consistent with the requirements of the Federal Rules of Criminal and Civil Procedure, the Federal Rules of Evidence, and all other applicable laws." Rule 16(a)(1)(C) of the Federal Rules of Criminal Procedure enables the defendants to obtain documents in the government's possession that are material to the preparation of their defense, or are intended for use by the government as evidence in chief at trial. These principles suggest that the district court should examine the relevant portions of the Bristol-Myers documents to assess the materiality of those portions of the documents sought to be withheld. *See United States v. Bocra*, 623 F.2d 281, 285 (3d Cir.1980) ("The submission of discovery materials to the court for an *in camera* inspection and decision as to which materials are discoverable is commonly used when the Government's need for preserving confidentiality over the materials must be balanced with the defendant's constitutional right to evidence material to his defense."). We leave to the district court the ultimate resolution of these issues if raised on remand by the defendants.

## IV. CONCLUSION

The district court's Order dated October 27, 1997, will be reversed, and the cause will be remanded for further proceedings consistent with this opinion.

# UNITED STATES v. HSU

40 F. Supp. 2d 623 (E.D. Pa. 1999)

DALZELL, DISTRICT JUDGE.

Defendant Kai-Lo Hsu argues that the recently-enacted Economic Espionage Act, 18 U.S.C. § 1831 *et seq.* ("EEA"), is unconstitutionally vague. Hsu's motion to dismiss the EEA charges in Counts Ten and Eleven of the Indictment raises serious concerns about the scope and clarity of the EEA that we at some length address here.

Defendant's Vagueness Argument

Hsu is charged in the Indictment with, *inter alia*, conspiracy to steal trade secrets in violation of 18 U.S.C. § 1832(a)(5) (Count Ten), and attempted theft of trade secrets in violation of 18 U.S.C. § 1832(a)(4) (Count Eleven). In his motion to dismiss Counts Ten and Eleven of the Indictment, Hsu argues that the EEA is unconstitutionally vague in two respects. First, he contends that the statute is unlawfully vague in that it fails to define the term "related to or included in" a product that is produced for or placed in interstate or foreign commerce. *See* 18 U.S.C. § 1832(a) (highlighted above). Second, Hsu argues that the definition of "trade secret" in 18 U.S.C. § 1839(3) offends due process with its vagueness because it does not define either "reasonable measures" to keep the information secret, or what is meant by information not being "generally known" or "readily ascertainable" to the public. *See* 18 U.S.C. § 1839(3) (highlighted above).

The Legal Landscape

It is well-recognized that due process requires a penal statute to "define [a] criminal offense with sufficient definiteness that ordinary people can understand what conduct is prohibited and in a manner that does not encourage arbitrary and discriminatory enforcement." *Kolender v. Lawson*, 461 U.S. 352, 357, 103 S.Ct. 1855, 75 L.Ed.2d 903 (1983); *see also United States v. National Dairy Prods. Corp.*, 372 U.S. 29, 32–33, 83 S.Ct. 594, 9 L.Ed.2d 561 (1963) ("Void for vagueness simply means that criminal responsibility should not attach where one could not reasonably understand that his contemplated conduct is proscribed"); *United States v. Pungitore*, 910 F.2d 1084, 1104 (3d Cir.1990) ("A statute is unconstitutionally vague when it either forbids or requires the doing of an act in terms so vague that men of ordinary intelligence must necessarily guess as to its meaning and differ as to its application." (internal quotations omitted)). The void for vagueness doctrine, however, does not mean that a statute is unconstitutionally vague where "Congress might, without difficulty, have chosen 'clearer and more precise language' equally capable of achieving the end which it sought." *United States v. Powell*, 423 U.S. 87, 94, 96 S.Ct. 316, 46 L.Ed.2d 228 (1975) (quoting *United States v. Petrillo*, 332 U.S. 1, 7, 67 S.Ct. 1538, 91 L.Ed. 1877 (1947)).

It has also been the experience, as Professor Anthony Amsterdam observed almost forty years ago, that "legislation creating 'new' crimes (which does not generically tend to be unclear, but is likely to represent affirmative legislative intrusion into realms previously left to individual freedom) is particularly vulnerable to vagueness attack." Anthony G. Amsterdam, *The Void-for-Vagueness Doctrine in the Supreme Court*, 109 U.Pa.L.Rev. 67, 84 (1960) (citing, *e.g., Winters v. New York*, 333 U.S. 507, 519–20, 68 S.Ct. 665, 92 L.Ed. 840 (1948); *United States v. Reese*, 92 U.S. 214, 219, 23 L.Ed. 563 (1875)). The EEA certainly constitutes such legislation, criminalizing, as it does, conduct that heretofore was thought best left to the civil law of unfair competition and cognate jurisprudence.

The developed case law recognizes that when, as here, the First Amendment is not implicated, a void for vagueness challenge must be unconstitutional as applied to the defendant and "must be examined in light of the facts of the case at hand." *United States v. Mazurie*, 419 U.S. 544, 550, 95 S.Ct. 710, 42 L.Ed.2d 706 (1975); *United States v. Pungitore*, 910 F.2d 1084, 1104 (3d Cir.1990) (explaining that "[o]utside the First Amendment context, a party has standing to raise a vagueness challenge only insofar as the statute is vague as applied to his or her specific conduct" and citing Supreme Court cases such as *New York v. Ferber*, 458 U.S. 747, 767–69, 102 S.Ct. 3348, 73 L.Ed.2d 1113 (1982)).

Analysis

Before addressing the merits of Hsu's vagueness arguments as applied to the facts of this case, we must address two contentions defense counsel pressed at the March 8 hearing on this motion.

First, this particular case does not implicate free expression and its attending First Amendment jurisprudence. This case only concerns Hsu's alleged pursuit of taxol technology, more specifically, the plant cell tissue culture technology to make Taxol, from an allegedly corrupt Bristol-Myers Squibb ("BMS") employee. At the hearing, defense counsel contended that free expression issues are implicated here because Tibor A. Rasz, the BMS employee who aided the Government "sting" operation on June 14, 1997 by posing as a corrupt employee, has a right freely to express himself and exchange information with the defendant, or with anyone else he thinks is a potential employer. This argument must fail because Hsu does not have standing to raise Mr. Rasz's First Amendment rights. *See, e.g.*, John E. Nowak and Ronald D. Rotunda, *Constitutional Law* § 2.12(f) (5th ed.1995) (explaining the law of standing). Furthermore, even if Hsu had standing to champion such rights, in this case Mr. Rasz was knowingly participating in a Government sting operation and did not, for example, believe he was on a job interview with a potential employer. No First Amendment interests are in play here.

Second, at the hearing and in his reply brief, Hsu also argues that the EEA is overbroad because it stifles the free flow of ideas. *See* Def.'s Omnibus Reply at 8. While we are sympathetic to Hsu's argument, *see infra*, the Supreme Court has made it clear that "outside the limited First Amendment context, a criminal statute may not be attacked as overbroad." *Schall v. Martin*, 467 U.S. 253, 268 n. 18, 104 S.Ct. 2403, 81 L.Ed.2d 207 (1984); *see also United States v. Salerno*, 481 U.S. 739, 745, 107 S.Ct. 2095, 95 L.Ed.2d 697 (1987); *United States v. Raines*, 362 U.S. 17, 21, 80 S.Ct. 519, 4 L.Ed.2d 524 (1960).

"Related to or included in"

We reject Hsu's argument that the term "related to or included in a product that is produced for or placed in interstate or foreign commerce" is unacceptably vague. The cases he cites in support of his argument are all First Amendment decisions in which the only connection to what is at stake here is the fact that the cases involve the use of the term *related. See* Def.'s Mot. at 20–21 (citing First Amendment cases involving "gang related" symbols and "airport related" activities). We believe the term "related to or included in" is readily understandable to one of ordinary intelligence, particularly here where the defendant appears to be well versed as to the relationship (and technological differences) between "first generation" and "second generation" taxol technology. *See, e.g.*, Transcript of Meeting between Hsu and FBI Agent Hartmann, (Feb. 27, 1996), at DOJ232–33 (in which Hsu explains to Agent Hartmann why he is specifically interested in the "tissue culture" technology to make Taxol).

"Reasonable Measures"

Similarly, we also find that the EEA's definition of "trade secret" — requiring, in part, that the owner take "reasonable measures" to keep such information secret — is also not for use of that locution void for vagueness. First, a statute is not void for vagueness merely because it uses the word "reasonable" or "unreasonable". *See, e.g.*, U.S. Const. amend. IV (prohibiting "unreasonable searches and seizures"); 18 U.S.C. § 922(d)(8) (making it unlawful for any person to sell to, or dispose of, a firearm or ammunition to any person who the seller knows or has "reasonable cause" to believe that such person is engaged in other conduct that would place an intimate partner in "reasonable fear" of bodily injury). In sustaining the antitrust "rule of reason" as sufficiently definite even in a criminal prosecution, Justice Holmes observed, with his customary sensitivity to human frailty, that "the law is full of instances where a man's fate depends on his estimating rightly, that is, as the jury subsequently estimates it, some matter of degree. If his judgment is wrong, not only may he incur a fine or a short imprisonment . . . ; he may incur the penalty of death." *Nash v. United States*, 229 U.S. 373, 377, 33 S.Ct. 780, 57 L.Ed. 1232 (1913).

The Government has here pointed out that the definition of "trade secret" is taken, "with only minor modifications", from the definition used in the Uniform Trade Secret Act (UTSA), which has apparently been adopted in forty states and the District of Columbia, and the language has withstood at least one vagueness attack. *See* Government's Resp. at 33–34; *see also People v. Serrata*, 62 Cal.App.3d 9, 133 Cal.Rptr. 144 (Cal.Ct.App.1976) (upholding the constitutionality of California's criminal trade secret statute and explaining that the term "measures" in the statute is not unconstitutionally vague).

Finally, as applied here, it is clear that Hsu and his alleged co-conspirator, Jessica Chou, were told on several occasions (in e-mails, telephone conversations, and in-person meetings) that the taxol technology in question was proprietary to BMS and Phyton, could not be acquired via a license or joint venture (as the cost would be too high), and that they would have to "get [it] another way", namely, through an allegedly corrupt BMS employee. *See, e.g.*, Transcript of Meeting between Hsu and FBI Agent Hartmann, (Feb. 27, 1996), at DOJ240–41 (in which Agent Hartmann explains that BMS is keeping the taxol technology "close to their chest" and that a license or joint venture would be too expensive, and in which Hsu responds that "[w]e'll get another way"); *see also* E-mail from FBI Agent Hartmann to Jessica Chou (Nov. 16, 1995) (in which Agent Hartmann explains that "BMS [has] exercised an exclusive option on Phyton's proprietary plant cell culture technology"). Hsu thus knew that BMS had taken many steps to keep its technology to itself, and therefore he will not be heard to quibble with the ductility of "reasonable measures" as applied to him in this case.

"Generally known to" and "not being readily ascertainable" through proper means by the public

At the outset, the issue of whether "second generation" taxol technology is "generally known to" and not "readily ascertainable" to the public is a question that we (and the parties) have struggled with since the inception of this case. *See United States v. Hsu*, Crim. No. 97-323-01, 1999 WL 80952, at *1–*4 (E.D. Pa. Feb. 16, 1999) (explaining the tortuous procedural *629 history of this case). After the June 14, 1997 sting operation at the Four Seasons Hotel, in August, 1997 two BMS scientists, Dr. Nikhil Mehta and Dr. Norman Lacroix, were enlisted by BMS and the Government to review the documents shown to the defendant at the Four Seasons Hotel ("the June 14th documents") and to redact all "confidential" information contained therein. As our February 16, 1999 Memorandum illustrates, even Dr. Mehta and Dr. Lacroix could not agree about what information in the June 14th documents was "confidential" and what information was public. *See id.* at *2 n. 9 (citing twenty-one examples of inconsistencies in the redactions to the June 14th documents).

After an interlocutory appeal in which the Government soothingly assured the Court of Appeals panel that the redactions to the June 14th documents "consist of technical information that constitutes trade secrets under any definition", *see Hsu*, 155 F.3d at 197–98 n. 11, BMS enlisted Dr. Pallaiah Thammana, the Associate Director of Biotechnical Development at BMS, to undertake a complete reevaluation of the redactions to the June 14th documents. After Dr. Thammana's reevaluation of the June 14th documents, over *one hundred* pages that had previously been redacted by Dr. Mehta and Dr. Lacroix were then unredacted as public information. *See Hsu*, 1999 WL 80952 at *3 n. 11.

Finally, at the urging of our Court of Appeals, we undertook an *in camera* review of the redactions made to the June 14th documents. While we (perhaps immodestly) consider ourselves of "ordinary" intelligence, after an *in camera* review of the June 14th documents, in both their newly-redacted and unredacted forms, it became clear to us that "the issue of whether the June 14th documents had been properly redacted to exclude only trade secret information required technical expertise far beyond our capabilities." *See id.* at *3. Accordingly, with the consent of the parties, we enlisted the assistance of Dr. Kenneth Snader from the National Cancer Institute as our technical advisor to review the June 14th documents in both their redacted and unredacted forms. After his exhaustive analysis, Dr. Snader suggested that we unredact yet another ten pages in the June 14th documents because they are truly public information. *See id.* at *6–*9.

At oral argument on the current motion, we asked counsel for the Government to explain how the terms "generally known" and not "readily ascertainable" by the public could be anything but vague in relation to taxol technology, particularly given the ever-shrinking redactions to the June 14th documents against the very same "trade secret" definition. *See supra.* In response, counsel for the Government argued that while it was a difficult undertaking to determine whether the June 14th documents actually contained trade secret information within the meaning of the EEA, ultimately the trade secret status of the June 14th documents did not matter to the outcome of this case because Hsu is charged only with the inchoate offenses of attempt and conspiracy. *See* 18 U.S.C. § 1832(a)(4), (5). At oral argument, the Government pointed to our Court of Appeals's August, 1998 decision in which the panel made it clear that the Government need not prove at trial that an actual trade secret was used during the investigation, because the defendant's culpability for a charge of attempt depends only on the circumstances as the defendant *believes* them to be and not as they really are. *See Hsu,* 155 F.3d at 203–04 (explaining that the defendant can be guilty of attempt and conspiracy to steal trade secrets even if the June 14th documents contained no confidential information at all).

While the Government's position is legally accurate, it is quite troubling in the context of this particular statute. Unlike statutes that prohibit, for example, murder (or attempted murder), bribery (or attempted bribery), or distribution of cocaine (or conspiracy to distribute cocaine), where there is a clearly defined end (*e.g.*, the definitions of murder, bribery, and cocaine are fixed), here, where a "trade secret" is based on intangible and evolving concepts and ideas, and where the definition of a "trade secret" is based, in part, on what is "generally known" or "readily ascertainable" to the public, the analysis is considerably more problematic.

A hypothetical illustrates the difficulty of the Government's argument. Assume Congress passed a statute making it a crime to be "bad" or to "attempt to be bad" and the definition of "bad" was "what people generally know as really bad or evil." On its face, such a statute is palpably and unlawfully vague. Yet as applied to Dr. Hannibal "the cannibal" Lecter (in *The Silence of the Lambs*), such a statute would not be unconstitutionally vague, as all but the criminally insane would agree that Dr. Lecter is "bad". As applied to Little Mary Sunshine, however, such a statute would be unconstitutionally vague because no reasonable person would call her morally "bad".

Turning specifically to the EEA, it is in many ways more problematic than our badness statute because, unlike our imagined law, what is "generally known" and "reasonably ascertainable" about ideas, concepts, and technology is constantly evolving in the modern age. With the proliferation of the media of communication on technological subjects, and (still) in so many languages, what is "generally known" or "reasonably ascertainable" to the public at any given time is necessarily never sure.

Furthermore, when the EEA states that the information must be generally known and not readily ascertainable "by the public", to whom does it refer? The "general" public? The "scientific" public? The "commercial" public? The "judicial" public? Prior to this case we had not heard of the cancer drug Taxol (and had never heard of the plant cell culture process to produce it) — does that ignorance in and of itself make taxol technology not "generally known"? If a large quantity of information about taxol technology is available on the Internet and in published journals (which it is), or if those subjects were discussed at scientific conferences abroad (they were), do those realities make it "readily ascertainable"?

While we are thus much troubled by the EEA's vaporous terms, as applied to the facts of *this* case and *this* defendant we nevertheless find that the term "generally known to, and not being readily ascertainable through proper means by, the public," 18 U.S.C. § 1839(3), is not unconstitutionally vague. Based upon a careful review of the evidence that the Government will offer at trial, including e-mails, telephone conversations, and tape recordings of in-person meetings, it appears that Hsu knew (or at a minimum believed) that the "second generation" taxol information he was seeking to acquire was not "generally*631 known to" or "readily ascertainable through proper means by, the public." 18 U.S.C. § 1839(3). The e-mails, telephone calls, and conversations show a pattern whereby Hsu, along with his indicted co-conspirator, Jessica Chou, realized that they could not license or acquire the "second generation" taxol technology through legal or public means, and that they would have to acquire it from an allegedly corrupt BMS employee. In several of the conversations Hsu and Chou are unambiguously told that this undertaking is illegal. *See, e.g.*, Transcript of Meeting between Hsu and FBI Agent Hartmann, (Feb. 27, 1996), at DOJ254 (in which Agent Hartmann explains that they are "talking about maybe even doing something, you know, that is against the law" and Hsu responds, "Right. Right. Right."). Yet, despite these warnings, Hsu and his co-conspirator continued with their pursuit of taxol technology and, on April 22, 1997, Jessica Chou offered undercover FBI Agent John Hartmann (posing as "John Mano") "US $400,000 which is a combination of cash payment, stock shares and royalties" for the taxol technology. *See* E-mail from Jessica Chou to FBI Agent John Hartmann a/k/a John Mano (Apr. 22, 1997).

Therefore, as applied to the conduct of this particular defendant and given the fact that he is charged *only* with the inchoate offenses of attempt and conspiracy (rather than completed offenses), we put aside our considerable disquiet about the EEA's language and deny defendant's motion to dismiss Counts Ten and Eleven of the Indictment.

## UNITED STATES v. MARTIN

228 F.3d 1 (1st Cir. 2000)

* * *

II. Conspiracy to Steal Trade Secrets

The jury found Martin guilty of count 13, which charged him with conspiracy to steal trade secrets in violation of the Economic Espionage Act of 1996, specifically 18 U.S.C. § 1832(a)(5). In order to find a defendant guilty of conspiracy, the prosecution must prove (1) that an agreement existed, (2) that it had an unlawful purpose, and (3) that the defendant was a voluntary participant. See United States v. Echeverri, 982 F.2d 675, 679 (1st Cir.1993). The government must prove that the defendant possessed both the "intent to agree and [the] intent to commit the substantive offense." United States v. Andújar, 49 F.3d 16, 20 (1st Cir.1995) (citing United States v. García, 983 F.2d 1160, 1165 (1st Cir.1993)). In addition, the government must prove that at least one conspirator committed an "overt act," that is, took an affirmative step toward achieving the conspiracy's purpose. See 18 U.S.C. § 1832(a)(5); United States v. Cassiere, 4 F.3d 1006, 1014 (1st Cir.1993).

The agreement need not be express, however, as long as its existence may be inferred from the "defendants' words and actions and the interdependence of activities and persons involved." Cassiere, 4 F.3d at 1015 (quoting United States v. Boylan, 898 F.2d 230, 241–42 (1st Cir.1990)). A so-called "tacit" agreement will suffice. See United States v. Woodward, 149 F.3d 46, 67 (1st Cir.1998). Moreover, the conspirators need not succeed in completing the underlying act, see United States v. Giry, 818 F.2d 120, 126 (1st Cir.1987), nor need that underlying act even be factually possible. See id.

As of yet, only the Third Circuit has had the opportunity to address § 1832(a), which specifically covers private corporate espionage. See United States v. Hsu, 155 F.3d 189 (3d Cir.1998). The statute criminalizes the knowing theft of trade secrets, as well as attempts or conspiracies to steal trade secrets. The Act defines a "trade secret" broadly, to include both tangible property and intangible information, as long as the owner "has taken reasonable measures to keep such information secret" and the information "derives independent economic value . . . from not being generally known to . . . the public." Id. at 196; 18 U.S.C. § 1839(3). This definition of trade secret "protects a wider variety" of information than most civil laws; however, "it is clear that Congress did not intend . . . to prohibit lawful competition such as the use of general skills or parallel development of a similar product," Hsu, 155 F.3d at 196–97, although it did mean to punish "the disgruntled former employee who walks out of his former company with a computer diskette full of engineering schematics," id. at 201 (citing H.R.Rep. No. 104–788, at 7). In other words, § 1832(a) was not designed to punish competition, even when such competition relies on the know-how of former employees of a direct competitor. It was, however, designed to prevent those employees (and their future employers) from taking advantage of confidential information gained, discovered, copied, or taken while employed elsewhere.

Martin contends that the evidence is factually insufficient to establish a "meeting of the minds" or agreement to violate § 1832(a), because (1) insufficient evidence exists to establish an agreement between Martin and Camp; (2) insufficient evidence exists to prove that Martin had the necessary intent to commit an act prohibited by § 1832(a), i.e., injure the owner of the trade secret (IDEXX); and (3) the information provided by Camp to Martin did not meet the statutory definition of a trade secret under § 1839(3). As we explain below, none of these arguments are persuasive.

First, the evidence is sufficient for a reasonable jury to conclude that Martin and Camp formed an agreement regarding the theft of trade secrets. Martin's argument against the existence of an agreement relies on the facts that (a) his early e-mails specifically requested that Camp not send him confidential information, and (b) Camp did not seem to know the distinction between confidential information, proprietary information, and office gossip. However, while Martin's disclaimer and Camp's confusion indicate the lack of an explicit agreement at that time, they do not necessarily negate the existence of an agreement. See Woodward, 149 F.3d at 67 (including tacit agreements within conspiracy requirements). A rational jury could have plausibly concluded on the basis of the evidence presented at trial that an agreement existed. By July 21, Martin had received extensive correspondence from Camp that she had either marked "confidential" or "proprietary," or had expressed some hesitation in forwarding. Despite his previous protestations that he wanted nothing to do with IDEXX or its confidential information, Martin asked Camp on July 21 to "absorb as much information, physically and intellectually, as you can," and included a set of questions to direct Camp's research. Throughout June and July, Martin referred to Camp as "Agent Ace," or as his "spy." Given the type of information that Martin had already received, a reasonable jury could have concluded that, whatever Martin's original intentions, as of July 21, Camp and Martin had reached a tacit agreement by which she would send him items and information that potentially fell under the trade secret definition of 18 U.S.C. § 1839(3). In other words, sufficient evidence exists to show an agreement between Camp and Martin to violate § 1832(a).

Second, the evidence is sufficient to show that Martin intended to injure IDEXX by obtaining IDEXX trade secrets and competing against IDEXX. Although Martin consistently claimed that he had no interest in developing products that competed with IDEXX, and hence had no intention of injuring IDEXX economically, his correspondence with Camp detailed a plan of competition. Martin had, among other things, considered the possibility of starting a competing veterinary lab, and had asked Camp to think, in particular, about ways to compete with tests that IDEXX manufactured. A reasonable jury could have found that Martin intended to use the information gained from Camp, particularly information on IDEXX's costs and customer dissatisfaction with IDEXX, to create a more successful competitor with greater capability to injure IDEXX.

Third, Martin's final argument — that he actually received no trade secrets — even if true, is irrelevant. Martin has only been found guilty of a conspiracy to steal trade secrets, rather than the underlying offense. See Giry, 818 F.2d at 126. The relevant question to determine whether a conspiracy existed was whether Martin intended to violate the statute. See id.; see also Hsu, 155 F.3d at 198 ("[T]he crimes charged — attempt and conspiracy — do not require proof of the existence of an actual trade secret, but, rather, proof only of one's attempt or conspiracy with intent to steal a trade secret."). The key question is whether Martin intended to steal trade secrets. A rational jury, considering the information Camp had already sent Martin, could have concluded that his further queries indicated such an intention.

A reasonable jury could therefore have concluded that Martin and Camp formed an agreement by which Camp conveyed information and property to Martin that potentially fell under the definition of a trade secret in 18 U.S.C. § 1839. As a result, sufficient evidence existed to convict Martin of conspiracy to steal trade secrets.

* * *

## UNITED STATES v. KRUMREI

258 F.3d 535 (6th Cir. 2001)

KENNEDY, CIRCUIT JUDGE.

Defendant-appellant Krumrei was indicted for violation of the Economic Espionage Act (EEA), 18 U.S.C. § 1832(a)(2). Defendant filed a motion to dismiss the indictment in the district court on the grounds that the provision of the Act defining a "trade secret" is unconstitutionally vague. The district court denied defendant's motion to dismiss, and defendant pleaded guilty pursuant to a Rule 11 conditional plea agreement. For the reasons stated below, we affirm the judgment of the district court and hold that the EEA is not unconstitutionally vague as applied to defendant.

I.

Defendant-appellant David Krumrei was indicted on one count of violating the EEA, 18 U.S.C. § 1832(a)(2), by knowingly and without authorization transmitting a trade secret to a competitor of the owner. According to the facts stipulated to by both parties, the indictment arose from a meeting between defendant and Ken Taylor, a private investigator, in Hawaii on January 10, 1997 at which defendant conveyed information that was a trade secret of Wilsonart International, Inc. (Wilsonart).

In the mid-1990s, Wilsonart developed a new process for applying hard coatings to the laminate contact surfaces of caul plates. Wilsonart contracted with a Michigan company, Vactec Coatings, Inc. (Vactec), to assist in research, development and testing of the new process. Vactec's owner, Robert Amis, in turn hired another Michigan company, Federal Industrial Services, Inc., to help prepare its planar magnetron sputter coating machine, a piece of equipment necessary for the testing process. Defendant Krumrei worked for Federal Industrial Services and helped Amis prepare the sputter coating machine.

The parties stipulated to the relevant facts. (J.A. 121-23.) Wilsonart expended substantial money and efforts to ensure that its employees properly safeguarded Wilsonart's proprietary technology and business information. In addition, Robert Amis and Wilsonart entered into a verbal agreement regarding the need for absolute confidentiality with regard to the work being performed by Amis. That agreement was later put in writing. During his employment, defendant's only access to confidential information was through observation at the facility and any questions he asked of Amis. Amis informed defendant of the confidential nature of the work they were doing.

In early 1996, defendant contacted CSR Limited (CSR), a competitor of Wilsonart, and offered to act as a consultant to CSR in developing the Wilsonart coating process for use by CSR. CSR contacted Wilsonart and advised them of defendant's proposal. Wilsonart then began an investigation into any breach of their corporate security and hired Ken Taylor to approach defendant, posing as a representative of CSR. Discussions between Taylor and defendant followed, and defendant offered to sell the information to Taylor for $350,000. Ultimately the two met in Hawaii at a meeting monitored by the FBI, during which defendant disclosed the information about the Wilsonart process.

Following his indictment, defendant filed a motion to dismiss the indictment claiming that the definition of "trade secret" in the EEA is unconstitutionally vague. The district court denied defendant's motion to dismiss. Defendant ultimately pleaded guilty to the one count indictment, according to the terms of a Rule 11 conditional plea agreement. The plea agreement reserved defendant's right to appeal the district court's denial of his motion to dismiss. Defendant thus brings this appeal, alleging that the Economic Espionage Act is unconstitutionally vague. For the following reasons, we affirm the ruling of the district court and hold the statute constitutional as applied to defendant.

II.

The constitutionality of a statute is a legal question which we review de novo. *United States v. Hill*, 167 F.3d 1055, 1063 (6th Cir.1999). As this court has explained, "[t]he standard for vagueness in a criminal statute is if it defines an offense in such a way that ordinary people cannot understand what is prohibited or if it encourages arbitrary or discriminatory enforcement." *United States v. Avant*, 907 F.2d 623, 625 (6th Cir.1990). Although a vagueness analysis in the context of first amendment rights may involve consideration of hypothetical facts not specifically before the court, "it is well established that vagueness challenges to statutes which do not involve First Amendment freedoms must be examined in the light of the facts of the case at hand." *United States v. Powell*, 423 U.S. 87, 92, 96 S.Ct. 316, 46 L.Ed.2d 228 (1975) [Citations omitted.]. Thus, defendant bears the burden of establishing that the statute is vague as applied to his particular case, not merely that the statute could be construed as vague in some hypothetical situation. *Avant*, 907 F.2d at 625.

The relevant portion of the EEA, 18 U.S.C. § 1832, provides as follows:

> (a) Whoever, with intent to convert a trade secret, that is related to or included in a product that is produced for or placed in interstate or foreign commerce, to the economic benefit of anyone other than the owner thereof, and intending or knowing that the offense will, injure any owner of that trade secret, knowingly-
>
> . . .
>
> (2) without authorization copies, duplicates, sketches, draws, photographs, downloads, uploads, alters, destroys, photocopies, replicates, transmits, delivers, sends, mails, communicates, or conveys such information;
>
> . . .
>
> shall, except as provided in subsection (b), be fined under this title or imprisoned for not more than 10 years, or both.

The term "trade secret" is defined in 18 U.S.C. § 1839(3) as follows:

> (3) the term "trade secret" means all forms and types of financial, business, scientific, technical, economic, or engineering information, including pat-

> terns, plans, compilations, program devices, formulas, designs, prototypes, methods, techniques, processes, procedures, programs, or codes, whether tangible or intangible, and whether or how stored, compiled, or memorialized physically, electronically, graphically, photographically, or in writing if-
>
> (A) the owner thereof has taken reasonable measures to keep such information secret; and
>
> (B) the information derives independent economic value, actual or potential, from not being generally known to, and not being readily ascertainable through proper means by, the public.

Defendant specifically alleges that the term "reasonable measures" in § 1839(3)(A) is unconstitutionally vague and that, therefore, the EEA does not allow an individual in defendant's position to adequately assess what constitutes a "trade secret." In addition, defendant alleges that the lack of clarity as to what constitutes "reasonable measures" has the potential to lead to arbitrary and discriminatory enforcement of the EEA. At oral argument, defendant's counsel also argued that defendant had no notice of any of the security measures taken by Wilsonart and that, in effect, there was no factual basis for defendant's guilty plea. The government contends that, regardless of whether there exist conditions under which the language of the EEA could be considered vague, those conditions are not before the court at this time. Under the factual scenario before this court, the government argues, there is no question that defendant knew what he was doing was prohibited and that, therefore, the statute is not unconstitutionally vague as applied to defendant.

The district court agreed with the government and denied defendant's motion to dismiss. The district court relied on the only other case to address a vagueness argument against the EEA, *United States v. Hsu*, 40 F.Supp.2d 623 (E.D.Pa.1999). There, the Pennsylvania district court explained that "a statute is not void for vagueness merely because it uses the word 'reasonable' or 'unreasonable.' " *Id.* at 628. Reviewing the particular facts of the case before it, the court held that:

> [A]s applied here, it is clear that [defendant] and his alleged co-conspirator . . . were told on several occasions . . . that the taxol technology in question was proprietary to BMS and Phyton, could not be acquired via a license or joint venture . . . and that they would have to "get [it] another way," namely through an allegedly corrupt . . . employee . . . . [Defendant] knew that BMS had taken many steps to keep its technology to itself, and therefore he will not be heard to quibble with the ductility of "reasonable measures" as applied to him in this case.

*Id.* Because the defendant knew that the information was proprietary and knew that his actions were illegal, the statute was constitutional as applied to him.

In the present case, the evidence shows that defendant Krumrei was aware that he was selling confidential information to which he had no claim. At defendant's guilty plea hearing, defendant made the following statements:

> THE DEFENDANT: . . .
>
> Subsequent to my employment with Robert Amos [sic] in the spring of 1995, I had chances to visit Mr. Amos [sic] and solicited information from

> Mr. Amos [sic] concerning the project that he was working on, on behalf of Wilsonart Corporation, a Texas Company.
>
> Through those conversations, I had the opportunity to glean information from Mr. Amos [sic] concerning the project that he was working on.
>
> From Mr. Amos's [sic] statements, it was clear to me that the information was proprietary in nature. I chose to ignore Mr. Amos's [sic] statements or the proprietariness of the information.
>
> THE COURT: Proprietary to whom?
>
> THE DEFENDANT: Proprietary to Wilsonart . . . .
>
> I then compiled a report and offered the same with information contained in the report for sale to an Australian corporation. That information was trade secret.
>
> THE COURT: And you knew that it was a trade secret?
>
> THE DEFENDANT: Through the information that I had from Mr. Amos [sic], I should have known it was a trade secret, Your Honor. I chose to ignore that fact.
>
> . . .
>
> THE COURT: And this was done to benefit someone other than the owner of the trade secret?
>
> THE DEFENDANT: That is correct.

(J.A. 246-47.) Thus, defendant admits that he knew the information was proprietary. The stipulated facts submitted by the parties to the district court also indicate that defendant knew the information was proprietary but that he sought to sell the information anyway, in order to profit personally, at the expense of the true owner of the information. (J.A. 121-23.) Furthermore, we hold that defendant need not have been aware of the particular security measures taken by Wilsonart. Regardless of his knowledge of those specific measures, defendant knew that the information was proprietary. As the Pennsylvania district court held in *Hsu*, defendant cannot claim that the statute is vague when he clearly was aware that his actions fell well within the activity proscribed by the statute. Thus, we affirm the ruling of the district court that the EEA is not unconstitutionally vague as applied to defendant.

## III.

For the foregoing reasons, we affirm the district court's judgment denying defendant's motion to dismiss.

## UNITED STATES v. LANGE

312 F.3d 263 (7th Cir. 2002)

Matthew Lange has been convicted of violating 18 U.S.C. § 1832, part of the Economic Espionage Act of 1996. This statute makes it a felony to sell, disseminate, or otherwise deal in trade secrets, or attempt to do so, without the owner's consent. Lange stole computer data from Replacement Aircraft Parts Co. (RAPCO), his former employer, and attempted to sell the data to one of RAPCO's competitors. He allows that his acts violated § 1832, if the data contained "trade secrets," but denies that the data met the statutory definition:

the term "trade secret" means all forms and types of financial, business, scientific, technical, economic, or engineering information, including patterns, plans, compilations, program devices, formulas, designs, prototypes, methods, techniques, processes, procedures, programs, or codes, whether tangible or intangible, and whether or how stored, compiled, or memorialized physically, electronically, graphically, photographically, or in writing if-(A) the owner thereof has taken reasonable measures to keep such information secret; and (B) the information derives independent economic value, actual or potential, from not being generally known to, and not being readily ascertainable through proper means by, the public[.]" 18 U.S.C. § 1839(3). Lange's appeal requires us to apply this definition.

RAPCO is in the business of making aircraft parts for the aftermarket. It buys original equipment parts, then disassembles them to identify (and measure) each component. This initial step of reverse engineering, usually performed by a drafter such as Lange, produces a set of measurements and drawings. See generally Pamela Samuelson & Suzanne Scotchmer, *The Law and Economics of Reverse Engineering*, 111 Yale L.J. 1575, 1582-94 (2002). Because this case involves an effort to sell the intellectual property used to make a brake assembly, we use brakes as an illustration.

Knowing exactly what a brake assembly looks like does not enable RAPCO to make a copy. It must figure out how to make a substitute with the same (or better) technical specifications. Brakes rely on friction to slow the airplane's speed by converting kinetic energy to heat. Surfaces that do this job well are made by sintering — the forming of solid metal, usually from a powder, without melting. Aftermarket manufacturers must experiment with different alloys and compositions until they achieve a process and product that fulfils requirements set by the Federal Aviation Administration for each brake assembly. Completed assemblies must be exhaustively tested to demonstrate, to the FAA's satisfaction, that all requirements have been met; only then does the FAA certify the part for sale. For brakes this entails 100 destructive tests on prototypes, bringing a spinning 60-ton wheel to a halt at a specified deceleration measured by a dynamometer. Further testing of finished assemblies is required. It takes RAPCO a year or two to design, and obtain approval for, a complex part; the dynamometer testing alone can cost $75,000. But the process of experimenting and testing can be avoided if the manufacturer demonstrates that its parts are identical (in composition and manufacturing processes) to parts that have already been certified. What Lange, a disgruntled former employee, offered for sale was all the information required to obtain certification of several components as identical to parts for which RAPCO held certification. Lange included with the package-which he offered via the Internet to anyone willing to pay his price of $100,000 — a pirated copy of AutoCAD®, the computer-assisted drawing software that RAPCO uses to maintain its drawings and specifications data. One person to whom Lange tried to peddle the data informed RAPCO, which turned to the FBI. Lange was arrested following taped negotiations that supply all the evidence necessary for conviction-if the data satisfy the statutory definition of trade secrets.

One ingredient of a trade secret is that "the owner thereof has taken reasonable measures to keep such information secret". Lange contends that the proof fell short, but a sensible trier of fact (in this bench trial, the district judge) could have concluded that RAPCO took "reasonable measures to keep [the] information secret". RAPCO stores all of its drawings and manufacturing data in its CAD room, which is protected by a special lock, an alarm system, and a motion detector. The number of copies of sensitive information is kept to a minimum; surplus copies are shredded. Some information in the plans is coded, and few people know the keys to these codes. Drawings and other manufacturing information contain warnings of RAPCO's intellectual-property rights; every employee receives a notice that the information with which he works is confidential. None of RAPCO's subcontractors receives full copies of the schematics; by dividing the work among vendors, RAPCO ensures that none can replicate the product. This makes it irrelevant that RAPCO does not require vendors to sign confidentiality agreements; it relies on *deeds* (the splitting of tasks) rather than *promises* to maintain confidentiality. Although, as Lange says, engineers and drafters knew where to get the key to the CAD room door, keeping these employees out can't be an ingredient of "reasonable measures to keep [the] information secret"; then no one could do any work. So too with plans sent to subcontractors, which is why dissemination to suppliers does not undermine a claim of trade secret. See *Rockwell Graphic Systems, Inc. v. DEV Industries, Inc.*, 925 F.2d 174, 177 (7th Cir.1991).

The second ingredient is that "the information derives independent economic value, actual or potential, from not being generally known to, and not being readily ascertainable through proper means by, the public[.]" According to Lange, all data obtained by reverse engineering some other product are "readily ascertainable . . . by the public" because everyone can do what RAPCO did: buy an original part, disassemble and measure it, and make a copy. The prosecutor responds to this contention by observing that "the public" is unable to reverse engineer an aircraft brake assembly.

The prosecutor's assumption is that the statutory reference in § 1839(3) to "the public" means the *general* public-the man in the street. Ordinary people don't have AutoCAD and 60-ton flywheels ready to hand. But is the general public the right benchmark? The statute itself does not give an answer: the word "public" could be preceded implicitly by "general" as the prosecutor supposes, but it also could be preceded implicitly by "educated" or "economically important" or any of many other qualifiers. Once we enter the business of adding words to flesh out the statute-and even the addition of "general" to "public" does this-it usually is best to ask what function the law serves. In criminal cases it also is important to inquire whether the unelaborated text is ambiguous, because if it is the language should be read to prevent surprises. That's the function of the Rule of Lenity. See *Staples v. United*

*States*, 511 U.S. 600, 619, 114 S.Ct. 1793, 128 L.Ed.2d 608 (1994). Some elaboration is needed. Although the third circuit assumed in *United States v. Hsu*, 155 F.3d 189, 196 (3d Cir.1998), that "general" belongs in front of "public," it did not explain why (nor was this important to, or a part of, *Hsu*'s holding). Commentators disagree about who "the public" includes. Compare Geraldine Szott Moohr, *The Problematic Role of Criminal Law in Regulating the Use of Information: The Case of the Economic Espionage Act*, 80 N.C. L.Rev. 853, 878-79 (2002), with Arthur J. Schwab & David J. Porter, *Guarding the Crown Jewels: A Guide to Protecting Your Trade Secrets* 85-86 (2002). It is therefore worth a look-though it turns out not to be dispositive here, any more than it was in *Hsu.*

A problem with using the general public as the reference group for identifying a trade secret is that many things unknown to the public at large are well known to engineers, scientists, and others whose intellectual property the Economic Espionage Act was enacted to protect. This makes the general public a poor benchmark for separating commercially valuable *secrets* from obscure (but generally known) information. Suppose that Lange had offered to sell Avogadro's number for $1. Avogadro's number, $6.02 \times 10^{23}$, is the number of molecules per mole of gas. It is an important constant, known to chemists since 1909 but not to the general public (or even to all recent graduates of a chemistry class). We can't believe that Avogadro's number could be called a trade secret. Other principles are known without being comprehended. Most people know that $E = mc^2$, but a pop quiz of the general public would reveal that they do not understand what this *means* or how it can be used productively.

One might respond that the context of the word "public" addresses this concern. The full text of § 1839(3)(B) is: "the information derives independent economic value, actual or potential, from not being generally known to, and not being readily ascertainable through proper means by, the public". Avogadro's number and other obscure knowledge is not "generally known to" the man in the street but might be deemed "readily ascertainable to" this hypothetical person. It appears in any number of scientific handbooks. Similarly one can visit a library and read Einstein's own discussion of his famous equation. See Albert Einstein, *Relativity: The Special and General Theory* (1920). Members of the general public can ascertain even abstruse information, such as Schrödinger's quantum field equation, by consulting people in the know-as high school dropouts can take advantage of obscure legal rules by hiring lawyers. But this approach uses the phrase "readily available" to treat the "general public" *as if* it were more technically competent, which poses the question whether it would be better to use a qualifier other than "general" in the first place.

Section 1839(3) was derived from the definition of a trade secret in the Uniform Trade Secrets Act, which many states have adopted. Section 1(4) of the Uniform Act provides:

> "Trade secret" means information, including a formula, pattern, compilation, program, device, method, technique, or process, that:
>
> (i) derives independent economic value, actual or potential, from not being generally known to, and not being readily ascertainable by proper means

> by, other persons who can obtain economic value from its disclosure or use, and
>
> (ii) is the subject of efforts that are reasonable under the circumstances to maintain its secrecy.

Section 1839(3)(B) replaces "persons who can obtain economic value from its disclosure or use" with "the public". The prosecutor believes that the substitution supports the conclusion that Congress referred to the *general* public. Yet one could say instead that "the public" is shorthand for the longer phrase, which then would be read as "the *economically relevant* public"-that is, the persons whose ignorance of the information is the source of its economic value. Let us recur to the statutory context of "the public":

> the information derives independent economic value, actual or potential, from not being generally known to, and not being readily ascertainable through proper means by, the public[.]

Section 1839(3)(B) as a whole refers to the source of economic value-that the information is not known to or easily discoverable by persons who could use it productively. To make this work, either the phrase "readily ascertainable" or the phrase "the public" must be understood to concentrate attention on either potential users of the information, or proxies for them (which is to say, persons who have the same ability to "ascertain" the information). And for purposes of this case those people would be engineers and manufacturers of aircraft parts, who have ample means to reverse engineer their competitors' products. It is by keeping secrets from its rivals that RAPCO captures the returns of its design and testing work. Thus it is unnecessary here to decide whether "general" belongs in front of "public"-for even if it does, the economically valuable information is not "readily ascertainable" to the general public, the educated public, the economically relevant public, or any sensible proxy for these groups.

Another line of prosecutorial argument starts with the fact that § 1832(a)(4) makes it a crime to attempt to sell trade secrets without the owner's permission. Even if Lange did not have real trade secrets in his possession, the argument goes, he *thought* he did and therefore may be penalized for an attempted sale. The argument finds support in *Hsu*, which held that in order to avoid graymail-the threat that to obtain a conviction the prosecutor must disclose the secret by putting it in the trial record-a case may be based on § 1832(a)(4) without disclosing all details of the trade secret. Accord, *United States v. Pin Yen Yang*, 281 F.3d 534, 543-44 (6th Cir.2002). We agree with the general approach of these decisions. *Hsu* analogized the attempted sale of information believed to be a trade secret to an attempt such as shooting a corpse, believing it to be alive, or selling sugar, believing it to be cocaine. Events of this sort underlie the maxim that factual impossibility is no defense to a prosecution for attempt. See *United States v. Bailey*, 227 F.3d 792, 797 (7th Cir.2000); *United States v. Saunders*, 166 F.3d 907, 916 (7th Cir.1999); *United States v. Cotts*, 14 F.3d 300, 307 (7th Cir.1994). This does not mean, however, that the defendant's belief *alone* can support a conviction. All attempt prosecutions depend on demonstrating that the defendant took a substantial step toward completion of the offense, which could have been carried out unless thwarted. *Braxton v. United States*, 500 U.S. 344, 111 S.Ct. 1854, 114 L.Ed.2d 385 (1991).

Although the American Law Institute recommends a definition of attempt linked closely to intent, *Model Penal Code* § 5.01(1)(c), the Supreme Court has not embraced this view and demands in cases under federal law that the prosecutor establish a probability of success. See, e.g., *Spectrum Sports, Inc. v. McQuillan*, 506 U.S. 447, 113 S.Ct. 884, 122 L.Ed.2d 247 (1993) ("dangerous probability" of success is an ingredient of attempted monopolization).

An attempted murder may be thwarted by substituting a sack of flour for the intended victim; a sale of drugs may be thwarted by substituting sugar for cocaine, or rock candy for crack. These situations present a good chance of success, but for the intervention. So does "the disgruntled former employee who walks out of his former company with a computer diskette full of engineering schematics" (*Hsu*, 155 F.3d at 201)-a fair description of Lange's conduct (though diskettes are obsolete). See also *United States v. Martin*, 228 F.3d 1, 10-12 (1st Cir.2000). A sale of trade secrets may be thwarted by substituting a disk with the collected works of Shakespeare for the disk that the defendant believed contained the plans for brake assemblies, or by an inadvertent failure to download the proper file. The attempted sale of the disk is a culpable substantial step. But it is far less clear that sale of information already known to the public could be deemed a substantial step toward the offense, just because the defendant is deluded and does not understand what a trade secret is. Selling a copy of *Zen and the Art of Motorcycle Maintenance* is not attempted economic espionage, even if the defendant thinks that the tips in the book are trade secrets; nor is sticking pins in voodoo dolls attempted murder. Booksellers and practitioners of the occult pose no social dangers, certainly none of the magnitude of those who are tricked into shooting bags of sand that have been substituted for targets of assassination. Lange was more dangerous than our bookseller but much less dangerous than our hypothetical assassin. Perhaps data purloined from an ex-employer is sufficiently *likely* to contain trade secrets to justify calling the preparation for sale a substantial step toward completion of the offense, and thus a culpable attempt, even if the employee stole the wrong data file and did not get his hands on the commercially valuable information. We need not pursue the subject beyond noting the plausibility of the claim and its sensitivity to the facts-what kind of data did the employee think he stole, and so on. For it is not necessary to announce a definitive rule about how dangerous the completed acts must be in trade secret cases: the judge was entitled to (and did) find that Lange had *real* trade secrets in his possession.

Lange wants us to proceed as if all he tried to sell were measurements that anyone could have taken with calipers after disassembling an original-equipment part. Such measurements could not be called trade secrets if, as Lange asserts, the assemblies in question were easy to take apart and measure. But no one would have paid $100,000 for metes and bounds, while Lange told his customers that the data on offer were worth more than that asking price. Which they were. What Lange had, and tried to sell, were the completed specifications and engineering diagrams that reflected all the work completed *after* the measurements had been taken: the metallurgical data, details of the sintering, the results of the tests, the plans needed to produce the finished goods, everything required to get FAA certification of a part supposedly identical to one that had been approved. Those details "derive[d] independent economic value, actual or potential, from not being generally known to, and not being readily ascertainable through proper means by, the public[.]" Every firm other than the original equipment manufacturer and RAPCO ha to pay dearly to devise, test, and win approval of similar parts; the details unknown to the rivals, and not discoverable with tape measures, had considerable "independent economic value . . . from not being generally known". A sensible trier of fact could determine that Lange tried to sell trade secrets. It was his customer's cooperation with the FBI, and not public access to the data, that prevented closing of the sale.

* * *

## UNITED STATES v. ALEYNIKOV

676 F.3d 71 (Fed. Cir. 2012)

Sergey Aleynikov appeals from his conviction, following a jury trial, for stealing and transferring proprietary computer source code of his employer's high frequency trading system in violation of the National Stolen Property Act, 18 U.S.C. § 2314, and the Economic Espionage Act of 1996, 18 U.S.C. § 1832. On appeal, defendant argues, *inter alia*, that his conduct did not constitute an offense under either statute. He argues that: [1] the source code was not a "stolen" "good" within the meaning of the National Stolen Property Act, and [2] the source code was not "related" to a product "produced for or placed in interstate or foreign commerce" within the meaning of the Economic Espionage Act. The judgment of the district court is reversed. Judge Calabresi concurs in the opinion and has filed an additional concurring opinion.

* * *

DENNIS JACOBS, CHIEF JUDGE:

Sergey Aleynikov was convicted, following a jury trial in the United States District Court for the Southern District of New York (Cote, J.), of stealing and transferring some of the proprietary computer source code used in his employer's high frequency trading system, in violation of the National Stolen Property Act, 18 U.S.C. § 2314 (the "NSPA"), and the Economic Espionage Act of 1996, 18 U.S.C. § 1832 (the "EEA"). On appeal, Aleynikov argues, *inter alia*, that his conduct did not constitute an offense under either statute. He argues that: [1] the source code was not a "stolen" "good" within the meaning of the NSPA, and [2] the source code was not "related to or included in a product that is produced for or placed in interstate or foreign commerce" within the meaning of the EEA. We agree, and reverse the judgment of the district court.

### BACKGROUND

Sergey Aleynikov, a computer programmer, was employed by Goldman Sachs & Co. ("Goldman") from May 2007 through June 2009, developing computer source code for the company's proprietary high-frequency trading ("HFT") system. An HFT system is a mechanism for making large volumes of trades in securities and commodities based on trading decisions effected in fractions of a second. Trades are executed on the basis of algorithms that incorporate rapid market developments and data from past trades. The computer programs used to operate Goldman's HFT system are of three kinds: [1] market connectivity programs that process realtime market data and execute trades; [2] programs that use algorithms to determine which trades to make; and [3] infrastructure programs that facilitate the flow of information throughout the trading system and monitor the system's performance. Aleynikov's work focused on developing code for this last category of infrastructure programs in Goldman's HFT system. High frequency trading is a competitive business that depends in large part on the speed with which information can be processed to seize fleeting market opportunities. Goldman closely guards the secrecy of each component of the system, and does not license the system to anyone. Goldman's confidentiality policies bound Aleynikov to keep in strict confidence all the firm's proprietary information, including any intellectual property created by Aleynikov. He was barred as well from taking it or using it when his employment ended.

By 2009, Aleynikov was earning $400,000, the highest paid of the twenty-five programmers in his group. In April 2009, he accepted an offer to become an Executive Vice President at Teza Technologies LLC, a Chicago-based startup that was looking to develop its own HFT system. Aleynikov was hired, at over $1 million a year, to develop the market connectivity and infrastructure components of Teza's HFT system. Teza's founder (a former head of HFT at Chicago based hedge fund Citadel Investment Group) emailed Aleynikov (and several other employees) in late May, conveying his expectation that they would develop a functional trading system within six months. It usually takes years for a team of programmers to develop an HFT system from scratch.

Aleynikov's last day at Goldman was June 5, 2009. At approximately 5:20 p.m., just before his going-away party, Aleynikov encrypted and uploaded to a server in Germany more than 500,000 lines of source code for Goldman's HFT system, including code for a substantial part of the infrastructure, and some of the algorithms and market data connectivity programs. Some of the code pertained to programs that could operate independently of the rest of the Goldman system and could be integrated into a competitor's system. After uploading the source code, Aleynikov deleted the encryption program as well as the history of his computer commands. When he returned to his home in New Jersey, Aleynikov downloaded the source code from the server in Germany to his home computer, and copied some of the files to other computer devices he owned.

On July 2, 2009, Aleynikov flew from New Jersey to Chicago to attend meetings at Teza. He brought with him a flash drive and a laptop containing portions of the Goldman source code. When Aleynikov flew back the following day, he was arrested by the FBI at Newark Liberty International Airport.

The indictment charged him with violating the EEA by downloading a trade secret "that is related to or included in a product that is produced for or placed in interstate or foreign commerce," with the intent to convert such trade secret and to injure its owner, to the economic benefit of anyone other than the owner, see 18 U.S.C. § 1832(a) (Count One); and with violating the NSPA, which makes it a crime to "transport[], transmit[], or transfer[] in interstate or foreign commerce any goods, wares, merchandise, securities or money, of the value of $5,000 or more, knowing the same to have been stolen, converted or taken by fraud," 18 U.S.C. § 2314 (Count Two). A third count charged him with unauthorized computer access and exceeding authorized access in violation of the Computer Fraud and Abuse Act, 18 U.S.C. § 1030.

Aleynikov moved to dismiss the indictment for failure to state an offense. See Fed. R. Crim. P. 12(b)(3)(B). The district court dismissed Count Three of the indictment but otherwise denied Aleynikov's motion. *United States v. Aleynikov*, 737 F. Supp.2d 173 (S.D.N.Y. 2010).

As to Count One, the district court concluded: [1] the stolen source code is a trade secret; [2] the HFT system constitutes a "product" to which the source code relates because the system was developed and modified through the labor of Goldman's computer programmers; and [3] the HFT system was "produced for" interstate commerce because it facilitates the rapid execution of trades on financial markets such as the New York Stock Exchange and NASDAQ. *Id.* at 177-79. The district court reasoned that the whole purpose of the HFT system was "to engage in interstate and foreign commerce." *Id.* at 179.

As to Count Two, the court held that the source code for Goldman's HFT system constitutes "goods" that were "stolen" within the meaning of the NSPA because, though source code is intangible, it "contains highly confidential trade secrets related to the Trading System" that "would be valuable for any firm seeking to launch, or enhance, a high frequency trading business." *Id.* at 187.

Count Three was dismissed on the ground that Aleynikov was authorized to access the Goldman computer and did not exceed the scope of his authorization, and that authorized use of a computer in a manner that misappropriates information is not an offense under the Computer Fraud and Abuse Act. *Id.* at 192-94.

The jury convicted Aleynikov on Counts One and Two. He was sentenced to 97 months of imprisonment followed by a three-year term of supervised release, and was ordered to pay a $12,500 fine. Bail pending appeal was denied because Aleynikov, a dual citizen of the United States and Russia, was feared to be a flight risk.

Aleynikov appealed his conviction and sentence, arguing, among other things, that the district court erred in denying his motion to dismiss the indictment in its entirety. The Government did not appeal the dismissal of Count Three of the indictment.

On February 17, 2012, following oral argument, we issued a short order reversing Aleynikov's convictions on both counts, and indicated that an opinion would follow.

DISCUSSION

On appeal, Aleynikov renews his challenge to the sufficiency of the indictment on both Counts One and Two. As to Count One, he argues that the source code is not "related to or included in a product that is produced for or placed in interstate or foreign commerce" within the meaning of the EEA. As to Count Two, Aleynikov argues that the source code — as purely intangible property — is not a "good" that was "stolen" within the meaning of the NSPA.

Aleynikov's challenge requires us to determine the scope of two federal criminal statutes. Since federal crimes are "solely creatures of statute," *Dowling v. United States*, 473 U.S. 207, 213 (1985) (internal quotation marks omitted), a federal indictment can be challenged on the ground that it fails to allege a crime within the terms of the applicable statute. *See United States v. Pirro*, 212 F.3d 86, 91-92 (2d Cir. 2000).3 The sufficiency of an indictment and the interpretation of a federal statute are both matters of law that we review de novo. See *Fiero v. Fin. Indus. Regulatory Auth., Inc.*, 660 F.3d 569, 573 (2d Cir. 2011); *Pirro*, 212 F.3d at 92.

Statutory construction "must begin with the language employed by Congress and the assumption that the ordinary meaning of that language accurately expresses the legislative purpose." *United States v. Albertini*, 472 U.S. 675, 680 (1985) (quoting *Park 'N Fly, Inc. v. Dollar Park & Fly, Inc.*, 469 U.S. 189, 194 (1985)). "Due respect for the prerogatives of Congress in defining federal crimes prompts restraint in this area, where we typically find a narrow interpretation appropriate." *Dowling*, 473 U.S. at 213 (internal quotation marks omitted).

We conclude that Aleynikov's conduct did not constitute an offense under either the NSPA or the EEA, and that the indictment was therefore legally insufficient. We consider the statutes in the order they were briefed: the NSPA first, the EEA second.

I

The NSPA makes it a crime to "transport[], transmit[], or transfer[] in interstate or foreign commerce any goods, wares, merchandise, securities or money, of the value of $5,000 or more, knowing the same to have been stolen, converted or taken by fraud." 18 U.S.C. § 2314. The statute does not define the terms "goods," "wares," or "merchandise." We have held that they provide "a general and comprehensive designation of such personal property or chattels as are ordinarily a subject of commerce." *In re Vericker*, 446 F.2d 244, 248 (2d Cir. 1971) (Friendly, C.J.) (quoting *United States v. Seagraves*, 265 F.2d 876, 880 (3d Cir. 1959)). The decisive question is whether the source code that Aleynikov uploaded to a server in Germany, then downloaded to his computer devices in New Jersey, and later transferred to Illinois, constituted stolen "goods," "wares," or "merchandise" within the meaning of the NSPA. Based on the substantial weight of the case law, as well as the ordinary meaning of the words, we conclude that it did not.

A.

We first considered the applicability of the NSPA to the theft of intellectual property in *United States v. Bottone*, 365 F.2d 389 (2d Cir. 1966) (Friendly, J.), in which photocopied documents outlining manufacturing procedures for certain pharmaceuticals were transported across state lines. Since the actual processes themselves (as opposed to photocopies) were never transported across state lines, the "serious question" (we explained) was whether "the papers showing [the] processes that were transported in interstate or foreign commerce were 'goods' which had been 'stolen, converted or taken by fraud' in view of the lack of proof that any of the physical materials so transported came from [the manufacturer's] possession." *Id.* at 393. We held that the NSPA was violated there, observing that what was "stolen and transported" was, ultimately, "tangible goods," notwithstanding the "clever intermediate transcription [and] use of a photocopy machine." *Id.* However, we suggested that a different result would obtain if there was no physical taking of tangible property whatsoever: "To be sure, where no tangible objects were ever taken or transported, a court would be hard pressed to conclude that 'goods' had been stolen and transported within the meaning of 2314." *Id.* Hence, we observed, "the statute would presumably not extend to the case where a carefully guarded secret formula was memorized, carried away in the recesses of a thievish mind and placed in writing only after a boundary had been crossed." *Id. Bottone* itself thus treats its holding as the furthest limit of a statute that is not endlessly elastic: Some tangible property must be taken from the owner for there to be deemed a "good" that is "stolen" for purposes of the NSPA.

*Bottone*'s reading of the NSPA is confirmed by the Supreme Court's opinion in *Dowling v. United States*, 473 U.S. 207 (1985), which held that the NSPA did not apply to an interstate bootleg record operation. Dowling rejected the Government's argument that the unauthorized use of the musical compositions rendered them "stolen, converted or taken by fraud." Cases prosecuted under the NSPA "have always involved physical 'goods, wares, [or] merchandise' that have themselves been 'stolen, converted or taken by fraud' " — even if the stolen thing does not "remain in entirely unaltered form," and "owes a major portion of its value to an intangible component." *Id.* at 216.

"This basic element" — the taking of a physical thing — "comports with the common-sense meaning of the statutory language: by requiring that the 'goods, wares [or] merchandise' be 'the same' as those 'stolen, converted or taken by fraud,' the provision seems clearly to contemplate a physical identity between the items unlawfully obtained and those eventually transported, and hence some prior physical taking of the subject goods." *Id.*

We join other circuits in relying on *Dowling* for the proposition that the theft and subsequent interstate transmission of purely intangible property is beyond the scope of the NSPA.

In a close analog to the present case, the Tenth Circuit affirmed the dismissal of an indictment alleging that the defendant transported in interstate commerce a computer program containing source code that was taken from his employer. *United States v. Brown*, 925 F.2d 1301, 1305, 1309 (10th Cir. 1991). Citing Dowling, the court held that the NSPA "applies only to physical 'goods, wares or merchandise' " and that "[p]urely intellectual property is not within this category. It can be represented physically, such as through writing on a page, but the underlying, intellectual property itself, remains intangible." *Id.* at 1307. The Court concluded that "the computer program itself is an intangible intellectual property, and as such, it alone cannot constitute goods, wares, merchandise, securities or moneys which have been stolen, converted or taken" for purposes of the NSPA. *Id.* at 1308.

Similarly, the Seventh Circuit has held that numerical "Comdata codes" used by truckers to access money transfers at truck stops constitute intangible property the theft of which is not a violation of the NSPA. *United States v. Stafford*, 136 F.3d 1109 (7th Cir. 1998). The court reasoned that the codes themselves were not "goods, wares, or merchandise," but rather "information"; that the defendant had not been charged with transporting pieces of paper containing the codes; and that the only conduct charged was "transferring the codes themselves, which are simply sequences of digits." *Id.* at 1114-15.

The First Circuit has also concluded that the NSPA does not criminalize the theft of intangible things: The NSPA "does not apply to purely 'intangible information,' the theft of which is punishable under copyright law and other intellectual property statutes" but "does apply when there has been 'some tangible item taken, however insignificant or valueless it may be, absent the intangible component.' " *United States v. Martin*, 228 F.3d 1, 14-15 (1st Cir. 2000) (quoting *Brown*, 925 F.2d at 1307, 1308 n.14).

The Government argues that a tangibility requirement ignores a 1988 amendment, which added the words "transmit[]" and "transfer[]" to the terms: "transport[], transmit[], or transfer[]." The Government contends that the added words reflect an intent to cover generally transfers and transmissions of non-physical forms of stolen property. The evident purpose of the amendment, however, was to clarify that the statute applied to non-physical electronic transfers of money. *See United States v. Piervinanzi*, 23 F.3d 670, 678 n.6 (2d Cir. 1994). Money, though it can be intangible, is specifically enumerated in § 2314 as a thing apart and distinct from "goods," "wares," or "merchandise." The addition to the possible means of transport does not bespeak an intent to alter or expand the ordinary meaning of "goods," "wares," or "merchandise" and therefore does not obviate the Government's need to identify a predicate good, ware, merchandise, security, or money that has been stolen.

B.

By uploading Goldman's proprietary source code to a computer server in Germany, Aleynikov stole purely intangible property embodied in a purely intangible format. There was no allegation that he physically seized anything tangible from Goldman, such as a compact disc or thumb drive containing source code, so we need not decide whether that would suffice as a physical theft. Aleynikov later transported portions of the source code to Chicago, on his laptop and flash drive. However, there is no violation of the statute unless the good is transported with knowledge that "the same" has been stolen; the statute therefore presupposes that the thing stolen was a good or ware, etc., *at the time of the theft.* The wording "contemplate[s] a physical identity between the items unlawfully obtained and those eventually transported." *Dowling*, 473 U.S. at 216. The later storage of intangible property on a tangible medium does not transform the intangible property into a stolen good.

The infringement of copyright in *Dowling* parallels Aleynikov's theft of computer code. Although "[t]he infringer invades a statutorily defined province guaranteed to the copyright holder alone[,] . . . he does not assume physical control over the copyright; nor does he wholly deprive its owner of its use." *Id.* at 217. Because Aleynikov did not "assume physical control" over anything when he took the source code, and because he did not thereby "deprive [Goldman] of its use," Aleynikov did not violate the NSPA.

As the district court observed, Goldman's source code is highly valuable, and there is no doubt that in virtually every case involving proprietary computer code worth stealing, the value of the intangible code will vastly exceed the value of any physical item on which it might be stored. *See Aleynikov*, 737 F. Supp.2d at 187. But federal crimes are "solely creatures of statute." *Dowling*, 473 U.S. at 213 (internal quotation marks omitted). We decline to stretch or update statutory words of plain and ordinary meaning in order to better accommodate the digital age.

## II

We next consider the sufficiency of the indictment as to the EEA. As with the NSPA count, we conclude that the indictment was insufficient as a matter of law.

### A.

The EEA contains two operative provisions. The first section (18 U.S.C. § 1831(a)), which is not charged in the indictment, applies to foreign espionage and is expressed broadly: "Whoever, intending or knowing that the offense will benefit any foreign government, foreign instrumentality, or foreign agent, knowingly . . . without authorization . . . downloads, uploads, . . . transmits, . . . or conveys a trade secret" is guilty of a federal offense, and may be imprisoned for up to 15 years. 18 U.S.C. § 1831(a).

Aleynikov, however, was charged with violating 18 U.S.C. § 1832, which imposes the italicized limitation (which is not found in § 1831): "Whoever, with intent to convert a trade secret, *that is related to or included in a product that is produced for or placed in interstate or foreign commerce*, to the economic benefit of anyone other than the owner thereof, and intending or knowing that the offense will, injure any owner of that trade secret, knowingly . . . without authorization . . . downloads, uploads, . . . transmits, . . . or conveys such information" is guilty of a federal offense, and may be imprisoned for up to 10 years. *Id.* § 1832(a) (emphasis added).

Thus there is a limitation — that products be "produced for" or "placed in" interstate or foreign commerce — in the statute Aleynikov is charged with violating, a limitation that does not appear in the otherwise parallel foreign espionage statute. "Where Congress includes particular language in one section of a statute but omits it in another section of the same Act, it is generally presumed that Congress acts intentionally and purposely in the disparate inclusion or exclusion." *Russello v. United States*, 464 U.S. 16, 23 (1983) (internal quotation marks and alteration omitted). The requirement that products be "produced for" or "placed in" interstate or foreign commerce therefore must be read as a term of limitation.

The legislative history confirms this. The version of § 1832 that appeared in the original Senate bill did not contain the limiting language. It applied to any person who steals "proprietary economic information having a value of not less than $100,000"; it did not specify whether that economic information relates to a product produced for or placed in interstate commerce, and instead contained a categorical finding that "the development and production of proprietary economic information involves every aspect of interstate commerce and business." S. 1556, 104th Cong.

§§ 2(a), 3 (2d Sess. 1996), *reprinted in* S. Rep. No. 104-359, at 1, 3. The limiting language was introduced in the House Bill. See H.R. Rep. No. 104-788, at 2 (1996), *reprinted in* 1996 U.S.C.C.A.N. 4021, 4021. The words of limitation in § 1832 were deliberately chosen.

The natural reading that takes account of the distinct meaning of the paired phrases ("produced for" and "placed in") is that § 1832(a) identifies two separate but related categories. Products "placed in" commerce have already been introduced into the stream of commerce and have reached the marketplace. Products that have not yet been "placed in" commerce but are still being developed or readied for the marketplace can properly be described as being "produced for," if not yet actually "placed in," commerce. Reading the statute in this way gives effect to both categories of product (those "produced for" commerce and those "placed in" commerce), without making one a subset of the other.

This interpretation has the added virtue of construing the two categories of product in relationship to one another (a sequential or temporal relationship), and finds support in the doctrine of statutory interpretation which instructs that words in a statute are known by the company they keep. *See Gustafson v. Alloyd Co., Inc.*, 513 U.S. 561, 575 (1995) (invoking this doctrine "to avoid ascribing to one word a meaning so broad that it is inconsistent with its accompanying words, thus giving unintended breadth to the Acts of Congress" (internal quotation marks omitted)). The statute would fall short of critical protections if it applied only to the theft of trade secrets relating to those products that had already been "placed in" the marketplace; left vulnerable would be the class of trade secrets inhering in products that have not yet been placed on the market, such as prototypes — precisely the kinds of trade secrets that are likely to attract espionage. Congress thus plugged a gap by extending the statute's coverage to include products "produced for" commerce as well as those already in the marketplace.

The district court interpreted the phrase "produced for" interstate or foreign commerce more broadly. It held that the HFT system was "produced for" interstate commerce because "the sole purpose for which Goldman purchased, developed, and modified the computer programs that comprise the Trading System was to engage in interstate and foreign commerce" and because "Goldman uses the Trading System to rapidly execute high volumes of trades in various financial markets" and "[t]he Trading System generates many millions of dollars in annual profits." *Aleynikov*, 737 F. Supp.2d at 179. Under that interpretation, a product is "produced for" interstate or foreign commerce if its purpose is to facilitate or engage in such commerce.

The district court erred by construing the phrase — "produced for . . . interstate or foreign commerce" — "in a vacuum." *See Davis v. Mich.Dep't of Treasury*, 489 U.S. 803, 809 (1989). "It is a fundamental canon of statutory construction that the words of a statute must be read in their context and with a view to their place in the overall statutory scheme." *Id.* That way, a statutory phrase "gathers meaning from the words around it." *Jones v. United States*, 527 U.S. 373, 389 (1999) (internal quotation marks omitted). The district court's broad interpretation of the phrase "produced for" commerce becomes untenable in light of the paired phrase "placed in" commerce. Since every product actually sold or licensed is by definition produced for the purpose of engaging in commerce, every product that is "placed in" commerce would necessarily also be "produced for" commerce — and the phrase "placed in" commerce would be surplusage. This interpretation is inconsistent with "one of the most basic interpretive canons, that a statute should be construed so that effect is given to all its provisions, so that no part will be inoperative or superfluous, void or insignificant." *Corley v. United States*, 556 U.S. 303, 314 (2009) (internal quotation marks and alteration omitted); *see also Duncan v. Walker*, 533 U.S. 167, 174 (2001) ("It is our duty to give effect, if possible, to every clause and word of a statute." (internal quotation marks omitted)). "Judges should hesitate to treat statutory terms in any setting as surplusage, and *resistance should be heightened when the words describe an element of a criminal offense.*" *Jones v. United States*, 529 U.S. 848, 857 (2000) (internal quotation marks and alterations omitted; emphasis added).

Even construed in isolation, the phrase "produced for . . . interstate or foreign commerce" cannot command the breadth that the district court and the Government ascribe to it. *See generally Fed. Commc'ns Comm'n v. AT & T Inc.*, 131 S. Ct. 1177, 1184 (2011) ("[C]onstruing statutory language is not merely an exercise in ascertaining 'the outer limits of [a word's] definitional possibilities' . . . ." (quoting *Dolan v. U.S. Postal Serv.*, 546 U.S. 481, 486 (2006)). At oral argument, the Government was unable to identify a single product that affects interstate commerce but that would nonetheless be excluded by virtue of the statute's limiting language. And even if one could identify one such example, or two, it would not be a category that would demand the attention of Congress, or be expressed in categorical terms.

If § 1832(a) was intended to have such a sweep, we would expect to see wording traditionally understood to invoke the full extent of Congress's regulatory power under the Commerce Clause. Notably, the EEA was enacted the year after the Supreme Court issued its landmark decision in *United States v. Lopez*, which held that Congress's Commerce Clause authority is limited to those activities that "substantially affect interstate commerce." 514 U.S.549, 558-59 (1995). The Supreme Court observes a distinction between "legislation invoking Congress' full power over activity substantially 'affecting . . . commerce' " and legislation which uses more limiting language, such as activities " 'in commerce,' " and thereby does not purport to exercise the full scope of congressional authority. Jones, 529 U.S. at 856 (quoting *Russell v. United States*, 471 U.S. 858, 859-60 & n.4 (1985)). The temporal proximity between the enactment of the EEA and the decision in Lopez makes significant the omission from the EEA of the language blessed in that case as invoking the outer limit of Congress's regulatory authority.

B.

Goldman's HFT system was neither "produced for" nor "placed in" interstate or foreign commerce. Goldman had no intention of selling its HFT system or licensing it to anyone. *Aleynikov*, 737 F. Supp.2d at 175. It went to great lengths to maintain the secrecy of its system. The enormous profits the system yielded for Goldman depended on no one else having it. Because the HFT system was not designed to enter or pass in commerce, or to make something that does, Aleynikov's theft of source code relating to that system was not an offense under the EEA.

Even if we were to conclude that the phrase "produced for . . . interstate or foreign commerce" is susceptible to a broader reading than we think it will bear, it would at most render § 1832(a) facially ambiguous, which would not assist the prosecution. "[A]mbiguity concerning the ambit of criminal statutes should be resolved in favor of lenity." *Rewis v. United States*, 401 U.S. 808, 812 (1971). And "when choice has to be made between two readings of what conduct Congress has made a crime, it is appropriate, before we choose the harsher alternative, to require that Congress should have spoken in language that is clear and definite." *United States v. Universal C.I.T. Credit Corp.*, 344 U.S. 218, 221-22 (1952).

The conduct found by the jury is conduct that Aleynikov should have known was in breach of his confidentiality obligations to Goldman, and was dishonest in ways that would subject him to sanctions; but he could not have known that it would offend this criminal law or this particular sovereign.

CONCLUSION

For the foregoing reasons, the judgment of the district court is reversed.

* * *

## NOTES AND QUESTIONS:

1. As noted by the court in *United States v. Hsu*, 155 F.3d 198 (3d Cir. 1998), the EEA has two separate trade secret provisions: section 1831, which requires that the offense "benefit" a foreign government, instrumentality or agent and "there is 'evidence of foreign government sponsorship of coordinated intelligence activity,' " and § 1832, which "applies to anyone who knowingly engages in the theft of trade secrets, or an attempt or conspiracy to do so, 'with intent to convert a trade secret, that is related to or included in a product that is produced for or placed in interstate or foreign commerce, to the economic benefit of anyone other than the owner thereof, and intending or knowing that the offense will, injure any owner of that trade secret.' " Although § 1831 is not applied very often, occasionally it is coupled with charges under § 1831. *See United States v. Jin*, No. 08 CR 192, 833 F. Supp. 2d 977 (N.D.Ill. Feb. 8, 2012), where, although the defendant was convicted of trade secret theft, she was acquitted of espionage charges.

2. Under the definition in § 1839(3), can there be theft of trade secret information that has not been stored electronically or recorded in or on a tangible medium? What about "negative information"?

3. On remand, the district court in *United States v. Hsu*, 40 F.Supp.2d 623, 630 (E.D.Pa.1999), found that the terms "generally known to" and "readily ascertainable through proper means by, the public," were not unconstitutionally vague. (Quoting 18 U.S.C. § 1893(3).) After considering these terms in the civil cases in previous chapters, are you convinced the judge was correct? If so, why? If not, why not?

4. In *Martin*, the defendant was convicted not only under the EEC but, as shown in the case excerpt from *Martin* included in the previous section, for

conspiracy to transport stolen property in interstate commerce and for violating the mail and wire fraud laws. *Martin* illustrates how a number of federal criminal laws can apply concurrently.

5. The court in *United States v. Krumrei*, 258 F.3d 535 (6th Cir.2001), found that it was not relevant that he did not know what security measures were taken to protect the trade secrets because he admitted that he knew the information was proprietary. Why thus was this admission contrary to his argument that the term "reasonable measures" was vague? What would have happened if he had thought he was stealing a trade secret, when it was not really a trade secret?

6. The *United States v. Lange*, 312 F.3d 263 (7th Cir.2002), court struggled with the definition of trade secret in § 1839(3), and eventually relied on the definition in the UTSA in holding that the specifications and engineering diagrams of equipment that could have been reverse-engineered were in fact trade secrets. How does this analysis compare with the discussions above in the civil cases regarding detailed information that could have been obtained by reverse engineering?

7. With the requirement that the trade secret be related to or included in a product, the obvious question is whether EEA applies to the theft of information relating to a manufacturing process or a computer program for a business method. The Second Circuit answered this question in *United States v. Aleynikov*, ___ F.3d ___, 2012 WL 1193611 (2d Cir. Apr. 11, 2012), as to source code, finding that it was not a product. How about a service such as the psychological profiling of individuals engaged in defined situations?

## D. COMPUTER FRAUD AND ABUSE ACT ("CFAA")

### UNITED STATES v. NOSAL

676 F.3d 854
(9th Cir. 2012)

KOZINSKI, CHIEF JUDGE:

Computers have become an indispensable part of our daily lives. We use them for work; we use them for play. Sometimes we use them for play at work. Many employers have adopted policies prohibiting the use of work computers for nonbusiness purposes. Does an employee who violates such a policy commit a federal crime? How about someone who violates the terms of service of a social networking website? This depends on how broadly we read the Computer Fraud and Abuse Act (CFAA), 18 U.S.C. § 1030.

FACTS

David Nosal used to work for Korn/Ferry, an executive search firm. Shortly after he left the company, he convinced some of his former colleagues who were still working for Korn/Ferry to help him start a competing business. The employees used their log-in credentials to download source lists, names and contact information from a confidential database on the company's computer, and then transferred that information to Nosal. The employees were authorized to access the database, but Korn/Ferry had a policy that forbade disclosing confidential information. The government indicted Nosal on twenty counts, including trade secret theft, mail fraud, conspiracy and violations of the CFAA. The CFAA counts charged Nosal with violations of 18 U.S.C. § 1030(a)(4), for aiding and abetting the Korn/Ferry employees in "exceed[ing their] authorized access" with intent to defraud.

Nosal filed a motion to dismiss the CFAA counts, arguing that the statute targets only hackers, not individuals who access a computer with authorization but then misuse information they obtain by means of such access. The district court initially rejected Nosal's argument, holding that when a person accesses a computer "knowingly and with the intent to defraud . . . [it] renders the access unauthorized or in excess of authorization." Shortly afterwards, however, we decided *LVRC Holdings LLC v. Brekka*, 581 F.3d 1127 (9th Cir. 2009), which construed narrowly the phrases "without authorization" and "exceeds authorized access" in the CFAA. Nosal filed a motion for reconsideration and a second motion to dismiss.

The district court reversed field and followed *Brekka*'s guidance that "[t]here is simply no way to read [the definition of 'exceeds authorized access'] to incorporate corporate policies governing use of information unless the word alter is interpreted to mean misappropriate," as "[s]uch an interpretation would defy the plain meaning of the word alter, as well as common sense." Accordingly, the district court dismissed counts 2 and 4-7 for failure to state an offense. The government appeals. We have jurisdiction over this interlocutory appeal. 18 U.S.C. § 3731; *United States v. Russell*, 804 F.2d 571, 573 (9th Cir. 1986). We review de novo. *United States v. Boren*, 278 F.3d 911, 913 (9th Cir. 2002).

DISCUSSION

The CFAA defines "exceeds authorized access" as "to access a computer with authorization and to use such access to obtain or alter information in the computer that the accesser is not entitled so to obtain or alter." 18 U.S.C. § 1030(e)(6). This language can be read either of two ways: First, as Nosal suggests and the district court held, it could refer to someone who's authorized to access only certain data or files but accesses unauthorized data or files — what is colloquially known as "hacking." For example, assume an employee is permitted to access only product information on the company's computer but accesses customer data: He would "exceed[ ] authorized access" if he looks at the customer lists. Second, as the government proposes, the language could refer to someone who has unrestricted physical access to a computer, but is limited in the use to which he can put the information. For example, an employee may be authorized to access customer lists in order to do his job but not to send them to a competitor.

The government argues that the statutory text can support only the latter interpretation of "exceeds authorized access." In its opening brief, it focuses on the word "entitled" in the phrase an "accesser is not *entitled* so to obtain or alter." *Id.* § 1030(e)(6) (emphasis added). Pointing to one dictionary definition of "entitle" as "to furnish with a right," *Webster's New Riverside University Dictionary* 435, the government argues that Korn/Ferry's computer use policy gives employees certain rights, and when the employees violated that policy, they "exceed[ed] authorized access." But "entitled" in the statutory text refers to how an accesser "obtain[s] or alter[s]" the information, whereas the computer use policy uses "entitled" to limit how the information is used after it is obtained. This is a poor fit with the statutory language. An equally or more sensible reading of "entitled" is as a synonym for "authorized." So read, "exceeds authorized access" would refer to data or files on a computer that one is not authorized to access.

In its reply brief and at oral argument, the government focuses on the word "so" in the same phrase. *See* 18 U.S.C. § 1030(e)(6) ("accesser is not entitled so to obtain or alter" (emphasis added)). The government reads "so" to mean "in that manner," which it claims must refer to use restrictions. In the government's view, reading the definition narrowly would render "so" superfluous.

The government's interpretation would transform the CFAA from an anti-hacking statute into an expansive misappropriation statute. This places a great deal of weight on a two-letter word that is essentially a conjunction. If Congress meant to expand the scope of criminal liability to everyone who uses a computer in violation of computer use restrictions — which may well include everyone who uses a computer — we would expect it to use language better suited to that purpose. Under the presumption that Congress acts interstitially, we construe a statute as displacing a substantial portion of the common law only where Congress has clearly indicated its intent to do so. *See Jones v. United States*, 529 U.S. 848, 858 (2000) ("[U]nless Congress conveys its purpose clearly, it will not be deemed to have significantly changed the federalstate balance in the prosecution of crimes." (internal quotation marks omitted)).

In any event, the government's "so" argument doesn't work because the word has meaning even if it doesn't refer to use restrictions. Suppose an employer keeps certain information in a separate database that can be viewed on a computer screen, but not copied or downloaded. If an employee circumvents the security measures, copies the information to a thumb drive and walks out of the building with it in his pocket, he would then have obtained access to information in the computer that he is not "entitled so to obtain." Or, let's say an employee is given full access to the information, provided he logs in with his username and password. In an effort to cover his tracks, he uses another employee's login to copy information from the database. Once again, this would be an employee who is authorized to access the information but does so in a manner he was not authorized "so to obtain." Of course, this all assumes that "so" must have a substantive meaning to make sense of the statute. But Congress could just as well have included "so" as a connector or for emphasis.

While the CFAA is susceptible to the government's broad interpretation, we find Nosal's narrower one more plausible. Congress enacted the CFAA in 1984 primarily to address the growing problem of computer hacking, recognizing that, "[i]n intentionally trespassing into someone else's computer files, the offender obtains at the very least information as to how to break into that computer system." S. Rep. No. 99-432, at 9 (1986) (Conf. Rep.). The government agrees that the CFAA was concerned with hacking, which is why it also prohibits accessing a computer "without authorization." According to the government, *that* prohibition applies to hackers, so the "exceeds authorized access" prohibition must apply to people who are authorized to use the computer, but do so for an unauthorized purpose. But it is possible to read both prohibitions as applying to hackers: "[W]ithout authorization" would apply to *outside* hackers (individuals who have no authorized access to the computer at all) and "exceeds authorized access" would apply to *inside* hackers (individuals whose initial access to a computer is authorized but who access unauthorized information or files). This is a perfectly plausible construction of the statutory language that maintains the CFAA's focus on hacking rather than turning it into a sweeping Internet-policing mandate.

The government's construction of the statute would expand its scope far beyond computer hacking to criminalize any unauthorized use of information obtained from a computer. This would make criminals of large groups of people who would have little reason to suspect they are committing a federal crime. While ignorance of the law is no excuse, we can properly be skeptical as to whether Congress, in 1984, meant to criminalize conduct beyond that which is inherently wrongful, such as breaking into a computer.

The government argues that defendants here did have notice that their conduct was wrongful by the fraud and materiality requirements in subsection 1030(a)(4), which punishes whoever:

> knowingly and with intent to defraud, accesses a protected computer without authorization, or exceeds authorized access, and by means of such conduct furthers the intended fraud and obtains anything of value, unless the object of the fraud and the thing obtained consists only of the use of the computer and the value of such use is not more than $5,000 in any 1-year period.

18 U.S.C. § 1030(a)(4). But "exceeds authorized access" is used elsewhere in the CFAA as a basis for criminal culpability without intent to defraud. Subsection 1030(a)(2)(C) requires only that the person who "exceeds authorized access" have "obtain[ed] . . . information from any protected computer." Because "protected computer" is defined as a computer affected by or involved in interstate commerce — effectively all computers with Internet access — the government's interpretation of "exceeds authorized access" makes every violation of a private computer use policy a federal crime. *See id.* § 1030(e)(2)(B).

The government argues that our ruling today would construe "exceeds authorized access" only in subsection 1030(a)(4), and we could give the phrase a narrower meaning when we construe other subsections. This is just not so: Once we define the phrase for the purpose of subsection 1030(a)(4), that definition must apply equally to the rest of the statute pursuant to the "standard principle of statutory construction . . . that identical words and phrases within the same statute should normally be given the same meaning." *Powerex Corp. v. Reliant Energy Servs., Inc.*, 551 U.S. 224, 232 (2007). The phrase appears five times in the first seven subsections of the statute, including subsection 1030(a)(2)(C). *See* 18 U.S.C. § 1030(a)(1), (2), (4) and (7). Giving a different interpretation to each is impossible because Congress provided a *single* definition of "exceeds authorized access" for all iterations of the statutory phrase. *See id.* § 1030(e)(6). Congress obviously meant "exceeds authorized access" to have the same meaning throughout section 1030. We must therefore consider how the interpretation we adopt will operate wherever in that section the phrase appears.

In the case of the CFAA, the broadest provision is subsection 1030(a)(2)(C), which makes it a crime to exceed authorized access of a computer connected to the Internet *without* any culpable intent. Were we to adopt the government's proposed interpretation, millions of unsuspecting individuals would find that they are engaging in criminal conduct.

Minds have wandered since the beginning of time and the computer gives employees new ways to procrastinate, by g-chatting with friends, playing games, shopping or watching sports highlights. Such activities are routinely prohibited by many computer-use policies, although employees are seldom disciplined for occasional use of work computers for personal purposes. Nevertheless, under the broad interpretation of the CFAA, such minor dalliances would become federal crimes. While it's unlikely that you'll be prosecuted for watching Reason. TV on your work computer, you *could* be. Employers wanting to rid themselves of troublesome employees without following proper procedures could threaten to report them to the FBI unless they quit. Ubiquitous, seldom-prosecuted crimes invite arbitrary and discriminatory enforcement.

Employer-employee and company-consumer relationships are traditionally governed by tort and contract law; the government's proposed interpretation of the CFAA allows private parties to manipulate their computer-use and personnel policies so as to turn these relationships into ones policed by the criminal law. Significant notice problems arise if we allow criminal liability to turn on the vagaries of private polices that are lengthy, opaque, subject to change and seldom read. Consider the typical corporate policy that computers can be used only for business purposes. What exactly is a "nonbusiness purpose"? If you use the computer to check the weather report for a business trip? For the company softball game? For your vacation to Hawaii? And if minor personal uses are tolerated, how can an employee be on notice of what constitutes a violation sufficient to trigger criminal liability?

Basing criminal liability on violations of private computer use polices can transform whole categories of otherwise innocuous behavior into federal crimes simply because a computer is involved. Employees who call family members from their work phones will become criminals if they send an email instead. Employees can sneak in the sports section of the *New York Times* to read at work, but they'd better not visit ESPN.com. And sudoku enthusiasts should stick to the printed puzzles, because visiting www.dailysudoku.com from their work computers might give them more than enough time to hone their sudoku skills behind bars.

The effect this broad construction of the CFAA has on workplace conduct pales by comparison with its effect on everyone else who uses a computer, smart-phone, iPad, Kindle, Nook, X-box, Blu-Ray player or any other Internetenabled device. The Internet is a means for communicating via computers: Whenever we access a web page, commence a download, post a message on somebody's Facebook wall, shop on Amazon, bid on eBay, publish a blog, rate a movie on IMDb, read www.NYT.com, watch YouTube and do the thousands of other things we routinely do online, we are using one computer to send commands to other computers at remote locations. Our access to those remote computers is governed by a series of private agreements and policies that most people are only dimly aware of and virtually no one reads or understands.

For example, it's not widely known that, up until very recently, Google forbade minors from using its services. *See* Google Terms of Service, effective April 16, 2007 — March 1, 2012, § 2.3, http://www.google.com/intl/en/policies/terms/archive/20070416 ("You may not use the Services and may not accept the Terms if . . . you are not of legal age to form a binding contract with Google . . . .") (last visited Mar. 4, 2012). Adopting the government's interpretation would turn vast numbers of teens and pre-teens into juvenile delinquents — and their parents and teachers into delinquency contributors. Similarly, Facebook makes it a violation of the terms of service to let anyone log into your account. *See* Facebook Statement of Rights and Responsibilities § 4.8 http://www.facebook.com/legal/terms ("You will not share your password, . . . let anyone else access your account, or do anything else that might jeopardize the security of your account.") (last visited Mar. 4, 2012). Yet it's very common for people to let close friends and relatives check their email or access their online accounts. Some may be aware that, if discovered, they may suffer a rebuke from the ISP or a loss of access, but few imagine they might be marched off to federal prison for doing so.

Or consider the numerous dating websites whose terms of use prohibit inaccurate or misleading information. *See, e.g.*, eHarmony Terms of Service § 2(I), http://www.eharmony.com/about/terms ("You will not provide inaccurate, misleading or false information to eHarmony or to any other user.") (last visited Mar. 4, 2012). Or eBay and Craigslist, where it's a violation of the terms of use to post items in an inappropriate category. *See, e.g.*, eBay User Agreement, http://pages.ebay.com/help/policies/useragreement.html ("While using eBay sites, services and tools, you will not: post content or items in an inappropriate category or areas on our sites and services . . . .") (last visited Mar. 4, 2012). Under the government's proposed interpretation of the CFAA, posting for sale an item prohibited by Craigslist's policy, or describing yourself as "tall, dark and handsome," when you're actually short and homely, will earn you a handsome orange jumpsuit.

Not only are the terms of service vague and generally unknown — unless you look real hard at the small print at the bottom of a webpage — but website owners retain the right to change the terms at any time and without notice. *See, e.g.*, YouTube Terms of Service § 1.B, http://www.youtube.com/t/terms ("YouTube may, in its sole discretion, modify or revise these Terms of Service and policies at any time, and you agree to be bound by such modifications or revisions.") (last visited Mar. 4, 2012). Accordingly, behavior that wasn't criminal yesterday can become criminal today without an act of Congress, and without any notice whatsoever.

The government assures us that, whatever the scope of the CFAA, it won't prosecute minor violations. But we shouldn't have to live at the mercy of our local prosecutor. *Cf. United States v. Stevens*, 130 S. Ct. 1577, 1591 (2010) ("We would not uphold an unconstitutional statute merely because the Government promised to use it responsibly."). And it's not clear we *can* trust the government when a tempting target comes along. Take the case of the mom who posed as a 17-year-old boy and cyber-bullied her daughter's classmate. The Justice Department prosecuted her under 18 U.S.C. § 1030(a)(2)(C) for violating MySpace's terms of service, which prohibited lying about identifying information, including age. *See United States v. Drew*, 259 F.R.D. 449 (C.D. Cal.2009). Lying on social media websites is common: People shave years off their age, add inches to their height and drop pounds from their weight. The difference between puffery and prosecution may depend on whether you happen to be someone an AUSA has reason to go after.

In *United States v. Kozminski*, 487 U.S. 931 (1988), the Supreme Court refused to adopt the government's broad interpretation of a statute because it would "criminalize a broad range of day-to-day activity." *Id.* at 949. Applying the rule of lenity, the Court warned that the broader statutory interpretation would "delegate to prosecutors and juries the inherently legislative task of determining what type of . . . activities are so morally reprehensible that they should be punished as crimes" and would "subject individuals to the risk of arbitrary or discriminatory prosecution and conviction." *Id.* By giving that much power to prosecutors, we're inviting discriminatory and arbitrary enforcement.

We remain unpersuaded by the decisions of our sister circuits that interpret the CFAA broadly to cover violations of corporate computer use restrictions or violations of a duty of loyalty. *See United States v. Rodriguez*, 628 F.3d 1258 (11th Cir. 2010); *United States v. John*, 597 F.3d 263 (5th Cir. 2010); *Int'l Airport Ctrs., LLC v. Citrin*, 440 F.3d 418 (7th Cir. 2006). These courts looked only at the culpable behavior of the defendants before them, and failed to consider the effect on millions of ordinary citizens caused by the statute's unitary definition of "exceeds authorized access." They therefore failed to apply the long-standing principle that we must construe ambiguous criminal statutes narrowly so as to avoid "making criminal law in Congress's stead." *United States v. Santos*, 553 U.S. 507, 514 (2008).

We therefore respectfully decline to follow our sister circuits and urge them to reconsider instead. For our part, we continue to follow in the path blazed by *Brekka*, 581 F.3d 1127, and the growing number of courts that have reached the same conclusion. These courts recognize that the plain language of the CFAA "target[s] the unauthorized procurement or alteration of information, not its misuse or misappropriation." *Shamrock Foods Co. v. Gast*, 535 F. Supp.2d 962, 965 (D. Ariz. 2008) (internal quotation marks omitted); *see also Orbit One Commc'ns, Inc. v. Numerex Corp.*, 692 F. Supp.2d 373, 385 (S.D.N.Y. 2010) ("The plain language of the CFAA supports a narrow reading. The CFAA expressly prohibits improper 'access' of computer information. It does not prohibit misuse or misappropriation."); *Diamond Power Int'l, Inc. v. Davidson*, 540 F. Supp.2d 1322, 1343 (N.D. Ga. 2007) ("[A] violation for 'exceeding authorized access' occurs where initial access is permitted but the access of certain information is not permitted."); *Int'l Ass'n of Machinists & Aerospace Workers v. Werner-Masuda*, 390 F. Supp. 2d 479, 499 (D. Md. 2005) ("[T]he CFAA, however, do[es] not prohibit the unauthorized disclosure or use of information, but rather unauthorized access.").

## CONCLUSION

We need not decide today whether Congress *could* base criminal liability on violations of a company or website's computer use restrictions. Instead, we hold that the phrase "exceeds authorized access" in the CFAA does not extend to violations of use restrictions. If Congress wants to incorporate misappropriation liability into the CFAA, it must speak more clearly. The rule of lenity requires "penal laws . . . to be construed strictly." *United States v. Wiltberger*, 18 U.S. (5 Wheat.) 76, 95 (1820). "[W]hen choice has to be made between two readings of what conduct Congress has made a crime, it is appropriate, before we choose the harsher alternative, to require that Congress should have spoken in language that is clear and definite." *Jones*, 529 U.S. at 858 (internal quotation marks and citation omitted).

The rule of lenity not only ensures that citizens will have fair notice of the criminal laws, but also that Congress will have fair notice of what conduct its laws criminalize. We construe criminal statutes narrowly so that Congress will not unintentionally turn ordinary citizens into criminals. "[B]ecause of the seriousness of criminal penalties, and because criminal punishment usually represents the moral condemnation of the community, legislatures and not courts should define criminal activity." *United States v. Bass*, 404 U.S. 336, 348 (1971). "If there is any doubt about whether Congress intended [the CFAA] to prohibit the conduct in which [Nosal] engaged, then 'we must choose the interpretation least likely to impose penalties unintended by Congress.' " *United States v. Cabaccang*, 332 F.3d 622, 635 n.22 (9th Cir. 2003) (quoting *United States v. Arzate-Nunez*, 18 F.3d 730, 736 (9th Cir. 1994)).

This narrower interpretation is also a more sensible reading of the text and legislative history of a statute whose general purpose is to punish hacking — the circumvention of technological access barriers — not misappropriation of trade secrets — a subject Congress has dealt with elsewhere. *See supra* note 3. Therefore, we hold that "exceeds authorized access" in the CFAA is limited to violations of restrictions on access to information, and not restrictions on its *use*.

Because Nosal's accomplices had permission to access the company database and obtain the information contained within, the government's charges fail to meet the element of "without authorization, or exceeds authorized access" under 18 U.S.C. § 1030(a)(4). Accordingly, we affirm the judgment of the district court dismissing counts 2 and 4-7 for failure to state an offense. The government may, of course, prosecute Nosal on the remaining counts of the indictment.

AFFIRMED.

SILVERMAN, CIRCUIT JUDGE, with whom TALLMAN, CIRCUIT JUDGE concurs, dissenting:

This case has nothing to do with playing sudoku, checking email, fibbing on dating sites, or any of the other activities that the majority rightly values. It has everything to do with stealing an employer's valuable information to set up a competing business with the purloined data, siphoned away from the victim, knowing such access and use were prohibited in the defendants' employment contracts. The indictment here charged that Nosal and his co-conspirators knowingly exceeded the access to a protected company computer they were given by an executive search firm that employed them; that they did so with the intent to defraud; and further, that they stole the victim's valuable proprietary information by means of that fraudulent conduct in order to profit from using it. In ridiculing scenarios not remotely presented by this case, the majority does a good job of knocking down straw men — far-fetched hypotheticals involving neither theft nor intentional fraudulent conduct, but innocuous violations of office policy.

The majority also takes a plainly written statute and parses it in a hyper-complicated way that distorts the obvious intent of Congress. No other circuit that has considered this statute finds the problems that the majority does.

18 U.S.C. § 1030(a)(4) is quite clear. It states, in relevant part:

(a) Whoever —

> (4) knowingly and with intent to defraud, accesses a protected computer without authorization, or exceeds authorized access, and by means of such conduct furthers the intended fraud and obtains anything of value . . .

shall be punished . . . .

Thus, it is perfectly clear that a person with *both* the requisite mens rea *and* the specific intent to defraud — but *only* such persons — can violate this subsection in one of two ways: first, by accessing a computer without authorization, or second, by exceeding authorized access. 18 U.S.C. § 1030(e)(6) defines "exceeds authorized access" as "to access a computer with authorization and to use such access to obtain or alter information in the computer that the accesser is not entitled so to obtain or alter."

"As this definition makes clear, an individual who is authorized to use a computer for certain purposes but goes beyond those limitations is considered by the CFAA as someone who has 'exceed[ed] authorized access.' " *LVRC Holdings LLC v. Brekka*, 581 F.3d 1127, 1133 (9th Cir. 2009).

"[T]he definition of the term 'exceeds authorized access' from § 1030(e)(6) implies that an employee can violate employer-placed limits on accessing information stored on the computer and still have authorization to access that computer. The plain language of the statute therefore indicates that 'authorization' depends on actions taken by the employer." *Id.* at 1135. In *Brekka*, we explained that a person "exceeds authorized access" when that person has permission to access a computer but accesses information on the computer that the person is not entitled to access. *Id.* at 1133. In that case, an employee allegedly emailed an employer's proprietary documents to his personal computer to use in a competing business. *Id.* at 1134. We held that one does not exceed authorized access simply by "breach[ing] a state law duty of loyalty to an employer" and that, because the employee did not breach a contract with his employer, he could not be liable under the Computer Fraud and Abuse Act. *Id.* at 1135, 1135 n.7.

This is not an esoteric concept. A bank teller is entitled to access a bank's money for legitimate banking purposes, but not to take the bank's money for himself. A new car buyer may be entitled to take a vehicle around the block on a test drive. But the buyer would not be entitled — he would "exceed his authority" — to take the vehicle to Mexico on a drug run. A person of ordinary intelligence understands that he may be totally prohibited from doing something *altogether*, or authorized to do something but prohibited from going *beyond* what is authorized. This is no doubt why the statute covers not only "unauthorized access," but also "exceed[ing] authorized access." The statute contemplates both means of committing the theft.

The majority holds that a person "exceeds authorized access" only when that person has permission to access a computer generally, but is *completely* prohibited from accessing a different portion of the computer (or different information on the computer). The majority's interpretation conflicts with the plain language of the statute. Furthermore, none of the circuits that have analyzed the meaning of "exceeds authorized access" as used in the Computer Fraud and Abuse Act read the statute the way the majority does. Both the Fifth and Eleventh Circuits have explicitly held that employees who knowingly violate clear company computer restrictions agreements "exceed authorized access" under the CFAA.

In *United States v. John*, 597 F.3d 263, 271-73 (5th Cir. 2010), the Fifth Circuit held that an employee of Citigroup exceeded her authorized access in violation of § 1030(a)(2) when she accessed confidential customer information in violation of her employer's computer use restrictions and used that information to commit fraud. As the Fifth Circuit noted in *John*, "an employer may 'authorize' employees to utilize computers for any lawful purpose but not for unlawful purposes and only in furtherance of the employer's business. An employee would 'exceed[ ] authorized access' if he or she used that access to obtain or steal information as part of a criminal scheme." *Id.* at 271 (alteration in original). At the very least, when an employee "knows that the purpose for which she is accessing information in a computer is both in violation of an employer's policies and is part of [a criminally fraudulent] scheme, it would be 'proper' to conclude that such conduct 'exceeds authorized access.' " *Id.* at 273.

Similarly, the Eleventh Circuit held in *United States v. Rodriguez*, 628 F.3d 1258, 1263 (11th Cir. 2010), that an employee of the Social Security Administration exceeded his authorized access under § 1030(a)(2) when he obtained personal information about former girlfriends and potential paramours and used that information to send the women flowers or to show up at their homes. The court rejected Rodriguez's argument that unlike the defendant in *John*, his use was "not criminal." The court held: "The problem with Rodriguez's argument is that his use of information is irrelevant if he obtained the information without authorization or as a result of exceeding authorized access." *Id.; see also EF Cultural Travel BV v. Explorica, Inc.*, 274 F.3d 577, 583-84 (1st Cir. 2001) (holding that an employee likely exceeded his authorized access when he used that access to disclose information in violation of a confidentiality agreement).

The Third Circuit has also implicitly adopted the Fifth and Eleventh circuit's reasoning. In *United States v. Teague*, 646 F.3d 1119, 1121-22 (8th Cir. 2011), the court upheld a conviction under § 1030(a)(2) and (c)(2)(A) where an employee of a government contractor used his privileged access to a government database to obtain President Obama's private student loan records.

The indictment here alleges that Nosal and his coconspirators knowingly exceeded the authority that they had to access their employer's computer, and that they did so with the intent to defraud and to steal trade secrets and proprietary information from the company's database for Nosal's competing business. It is alleged that at the time the employee coconspirators accessed the database they *knew* they only were allowed to use the database for a legitimate business purpose because the co-conspirators allegedly signed an agreement which restricted the use and disclosure of information on the database except for legitimate Korn/Ferry business. Moreover, it is alleged that before using a unique username and password to log on to the Korn/Ferry computer and database, the employees were notified that the information stored on those computers were the property of Korn/Ferry and that to access the information without relevant authority could lead to disciplinary action and criminal prosecution. Therefore, it is alleged, that when Nosal's co-conspirators accessed the database to obtain Korn/Ferry's secret source lists, names, and contact information with the intent to defraud Korn/Ferry by setting up a competing company to take business away using the stolen data, they "exceed[ed their] authorized access" to a computer with an intent to defraud Korn/Ferry and therefore violated 18 U.S.C. § 1030(a)(4). If true, these allegations adequately state a crime under a commonsense reading of this particular subsection.

Furthermore, it does not advance the ball to consider, as the majority does, the parade of horribles that might occur under *different* subsections of the CFAA, such as subsection (a)(2)(C), which does not have the scienter or specific intent to defraud requirements that subsection (a)(4) has. *Maldonado v. Morales*, 556 F.3d 1037, 1044 (9th Cir. 2009) ("The role of the courts is neither to issue advisory opinions nor to declare rights in hypothetical cases, but to adjudicate live cases or controversies.") (citation and internal quotation marks omitted). Other sections of the CFAA may or may not be unconstitutionally vague or pose other problems. We need to wait for an actual case or controversy to frame these issues, rather than posit a laundry list of wacky hypotheticals. I express no opinion on the validity or application of other subsections of 18 U.S.C § 1030, other than § 1030(a)(4), and with all due respect, neither should the majority.

The majority's opinion is driven out of a well meaning but ultimately misguided concern that if employment agreements or internet terms of service violations could subject someone to criminal liability, all internet users will suddenly become criminals overnight. I fail to see how anyone can seriously conclude that reading ESPN.com in contravention of office policy could come within the ambit of 18 U.S.C. § 1030(a)(4), a statute explicitly requiring an intent to defraud, the obtaining of something of value by means of that fraud, while doing so "knowingly." And even if an imaginative judge can conjure up far-fetched hypotheticals producing federal prison terms for accessing word puzzles, jokes, and sports scores while at work, well, . . . that is what an as-applied challenge is for. Meantime, back to this case, 18 U.S.C. § 1030(a)(4) clearly is aimed at, and limited to, knowing and intentional fraud. Because the indictment adequately states the elements of a valid crime, the district court erred in dismissing the charges.

I respectfully dissent.

* * *

## NOTES AND QUESTIONS:

1. The CFAA has broad applicability, including criminal conduct stemming from unauthorized access to a computer, which causes damage to computer systems, obtains information from a computer and executes a fraud through the use of a computer. As discussed above in Chapter 3(C), the civil provisions of the CFAA are gaining in importance in trade secret enforcement, particularly with the use of computers in all aspects of business. The criminal enforcement of trade secrets under the CFAA is in a state of flux with the Ninth Circuit's *en banc* decision in *United States v. Nosal*, 676 F.3d 854 (9th Cir. 2012), because, as the court noted, it disagreed with decisions in the Eleventh, Fifth, and Seventh Circuits that held that computer use outside of authorized access violated the CFAA.

2. After *Nosal*, we will have to wait for the U.S. Supreme Court to decide the issue or for Congress to amend the CFAA. In the meantime, employers would be wise to watch the law of the region in which they are located when drafting employment and consulting agreements that specify restrictions on employee access and computer systems use. Are there any restrictions that can be used to control rogue employees under *Nosal*?

# TABLE OF CASES

[References are to pages]

## A



## B



## C

[References are to pages]



## D



## E

[References are to pages]

## F



## G



## H



## I

[References are to pages]



## J



## K



## L



## M

[References are to pages]

[References are to pages]

[References are to pages]



## V



## W

# INDEX

[References are to sections.]

[References are to sections.]